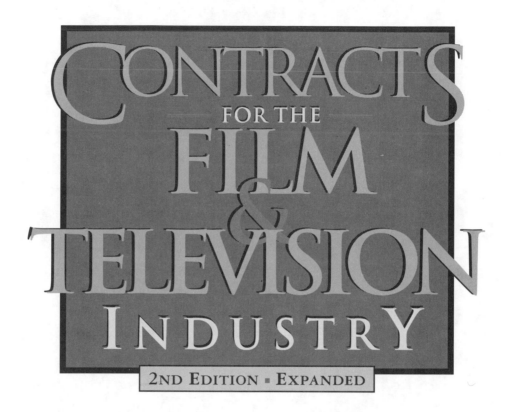

# CONTRACTS
## FOR THE
# FILM
# &
# TELEVISION
## INDUSTRY

2ND EDITION · EXPANDED

Other books by Mark Litwak

*Reel Power*
*Courtroom Crusaders*
*Dealmaking in the Film and Television Industry*
*Litwak's Multimedia Producer's Handbook*

# CONTRACTS FOR THE FILM & TELEVISION INDUSTRY

## 2ND EDITION · EXPANDED

### BY MARK LITWAK

**SILMAN-JAMES PRESS**
LOS ANGELES

First Edition
10 9 8 7 6 5 4 3 2

Library of Congress Cataloging-in-Publication Data

Litwak, Mark.
Contracts for the film & television industry / by Mark Litwak —
2nd ed., expanded
p.      cm.
Includes bibliographical references and index.
1. Motion pictures industry—Law and legislation—United States—Forms.
2. Television—Law and legislation—United States—Forms.
3. Artists' contracts—United States—Forms.  I. Title.  II. Title:
Contracts for the film and television industry.
KF4302.L58   1999          344.73'097—dc21          98-54341

ISBN: 1-879505-46-0

Cover design by Heidi Frieder

Printed and bound in the United States of America

SILMAN-JAMES  PRESS
1181 Angelo Drive
Beverly Hills, CA 90210

*For Glenn, Ellen and Denise.*

# DISCLAIMER

This book is designed to help readers understand legal issues frequently encountered in the entertainment industry. It will provide you with an understanding of basic legal principles, enabling you to better communicate with your attorney.

The information contained in this book is intended to provide general information and does not constitute legal advice. The content is not guaranteed to be correct, complete, or up-to-date. This book is not intended to create an attorney-client relationship between you and Mark Litwak or any of his associates, and you should not act or rely on any information in this book without seeking the advice of an attorney.

In using the material in this book please note that the information provided is not a substitute for consulting with an experienced attorney and receiving counsel based on the facts and circumstances of a particular transaction. Many of the legal principles mentioned are subject to exceptions and qualifications which may not be noted. Furthermore, case law and statutes are subject to revision and may not apply in every state. Because of the quick pace of technological change, some of the information in this book may be outdated by the time you read it. Readers should be aware that business practices, distribution methods and legislation continue to evolve in the rapidly changing entertainment industries.

THE INFORMATION IS PROVIDED "AS IS" AND MARK LITWAK MAKES NO EXPRESS OR IMPLIED REPRESENTATIONS OR WARRANTIES, INCLUDING WARRANTIES OF PERFORMANCE, MERCHANTABILITY, AND FITNESS FOR A PARTICULAR PURPOSE, REGARDING THIS INFORMATION. MARK LITWAK DOES NOT GUARANTEE THE COMPLETENESS, ACCURACY OR TIMELINESS OF THIS INFORMATION. YOUR USE OF THIS INFORMATION IS AT YOUR OWN RISK. YOU ASSUME FULL RESPONSIBILITY AND RISK OF LOSS RESULTING FROM THE USE OF THIS INFORMATION. MARK LITWAK WILL NOT BE LIABLE FOR ANY DIRECT, SPECIAL, INDIRECT, INCIDENTAL, CONSEQUENTIAL OR PUNITIVE DAMAGES OR ANY OTHER DAMAGES WHATSOEVER, WHETHER IN AN ACTION BASED UPON A STATUTE, CONTRACT, TORT (INCLUDING, WITHOUT LIMITATION NEGLIGENCE) OR OTHERWISE, RELATING TO THE USE OF THIS INFORMATION.

Mark Litwak can be contacted by e-mail. However, if you communicate with him electronically or otherwise in connection with a matter for which he does not already represent you, your communication may not be treated as privileged or confidential. An attorney-client relationship can only be created with Mark Litwak with a written retainer agreement signed by both parties. Purchase of this book does not include consultation or legal advice from Mark Litwak.

# CONTENTS

(Contracts are in **bold type**)

*All of the contracts in this book are available on CD-ROM or computer disc. See page 458 for information on how to order.*

# PREFACE

In 1979, I moved from New York to Los Angeles to work in the entertainment industry. As a young New York lawyer with a background in public-interest law, the movie industry was an alien culture. I came across strange practices, confusing jargon and odd people.

After nineteen years in the industry, I no longer qualify as an outsider. However, I remember my frustration in trying to learn the ropes of the business. I didn't have a mentor and there was no guidebook available. I wrote my first book, *Reel Power* (William Morrow) as an exploration into the practices and mores of the industry.

In 1993 I wrote *Dealmaking in the Motion Picture and Television Industry* (Silman-James Press), a guide to entertainment law that could be understood by non-lawyers. This book of contracts is a companion volume. The agreements and commentary illustrate many of the principles discussed in Dealmaking and explain how they are used in the industry.

As with *Dealmaking*, I have attempted to explain complex legal concepts simply, avoid jargon and explain terms of art. The sample contracts are adapted from actual agreements used in the industry. In some instances, only the names of the parties have been deleted.

While there is no such thing as a standard contract, many contracts have similar provisions—so-called "boilerplate clauses." The contracts in this book contain many such provisions. However, readers should not mindlessly use such provisions unless they understand them and modify them to fit the circumstances at hand.

Most of the contracts in this book can be used for production of either a television program or a feature film. The essential terms of depiction releases, option/purchase agreements or collaboration agreements are the same for television programs and feature films. Greater variation can be found in the area of artist employment and distribution agreements. In these areas, I have included samples of the different types of forms used in television and features.

I welcome comments and suggestions from readers. You can write me at P.O. Box 3226, Santa Monica, CA 90408, phone (310) 859-9595, fax (310) 859-0806, email: Litwak@ibm.net.

Readers are welcome to visit my website: Entertainment Legal Resources at **http://www.marklitwak.com** for recent information and articles on entertainment and multimedia law. If you would like to be placed on my mailing list for a free newsletter, please send me your name and address.

I hope this book will prove useful to you.

Mark Litwak
October 1998

# ACKNOWLEDGEMENTS

My special thanks to Robert L. Seigel, Gary Salt and Harris Tulchin for contributing sample contracts to this book.

Lonny Kaufman was instrumental in encouraging me to expand the first edition and publish a multimedia version of this book which is called: *Automated Contracts For The Film & Television Industry*. This software program can be ordered from my website: **http://www.marklitwak.com** or from my office at (310) 859-9595.

I appreciate the efforts of my helpful and competent assistant, Amy Lee, who helped me organize the material and make corrections. Thanks also to Lisa Katzman and Jennifer Denise Fitzpatrick for proofreading the manuscript.

I value the efforts of my book publishers, Gwen Feldman and Jim Fox, with whom I have now collaborated on four books.

# CHAPTER 1

# INTRODUCTION

## BASIC PRINCIPLES OF CONTRACT LAW

A contract is an agreement to do or not do a certain thing (Cal. Civil Code § 1549).[1] It gives rise to an obligation or legal duty, enforceable in an action at law (Cal. Civil Code § 1427, 1428). In other words, a contract is a promise. If the promise is broken, the law provides a remedy. A contract may consist of a single promise or a series of promises that the parties regard as one contract.

### ELEMENTS OF A CONTRACT

It is essential to the existence of a contract that there should be 1) parties capable of contracting, 2) mutual consent, 3) a lawful object, and 4) a sufficient cause or consideration (Cal. Civil Code § 1550).

### 1. Parties capable of contracting

Contracts made by minors, the insane and those who are intoxicated may not be enforceable. In California, minors are persons under age eighteen. Contracts entered into by minors may be either void or voidable (i.e., subject to disaffirmance). There are some exceptions. Contracts to pay for the reasonable value of necessities (i.e., food, shelter), and contracts approved by a court, can be enforced against minors (Cal. Civil Code § 36a).

Contracts made by persons of unsound mind may be completely void or voidable at the request of the person. Such people are not mentally competent to understand the nature and purpose of an agreement they may enter into. The burden of proof of insanity is on the party asserting it (Cal. Evidence Code § 522).

---

[1] The California Code sections cited in the text can be found in the Appendix.

Likewise, a person who is drunk might not have the capacity to understand the consequences of his actions. Of course, the person must be so intoxicated that he does not understand what he is doing.

### 2. Mutual consent

Every contract requires mutual agreement or consent. Usually a party must intend to enter a contract in order to be bound by it. However, if a person outwardly appears to agree to a contract, but does not want to be bound, the other party may be able to enforce the agreement. The law protects the party who reasonably relies on a manifestation of consent, even if the other party doesn't consent. Because people cannot look into other peoples' minds, contract law permits them to rely on the outward manifestation of consent.

Mutual consent typically arises when one party makes an offer and the other party accepts it. The accepting party must accept the terms of the offer as it has been proposed. If the accepting party attempts to vary an essential (i.e., important) term, the accepting party is deemed to be making a counter-offer. If the counter-offer is accepted, the parties have a contract.

Offers should be distinguished from "preliminary negotiations" that may lead to an agreement. Parties can discuss terms without being bound if that is their intent and they don't outwardly appear to enter an agreement. But if a party makes what appears to be an offer, and the other party accepts it, the offerer will be bound by the contract even if he doesn't want to make a contract.

Parties may engage in negotiations and reach an oral agreement with the understanding that a written contract will be signed later. If the parties intend the contract to be effective immediately, it may be enforceable before it is put in writing. On the other hand, the parties may intend that the "agreement" not be binding until it has been put in writing and signed by all parties.

What if the parties enter into an agreement but neglect to agree on all terms? If the essential terms are defined, then the contract will not be rendered unenforceable because of uncertainty as to some minor terms. However, if an essential element of the contract has not been agreed upon, a judge will not speculate as to what terms the parties might have agreed upon. The contract may be deemed fatally uncertain and unenforceable.

### 3. A lawful object

The object of a contract must be lawful (Cal. Civ. Code § 1550) and the consideration must be lawful. (Cal. Civ. Code § 1607). A contract to hire another to commit murder, for instance, would be void.

California classifies illegal contracts as either 1) those contrary to express statutes, 2) those contrary to the policy of express statutes, and 3) those otherwise contrary to good morals. (Cal. Civ. Code § 1667).

### 4. Sufficient cause or consideration

Consideration is often in the form of money or something of value. It can also be an act, forbearance from acting, or a promise. It may be a benefit agreed to be conferred on another, or a detriment agreed to be suffered. A contract is only binding with consideration. Consideration is what distinguishes a contract from a gift, which may be revocable.

Consideration must be something of value, although courts will not invalidate a contract simply because the value of what one party gives is not a fair exchange for what they receive. In other words, courts will not review the adequacy of consideration. Should you be foolish enough to sell your new Mercedes for $5,000, don't expect a judge to rescue you from the consequences of your poor judgment. Unless there was fraud or duress involved, the contract will be enforced, even if unfair. In extraordinary circumstances, courts may deem a contract unconscionable and refuse to enforce it.

The agreement should recite the consideration exchanged. This recital is evidence of consideration. To ensure that a contract is binding, agreements often state: "For ten dollars and other valuable consideration . . ." This establishes that there has been an exchange of value, even if it is nominal. Make sure that the consideration is actually paid. It is wise to pay by check so that you will have the canceled check as proof of payment.

Mutually exchanged promises can be adequate consideration. For example, a producer's efforts to develop a project could be deemed adequate consideration for an option. To be certain that their contracts are enforceable, however, producers often want to pay some money for an option. Promises may be enforced without consideration if a party makes a promise upon which another party justifiably relies. Here the party making the promise will be stopped from denying its existence. This doctrine is referred to as "promissory estoppel." The person who makes the promise must reasonably expect to induce the other party to act or rely on the promise.

## DEFENSES TO CONTRACT

If one or both parties consent to a contract that was induced by duress, undue influence, fraud or mistake, there may be a defense to formation of the contract. The innocent party may rescind the contract and/or sue for damages.

When one party uses physical force, threats of force or extortion to compel the other party to enter into an agreement, the contract may be invalidated on the grounds of DURESS. Similarly, if excessive pressure overcomes the will of a party, that party may raise UNDUE INFLUENCE as a defense. Usually courts require a confidential relationship between the parties for this defense.

If a person is tricked or defrauded into entering a contract, the party may have a defense of FRAUD or MISREPRESENTATION. When parties enter a contract under a MUTUAL MISTAKE about an important underlying fact, the contract may be invalidated. However, if one of the parties is merely mistaken as to the value of what he has bought or sold, mistake is usually not a defense.

If a contract is so one-sided and unfair that it is UNCONSCIONABLE, a court may refuse to enforce it. Often such an agreement is made between parties of unequal bargaining positions, and the weaker party is given an "adhesion" contract, the terms of which are not negotiable.

## TYPES OF CONTRACTS

Contracts can either be WRITTEN or ORAL. Contrary to popular belief, oral contracts may be valid and binding. Most states have a law, known as the Statute of Frauds,[2] requiring that certain kinds of agreements be in writing to be valid. For example, you cannot transfer real estate orally. Other kinds of agreements may be made orally, but take caution that oral contracts may prove difficult to enforce.

Let's assume that you made an oral agreement with a buyer to sell your car for $3,000. You shake hands on the deal but don't put anything in writing. One month later there is a dispute and eventually you end up in small claims court. The buyer informs the judge that you agreed to sell him your car for $3,000. You agree. The buyer then claims that you promised to fix a broken transmission before delivery. You disagree. There are no documents or witnesses or evidence to which the judge can look to determine the terms of the agreement. In this situation, whom should the judge believe? The judge may simply throw up her hands and refuse to enforce a contract for which she cannot ascertain its terms.

So while the law does not require that all contracts be in writing, it is usually advantageous to have a written agreement, if only for the sake of creating evidence. Otherwise, you risk having an unenforceable deal.

Another way to classify contracts is as EXPRESS or IMPLIED contracts. When parties make an express contract, it is explicit that they are making an agreement. Typically, they sign a piece of paper or shake hands. In other words, the parties to an express contract state its terms in words (Cal. Civ. Code § 1620).

An implied contract is a contract implied from conduct. It is implied wholly or partly from the behavior of the parties. Let's suppose that you enter a store and pick up a candy bar. Without saying a word to anyone, you remove the wrapper and begin eating it. Then you head for the door. The proprietor says, "Hey, wait a minute, you didn't pay for the candy bar." You reply, "I never said I would pay for it." Under these circumstances, a court might imply that an agreement exists, based on your conduct. It is understood that when a person consumes merchandise in a store, he has agreed to buy it.

Sometimes implied contracts are not based on behavior but are implied by law for reasons of equity and fairness, or to prevent the unjust enrichment of one party at the expense of another. These are called "Quasi-contracts." Unlike true contracts, they are not based on any intention of the parties to enter into an agreement. Their obligations arise from the law.

---

[2] See e.g., California Civil Code § 1624.

The law of oral and implied contracts can provide the basis for a successful lawsuit for story theft. A basic tenet of copyright law is that ideas are not copyrightable because they are not considered an "expression of an author." As courts sometimes observe, "ideas are as free as the air." Similarly, concepts, themes and titles are not protected by copyright law.

A copyright can protect embellishments upon ideas, however. So while a single word cannot be copyrighted, the particular manner in which a writer organizes words - his craft, his approach - can be protected. While other writers remain free to create work on the same topic, theme or idea, they cannot copy the particular expression of the first writer.

Since one cannot protect an idea under copyright law, a writer who pitches a story idea to another is vulnerable to theft. Fortunately, there is another way to protect ideas. An idea can be the subject of a contract. A writer can protect himself by getting the recipient of an idea to agree to pay for it.

The best way for the writer to protect himself would be to use a written agreement. However, it may be awkward to begin a meeting by asking a producer to sign a contract, even a short one. Such a request might offend some producers or make them uncomfortable. They might worry about liability or want to consult a lawyer. Since writers often have difficulty getting in the door to see influential producers, asking for a written agreement may not be possible.

A less-threatening approach would be to make an oral agreement. The writer begins the meeting by simply saying: "Before I tell you my idea, I want to make sure you understand that I am telling you this idea with the understanding that if you decide to use it, I expect to receive reasonable compensation." The producer most likely will nod her head "Yes," or say "Of course," in which case you have a deal. If the producer indicates that she does not agree to these terms, depart without pitching your story.

Since this contract is oral, there might be a problem proving its existence and terms. That is why it's advisable to have a witness or some documentation. You could bring a co-writer, agent or associate along to the meeting, and after the meeting you might send a letter to the producer reiterating your understanding. The letter should be cordial and non-threatening. You could write: "It was really a pleasure meeting with you to discuss my story about. . . . As we agreed, if you decide to exploit this material, I will receive reasonable compensation." If the terms set forth in your letter are not disavowed by the recipient, the letter could be used as evidence of your agreement.[3]

But what if the producer listening to your pitch doesn't steal your story but repeats it to another producer who uses it? You can protect yourself against this peril by saying: "I am telling you my idea with the understanding that you will keep it confidential and will not tell it to anyone else without my permission." If the producer nods her head okay or says yes, you have a deal, and you can sue if she breaches her promise.

---

[3] Since the letter has not been signed by the producer, his agreement is implied from the fact that he didn't object. Of course, if the producer confirms these terms in writing, that would be much better evidence.

# INTERPRETATION OF CONTRACTS AND CHOICE OF LAW

Suppose a contract is made by a California producer who wants to buy movie rights to a novel written by a Maine author. The agreement is negotiated by the author's New York agent, and the movie is shot in Florida. Sometime after the agreement is made, a dispute arises concerning the rights of the parties under the contract. Which state's law applies to interpret the contract?

If the parties in their agreement have not specified which state's law applies, the contract will be governed by the law of the state that has the most significant relationship with the transaction and the parties. The following factors are important: 1) the place where the contract was made, 2) the place where the contract is to be performed, 3) the location of the subject matter of the contract and 4) the residence of the parties.

Applying these factors to a particular situation may not clearly indicate which state's law should apply. Therefore, parties may want to designate before a dispute arises which law will apply. This will remove any ambiguity and potential litigation over the issue.

If the parties agree upon which state's law will govern their contract, courts will usually enforce that choice as long as there is some reasonable relationship between the law chosen and the parties or subject matter.

Many entertainment-industry disputes are resolved under New York or California law. Since there are numerous industry-related decisions in these states, the law is more settled and certain than in other states. Therefore, it is often advantageous for the parties to choose to have their contracts interpreted according to New York or California law.

# COMMON PROVISIONS OF ENTERTAINMENT CONTRACTS

Many industry contracts share certain "standard" or "boilerplate" provisions. Here are samples of such provisions and explanations of how they are used. These clauses have been taken from a variety of employment, literary-purchase and other agreements. Their form will vary depending on the type of agreement into which they are incorporated. For example, the assignment clause below is written in the context of an agreement between a writer and production company. If you wanted to use such a clause in a director employment agreement, appropriate changes would have to be made.

## ASSIGNMENT

(a) Assignability:  This Agreement is non-assignable by Writer.  Production Company and any subsequent assignee may freely assign this Agreement and grant its rights hereunder, in whole or in part, to any person, firm, or corporation, if such party assumes and agrees in writing to keep and perform all of the executory obligations of Production Company hereunder. Upon such assumption, Production Company is hereby released from all further obligations to Writer hereunder, except that unless the assignee or borrower is a so-called major motion-picture company, or mini-major, Production Company shall remain secondarily liable under this agreement.

(b) Right to Lend to Others:  Writer understands and acknowledges that the actual production entity of a motion picture to be made from the Product may be a party other than Production Company.  In such event, Writer's services shall be rendered hereunder for the actual production entity but without releasing Production Company from its obligations hereunder.

An assignment clause permits a party to an agreement to assign certain rights or obligations in the agreement to another. It would, for example, allow a buyer of a literary property to assign those rights.

A producer may need the flexibility to assign acquired rights because a distributor or financier may insist upon an assignment before financing a project. If the writer is concerned with whom the project may end up, he could try to limit the assignment to major studios and networks.

If the writer has a lot of clout, he could insist that no assignments be permitted without his prior approval. As a concession, the writer could agree to limit his discretion with a clause stating that his consent will "not be unreasonably withheld." The writer may want the assignment to require that any assignee assume all obligations owed the writer, and perhaps the assignor will remain liable as well.

On the other hand, a producer will not want a writer to be able to assign his writing obligations to another. Producers hire writers because they admire their writing, and they don't want the writer to subcontract the work to another. Producers usually don't mind, however, if the writer assigns his right to be paid money due him under an employment agreement.

## RIGHT OF FIRST NEGOTIATION

Buyer shall have a right of first negotiation. The term "Right of First Negotiation" means that if, after the expiration of an applicable time limitation, Seller wants to dispose of or exercise a particular right reserved to Seller herein ("Reserved Right"), whether directly or indirectly, then Seller shall notify Buyer in writing and immediately negotiate with Buyer regarding such Reserved Right. If, after the expiration of _____ days following the receipt of such notice, no agreement has been reached, then Seller may negotiate with third parties regarding such Reserved Right, subject to Clause ___.

A Right of First Negotiation requires a party to negotiate a matter with a second party before negotiating with third parties. In a literary-purchase agreement, for example, a buyer (studio) may agree to let a writer retain certain rights, subject to the writer giving the studio first shot at purchasing those rights, should the writer decide to sell them.

Suppose Writer A has sold the movie rights to his book to Paramount. The writer has retained all dramatic (play) rights. Paramount obtains a "Right of First Negotiation," giving it first opportunity to purchase the play rights if the Writer should choose to sell them. Paramount thinks that it is only fair for it to have such a right. It is investing millions of dollars in turning the writer's book into a movie, making the underlying property and all its derivative forms more valuable. The Right of First Negotiation only requires that the writer negotiate in good faith with Paramount first. If no agreement is reached within a set period (e.g., 30 days), the Writer can negotiate and sell the play rights to a third party.

## RIGHT OF LAST REFUSAL

Buyer shall have a right of last refusal. The term "Right of Last Refusal" means that if Buyer and Seller fail to agree pursuant to Buyer's right of first negotiation, and Seller makes and/or receives any bona fide offer to license, lease and/or purchase the particular Reserved Right or any interest therein ("Third-Party Offer"), and if the proposed purchase price and other material terms of a Third-Party Offer are no more favorable to Seller than the terms that were acceptable to Buyer during the first negotiation period, Seller shall notify Buyer, by registered mail or telegram, if Seller proposes to accept such Third-Party Offer. Seller shall disclose the name of the offerer, the proposed purchase price and other terms of such Third Party Offer.

During the period of _____ days after Buyer's receipt of such notice, Buyer shall have the exclusive option to license, lease and/or purchase, as the case may be, the particular Reserved Right or interest referred to in such Third-Party Offer, at the same purchase price and upon the same terms and conditions as set forth in such notice. If Buyer elects to exercise his right of last refusal, he shall notify Seller by registered mail or telegram within such _____ day period, failing which Seller shall be free to accept such Third-Party Offer.

If any such proposed license, lease and/or sale is not consummated with a third party within _____ days following the expiration of this _____ day period, Buyer's Right of Last Refusal shall revive and shall apply to every further offer or offers received by Seller relating to the particular Reserved Right or any interest therein; provided, further, that Buyer's option shall continue in full force and effect, upon all of the terms and conditions of this paragraph, while Seller retains any rights, title or interests in or to the particular Reserved Right. Buyer's Right of Last Refusal shall inure to the benefit of Buyer, its successors and assigns, and shall bind Seller and Seller's heirs, successors and assigns.

The Right of Last Refusal may be combined with, or used as an alternative to, the Right of First Negotiation. With the Right of Last Refusal, the buyer has the right to acquire a reserved right under the same terms and conditions as any offer made by a third party. If Paramount had a Right of Last Refusal, then the Writer would be free to offer the right to another buyer. Before closing the deal, however, the writer would have to offer Paramount the right on the same terms as the third-party's best offer.

As a practical matter, when a writer has given a studio a Right of Last Refusal, it can be difficult to interest third-party buyers. Why should Universal Pictures spend time negotiating the terms of a sale with the writer, only to have the deal supplanted at the last moment by Paramount? Thus, the Right of Last Refusal discourages third-party offers.

## ADDITIONAL DOCUMENTATION

Seller agrees to obtain and execute any other and further instruments necessary to transfer, convey, assign and copyright all rights in the Property granted herein by Seller to Buyer in any country throughout the world. If it shall be necessary under the laws of any country that copyright registration be acquired in the name of Seller, Buyer is authorized by Seller to apply for said copyright registration; and, in such event, Seller shall and does hereby assign and transfer the same unto Buyer, subject to the rights in the Property reserved hereunder by Seller. Seller further agrees, upon request, to duly execute, acknowledge, obtain and deliver to Buyer such short-form assignments as may be requested by Buyer for the purpose of copyright recordation in any country, or otherwise. If Seller shall fail to so execute and deliver, or cause to be executed and delivered, the assignments or other instruments herein referred to, Buyer is hereby irrevocably granted the power coupled with an interest to execute such assignments and instruments in the name of Seller and as Seller's attorney-in-fact.

In the industry, short-form contracts and deal memos are often used by the parties to expedite matters. Sometimes the long-form agreement doesn't get signed until after the parties have fulfilled their contractual obligations. Frequently, the long-form contracts are never signed. This provision protects the parties to a deal memo by providing that if additional documentation is needed later, the other party will cooperate.

The provision also states that if a party refuses to provide the additional documentation needed, the other party has a power of attorney, which enables him to sign the documents on behalf of the defaulting party.

Any additional documentation requested must comply with and not contradict the terms of the deal memo. A party cannot force another to agree to unreasonable and different terms than originally agreed to. All that should be left for future documentation is to fill in the details of the prior agreement.

## NOTICES

All notices to Buyer under this agreement shall be sent by United States registered mail, postage prepaid, or by telegram addressed to Buyer at _____ (address) with a courtesy copy to _____ (Buyer's attorney), and all notices to Seller under this agreement shall be sent by United States registered mail, postage prepaid, or by telegram addressed to _____ at _____(address) seller with a courtesy copy to _____ (Seller's attorney). The deposit of such notice in the United States mail or the delivery of the telegram message to the telegraph office shall constitute service of it, and the date of deposit shall be deemed to be the date of service of such notice.

A notice provision ensures that the parties know how and where to give notice to one another. Often, contracts require that one party notify the other of a default before an agreement can be terminated. To elimate confusion as to the manner of notice required, a notice clause is used.

## FORCE MAJEURE

"Force majeure" means superior force and it refers to certain events beyond control of the production company that may force suspension of a contract. Such forces typically include fire, earthquake, acts of God and death or illness of a principal member of the cast or the director.

A force-majeure clause will set forth the parties' obligations to each other in case of suspension. While the production company may have the right to suspend the contract, and suspend compensation due the artist, this right is usually limited. At a certain point, the artist will have a right to terminate the agreement and move on to other projects. The production company may have the right to terminate the employment agreement if the suspension lasts more than a certain number of weeks.

Note that the clause here is written as a loan-out agreement. The "Lender" is the artist's loan-out company.[4] This company, which is usually owned by the artist, is lending out the artist's services. There may be certain tax advantages in structuring a deal as a loan-out agreement rather than a direct employment agreement.

(a) Suspension:

If, (i) because of fire, earthquake, labor dispute or strike, act of God or public enemy, any municipal ordinance, any state or federal law, governmental order or regulation, or other cause beyond Production Company's control, Production Company is prevented from or hampered in the production of the Picture, or if,

(ii) because of the closing of substantially all the theaters in the United States for any of the aforesaid or other causes which would excuse Production Company's performance as a matter of law, Production Company's production of the Picture is postponed or suspended, or if,

(iii) because of any of the aforesaid contingencies or any other cause or occurrence not within Production Company's control, including but not limited to death, illness or incapacity of any principal member of the cast of the Picture or the director or individual producer, the preparation, commencement, production or completion of the Picture is hampered, interrupted or interfered with, and/or if,

(iv) Production Company's normal business operations are hampered or otherwise interfered with by virtue of any disruptive events which are beyond Production Company's control ("Production Company Disability"), then Production Company may postpone the commencement of or suspend the rendition of Writer's services and the running of time hereunder for such time as the Production Company Disability continues; and no compensation shall accrue or become payable to Lender hereunder during such suspension. Such suspension shall end upon the cessation of the cause of it.

(b) Termination:

(i) Production Company Termination Right: If a Production Company Disability continues for eight (8) weeks, Production Company may terminate this Agreement upon written notice to Lender.

(ii) Lender's Termination Right: If a Production Company Disability results in the payment of compensation being suspended hereunder for a period exceeding eight (8) weeks, Lender may terminate this Agreement upon written notice to Production Company.

(iii) Production Company Re-Establishment Right: Despite Lender's election to terminate this Agreement, within five (5) business days after Production Company's actual receipt of such written notice from Lender, Production Company may elect to re-establish the operation of this Agreement.

---

[4] See Chapter 4 for a discussion of loan-out companies.

# INCAPACITY

If, because of mental or physical disability, Writer shall be incapacitated from performing or complying with any of the terms or conditions hereof ("Writer's Incapacity") for a consecutive period exceeding fifteen days during the performance of Writer's services, then:

(a) Suspension:  Production Company may suspend the rendition of services by Writer and the running of time hereunder while Writer's Incapacity continues.

(b) Termination:  Production Company may terminate this Agreement and all of Production Company's obligations and liabilities hereunder upon written notice to Lender.

(c) Right of Examination:  If any claim of mental or physical disability is made by or for Writer, the Production Company may have Writer examined by such physicians as Production Company may designate. Writer's physician may be present at such examination, and shall not interfere with it. Any tests performed on Writer shall be related to and be customary for the treatment, diagnosis or examination to be performed concerning Writer's claim.

An artist may become incapacitated due to an injury or illness. This clause sets forth the rights of the production company upon incapacity. The artist will want to make sure that the agreement does not allow the production company to terminate for a short illness or minor injury.

# DEFAULT

If Lender or Writer fails or refuses to write, complete and deliver to Production Company the Product Form provided for herein within the respective periods specified, or if Lender or Writer otherwise fails or refuses to perform or comply with any of the terms or conditions hereof (other than because of Writer's Incapacity) ("Lender/Writer Default"), then:

(a) Suspension:  Production Company may suspend the rendition of services by Writer and the running of time hereunder as long as the Lender/Writer Default shall continue.

(b) Termination:  Production Company may terminate this Agreement and all of Production Company's obligations and liabilities hereunder upon written notice to Lender.

(c) Lender/Writer Default shall not include any failure or refusal of Writer to perform or comply with the material terms of this Agreement because of a breach or action by Production Company which makes the performance by Writer of his services impossible.

(d) Before termination of this Agreement by Production Company based upon Lender/Writer Default, Production Company shall notify Lender and Writer specifying the nature of the Lender/Writer Default, and Lender/Writer shall have a period of 72 hours after giving such notice to cure the Default. If the Lender/Writer Default is not cured within said period, Production Company may terminate this Agreement forthwith.

When one party fails to live up to his/her contractual obligations, they may be in default of the agreement. The innocent party may have a right to suspend performance of its obligations under the agreement and/or terminate the agreement. Often the innocent party is required, however, to first give notice of the default to the defaulting party.

## EFFECT OF SUSPENSION

No compensation shall accrue to Lender during any suspension. During any period of suspension hereunder, Lender shall not permit Writer to render services for any party other than Production Company. However, Writer shall have the right to render services to third parties during any period of suspension based upon a Production Company Disability subject, however, to Production Company's right to require Writer to resume the rendition of services hereunder upon three (3) days' prior notice. Production Company shall have the right (exercisable at any time) to extend the period of services of Writer hereunder for a period equal to the period of such suspension. If Production Company shall have paid compensation to Lender during any period of Writer's Incapacity or Lender/Writer Default, then Production Company shall have the right (exercisable at any time) to require Writer to render services hereunder without compensation for a period equal to that period of Writer's Incapacity or Lender/Writer Default.

This clause explains the effect suspension will have on the parties' rights and obligations.

## TERMINATION RIGHTS

A.        No failure by either party hereto to perform any of its obligations under this Agreement shall be deemed to be a breach of this Agreement until the non-breaching party has given the breaching party written notice of its failure to perform and such failure has not been corrected within thirty (30) days [fifteen (15) days for any non-payment of money] from and after the giving of such notice. Except with respect to the non-payment of the Advance hereunder, it is expressly understood and agreed that in the event of any breach or purported breach by DISTRIBUTOR hereunder, FILMMAKER's rights shall be limited to an action of law for money damages, if any, actually suffered by FILMMAKER as a result thereof, and in no event shall FILMMAKER be entitled to rescission, injunction, or other equitable relief of any kind.

B.        FILMMAKER shall have the right to terminate this Agreement and cause all rights herein conveyed to DISTRIBUTOR to revert to FILMMAKER subject, however, to third party agreements conveying rights in the Picture (in respect to which you shall be deemed an assignee of all of DISTRIBUTOR's rights therein in respect to the Picture), by written notice to DISTRIBUTOR in the event that DISTRIBUTOR files a petition in bankruptcy or consents to an involuntary petition in bankruptcy or to any reorganization under Chapter 11 of the Bankruptcy Act. Notwithstanding anything to the contrary which may be contained in the preceding sentence, in the event that DISTRIBUTOR files a petition in bankruptcy or consents to an involuntary petition in bankruptcy or to any reorganization under Chapter 11 of the Bankruptcy Act, FILMMAKER shall not be entitled to terminate this Agreement if thereafter: (1) DISTRIBUTOR shall segregate FILMMAKER's share of the moneys that DISTRIBUTOR receives in connection with the Picture and place the moneys segregated into a separate trust account that such moneys shall not be commingled with DISTRIBUTOR 's other funds, and FILMMAKER's share of such moneys shall become FILMMAKER 's property immediately upon the collection by DISTRIBUTOR and (2) this procedure is approved by the Bankruptcy Court. In connection with the foregoing, DISTRIBUTOR hereby grants to you a security interest in the Picture and the right to receive moneys from the exploitation of the Picture ("Security Interest"). FILMMAKER may by written notice to DISTRIBUTOR execute against your Security Interest if and only if DISTRIBUTOR files a petition in bankruptcy or consents to an involuntary bankruptcy or an organization under Chapter 11 and FILMMAKER is entitled to terminate this Agreement in accordance with the other provisions of this Paragraph.

This provision sets forth the grounds for termination, and the respective rights of the parties to a distribution agreement. Clause A restricts the filmmaker to a monetary award of damages, except in the event that the distributor goes into bankruptcy.

## EFFECT OF TERMINATION

Termination of this Agreement, whether by lapse of time, mutual consent, operation of law, exercise of right of termination or otherwise shall:

(a) Compensation: Terminate Production Company's obligation to pay Lender any further compensation. Nevertheless, if the termination is not for Lender/Writer Default, Production Company shall pay Lender any compensation due and unpaid prior to termination.

(b) Refund/Delivery: If termination occurs pursuant to Clauses _____, prior to Writer's delivery to Production Company of the Product Form on which Writer is then currently working, then Lender or Writer (or in the event of Writer's death, Writer's estate) shall, as Production Company requests, either forthwith refund to Production Company the compensation which may have been paid to Lender as of that time for such Product Form, or immediately deliver to Production Company all of the Product then completed or in progress, in whatever stage of completion it may be.

This clause explains the effect termination will have on the parties' rights and obligations.

# RIGHT TO CURE

Any Writer's Incapacity or Lender/Writer Default shall be deemed to continue until Production Company's receipt of written notice from Lender specifying that Writer is ready, willing and able to perform the services required hereunder; provided that any such notice from Lender to Production Company shall not preclude Production Company from exercising any rights or remedies Production Company may have hereunder or at law or in equity by reason of Writer's Incapacity or Lender/Writer Default.

After default or incapacity, the artist may be required to give written notice that she is now able and willing to perform her obligations.

# INDEMNIFICATION

Lender and Writer agree to indemnify Production Company, its successors, assigns, licensees, officers, directors and employees, and hold them harmless from and against any and all claims, liability, losses, damages, costs, expenses (including but not limited to attorneys' fees), judgments and penalties arising out of Lender's and Writer's breach of warranties under this Agreement. Production Company agrees to indemnify Lender, its successors, assigns, licensees, and employees, and hold them harmless from and against any and all claims, liability, losses, damages, costs, expenses (including but not limited to attorneys' fees), judgments and penalties arising out of any suit against Lender/Writer (arising from Lender's employment under this agreement) not based on Lender's/Writer's breach of her warranties under this Agreement.

The production company (buyer) of a literary property has no way of knowing for certain whether a literary property may infringe on another's rights. For example, a novelist may have plagiarized portions of his work from another. To protect the buyer, an indemnification clause will provide that the buyer has the right to be reimbursed any legal expenses and damages he may incur as a result of the seller (writer) breaching his warranties (promises).

# NAME AND LIKENESS

Production Company shall always have the right to use and display Writer's name and likeness for advertising, publicizing and exploiting the Picture or the Product. However, such advertising may not include the direct endorsement of any product (other than the Picture) without Writer's prior written consent. Exhibition, advertising, publicizing or exploiting the Picture by any media, even though a part of or in connection with a product or a commercially-sponsored program, shall not be deemed an endorsement of any nature.

The employer will want the right to use the artist's name and likeness in promoting the film. This right is particularly valuable if the artist is a star or important director. Studios rarely use a writer's name and likeness to promote a movie.

While the employer has the right to use the name and likeness of the artist to promote a picture, the employer doesn't have the right to use the artist's name and likeness to sell products such as celebrity coffee mugs or perfume.

## PUBLICITY RESTRICTIONS

Lender or Writer shall not, individually or jointly, or by any means of press agents, or publicity or advertising agencies or others, employed or paid by Lender or Writer or otherwise, circulate, publish or otherwise disseminate any news stories or articles, books or other publicity, containing Writer's name relating directly or indirectly to Lender's/Writer's employment by Production Company, the subject matter of this Agreement, the Picture, or the services to be rendered by Lender or Writer or others for the Picture, unless first approved by Production Company. Lender/Writer shall not transfer or attempt to transfer any right, privilege, title or interest in or to any of the aforestated things, nor shall Lender/Writer willingly permit any infringement upon the exclusive rights granted to Production Company. Lender and Writer authorize Production Company, at Production Company's expense, in Lender's or Writer's name or otherwise, to institute any proper legal proceedings to prevent such infringement.

Studios want to carefully orchestrate and time their movie's publicity campaigns. This clause is meant to deter artists from going off on their own and giving interviews that may not be helpful to the promotion of the movie.

## REMEDIES

(a) Remedies Cumulative:  All remedies of Production Company or Lender shall be cumulative, and no one such remedy shall be exclusive of any other. Without waiving any rights or remedies under this Agreement or otherwise, Production Company may from time to time recover, by action, any damages arising out of any breach of this Agreement by Lender and/or Writer and may institute and maintain subsequent actions for additional damages which may arise from the same or other breaches.  The commencement or maintaining of any such action or actions by Production Company shall not constitute or result in the termination of Lender's/Writer's engagement hereunder unless Production Company shall expressly so elect by written notice to Lender. The pursuit by Production Company or Lender of any remedy under this Agreement or otherwise shall not be deemed to waive any other or different remedy which may be available under this Agreement or otherwise.

(b) Services Unique:  Lender and Writer acknowledge that Writer's services to be furnished hereunder and the rights herein granted are of a special, unique, unusual, extraordinary and intellectual character which gives them a peculiar value, the loss of which cannot be reasonably or adequately compensated in damages in an action at law, and that Lender's or Writer's Default will cause Production Company irreparable injury and damage. Lender and Writer agree that Production Company shall be entitled to injunctive and other equitable relief to prevent default by Lender or Writer. In addition to such equitable relief,

Production Company shall be entitled to such other remedies as may be available at law, including damages.

Remedies are the means by which to enforce a right or obtain compensation. Remedies include money damages and injunctive relief (i.e., court orders). Subparagraph (a) above states that the election to use one remedy does not preclude other remedies.

Subparagraph (b) establishes the basis for injunctive relief. Courts usually won't grant injunctive relief if money damages can provide adequate relief. This clause acknowledges that the services of the artist are unique, loss of the services would cause irreparable harm, and money damages cannot adequately compensate the employer. Therefore, the employer might be able to obtain a court injunction ordering the artist not to work for another while the artist should be working for the employer. This could pressure the artist to return to work.

## GUILDS AND UNIONS

(a) Membership:  During Writer's engagement hereunder, as Production Company may lawfully require, Lender at Lender's sole cost and expense (and at Production Company's request) shall remain or become and remain a member in good standing of the then properly designated labor organization or organizations (as defined and determined under the then applicable law) representing persons performing services of the type and character required to be performed by Writer hereunder.

(b) Superseding Effect of Guild Arrangements:  Nothing contained in this Agreement shall be construed so as to require the violation of the applicable WGA Agreement, which by its terms is controlling with respect to this Agreement; and whenever there is any conflict between any provision of this Agreement and any such WGA Agreement, the latter shall prevail. In such event, the provisions of this Agreement shall be curtailed and limited only to the extent necessary to permit compliance with such WGA Agreement.

If a studio was able to circumvent the terms of a collective-bargaining agreement by getting an employee to agree to less favorable terms, then the collective-bargaining agreement would be worthless. This clause makes it clear that if there is any conflict between the collective-bargaining agreement and the individual employment agreement, the terms of the collective-bargaining agreement prevail.

Of course, the collective-bargaining agreement only applies to companies that sign it (signatory companies) and artists who are members of the union. Provisions similar to the sample above are found in DGA and SAG employment agreements.

## CREDITS

(a) Billing:  Provided that Lender and Writer fully perform all of Lender's/ Writer's obligations hereunder and the Picture is completed and distributed,

Production Company agrees that credits for authorship by Writer shall be determined and accorded pursuant to the provisions of the WGA Agreement in effect at the time of such determination.

(b) Inadvertent Non-Compliance: Subject to the foregoing provisions, Production Company shall determine, in Production Company's discretion, the manner of presenting such credits. No casual or inadvertent failure to comply with the provisions of this clause, nor any failure of any other person, firm or corporation to comply with its agreements with Production Company relating to such credits, shall constitute a breach by Production Company of Production Company's obligations under this clause. Lender and Writer hereby agree that if, through inadvertence, Production Company breaches its obligations pursuant to this Paragraph, the damages (if any) caused Lender or Writer by Production Company are not irreparable or sufficient to entitle Lender/Writer to injunctive or other equitable relief. Consequently, Lender's and/or Writer's rights and remedies in such event shall be limited to Lender's/Writer's rights, if any, to recover damages in an action at law, and Lender and Writer shall not be entitled to rescind this Agreement or any of the rights granted to Production Company hereunder, or to enjoin or restrain the distribution or exhibition of the Picture or any other rights granted to Production Company. Production Company agrees upon receipt of notice from Writer of Production Company's failure to comply with the provisions of this Paragraph, to take such steps as are reasonably practicable to cure such failure on future prints and advertisements.

The Writers Guild was formed as a result of writers' anger at studio moguls who assigned writing credit capriciously. Writers wanted to make sure that credit was given only to those who deserved it. The WGA's agreement with the studios provides that in the event of a credit dispute, the WGA will arbitrate and allocate credit among the writers involved.

While studios are willing to give up credit determination, they want to make sure that if they inadvertently drop a credit, the artist will not be able to go to court and get an injunction stopping distribution of the picture. Thus, the second paragraph of this clause limits the artist's remedies to money damages.

## INSURANCE

Production Company may secure life, health, accident, cast or other insurance covering Writer, the cost of which shall be included as a direct charge of the Picture. Such insurance shall be for Production Company's sole benefit and Production Company shall be the beneficiary thereof, and Lender/Writer shall have no interest in the proceeds thereof. Lender and Writer shall assist in procuring such insurance by submitting to required examinations and tests and by preparing, signing and delivering such applications and other documents as may be reasonably required. Lender and Writer shall, to the best of their ability, observe all terms and conditions of such insurance which Production Company notifies Lender is necessary for continuing such insurance in effect.

Production companies may want to secure insurance to protect their interests and investment if an artist they contract with becomes incapacitated and unable to perform. This clause requires the artist to submit to a medical examination if needed to secure insurance and makes it clear that the insurance is for the benefit of the employer.

## EMPLOYMENT OF OTHERS

Lender and Artist agree not to employ any person to serve in any capacity, nor contract for the purchase or renting of any article or material, nor make any agreement committing Production Company to pay any sum of money for any reason at all concerning the Picture or services to be rendered by Artist or provided by Lender hereunder, or otherwise, without written approval first being had and obtained from Production Company.

The employer doesn't want to be liable for persons hired by the artist, or any goods or services ordered by the artist. In some agreements, the studio may agree to hire members of a star's entourage, such as a favorite hairdresser, to work on the production.

## GOVERNING LAW

This Agreement shall be construed according to the laws of the State of California applicable to agreements which are executed and fully performed within said State.

As explained on page 6, the parties may want to choose which law will apply to any dispute that may arise under the contract. This provision is particularly important when the parties reside in different states, or when the subject/performance of a contract will take place in a state other than one in which the parties reside. In those situations, it may be unclear which state's law applies.

## CAPTIONS

The captions used concerning the clauses and subclauses of this Agreement are inserted only for reference. Such captions shall not be deemed to govern, limit, modify, or affect the scope, meaning or intent of the provisions of this Agreement or any part of it; nor shall such captions otherwise be given any legal effect.

This clause provides that the headlined paragraph captions are for ease of reading only and do not modify the detailed language of the agreement.

## SERVICE OF PROCESS

In any action or proceeding commenced in any court in the State of California to enforce this Agreement or any right granted herein or growing out hereof, or any order or decree predicated thereon, any summons, order to show cause, writ, judgment, decree, or other process, issued by such court, may be delivered to Lender or Writer personally without the State of California; and when so delivered, Lender and Writer shall be subject to the jurisdiction of such court as though the same had been served within the State of California, but outside the county in which such action or proceeding is pending.

With this clause the parties consent to service of process outside the state of California as if the parties were within the state. This provision comes into play if a dispute arises and one of the parties is outside the state.

## ILLEGALITY

Nothing contained herein shall require the commission of any act or the payment of any compensation which is contrary to an express provision of law or contrary to the policy of express law. If there shall exist any conflict between any provision contained herein and any such law or policy, the latter shall prevail; and the provision or provisions herein affected shall be curtailed, limited or eliminated to the extent (but only to the extent) necessary to remove such conflict; and as so modified the remaining provisions of this Agreement shall continue in full force and effect.

In the event a provision of the contract is found illegal, or requires the commission of an act that may be illegal, the question may arise whether the entire contract is nullified or just a part of it. The above clause says that if part of the contract is illegal, the parties want the remainder to be enforced.

## EMPLOYMENT ELIGIBILITY

All of Production Company's obligations herein are expressly conditioned upon Writer's completion, to Production Company's satisfaction, of the I-9 form (Employee Eligibility Verification Form), and upon Writer's submission to Production Company of original documents satisfactory to demonstrate to Production Company Writer's employment eligibility.

Recent changes in the law impose penalties on employers who hire illegal aliens. This provision makes it clear that the employer can rescind the agreement if the employee cannot be employed legally.

## ENTIRE AGREEMENT

This Agreement contains the entire agreement of the parties and all previous agreements, warranties and representations, if any, are merged herein.

Sometimes parties make several agreements concerning the same subject. For instance, the parties may make an oral agreement which is subsequently documented in a written one. If there is a dispute, a question may arise about which agreement should control. An "integration" clause provides that the earlier agreement(s) are merged and incorporated into the later agreement. The provisions of the later agreement will prevail over any inconsistent provisions in the earlier agreement(s).

## ARBITRATION (AFMA)

Arbitration and Jurisdiction. This Agreement shall be interpreted in accordance with the laws of the State of California, applicable to agreements executed and to be wholly performed therein. Any controversy or claim arising out of or in relation to this Agreement or the validity, construction or performance of this Agreement, or the breach thereof, shall be resolved by arbitration in accordance with the rules and procedures of AFMA, as said rules may be amended from time to time with rights of discovery if requested by the arbitrator. Such rules and procedures are incorporated and made a part of this Agreement by reference. If AFMA shall refuse to accept jurisdiction of such dispute, then the parties agree to arbitrate such matter before and in accordance with the rules of the American Arbitration Association under its jurisdiction in Los Angeles before a single arbitrator familiar with entertainment law. The parties shall have the right to engage in pre-hearing discovery in connection with such arbitration proceedings. The parties agree hereto that they will abide by and perform any award rendered in any arbitration conducted pursuant hereto, that any court having jurisdiction thereof may issue a judgment based upon such award and that the prevailing party in such arbitration and/or confirmation proceeding shall be entitled to recover its reasonable attorney's fees and expenses. The arbitration will be held in Los Angeles and any award shall be final, binding and non-appealable. The Parties agree to accept service of process in accordance with the AFMA Rules.

## ARBITRATION (AFMA WITH PERSONAL RIDER)

Arbitration and Jurisdiction. This Agreement shall be interpreted in accordance with the laws of the State of California, applicable to agreements executed and to be wholly performed therein. Any controversy or claim arising out of or in relation to this Agreement or the validity, construction or performance of this Agreement, or the breach thereof, shall be resolved by arbitration in accordance with the rules and procedures of AFMA, as said rules may be amended from time to time with rights of discovery if requested by the arbitrator. Such rules and procedures are incorporated and made a part of this Agreement by reference. If AFMA shall refuse to accept jurisdiction of such dispute, then the parties agree to arbitrate such matter before and in accordance with the rules of the American Arbitration Association under its jurisdiction in Los Angeles before a single arbitrator familiar with entertainment law. The parties shall have the right to engage in pre-hearing discovery in connection with such arbitration proceedings. The parties agree hereto that they will abide by and perform any award rendered in any arbitration conducted pursuant hereto, that any court having jurisdiction thereof may issue a judgment based upon such award and that the prevailing party in such arbitration and/or confirmation proceeding shall be entitled to recover its reasonable attorneys' fees and expenses. The arbitration will be held in Los Angeles and the award shall be final, binding and non-appealable. The Parties agree to accept service of process in accordance with AFMA Rules. The parties further agree that if an arbitration award is awarded against Distributor, and Distributor fails to pay the award after it is confirmed by a court, the AFMA market barring rule will apply against _____ as an officer of Distributor, and _____ agrees to sign the AFMA Rider attached to this agreement (attached as Exhibit B).

## AFMA RIDER

AFMA RIDER TO
    INTERNATIONAL DISTRIBUTION AGREEMENT

Licensor:_____

Distributor:_____

Picture:_____

Territory:_____

Contract Reference code:_____

Date:_____

The Undersigned, in order to induce the Licensor to enter into the "Agreement" with the Distributor for the Picture in the Territory with the date and Contract Reference Code listed above, executes this Rider to the Agreement and agrees and confirms as follows:

### 1. Arbitration

The Undersigned agrees that the Undersigned shall be a party respondent in any arbitration and related court proceedings which may be originally brought or brought in response by the Licensor against the Distributor under the Agreement.  The Undersigned shall have the right to raise in such proceedings only those defenses available to the Distributor.  No failure of Licensor to resort to any right, remedy or security will reduce or discharge the obligations of the Undersigned.  No amendment, renewal, extension, waiver or modification of the Agreement will reduce or discharge the obligation of the Undersigned.  The Undersigned waives all defenses in the nature of suretyship, including without limitation notice of acceptance, protest, notice of protest, dishonor, notice of dishonor and exoneration.  Subject to Paragraph 2 below, any award or judgment rendered as a result of such arbitration against the Distributor shall be deemed to be rendered against the Undersigned.  In the event that Licensor shall obtain an award for damages against Distributor, Licensor shall receive a similar award against the Undersigned.

### 2. Remedies.

Notwithstanding anything in this Rider, in the event of an award against the Distributor, Licensor shall have no remedy against the Undersigned other than the remedy provided under the Market Barring Rule of the American Film Marketing Association.  In that regard, the Undersigned hereby agrees to be bound by the provisions of the Market Barring Rule with respect to the Agreement, as though the Undersigned were the Distributor. Licensor confirms that its only remedy against the Undersigned in the event of breach of the Agreement by and an arbitration award for damages against the Distributor shall be application of the Market Barring Rule, to the same extent that the Market Barring Rule may be applied against the Distributor. Licensor waives any and all other remedies of every kind and nature which it may have with respect to the Undersigned's inducements and agreements herein.

3. Assignment.

This Rider will inure to the benefit of and be fully enforceable by Licensor and its successors and assigns.

4. Governing Law.

This Rider will be governed by and interpreted in accordance with the Agreement, including without limitation the arbitration provisions, governing law, and forum provisions therein stated.

The Undersigned confirms that service of arbitration notice, process, and other papers shall be made to the Undersigned at the address first set forth in the Agreement pertaining to Distributor, unless otherwise set forth below.

WHEREFORE, the Undersigned and the Licensor hereby execute this Rider as of the date first set forth above.

THE "UNDERSIGNED"

Name:_____

## ARBITRATION (AAA, long form)

ARBITRATION: Any controversy or claim arising out of or relating to this agreement or any breach thereof shall be settled by arbitration in accordance with the Rules of the American Arbitration Association; The parties select expedited arbitration using one arbitrator, to be a disinterested attorney specializing in entertainment law, as the sole forum for the resolution of any dispute between them. The venue for arbitration shall be Los Angeles, California. The arbitrator may make any interim order, decision, determinations, or award he deems necessary to preserve the status quo until he is able to render a final order, decision, determination or award. The determination of the arbitrator in such proceeding shall be final, binding and non-appealable. Judgment upon the award rendered by the arbitrator may be entered in any court having jurisdiction thereof. The prevailing party shall be entitled to reimbursement for costs and reasonable attorney's fees.

## ARBITRATION (AAA, short form)

Any controversy or claim arising out of or relating to this agreement or any breach of it shall be settled by arbitration according to the Rules of the American

Arbitration Association; and judgment upon the award rendered by the arbitrators may be entered in any court having jurisdiction thereof. The prevailing party shall be entitled to reimbursement for costs and reasonable attorneys' fees.

## OPTIONAL ARBITRATION PROVISIONS

The determination of the arbitrator in such proceeding shall be final, binding and non-appealable.

Nothing contained in this clause shall preclude any party from seeking and obtaining any injunctive relief or other provisional remedy available in a court of law.

Savvy filmmakers add arbitration clauses to their contracts. These provisions require that disputes be resolved through binding arbitration, not litigation. Arbitration is a much quicker, more informal and less expensive method of resolving disputes. Conflicts can be settled within a matter of months, rules of evidence don't apply and costs are much less.

It is particularly important to provide for arbitration if the party you are contracting with is wealthier than you. The wealthier party can finance a protracted court battle, which can impoverish the other party, forcing a settlement or dismissal. An arbitration clause levels the playing field.

The arbitration clause should provide that the prevailing party is entitled to reimbursement for costs and reasonable attorneys' fees. Without such a provision, the prevailing party in litigation or arbitration usually cannot recoup these expenses.

Binding arbitration awards are difficult to overturn. The grounds for appeal are quite limited. If the losing party does not voluntarily comply with the arbitration award, the prevailing party can go to court to seek confirmation of the award. Once confirmed, the award is no different from any court judgment. A Judgment Creditor can have the Sheriff seize the Judgment Debtor's assets to satisfy the award.

# CHAPTER 2

# DEPICTION RELEASES

When you buy the right to portray someone in a film or television program you buy a bundle of rights. These rights include protection from suits based on defamation, invasion of privacy and the right to publicity. You may also be buying the cooperation of the subject and his family or heirs. Perhaps you want access to a diary that is not otherwise available to you. The agreement used to purchase these rights is called a depiction release.

Before purchasing depiction rights, one should always consider the possibility of fictionalizing the story. If you change the names of the individuals involved, change the location and make other alterations so that real-life people are not recognizable to the public, you may forego the depiction release. However, if the story's appeal is based on the fact that it is a true story, and you want to be able to use the identities of real people, fictionalization is not a workable alternative.

Of course, a person's right to restrict the use of their name, likeness, and voice has to be balanced against the rights of others (e.g., journalists and filmmakers) under the First Amendment. Suppose a newspaper publisher wants to place a picture of a sports figure in its paper. Is permission required? What if 60 Minutes wants to broadcast an exposé of a corrupt politician? What if Kitty Kelley wants to write a critical biography of Nancy Reagan?

In each of these instances, a person's name and likeness are being used on a "product" sold to consumers. Products such as books, movies and plays, however, are also forms of expression protected by the First Amendment. The First Amendment allows journalists and writers to write freely about others without their consent. Otherwise, subjects could prevent any critical reporting of their activities. When one person's right of publicity conflicts with another person's rights under the First Amendment, the First Amendment is often, but not always, considered the dominant right.

When a use is newsworthy, or the use is in the context of a documentary, biography, or parody, the First Amendment will usually protect the producer. In Hicks v. Casablanca Records,[1] Casablanca Records made a movie called "Agatha" about the mystery writer Agatha Christie. The film portrayed her as an emotionally unstable criminal. An heir brought suit alleging infringement of Christie's right of publicity. The court held that Casablanca's rights under the First Amendment were paramount to the estate's rights. The court reasoned that the First Amendment outweighed the right of publicity because the subject was a public figure, and the events portrayed were obviously fictitious.

In negotiating for life-story rights, there are a number of important issues that need to be resolved. At the outset, the parties must determine the extent of the rights granted. Does the grant include remakes, sequels, television series, merchandising, novelization, live-stage rights and radio rights? Are the rights worldwide? Buyers will usually want as broad a grant as possible. The seller may want to retain certain rights.

The buyer should also think about other releases that may be necessary. Are releases needed from the subject's spouse, children, friends, etc.? Will these people consent to be portrayed? Will the subject ask his friends and relatives to cooperate? Can some or all of these secondary characters be fictionalized? If the producer is planning to tell the story of the domestic life of a mother, it may not make any sense to purchase her rights without obtaining similar rights from her immediate family.

The purchase of life-story rights can be structured as either an option/purchase or an outright sale, perhaps with a reversion clause. A reversion clause provides that if the buyer does not exploit the rights within a certain number of years (i.e., the movie is not made), then all rights revert to the seller (subject). This provision protects the subject if he has sold rights to his life story to a producer who is unable to produce the project. With a reversion clause, the subject eventually regains these rights and can later sell or option them to someone else.

Subjects are often paid a fixed fee for a depiction release. A producer could also give the subject points (percentage of net profits), consulting fees, and/or bonuses to be paid when the film is exploited in ancillary markets.

An important part of any depiction agreement is the "Warranties and Representations" clause. A warranty is a promise. The buyer will want the seller to promise never to sue for invasion of publicity, privacy or damage to reputation (defamation). The warranties must cover all 50 states and all conceivable situations. No one wants to buy a lawsuit.

Typically, the buyer has the right to embellish, fictionalize, dramatize and adapt the life story in any way he chooses. This is a frequent sticking point in negotiations. The subject is delighted to have her story told, but when presented with a depiction release, she becomes concerned. She may ask, "This document says you can change my story any way you like and I can't sue for defamation. How do I know you won't portray me as a criminal?" The subject may demand script approval.

---

[1] Hicks v. Casablanca Records, 464 F. Supp. 426 (S.D.N.Y. 1978).

Can a producer give script approval? No sane producer would. No producer is going to expend a lot of time and money developing a script only to find that the subject has changed his mind or is unreasonably withholding approval.

If the subject doesn't trust the producer, are any compromises possible? Yes. The subject could have approval over the treatment or selection of the writer. Perhaps the subject will figure that if he approves only a prestigious writer, his portrayal will be acceptable.

Alternatively, the producer could offer to make the subject a creative or technical consultant to the production. "You'll be right there by the side of the director," says the producer, "giving him advice and suggestions to ensure that everything is authentic." The producer may not mention that the director doesn't want the subject on the set and is not required to follow the subject's suggestions.

Another possible compromise could limit the subject matter and period portrayed. Perhaps the subject is concerned that an embarrassing incident in his life not be re-enacted in Panavision. The release could say that certain incidents, (e.g., a divorce), are not included in the release. Or the release could cover limited periods of the subject's life (e.g., only those incidents that occurred before 1947).

Finally, the subject might have the right to decide screen notice. He could decide if the film will be billed as a true story or a dramatized account. Alternatively, he could decide whether real names will be given to the characters.

# DEPICTION RELEASE
# GRANT WITH REVERSION FORMAT

## Consent And Release

To: _____

I understand that you desire to use all or parts of the events of my life in order to have one or more teleplays or screenplays written, and to produce, distribute, exhibit and exploit one or more television programs and/or motion pictures of any length in any media now known or hereafter devised and sound recordings in any media now known or hereafter devised. I have agreed to grant you certain rights in that connection. This Consent and Release confirms our agreement as follows:

**1. CONSIDERATION; GRANT OF RIGHTS:** In consideration of your efforts to produce my story, payment to me of $_____ upon the beginning of principal photography of a full-length Theatrical Motion Picture, and/or $_____ upon the beginning of production of a television movie, and/or $_____ upon the beginning of production of a pilot program and a royalty of $_____ for each episode thereafter, and for other valuable consideration, with full knowledge I hereby grant you, perpetually and irrevocably, the unconditional and exclusive right throughout the world to use, simulate and portray my name, likeness, voice, personality, personal identification and personal experiences, incidents, situations and events which heretofore occurred or hereafter occur (in whole or in part) based upon or taken from my life or otherwise in and in connection with motion pictures, sound recordings, publications and any other media of any nature at all, whether now known or hereafter devised. Without limiting the generality of the foregoing, it is understood and agreed that said exclusive right includes theatrical, television, dramatic stage, radio, sound recording, music, publishing, commercial tie-up, merchandising, advertising and publicity rights in all media of every nature whatsoever, whether now known or hereafter devised. I reserve no rights with respect to such uses. (All said rights are after this called the "Granted Rights"). It is further understood and agreed that the Granted Rights may be used in any manner and by any means, whether now known or unknown, and either factually or with such fictionalization, portrayal, impersonation, simulation and/or imitation or other modification as you, your successors and assigns, determine in your sole discretion. I further acknowledge that I am to receive no further payment with respect to any matter referred to herein. Any and all of the Granted Rights shall be freely assignable by you.

**2. PAYMENT OF CONSIDERATION; REVERSION OF RIGHTS:** I understand that you shall make the payments mentioned in paragraph 1 only if you begin production of a feature film or television movie or television pilot. In the event that you do not begin such a production within _____ years of the date this agreement was executed, all rights granted by me under this agreement shall revert to me. I understand that if you do begin production within _____ years of the date this agreement was executed, all rights granted by me under this agreement shall be perpetual.

**3. RELEASE:** I agree hereby to release and discharge you, your employees, agents, licensees, successors and assigns from any and all claims, demands or causes of actions that I may now have or may hereafter have for libel, defamation, invasion of privacy or right of publicity, infringement of copyright or violation of any other right arising out of or relating to any utilization of the Granted Rights or based upon any failure or omission to make use thereof.

**4. NAME - PSEUDONYM:** You have informed me and I agree that in exercising the Granted Rights, you, if you so elect, may refrain from using my real name and may use a pseudonym which will be dissimilar to my real name, however, such agreement does not preclude you from the use of my real name should you in your sole discretion elect and that in connection with it I shall have no claim arising out of the so-called right of privacy and/or right of publicity.

**5. FURTHER DOCUMENTS:** I agree to execute such further documents and instruments as you may reasonably request to effectuate the terms and intentions of this Consent and Release, and in the event I fail or am unable to execute any such documents or instruments, I hereby appoint you as my irrevocable attorney-in- fact to execute any such documents and instruments, if said documents and instruments shall not be inconsistent with the terms and conditions of this Consent and Release. Your rights under this Clause constitute a power coupled with an interest and are irrevocable.

**6. REMEDIES:** No breach of this Consent and Release shall entitle me to terminate or rescind the rights granted to you herein, and I hereby waive the right, in the event of any such breach, to equitable relief or to enjoin, restrain or interfere with the production, distribution, exploitation, exhibition or use of any of the Granted Rights granted, it being my understanding that my sole remedy shall be the right to recover damages with respect to any such breach.

**7. PUBLIC DOMAIN MATERIAL:** Nothing in this Consent and Release shall ever be construed to restrict, diminish or impair the rights of either you or me to use freely, in any work or media, any story, idea, pilot, theme, sequence, scene, episode, incident, name, characterization or dialogue which may be in the public domain from whatever source derived.

**8. ENTIRE UNDERSTANDING:** This Consent and Release expresses the entire understanding between you and me, and I agree that no oral understandings have been made with regard thereto. This Consent and Release may be amended only by written instrument signed by you and me. I acknowledge that in granting the Granted Rights I have not been induced to do so by any representations or assurances, whether written or oral, by you or your representatives concerning the manner in which the Granted Rights may be exercised and I agree that you are under no obligation to exercise any of the Granted Rights and agree I have not received any promises or inducements other than as herein set forth. The provisions hereof shall be binding upon me and my heirs, executors, administrators and successors. I acknowledge that you have explained to me that this Consent and Release has been prepared by your attorney and that you have recommended to me that I consult with my attorney concerning this Consent and Release. This Consent and Release shall be construed according to the laws of the State of California applicable to agreements which are fully signed and performed within the State of California and I hereby waive any rights I may have, known or unknown, pursuant to Section 1542 of the California Civil code which provides:

> "A general release does not extend to claims which the creditor does not know or suspect to exist in his favor at the time of executing the release, which if known by him must have materially affected his settlement with the debtor."

In witness hereof and in full understanding of the foregoing, I have signed this Consent and Release on this _____.

_____
(Signature)

_____
(Name, please print)

_____
(Address)

AGREED:

_____

by:_____ President
Production Company

# DEPICTION RELEASE, OPTION PURCHASE FORMAT
## (Deal Memo)

_____
Date

_____
Subject

_____
Address

_____
City, State, Zip

Dear _____:

It was a pleasure speaking to you recently. As I mentioned, I am interested in producing a television program or feature film about your life story.

This letter is intended to set forth the basic terms of our agreement regarding acquisition of the exclusive right and option to purchase all motion picture, television and allied rights in connection with your life story. Please feel free to consult an entertainment attorney or an agent before signing this document.

Our agreement is as follows:

1) In consideration of the mutual promises contained herein, _____ ($_____) and other valuable consideration, you grant my company _____, the exclusive and irrevocable right to option the motion picture, television and all allied, ancillary and subsidiary rights for the period of one year from the date of the signing of this agreement. _____ shall have the right to extend the initial option period for an additional year by sending notice to you prior to the expiration of the initial period, along with the payment of _____ ($_____) which sum shall be _____ against the full purchase price.

2) _____ promises to use its best efforts to produce a television program or feature film about your life story, and is acting in reliance upon your promises in this agreement.

3) If the option is exercised, _____ shall compensate you as full and final consideration for all rights conveyed as follows.

a) Television Movie-of-the-week or Mini-Series: A sum of _____ for a motion picture made for television based on the material.

b) Theatrical Motion Picture: A sum of _____ for a theatrical motion picture based on the material.

c) Television Series: A sum of _____ for the pilot episode and the sum of _____ for each episode after that.

Unless otherwise stated, all of the consideration described in this paragraph 3 shall be payable upon completion of principal photography.

4) Consulting Services: At my request, you agree to serve as a creative consultant in connection with any production made under this agreement at the option

of the producer. You shall receive _____ ($_____) per week for each week your services are required, not to exceed four weeks unless both parties agree otherwise. If you are asked to travel more than fifty miles from your home, _____ shall furnish you with round-trip transportation and accommodations. Prior to the time that the option is exercised, at _____ request you shall disclose, without compensation, any information in your possession or under your control relating to your life story, including newspaper and magazine clippings, photographs, transcripts and notes, and you will consult with any writer hired by _____, and share with him your observations, recollections, opinions and experiences concerning events and activities in your life story.

5) If the option is exercised, _____ will obtain the perpetual, exclusive and irrevocable worldwide right to depict you, whether wholly or partially factual or fictional, and to use your name or likeness and voice, and biography in connection with the material and any production and the advertising and exploitation thereof in any and all media. While it is _____'s intention to portray your story as factually as possible, _____ shall have the right to include such actual or fictional events, scenes, situations and dialogue s it may consider desirable or necessary in _____'s sole discretion.

6) You agree to use your best efforts to obtain for _____ at no additional cost, those releases _____ deems necessary from individuals who are a part of your life story or depicted in any information or materials you may supply _____. It is understood that you will not be expected to violate any confidences arising from any attorney-client relationship.

7) You understand that _____ shall not be obligated under this agreement to exercise any of its right or to initiate production.

8) _____ may sell, assign and/or license any of its rights under this agreement. You agree to execute any other assignments or other instruments necessary or expedient to carry out and effectuate the purposes and intent of this agreement. You agree to execute a complete long-form agreement with the customary language covering grants of biographical rights and a full release which will waive any claims or actions you may have against Producer arising from the exercise of any of its rights under this agreement.

13) This agreement shall be governed and controlled by the laws of the State of _____. This agreement constitutes the entire agreement between the parties and cannot be modified except in writing. Neither of the parties have made any promises or warranties not set forth herein.

    Sincerely,

_____
Production Company


AGREED TO AND ACCEPTED

_____
Subject

DATE: _____

# DEPICTION RELEASE
## DOCUMENTARY SHORT FORM

## Motion Picture and Television Release

I hereby irrevocably agree and consent that you _____
(Production Company Name), and your assigns, may use all or part of your videotaped or filmed interview of me for your documentary program about
_____.

You have the right to use my picture, silhouette and other reproductions of my likeness and voice in connection with any motion picture or television program in which this interview may be incorporated, and in any advertising material promoting it.

You may edit my appearance as you see fit.

You shall have all right, title and interest in any and all results and proceeds from said use or appearance.

The rights granted you are perpetual, worldwide, and include the use of this interview in any medium (all or part of the program may be shown), including broadcast and cable television, and videocassettes.

This consent is given as an inducement for you to interview me and I understand you will incur substantial expense in reliance thereof.

You are not obliged to make any use of this interview or exercise any of the rights granted you by this release.

I have read and understand the meaning of this release.


_____          _____
Signature                    Date


_____          _____
Print Name                   Phone

## FILM CLIPS

A film clip license is often used when a producer wants to incorporate some existing footage into a new production. This pre-existing footage may be purchased from an individual or from a stock footage house that is in the business of selling motion picture clips. A producer may find that it is more economical to purchase ten seconds of an airplane taking off, then to send a film crew to the airport and shoot original footage. Certain footage can be difficult or impossible to create. For instance, if a filmmaker wanted to incorporate 30 seconds of John F. Kennedy speaking, he would have to either license such footage or hire actors and try to re-create the scene.

The major studios often jealously guard their libraries of old films and may refuse to license footage from them. Broadcast networks may be willing to license old news footage but the price can be substantial. The networks may not own rights to the dramatic programs they broadcast; you may need to contact the producer of the program to secure the necessary rights.

Some footage is available for free. The National Archives in Washington D.C. has an extensive collection of public domain footage—mostly government funded films—that is available for the asking. The only cost is the expense of having a copy of the footage duplicated.

The purchaser of footage must be careful to ensure that all the necessary rights are being acquired from the seller. A motion picture may be based on a copyrighted book, and it could incorporate music, special effects, animation, stock footage and works of art. These underlying works were probably only licensed for a one-time use in the original feature film. Thus, the seller of stock footage may not have the right to make a new use of any underlying works.

If the purchaser cannot buy all the needed rights from the stock footage seller, then the purchaser can attempt to negotiate for these rights with the owner of the underlying material. The purchaser could, for example, secure his own license to make new use of the music in the clip. Alternatively, the purchaser could remove the music from the clip.

Movie studios may only be willing to license film clips on a quitclaim basis (i.e., without any warranties as to ownership of the various rights needed). It can be an arduous task for the producer to identify all rights owners and to license the appropriate rights. This may prove impossible if the film clip owner will not reveal the contents of its contracts, or if the contracts have been lost or destroyed.

If the film is based on another work, such as a book, the right to use the book may have expired unbeknownst to the film owner. Under federal copyright law, prior to 1978, a copyright lasted twenty-eight years and could be renewed for an additional twenty-eight years.[2] If the author of a book licensed movie rights to a studio, and if he died before the second copyright term began, his estate would own the copyright to the second term.[3] The studio would not own such rights,

---

[2] The Copyright Act of 1909, 35 Stat. 1075, 17 U.S.C. § 1 et seq. (1976 ed.).

[3] Assuming the estate renewed the copyright.

even if its contract with the author purported to transfer such rights. This is the issue discussed in the "Rear Window" case.[4]

The "Rear Window" case is of concern to producers because it may limit use of copyrighted material they license. If a producer incorporates work created before 1978, which is still in its first twenty-eight year copyright term, the producer may find that rights to the work can end abruptly if the author dies and his estate refuses to relicense it. The estate may refuse permission to use the work even if the author agreed to assign the second term to the producer.[5]

Another potential problem arises when distribution rights to a film clip are shared by several parties, as when a studio owns domestic rights and the foreign rights have been sold to other distributors. Can the owner of such foreign distribution rights prevent a producer from distributing a program with the clip in foreign territories? The answer is unclear.

An obstacle may arise when a producer wants to incorporate footage of a crowd scene. While filming a person in a public place is usually not an invasion of privacy,[6] incorporation of a recognizable person's identity in a film may be an infringement of their right of publicity.

Whether a use is infringing depends upon whether the image is used in a commercial context, such as in an entertainment program, or in a newsworthy context, such as in a documentary program.[7] The latter use is protected under the First Amendment. Thus, producers should avoid incorporating a person's image in a purely commercial program, or in advertising for such a program, unless a release has been obtained.

When a producer wants to license a motion picture clip portraying an actor, the producer should contact the Screen Actor's Guild (SAG) or the American Federation for Radio and Television Artists (AFTRA) to seek permission to use the actor's image. If the performance was first recorded on film, contact SAG; if the performance was first recorded on videotape, contact AFTRA.

The unions will supply the name of the actor's agent who can then be contacted to obtain permission to use the clip. When an actor's name is unknown, it may be difficult to match his or her image with the names listed in the credits. Moreover, if an actor is not a Guild member, or is deceased, it may be difficult to locate the holder of the rights.

---

[4] Stewart v. Abend, 495 U.S. 207, 219 (1990).

[5] There are some limitations on termination of derivative rights. See 17 U.S.C. § 304(c) (1994).

[6] Note that publication of a photograph of a person whose underwear was exposed in public was held an invasion of privacy. Daily Times Democrat v. Graham, 162 So.2d 474 (1964).

[7] See, e.g., Finger v. Omni Publications Intern, 566 N.E.2d 141 (N.Y. 1990).

# FILM CLIP LICENSE

This agreement (hereinafter referred to as the "Agreement") is entered into as of _____ by and between _____ (the "Production Company") and _____ (the "Licensor") regarding the use of a film clip from the motion picture "_____" (the "Film Clip"), by _____ (Distributor), released domestically in _____ (Release Year).

**1. GRANT OF LICENSE:** Subject to the provisions set forth in this Agreement and to the performance of all of the obligations by the Licensor to be performed hereunder, the Licensor hereby grants to the Production Company a non-exclusive license ("License") to use the Film Clip described in Exhibit "A" (attached hereto and incorporated herein) for the term, purpose, payment and territory specified. In connection therewith, the Licensor agrees to make the Film Clip available to the Production Company at no expense to the Licensor for use by the Production Company subject to the terms and conditions set forth in this Agreement below.

**2. LICENSOR'S REPRESENTATIONS & WARRANTIES:** The Licensor hereby represents and warrants that it is the legal owner of the Film Clip and warrants and represents that it has the right and power to enter into and perform this Agreement and to grant the License herein contained; provided, however, that the Production Company acknowledges that the Licensor makes no representations or warranties with respect to the rights of the Production Company to use any footage which contains the performances of any recognizable actor or actress without first obtaining the written consent of such person or persons.

**3. LIMITED LICENSE:** The Film Clip will be used solely for the term, purpose and territory specified in Exhibit "A", and for no other term, purpose or territory whatsoever. The Production Company will not make or permit the making of any reproduction of or from the Film Clip whatsoever, in whole or in part, except in connection with the purpose herein specified. The Production Company shall have no right to edit or otherwise alter the Film Clip or any portion thereof. The Production Company does not hereby gain a license or have the right to use the Film Clip or the right to license others to use the Film Clip to advertise or promote the Production Company or the Production Company's film which incorporates the Film Clip.

**4. COMPLIMENTARY COPIES OF THE FILM:** The Production Company hereby agrees to provide to the Licensor a print of the Production Company's film which incorporates the Film Clip for the purpose of verification of the Film Clip used. To the extent that the Licensor has provided the Production Company with physical materials of any sort, the Production Company shall return such physical materials to the Licensor within sixty (60) days of the domestic theatrical release of the film or the commercial exploitation of the film in any media or market. Concurrently therewith, the Production Company shall certify to the Licensor in writing, how many copies of such physical materials, if any, were made by the Production Company, and return all such copies to the Licensor or destroy the same and furnish to the Licensor a signed affidavit of destruction.

**5. AUTHORIZATIONS, CONSENTS & RELEASES:** The Production Company shall obtain all required written authorizations, consents and releases, in form and substance satisfactory to the Licensor, necessary for the use of the Film Clip hereunder including, without limitation, consents from those who appear recognizably in the Film Clip and those the results and proceeds of whose services are utilized in the Film Clip, as well as consents from unions and guilds including, if applicable and without limitation, the American Federation of Television and Radio Artists, the Screen Actors Guild, the Writers Guild of America and the Directors Guild of America, to the extent required under applicable collective bargaining agreements. If and to the extent required, the Production Company shall also obtain music synchronization agreements or licenses from the owners of the music and consents from those performing music in the Film Clip (including musicians), if any.

**6. MUSIC LICENSES:** It is also expressly understood and agreed that the Production Company shall not broadcast or cause to be broadcast any music contained in the Film Clip unless each local station, system or entity broadcasting the same shall have appropriate licenses therefor from ASCAP, BMI, SESAC or such other performing rights society having the right to license the performance and broadcast of such music, or the publisher of such music.

**7. COPIES TO LICENSOR:** The Production Company hereby agrees to deliver to the Licensor copies of all authorizations, consents, releases and licenses required to be obtained under clauses 5 and 6 above.

**8. RESERVATION OF RIGHTS:** Notwithstanding the limited license granted hereby, the Licensor reserves all of the Licensor's other rights in the Film Clip and the motion picture from which it came. The Licensor shall at all times, anywhere in the world and whether or not in conflict or competition with the Production Company, have the right to use or authorize others to use the Film Clip in any way the Licensor may choose.

**9. CREDIT:** The Production Company agrees that there shall be included in any use of the Film Clip a credit as specified and provided in Exhibit "A".

**10. REPRESENTATIONS & WARRANTIES:**

(a) The Production Company represents and warrants that the motion picture incorporating the Film Clip will have the notice required for copyright protection under the United States Copyright Act and in accordance with the requirements of the Berne and Universal Copyright treaties. Any copyright in the motion picture in which the Film Clip is used shall be held in trust for the Licensor and/or the copyright proprietor of the motion picture from which the Film Clip was taken, if other than the Licensor, to the extent that such Film Clip is used in such motion picture.

(b) The Production Company represents and warrants that nothing contained in the context in which the Film Clip is used will be in any way derogatory to the motion picture from which the Film Clip was taken, any person connected with the production thereof or depicted therein, the Licensor and/or the literary material upon which the Film Clip was based. Furthermore, the Film Clip will not be used in any way so as to constitute and express or implied endorsement of any product or service by, or a commercial tie-up involving, anyone associated with the motion picture from which the Film Clip was derived.

**11. INDEMNIFICATION:** The Production Company hereby agrees to indemnify, defend and hold the Licensor, its parent, affiliates, subsidiaries, agents, representatives and associates, and the officers, directors and employees of each of them harmless from and against all losses, costs, damages, judgments, liabilities and expenses (including, without limitation, attorneys' fees and any payments that may be due any music publisher, musician, writer, director, actor, union, guild or other party) arising from any claim whatsoever and whenever brought, which may be brought based directly or indirectly upon the Production Company's use of the Film Clip.

**12. EQUITABLE RELIEF:** The Production Company understands that a breach by the Production Company of any of its representations, warranties or undertakings hereunder may cause the Licensor damage which could not readily be remedied by an action at law and might, in addition, constitute an infringement of the Licensor's copyright. Any such breach would, therefore, entitle the Licensor to equitable remedies, costs and attorneys' fees in addition to any other rights provided for herein or by law.

**13. TERMINATION OF LICENSE:**

(a) The Production Company hereby agrees that upon its failure to comply with any of the foregoing terms and conditions, the License given the Production Company hereunder shall be automatically terminated and shall be deemed null and void relating back to the creation of this Agreement.

(b) The Production Company also agrees that the Licensor shall have the right to terminate this Agreement and withdraw the authorization it has granted hereby in the event any claim by a guild or other legal entity is submitted to the Licensor based upon the rights granted to the Production Company under this Agreement.

**14. MISCELLANEOUS PROVISIONS:**

(a) This Agreement contains the full and complete understanding and agreement between the parties with respect to the within subject matter, and supersedes all other agreements between the parties, whether written or oral, relating thereto, and may not be modified or amended except by written instrument executed by both of the parties hereto.

(b) A waiver by either party of any of the terms and conditions of this Agreement in any instance shall not be deemed or construed to be a waiver of such term or condition for the future or of any subsequent breach thereof.

(c) The parties agree that in the event of any dispute arising hereunder, such dispute shall be governed under the laws of the state of California. The parties further agree to be subject to the jurisdiction thereof.

(d) This Agreement shall not be binding on the parties until accepted by both parties and executed by a duly authorized officer of each such party. No additions, amendments or modifications to this Agreement shall be effective until accepted in a similar manner.

This Agreement is executed at _____ (Agreement City), _____, (Agreement State) as of the date first above written.

PRODUCTION COMPANY

(Its President)


LICENSOR

_____

Exhibit "A"


DESCRIPTION OF THE FILM CLIP:  That certain _____ (Film Clip Length) second segment of film from the motion picture "_____" produced by _____ (Second Film Producer Name) and released in _____ (Second Film Release Year) by _____ (Second Release Company) and consisting of the scene located approximately _____ minutes into the film in which the film's star, _____ (Scene Description), including the music, lyrics and all other audio content.

TERM:  Perpetuity.

PURPOSE:  Said Film Clip will be incorporated into the Motion Picture entitled "_____" produced by _____ (Production Company Name) and based on the screenplay written by _____ (Screenwriter Name) and starring _____ (Film's Star) which is intended to be exploited in all markets and media worldwide in perpetuity.

CREDIT:  An end title credit of a similar size and type of other similar end title credits as determined by the Production Company and substantially in the following form shall be accorded to the Licensor:

"_____" (Film Clip Film Name) film clip courtesy of _____ (Licensor Name).


LICENSE FEE:  $_____

# STILL PHOTOS

A photo release gives the buyer the right to incorporate a still photo in the buyer's motion picture. The release presented here is designed to give the producer the right to use a photo of the person giving the release. Care should be taken to ensure that the subject of the photo owns the copyright to it. In many instances, the photographer, or his employer, may own the copyright to the photo. If this is the case, then the producer needs to obtain a depiction release from the subject, and a release or license from the owner of photo.

Photography is copyrightable and the same of copyright, trademark, character, and tort liability that arise with the use of a motion picture clip will apply here as well. Likewise, copyright defenses predicated on fair use or the First Amendment can be invoked.

It can be especially difficult to determine whether a photograph is copyrighted, and to determine the identity of its owner. Many photographs are not registered with the Copyright Office. Even if registered, a search can be tiresome since a photograph may be untitled, or the title may not describe the image.

Some photographs are clearly in the public domain, such as those in the National Archives in Washington, D.C. For other photographs, the owner should be asked to warrant that he has all rights to a particular photograph, including releases from any identifiable persons in the photographs. Producers should ask that the photograph owner indemnify the producer, should a claim arise from a third party.

Keep in mind that while photographers may own the copyright to their photos, they may not have releases from their subjects granting the photographer the right to use the subject's image in a motion picture.

Permissions to use certain photographs may be obtained by contacting the Graphic Artists Guild or the American Society of Media Photographers.

# STILL PHOTO RELEASE

Subject: _____

Fee: $_____

Subject hereby grants to _____ ("Company") the exclusive right to use the photograph(s) depicting subject listed in Exhibit A, attached hereto, for inclusion in the motion picture _____ and any ancillary use or derivative works, and for all merchandising purposes. Subject acknowledges that the depiction of him in the Photo may be duplicated and distributed in any and all manner and media throughout the world in perpetuity.

Subject grants Company the exclusive right, license and privilege to utilize the names, characters, artist's portrayal of characters, likeness, and visual representations in the Photo in connection with the manufacture, advertising, distribution and sale of any motion pictures, articles or products. Such granted rights include the unconditional and exclusive right throughout the world to use, simulate and portray subject's likeness, voice, personality, personal identification and personal experiences, incidents, situations and events which heretofore occurred or hereafter occur (in whole or in part) in any and all other media of any nature whatsoever, whether now known or hereafter devised. Subject agrees that Company may elect to refrain from using subject's real name and may use a pseudonym.

Subject hereby releases and discharges Company, its employees, agents, licensees, successors and assigns from any and all claims, demands or causes of actions that it may have or may from now on for libel, defamation, invasion of privacy or right of publicity, infringement of copyright or trademark, or violation of any other right arising out of or relating to any utilization of the rights granted under this agreement.

Subject warrants and represents that Subject possesses all rights necessary for the grant of this license, and will indemnify and hold Company, its licensees and assigns, harmless from and against any and all claims, damages, liabilities, costs and expenses arising out of a breach of the foregoing warranty.

Subject agrees that Company shall have the unlimited right to vary, change, alter, modify, add to and/or delete from his depiction in the Photo, and to rearrange and/or transpose his depiction, and to use a portion or portions of his depiction or character together with any other literary, dramatic or other material of any kind.

Subject has not committed or omitted to perform any act by which such rights could or will be encumbered, diminished or impaired; Subject further represents and warrants that no attempt shall be made from now on to encumber, diminish or impair any of the rights granted herein and that all appropriate protection of such rights will continue to be maintained by Subject.

All rights, licenses and privileges herein granted to Company are irrevocable and not subject to rescission, restraint or injunction under any circumstances.

Nothing herein shall be construed to obligate Company to produce, distribute or use any of the rights granted herein.

This agreement shall be construed according to the laws of the State of _____ applicable to agreements which are executed and fully performed within said State.

This agreement contains the entire understanding of the parties relating to the subject matter, and this agreement cannot be changed except by written agreement executed by the party to be bound.

IN WITNESS WHEREOF, the parties hereto have signed this Agreement as of _____, 199__.

_____
(Subject Name)


_____
(Production Company Signer) on behalf of
(Production Company Name)



STATE OF                                  )
                                          ) ss.:
COUNTY OF                                 )


On the _____ day of _____, 199__, before me personally came _____ (Subject Name) to me known and known to be the individual described in and who executed the foregoing instrument, and he did duly acknowledge to me that he executed the same.


_____
Notary Public

# ARTWORK RELEASE

If artwork is incorporated in a motion picture, a license may be needed. Pictorial, graphic, and sculptural works of art are copyrightable,[8] and displaying them in a motion picture without permission could be an infringement.

Ownership of an item of art work does not necessarily include ownership of its copyright. Thus, the owner of the physical item may have the right to sell that item, but does not necessarily have the right to reproduce it. The latter right is part of the copyright. California law provides that when a work of art is sold, the right to reproduce it is reserved to the artist, unless that right is transferred in writing and the writing specifically refers to the right of reproduction.[9]

Suppose a piece of sculpture appears momentarily in the background of a scene. Is permission of the copyright owner necessary? Probably not. The maker of school room charts and wall decorations that appeared in the background as scenery in a "Barney and Sons" videotape recently sued for copyright infringement.[10] The charts and decorations appeared only fleetingly and were often obscured by the actors. The court refused to issue an injunction against the producers of the videotape on the grounds that the use was so minimal that it was not infringing. The fact that the video was educational in nature was an important factor in finding a fair use. If a producer features art work in the foreground, however, a release should be obtained.

When Congress passed the Visual Artists Rights Act of 1990,[11] the United States expressly recognized certain moral rights that artists have in works of visual art such as paintings, drawings, sculpture, and still photographs. Moral rights include the Right of Paternity, which is the right of an author to claim authorship to her work and prevent the use of her name on works she did not create, and the Right of Integrity, which prevents others from distorting or mutilating her work. A producer who incorporates art work in a program could be liable if the work is distorted, which may occur if the work is digitized and metamorphosed into a new form.

Moral rights differ from copyright. Even when an artist sells the copyright to his work, his moral rights may prevent others from removing the artist's name or modifying his work. While the United States does not recognize moral rights except as pertaining to fine art, many of the moral rights granted artists in other countries are protected in the United States as violation of our unfair competition and defamation laws. These laws have been applied to motion pictures and other works of authorship.

---

[8] 17 U.S.C. § 102a(5) (1982).

[9] Cal. Civil Code § 982(c) (1994). See Playboy Enterprises, Inc. v. Dumas, 831 F. Supp. 295 (S.D.N.Y. 1993).

[10] Frank Schaffer Publications, Inc. v. The Lyons Partnership, L.P., Civil Action No. CV 93 3614R (C.D. Cal. 1993).

[11] 17 U.S.C. § 106A (Supp. V 1993).

# ARTWORK RELEASE

For good and valuable consideration herein acknowledged as received, the undersigned, being the legal owner of, or having the right to permit the taking and use of motion picture depiction of certain artwork described as _____ (Artwork) does grant to _____ ("Producer"), and its legal representatives, agents, and assigns the full rights to incorporate images of said artwork in the motion picture tentatively titled: "_____." Producer shall solely own the copyright in the aforesaid motion picture, and any advertising or promotional materials for such motion picture. Producer shall have all rights to use said motion picture, including images of the aforementioned artwork, in all media now known or hereinafter devised, and in all territories worldwide, in perpetuity. The undersigned also consents to the use of images of said artwork in any printed matter and advertising and marketing materials used to promote said motion picture.

The undersigned hereby waives any right that he/she/it may have to inspect or approve the finished motion picture, or the advertising copy or printed matter that may be used in connection therewith, or the use to which it may be applied.

The undersigned hereby releases, discharges, and agrees to hold harmless Producer, its legal representatives, and assigns, and all persons acting under its permission or authority, or those for whom it is acting, from any liability by virtue of any blurring, distortion, alteration, optical illusion, or use in composite form, whether intentional or otherwise, that may occur or be produced in the taking of said motion picture image(s) or in any subsequent processing thereof, as well as any publication thereof, even though it may subject me to ridicule, scandal, reproach, scorn, and indignity.

The undersigned hereby warrants that he/she is of full age and has every right to contract in his/her own name in the above regard. The undersigned states further that he/she has read the above authorization, release, and agreement, prior to its execution, and that he/she is fully familiar with the contents thereof. If the undersigned is signing as an agent or employee of a firm or corporation, the undersigned warrants that he/she is fully authorized to do so. This release shall be binding upon the undersigned and his/her/its heirs, legal representatives, successors, and assigns.

DATE: _____

_____
WITNESS

_____
(Owner Name)

_____
(Owner Address)

_____
(Owner City, State, Zip)

# CHAPTER 3

# LITERARY SUBMISSION AND SALE

## SUBMISSION OF MATERIAL

Rights to literary property, like personal property, can be bought and sold. The buyer will want to make sure that the seller owns what he purports to sell. The seller may want to limit the rights sold.

Nowadays, buyers may not be willing to read a property without a submission release. Such a release makes it more difficult for a writer to successfully pursue a frivolous lawsuit for story theft. A release is usually not requested for submissions from veteran writers and those who submit through agents or attorneys.

# SUBMISSION RELEASE

_____ (Producer/Studio Executive Name)

_____ (Street Address of Producer)

_____ (Producer City State and Zip)

Dear _____:

I am submitting the enclosed material ("said material") to you: _____, an original screenplay. WGA REGISTRATION NO._____. Copyright Registration No._____.

The material is submitted on the following conditions:

1. I acknowledge that because of your position in the entertainment industry you receive numerous unsolicited submissions of ideas, formats, stories, suggestions and the like and that many such submissions received by you are similar to or identical to those developed by you or your employees or otherwise available to you. I agree that I will not be entitled to any compensation because of the use by you of any such similar or identical material.

2. I further understand that you would refuse to accept and evaluate said material in the absence of my acceptance of each and all of the provisions of this agreement. I shall retain all rights to submit this or similar material to persons other than you. I acknowledge that no fiduciary or confidential relationship now exists between you and me, and I further acknowledge that no such relationships are established between you and me by reason of this agreement or by reason of my submission to you of said material.

3. I request that you read and evaluate said material with a view to deciding whether you will undertake to acquire it.

4. I represent and warrant that I am the author of said material, having acquired said material as the employer-for-hire of all writers thereof; that I am the present and sole owner of all right, title and interest in and to said material; that I have the exclusive, unconditional right and authority to submit and/or convey said material to you upon the terms and conditions set forth herein; that no third party is entitled to any payment or other consideration as a condition of the exploitation of said material.

5. I agree to indemnify you from and against any and all claims, expenses, losses, or liabilities (including, without limitation, reasonable attorneys' fees and punitive damages) that may be asserted against you or incurred by you at any time in connection with said material, or any use thereof, including without limitation those arising from any breach of the warranties and promises given by me herein.

6. You may use without any obligation or payment to me any of said material which is not protectable as literary property under the laws of plagiarism, or which a third person would be free to use if the material had not been submitted to him or had not been the subject of any agreement with him, or which is in the public domain. Any of said material which, in accordance with the preceding sentence, you are entitled to use without obligation to me is hereinafter

referred to as "unprotected material." If all or any part of said material does not fall in the category of unprotected material it is hereinafter referred to as "protected material."

7. You agree that if you use or cause to be used any protected material provided it has not been obtained from, or independently created by, another source, you will pay or cause to be paid to me an amount which is comparable to the compensation customarily paid for similar material.

8. I agree to give you written notice by registered mail of any claim arising in connection with said material or arising in connection with this agreement, within 60 calendar days after I acquire knowledge of such claim, or of your breach or failure to perform the provisions of this agreement, or if it be sooner, within 60 calendar days after I acquire knowledge of facts sufficient to put me on notice of any such claim, or breach or failure to perform; my failure to so give you written notice will be deemed an irrevocable waiver of any rights I might otherwise have with respect to such claim, breach or failure to perform. You shall have 60 calendar days after receipt of said notice to attempt to cure any alleged breach or failure to perform prior to the time that I may file a Demand for Arbitration.

9. In the event of any dispute concerning said material or concerning any claim of any kind or nature arising in connection with said material or arising in connection with this agreement, such dispute will be submitted to binding arbitration. Each party hereby waives any and all rights and benefits which he or it may otherwise have or be entitled to under the laws of the State of _____ to litigate any such dispute in court, it being the intention of the parties to arbitrate all such disputes. Either party may commence arbitration proceedings by giving the other party written notice thereof by registered mail and proceeding thereafter in accordance with the rules and procedures of the American Arbitration Association. The arbitration shall be conducted in the County of _____, State of _____ , and shall be governed by and subject to the laws of the State of _____ and the then prevailing rules of the American Arbitration Association. The arbitrators' award shall be final and binding and a judgment upon the award may be enforced by any court of competent jurisdiction.

10. I have retained at least one copy of said material, and I release you from any and all liability for loss or other damage to the copies of said material submitted to you hereunder.

11. Either party to this agreement may assign or license its or their rights hereunder, but such assignment or license shall not relieve such party of its or their obligations hereunder. This agreement shall inure to the benefit of the parties hereto and their heirs, successors, representatives, assigns and licensees, and any such heir, successor, representative, assign or licensee shall be deemed a third party beneficiary under this agreement.

12. I hereby acknowledge and agree that there are no prior or contemporaneous oral agreements in effect between you and me pertaining to said material, or pertaining to any material (including, but not limited to, agreements pertaining to the submission by me of any ideas, formats, plots, characters, or the like). I further agree that no other obligations exist or shall exist or be deemed to exist unless and until a formal written agreement has been prepared and entered into by both you and me, and then your and my rights and obligations shall be only such as are expressed in said formal written agreement.

13. I understand that whenever the word "you" or "your" is used above, it refers to (1) you, (2) any company affiliated with you by way of common stock ownership or otherwise, (3) your subsidiaries, (4) subsidiaries of such affiliated companies, (5) any firm, person or corporation to whom you are leasing production facilities, (6) clients of any subsidiary or affiliated company of yours, and (7) the officers, agents, servants, employees, stockholders, clients, successors and assigns of you, and of all such person, corporations referred to in (1) through (6) hereof. If said material is submitted by more than one person, the word "I" shall be deemed changed to "we," and this agreement will be binding jointly and severally upon all the persons so submitting said material.

14. Should any provision or part of any provision be void or unenforceable, such provision or part thereof shall be deemed omitted, and this agreement with such provision or part thereof omitted shall remain in full force and effect.

15. This agreement shall be governed by the laws of the state of _____ applicable to agreements executed and to be fully performed therein.

16. I have read and understand this agreement and no oral representations of any kind have been made to me and this agreement states our entire understanding with reference to the subject matter hereof. Any modification or waiver of any of the provisions of this agreement must be in writing and signed by both of us.

Sincerely,

_____
(Writer's Name)

_____
(Writer's Street Address)

_____
(Writer's City State and Zip)

_____
(Writer's Phone Number)

ACCEPTED AND AGREED TO:

_____
(Producer/Studio Executive Name)

STATE OF _____)
                                                  ) ss.:
COUNTY OF_____)

On the _____day of _____,19___, before me personally came _____to me known and known to be the individual described in and who executed the foregoing instrument, and he did duly acknowledge to me that he executed the same.

_____
Notary Public

# NON-DISCLOSURE

A non-disclosure agreement serves the opposite purpose of a submission release. Here the discloser (e.g. the writer) seeks protection. The agreement provides that the recipient will keep certain information (i.e. a story or script) confidential. The producer cannot disclose the information to third parties without the writer's permission.

Because of the great many writers trying to break into the business, a fledgling writer may find it difficult to get an established producer or studio executive to read their script with any conditions. A non-disclosure agreement is more likely to be used by a sought-after writer who can demand that his work be kept confidential as a condition for submitting it.

## NON-DISCLOSURE AGREEMENT

This agreement made this _____ day of _____, 19__, by and between, _____, ("Writer"), and _____ ("Producer").

WHEREAS, Writer has written a script ("Submission") for a possible future theatrical or television motion picture production.

WHEREAS, Writer wishes Producer to evaluate said "Submission" for the sole purpose of determining whether said Submission may be further developed into a motion picture ("Project").

NOW, THEREAFTER, in consideration of the premises and mutual covenants herein contained, the parties agree as follows:

1. All information disclosed by Writer to Producer, in writing, whether or not such information is also disclosed orally, that relates or refers, directly or indirectly, to the Submission, including the Submission itself, shall be deemed confidential and shall constitute Confidential Information, and shall include (i) all documents generated by Producer which contain, comment upon, or relate in any way to any Confidential Information received form Writer, and (ii) any written samples of the Submission received from Writer together with any information derived by Producer therefrom.

2. Confidential Information shall not include any information:

(i) That Producer can show by documentary evidence was known to Producer prior to the date of its disclosure to Producer by Writer or

(ii) That becomes publicly known, by publication or otherwise, not due to any unauthorized act or omission of Producer or any other party having an obligation of confidentiality to Writer; or,

(iii) That is subsequently disclosed by Writer to any person, firm or corporation on a non-confidential basis; or

(iv) That Producer can conclusively show by documentary evidence that such information was developed independent of any access to the Confidential Information.

3. Writer discloses the Confidential Information to Producer solely for the purpose of allowing Producer to evaluate the Submission to determine, in its sole discretion, whether the Submission may be further developed into a Project.

4. Producer agrees to accept disclosure of the Confidential Information and to exercise the same degree of care to maintain the Confidential Information secret and confidential as is employed by Producer to preserve and safeguard its own materials and confidential information.

5. The Confidential Information shall remain the property of Writer and shall not be disclosed or revealed by Producer or to anyone else except employees of Producer who have a need to know the information in connection with Producer's evaluation of the Submission, and who have entered into a non-disclosure agreement with Producer under which such employees are required to keep confidential the Confidential Information of Writer, and such employees shall be advised by Producer of the confidential nature of the information and that the information shall be treated accordingly. Producer shall be liable for any improper disclosure of the Confidential Information by its employees.

6. (i) Producer shall notify Writer of any determination Producer may arrive at with respect to the further development of the Submission, provided, however, that, in doing so, Producer shall not directly or indirectly disclose any Confidential Information to any third party, without the consent of Writer.

(ii) If Producer determines that the Submission cannot be further developed into a Project, within _____ months of the receipt of the Submission, Producer shall within five (5) business days after such determination return any and all Confidential Information to Writer, along with all copies or derivatives thereof and all writings generated by Producer in connection with Producer's evaluation of the Submission of the Confidential Information.

7. If Producer determines that the Submission is suitable for further development into a Project, Producer and Writer will attempt to agree on a schedule for development, and compensation to Writer for the Submission.

8. Other than as specifically provided herein, Producer will not use the Confidential Information for any purpose whatsoever other than for the sole purpose permitted in paragraph 3 hereof, unless and until a further executed agreement is first made between the parties setting forth the terms and conditions under which rights to the Submission and the Confidential Information are to be licensed to, or acquired by, Producer.

9. Producer agrees that Producer will not contact any party or parties other than Writer concerning the Confidential Information without prior written authorization from Writer during the term of this agreement.

10. Producer's obligations under paragraphs 3, 4, and 9 of this agreement shall extend from the date of this agreement and shall survive the expiration or termination of this agreement, provided, however, that Producer's obligations under paragraphs 3 and 4 of this agreement shall terminate immediately in the event that Writer shall purposefully disclose the Confidential Information to any other person, firm, or corporation on a non-confidential basis, during the term of this Agreement.

11. Writer hereby expressly warrants that Writer has the full right and authority to disclose the Confidential Information to Producer, and that no prior public non-confidential disclosure of the Confidential Information has been made by Writer nor, to the best of Writer's knowledge, by any other party.

12. Nothing in this agreement shall be deemed a sale or offer for sale of the Submission, and nothing contained herein shall in any way obligate Writer to grant to Producer, a license or any other rights, directly or by implication, estoppel or otherwise to the Confidential Information or the Submission.

13. Subject to paragraph 10 above, this agreement shall terminate _____ years from the date of this agreement, unless extended by mutual agreement of the parties. This agreement may be terminated prior to the expiration of _____ years from the date of this agreement by either Writer or Producer upon thirty (30) days written notice to the other parties of an intention to terminate.

14. This agreement sets forth the entire agreement between the parties and may not be amended or modified, except by a writing signed by all of the parties.

15. This agreement shall be governed by the laws of the State of _____ without regard to the conflict of laws provisions thereof.

16. This agreement may be executed in counterparts.

IN WITNESS WHEREOF, the parties have executed this agreement as of the day and year first above written.

WRITER

PRODUCER

_____

_____
(Writer Name)

(Production Company Signer)


_____
(Title) on behalf of


_____
(Production Company Name)

# OPTION AND LITERARY PURCHASE

A literary acquisition contract is an agreement to acquire all or some rights in a literary property such as a novel or a play. Producers typically use it to obtain screenplays or movie rights to literary works.

Buyers, (e.g., producers) will want owners, (e.g., writers), to warrant that they own all the rights they are selling, free and clear of any other obligations (encumbrances). Sellers will disclose their copyright registration number so that buyers can check the copyright records and review the chain of title to ensure they obtain all the rights they desire.

Each agreement needs to define the extent of the rights being sold. Sometimes, all rights (the entire copyright) are sold. Other times limited rights, on either an exclusive or non-exclusive basis, are licensed.

If movie rights are sold, the buyer typically will have the right to adapt the work into a motion picture and release it in ancillary markets such as home video. The buyer may also obtain sequel and remake rights, although an additional payment may be due if and when these rights are exploited. The buyer is routinely granted the right to excerpt up to 7,500 words from the book for advertising and promotion purposes.

Writers may want to reserve certain rights. A writer who allows adaptation of his novel into film might want to retain publication rights, stage rights, radio rights and the right to use his characters in a new novel (a sequel book). The latter right should be distinguished from sequel motion picture rights which is the right to use the characters in sequel motion pictures.

Another point important to the buyer will be the unlimited right to make changes to the work when adapting it. Paramount Pictures is not going to invest large sums of money to develop a screenplay only to find itself in a vulnerable position later, unable to change a line of dialogue without the author's permission. Suppose the movie is in the midst of production and the author cannot be located? What if the author unreasonably withholds consent? No studio is going to let a writer hold a gun to its head by withholding permission to make changes.

On the other hand, authors frequently complain that studios and directors ruin their work. They are embarrassed when a studio releases a movie inferior to the original work it is based on. Some countries, such as France, grant artists so-called moral rights ("Droit Moral") which may prevent buyers from desecrating or changing an artist's work without his permission. The United States does not expressly recognize the doctrine of moral rights. However, a variety of state and federal laws accomplish much the same result in a more roundabout manner. At any rate, the buyer is going to ask the seller to waive any moral rights the seller may have.

Buyers want sellers to make certain warranties, or promises. For example, the writer will often warrant that the work does not defame or invade anyone's privacy, or infringe on another's copyright. Buyers prefer warranties to be absolute, while writers want the warranties to be based on the best of the writer's knowledge and belief. The difference is this: if the writer unknowingly defames another, he would be liable under an absolute warranty but not necessarily liable under one limited to the best of his knowledge and belief. Thus, if the writer in good faith believed he had not defamed anyone, he wouldn't be liable.

Buyers want writers to stand behind their warranties and indemnify them. When a writer indemnifies a buyer, the writer agrees to reimburse the buyer for any litigation costs and judgment that may be rendered as a result of the writer's breach of warranty.

Of course, an indemnity is only worth as much as the person standing behind it. It would be a waste of time for a studio to seek reimbursement from an impoverished writer.

To protect themselves from potential liability, producers and studios may purchase Errors and Omissions (E & O) insurance. Writers often ask that they be added as an additional named insured on the policy. This may add a few hundred dollars to the cost of the premium but will ensure that the insurance company defends the writer as well as the studio, and bears any litigation expense. A writer purchasing his own policy would pay much more.

Credit is another topic that needs to be addressed. The buyer wants the right to use the name and likeness of the author to promote the picture, although the writer is rarely featured in advertising. As for billing credit, the Writer's Guild agreement will usually determine who receives writing credits (assuming the Writer is in the guild and the production company is a guild signatory). The producer cannot arbitrarily assign credit. In case of a dispute over credits, the Writer's Guild will impanel a group of impartial writers to arbitrate. They will read all the drafts of the script and allocate credit.

The literary purchase agreement will also contain an explicit provision stating that the producer is under no obligation to actually produce a film. The producer wants the right to make a motion picture but not be obliged to make the picture. This prevents the writer from forcing the producer into production.

If the writer has a reversion clause, all rights to the script can revert to him if production is not commenced within a set time, (e.g., five years from the date the movie rights were bought). Thus the writer will regain rights to the property and have a chance to set it up elsewhere.

The acquisition of literary rights can be structured as an outright purchase or as an option/purchase agreement. Buyers typically prefer to take an option on a property to reduce their up-front risk. A party who buys an option on a literary property is obtaining the exclusive right to purchase the movie rights for a certain period into the future.

Suppose you are a producer and you read a wonderful novel written by Alice. You want to make a movie out of this book. You approach Alice and offer to buy the movie rights. She says "Fine, I would like $50,000." You cannot afford to pay $50,000 at this time. Even if you could afford it, an outright purchase would be risky. What if the screenwriter you hire doesn't produce a satisfactory screenplay? What if you cannot arrange production financing? There are many obstacles to getting a movie produced, and if you buy the movie rights and cannot get the movie produced, you have bought something you ultimately don't need.

Another way to structure the deal would be to option the rights instead of buying them. Let's say you offer Alice $5,000 for a one-year option. During that one-year period you have the exclusive right to exercise the option and buy the movie rights. Let's also suppose that the purchase price is $50,000. As a rule of thumb options are often 10% of the full purchase price, but the amount is negotiable. Sometimes sellers are willing to give a "free" option or an option for a nominal sum (e.g., "for ten dollars"). Of course, a seller is not required to give an option for movie rights, and if you are dealing with the author of a best seller, she may insist on an outright sale.

The option period can last for any length of time but it is often a year. The buyer may seek certain rights of renewal, which allow the buyer to extend the option upon payment of an additional sum. Let's suppose that you have taken a one-year option for $5,000, and have a right of renewal to extend the option for a second year for $6,000. The right of renewal must be exercised before the initial option period expires. If the parties agreed to give the buyer a second or third right of renewal, the buyer could extend the option further.

Renewals let the purchaser extend an option without exercising it. Assume Alice sells a producer a one-year option that is about to expire. The producer has commissioned a screenplay which she is pleased with, and she has the interest of an important director. But she doesn't have a star attached to the project and financing is not in place. At this time the producer doesn't want to buy the movie rights for $50,000, but she also doesn't want to lose the right to buy those rights in the future. If she has a right of renewal she can extend the option. Usually buyers don't want to purchase movie rights until the first day of principal photography, when they know for certain that a movie will be produced.

Note that an option gives the buyer the exclusive right to purchase movie rights within the option period. No one else can buy the movie rights during that time. The seller can do nothing that would interfere with the buyer purchasing those rights during the option period.

Once the option expires, however, the writer retains not only the option money but all movie rights as well. Some writers have sold options on the same property repeatedly because earlier options expired without being exercised. Of course, once an option is exercised, the buyer owns the movie rights outright, and the writer can't sell or option what he no longer owns.

The option payments, and any payments for rights of renewals, can be applicable or non-applicable. If the payments are applicable, they count as an advance against the purchase price. If they are non-applicable, they do not apply against the purchase price. For example, if an option was for $5,000 applicable against a purchase price of $50,000, a buyer wanting to exercise the option would pay an additional $45,000. If the $5,000 option was non-applicable, the buyer would pay an additional $50,000 because the $5,000 option payment would not count against the purchase price.

The most important point to remember when taking (purchasing) an option is that you must simultaneously negotiate the terms of the purchase agreement. Usually the option contract is a two- or three-page document with a literary purchase agreement attached as an exhibit. When the option is exercised, the literary purchase agreement automatically kicks in. A buyer who enters an option agreement without negotiating the underlying literary purchase agreement has purchased a WORTHLESS OPTION. All you have bought is the right to haggle with the seller in the future should you choose to buy the movie rights. The seller is under no obligation to sell on the terms you propose.

For example, you purchase an option for $500 for one year but don't work out the terms of the literary purchase agreement. Nine months later you decide to exercise the option and buy the movie rights. You send the writer a check for $10,000. She objects, wanting $20,000. Since the parties have not agreed to this essential term of the sale, the contract is unenforceable. You have a worthless option, and the time and money you spent developing the project may be wasted. The writer now has you over the barrel, and can demand any amount she wants for the rights.

# OPTION AND LITERARY PURCHASE AGREEMENT

THIS AGREEMENT, made and entered into as of _____, by and between _____ (hereinafter "Owner") and _____, (hereinafter "Purchaser").

## 1. OWNER'S REPRESENTATIONS AND WARRANTIES:

(a) Sole Proprietor: Owner represents and warrants to Purchaser that Owner is the sole and exclusive proprietor, throughout the world of the screenplay "_____," that certain original literary material written by Owner (the "Literary Material").

(b) Facts: Owner represents and warrants to Purchaser that the following statements are true and correct in all respects with respect to said Literary Material:

(i) Owner is the sole author of the Literary Material.

(ii) The Literary Material is unpublished and registered under Copyright number _____ in the Office of the United States Register of Copyrights, Washington D.C.

No Motion Picture or dramatic version of the Literary Material, or any part thereof, has been manufactured, produced, presented or authorized; no radio or television development, presentation or program based on the Literary Material, or any part thereof, has been manufactured, produced, presented, broadcast or authorized; and no written or oral agreements or commitments whatsoever with respect to the Literary Material or with respect to any right therein, have heretofore been made or entered into by or on behalf of Owner.

(c) No Infringement or Violation of Third Party Rights: Owner represents and warrants to Purchaser that Owner has not adapted the Literary Material from any other literary, dramatic or other material of any kind, nature or description, nor, excepting for material which is in the public domain, has Owner copied or used in the Literary Material the plot, scenes, sequence or story of any other literary, dramatic or other material; that the Literary Material does not infringe upon any common law or statutory rights in any other literary, dramatic, or other material; that insofar as Owner has knowledge, no material in the Literary Material is libelous or violative of the right of privacy of any person and the full use of the rights in the Literary Material which are covered by the within option would not violate any rights of any person, firm or corporation; and that the Literary Material is not in the public domain in any country in the world where copyright protection is available.

(d) No Impairment of Rights: Owner represents and warrants to Purchaser that Owner is the exclusive proprietor, throughout the world, of the rights in the Literary Material which are covered by the within option; that Owner has not assigned, licensed nor in any manner encumbered, diminished or impaired these rights; that Owner has not committed nor omitted to perform any act by which these rights could or will be encumbered, diminished or impaired; and that there is no outstanding claim or litigation pending against or involving the title, ownership and/or copyright in the Literary Material, or in any part thereof, or in the rights which are covered by the within option. Owner further represents and warrants that no attempt hereafter will be made to encumber, diminish or impair any of the rights herein granted and that all appropriate protections of such rights will continue to be maintained by Owner.

Without limiting any other rights Purchaser may have in the Literary Material, Owner hereby agrees that if there is any claim and/or litigation involving any breach or alleged breach of any such representations and warranties of Owner, the option period granted hereunder and any periods within which Purchaser may, pursuant to the provisions of Clause 3 hereof, extend the option, shall automatically be extended until no claim and/or litigation involving any breach or alleged breach of any such representation and warranties of Owner is outstanding. At any time after the occurrence of such a claim and/or litigation until the expiration of the option period, as extended, Purchaser may, in addition to any other rights and remedies Purchaser may have in the property, rescind this agreement and in such event, notwithstanding anything else to the contrary contained herein, Owner hereby agrees to repay Purchaser any monies paid by Purchaser to Owner hereunder in connection with the Literary Material and any reasonable amounts expended by Purchaser in developing or exploiting the Literary Material. Without limiting the generality of the foregoing, Owner agrees that Owner will not, at any time during the option period, exercise or authorize or permit the exercise by others of any of the rights covered by the option or any of the rights reserved by Owner under the provisions of Exhibit "A" which are not to be exercised or licensed to others during any period of time therein specified.

**2. CONSIDERATION FOR OPTION:** In consideration of the payment to Owner of the sum of _____ ($_____) receipt of which is hereby acknowledged, Owner agrees to and does hereby give and grant to Purchaser the exclusive and irrevocable option to purchase from Owner the rights in the Property as described in Exhibit "A" for the total purchase price specified and payable as provided in Exhibit "A," provided that any sums paid under this Clause 2 or any other provision of this agreement with respect to the option shall be credited against the first sums payable on account of such purchase price. If Purchaser shall fail to exercise this option, then the sums paid to Owner hereunder with respect to the option shall be and remain the sole property of Owner.

**3. OPTION PERIOD:** The within option shall be effective during the period commencing on the date hereof and ending _____ later (the "Initial Option Period"). The Initial Option Period may be extended for an additional _____ by the payment of _____ ($_____) on or before the expiration date specified above (the "Second Option Period").

**4. EXERCISE OF OPTION:**

(a) Notice of Exercise: If Purchaser elects to exercise the within option, Purchaser (at any time during the option period) shall serve upon Owner written notice of the exercise thereof by addressing such notice to Owner at his address as specified in Exhibit "A" and by depositing such notice, so addressed by certified mail, return receipt requested with postage prepaid, in the United States mail. The deposit of such notice in the United States mail as hereinabove specified shall constitute service thereof, and the date of such deposit shall be deemed to be the date of service of such notice.

(b) The purchase price shall be paid to Owner in accordance with Exhibit "A."

(c) The option may be exercised only by notice in writing as aforesaid; no conduct or oral statement by Purchaser or his agents, representatives or employees shall constitute an exercise of the option.

(d) Additional Documents: If Purchaser exercises the within option, Owner, without cost to Purchaser (other than the consideration provided for herein or in Exhibit "A") shall execute, acknowledge and deliver to Purchaser, or shall cause the execution, acknowledgment and delivery to Purchaser of, such further instruments as Purchaser may reasonably require in order to confirm unto Purchaser the rights, licenses, privileges and property which are the subject of the within option. If Owner shall fail to execute and deliver or to cause the execution and delivery to Purchaser of any such instruments, Purchaser is hereby irrevocably granted the power coupled with an interest to execute such instruments and to take such other steps and proceedings as may be necessary in connection therewith in the name and on behalf of Owner and as Owner's attorney-in-fact. Owner shall supply all supporting agreements and documentation requested by Purchaser.

Without limiting the generality of the foregoing, Owner agrees to execute and deliver to Purchaser concurrently herewith Exhibit "B" (Short Form Option Agreement), which instrument shall become effective immediately and may be recorded by Purchaser with the United States Copyright Office as evidence of the option herein granted to Purchaser, and Owner agrees to cause the publisher or publishers of the Property, if any, and any other person, firm or corporation having or claiming any interest in or to the Property, to execute, acknowledge and deliver to Purchaser promptly upon the execution hereof, quitclaims or assignments in form satisfactory to Purchaser, whereby such publisher or other parties quitclaim to Owner all their right, title and interest (or acknowledge and agree that they have no such right, title or interest) in or to any of the rights, licenses, privileges and property agreed to be granted to Purchaser upon the exercise of the option.

**5. EFFECTIVENESS OF EXHIBITS "A," "B" AND "C":** Concurrently with the execution of this agreement Owner has executed Exhibit "A" (Literary Purchase Agreement), Exhibit "B" (Short Form Option Agreement for Recordation) and Exhibit "C" (Assignment of the Copyright), which are undated, and it is agreed that if Purchaser shall exercise the option (but not otherwise) then the signature of Owner to Exhibits "A," "B" and "C" shall be deemed to be effective and these Exhibits shall constitute valid and binding agreements and assignment effective as of the date of exercise of such option, and Purchaser is hereby authorized and empowered to date such instruments accordingly. If Purchaser shall fail to exercise the option, then the signature of Owner to Exhibits "A," "B" and "C" shall be void and of no further force or effect whatever, and Purchaser shall not be deemed to have acquired any rights in or to the Property other than the option hereinabove provided for. If Purchaser exercises the option, Purchaser will execute and deliver to Owner copies of Exhibit "A," dated as of the date of the exercise of the option, and Owner will, if so requested by Purchaser, execute and deliver to Purchaser additional copies of Exhibits "A," "B" and "C." Notwithstanding the failure or omission of either party to execute and/or deliver such additional documents, it is agreed that upon the exercise of the option by Purchaser all rights in and to the Property agreed to be transferred to Purchaser pursuant to the provisions of Exhibit "A" shall be deemed vested in Purchaser, effective as of the date of exercise of the option, which rights shall be irrevocable.

**6. RIGHT TO ENGAGE IN PREPRODUCTION:** Owner acknowledges that Purchaser may during the option period, undertake production and preproduction activities in connection with any of the rights to be acquired hereunder including, without limitation, the preparation and submission of treatments and/or screenplays based on the Property.

**7. RESTRICTIONS:** During the option period, Owner shall not exercise or otherwise utilize any of the rights herein granted to Purchaser and as more particularly described in Exhibit "A" hereof nor the rights reserved to Owner pursuant to Clause 2 (Rights Reserved) of Exhibit "A," nor shall Owner permit the use of nor shall Owner use any other right Owner has reserved in a way that would in any manner or for any purpose unfairly compete with, interfere with or conflict with the full and unrestricted use of the rights herein granted to Purchaser and as described in Exhibit "A."

**8. ASSIGNMENT:** This Option Agreement and the rights granted hereunder may be assigned by Purchaser to any other person, firm or corporation.

**9. OPTION REVERSION:**

(a) If the Purchaser does not timely exercise the option during its original or extended term and timely pay the purchase price, the option shall terminate and all rights in the Literary Material shall immediately revert to the Owner. The Owner shall retain all sums therefore paid. Purchaser shall immediately execute and deliver to Owner any assignments and documents required to effectuate the Reversion. If Purchaser shall fail or be unable to do so, Purchaser hereby grants owner a power coupled with an interest to execute and deliver such documents as Purchaser's attorney-in-fact.

**10. GENDER AND NUMBER:** Terms used herein in the masculine gender include the feminine and neuter gender, and terms used in the singular number include the plural number, if the context may require.

**11. SECTION HEADINGS:** The headings of paragraphs, sections and other subdivisions of this agreement are for convenient reference only. They shall not be used in any way to govern, limit, modify, construe this agreement or any part or provision thereof or otherwise be given any legal effect.

**12. ENTIRE AGREEMENT:** This agreement, including the Exhibits attached hereto, contains the full and complete understanding and agreement between the parties with respect to the within subject matter, and supersedes all other agreements between the parties whether written or oral relating thereto, and may not be modified or amended except by written instrument executed by both of the parties hereto. This agreement shall in all respects be subject to the laws of the State of _____ applicable to agreements executed and wholly performed within such State. All the rights, licenses, privileges and property herein granted to Purchaser are irrevocable and not subject to rescission, restraint, or injunction under any or all circumstances.

**13. ARBITRATION:** This Agreement shall be interpreted in accordance with the laws of the State of _____, applicable to agreements executed and to be wholly performed therein. Any controversy or claim arising out of or in relation to this Agreement or the validity, construction or performance of this Agreement, or the breach thereof, shall be resolved by arbitration in accordance with the rules and procedures of AFMA, as said rules may be amended from time to time with rights of discovery if requested by the arbitrator. Such rules and procedures are incorporated and made a part of this Agreement by reference. If AFMA shall refuse to accept jurisdiction of such dispute, then the parties agree to arbitrate such matter before and in accordance with the rules of the American Arbitration Association under its jurisdiction in _____ before a single arbitrator familiar with entertainment law. The parties shall have the right to engage in pre-hearing discovery in connection with such arbitration proceedings. The parties agree hereto that they will abide by and perform any award rendered in any arbitration conducted pursuant hereto, that any court having jurisdiction thereof may issue a judgment based upon such award and that the prevailing party in such arbitration and/or confirmation proceeding shall be entitled to recover its reasonable attorneys' fees and expenses. The arbitration will be held in _____ and any award shall be final, binding and non-appealable. The Parties agree to accept service of process in accordance with the AFMA Rules.

IN WITNESS WHEREOF, the parties hereto have signed this Option Agreement as of the day and year first hereinabove written.

OWNER:


_____

PURCHASER:


_____ on behalf of
_____

# EXHIBIT A
## Purchase Agreement

This Agreement made on _____ by and between _____ (hereinafter referred to as "Owner") and _____ (hereinafter referred to as "Purchaser").

### WITNESSETH

WHEREAS, Owner is the sole and exclusive owner throughout the world of all rights in and to the literary work entitled: "_____," written by _____ which work has been filed in the United States Copyright Office under Copyright Registration Number _____; this work including all adaptations and/or versions, the titles, characters, plots, themes and story line is collectively referred to as the "Property"; and

WHEREAS, Purchaser wants to acquire certain rights of the Owner in consideration for the purchase price provided herein and in reliance upon the Owner's representations and warranties;

NOW, THEREFORE, the parties agree to as follows:

**1. RIGHTS GRANTED:** Owner hereby sells, grants, conveys and assigns to Purchaser, its successors, licensees and assigns exclusively and forever, all motion picture rights (including all silent, sound dialogue and musical motion picture rights), all television motion picture and other television rights, together with limited radio broadcasting rights and 7,500 word publication rights for advertisement, publicity and exploitation purposes, and certain incidental and allied rights, throughout the world, in and to the Property and in and to the copyright thereof and all renewals and extensions of copyright. Included among the rights granted to Purchaser hereunder (without in any way limiting the grant of rights hereinabove made) are the following sole and exclusive rights throughout the world:

(a) To make, produce, adapt and copyright one or more motion picture adaptations or versions, whether fixed on film, tape, disc, wire, audio-visual cartridge, cassette or through any other technical process whether now known or hereafter devised, based in whole or in part on the Property, of every size, gauge, color or type, including, but not limited to, musical motion pictures and remakes of and sequels to any motion picture produced hereunder and motion pictures in series or serial form, and for such purposes to record and reproduce and license others to record and reproduce, in synchronization with such motion pictures, spoken words taken from or based upon the text or theme of the Property and any and all kinds of music, musical accompaniments and/or lyrics to be performed or sung by the performers in any such motion picture and any and all other kinds of sound and sound effects.

(b) To exhibit, perform, rent, lease and generally deal in and with any motion picture produced hereunder:

(i) by all means or technical processes whatsoever, whether now known or hereafter devised including, by way of example only, film, tape, disc, wire, audio-visual cartridge, cassette or television (including commercially sponsored, sustaining and subscription or pay-per-view television, or any derivative thereof); and

(ii) in any place whatsoever, including homes, theaters and elsewhere, and whether or not a fee is charged, directly or indirectly, for viewing any such motion picture.

(c) To broadcast, transmit or reproduce the Property or any adaptation or version thereof (including without limitations to, any motion picture produced hereunder and/or any script or other material based on or utilizing the Property or any of the characters, themes or plots thereof), by means of television or any process analogous thereto whether now known or hereafter devised (including commercially sponsored, sustaining and subscription or pay-per-view television), through the use of motion pictures produced on films or by means of magnetic tape, wire, disc, audio-visual cartridge or any other device now known or hereafter devised and including such television productions presented in series or serial form, and the exclusive right generally to exercise for television purposes all the rights granted to Purchaser hereunder for motion picture purposes.

(d) Without limiting any other rights granted Purchaser, to broadcast and/or transmit by television or radio or any process analogous thereto whether now known or hereafter devised, all or any part of the Property or any adaptation or version thereof, including any motion picture or any other version or versions thereof, and announcements pertaining to said motion picture or other version or versions, for the purpose of advertising, publicizing or exploiting such motion picture or other version or versions, which broadcasts or transmissions may be accomplished through the use of living actors performing simultaneously with such broadcast or transmission or by any other method or means including the use of motion pictures (including trailers) reproduced on film or by means of magnetic tape or wire or through the use of other recordings or transcriptions.

(e) To publish and copyright or cause to be published and copyrighted in the name of Purchaser or its nominee in any and all languages throughout the world, in any form or media, synopses, novelizations, serializations, dramatizations, abridged and/or revised versions of the Property, not exceeding 7,500 words each, adapted from the Property or from any motion picture and/or other version of the Property for the purpose of advertising, publicizing and/or exploiting any such motion picture and/or other version.

(f) For the foregoing purposes to use all or any part of the Property and any of the characters, plots, themes and/or ideas contained therein, and the title of the Property and any title or subtitle of any component of the Property, and to use said titles or subtitles for any motion picture or other version of adaptation whether or not the same is based on or adapted from the Property and/or as the title of any musical composition contained in any such motion picture or other version or adaptation.

(g) To use and exploit commercial or merchandise tie-ups and recordings of any sort and nature arising out of or connected with the Property and/or its motion picture or other versions and/or the title or titles thereof and/or the characters thereof and/or their names or characteristics.

All rights, licenses, privileges and property herein granted Purchaser shall be cumulative and Purchaser may exercise or use any or all said rights, licenses, privileges or property simultaneously with or in connection with or separately and apart from the exercise of any other of said rights, licenses, privileges and property. If Owner hereafter makes or publishes or permits to be made or published any revision, adaptation, sequel, translation or dramatization or other versions of the Property, then Purchaser shall have and Owner hereby grants to

Purchaser without payment therefor all of the same rights therein as are herein granted Purchaser. The terms "Picture" and "Pictures" as used herein shall be deemed to mean or include any present or future kind of motion picture production based upon the Property, with or without sound recorded and reproduced synchronously therewith, whether the same is produced on film or by any other method or means now or hereafter used for the production, exhibition and/or transmission of any kind of motion picture productions.

**2. RIGHTS RESERVED:** The following rights are reserved to Owner for Owner's use and disposition, subject, however, to the provisions of this agreement:

(a) Publication Rights:  The right to publish and distribute printed versions of the Property owned or controlled by Owner in book form, whether hardcover or soft-cover, and in magazine or other periodicals, whether in installments or otherwise subject to Purchaser's rights as provided for in Clause 1, supra.

(b) Stage Rights:  The right to perform the Property or adaptations thereof on the spoken stage with actors appearing in person in the immediate presence of the audience, provided no broadcast, telecast, recording, photography or other reproduction of such performance is made. Owner agrees not to exercise, or permit any other person to exercise, said stage rights earlier than five (5) years after the first general release or telecast, if earlier, of the first Picture produced hereunder, or seven (7) years after the date of exercise of the purchaser's option to acquire the property, whichever is earlier.

(c) Radio Rights:  The right to broadcast the Property by sound (as distinguished from visually) by radio, subject however to Purchaser's right at all times to: (I) exercise its radio rights provided in Clause 1 supra for advertising and exploitation purposes by living actors or otherwise, by the use of excerpts from or condensations of the Property or any Picture produced hereunder; and (ii) in any event to broadcast any Picture produced hereunder by radio. Owner agrees not to exercise, or permit any other person to exercise, Owner's radio rights earlier than five (5) years after the first general release or initial telecast, if earlier, of the first Picture produced hereunder or seven (7) years after the date of exercise of purchaser's option to acquire the property, whichever is earlier.

(d) Author-Written Sequel:  A literary property (story, novel, drama or otherwise), whether written before or after the Property and whether written by Owner or by a successor in interest of Owner, using one or more of the characters appearing in the Property, participating in different events from those found in the Property, and whose plot is substantially different from that of the Property. Owner shall have the right to exercise publication rights (i.e., in book or magazine form) at any time. Owner agrees not to exercise, or permit any other person to exercise, any other rights (including but not limited to motion picture or allied rights) of any kind in or to any author-written sequel earlier than five (5) years after the first general release of the first Picture produced hereunder, or seven (7) years after the date of exercise of purchaser's option to acquire the property, whichever is earlier, provided such restriction on Owner's exercise of said author-written sequel rights shall be extended to any period during which there is in effect, in any particular country or territory, a network television broadcasting agreement for a television motion picture, (I) based upon the Property, or (ii) based upon any Picture produced in the exercise of rights assigned herein, or (iii) using a character or characters of the Property, plus one (1) year, which shall also be a restricted period in such country or territory, whether or not such period occurs wholly or partly during or entirely after the 5/7 year period first referred to in this clause.

(e) Inasmuch as the characters of the Property are included in the exclusive grant of motion picture rights to Purchaser, no sequel rights or television series rights may be granted to such other person or company, but such characters from the Property which are contained in the author-written sequel may be used in a motion picture and remakes thereof whose plot is based substantially on the plot of the respective author-written sequel.

It is expressly agreed that Owner's reserved rights under this subclause relate only to material written or authorized by Owner and not to any revision, adaptation, sequel, translation or dramatization written or authorized by Purchaser, even though the same may contain characters or other elements contained in the Property.

**3. RIGHT TO MAKE CHANGES:** Owner agrees that Purchaser shall have the unlimited right to vary, change, alter, modify, add to and/or delete from the Property, and to rearrange and/or transpose the Property and change the sequence thereof and the characters and descriptions of the characters contained in the Property, and to use a portion or portions of the Property or the characters, plots, or theme thereof in conjunction with any other literary, dramatic or other material of any kind. Owner hereby waives the benefits of any provisions of law known as the "droit moral" or any similar law in any country of the world and agrees not to permit or prosecute any action or lawsuit on the ground that any Picture or other version of the Property produced or exhibited by Purchaser, its assignees or licensees, in any way constitutes an infringement of any of the Owner's droit moral or is in any way a defamation or mutilation of the Property or any part thereof or contains unauthorized variations, alterations, modifications, changes or translations.

**4. DURATION AND EXTENT OF RIGHTS GRANTED:** Purchaser shall enjoy, solely and exclusively, all the rights licenses, privileges and property granted hereunder throughout the world, in perpetuity, as long as any rights in the Property are recognized in law or equity, except insofar as such period of perpetuity may be shortened due to any now existing or future copyright by Owner of the Property and/or any adaptations thereof, in which case Purchaser shall enjoy its sole and exclusive rights, licenses, privileges and property hereunder to the fullest extent permissible under and for the full duration of such copyright or copyrights, whether common law or statutory, and any and all renewals and/or extensions thereof, and shall thereafter enjoy all such rights, licenses, privileges and property non-exclusively in perpetuity throughout the world. The rights granted herein are in addition to and shall not be construed in derogation of any rights which Purchaser may have as a member of the public or pursuant to any other agreement. All rights, licenses, privileges and property granted herein to Purchaser are irrevocable and not subject to rescission, restraint or injunction under any circumstances.

**5. CONSIDERATION:** As consideration for all rights granted and assigned to Purchaser and for owner's representations and warranties, Purchaser agrees to pay to Owner, and Owner agrees to accept _____ ($_____) for all the rights granted including the production of one or more theatrical or television motion pictures.

(a) For any mini-series, _____ thousand dollars $_____ per hour, pro-rated for part hours.

(b) For any sequel or remake of a theatrical or television motion picture based on the Property, one-half and one-third, respectively, of the amount paid for the initial motion picture, payable upon commencement of principal photography of the subsequent production.

(c) For any television series produced, based on the Property, Purchaser will pay the following royalties per initial production upon completion of production of each program: up to 30 minutes, $_____; over 30, but not more than 60 minutes, $_____; over 60 minutes, $_____; and in addition to the foregoing, as a buy-out of all royalty obligations, one hundred percent (100%) of the applicable initial royalty amount, in equal installments over five (5) reruns, payable within thirty (30) days after each such rerun. Owner shall have a right of first negotiation to direct the pilot for any television series.

## 6. REPRESENTATIONS AND WARRANTIES:

(a) Sole Proprietor:  Owner represents and warrants to Purchaser that Owner is the sole and exclusive proprietor, throughout the universe, of that certain original literary material written by Owner entitled "_____."

(b) Facts:  Owner represents and warrants to Purchaser as follows:

(i)  Owner is the sole author and creator of the Property.

(ii)  The Property is unpublished and was registered for copyright in the name of _____ under copyright registration number _____ in the Office of the United States Register of Copyrights, Washington, D.C.

(iii)  No motion picture or dramatic version of the Property, or any part thereof, has been manufactured, produced, presented or authorized; no radio or television development, presentation, or program based on the Property, or any part thereof, has been manufactured, produced, presented, broadcast or authorized; and no written or oral agreements or commitments whatsoever with respect to the Property, or with respect to any rights therein, have been made or entered into by or on behalf of Owner.

(iv)  None of the rights herein granted and assigned to Purchaser have been granted and/or assigned to any person, firm or corporation other than Purchaser.

(c) No Infringement or Violation of Third Party Rights:  Owner represents and warrants to Purchaser that Owner has not adapted the Property from any other literary, dramatic or other material of any kind, nature or description, nor, except for material which is in the public domain, has Owner copied or used in the Property the plot, scenes, sequence or story of any other literary, dramatic or other material; that the Property does not infringe upon any common law or statutory rights in any other literary, dramatic or other material; that no material contained in the Property is libelous or violative of the right of privacy of any person; that the full utilization of any and all rights in and to the Property granted by Owner pursuant to this Agreement will not violate the rights of any person, firm or corporation; and that the Property is not in the public domain in any country in the world where copyright protection is available.

(d) No Impairment of Rights:  Owner represents and warrants to Purchaser that Owner is the exclusive proprietor, throughout the universe, of all rights in and to the Property granted herein to Purchaser; that Owner has not assigned, licensed or in any manner encumbered, diminished or impaired any such rights; that Owner has not committed or omitted to perform any act by which such rights could or will be encumbered, diminished or impaired; and that there is no outstanding claim or litigation pending against or involving the title, ownership and/or copyright in the Property, or in any part thereof, or in any rights granted herein to Purchaser. Owner further represents and warrants that no attempt shall be made hereafter to encumber, diminish or impair any of the rights granted herein and that all appropriate protection of such rights will continue to be maintained by Owner.

**7. INDEMNIFICATION:**

(a) Owner agrees to indemnify Purchaser against all judgments, liability, damages, penalties, losses and expense (including reasonable attorneys' fees) which may be suffered or assumed by or obtained against Purchaser by reason of any breach or failure of any warranty or agreement herein made by Owner.

(b) Purchaser shall not be liable to Owner for damages of any kind in connection with any Picture it may produce, distribute or exhibit, or for damages for any breach of this agreement (except failure to pay the money consideration herein specified) occurring or accruing before Purchaser has had reasonable notice and opportunity to adjust or correct such matters.

(c) All rights, licenses and privileges herein granted to Purchaser are irrevocable and not subject to rescission, restraint or injunction under any circumstances.

**8. PROTECTION OF RIGHTS GRANTED:** Owner hereby grants to Purchaser the free and unrestricted right, but at Purchaser's own cost and expense, to institute in the name and on behalf of Owner, or Owner and Purchaser jointly, any and all suits and proceedings at law or in equity, to enjoin and restrain any infringements of the rights herein granted, and hereby assigns and sets over to Purchaser any and all causes of action relative to or based upon any such infringement, as well as any and all recoveries obtained thereon. Owner will not compromise, settle or in any manner interfere with such litigation if brought; and Purchaser agrees to indemnify and hold Owner harmless from any costs, expenses, or damages which Owner may suffer as a result of any such suit or proceeding.

**9. COPYRIGHT:** Regarding the copyright in and to the Property, Owner agrees that:

(a) Owner will prevent the Property and any arrangements, revisions, translations, novelizations, dramatizations or new versions thereof whether published or unpublished and whether copyrighted or uncopyrighted, from vesting in the public domain, and will take or cause to be taken any and all steps and proceedings required for copyright or similar protection in any and all countries in which the same may be published or offered for sale, insofar as such countries now or hereafter provide for copyright or similar protection. Any contract or agreement entered into by Owner authorizing or permitting the publication of the Property or any arrangements, revisions, translations, novelizations, dramatizations or new versions thereof in any country will contain appropriate provisions requiring such publisher to comply with all the provisions of this clause.

(b) Without limiting the generality of the foregoing, if the Property or any arrangement, revision, translation, novelization, dramatization or new version thereof is published in the United States or in any other country in which registration is required for copyright or similar protection in accordance with the laws and regulations of such country, and Owner further agrees to affix or cause to be affixed to each copy of the Property or any arrangement, revision, translation, novelization, dramatization or new version thereof which is published or offered for sale such notice or notices as may be required for copyright or similar protection in any country in which such publication or sale occurs.

(c) At least six (6) months prior to the expiration of any copyright required by this provision for the protection of the Property, Owner will renew (or cause to be renewed) such copyright, as permitted by applicable law, and any and all rights granted Purchaser hereunder shall be deemed granted to Purchaser throughout the full period of such renewed copyright, without the payment of any additional consideration, it being agreed that the consideration payable to Owner under this agreement shall be deemed to include full consideration for the grant of such rights to Purchaser throughout the period of such renewed copyright.

(d) If the Property, or any arrangement, revision, translation, novelization, dramatization or new version thereof, shall ever enter the public domain, then nothing contained in this agreement shall impair any rights or privileges that the Purchaser might be entitled to as a member of the public; thus, the Purchaser may exercise any and all such rights and privileges as though this agreement were not in existence. The rights granted herein by Owner to Purchaser, and the representations, warranties, undertakings and agreements made hereunder by Owner shall endure in perpetuity and shall be in addition to any rights, licenses, privileges or property of Purchaser referred to in this subclause (d).

(e) All rights granted or agreed to be granted to Purchaser under this Agreement shall be irrevocably vested in Purchaser and shall not be subject to rescission by Owner or any other party for any cause, nor shall said rights be subject to termination or reversion by operation of law or otherwise, except to the extent, if any, that the provisions of any copyright law or similar law relating to the right to terminate grants of, or recapture rights in, literary property may apply. If, pursuant to any such copyright law or similar law, Owner or any successor or any other legally designated party (all herein referred to as "the terminating party") becomes entitled to exercise any right to reversion, recapture or termination ( the "termination right") with respect to all or any part of the rights granted or to be granted under this Agreement, and if the terminating party exercises said termination right with respect to all or part of said rights (the "recaptured rights"), then from and after the date on which the terminating party has the right to transfer to a third party all or part of the recaptured rights, Purchaser shall have the first right to purchase and acquire the recaptured rights from the terminating party. If the terminating party is prepared to accept a bona fide offer from a third party with respect to all or part of the recaptured rights, then in each such instance the terminating party shall notify Purchaser of such offer which the terminating party is prepared to accept and the name of the third party who made the offer to the terminating party, and the terminating party shall offer Purchaser the right to enter into an agreement with the terminating party with respect to the recaptured rights on the aforesaid terms and conditions. Purchaser shall have 30 days from the date of its receipt of such written offer within which to notify the terminating party of its acceptance of such offer (provided, however, the

Purchaser shall not be required to meet any terms or conditions which cannot be as easily met by one person as another, including, without limitation, the employment of a specified person, etc.) If Purchaser shall acquire from the terminating party all or part of the recaptured rights, then the terminating party agrees to enter into appropriate written agreements with Purchaser covering said acquisition. If Purchaser shall elect not to purchase the recaptured rights from the terminating party, then the terminating party may dispose of said recaptured rights, but only to the aforesaid third party and only upon the terms and conditions specified in the aforesaid written notice given by the terminating party to Purchaser, it being understood and agreed that the terminating party may not dispose of said recaptured rights either to: (a) any other proposed transferee; or (b) upon terms and conditions which are more favorable to any transferee than the terms and conditions previously offered to Purchaser hereunder, without again offering to enter into an agreement with Purchaser on: (I) the terms offered to such other transferee; or (ii) such more favorable terms and conditions offered to said proposed transferee, whichever of (a) or (b) shall apply. Any such required offer made to Purchaser by the terminating party shall be governed by the procedure set forth in the preceding four sentences of this Paragraph. The unenforceability of any portion of this Paragraph shall not invalidate or affect the remaining portions of this Paragraph of this Agreement.

**10. CREDIT OBLIGATIONS:** Purchaser shall have the right to publish, advertise, announce and use in any manner or medium, the name, biography and photographs or likenesses of Owner in connection with any exercise by Purchaser of its rights hereunder, provided such use shall not constitute an endorsement of any product or service.

During the term of the Writer's Guild of America Minimum Basic Agreement ("WGA Agreement"), as it may be amended, the credit provisions of the WGA Agreement shall govern the determination of credits, if any, which the Purchaser shall accord the Owner hereunder in connection with photoplays. If the Purchaser or his assignee is not a party to said WGA Agreement, the provisions of the WGA Agreement shall no longer directly govern the determination of such credits, and when the WGA Agreement or any amendment is not effective as between the Purchaser or assignee and Writer's Guild of America, such credits shall be determined with reference to the Credit rules of the WGA, with any dispute arbitrated by the American Arbitration Association.

Subject to the foregoing, Owner shall be accorded the following credit on a single card on screen and in paid ads controlled by Purchaser and in which any other writer is accorded credit, and in size of type (as to height, width, thickness and boldness) equal to the largest size of type in which any other writer is accorded credit:

WRITTEN BY _____

Additionally, if Purchaser shall exploit any other rights in and to the Property, then Purchaser agrees to give appropriate source material credit to the Property, to the extent that such source material credits are customarily given in connection with the exploitation of such rights.

No casual or inadvertent failure to comply with any of the provisions of this clause shall be deemed a breach of this agreement by the Purchaser. Owner hereby expressly acknowledges that in the event of a failure or omission constituting a breach of the provisions of this paragraph, the damage (if any) caused Owner thereby is not irreparable or sufficient to entitle Owner to injunctive or other equitable relief. Consequently, Owner's rights and remedies in the event of such breach shall be limited to the right to recover damages in an action at law.

**11. RIGHT OF FIRST NEGOTIATION:** Purchaser shall have a right of first negotiation on all Reserved Rights. The term "Right of First Negotiation" means that if, after the expiration of an applicable time limitation, Owner desires to dispose of or exercise a particular right reserved to Owner herein ("Reserved Right"), whether directly or indirectly, then Owner shall notify Purchaser in writing and immediately negotiate with Purchaser regarding such Reserved Right. If, after the expiration of thirty (30) days following the receipt of such notice, no agreement has been reached, then Owner may negotiate with third parties regarding such Reserved Right subject to Clause 12 infra.

**12. RIGHT OF LAST REFUSAL:** The Purchaser shall have a right of last refusal on all Reserved Rights. The term "Right of Last Refusal" means that if Purchaser and Owner fail to reach an agreement pursuant to Purchaser's right of first negotiation, and Owner makes and/or receives any bona fide offer to license, lease and/or purchase the particular Reserved Right or any interest therein ("Third Party Offer"), and if the proposed purchase price and other material terms of a Third Party Offer are no more favorable to Owner than the terms which were acceptable to Purchaser during the first negotiation period, Owner shall notify Purchaser, by registered mail or telegram, if Owner proposes to accept such Third Party Offer, the name of the offerer, the proposed purchase price, and other terms of such Third Party Offer. During the period of thirty (30) days after Purchaser's receipt of such notice, Purchaser shall have the exclusive option to license, lease and/or purchase, as the case may be, the particular Reserved Right or interest referred to in such Third Party Offer, at the same purchase price and upon the same terms and conditions as set forth in such notice. If Purchaser elects to exercise thereof by registered mail or telegram within such thirty (30) day period, failing which Owner shall be free to accept such Third Party Offer; provided that if any such proposed license, lease and/or sale is not consummated with a third party within thirty (30) days following the expiration of the aforesaid thirty (30) day period, Purchaser's Right of Last Refusal shall revive and shall apply to each and every further offer or offers at any time received by Owner relating to the particular Reserved Right or any interest therein; provided, further, that Purchaser's option shall continue in full force and effect, upon all of the terms and conditions of this paragraph, so long as Owner retains any rights, title or interests in or to the particular Reserved Right. Purchaser's Right of Last Refusal shall inure to the benefit of Purchaser, its successors and assigns, and shall bind Owner and Owner's heirs, successors and assigns.

**13. NO OBLIGATION TO PRODUCE:** Nothing herein shall be construed to obligate Purchaser to produce, distribute, release, perform or exhibit any motion picture, television, theatrical or other production based upon, adapted from or suggested by the Property, in whole or in part, or otherwise to exercise, exploit or make any use of any rights, licenses, privileges or property granted herein to Purchaser.

**14. ASSIGNMENT:** Purchaser may assign and transfer this agreement or all or any part of its rights hereunder to any person, firm or corporation without limitation, and this agreement shall be binding upon and inure to the benefit of the parties hereto and their successors, representatives and assigns forever.

**15. NO PUBLICITY:** Owner will not, without Purchaser's prior written consent in each instance, issue or authorize the issuance or publication of any news story or publicity relating to (I) this Agreement, (ii) the subject matter or terms hereof, or to any use by Purchaser, its successors, licensees and assigns, and (iii) any of the rights granted Purchaser hereunder.

**16. AGENT COMMISSIONS:** Purchaser shall not be liable for any compensation or fee to any agent of Owner in connection with this Agreement.

**17. ADDITIONAL DOCUMENTATION:** Owner agrees to execute and procure any other and further instruments necessary to transfer, convey, assign and copyright all rights in the Property granted herein by Owner to Purchaser in any country throughout the world. If it shall be necessary under the laws of any country that copyright registration be acquired in the name of Owner, Purchaser is hereby authorized by Owner to apply for said copyright registration thereof; and, in such event, Owner shall and does hereby assign and transfer the same unto Purchaser, subject to the rights in the Property reserved hereunder by Owner. Owner further agrees, upon request, to duly execute, acknowledge, procure and deliver to Purchaser such short form assignments as may be requested by Purchaser for the purpose of copyright recordation in any country, or otherwise. If Owner shall fail to so execute and deliver, or cause to be executed and delivered, the assignments or other instruments herein referred to, Purchaser is hereby irrevocably granted the power coupled with an interest to execute such assignments and instruments in the name of Owner and as Owner's attorney-in-fact.

**18. NOTICES:** All notices to Purchaser under this agreement shall be sent by United States registered mail, postage prepaid, or by telegram addressed to Purchaser at _____ and all notices to Owner under this agreement shall be sent by United States registered mail, postage prepaid, or by telegram addressed to _____. The deposit of such notice in the United States mail or the delivery of the telegram message to the telegraph office shall constitute service thereof, and the date of such deposit shall be deemed to be the date of service of such notice.

**19. MISCELLANEOUS:**

 (a) Relationship: This agreement between the parties does not constitute a joint venture or partnership of any kind.

 (b) Cumulative Rights and Remedies: All rights, remedies, licenses, undertakings, obligations, covenants, privileges and other property granted herein shall be cumulative, and Purchaser may exercise or use any of them separately or in conjunction with any one or more of the others.

(c) Waiver: A waiver by either party of any term or condition of this agreement in any instance shall not be deemed or construed to be a waiver of such term or condition for the future, or any subsequent breach thereof.

(d) Severability: If any provision of this agreement as applied to either party or any circumstances shall be adjudged by a court to be void and unenforceable, such shall in no way affect any other provision of this agreement, the application of such provision in any other circumstance, or the validity or enforceability of this agreement.

(e) Governing Law:  This agreement shall be construed in accordance with the laws of the State of _____ applicable to agreements which are executed and fully performed within said State.

(f) Captions:  Captions are inserted for reference and convenience only and in no way define, limit or describe the scope of this agreement or intent of any provision.

(g) Entire Understanding:  This agreement contains the entire understanding of the parties relating to the subject matter, and this agreement cannot be changed except by written agreement executed by the party to be bound.

(h) Arbitration: This Agreement shall be interpreted in accordance with the laws of the State of _____, applicable to agreements executed and to be wholly performed therein. Any controversy or claim arising out of or in relation to this Agreement or the validity, construction or performance of this Agreement, or the breach thereof, shall be resolved by arbitration in accordance with the rules and procedures of AFMA, as said rules may be amended from time to time with rights of discovery if requested by the arbitrator. Such rules and procedures are incorporated and made a part of this Agreement by reference. If AFMA shall refuse to accept jurisdiction of such dispute, then the parties agree to arbitrate such matter before and in accordance with the rules of the American Arbitration Association under its jurisdiction in _____ before a single arbitrator familiar with entertainment law. The parties shall have the right to engage in pre-hearing discovery in connection with such arbitration proceedings. The parties agree hereto that they will abide by and perform any award rendered in any arbitration conducted pursuant hereto, that any court having jurisdiction thereof may issue a judgment based upon such award and that the prevailing party in such arbitration and/or confirmation proceeding shall be entitled to recover its reasonable attorneys' fees and expenses. The arbitration will be held in _____ and any award shall be final, binding and non-appealable. The Parties agree to accept service of process in accordance with the AFMA Rules.

IN WITNESS WHEREOF, the parties hereto have signed this Agreement as of the day and year first above written.


_____
 ("Owner")


_____ on behalf of


_____
("Purchaser")

# EXHIBIT B
# OPTION AGREEMENT
## (Short Form for Recordation at U.S. Copyright Office)

For good and valuable consideration, receipt of which is hereby acknowledged, the undersigned hereby grants to _____ (the "Purchaser"), its successors and assigns, the sole and exclusive option to purchase all motion picture and certain allied rights, in the original literary and/or dramatic work (the "Work") described as follows:

Title: _____
Author: _____
Copyright Registration: _____

The Work includes but is not limited to: (I) all contents; (ii) all present and future adaptations and versions; (iii) the title, characters and theme; and (iv) the copyright and all renewals and extensions of copyright.

This instrument is executed in accordance with and is subject to the agreement (the "Option Agreement") between the undersigned and the Purchaser dated as of _____ relating to the option granted to the Purchaser to purchase the above-mentioned rights in the Work, which rights are more fully described in the Purchase Agreement, attached to the Option Agreement.

Date:

Attest _____
                (name of witness)


_____

# EXHIBIT C
## SHORT FORM COPYRIGHT ASSIGNMENT

KNOW ALL MEN BY THESE PRESENTS that, in consideration of one dollar ($1.00) and other good and valuable consideration, receipt of which is hereby acknowledged, the undersigned _____ ("Assignor") do(es) hereby sell, grant, convey and assign unto _____ ("Assignee"), its successors, assigns and licensees forever, all right, title and interest including but not limited to the exclusive worldwide Motion Picture and allied rights of Assignor in and to that certain literary work to wit: that certain original screenplay written by _____ entitled "_____," ("Literary Material"), and all drafts, revisions, arrangements, adaptations, dramatizations, translations, sequels and other versions of the Literary Material which may heretofore have been written or which may hereafter be written with the sanction of Assignor.

Dated this _____ day of _____, 199__.


_____
("Assignor")


AGREED TO:


_____ on behalf of

_____
("Assignee")


STATE OF _____   )
                                                        )ss
COUNTY OF _____   )

On the    day of    , 199__, before me personally came _____ to me known and known to be the individual described in and who executed the foregoing instrument, and he did duly acknowledge to me that he executed the same.

Notary Public

# OPTION AND LITERARY PURCHASE AGREEMENT
## (Short Form)

This contract, when countersigned by you, will confirm the agreement between _____ ("PURCHASER") and _____ ("WRITER") for the acquisition of that original screenplay entitled "_____" (hereinafter called "the Literary Property"). As used herein, the reference to "PURCHASER" includes PURCHASER's assignees.

**1. OPTION.** In consideration of PURCHASER's effort to produce the literary property, WRITER hereby grant to PURCHASER a _____ (Duration of Option) exclusive and irrevocable option to acquire any and all motion picture, allied and ancillary rights in order to develop and produce an original motion picture based on the Literary Property ("the Picture") and exploit the Picture and all rights acquired herein. The initial option period shall commence on the date of WRITER's and PURCHASER's execution hereof, and may be extended for an additional _____ year period by the giving of written notice and the payment to WRITER of $_____ (Renewal Payment), applicable against the purchase price, at any time prior to the expiration of the initial option period.

**2. ACQUISITION AND COMPENSATION:** If PURCHASER timely exercises its option and pays the Purchase Price during the option period, including any extension, the following terms shall apply:

(a) The WRITER shall grant to PURCHASER the right to produce an original motion picture including remakes and sequels, television long-form and series rights, and 7,500 word promotional publishing rights and ancillary rights thereto.

(b) The PURCHASER, or its assignee, shall pay WRITER a Purchase Price of _____ (__%) of the film's negative cost (exclusive of financing costs), with a floor of $_____ and a ceiling of $_____.

(c) In addition to the aforesaid Purchase Price, WRITER shall receive Bonus compensation as follows:

i. Budget Bonus: If a motion picture is produced based on the Literary Property with a final production budget of _____ ($) or more, and if WRITER receives sole or shared screenplay credit, a bonus of _____ ($), shall be paid to WRITER, payable 90 days after the first day of principal photography.

ii. Box Office Bonus: If a motion picture is produced based on the Literary Property, and if WRITER receives sole or shared screenplay credit, and if the Picture generates U.S. theatrical box office receipts of _____ ($) or more in the first year of theatrical release, then an additional bonus of _____ ($) shall be paid to WRITER.

(d) For any sequel produced based on the Literary Property, in whole or in part, PURCHASER will pay or cause WRITER to be paid one-half (½) of the original compensation payable under Subclauses 2(b) and 2(c) of this agreement; and for any remake produced based on the Literary Property, in whole or in part, PURCHASER will pay or cause WRITER to be paid one-third 1/3 of the original compensation payable under Subclauses 2(b) and 2(c) of this agreement. The compensation described in 2(b) shall be paid to WRITER upon commencement of principal photography of any such sequel and/or remake.

(e) For any television series produced, based on the Literary Property, PUR-CHASER will pay or cause to be paid to WRITER the following royalties per initial production upon completion of production of each program: programs up to 30 minutes--$1,500; over thirty (30) minutes but not more than sixty (60) minutes--$1,750; over sixty (60) minutes but not more than ninety (90) minutes--$2,000; over ninety (90) minutes--$2,500; and in addition to the foregoing, as a buy out of all royalty obligations, one hundred percent (100%) in equal installments over five (5) reruns, payable within thirty (30) days after each such rerun, or subject to the WGA minimum, whichever is greater.

(f) PURCHASER shall pay WRITER a percentage participation of four percent of one hundred percent (4% of 100%) of the net profits (including all allied rights and exploitation of ancillary markets) of each motion picture and television program or series based on the Literary Property if WRITER receives sole Screenplay credit. If WRITER receives shared credit, she shall receive two percent of one hundred percent (2% of 100%) of the net profits. The percentage participation shall be defined in the same as the net profit participation granted to PURCHASER.

(g) EMPLOYMENT OF WRITER: If in Producer's sole discretion, Producer decides to have the script re-written, WRITER will be offered the first opportunity to be employed to do a re-write for a flat fee of $_____, which shall be full and complete compensation for WRITER. Producer shall have no obligation to employ WRITER for any subsequent rewrites or polishes. Any work created by WRITER for such a rewrite shall be a work for hire and all rights to WRITER's work shall be owned by Producer or his assignee.

All of the sums set forth as compensation in this paragraph are for the total amount of monies payable by PURCHASER. Unless WRITER instruct PURCHASER otherwise, said sums shall be payable fifty percent to each WRITER.

3. REPRESENTATIONS AND WARRANTIES: WRITER hereby represent and warrant that: WRITER has the sole, exclusive and unencumbered ownership of all rights of every kind and character throughout the world in and to the Literary Property and (a) the Literary Property was written solely by and is original with WRITER; (b) neither the Literary Property nor any element thereof infringes upon any other literary property; (c) the production or exploitation of any motion picture or other production based on the Literary Property will not violate the rights to privacy of any person or constitute a defamation against any person, nor will production or exploitation of any motion picture or other production based thereon in any other way violate the rights of any person; (d) WRITER owns all rights in the Literary Property as specified hereinabove free and clear of any liens, encumbrances, claims or litigation, whether pending or threatened; (e) WRITER has full right and power to make and perform this agreement; and (f) the Literary Property has not previously been exploited as a motion picture, television production, play or otherwise, and no rights have been granted to any third party to do so. WRITER hereby indemnifies PURCHASER against any loss or damage (including reasonable attorneys' fees) incurred by reason of any breach or claim of breach of the foregoing representations and warranties. The term "person" as used herein shall mean any person, firm, corporation or other entity.

4. RIGHTS ACQUIRED/RESERVED: The foregoing option covers the sole, exclusive, perpetual and worldwide motion picture, television and allied and incidental rights in the Literary Property and any and all screenplays or other adaptations thereof, whether heretofore or hereafter written by WRITER or any other person, including

theatrical, television (whether filmed, taped or otherwise recorded, and including series rights), cassette and other compact devices, sequel, remake and advertising rights (including 7,500-word synopsis publication rights); all rights to exploit, distribute and exhibit any motion picture or other production produced hereunder in all media now known or hereafter devised; all rights to make any and all changes to and adaptations of the Literary Property; merchandising, sound track, music publishing and exploitation rights; the right to use WRITER'S name in and in connection with the exploitation of the rights granted hereunder; and all other rights customarily obtained in connection with formal literary purchase agreements, as referred to in Clause 9 below. PURCHASER hereby acknowledges that WRITER reserves live television, radio, book publication and legitimate stage rights, subject to PURCHASER's customary limited advertising and promotion rights. WRITER will not exercise or dispose of, or permit the exercise or disposition of such reserved rights for a period of five (5) years after release of the first motion picture based upon the Literary Property (herein the "Picture"), or five (5) years from the date on which PURCHASER exercises its option, whichever first occurs.

**5. EXECUTION OF ADDITIONAL DOCUMENTS:** WRITER agrees to execute any and all additional documents or instruments, including a short form option agreement (Exhibit A) and a short form assignment for purposes of recording in the Copyright Office (Exhibit B), and to do any and all things necessary or desirable to effectuate the purposes of this agreement. If such short form assignment is undated, PURCHASER is authorized to date such short form assignment and to file the same in the Copyright Office immediately upon exercise of the option herein granted. If WRITER fails to do anything necessary or desirable to effectuate the purposes of this agreement, including, but not limited to, renewing copyrights and instituting and maintaining actions for infringement of any rights herein granted to PURCHASER under copyright or otherwise, WRITER hereby irrevocably appoints PURCHASER as WRITER's attorney-in-fact with the right, but not the obligation, to do any such things and renew copyrights and institute and maintain actions in WRITER's name and behalf, but for PURCHASER's benefit, which appointment shall be coupled with an interest and shall be irrevocable.

**6. CREDIT:**

In determining whether WRITER is awarded sole, shared or no writing credit, reference shall be made to the principles of the WGA credit arbitration rules. Although PURCHASER is not a WGA signatory, and WRITER is not a member of the WGA, to the extent possible, the principles of the WGA credit arbitration rules shall be followed by the parties. In the event of a credit dispute, the arbitrator of such a dispute shall follow the WGA credit rules to the extent they do not conflict with the rules of AAA arbitration.

Subject to the foregoing provision, Purchaser agrees to accord WRITER credit on the positive prints of the Picture substantially as follows:

"WRITTEN BY _____."

Such credit shall also be provided in paid advertising, subject to any distributor's and customary exclusions for award, congratulatory and similar ads. Subject to the foregoing, the presentation of such credits shall be determined by PURCHASER. Any casual or inadvertent failure by PURCHASER, or any failure by any third party, to comply with the provisions of this clause shall not be deemed to be a breach of this agreement. In the event of a failure or omission of PURCHASER's obligations under this clause, it is expressly agreed that WRITER's sole remedy shall be to seek damages in arbitration, and that in no event shall WRITER be entitled to obtain any injunctive or other equitable relief or undertake any legal efforts to restrict PURCHASER's right to exploit the Literary Property.

**7. ASSIGNMENT: PURCHASER** has the right to assign this agreement or any part hereof to a third party motion picture company or motion picture production company upon the terms and conditions set forth in this agreement, and any such assignment and transfer shall be made specifically subject to the terms and conditions and payments of this agreement, regardless of whether or not PURCHASER becomes or remains involved in the production of the Literary Property as producer or otherwise.

**8. NOTICES :** All checks and notices from PURCHASER to WRITER shall be sent to WRITER by mail at the following address:

———————————————————
(WRITER)

———————————————————
(Address)

———————————————————

with a courtesy copy to:

———————————————————

———————————————————

———————————————————

All notices from WRITER to PURCHASER shall be sent to the PURCHASER at the following address:

———————————————————
(PURCHASER)

———————————————————
(Purchaser Address)

———————————————————
(Purchaser City, State, Zip)

with a courtesy copy to:

———————————————————

———————————————————

———————————————————

All notices shall be deemed given upon receipt by the party to whom they are addressed or upon deposit in the ordinary course of the U.S. mail by the method specified above.

**9. MORE FORMAL AGREEMENT:** Until such time as a more formal agreement may be executed incorporating all of the foregoing and additional detailed representations, warranties and other provisions customarily included in such formal literary purchase agreements, this agreement shall be binding upon and inure to the benefit of the parties hereto and their successors, representatives, assigns and licensees.

**10. RIGHT TO ENGAGE IN PREPRODUCTION:** During said option period or extension thereof, PURCHASER shall have the right (at its own expense) to engage in preproduction with respect to a motion picture or other production intended to be based on the Literary Property.

**11. FORCE MAJEURE:** "Force Majeure" means any fire, flood, earthquake, or public disaster; strike, labor dispute or unrest; embargo, riot, war, insurrection or civil unrest; any act of God, any act of legally constituted authority; or any other cause beyond PURCHASER's control which would excuse PURCHASER's performance as a matter of law. If by reason of force majeure, PURCHASER's performance hereunder is delayed, hampered or prevented, then the option period provided herein (and any performance by PURCHASER) shall be extended for the amount of time of such delay or prevention up to a maximum of six months.

**12. ARBITRATION:** Any controversy or claim arising out of or relating to this agreement or any breach thereof shall be settled by arbitration in accordance with the Rules of the American Arbitration Association; The parties select expedited arbitration using one arbitrator, to be a disinterested attorney specializing in entertainment law, as the sole forum for the resolution of any dispute between them. The venue for arbitration shall be _____ (Venue). The arbitrator may make any interim order, decision, determinations, or award he deems necessary to preserve the status quo until he is able to render a final order, decision, determination or award. The determination of the arbitrator in such proceeding shall be final, binding and non-appealable. Judgment upon the award rendered by the arbitrator may be entered in any court having jurisdiction thereof. The prevailing party shall be entitled to reimbursement for costs and reasonable attorney's fees.

Please signify your agreement to the foregoing by signing where indicated below and returning this letter.

AGREED TO AND ACCEPTED:


PURCHASER:                              WRITER:



By:_____           _____
   (PURCHASER)                         (WRITER)

# EXHIBIT "A"
## SHORT FORM COPYRIGHT ASSIGNMENT

**KNOW ALL PERSONS BY THESE PRESENTS** that, in consideration of Ten Dollars ($10.00) and other good and valuable consideration, receipt of which is hereby acknowledged, the undersigned _____ ("Assignors") do hereby sell, grant, convey and assign unto _____ ("Purchaser/Assignee"), his successors, assigns and licensees forever, all right, title and interest including but not limited to the exclusive worldwide Motion Picture and allied rights of Assignor in and to that certain literary work to wit: that certain original screenplay written by _____ entitled "_____" ("Literary Property"), and all drafts, revisions, arrangements, adaptations, dramatizations, translations, sequels and other versions of the Literary Property which may heretofore have been written or which may hereafter be written with the sanction of the Assignors.

This instrument is executed in accordance with and is subject to the agreement (the "Option/Acquisition Agreement") between the undersigned and the Assignee dated as of the _____ (Date of Agreement) relating to the purchase of certain rights in the Literary Property, which rights are more fully described in said Option/Acquisition Agreement.

Dated this the _____ (Date of Agreement).

ASSIGNORS:

_____
(WRITER)


## ACKNOWLEDGMENT


THE STATE OF                                        }
                                                   } ss:
COUNTY OF                                          }


This instrument was acknowledged before me on the _____ day of _____, 19__, by _____, Writer of the above named screenplay and assignor for this document and they are known by me to be the persons represented.

                                        Notary Public in and for
                                        the State of _____

(Notary Seal)


                                        _____
My Commission Expires                   Printed Name of Notary

_____

# QUITCLAIM RELEASE

I, _____, (Name of grantor) residing at _____, City of _____, State of _____, for good and valuable considerations received from _____, residing at _____, City of _____, State of _____.

Have remised, released and forever quitclaimed, and do by these presents justly and absolutely remise, release and forever quitclaim unto _____ (Person obtaining rights) any and all right, title or interest, including but not limited to any copyright or trademark interests that I may have in or to the following:

_____,
(Literary property)

To have and to hold the same unto _____ (Person obtaining rights) for his sole use and benefit, so that neither I nor any other person or persons in my name and behalf shall or will hereafter claim or demand any right, title or interest in or to the above-described property or any part thereof, but they and every one of them shall by these presents be excluded and forever barred therefrom.

[I am executing this quitclaim pursuant to the provisions of a certain agreement which I entered into with _____ (Person obtaining rights) under date of _____ (Date of previous agreement)]

This quitclaim shall bind my heirs, executors, administrators and assigns, and shall endure to the benefit of _____ (Person obtaining rights), heirs, executors, administrators and assigns.

IN WITNESS WHEREOF I have hereunto set my hand and seal as of _____ (Date of Quitclaim Release).


_____
(Name of Grantor)


Witnessed by:

_____

STATE OF _____ )
                                ) ss.:
COUNTY OF_____ )


On the __ day of _____, 199_, before me personally came _____ to me known and known to be the individual described in and who executed the foregoing instrument, and he did duly acknowledge to me that he executed the same.


_____
Notary Public

# CHAPTER 4

# ARTIST EMPLOYMENT

## LOAN-OUT COMPANIES

A producer seeking to employ an artist can either hire that person directly or contract with his company for his services. Many writers, directors and actors have incorporated themselves by setting up "loan out" companies. At one time there were significant tax advantages to establishing such companies. Most of these benefits have now been abolished, although some pension and health plan benefits remain.

The company is called a "loan-out" company because it lends the talent's services first to studio A, then to studio B, and so on. All the money earned from the talent's services are paid to the company. The loan-out company pays the talent's business expenses and a salary.

Studios don't object to paying talent through their loan-out companies if the studio's interests are protected. The studio will want the talent to sign an "Inducement Agreement." This is a contract between the studio and the talent guaranteeing that the talent will abide by the terms of the loan-out agreement. Otherwise, the studio's only remedy for breach of contract is to sue the loan-out company which may not have any assets and which cannot perform the promised acts (i.e., corporations cannot act, write, or direct, only people can).

When talent requests that the deal be structured as a loan-out deal, three agreements are needed. First is the employment contract between the studio and the loan-out company. Second is the agreement between the studio and the talent, the so-called inducement agreement. And third is an employment agreement between the loan-out company and the talent.

The terms of a loan-out agreement are not much different than a direct employment agreement. One can immediately recognize a loan-out deal because it refers to one party as the "Lender." The "Lender" is the loan-out company, not a bank.

## ACTOR EMPLOYMENT

Actor employment agreements contain many provisions similar to those found in writer and director agreements. Agreements often refer to the employer as the "Producer" and the employee as the "Player."

The actor's employment agreement will grant the producer the right to use the name and likeness of the actor in the film. The producer may obtain the right to use the actor's name and likeness for merchandising, in which case the actor will be entitled to a percentage participation in the revenues received by the producer.

Typically the producer will supply any costumes required for a role. If a contemporary story is being filmed, the producer may ask the player to provide his own clothing. In this case, the actor should receive a cleaning allowance.

Employment of child actors raises special concerns because minors can repudiate contracts.[1] A producer cannot enforce a disaffirmed contract. However, the law provides that when a minor is employed as an entertainer, he cannot disaffirm a contract if that contract has been approved by the Superior Court beforehand. The minor or the employer must petition the Superior Court to determine if the contract is fair to the minor. The court may require that part of the minor's earnings be set aside in a trust fund for him.

In hiring a minor, the employer must also comply with provisions of the California Labor Code and regulations of the Labor Commission. For example, an employer must obtain a work permit from the Division of Labor Standards Enforcement.[2] Minors cannot perform work that is hazardous or detrimental to their health, safety, morals or education.[3]

Actor employment agreements may contain a "morals" clause which requires the actor to conduct himself so as not to violate public conventions or subject himself to public hatred, contempt or ridicule. If the actor violates this clause, the employer has the right to terminate the agreement.

The employer may want to purchase life, accident or health insurance covering the actor. The actor is typically required to submit to a medical examination to obtain this coverage. If the employer is unable to obtain insurance at standard rates, the employer may have the right to terminate the agreement. If the actor fails the medical exam or insurance coverage is denied, the employer may be required to give prompt notice to the actor.

Negotiators sometimes try to resolve issues by agreeing to a "favored nations" clause. Such a provision guarantees that no other actor on the picture will obtain more advantageous terms. If another actor negotiates a better deal, there is an automatic upgrade for actors who have a favored nations clause in their contracts. Such a clause makes sense for a fledgling actor. If an actor with more clout gets a better deal, the fledgling actor will benefit.

---

[1] See California Civil Code § 35.

[2] California Administrative Code, Title 8, §11753

[3] California Administrative Code, Title 8, §11751

A producer who hires an actor for a television series will want to have an option on that actor's services for five to seven years. The actor may have to turn down attractive offers that conflict with this commitment. Before an actor enters an exclusive agreement he needs to consider whether it will restrict him from performing in such related fields as theatrical motion pictures, the legitimate stage and commercials.

When a novice signs a series deal he has little bargaining power. The agreement will set the amount of compensation due in subsequent years. If the series becomes a hit, and the actor becomes a star, he may chafe under the terms of an agreement that he now considers unfair. With his newfound clout he may try to renegotiate the deal. Sometimes he will refuse to work or become uncooperative or "sick" to pressure the employer to sweeten the deal. The employer may threaten to sue. Often a compromise is reached as neither party wants to kill the goose that lays the golden eggs.

What can the employer do if the actor refuses to perform under the contract? Certainly the employer can sue for money damages to compensate the employer for any loss incurred as a result of a wrongful breach. However, the actor may not have enough assets to satisfy any damages awarded the employer.

The employer cannot get a court order forcing the employee to perform because that would be form of involuntary servitude prohibited by the Constitution. However, if the services are of a special, unique, extraordinary or intellectual character so that the loss of these services cannot be reasonably or adequately compensated by money, a court may enjoin the employee from working for others during the term of the agreement. This is often referred to as a "negative injunction."

Note that under California Labor Code personal service contracts cannot exceed seven years (Cal. Labor Code § 2855) and injunctions will not be granted to enforce contracts unless the agreement is in writing and the minimum compensation is not less than six thousand dollars a year [Cal. Civil Code 3423, Cal. Code of Civil Procedure 526(5).] In New York personal services contracts have been enforced with court orders when the performer's services are special, unique or extraordinary and the terms are sufficiently definite.

## ACTOR OFFER

Producers often seek to attach one or more name actors to their project in order to obtain financing. Agents may be reluctant to read scripts, or forward them to their clients, unless the producer has secured financing. Agents see little advantage in allowing a producer to attach their client's names to projects that the producer will then shop to potential financiers.

Consequently, many agents will refuse to consider a project unless the producer can make a firm offer on a pay-or-play basis. A firm offer, if accepted, results in a binding agreement between the parties. If the offer of employment is on a pay-or-play basis, then the producer is obliged to compensate the actor regardless of whether the project goes into production. Producers need to be careful in making offers because a contract is formed upon acceptance and the offeror is bound by its terms.

A firm offer is one which includes the material (i.e., important) terms. The essential terms for artist employment agreements would include the start date of the motion picture, the compensation, and the credit to be given the artist. It is good practice to include an expiration date in an offer so that the artist cannot accept the offer months later — after the Producer has assumed the actor has declined the offer and the Producer has employed someone else. An offer, if accepted, will typically be followed by a more detailed employment agreement.

Producers often try to attach actors to projects without making a firm offer. If the producer has a personal relationship with an actor or if the producer has an impressive track-record, an actor may permit a producer to tell third parties that the actor is willing to accept a role in a proposed project. Sometimes actors will allow a Producer to use their names on prototype posters, advertising the yet-to-be made motion picture. Here the credits usually include the notation "credits not contractual," which means the actors are not under contract.

To document an actor's permission to use his name, a producer may ask the actor to sign a "Letter of Intent." Such a letter merely expresses the actor's interest in the project, but it is not a binding commitment on the actor (nor does it commit the producer). A letter of intent may say that the actor has read the script and is interested in playing the role subject to the actor's availability, and subject to the actor and the producer agreeing on the terms of employment.

# ACTOR OFFER LETTER

—————
(Letter Date)

—————————————
(Agent)

—————————————
(Agency)

—————————————
(Agency Address)

—————————————
(Agency City State Zip)

    **Re:  "——————" (Motion Picture) - Offer for ————— (Actor)**

Dear ——————————:

    I represent producer —————— ("Producer") in regard to the up-coming production "————————." Producer would like to employ —————— ("Artist") for shooting for a —————— (Shooting Duration) week (six (6) day weeks) period between the dates of ——— and ———. Producer would like to have the option to employ Artist for an additional ——— (Option) week (six (6) day week) period from ——— to ———.

    The role is playing ——————. The shooting will take place in ——————.

    Fixed Compensation: For the first two (2) weeks, Producer is willing to pay $——— per six (6) day week of shooting on a pay or play basis. Producer is willing to pay $——— for an additional week, if needed, at Producer's option.

    Deferment: Provided that Artist shall appear recognizably in the Picture as released in the role in which Artist is engaged hereunder, Artist shall receive a contingent deferment ("Deferment") in the amount of $——— Dollars (Deferment) payable, if at all, out of the first sums which would otherwise constitute "net proceeds" of the Picture. The Deferment shall be payable pari passu with all other contingent deferments.

    Contingent Compensation: Upon condition that Artist appears recognizably in the Picture as released in the role in which he is engaged hereunder, Artist shall be entitled to receive an amount equal to (Contingent Compensation) percent of one hundred percent (——— of 100%) of the net proceeds, if any, of the Picture.

    Credit: Upon condition that Artist shall appear recognizably in the Picture as released, the Producer shall accord the Artist credit in connection with the Picture as follows:

    (a) On Screen—On screen on a separate card, in the main titles, below or after the title of the Picture, in first or second position to be determined by alphabetical order with the other cast member guaranteed credit in first or second position, in a size of type no smaller than seventy-five percent (75%) of the size of type used to display the title of the Picture and in a size of type no smaller than the size of type used to accord an individual "directed by" credit to the director of the Picture;

(b) Paid Advertising—In all paid advertising for the Picture issued by or under the control of the Producer (subject to the customary exclusions of each distributor/broadcaster of the Picture), below or after the title of the Picture, in first or second position to be determined by alphabetical order with the other cast member guaranteed credit in first or second position, in a size of type no less than thirty-five percent (35%) of the size of type used to display the title of the Picture, and in a size of type no smaller than the size used to accord an individual "directed by" credit to the director of the Picture. Notwithstanding the foregoing, the Artist shall receive such credit in all excluded advertising issued by or under the control of Producer in which any other cast member is accorded credit, other than award, nomination, congratulatory, institutional or film market or festival advertising.

Travel and Expenses: Producer shall either provide Artist with transportation, or reimburse Artist the cost of the following in connection with services at any place outside of _____ ("Location"):

(a) Transportation—Three (3) round-trip air fares, first-class, if available, between _____ and any Location where Artist is required to render services hereunder in connection with the Picture, plus one (1) additional round-trip airfare, first-class, if available, on an if-used and one-time basis only, between _____ and any Location;

(b) Expenses—The sum of $_____ Dollars (Expenses) for each week the Producer shall require Artist to be at a Location in order to render services here-under, commencing on the date of Artist's arrival at the Location and continuing until Artist's departure therefrom. Sums specified in this Paragraph 5(b) shall be payable at the beginning of each week, in lieu of payment for any and all expenses incurred by the Artist while at the Location and shall be prorated on the basis of a seven (7) day week in the event of any partial week.

(c) Motor Home—One (1) small motor home during any period in which the Producer shall require the Artist's services at a Location;

(d) Car—The use of a car during any period when the Producer shall require the Artist's services at a Location, which car may be shared.

Dressing Facilities—At all times when the Artist is required to render services hereunder, the Producer shall provide the Artist with separate dressing facilities, if available.

Arbitration: Any dispute under this Agreement shall be settled by arbitration in _____ (Arbitration State) with the prevailing party being entitled to re-imbursement of attorneys' fees.

Additional Terms and Conditions: The parties will enter into a more formal agreement, which agreement shall incorporate the foregoing terms as well as other customary terms and conditions contained in comparable agreements, including customary representations and warranties, mutual indemnification, Actor's waiver of injunctive and other equitable relief, full depiction release including merchandising rights, Producer's right to assign rights, extensions for force majeure including any period in which a member of the principal cast and/or a director is unavailable, and application of _____ (Arbitration State) law.

Please discuss this offer with your client. If your client is willing to accept this offer, please contact me by _____. If I do not hear from you by that date, this offer will lapse. If the offer is accepted, unless and until such more formal Agreement is executed, this letter agreement, supplemented by the aforementioned customary terms and conditions, shall constitute the parties' agreement.

Thank you and I look forward to hearing from you.

Sincerely,

_____
(Representative)

_____
(Representative Title)

# ACTOR EMPLOYMENT AGREEMENT
## (Loanout Format To Employ S.A.G. Actor)

The following agreement ("Agreement"), dated as of _____, shall constitute the basic terms and conditions of the agreement between _____ ("Producer") and _____ ("Lender"), a _____ Corporation, relating to the services of _____ ("Employee"):

**1. Engagement:** The Producer hereby engages the Lender to furnish the services of the Employee as an actor portraying the role of "_____" in connection with the feature-length motion picture presently entitled "_____" ("Picture") pursuant to the terms and conditions hereof and the Lender hereby accepts such engagement.

**2. Services:** The Lender agrees to cause the Employee to render all such services as are required by the Producer and customarily rendered by actors in first-class feature-length theatrical motion pictures in the motion picture and television industry, at such times and places required by the Producer, and to comply with all reasonable directions, requests, rules and regulations of the Producer in connection therewith, whether the same involve matters of artistic taste or judgment.

**3. Start Date:** The Lender agrees to cause the Employee to render services hereunder exclusively to the Producer in connection with the principal photography of the Picture commencing on a date to be designated by the Producer ("Start Date") and continuing for ten (10) consecutive weeks thereafter ("Guaranteed Period") or until completion of principal photography of the Picture, whichever is later. The Start Date is presently contemplated by the Producer to be on or about _____. In addition, the Lender agrees to cause the Employee to render services in connection with rehearsals and pre-production of the Picture [as more fully described in Paragraph 4(c) hereof] commencing on a date to be designated by the Producer and continuing until the Start Date.

**4. Compensation:** Upon condition that the Lender and the Employee shall fully perform all services required of each of them hereunder and that the Lender and the Employee are not in default hereunder, the Producer agrees to pay to the Lender, as full and complete consideration for such services and for all rights transferred by the Lender and the Employee to the Producer hereunder, the following:

(a) Guaranteed Compensation: The sum of _____ Dollars ("Guaranteed Compensation") accruing in ten (10) equal weekly installments commencing on the Start Date. No additional compensation shall accrue or be payable with regard to the first two (2) weeks ("Free Weeks") of Employee's services hereunder immediately following the Guaranteed Period. The Guaranteed Period and the Free Weeks are sometimes referred to collectively herein as the "Minimum Employment Period."

(b) Additional Compensation: If the Producer shall require the Lender to furnish the Employee's services hereunder in connection with the principal photography of the Picture beyond the expiration of the Minimum Employment Period, the Producer shall pay the Lender the sum of _____ Dollars ("Weekly Compensation") for each additional week of such services, prorated as hereinafter provided.

(c) Pre-Production Services: The Lender shall cause the Employee to render such exclusive services in connection with rehearsals, pre-production meetings, costume fittings, make-up and other customary pre-production services as may be required by the Producer. Notwithstanding anything to the contrary contained in this Agreement, the Fixed Compensation specified in Paragraph 4(a) hereof shall also constitute full and complete consideration to the Lender for any such pre-production services.

(d) Post-Production Services: The Lender shall cause the Employee to render such customary services (including, without limitation, looping, added scenes and retakes) in connection with the post-production of the Picture as may be required by the Producer, subject to the Employee's prior conflicting professional commitments. Notwithstanding anything to the contrary contained in this Agreement, the Guaranteed Compensation specified in Paragraph 4(a) hereof shall also constitute full and complete consideration to the Lender for the first two (2) days (consecutive or non-consecutive) of such post-production services, and the Producer shall pay the Lender the Weekly Compensation set forth in subparagraph (b) above for each additional week of post-production services which the Producer may require hereunder beyond the Minimum Employment Period and the two (2) additional days described in this paragraph, prorated as hereinafter provided.

(e) Deferment: Provided that the Employee shall appear recognizably in the Picture as released in the role in which the Employee is engaged hereunder, a contingent deferment ("Deferment") in the amount of _____ Dollars payable, if at all, out of the first sums which would otherwise constitute "net proceeds" of the Picture ("Net proceeds" shall be defined, computed, accounted for and paid in accordance with the provisions of Exhibit "A" attached hereto). The Deferment shall be payable pari passu with all other contingent deferments which are payable out of first sums which would otherwise constitute "net proceeds" of the Picture.

(f) Contingent Compensation: Upon condition that the Employee appears recognizably in the Picture as released in the role in which the Employee is engaged hereunder, the Lender shall be entitled to receive an amount equal to _____ percent of one hundred percent (_____% of 100%) of the net proceeds, if any, of the Picture.

The parties hereto acknowledge that the Producer has granted to _____ ("Distributor") the right to distribute the Picture, in perpetuity, in any and all media by any means whatsoever, throughout the universe. The Producer shall cause _____ (Distribution Company) to compute, account for and pay the Lender's share of "net proceeds" hereunder directly to the Lender in accordance with the terms and provisions hereof.

Notwithstanding anything to the contrary contained in this Agreement, to the maximum extent permitted under the 1989 Producer's Screen Actors Guild Codified Basic Agreement, as amended in 1992 ("Basic Agreement"), all amounts paid to the Lender pursuant to this Paragraph 4(f) shall be applied against and in reduction of any so-called residual, reuse or supplemental market use payments required to be paid to the Lender pursuant to the Basic Agreement on account of the Employee's services hereunder and all such residual, reuse or supplemental market use payments required to be paid to the Lender pursuant to the Basic Agreement shall be applied against and in reduction of any amounts payable to the Lender pursuant to this Paragraph 4(f).

(g) Payday: All payments to the Lender hereunder shall be payable on the Producer's regular payday in the week following that week during which such payments shall have accrued.

(h) Employee's Services: The Employee's services hereunder shall be rendered as the Lender's employee. The Lender hereby agrees that the Lender will fully perform and discharge, and that the Producer shall have no responsibility or liability on account of, any and all obligations of an employer with respect to the Employee and the Employee's services hereunder, including, but not limited to, the withholding and/or payment of any sums required to be withheld and/or paid by such employer to any governmental authority, or pursuant to any guild or union health, welfare, or pension plan, or on account of any other so-called fringe benefits, based on or resulting from the services rendered by the Employee hereunder or the compensation paid to the Lender for such services, and the Lender agrees to and does hereby indemnify and hold the Producer harmless from and against any such liability or obligation.

Notwithstanding the foregoing, the Producer shall, upon receipt of appropriate invoices from the Lender, reimburse the Lender the amount, if any, which the Lender actually pays to any applicable collective bargaining organization's pension plan and health and welfare plan on account of the services rendered by the Employee hereunder. In no event shall the amount required to be paid by the Producer pursuant to this subparagraph exceed the amount which the Producer would have been required to pay if the Employee rendered services hereunder as the Producer's employee-for-hire.

(i) Agency Payment: All payments to the Lender hereunder shall be made to the Lender's Agent: _____, and the Lender hereby authorizes the Producer to make all such payments as aforesaid.

**5. Travel and Expenses:** The Producer shall either provide the Lender or the Employee, as the case may be, with, or reimburse the Lender for (as Producer shall determine), the cost of the following in connection with the Employee's services at any place outside of _____ ("Location"):

(a) Transportation: Three (3) round-trip air fares, first-class, if available, between _____ and any Location where the Employee is required to render services hereunder in connection with the Picture, plus one (1) additional round-trip airfare, first-class, if available, on an if-used and one-time basis only, between _____ and any Location;

(b) Expenses: The sum of _____ Dollars for each week the Producer shall require the Employee to be at a Location in order to render services hereunder, commencing on the date of the Employee's arrival at the Location and continuing until the Employee's departure therefrom. Sums specified in this Paragraph 5(b) shall be payable at the beginning of each week, in lieu of payment for any and all expenses incurred by the Employee while at the Location and shall be prorated on the basis of a seven (7) day week in the event of any partial week. The Lender hereby authorizes the Producer to pay the foregoing expense allowance directly to the Employee;

(c) Motor Home: One (1) small motor home during any period in which the Producer shall require the Employee's services at a Location;

(d) Car: The use of a car during any period when the Producer shall require the Employee's services at a Location;

**6. Dressing Facilities:** At all times when the Employee is required to render services hereunder, the Producer shall provide the Employee with separate dressing facilities, if available.

**7. Credit:** Upon condition that the Employee shall appear recognizably in the Picture as released, the Producer shall accord the Employee credit in connection with the Picture as follows:

(a) On Screen: On screen on a separate card, in the main titles, below or after the title of the Picture, in first or second position to be determined by alphabetical order with the other cast member guaranteed credit in first or second position, in a size of type no smaller than seventy-five percent (75%) of the size of type used to display the title of the Picture and in a size of type no smaller than the size of type used to accord an individual "directed by" credit to the director of the Picture;

(b) Paid Advertising: In all paid advertising for the Picture issued by or under the control of the Producer (subject to the customary exclusions of each distributor/broadcaster of the Picture), below or after the title of the Picture, in first or second position to be determined by alphabetical order with the other cast member guaranteed credit in first or second position, in a size of type no less than thirty-five percent (35%) of the size of type used to display the title of the Picture, and in a size of type no smaller than the size used to accord an individual "directed by" credit to the director of the Picture. Notwithstanding the foregoing, the Employee shall receive such credit in all excluded advertising issued by or under the control of Producer in which any other cast member is accorded credit, other than award, nomination, congratulatory, institutional or film market or festival advertising.

All other matters with respect to the Employee's credit, including the position in which the Employee will receive credit in paid advertising if the Employee shall be entitled to receive such credit, shall be in the Producer's sole discretion. The Producer agrees to use its good faith efforts to cause all third-party distributors to comply with the provisions of this Paragraph 7. No casual or inadvertent failure to comply with the provisions of this paragraph nor any failure by third parties to comply with their agreements with the Producer shall constitute a breach of this Agreement by the Producer. Upon notice to the Producer of its failure to comply with the provisions of this Paragraph, the Producer agrees to correct such error in paid advertising issued by or under the control of the Producer prepared after the Producer's receipt of such notice (allowing for an adequate period of time after receipt of such notice to implement such correction).

**8. Breach of Agreement:** In the event of any breach by the Producer of this Agreement, including, without limitation, any breach of the provisions of Paragraph 7, the Lender and the Employee shall be limited to the Lender's remedy at law for damages, if any, and shall not have the right to terminate or rescind this Agreement or to enjoin or restrain in any way the production, distribution, advertising or exploitation of the Picture.

**9. Name and Likeness:** The Lender hereby grants to the Producer the exclusive right to use the Employee's name, likeness, voice and/or biography in connection with the production, exhibition, advertising and other exploitation of the Picture and all subsidiary and ancillary rights therein, including, but not limited to, sound recordings (in any configuration) containing all or any part of the original or re-recorded soundtrack, music, lyrics and/or dialogue from the Picture, publications, merchandising and commercial tie ups; provided, however, that in no event shall the Employee be depicted as using or endorsing any product, commodity or service other than the Picture without the Lender's prior consent. In the event the Employee's name and/or likeness is used in connection with merchandising, the Producer shall pay or cause to be paid to the Employee a pro rata share (payable among all members of the cast of the Picture whose name and likeness is used) of _____ percent of the "net receipts," if any, actually received by the Producer from the exploitation of merchandising utilizing the Employee's name and/or likeness, other than in any listing of cast credits for the Picture. "Net receipts" shall be computed and accounted for in accordance with the customary accounting practices of the distributor of the Picture.

**10. Promotion and Publicity Services:**  The Lender agrees to cause the Employee, subject to the Employee's prior conflicting professional commitments, to participate in such promotional activities, including, without limitation, television and radio appearances, photo sessions, interviews, appearances at premieres and similar activities, as the Producer may reasonably request and the Guaranteed Compensation specified in Paragraph 4(a) hereof shall also constitute full and complete consideration to the Lender for such services. The provisions of Paragraph 5 hereof shall be applicable with respect to any services required of the Employee pursuant to this Paragraph 10. The Lender acknowledges the importance of conducting such promotional and publicity services, and agrees to cause the Employee to cooperate fully in connection therewith.

**11. Insurance/Air Transport:**  The Producer shall have the right to apply for and take out, at the Producer's expense, life, health, accident, cast or other insurance covering the Employee, in any amount the Producer deems necessary to protect the Producer's interest hereunder. Neither the Lender nor the Employee shall have any right, title or interest in or to such insurance. The Lender and the Employee shall assist the Producer in obtaining such insurance by submitting to usual and customary medical and other examinations and by signing such applications, statements and other instruments as may be required by any insurance company. In the event the Employee fails or is unable to qualify for such insurance at customary rates, the Producer shall have the right to terminate this Agreement by written notice to the Lender, given on or before the Start Date.

Employee shall not engage in any conduct prohibited by any policy of insurance obtained by the Producer in accordance with this Paragraph 11 (to the extent that the Lender or the Employee knows or should have known of such prohibition).

**12. Default:**  No act or omission of the Producer hereunder shall constitute an event of default or breach of this Agreement unless the Lender and the Employee shall first notify the Producer in writing setting forth such alleged breach or default and the Producer shall not commence reasonable efforts to cure said alleged breach or default within thirty (30) days after receipt of such notice. Upon any breach by the Lender and/or the Employee of any of the terms and conditions of this Agreement, the Producer shall immediately have the right, exercisable at any time after becoming aware of such breach, to suspend the Lender's engagement hereunder and/or to terminate this Agreement by so notifying the Lender in writing; provided, however, that if such breach shall occur after principal photography of the Picture, the Producer will notify the Employee of such breach and will afford the Employee forty-eight (48) hours after such notice to cure the alleged breach. The Producer's election to suspend this Agreement shall not affect its right to thereafter terminate this Agreement.

In the event of a suspension pursuant to this Paragraph 12, the Producer's obligation to make the payments described in Paragraph 4 hereof shall likewise be suspended. In the event of a termination pursuant to this Paragraph 12, the Lender shall be entitled to no further compensation hereunder. The foregoing shall in no way limit any other remedy which the Producer may have against the Lender.

**13. No Obligation to Proceed:** Nothing herein contained shall in any way obligate the Producer to use the Employee's services hereunder or to include the results and proceeds of the Employee's services in the Picture or to produce, exhibit, advertise or distribute the Picture. Not withstanding the foregoing, upon the condition that the Lender and the Employee shall fully perform all of the material terms and conditions hereof, nothing contained in this Paragraph shall relieve the Producer of its obligation to pay to the Lender the Guaranteed Compensation specified in Paragraph 4(a) hereof and the Producer's obligations to the Lender hereunder shall be deemed fully performed by payment to the Lender of said amount. Notwithstanding the foregoing, if the Producer shall suspend production of the Picture due to an event of force majeure and shall fail to recommence said production, the Producer shall pay to the Lender only that portion of the Guaranteed Compensation which shall have accrued prior to such suspension.

**14. Notices:** All notices hereunder shall be in writing and shall be given either by personal delivery, telegram or telex (toll prepaid) or by registered or certified mail (postage prepaid), and shall be deemed given here under on the date delivered, telegraphed or telexed or a date forty-eight (48) hours after the date mailed. Until further notice, the addresses of the parties shall be as follows:

LENDER: _____
(Lender)

_____
(Address)

_____
Fax:

With copy to: _____

_____

_____
Fax:

PRODUCER: _____
(Producer)

_____
(Producer Address)

_____
Fax:

With copy to: _____

_____

_____
Fax:

**15. Assignment:** The Lender agrees that the Producer may assign this Agreement, in whole or in part, at any time to any party, as the Producer shall determine in its sole discretion.

**16. Miscellaneous:** This Agreement shall be governed by the laws of the State of _____ applicable to agreements executed and wholly performed therein and all parties hereby consent to the jurisdiction of the courts of said State in the event of any dispute hereunder. This Agreement shall not be modified except by a written document executed by both parties hereto. The Paragraph headings used herein are for the convenience of the parties only and shall have no legal effect whatsoever.

**17. Lender's Agreement with Employee:** The Lender hereby represents and warrants that the Lender is a duly organized and existing corporation and is presently in good standing under the laws of the state of its incorporation, that the Lender has a valid, binding and subsisting agreement with the Employee pursuant to which the Employee is obligated to render services exclusively to the Lender for at least the full term of this Agreement and that, by the terms of such agreement, the Lender has the right to enter into this Agreement with the Producer for the furnishing of the Employee's services hereunder and to grant to the Producer any and all of the services and rights herein set forth. The Producer shall pay directly to the Lender all of the compensation that would have been payable to the Employee had the Employee rendered services directly to the Producer in the first instance, and the Producer shall not be obligated to make any payments of any nature whatsoever to the Employee. In no event shall the Lender's failure to pay any amounts to the Employee be deemed to constitute a breach of this Agreement by the Producer.

**18. Entire Agreement:** This Agreement (including Exhibit "A" attached hereto and by this reference made a part hereof) contains the full and complete understanding between the parties with reference to the within subject matter, supersedes all prior agreements and understandings whether written or oral pertaining thereto, and cannot be modified except by a written instrument signed by each party. The Lender acknowledges that in entering into this Agreement neither it nor the Employee has relied upon any representation or promise not expressly contained herein.

IN WITNESS WHEREOF, the parties have hereunto set their hands as of the date and year first indicated above.

_____          _____
("Lender")                                ("Producer")


By: _____          By:_____

Its:_____          Its:_____

# EXHIBIT A
## INDUCEMENT LETTER

Date: _____

_____
(Producer)

_____
(Producer Address)

Re: "_____" (Motion Picture)

Dear Sirs/Mesdames:

Reference is made to the agreement (herein the "Agreement") dated concurrently herewith between _____ (herein the "Producer") and _____ (herein the "Lender") for my services in the above-referenced motion picture.

As an inducement to you to enter into the Agreement and as a material part of the consideration moving to you for so doing, I hereby represent, warrant and agree as follows:

1. That I have entered into an agreement ("Actor's Employment Agreement") with the Lender covering the rendition of my services for the Lender, and that the Lender has the right and authority to enter into the Agreement and to furnish to you my services upon the terms and conditions therein specified.

2. I am familiar with each and all of the terms, covenants and conditions of the Agreement and hereby consent to the execution thereof; that I will be bound by and will duly observe, perform and comply with each and all of the terms, covenants and conditions of the Agreement on my part to be performed and complied with, even if the Actor's Employment Agreement should hereafter expire, be terminated (whether by the Lender or myself) or suspended; that I shall render to you all of the services which are to be rendered by me pursuant to the Agreement even if the Lender shall be dissolved or should otherwise cease to exist; and that I hereby confirm that there have been granted to the Lender all of the rights granted by the Lender to you under the Agreement.

3. That I am under no obligation or disability by law or otherwise which would prevent or restrict me from performing and complying with all of the terms, covenants and conditions of the Agreement to be performed or complied with by me.

4. That I will look solely to the Lender or its associated or subsidiary companies and not to you for all compensation and other remuneration for any and all services and rights which I may render and grant to you under the Agreement.

5. That you shall be entitled to equitable relief against me by injunction or otherwise to restrain, enjoin and/or prevent the violation or breach by me of any obligation of mine to be performed as provided in the Agreement, and/or the violation or breach by me of any obligations or agreements under this present instrument. You shall have all rights and remedies against me which you would have if I were your direct employee under the Agreement and you shall not be required to first resort to or exhaust any rights or remedies which you may have against the Lender before exercising your rights and remedies against me.

6. That I will indemnify and hold you, your employees, officers and assigns harmless from and against any and all taxes which you may have to pay and any and all liabilities (including judgments, penalties, interest, damages, costs and expenses including reasonable attorneys' fees, whether or not litigation is actually commenced) which may be obtained against, imposed or suffered by you or which you may incur by reason of your failure to deduct and withhold from the compensation payable under the Agreement any amounts required or permitted to be deducted and withheld from the compensation of an employee under the provisions of the Federal and _____ Income Tax acts, the Federal Social Security Act, the _____ Unemployment Insurance Act and/or any amendments thereof and/or any other statutes or regulations heretofore or hereafter enacted requiring the withholding of any amount from the compensation of an employee.

7. That I will not amend or modify the Actor's Employment Agreement with the Lender in any particular manner that would prevent or interfere with the performance of my services for you or the use and ownership of the results and proceeds thereof, pursuant to the Agreement.

_____
"Employee"
Actor

# ACTOR EMPLOYMENT AGREEMENT
## (Low-budget, Non-Union Day Player)

THIS AGREEMENT is made and entered into as of the _____ (Date), by and between _____ (Production Company), a _____ (State) corporation, (hereinafter "Producer"), and _____ (hereinafter "Player").

A. Producer intends to produce a theatrical motion picture (hereinafter the "Picture") based upon that certain screenplay tentatively entitled "_____" (hereinafter the "Screenplay") which Picture is intended for initial theatrical exhibition.

B. Producer wishes to utilize the services of Player in connection with the Picture upon the terms and conditions herein contained.

ACCORDINGLY, IT IS AGREED AS FOLLOWS:

**1. PHOTOPLAY, ROLE, SALARY AND GUARANTEE:** Producer hereby engages Player to render services as such in the role of _____, in the Screenplay, at the salary of $_____ Dollars per day. Player accepts such engagement upon the terms herein specified. Producer guarantees that it will furnish Player not less than _____ (Days of Employment).

**2. TERM:** The term of employment hereunder shall begin on or about _____ (the "Start Date") and continue until _____, or until the completion of the photography and recordation of said role.

**3. PLAYER'S ADDRESS:** All notices which the Producer is required or may desire to give to the Player may be given either by mailing the same addressed to the Player at the address listed at the end of this agreement, or such notice may be given to the Player personally, either orally or in writing.

**4. PLAYER'S TELEPHONE:** The Player must keep the Producer's casting office or the assistant director of said photoplay advised as to where the Player may be reached by telephone without unreasonable delay. The current telephone number of the Player is listed at the end of this agreement.

**5. FURNISHING OF WARDROBE:** The Player agrees to furnish all modern wardrobe and wearing apparel reasonably necessary for the portrayal of said role; it being agreed, however, that should so-called "character" or "period" costumes be required, the Producer shall supply the same. When Player furnishes any wardrobe, Player shall receive a reasonable cleaning allowance and reimbursement for any soiled or damaged clothes.

Number of outfits furnished by Player:

_____ (Informal Outfits) @ $_____ (Informal Cost)

**6. NEXT STARTING DATE:** The starting date of Player's next engagement is: _____.

**7. NON-UNION PICTURE:** Producer makes the material representation that it is not a signatory to the Screen Actors Guild collective bargaining agreement or any other union or guild agreement. Player warrants that Player is not a member of any union or guild, memberships in which would prevent Player from working in this picture.

**8. PROMOTIONAL FILM:** Producer shall have the exclusive right to make one or more promotional films of thirty (30) minutes or less and to utilize the results and proceeds of Player's services therein. Player agrees to render such services for said promotional films during the term of his employment hereunder as Producer may request and Player further agrees to use by Producer of film clips and behind-the-scenes shots in which Player appears in such promotional films. Provided Player appears therein, Producer shall pay to Player the sum of _____ within 30 days after the first use of each such promotional film on television or before a paying audience.

**9. NAME AND LIKENESS:** Producer shall have the exclusive right to use and to license the use of Player's name, sobriquet, photograph, likeness, voice and/or caricature and shall have the right to simulate Player's voice, signature and appearance by any means in and in connection with the film and the advertising, publicizing, exhibition, and/or other exploitation thereof in any manner and by any means and in connection with commercial advertising and publicity tie-ups.

**10. MERCHANDISING:** Producer is also granted the further exclusive right and license, but only in connection with the role portrayed by Player in the film to use and to license the use of Player's name, sobriquet, photograph, likeness, caricature and/or signature (collectively referred to herein as "name and likeness") in and in connection with any merchandising and/or publishing undertakings. In consideration therefore, Producer shall pay Player a pro rata share (payable among all players whose name, etc. is used on a piece of merchandise) of 2 1/2% of the gross monies actually derived by Producer after deducting therefrom a distribution fee of fifty percent (50%) thereof and a sum equal to all Producer's actual out-of-pocket expenses in connection therewith, for the use of such name or likeness on merchandising and publishing items which utilize Player's name and likeness, other than in a listing of cast credits.

**11. TRAVEL EXPENSES:** Any right of Player to transportation and expenses pursuant to this Agreement shall be effective when and only when Player is required by Producer to render services more than seventy-five (75) miles from Player's principal place of residence. Any weekly expense allowance provided Employee under this Agreement shall be prorated at one-seventh (1/7th) thereof per day. Player shall be reimbursed at the rate of _____ per mile for use of Player's car to travel to distant locations.

**12. INCLUSIVE PAYMENTS:** All payments to Player hereunder shall be deemed to be equitable and inclusive remuneration for all services rendered by Player in connection with the Picture and to be paid by way of a complete buy-out of all rights granted to Producer hereunder and no further sums shall be payable to Player by Producer by reason of the exploitation of the Picture and all results and proceeds of Player's services hereunder in any and all media throughout the universe pursuant to any collective bargaining agreement, if any, or otherwise, by way of residuals, repeat fees, pension contributions, or any other monies whatsoever.

**13. ARBITRATION:** Any controversy or claim arising out of or relating to this agreement or any breach thereof shall be settled by arbitration in accordance with the Rules of the American Arbitration Association; and judgment upon the award rendered by the arbitrators may be entered in any court having jurisdiction thereof. The prevailing party shall be entitled to reimbursement for costs and reasonable attorney's fees. The determination of the arbitrator in such proceeding shall be final, binding and non-appealable. In the event of any breach by the

Producer of this Agreement, the Player shall be limited to the Player's remedy at law for damages, if any, and shall not have the right to terminate or rescind this Agreement or to enjoin or restrain in any way the production, distribution, advertising or exploitation of the Picture.

**14. EMPLOYMENT ELIGIBILITY:** All of Producer's obligation herein are expressly conditioned upon Performer's completion, to Producer's satisfaction, of the I-9 form (Employee Eligibility Verification Form), and upon Performer's submission to Producer of original documents satisfactory to demonstrate to Production Producer Performer's employment eligibility.

IN WITNESS WHEREOF, the parties have executed this agreement on the day and year first above written.

AGREED TO AND ACCEPTED:


_____
(Actor), "Player"


Player address: _____

Player Phone number: _____

Player Social Security # _____


AGREED TO AND ACCEPTED:


(Producer),

By:_____


RIDER TO DAY PLAYER AGREEMENT
_____ (Production Company)

**1. SERVICES/TERM:** Producer engages Player as an actor in the Role set forth in the Principal Agreement and shall cause Player to render all services customarily rendered by actors in feature-length motion pictures at such times and places designated by Producer and in full compliance with Producer's instructions in all matters. Without limiting the foregoing, Player's services shall be in accordance with the following:

(a) Start Date : Principal Photography of the Picture shall commence on or about _____ but no later than _____. The Start Date shall be automatically extended without notice for a period equal to the duration of any default, disability and/or force majeure (as such terms are defined below and regardless of whether Player's services are suspended therefore), or due to any location requirements, director and/or cast unavailability, weather conditions, and/or other similar contingencies.

CONTRACTS
FOR THE
FILM AND
TELEVISION
INDUSTRY

100

(b) Exclusivity: Player's services hereunder shall be non-exclusive first priority during the Pre-Production, exclusive during Production Periods, and non-exclusive, but on a first-priority basis, during the Post-Production Period.

(c) Retakes and Other Additional Services : During and after the Term, Player shall render such services as Producer may desire in producing retakes, added scenes, transparencies, closeups, sound track (including dubbing and looping), process shots, trick shots and trailers for changes in and foreign versions of the Picture. Compensation for such additional services shall be payable pursuant to Paragraph 1 of the principal agreement; provided, however, that no compensation shall be payable for such additional services to the extent they are rendered during any period for which Producer is otherwise obligated to pay or has paid Player compensation, or is entitled to Player's services without compensation.

(d) Nights, Weekends, Holidays, Work Time : No increased or additional compensation shall accrue or be payable to Player for services rendered by Player at night or on weekends or holidays, or after the expiration of any number of hours of service in any period.

**2. CREDIT:** There shall be no obligation to accord Player credit in paid advertising and/or publicity, although Producer may from time to time elect, in its sole discretion, to accord Player such credit. Producer shall accord Player customary shared screen credit.

**3. RIGHTS:** Player grants, and Producer shall have, the perpetual and universal right to photograph and re-photograph Player (still and moving) and to record and re-record, double and dub Player's voice and performances, by any present or future methods or means and to use and authorize others to use Player's name, voice and likeness for and in connection with the Picture, the soundtrack (including a soundtrack album), trailers, and documentary and/or "making of" pictures, and all advertising (including Player's name and likeness on sleeves, jackets and other packaging for soundtrack albums, video cassettes, videodiscs, written publications and the like), merchandising, commercial tie-ups, publicity, and other means of exploitation of any and all rights pertaining to the Picture and any element thereof. Producer shall own all results and proceeds of Player's services hereunder, including the copyrights thereof, and as such owner shall have the right (among all other rights of ownership): (i) to include such results and proceeds in the Picture and in advertising and publicity relating to the Picture, (ii) to reproduce such results and proceeds by any present or future means, (iii) to combine such results and proceeds with photographs and recordings made by others for use in the Picture, (iv) to exhibit and perform such results and proceeds in theaters, on the radio and television, and in or by any other present or future media, for profit and otherwise, and for commercial or non-commercial purposes and purposes of trade, and (v) to license and assign its rights to any other person or producer. Without in any way limiting the foregoing, the results and proceeds of Player's services hereunder include any and all material, words, writings, ideas, "gags", dialogue, melody and lyrics composed, submitted or interpolated by Player in connection with the preparation or production of the Picture (hereinafter referred to as "material"). All said material, the copyright therein, and all renewals, extensions or reversions of copyright now or hereafter provided, shall automatically become the property of Producer, which shall be deemed the author thereof, it being agreed and acknowledged that all of the results and proceeds of Player's services hereunder are a specially ordered and commissioned "work made for hire" within the meaning of the 1976 Copyright Act for the compensation provided in the Principal Agreement.

Player hereby expressly waives and relinquishes any moral rights or "droit morale" in and to any material created by or contributed to the Picture by Player including all of Player's performance.

**4. FORCE MAJEURE:** As used herein the term "force majeure" means epidemic, act of God, strike, lockout, labor condition, unavailability of materials, transportation, power or other commodity, delay of common carrier, civil disturbance, riot, war or armed conflict (whether or not there has been an official declaration of war), the enactment of any law, the issuance of any executive or judicial order or decree, breach of contract by, or disability of, the Producer, Director, other principal cast member, breach of contract by a financier or completion guarantor, or other similar occurrence beyond the control of Producer, which causes an interruption of or materially hampers or materially interferes with the production of the Picture.

**5. INSURANCE:** Player warrants that to the best of Player's knowledge Player is in good health and has no condition which would prevent Producer from obtaining life, health, accident, cast or other insurance covering Player at premium rates normal to Player's age and sex, without any unusual exclusion or limitation of liability on the part of the insurer.

**6. WITHHOLDING:** Producer may deduct and withhold from any monies otherwise payable under this Agreement such amounts as Producer may reasonably believe it is legally required to deduct and withhold.

**7. ASSIGNMENT:** Producer shall have the right to assign this Agreement and any of the rights granted herein, in whole or in part, to any person, firm, corporation or entity, and nothing contained herein shall imply anything to the contrary. Upon the assignee's assumption of the obligations of Producer with respect to the rights so assigned, Producer shall be relieved of all such obligations. Producer shall also have the right to lend the services of Player to any person, firm or corporation which is a subsidiary, parent or affiliate of Producer or the successor to Producer by a merger or by a transfer of substantially all of Producer's assets hereunder. In the event of any such lending, Player agrees to render his services to the best of his ability to the person, firm, or corporation to whom his services are loaned hereunder. Player may not assign Player's rights or obligations hereunder.

AGREED TO AND ACCEPTED:

———————————————
(Actor)

CONTRACTS
FOR THE
FILM AND
TELEVISION
INDUSTRY

102

# EXTRA AGREEMENT

Producer: _____ (Production Company Name)

MOTION PICTURE: _____

EMPLOYEE EMPLOYMENT DATE(S): _____ through _____

ROLE: _____

EMPLOYEE NAME: _____

ADDRESS: _____

PHONE: Home: _____ Work: _____

SOCIAL SECURITY #: _____

RATE: $_____ per day

OTHER TERMS: _____

## TERMS AND CONDITIONS OF EMPLOYMENT

1. Payment of Wages: Wages shall be paid to all employees no later than Friday following the week in which services were performed. Pay date may be delayed by reason of an intervening federal or state holiday. Employee is responsible for submitting her/his time card at the end of the work week to insure timely payment. No employee will be paid without fully completing these forms.

2. All payments to Employee hereunder shall be deemed to be equitable and inclusive remuneration for all services rendered by Employee in connection with the Picture and to be paid by way of a complete buy-out of all rights granted to Producer hereunder and no further sums shall be payable to Employee by Producer by reason of the exploitation of the Picture and all results and proceeds of Employee's services hereunder in any and all media throughout the universe pursuant to any collective bargaining agreement, if any, or otherwise, by way of residuals, repeat fees, pension contributions, or any other monies whatsoever.

3. Nights, Weekends, Holidays, Work Time: Unless expressly provided elsewhere in this deal memo, no increased or additional compensation shall accrue or be payable to employee for the rendering of services at night or on weekends or holidays, or after the expiration of any particular number of hours of service in any period.

4. The Producer will provide meal breaks and/or food service at approximately six (6) hour intervals.

5. Immigration Reform and Control Act of 1986 (IRCA): Employment (or the engagement of services) hereunder is subject to employee providing the requisite documents required by IRCA and completing and signing the required Form I-9 pursuant to IRCA Section 274a.2. Employee shall comply with the immigration verification employment eligibility provisions required by law.

6. Use of alcohol or drugs during hours of employment will result in employee's immediate termination.

7. Employee's services are on an exclusive basis to the production of the motion picture (the "Picture") referred to in this deal memo for such period of time as required unless otherwise specified in this deal memo.

8. Screen credit is at Producer's discretion subject to employee's performing all services required through completion of term.

9. Unless expressly provided elsewhere in this agreement, employee's employment hereunder shall not be for a "run of the show" or for any guaranteed period of employment. Production reserves the right to discharge employee at any time, subject only to the obligation to pay the balance of any guaranteed compensation due. Producer will attempt to notify employees a minimum of twenty-four (24) hours in advance of layoff. This agreement is subject to immediate suspension and/or termination (at Production's election) without further obligation on the part of Production in the event of any incapacity or default of employee or in the case of any suspension, postponement or interference with the production by reason of labor controversy, strike, earthquake, act of God, governmental action, regulation, or decree or for any other customary force majeure reason.

10. The terms and conditions of this deal memo are binding on Producer and Employee and shall not be waived or altered by any method.

11. Producer shall be the owner of all of the results and proceeds of Employee's services and shall have the right to use employee's name, voice, picture and likeness in connection with the Picture, the advertising and publicizing thereof, and any promotional films or clips respecting the Picture without additional compensation therefore. Employee hereby grants to Producer and to its licensees, assignees, and other successors-in-interest all rights of every kind and character whatsoever, throughout the universe, in perpetuity in and to Employee's performance, appearance, name and/or voice and the results and proceeds thereof ("the Performance") in connection with the Picture, and hereby authorizes Producer to photograph and record (on film, tape, or otherwise), the Performance; to edit same at its discretion and to include it with the performance of others and with sound effects, special effects and music; to incorporate same into Picture or other program or not; to use and to license others to use such recordings and photographs in any manner or media whatsoever, including without limitation unrestricted use for purposes of publicity, advertising and sales promotion; and to use Employee's name, likeness, voice, biographic or other information concerning Employee in connection with the Picture, commercial tie-ups, merchandising, and for any other purpose.

12. This Agreement shall be interpreted in accordance with the laws of the State of _____, applicable to agreements executed and to be wholly performed therein. Any controversy or claim arising out of or in relation to this Agreement or the validity, construction or performance of this Agreement, or the breach thereof, shall be resolved by arbitration in accordance with the rules and procedures of AFMA, as said rules may be amended from time to time with rights of discovery if requested by the arbitrator. Such rules and procedures are incorporated and made a part of this Agreement by reference. If AFMA shall refuse to accept jurisdiction of such dispute, then the parties agree to arbitrate such matter before and in accordance with the rules of the American Arbitration Association under its jurisdiction in _____ (State Law) before a single arbitrator familiar with entertainment law. The parties shall have the right to engage in pre-hearing discovery in connection with such arbitration proceedings. The parties

CONTRACTS
FOR THE
FILM AND
TELEVISION
INDUSTRY

104

agree hereto that they will abide by and perform any award rendered in any arbitration conducted pursuant hereto, that any court having jurisdiction thereof may issue a judgment based upon such award and that the prevailing party in such arbitration and/or confirmation proceeding shall be entitled to recover its reasonable attorneys' fees and expenses. The arbitration award shall be final, binding and non-appealable. The Parties agree to accept service of process in accordance with the AFMA Rules.

EMPLOYEE ACCEPTS ALL CONDITIONS OF EMPLOYMENT AS DESCRIBED ABOVE.

AGREED TO AND ACCEPTED:

EMPLOYEE SIGNATURE: _____DATE: _____

PRODUCER SIGNATURE: _____DATE: _____

# EXTRA RELEASE

FOR GOOD AND VALUABLE CONSIDERATION, I hereby grant to _____ ("Producer") and to its licensees, assignees, and other successors-in-interest all rights of every kind and character whatsoever in perpetuity in and to my performance, appearance, name and/or voice and the results and proceeds thereof (the "Performance") in connection with the motion picture currently entitled _____ ("The Picture"), and I hereby authorize Producer to photograph and record (on film, tape, or otherwise), the Performance; to edit same at its discretion and to include it with the performance of others and with sound effects, special effects and music; to incorporate same into Picture or other program or not; to use and to license others to use such recordings and photographs in any manner or media whatsoever, including without limitation unrestricted use for purposes of publicity, advertising and sales promotion; and to use my name, likeness, voice, biographic or other information concerning me in connection with the Picture, commercial tie-ups, merchandising, and for any other purpose. I agree that Producer owns all rights and proceeds of my services rendered in connection herewith as a work–made for hire.

AGREED TO AND ACCEPTED:

_____          DATE: _____
(Extra's Name)

# EMPLOYING MINORS

Note that a minor may be able to repudiate or dissafirm contracts in certain circumstances. See the discussion concerning employment of minors under Actor Employment in this Chapter.

## MINOR RELEASE

The undersigned, being the legal parent(s) or guardian(s) of _____, a minor child (hereinafter referred to as the "Child"), being of legal age and residents of the state of _____, at _____, do hereby consent and grant to _____ (Production company name), permission (1) to take photographs and record the voice of the Child in connection with the motion picture "_____" (the "Picture"), (2) to put the finished pictures, negatives, reproductions and copies or the original prints and negatives of the Child and any sound track recordings, and recordings which may be made of the Child's voice, including the right to substitute the voice of other persons for the Child's voice, the Child's name, or likeness, (collectively "Tangible and Intangible Items"), in said Picture and (3) to use said Tangible and Intangible Items in any manner deemed proper by _____ (Production Company Name) so long as such use is in connection with the exhibition, advertising, promotion, distribution and/or exploitation of said Picture

The undersigned further agree and warrant that the above-mentioned minor Child, will not disaffirm or disavow this consent and permission on the ground that the Child was a minor on the date of execution thereof or any similar grounds whatsoever, or endeavor to recover from _____ (Production Company Name) or any of its individual shareholders, directors, officers, employees or other associated persons, or through any guardian, any sums for participating in the Picture, other than those sums specified in the Child Actor Employment Agreement which accompanies this Minor Release.

PARENT/GUARDIAN

_____        Date: _____

PARENT/GUARDIAN

_____        Date: _____

CONTRACTS
FOR THE
FILM AND
TELEVISION
INDUSTRY

106

# NUDITY RIDER TO PLAYER AGREEMENT

DATED AS OF _____,
BETWEEN _____ ("PRODUCTION COMPANY")
AND _____ ("PLAYER") IN CONNECTION WITH THE MOTION
PICTURE CURRENTLY ENTITLED "_____" ("PICTURE")

Reference is made to the Agreement dated _____ (the "Agreement") between you, ("Player") and _____ ("Production Company") with respect to your acting services in connection with the theatrical motion picture currently entitled _____ (the "Picture").

**1. NUDITY SEX ACTS:** It is understood between the parties that, with respect
to the services to be rendered by Player, for the consideration set forth in the
Agreement, such services shall require Player to appear nude and/or semi-nude,
and/or perform designated sexual act(s), as the case may be, in the Picture. The
general description of the extent of such nudity, and the type of physical contact
required in such designated sex acts, is attached as Exhibit "A."

**2. PLAYER'S CONSENT:** Player agrees and consents to render the services set
forth above and hereby affirms that Player agrees to appear nude and/or semi-
nude and to perform such designated sex act(s).

**3. OWNERSHIP OF PERFORMANCE:** Pursuant to terms and conditions of the
Agreement, Production Company owns all results and proceeds of Player's services
rendered pursuant to the Agreement and has the exclusive right to use, license and
exploit the Picture and Player's performance therein, throughout the world in
perpetuity in any and all media whether now known or hereafter devised.

All terms and provisions of the Agreement remain in full force and effect without modification or change and the Agreement is hereby affirmed.

I acknowledge my agreement to the foregoing by signing below:

AGREED TO AND ACCEPTED:


_____
"PLAYER"



## EXHIBIT "A"

1) _____ (Description of Sex Acts #1)

2) _____ (Description of Sex Acts #2)

3) _____ (Description of Sex Acts #3)

# STUNT PERFORMER'S AGREEMENT

This agreement (hereinafter referred to as the "Agreement") is entered into on this _____ by and between _____, whose offices are located at _____ (the "Production Company") and _____ (SS# _____) whose residence address is _____ (the "Stunt Performer").

**1. DESCRIPTION OF SERVICES:** The Production Company hereby engages the Stunt Performer to render services as _____ (Role) in conjunction with the motion picture entitled "_____" (the "Picture") and to perform such activities as required by the Production Company and further described in the shooting script for the Picture. The Stunt Performer accepts such engagement upon the terms herein specified.

**2. COMPENSATION, TERM AND GUARANTEE:** The Production Company agrees to pay the Stunt Performer and the Stunt Performer agrees to accept the following weekly compensation (excluding location premiums) of _____ Dollars (and pro rata for each additional day beyond the guarantee until completion of the Stunt Performer's services). The total guaranteed compensation shall be _____ Dollars for the total guaranteed period of _____ weeks. The Stunt Performer shall receive sixth day location premiums where applicable.

**3. START DATE:** The term of the Stunt Performer's engagement shall begin on _____ or in the alternative on or about _____, (the "Start Date") if this Agreement is signed by both parties and delivered to the Stunt Performer at least _____ days before the Start Date.

**4. NEXT START DATE:** The start date of the Stunt Performer's next engagement is _____.

**5. STUNT ADJUSTMENTS:** It is understood that the rate of compensation specified may be adjusted depending upon the nature of the stunt activities the Production Company may require. If so, a stunt adjustment will be agreed upon between the parties through good faith bargaining, said adjustments shall be noted on the Stunt Performer daily time report or time card and said reports and/or time cards shall be signed or initialed by the Stunt Performer. Production time reports and/or time cards shall be made available by the Production Company on the set at the beginning and end of each day.

In all such instances, the parties shall agree upon such compensation adjustments before the stunt is performed if they may readily do so; however, it is expressly agreed that production shall not be delayed for the purpose of first determining the compensation for a stunt. Such adjustments shall increase the Stunt Performer's compensation for the week in the manner prescribed in Schedule H-II or H-III of the Screen Actors Guild Codified Basic Agreement.

**6. INCORPORATION OF PRODUCER/SAG COLLECTIVE BARGAINING AGREEMENT:** All provisions of the Screen Actors Guild Codified Basic Agreement as the same may be supplemented and/or amended to date shall be deemed incorporated herein. The Stunt Performer's engagement shall be upon the terms, conditions and exceptions of said provisions applicable to the rate of compensation and guarantee specified.

CONTRACTS
FOR THE
FILM AND
TELEVISION
INDUSTRY

108

**7. OWNERSHIP OF RESULTS AND PROCEEDS:** The Production Company shall have the unlimited right throughout the universe and in perpetuity to exhibit the Picture in all media, now or hereafter known, and the Production Company, as the employer-for-hire of the Stunt Performer, shall own all rights in the results and proceeds of the Stunt Performer's services hereunder.

**8. ADDITIONAL COMPENSATION:** If the Picture covered hereby is exhibited, containing any of the results and proceeds of the Stunt Performer's services hereunder, in any of the following media:

(a)     "Free" television re-runs in the United States or Canada, or both;

(b)     Television exhibition anywhere in the universe outside the United States and Canada;

(c)     Theatrical exhibition anywhere in the universe;

(d)     Supplemental Market exhibition anywhere in the universe; or

(e)     Basic Cable exhibition anywhere in the universe.

As to each such medium in which the Picture is so exhibited, the Production Company will pay, and the Stunt Performer hereby agrees to accept as payment in full, the minimum additional compensation provided therefor in the SAG Codified Basic Agreement or Television Agreement, as the case may be.

**9. CONTINUOUS EMPLOYMENT AND RIGHT TO ROLE:** If the Stunt Performer portrays a role or has dialogue, the Stunt Performer shall be entitled to "Continuous Employment" and "Right to Role", if any, (as such terms are defined by the SAG Codified Basic Agreement and only to the extent prescribed such agreement). The Stunt Performer shall receive a separate contract for such services.

**10. MOTION PICTURE AND TELEVISION FUND:** The Stunt Performer hereby authorizes the Production Company to deduct from the compensation hereinabove specified an amount equal to two percent (2%) of each installment of compensation due the Stunt Performer hereunder, and to pay the amount so deducted to the Motion Picture and Television Fund of America, Inc.

**11. WAIVER:** The Stunt Performer may not waive any provision of the SAG Codified Basic Agreement or Television Agreement, whichever is applicable, without the written consent of the Screen Actors Guild, Inc.

**12. SIGNATORY:** The Production Company makes the material representation that either it is presently a signatory to the Screen Actors Guild collective bargaining agreement covering the engagement contract for herein, or that the Picture is covered by such collective bargaining agreement under the "Independent Production" provisions (Section 24) of the General Provisions of the SAG Codified Basic Agreement.

The signing of this Agreement in the spaces below signifies acceptance by the Production Company and the Stunt Performer of all of the above terms and conditions as of the date first above written.

PRODUCTION COMPANY

———————————————————————

STUNT PERFORMER

———————————————————————

# TELEVISION HOST AGREEMENT

This Agreement made between_____, a _____ corporation, herein called the Corporation, with principal place of business at _____, and _____ (Host Name), herein called the Employee, residing at _____,

For and in consideration of the mutual undertakings herein set forth, the parties agree as follows:

**1. EMPLOYMENT:** The Corporation hereby engages Employee to render his exclusive services to the Corporation during the term of this agreement. The Employee hereby accepts such employment, and undertakes to perform all the duties and obligations assumed by him hereunder.

**2. DUTIES AND SERVICES:** The Employee's services shall consist of the following: host of a television show about _____ tentatively titled "_____." Show length: approximately _____ minutes.

**3. TERM:** The term of this agreement shall commence on _____, and shall continue for a period of one year from such date, unless further extended as provided in clauses 5 and 13, or sooner terminated as provided in clauses 14 and 15. The aforesaid one-year period is herein called the Initial Term.

**4. COMPENSATION:** Provided the Employee duly performs his obligations hereunder, the Corporation shall pay him for his services and for all rights herein granted and agreed to be granted by him to the Corporation, the sum of $_____ for the initial pilot. Once the show goes into production, Employee shall be paid $_____ per episode or $_____ per day with _____ episodes shot each day, whichever is less. Such compensation shall be payable one week after the services are rendered.

**5. OPTION TO EXTEND TERM:** In consideration of the execution of this agreement by the Corporation, the Employee hereby grants to the Corporation the following rights or options:

(a) To extend the term of the Employee's employment for an additional period of one year (herein called the First Extension Period) from the expiration of the Initial Term, upon the same terms and conditions as those herein contained, except that the Employee's compensation during the First Extension Period shall be at the rate of $_____ per day which includes the production of _____ episodes.

(b) To extend the term of the Employee's employment for an additional period of one year (herein called the Second Extension Period) from the expiration of the First Extension Period, upon the same terms and conditions as those herein contained, except that the Employee's compensation during the Second Extension Period shall be at the rate of $_____ per day which includes the production of _____ episodes.

(c) To extend the term of the Employee's employment for an additional period of one year (herein called the Third Extension Period) from the expiration of the Second Extension Period, upon the same terms and conditions as those herein contained, except that (1) the Employee's compensation during the Third Extension Period shall be at the rate of $_____ per

CONTRACTS
FOR THE
FILM AND
TELEVISION
INDUSTRY

110

day which includes the production of _____ episodes, and except that (2) there shall be no further right and option to extend.

Each of the foregoing options may be exercised separately at any time, but not later than thirty days prior to the expiration of the then current period. No option shall be exercisable unless all preceding options have been exercised. The exercise by the Corporation of any option shall not be deemed to be (1) an exercise of any subsequent option or options, nor (2) a waiver by the Corporation of any prior breach of this agreement by the Employee, whether known or unknown, nor (3) a ratification by the Corporation of any prior course of conduct on the part of the Employee. The exercise of any option shall be by notice served upon the Employee within the periods above specified.

Whenever in this agreement the words "the term hereof" or "the term of this agreement" are used, such words shall mean and include not only the Initial Term, but also all Extension Periods if the options with respect thereto are exercised.

**6. PERFORMANCE:** The Employee shall devote his full time, attention and energy to the performance of his services hereunder. He shall perform the same conscientiously and to the full limit of his ability at all times. He shall promptly and faithfully comply with all the instructions, directions, requests, rules and regulations of the Corporation in connection therewith.

**7. PLACE OF PERFORMANCE:** The Employee's services shall be rendered in _____ and, on a temporary basis, at such place or places outside _____ as the Corporation may designate from time to time. If the Employee is required to perform services outside _____, the Corporation shall at its cost supply such transportation (first class if available) and suitable meals and lodgings for the Employee as may be necessitated thereby.

**8. SERVICES EXCLUSIVE:** The Employee shall render his services solely and exclusively for the Corporation throughout the term hereof on those days when Corporation is videotaping episodes. The shooting schedule shall be proposed by the Corporation which shall endeavor to schedule production so that there is no conflict with Employee's other professional commitments. Employee shall make himself reasonably available for production of episodes.

(a) The Corporation recognizes that the Employee has, in connection with his prior performances on television, granted to others the right to use his name, voice and likeness for the purpose of promoting and advertising the same. However, the Employee shall not, during the term hereof, grant any such right to others in connection with any show similar to Corporation's without the Corporation's prior written consent.

(b) Except as above stated, the Employee shall not during the term of this agreement permit the issuance of any advertising, exploitation or publicity whatsoever concerning him and the Corporation's show without the Corporation's prior written consent, nor shall he announce or make known, directly or indirectly, by paid advertisement, press notice or otherwise, that he has contracted to perform any services contrary to the terms hereof.

**9. EMPLOYEE'S CONDUCT:** The Employee shall not during the term hereof act in a manner tending to be offensive to decency, morality, or social propriety, or tending to result in scandal, ridicule or contempt, or tending to provoke any retaliatory action or boycott against himself or the Corporation.

**10. OWNERSHIP OF RESULTS AND PROCEEDS:** In addition to the Employee's services, the Corporation shall be entitled to, and shall own, solely and exclusively, all the results and proceeds thereof as a work-for-hire, and all rights of every kind therein.

(a) The Employee hereby assigns and transfers to the Corporation all his right, title and interest in such results and proceeds, without reservation, condition or limitation. If the Corporation desires to secure separate assignments thereof, the Employee shall promptly execute and deliver the same to the Corporation upon request.

(b) The Employee shall not transfer or attempt to transfer to anyone other than the Corporation, any right, title or interest in or to any of the foregoing, nor shall he at any time make or purport to make any grant to any third party in derogation thereof.

(c) The provisions of this clause 10 shall remain in full force and effect regardless of the termination of this agreement, and regardless of whether such termination occurs through expiration or as a result of cancellation by the Corporation.

**11. USE OF NAME AND LIKENESS:** Except as otherwise specifically provided in clause 8(a), the Corporation shall have:

(a) The exclusive right during the term hereof to use the Employee's name, voice and likeness for advertising and promoting the television programs in which he has rendered services to the Corporation; and

(b) The non-exclusive right to use the same after the termination of this agreement in connection with such programs.

(c) The use hereinabove referred shall not, without the Employee's written consent, include the use of his name, voice or likeness for general commercial purposes, such as the advertising or promotion of a product or service by way of endorsement or otherwise.

**12. INSURANCE:** The Corporation shall have the right to apply, at any time or from time to time, in its own name or otherwise, and at its own expense, for life, health, accident or other insurance covering the Employee, in order to protect its interest hereunder. The Employee shall assist the Corporation in procuring such insurance by submitting to the customary medical examination and by signing such papers as may reasonably be required in connection therewith. The Employee shall have no right, title or interest in or to such insurance.

**13. CORPORATION'S RIGHT TO SUSPEND:** The Corporation shall have the right to suspend the operation of this agreement, both as to services and compensation, for a period equal to all or any part of the period or aggregate of periods during which any contingency mentioned in clause 16 occurs.

(a) The Corporation shall give the Employee immediate notice of any suspension.

(b) Upon the resumption of the operation of this agreement, the Corporation shall have the right to extend the term hereof for a period equal to all or any part of the period of suspension.

CONTRACTS
FOR THE
FILM AND
TELEVISION
INDUSTRY

112

(c) Any such right of extension shall be exercised by notice served upon the Employee prior to the expiration of the then current term.

**14. CORPORATION'S RIGHT TO TERMINATE:** The Corporation shall have the right, at its option, to terminate this agreement at any time upon or during the occurrence of:

(a) Any contingency mentioned in subdivision (a) of clause 16 if it continues for more than two weeks; or

(b) Any contingency mentioned in subdivision (b) of clause 16 if it continues for more than six weeks; or

(c) Any contingency mentioned in subdivision (c), (d) or (e) of clause 16.

In the event of the termination of this agreement in accordance with the foregoing provisions, the Corporation shall upon such termination be released from all further obligations to the Employee hereunder, except that it shall be liable to the Employee for such compensation as may have been unpaid prior thereto. Termination by the Corporation shall not be deemed to be a waiver on its part of any other rights or remedies it may have by reason of the circumstances on which the termination is predicated.

**15. EMPLOYEE'S RIGHT TO TERMINATE:** The Employee shall have the right to terminate this agreement at any time during the occurrence of any contingency mentioned in subdivision (b) of clause 16 if the Corporation has suspended this agreement for such contingency and such suspension continues for a period of six weeks or more.

(a) If the Employee elects to terminate as aforesaid, he shall do so by notifying the Corporation to that effect upon the expiration of the six-week period.

(b) If within five days after receipt of the Employee's notice of termination, the Corporation resumes the payment of compensation to the Employee and continues such payment during the remainder of the continuance of the contingency, then notwithstanding the Employee's notice this agreement shall not be terminated, but shall remain in full force and effect. However, in that event the Corporation shall not thereafter have the right to suspend or terminate this agreement for the same contingency, whether occurring during the same period of the term hereof or during any subsequent option period.

**16. CONTINGENCIES:** The contingencies mentioned in clauses 13, 14 and 15 shall be as follows:

(a) The inability of the Employee to fully perform his obligations hereunder by reason of mental or physical incapacity or accident or any other cause that renders such non-performance excusable at law.

(b) The hampering or interruption of the operation of the Corporation's business by force majeure or any other cause beyond the Corporation's control.

(c) The failure or refusal of the Employee to render his required services hereunder to the best of his ability as, when and wherever instructed by the Corporation, except for any cause mentioned in subdivision (a) or (b) of this clause 16.

(d) The Employee's failure or inability to qualify for insurance at any time during the original term hereof or during any option period.

(e) The breach by the Employee of any material provision of this agreement.

**17. NO OBLIGATION TO USE SERVICES:** Subject to Corporation's obligation to pay the Employee the compensation specified in clause 4 or clause 5, as the case may be (except as otherwise provided in clause 13) the Corporation shall not be obligated to use the Employee's services, and shall not be liable to the Employee in any way for failure to do so in whole or in part.

**18. EQUITABLE RELIEF:** The Employee acknowledges that the services he is to render to the Corporation are of a special and extraordinary character that gives them a unique value; that the loss of such services could not be reasonably or adequately compensated by damages in an action at law; and that a breach by him of any provision hereof would cause the Corporation irreparable injury.

(a) Accordingly the Corporation shall be entitled to injunctive or other equitable relief to prevent such breach.

(b) Resort by the Corporation to such relief shall not be construed as a waiver by it of any other rights it might have for damages or otherwise.

(c) If the Employee at any time indicates to the Corporation that he does not intend to perform his obligations hereunder, such indication shall constitute a breach thereof on his part.

(d) The Corporation's rights and remedies by reason of the Employee's breach of his obligations hereunder shall be cumulative; and the exercise of any one or more of them shall not be exclusive of any other or others the Corporation might have under this agreement or by law.

**19. DEDUCTIONS:** The Corporation shall have the right to deduct and withhold from the Employee's compensation any amounts required to be deducted and withheld by it pursuant to any present or future law.

(a) If the Corporation makes any payments or incurs any charges for the Employee's account or if the Employee incurs any charges with the Corporation, the Corporation shall have the right to recoup such payments or charges by deducting the aggregate amount thereof from any compensation then or thereafter payable to the Employee hereunder. This provision shall not limit or exclude any other right of recovery that the Corporation may have.

(b) Nothing herein contained shall be construed to obligate the Corporation to make such payments or incur such charges or to permit the Employee to incur such charges.

CONTRACTS
FOR THE
FILM AND
TELEVISION
INDUSTRY

114

(c) If the Employee claims that any such deduction is unauthorized, he shall so notify the Corporation, and due consideration shall be given to the merits of his claim; but the making of any such deduction shall not constitute a breach of this agreement by Corporation, even though it may ultimately be found to have been unwarranted.

(d) If the Corporation pays the Employee any compensation that the Employee is not entitled to receive, the Employee shall repay such compensation to the Corporation on demand, or the Corporation may at its option recoup the amount thereof by deducting the same from any compensation thereafter payable to the Employee.

**20. GUILD MEMBERSHIP:** During the entire term of this agreement, the Employee shall become and remain a member in good standing of the properly designated labor organization or organizations (as defined and determined under applicable law) representing persons performing services of the type and character that the Employee is required to perform hereunder.

**21. EMPLOYEE'S RIGHT TO CONTRACT:** The Employee represents and warrants to the Corporation that he has the full right and power to enter into this agreement; that he does not now have, nor will at any time hereafter enter into, any contract or commitment with any third party that will prevent or interfere with the full and complete performance of his obligations hereunder, or with the full exercise and enjoyment by the Corporation of its rights hereunder.

**22. RELATIONSHIP OF PARTIES:** Nothing herein contained shall be deemed to constitute a partnership between, or a joint venture by, or an agency relationship between, the parties. Neither party shall hold itself or himself out contrary to the terms of this clause, by any means whatsoever. Neither party shall be bound by, or become liable for, any representation, commitment, act or omission whatsoever of the other contrary to the provisions hereof.

**23. NOTICES:** All notices hereunder shall be in writing, and shall be served by mail, telegraph or cable, duly addressed to the parties at their respective addresses hereinabove given. Either party may specify a different address for such purpose by notice given to the other in the same manner.

**24. CLAUSE HEADINGS:** The headings of the clauses of this agreement are solely for the purpose of convenience. They are not a part hereof, and shall not be used in the construction of any provision.

**25. CONSTRUCTION:** This agreement shall be construed in accordance with the laws of the State of (State Law).

**26. WAIVER:** No waiver by either party of the breach of any provision of this agreement shall be deemed to be a waiver of any preceding or succeeding breach of the same or similar nature.

**27. MODIFICATION:** This agreement may not be changed or modified, nor may any provision hereof be waived, except by an agreement in writing signed by the party against whom enforcement of the change or modification is asserted.

**28. ASSIGNMENT, Etc.:** This agreement shall inure to the benefit of, and shall be binding on, the Corporation's successors and assigns.

**29. AGREEMENT COMPLETE:** This agreement constitutes the entire understanding between the parties. All previous representations and undertakings, whether oral or written, have been merged herein.

In Witness Whereof the parties have executed this agreement this
_____ (Agreement Date).


_____
(Corp. Name)


_____
By:
Authorized Officer


_____
(Host Name)


ACKNOWLEDGMENT


STATE OF                              )
                                     ) ss.
COUNTY OF                            )


On _____, 199__, before me personally appeared
_____ who proved to me on the basis of satisfactory evidence
to be the person whose name is subscribed to the within instrument and acknowledged to me that she executed the same in her authorized capacity, and that by
her signature on the instrument the person, or the entity upon behalf of which
the person acted, executed the instrument.

WITNESS my hand and official seal.


_____
Notary Public in and for said
County and State

CONTRACTS
FOR THE
FILM AND
TELEVISION
INDUSTRY

116

# TELEVISION PERFORMER EMPLOYMENT AGREEMENT

This Agreement made between _____ (Employer Name), a _____, herein called the Company, with principal place of business at _____, City of _____, State of _____, and _____ (Employee Name), herein called the Employee, residing at _____, City of _____, State of _____.

For and in consideration of the mutual undertakings herein set forth, the parties agree as follows:

**1. EMPLOYMENT:** The Company hereby engages the Employee to render his exclusive services to the Company during the term of this Agreement. The Employee hereby accepts such employment, and undertakes to perform all the duties and obligations assumed by him hereunder.

**2. DUTIES AND SERVICES:** The Employee's services shall consist of the following:

**3. TERM:** The term of this Agreement shall commence on _____, and shall continue for a period of _____ year from such date, unless further extended as provided in clauses 5 and 13, or sooner terminated as provided in clauses 14 and 15. The aforesaid_____ year period is herein called the Initial Term.

**4.COMPENSATION:** Provided the Employee duly performs his obligations hereunder, the Company shall pay him for his services and for all rights herein granted and agreed to be granted by him to the Company, the sum of $_____ per week. Such compensation shall be payable on Monday of each week for services rendered during the preceding week.

**5. OPTION TO EXTEND TERM:** In consideration of the execution of this agreement by the Company, the Employee hereby grants to the Company the following rights or options:

(a) To extend the term of the Employee's employment for an additional period of _____ year(s) (herein called the First Extension Period) from the expiration of the Initial Term, upon the same terms and conditions as those herein contained, except that the Employee's compensation during the First Extension Period shall be at the rate of $_____ per week.

(b) To extend the term of the Employee's employment for an additional period of _____ year(s) (herein called the Second Extension Period) from the expiration of the First Extension Period, upon the same terms and conditions as those herein contained, except that the Employee's compensation during the Second Extension Period shall be at the rate of $_____ per week.

(c) To extend the term of the Employee's employment for an additional period of _____ year(s) (herein called the Third Extension Period) from the expiration of the Second Extension Period, upon the same terms and conditions as those herein contained, except that (1) the Employee's compensation during the Third Extension Period shall be at the rate of $_____ per week, and except that (2) there shall be no further right and option to extend.

Each of the foregoing options may be exercised separately at any time, but not later than _____ days prior to the expiration of the then current period. No option shall be exercisable unless all preceding options have been exercised. The exercise by the Company of any option shall not be deemed to be (1) an exercise of any subsequent option or options, nor (2) a waiver by the Company of any prior breach of this Agreement by the Employee, whether known or unknown, nor (3) a ratification by the Company of any prior course of conduct on the part of the Employee. The exercise of any option shall be by notice served upon the Employee within the periods above specified.

Whenever in this Agreement the words "the term hereof" or "the term of this Agreement" are used, such words shall mean and include not only the Initial Term, but also all Extension Periods if the options with respect thereto are exercised.

**6. PERFORMANCE:** The Employee shall devote his full time, attention and energy to the performance of his services hereunder. He shall perform the same conscientiously and to the full limit of his ability at all times. He shall promptly and faithfully comply with all the instructions, directions, requests, rules and regulations of the Company in connection therewith.

**7. PLACE OF PERFORMANCE:** The Employee's services shall be rendered in _____ (Performing City), _____ (Performing State) and, on a temporary basis, at such place or places outside _____ (Performing City), _____ (Performing State) as the Company may designate from time to time. If the Employee is required to perform services outside _____ (Performing City), _____ (Performing State), the Company shall at its cost supply such transportation (first class if available) and suitable meals and lodgings for the Employee as may be necessitated thereby.

**8. SERVICES EXCLUSIVE:** The Employee shall render his services solely and exclusively for the Company throughout the term hereof.

(a) The Company recognizes that the Employee has, in connection with his prior performances on television, granted to others the right to use his name, voice and likeness for the purpose of promoting and advertising the same. However, the Employee shall not, during the term hereof, grant any such right to others without the Company's prior written consent.

(b) Except as above stated, the Employee shall not during the term of this Agreement permit the issuance of any advertising, exploitation or publicity whatsoever concerning him without the Company's prior written consent, nor shall he announce or make known, directly or indirectly, by paid advertisement, press notice or otherwise, that he has contracted to perform any services contrary to the terms hereof.

**9. EMPLOYEE'S CONDUCT:** The Employee shall not during the term hereof act in a manner tending to be offensive to decency, morality, or social propriety, or tending to result in scandal, ridicule or contempt, or tending to provoke any retaliatory action or boycott against himself or the Company.

**10. OWNERSHIP OF RESULTS AND PROCEEDS:** In addition to the Employee's services, the Company shall be entitled to, and shall own, solely and exclusively, all the results and proceeds thereof, and all rights of every kind therein.

CONTRACTS
FOR THE
FILM AND
TELEVISION
INDUSTRY

118

(a) The Employee hereby assigns and transfers to the Company all his right, title and interest in such results and proceeds, without reservation, condition or limitation. If the Company desires to secure separate assignments thereof, the Employee shall promptly execute and deliver the same to the Company upon request.

(b) The Employee shall not transfer or attempt to transfer to anyone other than the Company, any right, title or interest in or to any of the foregoing, nor shall he at any time make or purport to make any grant to any third party in derogation thereof.

(c) The provisions of this clause 10 shall remain in full force and effect regardless of the termination of this Agreement, and regardless of whether such termination occurs through expiration or as a result of cancellation by the Company.

**11. USE OF NAME AND LIKENESS:** Except as otherwise specifically provided in clause 8 (a), the Company shall have:

(a) The exclusive right during the term hereof to use the Employee's name, voice and likeness for advertising and promoting the television programs in which he has rendered services to the Company; and

(b) The non-exclusive right to use the same after the termination of this Agreement in connection with such programs.

(c) The use hereinabove referred shall not, without the Employee's written consent, include the use of his name, voice or likeness for general commercial purposes, such as the advertising or promotion of a product or service by way of endorsement or otherwise.

**12. INSURANCE:** The Company shall have the right to apply, at any time or from time to time, in its own name or otherwise, and at its own expense, for life, health, accident or other insurance covering the Employee, in order to protect its interest hereunder. The Employee shall assist the Company in procuring such insurance by submitting to the customary medical examination and by signing such papers as may reasonably be required in connection therewith. The Employee shall have no right, title or interest in or to such insurance.

**13. COMPANY'S RIGHT TO SUSPEND:** The Company shall have the right to suspend the operation of this Agreement, both as to services and compensation, for a period equal to all or any part of the period or aggregate of periods during which any contingency mentioned in clause 16 occurs.

(a) The Company shall give the Employee immediate notice of any suspension.

(b) Upon the resumption of the operation of this Agreement, the Company shall have the right to extend the term hereof for a period equal to all or any part of the period of suspension.

(c) Any such right of extension shall be exercised by notice served upon the Employee prior to the expiration of the then current term.

**14. COMPANY'S RIGHT TO TERMINATE:** The Company shall have the right, at its option, to terminate this Agreement at any time upon or during the occurrence of:

(a) Any contingency mentioned in subdivision (a) of clause 16 if it continues for more than *two* weeks; or

(b) Any contingency mentioned in subdivision (b) of clause 16 if it continues for more than *six* weeks; or

(c) Any contingency mentioned in subdivision (c), (d) or (e) of clause 16.

In the event of the termination of this Agreement in accordance with the foregoing provisions, the Company shall upon such termination be released from all further obligations to the Employee hereunder, except that it shall be liable to the Employee for such compensation as may have been unpaid prior thereto. Termination by the Company shall not be deemed to be a waiver on its part of any other rights or remedies it may have by reason of the circumstances on which the termination is predicated.

**15. EMPLOYEE'S RIGHT TO TERMINATE:** The Employee shall have the right to terminate this Agreement at any time during the occurrence of any contingency mentioned in subdivision (b) of clause 16 if the Company has suspended this Agreement for such contingency and such suspension continues for a period of six weeks or more.

(a) If the Employee elects to terminate as aforesaid, he shall do so by notifying the Company to that effect upon the expiration of the six-week period.

(b) If within five days after receipt of the Employee's notice of termination, the Company resumes the payment of compensation to the Employee and continues such payment during the remainder of the continuance of the contingency, then notwithstanding the Employee's notice this Agreement shall not be terminated, but shall remain in full force and effect. However, in that event the Company shall not thereafter have the right to suspend or terminate this Agreement for the same contingency, whether occurring during the same period of the term hereof or during any subsequent option period.

**16. CONTINGENCIES:** The contingencies mentioned in clauses 13, 14 and 15 shall be as follows:

(a) The inability of the Employee to fully perform his obligations hereunder by reason of mental or physical incapacity or accident or any other cause that renders such non-performance excusable at law.

(b) The hampering or interruption of the operation of the Company's business by *force majeure* or any other cause beyond the Company's control.

(c) The failure or refusal of the Employee to render his required services hereunder to the best of his ability as, when and wherever instructed by the Company, except for any cause mentioned in subdivision (a) or (b) of this clause 16.

(d) The Employee's failure or inability to qualify for insurance at any time during the original term hereof or during any option period.

(e) The breach by the Employee of any material provision of this Agreement.

**17. NO OBLIGATION TO USE SERVICES:** Subject to Company's obligation to pay the Employee the compensation specified in clause 4 or clause 5, as the case may be (except as otherwise provided in clause 13) the Company shall not be obligated to use the Employee's services, and shall not be liable to the Employee in any way for failure to do so in whole or in part.

CONTRACTS
FOR THE
FILM AND
TELEVISION
INDUSTRY

120

**18. EQUITABLE RELIEF:** The Employee acknowledges that the services he is to render to the Company are of a special and extraordinary character that gives them a unique value; that the loss of such services could not be reasonably or adequately compensated by damages in an action at law; and that a breach by him of any provision hereof would cause the Company irreparable injury.

(a) Accordingly the Company shall be entitled to injunctive or other equitable relief to prevent such breach.

(b) Resort by the Company to such relief shall not be construed as a waiver by it of any other rights it might have for damages or otherwise.

(c) If the Employee at any time indicates to the Company that he does not intend to perform his obligations hereunder, such indication shall constitute a breach thereof on his part.

(d) The Company's rights and remedies by reason of the Employee's breach of his obligations hereunder shall be cumulative; and the exercise of any one or more of them shall not be exclusive of any other or others the Company might have under this Agreement or by law.

**19. DEDUCTIONS:** The Company shall have the right to deduct and withhold from the Employee's compensation any amounts required to be deducted and withheld by it pursuant to any present or future law.

(a) If the Company makes any payments or incurs any charges for the Employee's account or if the Employee incurs any charges with the Company, the Company shall have the right to recoup such payments or charges by deducting the aggregate amount thereof from any compensation then or thereafter payable to the Employee hereunder. This provision shall not limit or exclude any other right of recovery that the Company may have.

(b) Nothing herein contained shall be construed to obligate the Company to make such payments or incur such charges or to permit the Employee to incur such charges.

(c) If the Employee claims that any such deduction is unauthorized, he shall so notify the Company, and due consideration shall be given to the merits of his claim; but the making of any such deduction shall not constitute a breach of this Agreement by Company, even though it may ultimately be found to have been unwarranted.

(d) If the Company pays the Employee any compensation that the Employee is not entitled to receive, the Employee shall repay such compensation to the Company on demand, or the Company may at its option recoup the amount thereof by deducting the same from any compensation thereafter payable to the Employee.

**20. GUILD MEMBERSHIP:** During the entire term of this Agreement, the Employee shall become and remain a member in good standing of the properly designated labor organization or organizations (as defined and determined under applicable law) representing persons performing services of the type and character that the Employee is required to perform hereunder.

**21. EMPLOYEE'S RIGHT TO CONTRACT:** The Employee represents and warrants to the Company that he has the full right and power to enter into this

Agreement; that he does not now have, nor will at any time hereafter enter into, any contract or commitment with any third party that will prevent or interfere with the full and complete performance of his obligations hereunder, or with the full exercise and enjoyment by the Company of its rights hereunder.

**22. RELATIONSHIP OF PARTIES:**  Nothing herein contained shall be deemed to constitute a partnership between, or a joint venture by, or an agency relationship between, the parties. Neither party shall hold itself or himself out contrary to the terms of this clause, by any means whatsoever. Neither party shall be bound by, or become liable for, any representation, commitment, act or omission whatsoever of the other contrary to the provisions hereof.

**23. NOTICES:**  All notices hereunder shall be in writing, and shall be served by mail, telegraph or cable, duly addressed to the parties at their respective addresses hereinabove given. Either party may specify a different address for such purpose by notice given to the other in the same manner.

**24. HEADINGS:**  The headings of the clauses of this Agreement are solely for the purpose of convenience. They are not a part hereof, and shall not be used in the construction of any provision.

**25. CONSTRUCTION:**  This Agreement shall be construed in accordance with the laws of the State of _____.

**26. WAIVER:**  No waiver by either party of the breach of any provision of this Agreement shall be deemed to be a waiver of any preceding or succeeding breach of the same or similar nature.

**27. MODIFICATION:**  This Agreement may not be changed or modified, nor may any provision hereof be waived, except by an agreement in writing signed by the party against whom enforcement of the change or modification is asserted.

**28. ASSIGNMENT:**  This Agreement shall inure to the benefit of, and shall be binding on, the Company's successors and assigns.

**29. AGREEMENT COMPLETE:**  This Agreement constitutes the entire understanding between the parties. All previous representations and undertakings, whether oral or written, have been merged herein.

In Witness Whereof the parties have executed this Agreement as of _____.

_____

"Company"

_____

By its President

_____

"Employee"

CONTRACTS
FOR THE
FILM AND
TELEVISION
INDUSTRY

122

# WRITER EMPLOYMENT

Writers can create screenplays on their own and sell them to a studio (or a producer). Screenplays are a form of intellectual property and can be sold like personal property. As discussed in Chapter 3, option agreements and literary purchase agreements are contracts for the sale of a writer's rights in literary property.

Another method studios use to acquire screenplays entails hiring someone to write one for them. The idea for the screenplay may be suggested by the writer in a pitch meeting, or it may come from the studio.[4]

Writers often prefer to be hired to write rather than create scripts on their own. That is because the employer takes the risk of the project not turning out well. A writer who spends six months on his own creating a screenplay that he can't sell has no income to show for his work. The employed writer, on the other hand, receives a guaranteed payment for his labor, even if the script never gets produced. And if the script is produced, the writer may receive additional compensation in the form of a bonus or a percentage of profits.

Studios employ writers to create scripts because they may not be able to acquire enough finished scripts to maintain their desired level of production. Also, a hot "spec" script can be quite expensive to acquire because several studios may be competing for it.

An employment contract is used to hire a writer. As a "work for hire," the employer owns the copyright. The writer gets the money; the studio gets the script. Since the studio owns the work, it can shelve the project or hire someone else to rewrite it.

Many of the provisions found in a writer's employment agreement are also present in actor and director employment agreements. The methods of structuring compensation, force majeure conditions and credit provisions are quite similar.

A producer can hire a writer on a step deal or a flat deal. In a step deal the employer has the right to terminate the writer's services after each step. Step deals are often used when an employer is hiring a novice writer. The employer reduces his financial risk by proceeding in a series of steps instead of hiring the writer to write a finished script.

Suppose a producer wants to hire a writer to create a romantic comedy but the writer has never written in that genre. The producer doesn't want to risk $50,000 (approximately WGA scale for a feature) to hire him. So the producer hires the writer on a step deal. The steps could be:

    a) treatment/outline

    b) first draft screenplay

    c) second draft

    d) rewrite

    e) polish

---

[4] The idea could be an original one or one based on another work, such as play, magazine article or book, that the studio wants to adapt as a movie.

The writer receives a payment for each step. After each step the producer has the option of whether to proceed to the next step. After any step the producer can decide to shelve the project or bring in another writer. As the employer, the producer owns all the writer's work. The writer retains the money for the steps completed.

The Writer's Guild sets minimums for each step, and the total compensation paid for the steps will be no less than the minimum scale payment for a flat deal for a complete screenplay.

A step deal will provide for "reading periods." These are periods, usually a couple of weeks, in which the producer has the opportunity to decide whether he wants to go on to the next step. If the producer does not exercise his right to proceed within the reading period, he risks losing the writer. During the reading period the writer cannot accept outside assignments that might prevent her from completing the remaining steps.

The writer's employment agreement will also set out the time requirements when various items are due. Usually the writer gets one to three months to complete a first draft.

CONTRACTS
FOR THE
FILM AND
TELEVISION
INDUSTRY

124

# WRITER EMPLOYMENT AGREEMENT
## (LOW-BUDGET, NON-UNION)

Agreement effective _____ (19__), between _____ ("Production Company"), and _____ ("Writer").

**1. EMPLOYMENT:** Production Company employs Writer to perform and Writer agrees to perform writing services for Production Company's proposed motion picture currently entitled _____ ("The Picture"), based on an original story by _____. All of Production Company's obligations under this Agreement are expressly conditioned upon Writer's completion, to Production Company's satisfaction, of Form I-9 (Employment Eligibility Verification Form) and Writer's submission to Production Company of original documents satisfactory to Production Company to prove Writer's employment eligibility.

**2. SERVICES/FORM OF WORK:** The completed results and product of Writer's services (including all material created, added, interpolated and submitted by Writer) shall be deemed the "Work" which shall be created in each of the applicable forms listed below ("Forms of Work"):

Form of Work: _____

(a) Use of Work: In Production Company's sole, absolute and unfettered discretion, Production Company may use or not use the Work and may make any changes in, deletions from or additions to the Work.

(b) Underlying Property: If the Work is based on an original idea or material ("Property") created by Writer, Writer hereby grants Production Company the same rights in the Property as Production Company is acquiring hereunder in the Work. The compensation payable to Writer pursuant to Paragraph 5 includes payment for said rights in the Property and for the writing services of Writer hereunder.

**3. DELIVERY:** Writer agrees to complete and deliver each Form of Work and the Work, including any changes and revisions required by Production Company as follows:

_____ (Form of Work) due: _____ (Work Date).

**4. PERFORMANCE STANDARDS:** All of Writer's services shall be rendered promptly in a diligent, conscientious, artistic and efficient manner and Writer shall devote Writer's entire time and attention and best talents and abilities to the services to be rendered, either alone or in collaboration with others. Writer's services shall be rendered in such manner as Production Company may reasonably direct pursuant to the instructions, suggestions and ideas of, and under the control of, and at the times and places reasonably required by, Production Company's duly authorized representatives. Writer, as and when reasonably requested by Production Company, shall consult with Production Company's duly authorized representatives and shall be available for conferences with such representatives for such purposes at such times and places during Writer's employment as may be required by such representatives.

**5. COMPENSATION:** Conditioned upon Writer's full performance of all of Writer's obligations hereunder, Production Company will pay Writer as full compensation for all services rendered and rights granted as follows:
(a) Fixed compensation: $_____ which shall be paid as follows:

i. _____% upon execution of this Agreement.

ii. ____% upon delivery of the last Form of Work due Production Company.

In addition:

(b) Bonus compensation as follows:

i. If a motion picture is produced based on the Work with a final production budget of _____ (Production Budget 1) or less, and if Writer receives sole or shared screenplay credit, a bonus of _____ (First Level) dollars, shall be paid to Writer, payable on the first day of principal photography, or

ii. If a motion picture is produced based on the Work with a final production budget more than _____ (Production Budget 1) dollars but less than _____ (Production Budget 2) dollars, and if Writer receives sole or shared screenplay credit, a bonus of _____ (Second Level) dollars, shall be paid to Writer, payable on the first day of principal photography, or

iii. If a motion picture is produced based on the Work with a final production budget of _____ (Second Level) dollars or more, but less than _____ (Third Level) dollars, and if Writer receives sole or shared screenplay credit, a bonus of _____ (Third Payment) dollars, shall be paid to Writer, payable on the first day of principal photography, or

iv. If a motion picture is produced based on the Work with a final production budget of _____ (Third Level) dollars or more, but less than _____ (Fourth Level) dollars, and if Writer receives sole or shared screenplay credit, a bonus of _____ (Fourth Payment) dollars, shall be paid to Writer, payable on the first day of principal photography, or

v. If a motion picture is produced based on the Work with a final production budget of _____ (Fourth Level) dollars or more, but less than _____ (Fifth Level) dollars and if Writer receives sole or shared screenplay credit, a bonus of _____ (Fifth Payment) dollars, shall be paid to Writer, payable on the first day of principal photography, or

vi. If a motion picture is produced based on the Work with a final production budget of _____ (Fifth Level) dollars or more, and if Writer receives sole or shared screenplay credit, a bonus of _____ (Sixth Payment) dollars, shall be paid to Writer, payable on the first day of principal photography.

(c) Contingent Compensation: In addition to the Fixed Compensation payable under Clause 5(a), and any Bonus Compensation payable under Clause 5(b), subject to the production and release of the Picture and subject to the performance of Writer's obligations hereunder, Writer shall be entitled to receive as Contingent Compensation an amount equal to _____ (Contingent Compensation) percent of one hundred percent of 100% of the Net Profits of the Picture, if any.

(d) Net Profits Definition: Net Profits shall be computed, determined and paid in accordance with the distribution agreements entered into by Production Company and any distributor.

(e) Sequels and Remakes: If Writer, pursuant to final credit determination, receives sole or shared screenplay credit, and Production Company produces a

CONTRACTS
FOR THE
FILM AND
TELEVISION
INDUSTRY

126

sequel of a theatrical motion picture based on the Property, Production Company shall pay Writer an additional payment equal to one half (1/2) of the total fixed and bonus compensation paid to Writer for the Original work. If Writer pursuant to final credit determination receives sole or shared screenplay credit, and Production Company produces a remake of a theatrical motion picture based on the Property, an additional payment equal to one third (1/3) of the total fixed and bonus compensation paid to Writer for the Original Work. Said payments are payable on the first day of principal photography for said sequel or remake, and are payable only for the first sequel or remake.

(f) Series spin-off: If Production Company produces and licenses a television series based on the Work and Writer, pursuant to final credit determination, receives sole or shared screenplay credit, Production Company will pay Writer the applicable royalties as follows:

(i) Pilot program: _____ (Pilot Compensation) dollars.

(ii) Additional episodes of any length: _____ (Episode compensation) dollars per episode.

(iii) Reruns payments: 20% of the payment for original broadcast for each rerun, up to five runs. Thereafter no payments.

These payments shall be made within 30 days of completion of principal photography of any pilot or episode.

## 6. WARRANTIES, REPRESENTATIONS, INDEMNITIES:

(a) Writer Warranties and Representations: Writer warrants and represents that each Form of Work and the Work shall be wholly original with Writer, except as to matters within the public domain and except as to material inserted by Writer pursuant to specific instructions of Production Company, and shall not infringe upon or violate the rights of privacy or publicity of, or constitute a libel or slander against, or violate any common law or any other rights of, any person, firm or corporation.

(b) Writer's Indemnities: Writer shall indemnify Production Company and Production Company's licensees and assigns and its or their officers, agents and employees, from all liabilities, actions, suits or other claims arising out of any breach by Writer of Writer's warranties and representations and out of the use by Production Company of the Work and from reasonable attorneys' fees and costs in defending against the same. The foregoing shall apply only to material created or furnished by Writer, and shall not extend to changes or additions made therein by Production Company, or to claims for defamation or invasion of the privacy of any person unless Writer knowingly uses the name or personality of such person or should have known, in the exercise of reasonable prudence, that such person would or might claim that such person's personality was used in the Work.

(c) Production Company's Indemnities: Production Company shall indemnify Writer to the same extent that Writer indemnifies Production Company hereunder, as to any material supplied by Production Company to Writer for incorporation into the Work.

(d) Notice and Pendency of Claims: The party receiving notice of any claim or action subject to indemnity hereunder shall promptly notify the other party.

**7. OWNERSHIP:** As Writer's employer, Production Company shall solely and exclusively own throughout the world in perpetuity all rights of every kind and nature in the Work, and all of the results and proceeds thereof in whatever stage of completion as may exist from time to time, together with the rights generally known as the "moral rights of authors." Writer acknowledges that the Work is being written by Writer for use as a Motion Picture and that each Form of Work is being written by Writer as a "work made for hire" within the scope of Writer's employment by Production Company, and, therefore, Production Company shall be the author and copyright owner of the Work.

**8. FCC:** Writer understands that, as to any Television Program based on the Work, it is a Federal offense, unless disclosed prior to broadcast to Production Company or to the station or licensee which broadcasts the Program, to:

(a) Give or agree to give any member of the production staff, anyone associated in any manner with the Program or any representative of the Production Company, the station or network, any portion of compensation payable to Writer or anything else of value for arranging Writer's employment in connection with the Program.

(b) Accept or agree to accept anything of value, other than compensation payable to Writer under this Agreement, to promote any product, service or venture on the air, or to incorporate any material containing such a promotion in the Program.

Writer is aware that Production Company prohibits such conduct with or without disclosure to Production Company, and any such conduct or failure to disclose shall be a material breach of this Agreement.

**9. NOTICES/PAYMENT:**

(a) To Writer: All notices from Production Company to Writer may be given in writing by mailing the notice to Writer, postage prepaid, or at Production Company's option, Production Company may deliver such notice to Writer personally, either orally or in writing. The date of mailing or of personal delivery shall be deemed to be the date of service. Payments and written notice to Writer shall be sent to Writer at _____.

(b) To Production Company: All notices from Writer to Production Company shall be given in writing by mail, messenger, cable, telex or telecopier addressed as indicated below. The date of mailing, messengering, cabling, telexing or telecopying shall be deemed to be the date of service. Notice to the Production Company shall be sent to _____.

(c) Change of Address: The address of Writer and of Production Company set forth herein may be changed to such other address as Writer or Production Company may hereafter specify by written notice given to the other Party.

**10. ASSIGNMENT:** This Agreement is non-assignable by Writer. This Agreement shall inure to the benefit of Production Company's successors, assignees, licensees and grantees and associated, affiliated and subsidiary companies. Production Company and any subsequent assignee may freely assign this Agreement, in whole or in part, to any party provided that such party assumes and agrees in writing to keep and perform all of the executory obligations of Production Company hereunder.

CONTRACTS
FOR THE
FILM AND
TELEVISION
INDUSTRY

128

**11. NAME AND LIKENESS:** Production Company shall have the right to use and permit others (including any exhibitor or sponsor of the Program or Series) to use Writer's name and likeness for the purpose of advertising and publicizing the Work, any Program based on the Work, and any of exhibitor's or sponsor's products and services, but not as an endorsement or testimonial.

**12. PAY OR PLAY:** The rights in this Paragraph shall be in addition to and shall not in any way diminish or detract from Production Company's rights as otherwise set forth. Production Company shall not be obligated to use Writer's services, nor use the results and product of Writers services, nor produce, release, distribute, exhibit, advertise, exploit or otherwise make use of the Program. Production Company may at any time, without legal justification or excuse, elect not to use Writer's services or to have any further obligations to Writer under this Agreement. If Production Company elects not to use Writer's services pursuant to this Paragraph, Writer shall be paid the Compensation set forth in Paragraph 5 (a) if Writer performs those services.

**13. CREDIT:**

(a) The writing credits shall read: "Story by _____," and "Written by _____ (Writer's Name)," (or another name chosen by Writer), if a substantial amount of Writer's work is incorporated in the Picture. In determining whether Writer is awarded sole, shared or no writing credit, reference shall be made to the principles of the WGA credit arbitration rules. Although Production Company is not a WGA signatory, to the extent possible, the principles of the WGA credit arbitration rules shall be followed by the parties. In the event of a credit dispute, the arbitrator of such a dispute shall follow the WGA credit rules to the extent they do not conflict with the rules of the AFMA or the American Arbitration Association.

(b) In the event that writer also directs the picture, writer shall receive an appropriate directing credit in accordance with the rules of the DGA. Although Production Company is not a DGA signatory, and writer is not a DGA member, to the extent possible, the principles of the WGA credit rules shall be followed by the parties. In the event of a credit dispute, the arbitrator of such a dispute shall follow the DGA credit rules to the extent they do not conflict with the rules of AFMA or the American Arbitration Association.

**14. CONDITIONS AFFECTING OR RELATED TO COMPENSATION :**

(a) Method of Payment: All compensation which shall become due to Writer shall be paid by Production Company by check and sent to Writer at the address provided in the Notices and Payments provision of this Agreement.

(b) Governmental Limitation: No withholding, deduction, reduction or limitation of compensation by Production Company which is required or authorized by law ("Governmental Limitation") shall be a breach by Production Company or relieve Writer from Writer's obligations. Payment of compensation as permitted pursuant to the Governmental Limitation shall continue while such Governmental Limitation is in effect and shall be deemed to constitute full performance by Production Company of its obligations respecting the payment of compensation. The foregoing notwithstanding, if at such time as the Governmental Limitation is no longer in effect there is compensation remaining unpaid to Writer, Production Company shall cooperate with Writer in connection with the processing of any applications relative to the payment of such unpaid compensation and Production Company shall pay such compensation to Writer at such times as Production Company is legally permitted to do so.

(c) Garnishment/Attachment: If Production Company shall be required, because of the service of any garnishment, attachment, writ of execution, or lien, or by the terms of any contract or assignment executed by Writer, to withhold, or to pay to any other Party all or any portion of the compensation due Writer, the withholding or payment of such compensation or any portion thereof in accordance with the requirements of any such attachment, garnishment, writ of execution, lien, contract or assignment shall not be construed as a breach by Production Company.

(d) Overpayment/Offset: If Production Company makes any overpayment to Writer for any reason or if Writer is indebted to Production Company for any reason, Writer shall pay Production Company such overpayment or indebtedness on demand, or at the election of Production Company, Production Company may deduct and retain for its own account an amount equal to all or any part of such overpayment or indebtedness from any sums that may be due or become due or payable by Production Company to Writer or for the account of Writer and such deduction or retention shall not be construed as a breach by Production Company.

**15. ARBITRATION:** This Agreement shall be interpreted in accordance with the laws of the State of _____, applicable to agreements executed and to be wholly performed therein. Any controversy or claim arising out of or in relation to this Agreement or the validity, construction or performance of this Agreement, or the breach thereof, shall be resolved by arbitration in accordance with the rules and procedures of AFMA, as said rules may be amended from time to time with rights of discovery if requested by the arbitrator. Such rules and procedures are incorporated and made a part of this Agreement by reference. If AFMA shall refuse to accept jurisdiction of such dispute, then the parties agree to arbitrate such matter before and in accordance with the rules of the American Arbitration Association under its jurisdiction in _____ (city) before a single arbitrator familiar with entertainment law. The parties shall have the right to engage in pre-hearing discovery in connection with such arbitration proceedings. The parties agree hereto that they will abide by and perform any award rendered in any arbitration conducted pursuant hereto, that any court having jurisdiction thereof may issue a judgment based upon such award and that the prevailing party in such arbitration and/or confirmation proceeding shall be entitled to recover its reasonable attorneys' fees and expenses. The arbitration will be held in _____ (city) and any award shall be final, binding and non-appealable. The Parties agree to accept service of process in accordance with the AFMA Rules.

IN WITNESS WHEREOF, the parties hereto have signed this Agreement as of the day and year first above written.

"Production Company"          "Writer"

_____     _____
(Production Company Signer),        (Writer's Name)

_____
(Production Company Signer's Title)

_____
on behalf of (Employer Name)

CONTRACTS
FOR THE
FILM AND
TELEVISION
INDUSTRY

130

# TYPES OF COMPENSATION

There are different ways to compensate writers. Fixed compensation is a guaranteed sum. Typically, producers pay half the fee up-front, and half when the work is delivered. If the writer doesn't produce a craftsman-like work, the producer doesn't have to pay. But the producer must pay if a craftsman-like work is turned in even if the producer doesn't like the script. The producer takes the risk if the script turns out poorly.

The Writer's Guild prohibits its members from working on speculation without a guarantee of fixed compensation. The amount of fixed compensation is often minimum WGA scale for a novice writer. For more experienced writers, the amount is usually a modest increase over their last deal. Of course, if the writer wins an Academy Award or his last movie was a blockbuster hit, his price will skyrocket.

Bonus compensation is another form of payment. Let's say you are a producer and a writer asks to be paid $90,000. You can't afford to pay that up front so you counter by offering $60,000 fixed compensation, and another $30,000 as bonus compensation. Bonus compensation is not guaranteed. Payment is contingent on a certain event, such as the script going into production. If the script isn't produced, the bonus need not be paid. Thus, bonus compensation is more iffy than fixed compensation.

Deferred compensation is more iffy than bonus compensation. Deferments are often used in low-budget films when the producer can't afford to pay his cast and crew their usual wages. Perhaps the producer offers to hire everyone for $250 a week, and to defer the rest of the salary that they would normally earn. Deferments are usually not payable unless the script gets produced, the movie is released and revenue is received. Deferments can be payable before or after investors recoup their investment. The agreement may give priority to some deferment holders over others or it may provide that everyone shares equally (in pari passu).

The most iffy kind of payment is contingent compensation, or net profits (points). Here the employee will receive payment only if the script is produced, released, and it generates enough revenue to cover all expenses and deductions, including distribution fees and marketing costs. Net profit participants rarely see any money from their net points. Artists often complain that studios use creative accounting to deny them their share of profits.

Writers typically receive between 1 and 5 percent of 100 percent of net profits. Why do we state the writer's share in terms of a percent of one hundred percent? So that there won't be any confusion as to the size of the writer's slice of net profits. If we simply said that the writer gets 5% of net profits, it would be unclear whether she gets 5% of all the net profits or 5% of the producer's share of net profits.

Typically, the studio and the producer split net profits 50/50. The producer, however, often must give a writer, director and star a portion of his net profits. These profit participants take from the producer's half of net profits. Nevertheless, the custom in the industry is to express net profits in terms of the whole (all profits) to avoid ambiguity. Of course, rather than giving a writer 5% of 100% of the net profits, one could give her 10% of 50%. It would be the same amount.

Another form of payment is known as "additional" compensation. This fee is payable if the producer makes a sequel, remake or television spin-off series based on the original work (assuming he has the right to make those works). Writers often receive 50 percent of what they were paid for the original movie for a sequel, and 33 percent for a remake. For a television spin-off series the writer usually gets a royalty for every episode. If the series is a hit, the writers may earn more in royalties from the series than they received for writing the film.

The series royalty is a passive one. That means the writer is not obliged to work on the series. The payment is compensation for his work on the original. So the writer is entitled to the royalty even if he is not involved in the series. If the writer is hired to work on the series, he would receive additional compensation for his services.

## CREDIT

A writer's employment agreement will have a credit clause. For a WGA writer and a signatory company, the WGA credit rules determine how credit is allocated. Consequently, the producer does not have the discretion to allocate writing credits as he may choose. After the "Notice of Tentative Credits" is given, every writer on the project has the opportunity to object and request credit arbitration.

Credit is important for reasons besides ego and professional stature. The determination of credit can have financial repercussions. Often the amount of points a writer receives will vary depending on whether he receives sole, shared or no credit.

Writers sometimes complain about directors who have their writer friends needlessly rewrite a script. The first writer is forced to share credit and profits with another writer. However, the Writer's Guild credit guidelines give a strong preference to the first writer. The second writer will only obtain credit if his contribution is 50% or more of the completed script. Unfortunately this may encourage the second writer to extensively revise the work and throw out good material.

Performance standards will also be addressed in the agreement. The writer will be required to perform diligently and efficiently, to follow the suggestions and instructions of the company, and to devote all of his time exclusively to the project during the term of the agreement.

CONTRACTS
FOR THE
FILM AND
TELEVISION
INDUSTRY

132

# WRITER EMPLOYMENT AGREEMENT
## (Theatrical WGA Writer)
## (To Employ Writing Team Member)
## (Step deal)

Agreement dated _____ (Date of Agreement) between _____ ("Writer"), and _____ ("Production Company").

**1. EMPLOYMENT:** Production Company agrees to employ Writer to perform and Writer agrees to perform, upon the terms and conditions herein specified, writing services for the proposed Theatrical Motion Picture currently entitled _____ ("Picture"), based upon a treatment of the same name supplied by Production Company ("Basic Property"). Writer shall perform such writing services in collaboration with Writer _____ (Second Writer) pursuant to the Employment Agreement dated _____ (Agreement date with second Writer), between _____ (Second Writer) and Production Company ("Agreement"). Writer and _____ (Second Writer) are hereinafter collectively referred to as the "_____" team (Writers' team short name). All of the compensation to be paid under this agreement is compensation solely for the services of Writer. Compensation for _____ (Second Writer) is set forth in _____'s (Second Writer's) agreement with Production Company.

**2. THE PRODUCT AGREEMENT WITH OPTIONS:** The completed results of Writer's services hereunder shall be deemed collectively the "Product" and individually the "Product Form," and shall be created as follows:

First Draft screenplay with option for one Revision/Draft thereof and dependent option for one polish.

**3. COMMENCEMENT OF SERVICES:** Writer shall commence services in writing the first draft of the screenplay upon execution of this agreement and Production Company becoming a signatory of the Writers Guild of America. Writer shall commence writing each subsequent Product Form on a date to be designated by Production Company, which date may be earlier, but shall not be later than the first business day after expiration of the then current Reading Period or Option Period, as the case may be, described in Clause 4.

**4. TIME REQUIREMENTS** (Agreement with Options) — Writer's services shall be rendered pursuant to the following time requirements:

(a) Delivery Periods: Writer shall deliver each Product Form within the period ("Delivery Period") which commences on the date Writer is obligated to commence writing each designated Product Form and which ends upon expiration of the applicable time period listed in Clause 4(e).

(b) Reading Periods: Each time Writer delivers any Product Form, if Writer's engagement herein requires additional writing services, Production Company shall have a period ("Reading Period"), which commences on the first business day following the delivery of such Product Form and which continues for the length of time listed in Clause 4(e) opposite the description of the Product Form delivered, within which to read such Product Form and advise Writer to commence writing the next Product Form.

(c) Postponement of Services: If Production Company does not exercise within the applicable Reading Period its right to require Writer to commence writing either the first set of revisions or the polish, Production Company may nonetheless require Writer to render such services at any time within the one (1) year period commencing upon delivery of the immediately preceding Product Form, subject to Writer's availability and provided: 1) Writer's services are to be rendered during the one year period, and 2) Production Company shall furnish Writer with thirty (30) days' prior written notice of the date designated for the commencement of such services, and 3) that Production Company has paid Writer in a timely manner for the postponed product forms if those services were timely rendered.

(d) Option Periods: Each Option, if any, under Clause 4(e), shall be exercised, if at all, in writing within the period ("Option Period") which commences on the first business day following the delivery of the Product Form immediately preceding that for which an Option may be exercised, or upon the expiration of the Delivery Period applicable to such Product Form, whichever is later, and which continues for the length of time listed in Clause 4(e) opposite the description of the Product Form delivered.

(e) Length of Periods — Delivery, Reading and Option Periods shall be the following lengths:

(a) FIRST DRAFT: The Delivery Period for the First Draft is _____ (Delivery Period-First Draft). The Reading/Option Period for the First Draft is Two (2) Weeks.

(b) FIRST REVISION/SECOND DRAFT: The Delivery Period for the Second Draft is _____ (Delivery Period-Second Draft). The Reading/Option Period for the Second Draft is Two (2) Weeks.

(c) POLISH: The Delivery Period for the Polish is _____ (Delivery Period-Polish). The Reading/Option Period for the Polish is Two (2) Weeks.

## 5. DELIVERY: TIME OF THE ESSENCE:

(a) Effective Delivery: Delivery of Product Form to any person other than _____ (Producer Representative) shall not constitute delivery of such Product Form as required by this Agreement.

(b) Time of the Essence: Writer shall write and deliver each Product Form for which Writer is engaged as soon as reasonably possible after commencement of Writer's services thereon, but not later than the date upon which the applicable Delivery Period expires. Time of delivery is of the essence.

(c) Revisions: For each Product Form which is in the nature of a Revision, Writer's services shall include the writing and delivery of such changes as may be required by Production Company within a reasonable time prior to the expiration of the Delivery Period applicable to such Product Form.

## 6. COMPENSATION:

(a) Fixed Compensation — Production Company shall pay Writer as set forth below for Writer's services and all rights granted by Writer:

CONTRACTS
FOR THE
FILM AND
TELEVISION
INDUSTRY

134

1. For First Draft Screenplay: $\_\_\_\_, payable half upon commencement, half upon delivery.

2. For First Revision/Second Draft Screenplay: $\_\_\_\_, payable half upon commencement, half upon delivery.

3. For Polish of Screenplay: $\_\_\_\_, payable half upon commencement, half upon delivery.

(b) Payment: Production Company shall have no obligation to pay Writer any compensation with respect to any Product Form for which Production Company has failed to exercise its Option under Clause 4.

(c) Bonus Compensation: Subject to the production and release of the Picture, and to the Writer not being in material default hereunder, in addition to the Fixed Compensation set forth above, Writer shall be entitled to be paid the following:

(i) If _____ (Writers' team short name) receives sole or shared screenplay credit pursuant to final Writer's Guild of America ("WGA") credit determination with respect to the Picture, Writer shall be entitled to receive as Bonus Compensation the sum of $\_\_\_\_ (Bonus Compensation) over the compensation provided by Clause 6(a), less the aggregate of all sums paid to Writer pursuant to Clause 6(a) above, and shall be payable upon commencement of principal photography.

(ii) Repayment: If Bonus Compensation set forth in Clause 6(c) above is paid to Writer as set forth hereinabove, and if _____ (Writers' team short name) receives neither sole screenplay credit nor shared screenplay credit pursuant to final WGA credit determination for the Picture, the Writer shall repay to Production Company such sum so paid to Writer within five (5) days of such determination.

(d) Contingent Compensation: Subject to the production and release of the Picture and subject to Writer not being in default of his obligations hereunder, in addition to the Fixed Compensation and Bonus Compensation set forth above, Writer shall be entitled to be paid the following:

(i) Sole Screenplay Credit: If the _____ (Writers' team short name) receives sole screenplay credit pursuant to final WGA credit determination for the Picture, Writer shall be entitled to receive as Contingent Compensation an amount equal to \_\_\_\_\_ (Sole Credit Compensation) percent of one hundred percent of the Net Profits of the Picture.

(ii) Shared Screenplay Credit: If the _____ (Writers' team short name) receives shared screenplay credit pursuant to final WGA credit determination for the Picture, Writer shall be entitled to receive as Contingent Compensation an amount equal to \_\_\_\_\_ (Shared Credit Compensation) percent of one hundred percent of the Net Profits of the Picture.

(e) For purposes of this Agreement, "Net Profits" shall be computed, determined and paid in accordance with definition of net profits defined in the production/distribution agreement between production company and the distributor of the Picture, provided that Writer's definition shall be as favorable as any other net profit participant.

(f) Additional payments to Writer for Sequel, Remake and Television Use of the Work; Right of First Negotiation: Subject to the provisions of Clauses 6(g) and 6(h) below, and subject to the production and release of the Picture and the performance of all obligations of Writer hereunder:

(i) Sequel Theatrical Motion Picture: If the _____ (Writers' team short name) receives sole/shared screenplay credit or is accorded separation of rights pursuant to applicable WGA determination with respect to the Picture, then for each Sequel Theatrical Motion Picture based on the Picture produced and released, Writer shall be entitled to be paid an amount equal to fifty percent of one hundred percent (50% of 100%) of the sum paid to Writer as Compensation pursuant to Clause 6(a) and 6(c) supra, and a percentage participation in the Net Profits of such Sequel Theatrical Motion Picture in an amount equal to fifty percent of one hundred percent (50% of 100%) of the rate of percentage participation in Net Profits of the Picture payable to Writer as Contingent Compensation pursuant to Clauses 6(d)(i) or 6(d)(ii) above, if any.

(ii) Theatrical Remakes: If the _____ (Writers' team short name) receives sole/shared screenplay credit or is accorded separation of rights pursuant to applicable WGA determination for the Picture, then for each Theatrical Remake of the Picture produced and released, Writer shall be entitled to be paid an amount equal to thirty three percent (33%) of one hundred percent (100%) of the sum paid to Writer as Compensation pursuant to Clause 6(a) and 6(c) supra, and thirty three percent (33%) of one hundred percent (100%) of the percentage participation in Net Profits of the Picture payable to Writer as Contingent Compensation pursuant to Clauses 6(d)(i) or 6(d)(ii) above, if any.

(iv) Sequel Television Motion Pictures and Television Remakes:

(A) Pilot and Series: If Writer is accorded separation of rights pursuant to applicable WGA determination with respect to the Picture, then for each Studio Sequel Television Motion Picture based upon the Picture and/or Television Remake of the Picture which is produced and licensed for exhibition by Production Company and which is a Pilot or an episode of an episodic or anthology television series (collectively "TV Program"), Writer shall be entitled to receive the following royalties:

(1) $_____ for each TV Program of not more than thirty (30) minutes in length.

(2) $_____ for each TV Program in excess of thirty (30) minutes but not more than sixty (60) minutes in length.

(3) $_____ for each TV Program in excess of sixty (60) minutes in length.

(4) If any TV Program is rerun, Writer shall be paid twenty percent (20%) of the applicable sum initially paid Writer pursuant to Subclauses (1), (2) or (3) above for the second run, third run, fourth run, fifth run, and sixth run respectively. No further rerun payments shall be due or payable for any rerun after the sixth run.

(B) Movies of the Week and Mini-Series: If Writer is accorded separation of rights pursuant to applicable WGA determination for the Picture, then for each Sequel Television Motion Picture or Television Remake of the Picture which is produced and licensed for exhibition by Production Company and which is a

CONTRACTS
FOR THE
FILM AND
TELEVISION
INDUSTRY

136

so-called "Movie of the Week" or so-called "Mini-Series," Writer shall be entitled to receive the following royalties which sum shall constitute full payment for all rerun use and/or other exploitation thereof:

(1) $_____ for the first two (2) hours of running time of each such Movie of the Week and/or each such Mini-Series.

(2) $_____ for every hour of running time, if any, exceeding the first two (2) hours of running time of such Movie of the Week and/or such Mini-Series up to a maximum of $_____.

(vi) Definitions — The following terms as utilized in connection with this Agreement, shall be defined as set forth below:

(a) "Television Remake": A remake primarily intended to be initially distributed for free-television exhibition.

(b) "Television Studio Sequel Motion Picture": A studio sequel motion picture primarily intended to be initially distributed for free-television exhibition.

(c) "Theatrical Remake": A remake primarily intended to be initially distributed for theatrical exhibition.

(d) "Theatrical Studio Sequel Motion Picture": A studio sequel motion picture primarily intended to be initially distributed for theatrical exhibition.

(e) WGA Agreement: All sums payable to Writer pursuant to this Agreement shall be in lieu of, and not in addition to, any similar payment to which Writer may be entitled pursuant to the current Writers Guild of America Theatrical and Television Agreement ("WGA Agreement").

## 7. CONDITIONS AFFECTING OR RELATED TO COMPENSATION:

(a) Method of Payment: All compensation which shall become due to Writer hereunder shall be sent to Writer at the address provided in Clause 26. Such address may be changed to such other address as Writer may hereafter notify Production Company in accordance with Clause 26.

(b) Performance: Production Company's obligation to pay compensation or otherwise perform hereunder shall be conditioned upon Writer not being in default of his obligations under the Agreement. No compensation shall accrue to Writer during Writer's inability, failure or refusal to perform, according to the terms and conditions of this Agreement, the services contracted for herein, nor shall compensation accrue during any period of Force Majeure, Suspension or upon Termination except as otherwise herein provided.

(c) Governmental Limitation: No withholding, deduction, reduction or limitation of compensation by Production Company which is required or authorized by law ("Governmental Limitation") shall be a breach of this Agreement by Production Company or relieve Writer from Writer's obligations hereunder. Payment of compensation as permitted pursuant to the Governmental Limitation shall continue while such Governmental Limitation is in effect and shall be deemed to constitute full performance by Production Company of its obligation to pay compensation hereunder.

(d) Garnishment/Attachment: If Production Company is required, because of the service of any garnishment, writ of execution or lien, or by the terms of any contract or assignment executed by Writer, to withhold, or to pay all or any portion of the compensation due Writer hereunder to any other person, firm or corporation, the withholding or payment of such compensation or portion thereof, pursuant to the requirements of any such garnishment, writ of execution, lien, contract or assignment shall not be construed as a breach by Production Company of this Agreement.

(e) Overpayment/Offset: If Production Company makes any overpayment to Writer hereunder for any reason or if Writer is indebted to Production Company for any reason, Writer shall pay Production Company such overpayment or indebtedness on demand, or at the election of Production Company may deduct and retain for its own account an amount equal to all or any part of such overpayment or indebtedness from any sums that may be due or become due or payable by Production Company to Writer or for the account of Writer and such deduction os allention shallen a breach of this Agreement.

(f) Pay or Play: Production Company shall not be obligated to use Writer's services for the Picture, nor shall Production Company be obligated to produce, release, distribute, advertise, exploit or otherwise make use of the results and proceeds of Writer's services if such services are used. Production Company may elect to terminate Writer's services at any time without legal justification or excuse provided that the Fixed Compensation provided in Clause 6(a), which shall have been earned and accrued prior to such termination shall be paid to Writer. In the event of such termination, all other rights of Writer herein shall be deemed void ab initio except such rights as may have accrued to Writer in accordance with the terms of Clauses 21 (relating to Guilds and Unions), 22 (relating to Credits) and 6(c)&(d) (relating to Bonus & Contingent Compensation).

**8. PERFORMANCE STANDARDS:** Writer's services hereunder shall be rendered promptly in collaboration with _____ (Second Writer) in a diligent, conscientious, artistic and efficient manner to Writer's best ability. Writer shall devote all of Writer's time and shall render Writer's services exclusively (during writing periods only) to Production Company in performing the writing services contemplated hereunder, and shall not render services for any other party during the period of Writer's engagement. Writer's services shall be rendered in such manner as Production Company may direct pursuant to the instructions, suggestions and ideas of and under the control of and at the times and places required by Production Company's authorized representatives. Writer shall, as and when requested by Production Company, consult with Production Company's daily authorized representatives and shall be available for conferences in person or by telephone with such representatives for such purposes at such times during Writer's engagement as may be required by such representatives.

**9. RESULTS AND PROCEEDS OF SERVICES:**

(a) Ownership: Production Company shall solely and exclusively own, the Product, each Product Form and all of the results and proceeds thereof, in whatever stage of completion as may exist from time to time (including but not limited to all rights of whatever kind and character, throughout the world, in perpetuity, in any and all languages of copyright, trademark, patent, production, manufacture, recordation, reproduction, transcription, performance, broadcast and exhibition by any art, method or device, now known or hereafter devised, including without limitation radio broadcast, theatrical and non-theatrical exhibition, and television exhibition or otherwise) whether such results and proceeds

CONTRACTS
FOR THE
FILM AND
TELEVISION
INDUSTRY

138

consist of literary, dramatic, musical, motion picture, mechanical or any other form or works, themes, ideas, compositions, creations or products. Production Company's acquisition hereunder shall also include all rights generally known in the field of literary and musical endeavor as the "moral rights of authors" in and/ or to the Product, each Product Form, and any musical and literary proceeds of Writer's services. Production Company shall have the right but not the obligation, with respect to the Product, each Product Form, the results and proceeds thereof, to add to, subtract from, change, arrange, revise, adapt, rearrange, make variations, and to translate the same into any and all languages, change the sequence, change the characters and the descriptions thereof contained therein, change the title of the same, record and photograph the same with or without sound (including spoken words, dialogue and music synchronously recorded), use said title or any of its components in connection with works or motion pictures wholly or partially independent thereof, to sell, copy and publish the same as Production Company may desire and to use all or any part thereof in new versions, adaptations and sequels in any and all languages and to obtain copyright therein throughout the world. Writer hereby expressly waives any and all rights which Writer may have, either in law, in equity, or otherwise, which Writer may have or claim to have as a result of any alleged infringements of Writer's so-called "moral rights of authors." Writer acknowledges that the results and proceeds of Writer's services are works specially ordered by Production Company for use as part of a motion picture and the results and proceeds of Writer's services shall be considered to be works made for hire for Production Company, and, therefore, Production Company shall be the author and copyright owner of the results and proceeds of Writer's services.

(b) Assignment and Vesting of Rights: All rights granted or agreed to be granted to Production Company hereunder shall vest in Production Company immediately and shall remain vested whether this Agreement expires in normal course or is terminated for any cause or reason, or whether Writer executes the Certificate of Authorship required infra. All material created, composed, submitted, added or interpolated by Writer hereunder shall automatically become Production Company's property, and Production Company, for this purpose, shall be deemed author thereof with Writer acting entirely as Production Company's employee. Writer does hereby assign and transfer to Production Company all of the foregoing without reservation, condition or limitation, and no right of any kind, nature or description is reserved by Writer. The said assignment and transfer to Production Company by Writer are subject to the limitations contained in the current Writer's Guild of America Theatrical and Television Film Basic Agreement ("WGA Agreement").

(c) Execution of Other Documents:

(i) Certificate of Authorship: Writer further agrees, if Production Company requests Writer to do so, to execute and deliver to Production Company, in connection with all material written by writer hereunder, a Certificate of Authorship in substantially the following form:

I hereby certify that I wrote the manuscript hereto attached, entitled (Motion Picture Title) based upon a screenplay of the same name written by me, as an employee of (Production Company) pursuant to an employment Agreement between myself and (Production Company) dated (Date of Agreement), in performance of my duties thereunder and in the regular course of my employment, and that Production Company is the author thereof and entitled to the copyright therein and thereto, with the right to make such changes therein and such uses thereof as it may from time to time determine as such author.

IN WITNESS WHEREOF, I have hereto set my hand this _____ (date).

If Production Company desires to secure separate assignments or Certificates of Authorship of or for any of the foregoing, Writer agrees to execute such certificate upon Production Company's request therefor. Writer irrevocably grant(s) Production Company the power coupled with an interest to execute such separate assignments or Certificates of Authorship in Writer's name and as Writer's attorney-in-fact.

(ii) Writer recognizes that the provisions in Clause 9(c)(iii) dealing with any other documents to be signed by Writer are not to be construed in derogation of Production Company's rights arising from the employer-employee relationship but are included because in certain jurisdictions and in special circumstances the rights in and to the material which flow from the employer-employee relationship may not be sufficient in and of themselves to vest ownership in Production Company.

(iii) If Production Company desires to secure further documents covering, quitclaiming or assigning all or any of the results and proceeds of Writer's services; or all or any rights in and to the same, then Writer agrees to execute and deliver to Production Company any such documents at any time and from time to time upon Production Company's request, and in such form as may be prescribed by Production Company; without limiting the generality of the foregoing Writer agrees to execute and deliver to Production Company upon Production Company's request therefor an assignment of all rights, it being agreed that all of the representations, warranties and agreements made and to be made by Writer under this Exhibit shall be deemed made by Writer as part of this agreement. If Writer shall fail or refuse to execute and deliver the certificate above described and/or any such documents within ten business days of a written request, the Writer hereby irrevocably grants Production Company the power coupled with an interest to execute this certificate and/or documents in Writer's name and as Writer's attorney-in-fact. Writer's failure to execute this certificate and/or documents shall not affect or limit any of Production Company's rights in and to the results and proceeds of Writer's services.

(iv) Separation of Rights: Since Writer has been assigned material, he is not expected to be entitled to separation of rights under the WGA Agreement. Notwithstanding anything to the contrary contained herein, Production Company shall have the right to publish and copyright, or cause to be published and copyrighted, screenplays, teleplays and scripts adapted from or based upon the Product and the novelization of screenplays, teleplays and scripts adapted from or based upon the Product or any Product Form created hereunder.

## 10. WRITER'S WARRANTIES:

Subject to Article 28 of the WGA basic agreement Writer warrants:

(a) that, except as provided in the next sentence hereof, all material composed and/or submitted by Writer for or to Production Company shall be wholly original with Writer and shall not infringe upon or violate the right of privacy of, nor constitute a libel or slander against, nor violate any common law rights or any other rights of any person, firm or corporation. The same agreements and

CONTRACTS
FOR THE
FILM AND
TELEVISION
INDUSTRY

140

warranties are made by Writer regarding any and all material, incidents, treatments, characters and action which Writer may add to or interpolate in any material assigned by Production Company to Writer for preparation, but are not made regarding violations or infringements contained in the material so assigned by Production Company to Writer. The said agreements and warranties on Writer's part are subject to the limitations contained in the WGA Agreement.

(b) Further Warranties: Writer hereby warrants that Writer is under no obligation or disability, created by law or otherwise, which would in any manner or to any extent prevent or restrict Writer from entering into and fully performing this Agreement, and Writer hereby accepts the obligations hereunder. Writer warrants that Writer has not entered into any agreement or commitment that would prevent his fulfilling Writer's commitments with Production Company hereunder and that Writer will not enter into any such agreement or commitment without Production Company's specific approval. Writer hereby agrees that Writer shall devote his entire time and attention and best talents and ability exclusively to Production Company as specified herein and observe and be governed by the rules of conduct established by Production Company for the conduct of its employees.

(c) Indemnification: Writer agrees to indemnify Production Company, its successors, assigns, licensees, officers, directors and employees, and hold them harmless from and against any and all claims, liability, losses, damages, costs, expenses (including but not limited to attorneys' fees), judgments and penalties arising out of Writer's breach of warranties under this Agreement. Production Company agrees to indemnify Writer, its successors, assigns, licensees, and employees, and hold them harmless from and against any and all claims, liability, losses, damages, costs, expenses (including but not limited to attorneys' fees), judgments and penalties arising out of any suit against Writer (arising from Writer's employment under this agreement) not based on Writer's breach of his warranties under this Agreement.

**11. NAME AND LIKENESS:** Production Company shall always have the right to use and display Writer's name and likeness for advertising, publicizing and exploiting the Picture or the Product. However, such advertising may not include the direct endorsement of any product (other than the Picture) without Writer's prior written consent. Exhibition, advertising, publicizing or exploiting the Picture by any media, even through a part of or in connection with a product or a commercially-sponsored program, shall not be deemed an endorsement of any nature.

**12. PUBLICITY RESTRICTIONS:** Writer shall not, individually or jointly, or by any means of press agents or publicity or advertising agencies or others, employed or paid by Writer or otherwise, circulate, publish or otherwise disseminate any news stories or articles, books or other publicity, containing Writer's name relating directly or indirectly to Writer's employment by Production Company, the subject matter of this Agreement, the Picture, or the services to be rendered by Writer or others for the Picture , unless first approved by Production Company. Writer shall not transfer or attempt to transfer any right, privilege, title or interest in or to any of the aforestated things, nor shall Writer willingly permit any infringement upon the exclusive rights granted to Production Company. Writer authorizes Production Company, at Production Company's expense, in Writer's name or otherwise, to institute any proper legal proceedings to prevent such infringement.

## 13. REMEDIES:

(a) Remedies Cumulative: All remedies of Production Company or Writer shall be cumulative, and no one such remedy shall be exclusive of any other. Without waiving any rights or remedies under this Agreement or otherwise, Production Company may from time to time recover, by action, any damages arising out of any breach of this Agreement by Writer and may institute and maintain subsequent actions for additional damages which may arise from the same or other breaches. The commencement or maintaining of any such action or actions by Production Company shall not constitute or result in the termination of Writer's engagement hereunder unless Production Company shall expressly so elect by written notice to Writer. The pursuit by Production Company or Writer of any remedy under this Agreement or otherwise shall not be deemed to waive any other or different remedy which may be available under this Agreement or otherwise.

(b) Services Unique: Writer acknowledges that Writer's services to be furnished hereunder and the rights herein granted are of a special, unique, unusual, extraordinary and intellectual character which gives them a peculiar value, the loss of which cannot be reasonably or adequately compensated in damages in an action at law, and that Writer's Default will cause Production Company irreparable injury and damage. Writer agrees that Production Company shall be entitled to injunctive and other equitable relief to prevent default by Writer. In addition to such equitable relief, Production Company shall be entitled to such other remedies as may be available at law, including damages.

## 14. FORCE MAJEURE:

(a) Suspension: If, (i) by reason of fire, earthquake, labor dispute or strike, act of God or public enemy, any municipal ordinance, any state or federal law, governmental order or regulation, or other cause beyond Production Company's control, Production Company is prevented from or hampered in the production of the Picture, or if, (ii) by reason of the closing of substantially all the theatres in the United States for any of the aforesaid or other causes which would excuse Production Company's performance as a matter of law, Production Company's production of the Picture is postponed or suspended, or if, (iii) by reason of any of the aforesaid contingencies or any other cause or occurrence not within Production Company's control, including but not limited to the death, illness or incapacity of any principal member of the cast of the Picture or the director or individual producer, the preparation, commencement, production or completion of the Picture is hampered, interrupted or interfered with, and/or if, (iv) Production Company's normal business operations are hampered or otherwise interfered with by virtue of any disruptive events which are beyond Production Company's control ("Production Company Disability"), then Production Company may postpone the commencement of or suspend the rendition of Writer's services and the running of time hereunder for such time as the Production Company Disability continues; and no compensation shall accrue or become payable to Writer hereunder during such suspension. Such suspension shall end upon the cessation of the cause thereof.

(b) Termination:

(i) Production Company Termination Right: If a Production Company Disability continues for a period of eight (8) weeks, Production Company may terminate this Agreement upon written notice to Writer.

CONTRACTS
FOR THE
FILM AND
TELEVISION
INDUSTRY

142

(ii) Writer's Termination Right: If a Production Company Disability results in the payment of compensation being suspended hereunder for a period exceeding eight (8) weeks, Writer may terminate this Agreement upon written notice to Production Company.

(iii) Production Company Re-Establishment Right: Despite Writer's election to terminate this Agreement, within five (5) business days after Production Company's actual receipt of such written notice from Writer, Production Company may elect to re-establish the operation of this Agreement.

**15. WRITER'S INCAPACITY:** If, by reason of mental or physical disability, Writer shall be incapacitated from performing or complying with any of the terms or conditions hereof ("Writer's Incapacity") for a consecutive period exceeding fifteen (15) days during the performance of Writer's services, then:

(a) Suspension: Production Company may suspend the rendition of services by Writer and the running of time hereunder so long as Writer's Incapacity shall continue.

(b) Termination: Production Company may terminate this Agreement and all of Production Company's obligations and liabilities hereunder upon written notice to Writer.

(c) Right of Examination: If any claim of mental or physical disability is made by Writer or on Writer's behalf, the Production Company may have Writer examined by such physicians as Production Company may designate. Writer's physician may be present at such examination, and shall not interfere therewith. Any tests performed on Writer shall be related to and be customary for the treatment, diagnosis or examination to be performed in connection with Writer's claim.

**16. WRITER DEFAULT:** If Writer fails or refuses to write, complete and deliver to Production Company the Product Form provided for herein within the respective periods specified or if Writer otherwise fails or refuses to perform or comply with any of the terms or conditions hereof (other than by reason of Writer's Incapacity) ("Writer's Default"), then:

(a) Suspension: Production Company may suspend the rendition of services by Writer and the running of time hereunder as long as the Writer Default shall continue,

(b) Termination: Production Company may terminate this Agreement and all of Production Company's obligations and liabilities hereunder upon written notice to Writer.

(c) Writer Default shall not include any failure or refusal of Writer to perform or comply with the material terms of this Agreement by reason of a breach or action by Production Company which makes the performance by Writer of his services impossible.

(d) Prior to termination of this Agreement by Production Company based upon Writer Default, Production Company shall notify Writer specifying the nature of the Writer Default and Writer shall have a period of 72 hours after giving of such notice to cure the Writer Default. If the Writer Default is not cured within said period, Production Company may terminate this Agreement forthwith.

**17. EFFECT OF TERMINATION:** Termination of this Agreement, whether by lapse of time, mutual consent, operation of law, exercise of right of termination or otherwise shall:

(a) Compensation: Terminate Production Company's obligation to pay Writer any further compensation. Nevertheless, if the termination is not for Writer Default, Production Company shall pay Writer any compensation due and unpaid prior to termination;

(b) Refund/Delivery: If termination occurs pursuant to Clauses 14, 15, or 16, prior to Writer's delivery to Production Company of the Product Form on which Writer is then currently working, then Writer (or in the event of Writer's death, Writer's estate) shall, as Production Company requests, either forthwith refund to Production Company the compensation which may have been paid to Writer as of that time for such Product Form, or immediately deliver to Production Company all of the Product then completed or in progress, in whatever stage of completion it may be.

**18. EFFECT OF SUSPENSION:** No compensation shall accrue to Writer during any suspension. During any period of suspension hereunder, Writer shall not render services for any party other than Production Company. However, Writer shall have the right to render services to third parties during any period of suspension based upon a Production Company Disability subject, however, to Production Company's right to require Writer to resume the rendition of services hereunder upon three (3) days' prior notice. Production Company shall have the right (exercisable at any time) to extend the period of services of Writer hereunder for a period equal to the period of such suspension. If Production Company shall have paid compensation to Writer during any period of Writer's Incapacity or Writer Default, then Production Company shall have the right (exercisable at any time) to require Writer to render services hereunder without compensation for a period equal to that period of Writer's Incapacity or Default.

**19. WRITER'S RIGHT TO CURE:** Any Writer's Incapacity or Writer Default shall be deemed to continue until Production Company's receipt of written notice from Writer specifying that Writer is ready, willing and able to perform the services required hereunder; provided that any such notice from Writer to Production Company shall not preclude Production Company from exercising any rights or remedies Production Company may have hereunder or at law or in equity by reason of Writer's Incapacity or Writer Default.

**20. TEAM OF WRITERS:** The obligations of the Writers' team under this Agreement shall be joint and several, and references in this Agreement to Writer shall be deemed to refer to the Team of Writers jointly and severally. Should any right of termination arise as a result of the Incapacity or Default of any one of the Team of Writers, the remedies of the Production Company may be exercised either as to such Writer or as to the Team of Writers, at Production Company's election. Should Production Company elect to exercise its remedies only as to the Writer affected, the engagement of the other Writer or Writers shall continue and such remaining Writer shall receive only his share of the compensation provided herein.

**21. GUILDS AND UNIONS:**

(a) Membership: During Writer's engagement hereunder, as Production Company may lawfully require, Writer at Writer's sole cost and expense (and at

CONTRACTS
FOR THE
FILM AND
TELEVISION
INDUSTRY

144

Production Company's request) shall remain or become and remain a member in good standing of the then properly designated labor organization or organizations (as defined and determined under the then applicable law) representing persons performing services of the type and character required to be performed by Writer hereunder.

(b) Superseding Effect of Guild Arrangements: Nothing contained in this Agreement shall be construed so as to require the violation of the applicable WGA Agreement, which by its terms is controlling with respect to this Agreement; and whenever there is any conflict between any provision of this Agreement and any such WGA Agreement, the latter shall prevail. In such event the provisions of this Agreement shall be curtailed and limited only to the extent necessary to permit compliance with such WGA Agreement.

## 22. CREDITS:

(a) Billing: Provided that Writer fully performs all of Writer's obligations hereunder and the Picture is completed and distributed, Production Company agrees that credits for authorship by Writer shall be determined and accorded pursuant to the provisions of the WGA Agreement in effect at the time of such determination.

(b) Inadvertent Non-Compliance: Subject to the foregoing provisions, Production Company shall determine, in Production Company's discretion, the manner of presenting such credits. No casual or inadvertent failure to comply with the provisions of this clause, nor any failure of any other person, firm or corporation to comply with its agreements with Production Company relating to such credits, shall constitute a breach by Production Company of Production Company's obligations under this clause. Writer hereby agrees that if through inadvertence Production Company breaches its obligations pursuant to this Paragraph, the damages (if any) caused Writer by Production Company are not irreparable or sufficient to entitle Writer to injunctive or other equitable relief. Consequently, Writer's rights and remedies in such event shall be limited to Writer's rights, if any, to recover damages in an action at law, and Writer shall not be entitled to rescind this Agreement or any of the rights granted to Production Company hereunder, or to enjoin or restrain the distribution or exhibition of the Picture or any other rights granted to Production Company. Production Company agrees upon receipt of notice from Writer of Production Company's failure to comply with the provisions of this Paragraph, to take such steps as are reasonably practicable to cure such failure on future prints and advertisements.

**23. INSURANCE:** Production Company may secure life, health, accident, cast or other insurance covering Writer, the cost of which shall be included as a direct charge of the Picture. Such insurance shall be for Production Company's sole benefit and Production Company shall be the beneficiary thereof, and Writer shall have no interest in the proceeds thereof. Writer shall assist in procuring such insurance by submitting to required examinations and tests and by preparing, signing and delivering such applications and other documents as may be reasonably required. Writer shall, to the best of Writer's ability, observe all terms and conditions of such insurance of which Production Company notifies Writer as necessary for continuing such insurance in effect.

**24. EMPLOYMENT OF OTHERS:** Writer agrees not to employ any person to serve in any capacity, nor contract for the purchase or renting of any article or material, nor make any agreement committing Production Company to pay any sum of money for any reason whatsoever in connection with the Picture or services to be rendered by Writer hereunder, or otherwise, without written approval first being had and obtained from Production Company.

## 25. ASSIGNMENT AND LENDING:

(a) Assignability: This Agreement is non-assignable by Writer. Production Company and any subsequent assignee may freely assign this Agreement and grant its rights hereunder, in whole or in part to any person, firm, or corporation provided that such party assumes and agrees in writing to keep and perform all of the executory obligations of Production Company hereunder. Upon such assumption, Production Company is hereby released from all further obligations to Writer hereunder, except that unless the assignee or borrower is a so-called major motion picture company, or mini-major, Production Company shall remain secondarily liable under this agreement.

(b) Right to Lend to Others: Writer understands and acknowledges that the actual production entity of a motion picture to be made from the Product may be a party other than Production Company. In such event, Writer's services shall be rendered hereunder for the actual production entity but without releasing Production Company from its obligations hereunder.

## 26. NOTICES:

(a) Writer's Address: All notices from Production Company to Writer, in connection with this Agreement, may be given in writing by addressing the same to Writer _____ (Writer address). Production Company may deliver such notice to Writer personally, either orally or in writing. A courtesy copy shall be given to _____ at _____ . If such notice is sent by mail, the date of mailing shall be deemed to be the date of service of such notice.

(b) Writing Requirement: Any oral notice given in respect to any right of termination, suspension or extension under this Agreement shall be confirmed in writing. If any notice is delivered to Writer personally, a copy of such notice shall be sent to Writer at the above address.

(c) Producer's Address: All notices from Writer to Production Company hereunder shall be given in writing addressed to Production Company as follows: _____, _____ and by depositing the same, so addressed, postage prepaid, in the mail. A courtesy copy shall be given to _____. Unless otherwise expressly provided, the date of mailing shall be deemed to be the date of service of such notice.

**27. TRANSPORTATION AND EXPENSES:** When Writer's services are required by Production Company to be rendered hereunder at a place more than fifty (50) miles from Writer's domicile, Production Company shall furnish Writer transportation to and from such places and meals and lodging accommodations while Writer is on location to render Writer's services.

**28. GOVERNING LAW:** This Agreement shall be construed in accordance with the laws of the State of _____ applicable to agreements which are executed and fully performed within said State.

CONTRACTS
FOR THE
FILM AND
TELEVISION
INDUSTRY

146

**29. CAPTIONS:** The captions used in connection with the clauses and subclauses of this Agreement are inserted only for the purpose of reference. Such captions shall not be deemed to govern, limit, modify, or in any other manner affect the scope, meaning or intent of the provisions of this Agreement or any part thereof; nor shall such captions otherwise be given any legal effect.

**30. SERVICE OF PROCESS:** In any action or proceeding commenced in any court in the State of _____ for the purpose of enforcing this Agreement or any right granted herein or growing out hereof, or any order or decree predicated thereon, any summons, order to show cause, writ, judgment, decree, or other process, issued by such court, may be delivered to Writer personally without the State of _____; and when so delivered, Writer shall be subject to the jurisdiction of such court as though the same had been served within the State of _____ (State Law), but outside the county in which such action or proceeding is pending.

**31. ILLEGALITY:** Nothing contained herein shall require the commission of any act or the payment of any compensation which is contrary to an express provision of law or contrary to the policy of express law. If there shall exist any conflict between any provision contained herein and any such law or policy, the latter shall prevail; and the provision or provisions herein affected shall be curtailed, limited or eliminated to the extent (but only to the extent) necessary to remove such conflict; and as so modified the remaining provisions of this Agreement shall continue in full force and effect.

**32. EMPLOYMENT ELIGIBILITY:** All of Production Company's obligations herein are expressly conditioned upon Writer's completion, to Production Company's satisfaction, of the I-9 form (Employee Eligibility Verification Form), and upon Writer's submission to Production Company of original documents satisfactory to demonstrate to Production Company Writer's employment eligibility.

**36. ENTIRE AGREEMENT:** This Agreement contains the entire agreement of the parties and all previous agreements, warranties and representations, if any, are merged herein.

By signing in the spaces provided below, Writer and Production Company accept and agree to all of the terms and conditions of this Agreement.

_____     Date: _____
("Writer")


_____
("Production Company")


By: _____     Date: _____
(Production Company Representative)

# DIRECTOR EMPLOYMENT

Director employment agreements share many provisions of writer employment agreements. Once again, the deal may be structured as direct employment or through a loan-out arrangement.

Directors are hired for the period of principal photography as well as the time needed beforehand to prepare for filming (pre-production) and time afterwards to supervise editing (post-production). The director may also work with the writer during development.

Often the director is hired on a flat fee basis that covers all these phases. Payments are made in installments with most of the fee paid during principal photography. A director is typically hired on an exclusive basis, preventing her from accepting outside employment and working on more than one film at a time.

The agreement is frequently a "pay-or-play" deal which means that if the studio does not use the director's services, or replaces her, the director is still entitled to fixed compensation. The director may also receive bonus, deferred, contingent, and additional compensation, although these payments may not vest until and unless the person is entitled to a director credit.

Usually the director does not have the right of "final cut," which is the power to determine the composition of the final edited version of the picture. Studios may insist on reserving this right to protect their investment and make sure that the director does not create an artistic masterpiece that is a commercial flop. The agreement will also specify that the film be a certain length (e.g., within 90-120 minutes). Directors may be required to produce two versions of the film: one for theatrical release and another for television broadcast.

The director may have the right to select key personnel such as the Director of Photography, Production Manager and Editor. A veteran director with clout will have the power to hire certain cast and crew members without studio approval.

CONTRACTS
FOR THE
FILM AND
TELEVISION
INDUSTRY

148

# DIRECTOR'S AGREEMENT (THEATRICAL, LOAN-OUT)

THIS AGREEMENT and attached Exhibits, effective as of _____ (Agreement Date) between _____ (Producer), incorporated in the state of _____ ("Producer") and, _____ (Lender), incorporated in the state of _____, for the director services of _____ ("Director"), with regard to the theatrical motion picture entitled "_____" ("Picture").

**1. ENGAGEMENT AND SERVICES:** Producer hereby agrees to borrow from Lender, and Lender agrees to lend to Producer, Director to render directing services in connection with the Picture, on a pay or play basis effective _____(Date), such services to include such pre-production, production and post-production services and such other services as a director is usually required to perform in order to make the negative of the Picture ready for final release printing. All such services shall be rendered for and under the control of the Producer at such studios, locations and other places as the Producer may designate, which services shall include, without limitation, the following:

Pre-Production: Director shall be available and undertake a location search on or about _____.

Photography: Director's exclusive services for the Picture shall commence _____ weeks prior to the start of principal photography, for preparation, and shall be rendered exclusively thereafter until completion of the _____week scheduled period of photography. The scheduled start date of principal photography is _____.

Post-Production: Director's post-production services shall be rendered on an exclusive basis in order to work during the _____ week post-production period with the editor until completion of the final corrected answer print. In connection with post-production:

Cooperation with Editor: Lender hereby warrants and agrees that Director will cooperate with the picture editor and other post-production personnel so that the assemblage of sequences and other elements of post-production shall be conducted in conformance with the schedule described herein.

Post-Production Schedule: Lender agrees that the post-production schedule, which has or shall be agreed to in writing by Lender and Producer, shall be followed by Director.

Final Cutting Authority: _____ is designated as the person with final cutting authority over the Picture.

Dailies: Producer shall have the right to view the dailies during the production of the Picture, the rough cut and all subsequent cuts of the Picture.

Television Cover Shots: When protective cover shots are requested for any particular scene, Director shall furnish Producer with such cover shots necessary for the release of the Picture on television, based on network continuity standards in existence at the time of commencement of principal photography.

Additional Post-Production Services: If after the completion of principal photography, Producer requires retakes, changes, dubbing, transparencies, added scenes, further photography, trailers, sound track, process shots or other language versions (herein collectively called "Retakes") for the Picture, Director shall report to Producer for such Retakes, at such place or places and on such consecutive or non-consecutive days as Producer may designate, subject only to Director's prior contractual commitments. Director shall not be entitled to additional compensation for any such additional services performed.

**2. TERM:**  The term of this agreement shall commence on or about \_\_\_\_\_ and shall continue until the completion of all of Director's required services on the Picture.

**3. RESULTS AND PROCEEDS OF SERVICES:**  Producer shall be entitled to and shall solely and exclusively own, in addition to Director's services hereunder, all of the results and proceeds thereof (including but not limited to all rights, throughout the world, of copyright, trademark, patent, production, manufacture, recordation, reproduction, transcription, performance, broadcast and exhibition of any art or method now known or hereafter devised, including radio broadcasting, theatrical and non-theatrical exhibition, and exhibition by medium of television or otherwise), whether such results and proceeds consist of literary, dramatic, musical, motion picture, mechanical or any other form of works, themes, ideas, compositions, creations, or productions, together with the rights generally known in the field of literary and musical endeavor as the "moral rights of authors" in and/or to any musical and/or literary proceeds of Director's services, including but not limited to the right to add to, subtract from, arrange, revise, adapt, rearrange, make variations of said property, and to translate the same into any and all languages, change the sequence, change the characters and the descriptions thereof contained in said property, change the title of the same, use said title or any of its components in connection with works or motion pictures wholly or partially independent of said property, and to use all or any part of said property in new versions, adaptations and sequels in any and all languages, and to obtain copyright therein throughout the world. Lender does hereby assign and transfer to Producer all of the foregoing without reservation, condition, or limitation, and no right of any kind, nature, or description is reserved by Lender. If Producer shall desire to secure separate assignments of or other documents on or for any of the foregoing, Lender shall execute the same upon Producer's request therefor, and if Lender fails or refuses to execute and deliver any such separate assignments or other documents, Producer shall have and is hereby granted the right and authority to execute the same in Lender's name and as Lender's attorney-in-fact.

**4. WARRANTIES AND INDEMNIFICATION:**

Lender warrants and represents that Lender (1) has the right to enter into this Agreement, (2) has entered into a written contract with Director which is now in full force and effect and pursuant to which Lender has the full right and authority to provide Director's services to Producer in accordance with the terms and conditions hereof; (3) is not subject to any obligation or disability which would interfere with or prevent the providing of Director's services hereunder; (4) shall, with respect to any compensation received pursuant to this Agreement, make all tax payments required of independent contractors by federal, state, and local laws, including without limitation all income and estimated tax payments; and that (5) any material created, composed, submitted, added or interpolated by Director hereunder shall be wholly original with Director and shall not, to the best of Director's knowledge, infringe upon or violate the copyright, literary, dramatic or photoplay rights, the right of privacy or publicity of, nor constitute a liable or slander against, nor violate any common law rights or any other rights of any person, firm or corporation.

CONTRACTS
FOR THE
FILM AND
TELEVISION
INDUSTRY

150

Lender agrees to indemnify Producer, its successors, assigns, licensees, employees and agents, and hold them harmless from and against any and all claims, liability, losses, damages, costs, and expenses (including reasonable attorneys' fees), judgment and penalties arising out of, resulting from, or based upon the breach by Lender of any representation, warranty or covenant made under this Agreement.

Producer agrees to indemnify Lender, its successors, assigns, licensees, employees and agents, and hold them harmless from and against any and all claims, liability, losses, damages, costs, and expenses (including reasonable attorneys' fees), judgment and penalties arising out of, resulting from, or based upon the breach by Producer of any representation, warranty or covenant made under this Agreement.

**5. COMPENSATION:** As full and complete consideration for Director's services hereunder, and for all rights herein granted to Producer, and subject to Lender's full compliance with the terms and conditions of this Agreement, Producer agrees to pay to Lender the following sums in the following manner:

Guaranteed Compensation: Salary at the rate of _____ dollars per week, _____ percent of which shall be payable, pursuant to the "Low Budget" Side letter attached hereto as Exhibit "B" and made a part hereof by this reference, for the thirteen (13) week minimum guaranteed period hereof (the "Guaranteed Period") in three (3) equal installments of _____ dollars, with the first upon the effective date hereof, the second upon commencement of principal photography and the third upon completion of principal photography.

Deferred Compensation: In addition to the Guaranteed Compensation payable above, Lender shall be entitled to receive an amount equal to _____ percent of said salary on a deferred basis pursuant to the aforementioned "Low Cost" Side letter.

Contingent Compensation: In addition to the Guaranteed and Deferred Compensation payable above, subject to the production and release of the Picture, Lender shall be entitled to receive as Contingent Compensation an amount equal to _____ percent of one-hundred percent of the Net Profits of the Picture, if any.

Net Profits Definition: "Net Profits" shall be computed, determined and paid in accordance with the definition of net profits between Producer and the distributor of the Picture, unless none exists, in which case Producer's standard definition shall apply, the terms and conditions of which shall be subject to good faith negotiation within customary United States motion picture industry parameters.

Flat Fee Basis: Producer and Lender hereby mutually acknowledge that the Guaranteed Compensation as hereinabove specified is a "flat fee." The Guaranteed Compensation shall be the prevailing minimum wage, subject to the "Low Cost" Side letter, so that Lender shall not be entitled to any additional and/or so-called "overage" compensation for any services rendered by Director during the development, pre-production, production, or post-production phases, or for additional post-production services rendered by Director.

Pay or Play: Producer shall not be obligated to utilize Director's services in connection with the Picture, nor be obligated to produce, release, distribute, advertise, exploit or otherwise make use of the Picture, provided, however, that, as of _____ (Guranteed Compensation Pay Date), the full amount of the Guaranteed Compensation shall be paid to Lender as provided under Paragraph 5(a) should Producer (without legal justification or excuse as elsewhere provided in this agreement or by operation of law), abandon the Picture or otherwise elect not to utilize Director's services.

Guild Plans: Producer shall pay all required Director's Guild of America, Inc. ("DGA") Pension, Health and Welfare contributions directly to the respective Plans on behalf of Director.

**6. TRANSPORTATION AND EXPENSES:** If Director's services are required at Producer's request to be rendered on location more than fifty (50) miles from the City of _____, Producer shall furnish Director, or reimburse Lender for (i) first-class round trip airfare for one (1) to such location (if available and if used), (ii) Director's reasonable and necessary living expenses in the amount of _____ dollars per day (payable on a weekly basis at the beginning of each week), and (iii) a first-class or best obtainable hotel suite. Producer shall also provide Director with a rental car while at such location, at Producer's expense. All travel arrangements, including, without limitation, the acquisition of airline tickets and booking of accommodations, shall be made through Producer, or its designated agent, unless Lender obtains Producer's prior written approval to vary from said procedure. Lender shall be reimbursed for any necessary out-of-pocket expenses incurred hereunder by Director with the prior written approval of Producer.

**7. CREDIT:** Provided the Picture is released, and provided Director shall have rendered and completed Director's services in principal photography of the Picture, Producer agrees to accord Director credit, in accordance with the requirements contained in the Directors Guild of America, Inc. Basic Agreement of 1987, substantially as follows:

"Directed by _____"

Such credit shall be accorded on a separate card in the main titles on all positive prints of the Picture, and in all paid advertising issued by Producer in connection therewith, except advertisements of eight (8) column inches or less; group and list advertisements; teasers; publicity; special advertising; billboards; television trailers; film clips or other advertising on the screen, radio or television ("excluded Ads"); except however, Director shall be entitled to a credit in any said excluded Ad in which any other person receives credit in connection with the Picture, with the exception of _____. Nothing contained in this Paragraph shall be construed to prevent the use of so-called "teaser," trailer, award and congratulatory ads, or other special advertising, publicity or exploitation relating to the story or screenplay, any members of the cast, or similar matters, without mentioning Director's name.

Director shall not receive a possessory credit unless Producer, in its sole discretion, deems such credit to be appropriate.

No casual or inadvertent failure to comply with the provisions of this clause shall be deemed to be a breach of this Agreement by Producer. Upon receipt of written notice of such failure from Lender, Producer shall use Producers best efforts to cure any such curable failure, to the extent reasonably possible. Lender hereby recognizes and confirms that in the event of failure or omission by Producer constituting a breach of its obligations under this clause, the damage, if any, caused Lender by Producer is not irreparable or sufficient to entitle Lender to

CONTRACTS
FOR THE
FILM AND
TELEVISION
INDUSTRY

152

injunctive or other equitable relief. Consequently, Lender's rights and remedies hereunder shall be limited to the right, if any, to obtain damages at law and Lender shall have no right in such event to rescind this Agreement or any of the rights granted to Producer hereunder or to enjoin or restrain the distribution or exhibition of the Picture.

**8. PERFORMANCE STANDARDS:** During the Term of this Agreement, Director shall render his services exclusively to Producer in directing and, to such extent as usually required, in otherwise assisting in the production of the Picture; except, however, Director's services in connection with any additional Post-Production Services shall be rendered on a non-exclusive basis, but in first priority following Director's prior contractual commitments. Said services shall be rendered either alone or in collaboration with other artists in such manner as Producer may reasonably direct, pursuant to the instructions, controls and schedules established by Producer and at the times, places and in the manner required by Producer. Such services shall be rendered in a directoric, conscientious, efficient and punctual manner, to the best of Director's ability and with full regard to the careful, efficient, economical and expeditious production of the Picture within the budget and shooting schedule established by Producer immediately prior to the commencement of principal photography; it being further understood that the production of motion pictures by Producer involves matters of discretion to be exercised by Producer with respect to art and taste, and Director's services and the manner of rendition thereof is to be governed entirely by Producer.

**9. FORCE MAJEURE:**

Suspension: If, by reason of fire, earthquake, labor dispute or strike, act of God or public enemy, any municipal ordinance, any state or federal law, governmental order or regulation, or other cause beyond Producer's control, Producer is prevented from or hampered in the production of the Picture, or if, by reason of the closing of substantially all of the theatres in the United States for any of the aforesaid or other causes, Producer's production of the Picture is postponed or suspended, or if, by reason of any of the aforesaid contingencies or any other cause or occurrence not within Producer's control, including but not limited to the death, illness or incapacity of any principal member of the cast of the Picture, the preparation, commencement, production or completion of the Picture is hampered, interrupted or interfered with ("Producer Disability"), then Producer may postpone the commencement of or suspend the rendition of services by Director and the running of time hereunder for such time as the Producer Disability shall continue; and no compensation shall accrue or become payable to Lender hereunder during the period of such suspension. Such suspension shall end upon the cessation of the cause thereof.

Termination:

Producer Termination Right: If a Producer Disability continues for a period in excess of eight (8) weeks, Producer shall have the right to terminate this Agreement upon written notice thereof to Lender.

Lender's Termination Right: If a Producer Disability results in the payment of compensation being suspended hereunder for a period in excess of eight (8) weeks, Lender shall have the right to terminate this Agreement upon written notice thereof to Producer.

Producer Re-Establishment Right: Despite Lender's election to terminate this Agreement, within five (5) days after Producer's actual receipt of such written notice from Lender, Producer shall have the right to elect to reestablish the operation of this Agreement upon written notice hereof to Lender.

## 10. DIRECTOR'S INCAPACITY

Effect of Director's Incapacity: If, by reason of mental or physical disability, Director shall be incapacitated from performing or complying with any of the terms or conditions hereof ("Director's Incapacity") for a consecutive period in excess of seven (7) days or aggregate period in excess of ten (10) days, then Producer shall have the right to terminate this Agreement upon written notice thereof to Lender.

Right of Examination: If any claim of mental or physical disability is made by Director or on Director's behalf, Producer shall have the right to have Director examined by such physicians as Producer may designate. Director's physician may be present at such examination, but such physician shall not interfere therewith.

**11. LENDER/DIRECTOR DEFAULT:** If Lender and/or Director fails or refuses to perform or comply with any of the terms or conditions hereof (other than by reason of Director's Incapacity) ("Lender/Director Default"), then Producer shall have the right to terminate this Agreement upon written notice thereof to Lender. Prior to termination of this Agreement by Producer based upon Lender/Director Default, Producer shall notify Lender specifying the nature of the Lender/Director Default and Lender shall have 48 hours after the giving of such notice within which to cure the Lender/Director Default. If the Lender/Director Default is not cured within the 48-hour period, Producer may terminate this Agreement forthwith.

**12. EFFECT OF TERMINATION:** Termination of this Agreement, whether by lapse of time, mutual consent, operation of law, exercise of a right of termination, or otherwise shall:

Terminate Producer's obligation to pay Lender any further compensation. Nevertheless, if the termination is not for Lender/Director Default, Producer shall pay Lender any compensation due and unpaid prior to the termination, and

Producer shall not be deemed to have waived any rights it may have or alter Producer's right or any of Lender's agreements or warranties in connection with the rendition of Director's services prior to termination.

**13. PRODUCER RIGHT TO SUSPEND:** In the event of Director's Incapacity or Lender/Director Default, Producer may postpone the commencement of or suspend the rendition of services by Director and the running of time hereunder so long as any such Director's Incapacity or Lender/Director Default shall continue; and no compensation shall accrue or become payable to Lender during the period of such suspension.

Lender's Right to Cure: Any Director's Incapacity or Lender/Director Default shall be deemed to continue until Producer's receipt of written notice from Lender specifying that Director is ready, willing and able to perform the services required hereunder; provided that any such notice from Lender to Producer shall not preclude Producer from exercising any rights or remedies Producer may have hereunder or at law or in equity by reason of Director's Incapacity or Lender/Director Default.

CONTRACTS
FOR THE
FILM AND
TELEVISION
INDUSTRY

154

Alternative Services Restricted: During any period of suspension hereunder, Director shall not render services for any party other than Producer.

Producer Right to Extend: If Producer elects to suspend the rendition of services by Director as herein specified, then Producer shall have the right (exercisable at any time) to extend the period of services required of Director hereunder for a period equal to the period of such suspension.

Additional Services: If Producer shall have paid compensation to Lender during any period of Director's Incapacity or Lender/Director Default, then Producer shall have the right (exercisable at any time) to require Lender to furnish Director's services hereunder without compensation for a period equal to the period for which Producer shall have paid compensation to Lender during such Director's Incapacity or Lender/Director Default; except, however, said Additional Services necessitated by Director's Incapacity shall be subject only to Director's prior contractual commitments, and if Director is unable to report to Producer at such time(s) as Producer may require, Lender shall make such services available to Producer at the earliest possible date thereafter.

**14. FURTHER WARRANTIES:** Lender hereby warrants that neither Lender nor Director is under any obligation or disability, created by law or otherwise, which would in any manner or to any extent prevent or restrict Lender or Director from entering into and fully performing this Agreement; and Lender agrees that Director shall devote Director's entire time and attention and best talents and abilities exclusively to Producer as specified herein, and to observe and to be governed by the rules of conduct established by Producer for the conduct of Producer's employees.

**15. UNIQUE SERVICES:** Except as specifically provided to the contrary hereinabove, Director's Services shall be rendered exclusively to Producer until expiration of the Term of this Agreement, it being mutually understood and agreed that Director's services are extraordinary, unique and not replaceable, and that there is no adequate remedy at law for any breach of this Agreement by Director and/or Lender, and that Producer, in the event of breach by Director and/or Lender, shall be entitled to seek equitable relief by way of injunction or otherwise.

**16. REMEDIES:** All remedies accorded herein or otherwise available to either Producer or Lender shall be cumulative, and no one such remedy shall be exclusive to any other. Without waiving any of Producer's rights or remedies under this Agreement or otherwise, Producer may from time to time recover, by action, any damages arising out of any breach of this Agreement by Lender, and may institute and maintain subsequent actions for additional damages which may arise from the same or other breaches. The commencement or maintaining of any such action or actions by Producer shall not constitute an election on Producer's part to terminate this Agreement nor constitute or result in termination of Director's employment hereunder unless Producer shall expressly so elect by written notice to Lender. The pursuit by either Producer or Lender of any remedy under this Agreement or otherwise shall not be deemed to waive any other or different remedy which may be available under this Agreement or otherwise, either at law or in equity. Lender acknowledges and agrees that Lender's sole remedy for any breach or alleged breach of this Agreement by Producer shall be an action at law to recover money damages; in no event shall Lender seek or be entitled to injunctive or other equitable relief on account of any breach or alleged breach of this Agreement by Producer.

**17. NAME AND LIKENESS:** Lender grants to Producer the right to use Director's name and likeness for advertising, publicizing, and exploiting the Picture; provided, however, that such advertising and publicity may not include the direct endorsement of any product (other than the Picture) without the Lender's written consent. Exhibition, advertising, publicizing or exploiting the Picture by any media, even though a part of or in connection with a product or commercially sponsored program, shall not be deemed an endorsement of any nature.

**18. PUBLICITY RESTRICTIONS:** Lender or Director shall not individually or jointly, by means of press agents or publicity or advertising agencies or others, employed or paid by Lender or Director or otherwise, circulate, publish or otherwise disseminate any news stories or articles, books or other publicity, containing Director's name and relating directly or indirectly to Director's employment, the subject matter of this Agreement, the Picture or the services to be rendered by Director or others in connection with the Picture unless the same are first approved by Producer. Notwithstanding the foregoing, Lender or Director may disseminate publicity which contains Director's name and identifies the Picture or Director's services in connection therewith so long as such publicity (a) is not an advertisement for the Picture, (b) is not derogatory, and (c) does not disclose confidential information. Lender or Director shall not transfer or attempt to transfer any right, privilege, title, or interest in or to any of the things above specified, nor shall Lender or Director at any time grant the right to or authorize any person, firm or corporation in any way to infringe upon such rights hereby granted to Producer, and Lender or Director authorize Producer, at Producer's expense, in Lender's or Director's name or otherwise, to institute any proper legal proceedings to prevent any infringement.

**19. GUILDS AND UNIONS:**

During the periods when Director is required to render services hereunder, as Producer may lawfully require, Lender shall cause Director, at Lender's or Director's sole cost and expense, to remain or become and remain a member in good standing of the then properly designated labor organization or organizations (as defined and determined under the then applicable law) representing persons performing services of the type and character required to be performed by Director hereunder.

Nothing contained in this Agreement shall be construed so as to require the violation of the Directors Guild of America, Inc. Basic Agreement of 1987, as amended from time-to-time, or any other written agreement between Producer and the DGA, which may from time-to-time be in effect and by its terms controlling with respect to this Agreement; and wherever there is any conflict between any provision of this Agreement and any such agreement, the latter shall prevail, but in such event the provisions of this Agreement shall be curtailed and limited only to the extent necessary to permit compliance with such agreement with the DGA.

**20. EMPLOYER TAXES:** Producer shall have no obligation to reimburse Lender for employer taxes of any kind or nature.

**21. MOTION PICTURE RELIEF FUND OF AMERICA, INC.:** Lender does not authorize Producer, and Producer shall not be obligated, to pay on Director's behalf any amounts to the Motion Picture Relief Fund of America, Inc. in connection with any compensation accruing to Lender hereunder.

CONTRACTS
FOR THE
FILM AND
TELEVISION
INDUSTRY

156

**22. ATTACHMENT:** If Producer shall be required, because of the service of any garnishment or by the terms of any contract or assignment executed by Lender, to pay all or any portion of the compensation hereunder to any other person, firm or corporation, the withholding of payment of such compensation or any portion thereof, in accordance with the requirements of any such attachment, contract or assignment shall not be construed as a breach by Producer of this Agreement. Producer will advise Lender of any such attachment, garnishment or other obligation within a reasonable period after receipt thereof. Lender shall have the right to discharge any such attachment, garnishment, or other obligation before Producer acts in compliance therewith. Lender agrees to indemnify and hold harmless Producer, its successors and assigns, from any cost, expense, penalty, or liability arising out of, resulting from, or based upon said attachment, contract or assignment.

**23. GOVERNMENTAL LIMITATION:** If the compensation provided for by this Agreement shall exceed the amount permitted by any present or future law or governmental order or regulation, such stated compensation shall be reduced, while such limitation is in effect, to the amount which is so permitted, and the payment of such reduced compensation shall be deemed to constitute full performance by Producer of Producer's obligations respecting the payment of compensation hereunder.

**24. INSURANCE:** Producer may secure life, health, accident, or other insurance covering Director, the cost of which shall be included as a Direct Charge of the Picture. Such insurance shall be for Producer's sole benefit and Producer shall be the beneficiary thereof, and Lender and Director shall have no interest in the proceeds thereof. Director shall assist in procuring such insurance by submitting to required examinations and tests and by preparing, signing, and delivering such applications and other documents as may reasonably be required. Lender and Director shall, to the best of Lender's and Director's ability, observe all terms and conditions of such insurance of which Producer notifies the Lender or Director as necessary for continuing such insurance in effect. If Producer is unable to obtain any such insurance covering Director at prevailing standard rates and without any exclusions, restrictions, conditions, or exceptions of any kind, Lender shall have the right to pay any premium in excess of the prevailing standard rates in order for Producer to obtain such insurance. If Lender fails, refuses or is unable for any reason whatsoever to pay such excess premiums, or if Producer having obtained such insurance, Lender or Director fails to observe all terms or conditions necessary to maintain such insurance in effect, Producer shall have the right to terminate this Agreement without any obligation to Lender or Director by giving Lender written notice of termination.

**25. EMPLOYMENT OF OTHERS:** Lender and Director agree not to employ any person to serve in any capacity, nor contract for the purchase or renting of any article or material, nor make any agreement committing Producer to pay any sum of money for any reason whatsoever in connection with the Picture or services to be rendered by Director hereunder or otherwise, without written approval first being had and obtained from Producer.

**26. RIGHT TO LEND TO OTHERS:** Producer shall have the right to lend Director's services hereunder to (a) any of Producer's subsidiary or affiliated companies, or (b) any other producer of motion pictures provided such producer shall have granted to Producer the right to distribute the Picture. No such lending of Director's services shall relieve Producer of its obligations hereunder.

**27. ASSIGNMENT:** This Agreement, at the election of Producer, shall inure to the benefit of Producer's administrators, successors, assigns, licensees, grantees, and associated, affiliated and subsidiary companies, and Lender agrees that Producer and any subsequent assignee may freely assign this Agreement and grant its rights hereunder, in whole or in part, to any party.

**28. NOTICES:** Any notice required or desired to be given to Producer or to Lender shall be given in one of the following ways:

By personal delivery or telecopier;

By deposit, addressed as specified below, registered or certified mail, return receipt requested, postage prepaid, in the United States mail; or

By delivery, addressed as specified below, toll prepaid to a cable company.

If so delivered, mailed, telegraphed or cabled, each such notice, statement or other document shall be conclusively deemed to have been given when personally delivered, or on the day of telecopying or delivery to the telegraph or cable company or on the third day after mailing, as the case may be. The addresses of the parties shall be those at which the other party actually receives written notice and, until further notice are:

To Production
Company:
_____
(Producer)

_____
(Address)

_____
Fax:

With copies to:
_____
(Courtesy Copy)

_____
(Address)

_____
Fax:

To Lender:
_____
(Lender)

_____
(Address)

_____
Fax:

**29. MISCELLANEOUS:** This Agreement and Exhibits attached hereto supersede any and all prior agreements between the parties relating hereto, constitute the entire agreement between the parties and cannot be modified except by written instrument. Neither Producer nor Lender and Director have made any representations, promises or warranties not set forth herein. This Agreement shall be binding upon and inure to the benefit of the parties hereto, and their respective heirs, executors, administrators, successors, and assigns. This Agreement shall in all respects be governed and construed in accordance with the laws of the State

CONTRACTS
FOR THE
FILM AND
TELEVISION
INDUSTRY

158

of \_\_\_\_\_. This Agreement may be signed in counterparts and if so signed shall have the same force and effect as though all signatures appeared on the same document.

IN WITNESS WHEREOF, the parties hereto have executed this Agreement as of the date first above written.


By _____

Its_____
  (Producer)


AGREED AND ACCEPTED:

_____
Company


By_____

Its_____
  (Lender)

**EXHIBIT "A"**

**DIRECTOR'S LOANOUT AGREEMENT
ADDITIONAL TERMS AND CONDITIONS**

## 1. RELATIONSHIP OF PARTIES:

The parties hereto are entering into this Agreement as independent contractors, and no partnership or joint venture or other association shall be deemed created by this Agreement. Lender will have the entire responsibility as the employer of Director and will discharge all of the obligations of any employer under federal, state or local laws, regulations or order, now or hereafter in force, including, but not limited to, those relating to taxes, unemployment compensation or insurance, social security, workmen's compensation, disability pensions, tax withholding and including the filing of all returns and reports required of an employer and the payment of all taxes, assessments and contributions and other sums required of an employer. Lender will deduct and withhold from the consideration payable by Lender to Director all amounts required to be deducted and withheld under employment agreements, under the provisions of any statute, regulation, ordinance or order requiring the withholding or deduction of compensation. Notwithstanding anything to the contrary set forth herein, it is agreed that Producer will pay all employer contributions to any Pension, Health and Welfare plans required by reason of the services rendered hereunder by Director, as set forth in the applicable Directors Guild of America, Inc. Theatrical and Television Basic Agreement (the "Basic Agreement").

Wherever reference is made to payments to Director herein, such reference shall be deemed to refer to payments to Lender; and

All rights granted by and/or accruing to Director herein shall be deemed granted by and/or accruing to Lender as well, and all warranties, agreements, duties, liabilities, obligations, waivers and indemnifications given, made and/or assumed by Director shall be deemed given, made and/or assumed by Lender as well.

## 2. DEFINITIONS

Main Agreement: The Agreement to which these Additional Terms and Conditions are attached.

Material: as herein used shall be deemed to include, but not by way of limitation, all material created, prepared, written and delivered under the Main Agreement to which these Additional Terms and Conditions are attached and otherwise in connection with this Agreement and the titles thereof, and all formats, treatments, themes, dialogue, plots, idea, characters and characterizations therein contained.

Picture: The motion picture defined under the terms of the Main Agreement, in any medium or format, including without limitation silent motion pictures, sound and talking motion pictures, produced, transmitted or exhibited with or accompanied by sound and voice recording, transmitting or reproducing devices and all developments and improvements of such devices, and all motion picture productions of every kind produced, transmitted or exhibited by any means now known or hereafter to become known.

CONTRACTS
FOR THE
FILM AND
TELEVISION
INDUSTRY

160

Pre-Production Services: Tests (including photographic and recording tests), readings, rehearsals, pre-recording, location searches and visits, publicity stills, sittings and interviews, conferences, and similar services, relating to the Picture, required by the Producer prior to the commencement of the term. Such services may also be required and if so shall be rendered, during the term.

Post-Production Services: Such services of the Director in connection with the Picture (including but not limited to trailers and foreign versions) as may be required by the Producer after the expiration of the term, including but not limited to photography, recording, editing, scoring, looping, dubbing and publicity (but required publicity services shall be limited to interviews, voice transcriptions and stills).

Term: The continuous period starting with the commencement date and continuing until the Producer releases the Director from the obligation to remain available to render services hereunder (other than post-production services). The Producer shall have the right to postpone the commencement date by a period of time equivalent to any period(s) of incapacity, cast incapacity, force majeure or default, plus a period of time after the termination of such situation reasonably necessary to prepare for the commencement date. Unless sooner terminated pursuant to any right of termination set forth in these Additional Terms and Conditions, the term shall consist of the minimum period of employment, immediately followed by the free period, if any, immediately followed by the remainder of the term, if any. If no free period is provided for, then the remainder of the term, if any, shall immediately follow the minimum period of employment.

**3. DURATION OF TERM:** The term shall continue for such continuous period as the Producer desires the Director to remain available to perform services in connection with the production of the Picture. If the terms of Article 6-104 (or a successor provision) of the Basic Agreement are applicable in the event of termination of the Director's employment hereunder, then it is agreed that the Director shall be entitled to receive the sum of One Hundred Dollars ($100) as the "additional negotiated sum" payable pursuant to the terms of said Article 6-104.

### 4. EXCLUSIVITY:

The Director's services hereunder during the term and during any continuous period of employment provided for in Article 7 hereof regarding post-production services are exclusive; that is to say that during the term and during said other continuous periods of employment, if any, the Director will be at all times available for the Producer, will render services exclusively for the Producer, and will not render services for himself (herself) or any other person or company, without prior written consent of the Producer, which the Producer shall be under no obligation to give.

### 5. SERVICES:

The Director shall (i) perform hereunder such services as a Director in connection with the Picture as may be required by the Producer; (ii) comply with the Producer's reasonable rules and regulations; and (iii) perform his (her) services and comply with his (her) other obligations promptly, faithfully, conscientiously, and to the full limit of his (her) talents and capabilities, whenever required by the Producer during the term, and at such other times as are provided herein, and in accordance with the Producer's instructions and directions in all matters, including those involving artistic taste and judgment. Services as a Director may include, if so required by the Producer, and in addition to actual direction as such, assistance in the preparation of the screenplay, assistance in cutting and editing, and such other services as may be required of a Director in accordance with the custom of the industry.

The Director has no rights of approval, of cast, script, other employees, or other matters whatsoever. The title of the Picture may be changed by the Producer or its assigns.

The Producer shall not be obligated (i) to cause or permit the Director to commence, continue or complete the performance of his (her) services hereunder, or (ii) to use the Director's name, voice or likeness in advertising or publicity, except as provided in the Main Agreement, (iii) to use any results of proceeds of the Director's services, or (iv) to produce, complete the production of, release, distribute, exhibit, advertise or exploit the Picture. Nothing in this paragraph is intended to release the Producer from its obligations hereunder with reference to the Director's compensation. The screenplay, and characters embodied therein, may be changed and rewritten by the Producer to such extent as it may determine, and without any necessity of obtaining the Director's approval.

## 6. PRE-PRODUCTION SERVICES:

The Director shall perform such pre-production services as may be required by the Producer, but only at such times as the Director is not otherwise employed. No compensation shall be payable for pre-production services, except to the extent, if any, required by the Basic Agreement; and if so required, then any such compensation paid shall be deemed paid against the minimum compensation, and the minimum period of employment shall be deemed to be correspondingly shortened.

## 7. POST-PRODUCTION SERVICES:

The Director shall perform such post-production services as may be required by the Producer, in accordance with the Main Agreement at the compensation prescribed therein, but only at such times as the Director is not otherwise employed. No compensation shall be payable for post-production publicity services. Compensation shall be payable for other post-production services, at the weekly rate of compensation provided for the minimum period of employment, but only for the days on which the Director is instructed to and does report to the Producer for such services and performs such services as are required.

## 8. LOCATION:

The Director's services shall be rendered, and the Director shall be available, at such times during the term (and at such other times as herein provided) and place(s) as the Producer may designate from time to time, including Saturdays, Sundays, holidays and nights if so required by the Producer. No overtime or other additional compensation or penalties shall be payable for work on Saturdays, Sundays, holidays or at night except as and then only to the minimum extent provided in the Basic Agreement.

The Director shall, if so required by the Producer, promptly apply for all passports, visas, work permits, membership in foreign labor organizations, and the like, and promptly take all such other steps as may be necessary to permit him (her) to enter, remain in, leave and work in any country where his (her) services

CONTRACTS
FOR THE
FILM AND
TELEVISION
INDUSTRY

162

may be required hereunder. The Producer shall pay or reimburse the Director for any fees or costs incurred in connection therewith, except taxes, and except such fees and costs as are applicable in the United States or in the Director's country of residence if other than the United States.

### 9. GUILD:

The Director represents that Director is (or if Director is not, Director agrees to become) a member in good standing of the Directors Guild of America, Inc. (the "Guild"), and agrees that during such period or periods as it may be lawful for the Producer to require the Director so to do, Director will remain a member in good standing of the Guild. If legally permissible, the Producer may pay any dues which may be or become payable by the Director to the Guild, and may deduct the amount of such payment from any compensation then or thereafter due from the Producer to the Director. The Director expressly authorizes the Producer to make such deductions and payments. The Producer shall be entitled to rely upon information furnished by the Guild with respect to Director's dues to the Guild, and shall not be liable to the Director for any payment or overpayment to the Guild based on such information, nor shall the Producer be obligated to take any steps whatsoever to reclaim or recover any such payment or overpayment.

If Director fails or refuses to become or remain a member in good standing of the Guild as required hereunder, Producer shall have the right at any time thereafter to terminate this Agreement and all of Producer's obligations to Director hereunder without prejudice to any other rights Producer may have hereunder for damages or otherwise by reason of such failure, but no such termination shall affect or limit Producer's right to use all the results and proceeds of Director's services performed hereunder.

If the Basic Agreement requires incorporation of any of its provisions in this Agreement, such provisions are hereby incorporated herein, but only to the extent they are so required to be so incorporated by the Basic Agreement.

### 10. PAYMENT:

Producer's obligation to pay compensation or otherwise perform herein shall be conditioned upon full performance by Director of all of Director's obligations.

No withholding, deduction, reduction or limitation of compensation by Producer which is required or authorized by law, including any garnishment, attachment, writ of execution, or lien, ("Governmental Limitation") shall be a breach of this Agreement by Producer or relieve Director from Director's obligations hereunder. Payment of compensation as permitted pursuant to the Governmental Limitation shall continue while such Governmental Limitation is in effect and shall be deemed to constitute full performance by Producer of its obligation respecting the payment of compensation hereunder.

In the event the rules or regulations of any union or guild having jurisdiction over this employment require payments of minimum scale amounts at certain specified times or for certain uses, benefits or privileges in connection with the services and materials which may be required of Director herein, or for the rights granted hereunder, the parties hereby agree that the portions of any preceding payment made pursuant to this Agreement in excess of such applicable minimum scale for the services, materials or rights then or thereafter rendered or delivered shall be deemed credited against any such minimum scale payment, and such minimum scale payment shall therefore be deemed paid to the extent of such application at or prior to the time required under such rules or regulations.

If Producer makes any overpayment to Director hereunder for any reason or if Director is indebted to Producer for any reason, Director shall pay Producer such overpayment or indebtedness on demand, or, at the election of Producer, Producer may deduct and retain for its own account, an amount equal to all or any part of such overpayment or indebtedness from any sums that may be due or become due or payable by Producer to Director or for the account of Director and such deduction or retention shall not be deemed a breach of this Agreement.

## 11. RIGHTS IN MATERIAL:

The Producer shall own all material furnished by Director and all results and proceeds of Director's services hereunder, including the copyrights thereof, and all renewals and extensions, and rights to renewal and extension, of copyright, and as such owner shall have the right (among all other rights of ownership, but subject to the provisions of this Agreement): (i) to include them in the Picture and in advertising and publicity relating to the Picture, (ii) to reproduce them by any present or future means, (iii) to combine them with photographs and recordings made by others, (iv) to exhibit and perform them in theatres, on the radio and television, and in or by any other present or future media, for profit and otherwise, and for commercial or non-commercial purposes and purposes of trade, and (v) to license and assign its rights to any other person or company.

The Producer shall have the right to use and authorize others to use the name, voice and likeness of the Director, and all material furnished by Director and all results and proceeds of the Director's services hereunder, to advertise and publicize the Picture, including but not limited to the right to use and authorize others to use the same in the credits of the Picture, in trailers, in commercial tie-ups, and in all other forms and media of advertising and publicity.

Director agrees to execute such assignments or other instruments as Producer may from time-to-time deem necessary or desirable to evidence, establish, maintain, protect, enforce or defend its right, title and interest in or to any such material and the results and proceeds of Director's services hereunder. Director hereby appoints Producer the true and lawful attorney-in-fact of Director irrevocably to execute, verify, acknowledge and deliver any and all such instruments or documents which Director shall fail or refuse to execute, verify, acknowledge or deliver.

Without in any way limiting any of the other provisions hereof, Producer shall have the absolute and unlimited right for all uses of the material and the results and proceeds of Director's services hereunder, or produced or distributed hereunder, to make such changes, variations, revisions, modifications, alterations, adaptations, arrangements, additions, deletions in and/or to the characters, plot, dialogue, scenes, incidents, situations, action, language and themes thereof, and the music and lyrics, if any, thereof, in whole or in part, and to add to and/or include in any of same such language, speech, songs, music, lyrics, dancing, choreography, sound, action, situation, scenes, plot, dialogue, incidents and characters as Producer, in its uncontrolled discretion may deem advisable, it being the intention hereof that Producer shall have the absolute and unlimited right to use said material and results and proceeds of Director Services hereunder, and each and every part thereof in any manner

CONTRACTS
FOR THE
FILM AND
TELEVISION
INDUSTRY

164

or may in its uncontrolled discretion deem advisable, without in any way being accountable or liable to Director for any use it may make of the material and results and proceeds of Director Services hereunder, or any part thereof, for any permitted purposes. Director hereby waives the benefits of any provision of law known as the "droit moral" or any similar laws and Director agrees not to institute, support, maintain, or permit any action or lawsuit on the ground that any use made by Producer, its assignees or licensees, or under the authority of any of them, in any way constitutes an infringement of any of Director's "droit moral" or is in any way, without limitation, a defamation or mutilation of said material, and results and proceeds of Director Services hereunder, or any part thereof, or contains unauthorized variations, alterations, modifications, changes or translations.

All rights of the Producer hereunder are perpetual, exclusive and freely assignable, and vest in the Producer whether the Director's employment expires in normal course or is otherwise terminated.

## 12. CREDIT:

The Main Agreement is subject to the provisions of this Article 12, unless specifically provided to the contrary therein or unless and to the extent that the following provisions are inconsistent with the Basic Agreement.

The Producer shall be obligated to give credit to the Director only if a substantial part of the results and proceeds of the Director's services are retained in the Picture as generally released. No casual or inadvertent failure by the Producer to comply with the provisions of the Main Agreement shall constitute a breach of this Agreement.

If the Main Agreement provides for credit in paid advertising and/or publicity, then notwithstanding such provision the Producer shall not be obligated to give the Director credit in any of the following: (i) teaser advertising or publicity, (ii) group, list or institutional advertising or publicity, (iii) advertising of eight column inches or less, or its equivalent in the SAU (Standard Advertising Units) system of measurement, (iv) commercial tie-ups, (v) trailers or other advertising on the screen, and (vi) radio or television advertising or publicity.

If the Main Agreement provides for credit in paid advertising and if the size of type of such credit is based upon the size of type used for the title of the Picture and/or the name(s) of the star(s), then in the event the title and/or the name(s) of the star(s) are used more than once in a so-called "regular" use and a so-called "artwork" use, the references in the Main Agreement to the size of type shall be to the "regular" use as distinguished from the "artwork" use.

Any provision of the Main Agreement relating to the size of type, position or other manner in which the Director's name shall appear shall not apply as to any advertising or publicity written in narrative form.

No casual or inadvertent failure by Producer to comply with the provisions of the Main Agreement or this Article 12 shall constitute a breach of this Agreement. The rights and remedies of Director, in the event of a failure or omission by Producer constituting a breach, shall be limited to Director's rights, if any, to recover damages at law, but in no event shall Director be entitled by reasons of any such breach to terminate this Agreement or to enjoin or restrain the distribution or exhibition of the Picture.

## 13. PRODUCER'S PUBLICITY:

Director hereby grants to Producer the irrevocable and perpetual right to use and authorize others to use Director's name, photograph, likeness, voice, facsimile signature and biographical material for advertising and purposes of trade, and as news or informative matter, in connection with the material delivered and services performed hereunder and the exercise of all rights therein and all dealings therewith, and in connection with the exercise of any rights granted by Director hereunder, and in connection with publicity and institutional advertising of Producer and any other parties who may be involved in the production, exploitation, exhibition or use of the material, or any rights therein, and all commercial and promotional tie-ins in connection with any of the foregoing, but in no event shall Producer authorize any direct endorsement by Director of any product or service whatsoever without Director's prior written consent.

## 14. OTHER PUBLICITY:

Director agrees that, except as merely incidental to Director's personal publicity endeavors, Director shall not issue or authorize or permit the issuance of any advertising or publicity of any kind or nature relating to this Agreement, Producer, the material delivered by Director and results and proceeds of Director's services hereunder, any exercise of any rights therein, or any versions or productions based in whole or in part thereon, without the express prior written consent of Producer in each case.

## 15. REPRESENTATIONS AND WARRANTIES:

Director represents and warrants that:

Director is free to enter into and fully perform this Agreement, and that Director has full authority to grant the rights herein granted and that Director has not conveyed, granted, mortgaged, encumbered or otherwise disposed of, to or in favor of any other person, firm or corporation the rights so granted;

Director will not do and has not done any act or thing, by grant or otherwise, impairing the rights herein conveyed or that can prevent, or in any manner interfere with, the full enjoyment by Producer of the rights granted to Producer hereunder;

All material to be created, written and furnished hereunder by Director and all results and proceeds of Director's services hereunder shall be new and original with Director and Director will be the sole creator thereof;

No incident contained in the material to be created and furnished hereunder by Director and all results and proceeds of Director's services hereunder, and no part thereof, will be taken from or based upon any other literary material, or any dramatic work, or any motion picture, or any writing, or shall in anyway infringe upon the trademark, copyright or the literary, dramatic or motion picture rights, or any other rights of any person, entity, whatsoever; and

The reproduction and exhibition of such material and results and proceeds in photoplays, either with or without the reproduction in synchronism with such exhibition of recorded language, speech, songs, dance and other sounds, and the exercise of the rights herein granted to Producer, or any of them, will not in any way, directly or indirectly, infringe upon any rights of any person, or entity whatsoever.

CONTRACTS
FOR THE
FILM AND
TELEVISION
INDUSTRY

166

## 16. INDEMNIFICATION:

Director agrees to defend, indemnify, make good, save and hold harmless Producer, its successors, assigns and licensees, and the officers, agents, directors and employees of Producer and all such parties, from and against any and all losses, damages, claims, costs, charges, reasonable legal fees, recoveries, actions, judgments, penalties, expenses and/or other losses whatsoever which may be obtained against, imposed upon or suffered by Producer or any of them by reason of or relating to the breach or alleged breach of any warranty, covenant, agreement and/or representation herein made by Director. Producer may at its election assume the defense of any such claim or action which names or otherwise affects Producer.

With respect to the warranties and indemnifications set forth above, it is agreed that upon the presentation of any claim or the institution of any action involving a breach of warranty, or the institution of any action involving a breach of warranty, Director will promptly notify Producer in regard thereof. Producer agrees that the pendency of any such claim or action shall not relieve Producer of its obligation to pay Director any monies due hereunder and Producer shall not have the right to withhold such monies until Producer has sustained a loss or suffered an adverse judgment or decree by reason of such claim or action.

## 17. SUSPENSION RIGHTS:

No compensation shall accrue or become payable to Director during the period of any suspension. During any period of suspension hereunder, Director shall not render services for any party other than Producer. Producer shall have the right (exercisable at any time) to extend the period of services of Director hereunder for a period equal to the period of such suspension. If Producer shall have paid compensation to Director during any period of Director's Incapacity or Director's Default, then Producer shall have the right (exercisable at any time) to require Director to render services hereunder without compensation for a period equal to the period for which Producer shall have paid compensation to Director during such Director's Incapacity or Director's Default.

Any Director's Incapacity or Director's Default shall be deemed to continue until Producer's receipt of written notice from Director specifying that Director is ready, willing and able to perform the services required hereunder; provided that any such notice from Director to Producer shall not preclude Producer from exercising any rights or remedies Producer may have hereunder or at law or in equity by reason of Director's Incapacity or Director's Default.

## 18. RIGHTS/REMEDIES:

The rights herein granted to Producer are irrevocable and without right of rescission by Director or reversion to Director under any circumstances whatsoever. The expiration or termination of this Agreement on whatever grounds and by whomsoever effected shall not affect or impair the exclusive ownership by Producer of any results, proceeds or benefits of services theretofore rendered hereunder. In connection with the foregoing, it is expressly understood and agreed, and Director hereby expressly confirms that, in the event Producer terminates or cancels (or purports to terminate or cancel) this Agreement or any other agreement entered into by and between Producer and Director concurrently herewith, or as part of the same transaction (and even if such cancellation or termination is ultimately determined by a court to have been without proper or legal cause, or if it be ultimately determined by such court that Producer committed any material breach of any such agreement), the damage (if any) caused Director by Producer thereby is not irreparable or sufficient to entitle Director to seek injunctive or other equitable relief. Consequently, Director's rights and remedies in any such event shall be strictly limited to Director's right and remedy, otherwise available, to recover damages, and Director shall not have the right to rescind this Agreement or any such other agreement, or any of Producer's rights hereunder or thereunder, with respect to any such results, proceeds or benefits of Director's services.

## 19. NO PARTNERSHIP:

Nothing herein contained shall be construed to create a partnership or joint venture between the parties or to make either party the agent of the other. Neither party shall be or become liable or bound by any representation, act, omission or agreement whatsoever of the other which may be contrary to the provisions of this Agreement.

## 20. ASSIGNMENT:

Producer may assign this Agreement and/or any or all of its rights hereunder, and/or delegate any or all of its duties hereunder, at any time and from time-to-time, to any person, firm or corporation, but Producer shall not be relieved of its obligations hereunder by reason of any such assignment and/or delegation unless the assignee and/or delegate assumes in writing all of Producer's obligations to Director then remaining to be performed. This Agreement shall inure to the benefit of Producer, its successors and assigns. This Agreement shall be personal and non-assignable as to Director.

## 21. INJUNCTIVE RELIEF:

It is mutually acknowledged that the services to be performed and the rights granted by Director are of a special, unique, extraordinary, and intellectual character giving them a peculiar value, the loss of which cannot be reasonably or adequately compensated for in damages in an action at law, and breach by Director of any provision hereof will cause Producer irreparable injury and damage. Producer shall be entitled, as a matter of right, without further notice, to injunctive and other equitable relief to prevent the violation of any provision hereof by Director, in addition to any and all other rights and remedies which Producer may have to damages or otherwise.

## 22. NOTICES:

All notices and statements which either party shall be required or shall desire to give to the other party shall be given in one of the following ways: by personal delivery or telecopier; by deposit, registered or certified mail, return receipt requested, postage prepaid, in the United States mail; by delivery, toll prepaid, to a cable company; or by deposit with Federal Express or other comparable overnight courier.

If so delivered, mailed, telegraphed or cabled, each such notice, statement or other document shall be conclusively deemed to have been given when personally delivered, or on the day of telecopying or delivery to the telegraph or cable company, or on the first day following deposit with the overnight carrier, or on the third day after mailing, as the case may be. The addresses of the parties shall be those of which the other party actually receives written notice and, until further notice, are those addresses set forth at the beginning of this Agreement.

CONTRACTS
FOR THE
FILM AND
TELEVISION
INDUSTRY

168

## 23. WAIVER:

No waiver by either of the parties hereto of any failure by the other party to keep or perform any covenants or conditions of this Agreement shall be deemed to be a waiver of any preceding or succeeding breach of the same or any other covenant or condition of this Agreement. Each and all of the several rights and remedies provided for in this Agreement shall be construed as being cumulative and no one of them shall be deemed to be exclusive of the others or of any right or remedy allowed by law.

## 24. GOVERNING LAW:

This Agreement shall be construed and enforced in accordance with the laws and procedures of the State of _____, and this transaction is made in _____.

## 25. CONFLICT:

Notwithstanding anything to the contrary contained herein, in the event of any conflict between the terms and provisions of these Additional Terms and Conditions and the Main Agreement to which they are attached, the terms and provisions of the Main Agreement shall prevail.

## 26. FCC:

Director understands that it is a Federal offense, unless disclosed to Producer or to the network (and/or stations) broadcasting the material prior to broadcast, to: (i) give or agree to give any member of the production staff, anyone associated in any manner with the material or any representative of the network and/or stations broadcasting the material, any portion of Director's compensation or anything else of value for arranging Director's engagement to prepare the material; and/or (ii) accept or agree to accept anything of value, other than Director's regular compensation for services on or in connection with the material, to promote any product, services or venture on the air, or to use any prepared material containing such a promotion where Director knows that the Director or supplier of such material received a consideration for it. Director understands further that the policy of the Producer and the network and/or stations broadcasting the material prohibits such conduct with or without disclosure and any violation shall be a material breach and cause for dismissal and termination. Director affirms and represents that neither Director nor anyone acting in Director's behalf has made or will make any such arrangements.

## 27. ENTIRE AGREEMENT:

This Agreement expresses the entire understanding of the parties hereto and replaces any and all former agreements, understandings, representations or warranties relating to Director's employment hereunder and contains all of the terms, conditions, understandings, representations, warranties and promises of the parties hereto in connection with such employment. No modification, alteration or amendment of this Agreement shall be valid or binding unless in writing and signed by the party to be charged with such modification, alteration or amendment. No officer, employee or representative of Producer has any authority to make any representation, warranty or promise not contained in this Agreement, and Director acknowledges that Director has not executed this Agreement in reliance upon any promise, representation or warranty not expressly set forth in this Agreement. No waiver of any term or condition of this Agreement shall be construed as a waiver of any other term or condition; nor shall exercise of any option hereunder be deemed a waiver of any preceding default. Headings or titles of paragraphs herein are for convenience only and shall not in any way affect the construction or interpretation thereof.

## INDUCEMENT LETTER

Date: _____

_____
(Producer)

_____
(Address)

Re: "_____"

Dear Sirs/Mesdames:

Reference is made to the agreement (herein the "Agreement") dated concurrently herewith between _____ (herein the "Producer") and _____ (herein the "Lender") for my services in the above-referenced motion picture.

As an inducement to you to enter into the Agreement and as a material part of the consideration moving to you for so doing, I hereby represent, warrant and agree as follows:

1. That I have entered into an agreement ("Director's Employment Agreement") with the Lender covering the rendition of my services for the Lender, and that the Lender has the right and authority to enter into the Agreement and to furnish to you my services upon the terms and conditions therein specified.

2. I am familiar with each and all of the terms, covenants and conditions of the Agreement and hereby consent to the execution thereof; that I will be bound by and will duly observe, perform and comply with each and all of the terms, covenants and conditions of the Agreement on my part to be performed and complied with, even if the Director's Employment Agreement should hereafter expire, be terminated (whether by the Lender or myself) or suspended; that I shall render to you all of the services which are to be rendered by me pursuant to the Agreement even if the Lender shall be dissolved or should otherwise cease to exist; and that I hereby confirm that there have been granted to the Lender all of the rights granted by the Lender to you under the Agreement.

3. That I am under no obligation or disability by law or otherwise which would prevent or restrict me from performing and complying with all of the terms, covenants and conditions of the Agreement to be performed or complied with by me.

4. That I will look solely to the Lender or its associated or subsidiary companies and not to you for all compensation and other remuneration for any and all services and rights which I may render and grant to you under the Agreement.

CONTRACTS
FOR THE
FILM AND
TELEVISION
INDUSTRY

170

5. That you shall be entitled to equitable relief against me by injunction or otherwise to restrain, enjoin and/or prevent the violation or breach by me of any obligation of mine to be performed as provided in the Agreement, and/or the violation or breach by me of any obligations or agreements under this present instrument. You shall have all rights and remedies against me which you would have if I were your direct employee under the Agreement and you shall not be required to first resort to or exhaust any rights or remedies which you may have against the Lender before exercising your rights and remedies against me.

6. That I will indemnify and hold you, your employees, officers and assigns harmless from and against any and all taxes which you may have to pay and any and all liabilities (including judgments, penalties, interest, damages, costs and expenses including reasonable attorneys' fees, whether or not litigation is actually commenced) which may be obtained against, imposed or suffered by you or which you may incur by reason of your failure to deduct and withhold from the compensation payable under the Agreement any amounts required or permitted to be deducted and withheld from the compensation of an employee under the provisions of the Federal and _____ Income Tax acts, the Federal Social Security Act, the _____ Unemployment Insurance Act and/or any amendments thereof and/or any other statutes or regulations heretofore or hereafter enacted requiring the withholding of any amount from the compensation of an employee.

7. That I will not amend or modify the Director's Employment Agreement with the Lender in any particular manner that would prevent or interfere with the performance of my services for you or the use and ownership of the results and proceeds thereof, pursuant to the Agreement.

_____
"Employee"
Director

## EXHIBIT "B"
## "LOW BUDGET" SIDE LETTER

# DIRECTOR EMPLOYMENT AGREEMENT
## (Non-union)

Agreement dated _____, between _____ ("Director") and _____ ("Production Company").

**1. EMPLOYMENT:** Production Company agrees to employ Director to perform and Director agrees to perform, upon the terms and conditions herein specified, directing services in connection with the Theatrical Motion Picture currently entitled "_____" (the "Picture").

**2. TERM:** The Term of this agreement shall commence on (commence) and shall continue until the completion of all of Director's required services on the Picture.

**3. SERVICES:**

(a) Pre-Production: Director shall be available and undertake a location search on or about _____.

(b) Photography: Director's exclusive services for the Picture shall commence _____ weeks prior to the start of principal photography and shall be rendered exclusively after that until completion of all photography. The start date of principal photography shall be as Production Company designates. The scheduled start date of principal photography is _____.

(c) Post-Production: Director's post-production services shall be rendered on a non-exclusive but first-call basis, if Production Company so requires, in order to work during the post-production period with the editor until completion of the final corrected answer print.

(i) Cooperation with Editor: Director hereby warrants and agrees that Director will cooperate with the picture editor and other post-production personnel and will do nothing to hinder or delay the assemblage of film by the editor during the photography of the Picture so that the assembled sequences will be completed immediately following the completion of principal photography.

(ii) Post-Production Schedule: Director agrees that the post-production schedule, which shall be agreed to in writing by Director and Production Company, shall be followed by Director.

(iii) Final Cutting Authority: _____ is designated as the Production Company Executive with final cutting authority over the Picture. The foregoing shall be subject to applicable guild and union requirements, if any.

(d) Dailies: Production Company shall have the right to view the dailies during the production of the Picture, the rough cut and all subsequent cuts of the Picture.

(e) Television Cover Shots: When protective cover shots are requested for any particular scene, Director shall furnish Production Company with such cover shots necessary for the release of the Picture on television, based on network continuity standards in existence at the time of commencement of principal photography.

CONTRACTS
FOR THE
FILM AND
TELEVISION
INDUSTRY

172

(f) Additional Post-Production Services: If after the completion of principal photography Production Company requires retakes, changes, dubbing, transparencies, added scenes, further photography, trailers, sound track, process shots or other language versions (herein collectively called "retakes, etc.") for the Picture, Director shall report to Production Company for such retakes, etc., at such place or places and on such consecutive or non-consecutive days as Production Company may designate. Provided Director is not then rendering services (pursuant to a contractual commitment) for another party, Director shall cooperate to make such services available to Production Company at the earliest possible date.

**4. COMPENSATION:** As full and complete consideration for Director's services and Director's undertakings hereunder and for all rights granted to Production Company hereunder, and subject to Director's full compliance with the terms and conditions of this Agreement, Production Company agrees to pay Director as follows:

(a) Fixed Compensation:

(i) The total sum of _____ payable in equal weekly installments over the course of pre-production, principal photography and post-production.

(ii) Flat Fee Basis: Production Company and Director hereby mutually acknowledge that the Fixed Compensation as hereinabove specified is a "flat fee" and Director shall not be entitled to any additional and/or so-called "overage" compensation for any services rendered by Director during the development, pre-production, production or post-production phases, or for additional post-production services rendered by Director. Without limiting the generality of the foregoing, no additional compensation shall be payable to Director if the actual principal photography period for the Picture exceeds the scheduled principal photography period, nor for any services rendered pursuant to Clause 3(f).

(b) Deferred Compensation: In addition to the Fixed Compensation payable under Clause 4(a), subject to the production and release of the Picture, and subject to the performance of all obligations of Director, the Director shall receive and an amount equal to $_____ per week, in first position of all contingent deferments payable out of no more than fifty percent (50%) of the Production Company's gross revenues from the Picture, after the investors in the Picture have recouped their entire investment plus ten percent, after recoupment of all costs of production, financing and repayment of loans, and after any deferments payable to any laboratories, post-production services and cost of becoming a signatory to any Guild agreements. The aforesaid payment shall be deferred and paid pari passu with all similar deferments.

(c) Contingent Compensation: In addition to the Fixed Compensation payable above, subject to the production and release of the Picture and subject to the performance of Director's obligations hereunder, Director shall be entitled to receive as Contingent Compensation an amount equal to _____ percent of one hundred percent (_____% of 100%) of the Net Profits of the Picture, if any (and after d cust ng bhcocost of becoming a signatory to any guild agreements).

(d) Net Profits Definition: All income actually received by Production Company from the exploitation of the Picture after deducting all expenses and deferments incurred by Production Company in connection with the financing (including all interest and fees owed), pre-production, production, post-production, investor recoupment, marketing, distribution and exploitation of the Picture; this shall also include any attorneys' fees, expenses incurred by Production Company in connection with the Picture, residuals, union payments and the like. Also included within the Net Profits definition is a one percent (1%) deduction of the Production Company's gross income for Production Company operating expenses.

(e) Conditions Related to Compensation: Notwithstanding anything to the contrary contained in any of the above compensation provisions:

(i) Performance: No compensation shall accrue or become payable to Director during Director's inability, failure or refusal to perform the services contracted for herein according to the terms and conditions of this Agreement.

(ii) Pay or Play: Production Company shall not be obligated to use Director's services on the Picture, nor shall Production Company be obligated to produce, release, distribute, advertise, exploit or otherwise make use of the Picture; provided, however, that the full amount of the Fixed Compensation hereinabove specified shall be paid to Director should Production Company elect not to utilize Director's services.

(f) Vesting: The Fixed Compensation and Contingent Compensation hereinabove specified shall be deemed fully vested if, notwithstanding the termination of Director's services due to Production Company Disability or Director's Incapacity or Director Default, Director shall be entitled to receive "Directed by" credit by reference to the principles of the Director's Guild of America, Basic Agreement as same is amended and supplemented from time to time ("Basic Agreement").

If the services of Director are terminated by Production Company due to Production Disability or Director's Incapacity or Director Default, as defined below, and Director is not entitled to receive credit pursuant to the Basic Agreement, then the Fixed Compensation shall vest and accrue in the same manner as set forth herein and the Contingent Compensation shall accrue and vest in the same ratio that the number of linear feet in the completed Picture as released, which was directed by Director, bears to the total number of linear feet in the completed Picture as released. Notwithstanding the foregoing, if principal photography has not commenced on the scheduled start date as set forth in Clause 3(b) hereof, then the total Fixed Compensation shall vest and accrue on the aforesaid scheduled start date and production of the Picture is thereafter terminated prior to completion of principal photography and/or delivery of the final answer print to Production Company, then that portion of the Fixed Compensation not theretofore accrued shall fully vest and accrue on the date of such termination. If Production Company terminates this Agreement by reason of a Director Default, notwithstanding any vesting of Fixed Compensation and/or Contingent Compensation as set forth above, such vesting shall be subject to any and all the rights accorded to Production Company at law and in equity.

(g) Mitigation: If Production Company elects to exercise its pay or play right as set forth above and/or fails to produce the Picture, Director shall be obligated to mitigate damages.

## 5. CREDITS:

(a) Credit: Subject to the production and release of the Picture and provided Director performs his material obligations hereunder, then Production Company

CONTRACTS
FOR THE
FILM AND
TELEVISION
INDUSTRY

174

shall accord Director credit in connection with the Picture in accordance with the credit allocation rules of the Directors Guild of America, as amended and supplemented from time to time. Subject to the foregoing, said credit shall read:

"Directed by _____"

In determining credit, reference shall be made to the principles of the DGA credit arbitration rules. Although Production Company is not a DGA signatory, and writer is not a DGA member, to the extent possible, the principles of the DGA credit rules shall be followed by the parties. In the event of a credit dispute, the arbitrator of such a dispute shall follow the DGA credit rules to the extent they do not conflict with the rules of the arbitration proceeding used to resolve disputes under this agreement.

(b) Artwork Title Exception: If both a regular (or repeat) title and an artwork title are used, the position and percentage requirements above, as they relate to the title of the Picture, shall relate to the regular (or repeat) title. If only an artwork title is used, the percentage requirements above, as they relate to the title, shall be not less than ten percent (10%) of the average size of the letters used in the artwork title.

(c) Credit Limitation: Production Company agrees that no other individual and/or entity (other than members of the cast receiving "starring" billing before or after the title of the Picture or the company distributing and/or financing the Picture) shall receive credit larger than that used to display the credit accorded to Director and no other individual or entity shall receive a credit that is larger.

(d) Inadvertent Non-Compliance: No casual or inadvertent failure to comply with the provisions of this Paragraph shall be deemed to be a breach of this Agreement by Production Company. Director hereby recognizes and confirms that in the event of a failure or omission by Production Company constituting a breach of Production Company obligations under this Paragraph, the damages, if any, caused Director by Production Company are not irreparable or sufficient to entitle Director to injunctive or other equitable relief. Consequently, Director's rights and remedies hereunder shall be limited to the right, if any, to obtain damages at law and Director shall have no right in such event to rescind this Agreement or any of the rights assigned to Production Company hereunder or to enjoin or restrain the distribution or exhibition of the Picture. Production Company agrees to advise its assignees and licensees of the credit requirements herein. If Production Company shall learn of such failure of a third party to give such credit, Production Company shall notify such party of such failure and Production Company may, but shall not be obligated to, take action to cause such party to prospectively cure such failure.

## 6. TRANSPORTATION AND EXPENSES:

(a)     Local Transportation/Expenses: no reimbursement.

(b)     Distant Location expenses: Any expense allowance is limited to reimbursement of out-of-pocket gasoline expense. Location lodging (including a bed, sheets, pillow and blanket) and meals (continental breakfast and 2 meals per day) shall be provided by Production Company. A distant location shall be defined as one which is more than 75 miles from Director's residence. Any location expenses for purposes unrelated to the production are not reimbursable.

**7. PERFORMANCE STANDARDS:** Except as specifically provided to the contrary herein, during the Term of this Agreement, Director shall render his directing services exclusively to Production Company and, to such extent as Production Company may require, in otherwise assisting in the production of the Picture. Said services shall be rendered either alone or in collaboration with another or other artists in such manner as Production Company may direct, pursuant to the instructions, controls and schedules established by Production Company, and at the times, places and in the manner required by Production Company. Such manners, instructions, directions, and controls shall be exercised by Production Company in accordance with standards of reasonableness and also with what is customary practice in the Motion Picture industry. Such services shall be rendered in an artistic, conscientious, efficient and punctual manner, to the best of Director's ability and with full regard to the careful, efficient, economical and expeditious production of the Picture within the budget and shooting schedule established by Production Company immediately prior to the commencement of principal photography, it being further understood that the production of motion pictures by Production Company involves matters of discretion to be exercised by Production Company with respect to art and taste, and Director's services and the manner of rendition thereof is to be governed entirely by Production Company.

**8. UNIQUE SERVICES:** Except as specifically provided to the contrary hereinabove, Director's services shall be rendered exclusively to Production Company until expiration of the Term of this Agreement, it being mutually understood that said services are extraordinary, unique and not replaceable, and that there is no adequate remedy at law for breach of this contract by Director, and that Production Company, in the event of such breach by Director, shall be entitled to equitable relief by way of injunction or otherwise to prevent default by Director.

**9. RESULTS AND PROCEEDS OF SERVICES:** Production Company shall be entitled to and shall solely and exclusively own, in addition to Director's services hereunder, all results and proceeds thereof (including but not limited to all rights, throughout the world, of copyright, trademark, patent, production, manufacture, recordation, reproduction, transcription, performance, broadcast and exhibition of any art or method now known or hereafter devised, including radio broadcasting, theatrical and nontheatrical exhibition, and exhibition by the medium of television or otherwise), whether such results and proceeds consist of literary, dramatic, musical, motion picture, mechanical or any other forms of works, themes, ideas, compositions, creations or production, together with the rights generally known in the field of literary and musical endeavor as the "moral rights of authors" in and/or to any musical and/or literary proceeds of Director's services, including but not limited to the right to add to, subtract from, arrange, revise, adapt, rearrange, make variations of the property, and to translate the same into any and all languages, change the sequence, change the characters and the descriptions thereof contained in the property, change the title of the same, record and photocopy the same with or without sound (including spoken words, dialogue and music synchronously recorded), use this title or any of its components in connection with works or motion pictures wholly or partially independent of said property, and to use all or any part of the property in new versions, adaptations and sequels in any and all languages, and to obtain copyright therein throughout the world, and Director does assign and transfer to Production Company all the foregoing without reservation, condition, or limitation, and no right of any kind, nature, or description is reserved by Director. If Production Company shall desire separate assignments or other documents to implement the foregoing, Director shall execute the same upon Production Company's request, and if Director fails or refuses

CONTRACTS
FOR THE
FILM AND
TELEVISION
INDUSTRY

176

to execute and deliver any such separate assignments or other documents, Production Company shall have and is granted the right and authority to execute the same in Director's name and as Director's attorney-in-fact. Production Company shall supply Director with a copy of any document so executed.

**10. WARRANTIES RELATED TO CREATED MATERIAL:** Director hereby warrants and agrees that all material, works, writings, idea, "gags" or dialogue written, composed, prepared, submitted or interpolated by Director in connection with the Picture or its preparation or production, shall be wholly original with Director and shall not be copied in whole or in part from any other work, except that submitted to Director by Production Company as a basis for such material. Director further warrants that neither said material nor any part thereof will violate the rights of privacy or constitute a libel or slander against any person, firm, or corporation, and that the material will not infringe upon the copyright, literary, dramatic or photoplay rights of any person. Director further warrants and agrees to hold Production Company and its successors, licensees, and assigns harmless against all liability or loss which they or any of them may suffer by reason of the breach of any of the terms or warranties of this Clause.

**11. VESTING OF PRODUCTION COMPANY'S RIGHTS:** All rights granted or agreed to be granted to Production Company hereunder shall vest in Production Company immediately and shall remain so vested whether this Agreement expires in normal course or is terminated for any cause or reason.

**12. NAME AND LIKENESS:** Production Company shall always have the right to use and display Director's name and likeness for advertising, publicizing, and exploiting the picture. However, such advertising may not include the direct endorsement of any product (other than the Picture) without Director's consent. Exhibition, advertising, publicizing or exploiting the Picture by any media, even though a part of or in connection with a product or a commercially sponsored program, shall not be deemed an endorsement of any nature.

**13. PUBLICITY RESTRICTIONS:** Director shall not by means of press agents or publicity or advertising agencies or others, employed or paid by Director or otherwise, circulate, publish or otherwise disseminate any news stories or articles, books or other publicity, containing Director's name relating to Director's employment by Production Company, the subject matter of this contract, the Picture or the services to be rendered by Director or others in connection with the Picture unless first approved by Production Company.

**14. FORCE MAJEURE:**

(a) Suspension: If, by reason of fire, earthquake, labor dispute or strike, act of God or public enemy, any municipal ordinance, any state or federal law, governmental order or regulation, or other cause beyond Production Company's control which would excuse Production Company's performance as a matter of law, Production Company is prevented from or hampered in the production of the Picture, or if, by reason of the closing of substantially all theatres in the United States, Production Company's production of the Picture is postponed or suspended, or if, by reason of any of the aforesaid contingencies or any other cause or occurrence not within Production Company's control, including but not limited to the death, illness or incapability of any principal member of the cast of the Picture, the preparation or production of the Picture is interrupted or delayed and/or, if Production Company's normal business operations are interrupted or otherwise interfered with by virtue of any disruptive events which are beyond Production Company's control ("Production Company Disability"), then Production Company may postpone the commencement of or suspend the rendition of services by Director and the running of time hereunder for such time as the Production Company Disability shall continue; and no compensation shall accrue or become payable to Director hereunder during the period of such suspension. Such suspension shall end upon the cessation of the cause thereof.

(b) Termination:

(i) Production Company Termination Right: If a Production Company Disability continues for a period in excess of _____ (Producer Disability) _____ (week), Production Company shall have the right to terminate this Agreement upon written notice to Director.

(ii) Director's Termination Right: If a Production Company Disability results in compensation being suspended hereunder for a period in excess of _____ (Dir Termination) _____ (weeks), Director shall have the right to terminate this Agreement upon written notice to Production Company.

(iii) Production Company Re-Establishment Right: Despite Director's election to terminate this Agreement, within five (5) days after Production Company's actual receipt of such written notice from Director, Production Company shall have the right to elect to re-establish the operation of this Agreement.

## 15. DIRECTOR'S INCAPACITY:

(a) Effect of Director's Incapacity: If, by reason of mental or physical disability, Director is incapacitated from performing or complying with any of the terms of conditions hereof ("Director's Incapacity") for a consecutive period in excess of seven (7) days or aggregate period in excess of ten (10) days, then Production Company shall have the right to terminate this Agreement upon written notice to Director.

## 16. DIRECTOR'S DEFAULT: If Director fails or refuses to perform or comply with any of the terms or conditions hereof (other than by reason of Director's Incapacity) ("Director's Default"), then Production Company may terminate this Agreement upon written notice to Director. Director Default shall not include any failure or refusal of Director to perform or comply with the material terms of this Agreement due to a breach or action by Production Company which makes the performance by Director of his services impossible. Prior to termination of this Agreement by Production Company based upon Director Default, Production Company shall notify Director specifying the nature of the Director Default and Director shall have a period of 24 hours to cure the Director Default. If the Director Default is not cured within said 24 hour period, Production Company may terminate this Agreement forthwith.

## 17. EFFECT OF TERMINATION: Termination of this Agreement, whether by lapse of time, mutual consent, operation of law, exercise of a right of termination or otherwise shall:

(a) Terminate Production Company's obligation to pay Director any further compensation. Nevertheless, if the termination is not for Director's Default, Production Company shall pay Director any compensation due and unpaid prior to the termination, and;

CONTRACTS
FOR THE
FILM AND
TELEVISION
INDUSTRY

178

(b) Production Company shall not be deemed to have waived any other rights it may have or alter Production Company's rights or any of Director's agreements or warranties relating to the rendition of Director's services prior to termination.

**18. PRODUCTION COMPANY RIGHT TO SUSPEND:** In the event of Director's Incapacity or Director's Default, Production Company may postpone upon written notice the commencement of or suspend the rendition of services by Director and the running of time hereunder so long as any Director's Disability or Director's Default shall continue; and no compensation shall accrue or become payable to Director during the period of such suspension.

(a) Director's Right to Cure: Any Director's Incapacity or Director's Default shall be deemed to continue until Production Company's receipt of written notice from Director specifying that Director is ready, willing and able to perform the services required hereunder; provided that any such notice from Director to Production Company shall not preclude Production Company from exercising any rights or remedies Production Company may have hereunder or at law or in equity by reason of Director's Incapacity or Director's Default.

(b) Alternative Services Restricted: During any period of suspension hereunder, Director shall not render services for any person, firm or corporation other than Production Company. However, Director shall have the right to render services to third parties during any period of suspension based upon a Production Company Disability, subject, however, to Production Company's right to require Director to resume the rendition of services hereunder.

(c) Production Company Right to Extend: If Production Company elects to suspend the rendition of services by Director as herein specified, then Production Company shall have the right (exercisable at any time) to extend the period of services of Director hereunder for a period equal to the period of such suspension.

(d) Additional Services: If Production Company shall have paid compensation to Director during any period of Director's Incapacity or Director's Default, then Production Company shall have the right (exercisable at any time) to require Director to render services hereunder without compensation for a period equal to the period for which Production Company shall have paid compensation to Director during such Director's Incapacity or Director's Default.

**19. FURTHER WARRANTIES:** Director hereby warrants that Director is not under any obligation or disability, created by law or otherwise, which would in any manner or to any extent prevent or restrict Director from entering into and fully performing this Agreement; Director warrants that Director has not entered into any agreement or commitment that would prevent Director fulfilling Director's commitments with Production Company hereunder and that Director will not enter into any such agreement or commitment without Production Company's specific approval; and Director hereby accepts the obligation hereunder and agrees to devote Director's entire time and attention and best talents and abilities exclusively to Production Company as specified herein, and to observe and to be governed by the rules of conduct established by Production Company for the conduct of its employees.

(a) Indemnity: Director shall at all times indemnify Production Company, its successors, assignees and licensees, from and against any and all costs, expenses, losses, damages, judgments and attorneys' fees arising out of or connected with or resulting from any claims, demands or causes of action by any person or entity which is inconsistent with any of Director's representations, warranties or agreements hereunder. Director will reimburse Production Company on demand for any payment made by Production Company at any time after the date hereof in respect of any liability, loss, damage, cost or expense to which the foregoing indemnity relates.

**20. REMEDIES:** All remedies accorded herein or otherwise available to either Production Company or Director shall be cumulative, and no one such remedy shall be exclusive of any other. Without waiving any rights or remedies under this Agreement or otherwise, Production Company may from time to time recover, by action, any damages arising out of any breach of this Agreement by Director, and may institute and maintain subsequent actions for additional damages which may arise from the same or other breaches. The commencement or maintenance of any such action or actions by Production Company shall not constitute an election on Production Company's part to terminate this Agreement nor constitute or result in termination of Director's services hereunder unless Production Company shall expressly so elect by written notice to Director. The pursuit by either Production Company or Director of any remedy under this Agreement or otherwise shall not be deemed to waive any other or different remedy which may be available under this Agreement or otherwise, either at law or in equity.

**21. INSURANCE:**

(a) Production Company may secure life, health, accident, cast, or other insurance covering Director, the cost of which shall be included as a Direct Charge of the Picture. Such insurance shall be for Production Company's sole benefit and Production Company shall be the beneficiary thereof, and Director shall have no interest in the proceeds thereof. Director shall assist in procuring such insurance by submitting to required examinations and tests and by preparing, signing, and delivering such applications and other documents as may be reasonably required. Director shall, to the best of Director's ability, observe all terms and conditions of such insurance of which Production Company notifies Director as necessary for continuing such insurance in effect.

(b) If Production Company is unable to obtain pre-production or cast insurance covering Director at prevailing standard rates and without any exclusions, restrictions, conditions, or exceptions of any kind, Director shall have the right to pay any premium in excess of the prevailing standard rate in order for Production Company to obtain such insurance. If Director fails or refuses to pay such excess premium, or if Production Company having obtained such insurance Director fails to observe all terms and conditions necessary to maintain such insurance in effect, Production Company shall have the right to terminate this Agreement without any obligation to Director by giving Director written notice of termination.

**22. EMPLOYMENT OF OTHERS:** Director agrees not to employ any person to serve in any capacity, nor contract for the purchase or renting of any article or material, nor make any agreement committing Production Company to pay any sum of money for any reason whatsoever in connection with the Picture or services to be rendered by Director hereunder or otherwise, without written approval first being had and obtained from Production Company.

**23. ASSIGNMENT:** This Agreement, at the election of Production Company, shall inure to the benefit of Production Company's administrators, successors, assigns, licensees, grantees, and associated, affiliated and subsidiary companies,

CONTRACTS
FOR THE
FILM AND
TELEVISION
INDUSTRY

180

and Director agrees that Production Company and any subsequent assignee may freely assign this Agreement and grant its rights hereunder, in whole or in part, to any person, firm or corporation.

### 24. NOTICES AND PAYMENT:

(a) To Director: All notices from Production Company to Director may be given in writing by mailing the notice to Director, postage prepaid, or at Production Company's option, Production Company may deliver such notice to Director personally, either orally or in writing. The date of mailing or of personal delivery shall be deemed to be the date of service. Payments and written notice to Director shall be sent to Director at (Director Address).

(b) To Production Company: All notices from Director to Production Company shall be given in writing by mail, messenger, cable, telex or telecopier addressed as indicated below. The date of mailing, messengering, cabling, telexing or telecopying shall be deemed to be the date of service.

Mail: _____

(Producer)

_____

(Producer Address)

FAX: _____

(Producer's Fax)

(c) Writing Requirement: Any oral notice given by Production Company in respect to any right of termination, suspension or extension under this Agreement shall be confirmed in writing.

(d) Change of Address: The address of Director and of Production Company set forth herein may be changed to such other address as Director or Production Company may hereafter specify by written notice given to the other Party.

### 25. UNION/GUILD AGREEMENT: If Production Company becomes a signatory with the DGA, the provisions of the Basic Agreement as same is amended and supplemented from time to time, and any side letters shall control should they conflict with any of the terms of this agreement.

### 26. VIDEOCASSETTE: After domestic distribution of the Picture has been secured, Company shall provide Director with one VHS videocassette copy of the entire Picture, at Company's expense.

### 27. CONDITIONS AFFECTING OR RELATED TO COMPENSATION:

(a) Method of Payment: All compensation which shall become due to Director shall be paid by Production Company by check and sent to Director at the address provided in the Notices and Payments provision of this Agreement.

(b) Governmental Limitation: No withholding, deduction, reduction or limitation of compensation by Production Company which is required or authorized by law ("Governmental Limitation") shall be a breach by Production Company or relieve Director from Director's obligations. Payment of compensation as permitted pursuant to the Governmental Limitation shall continue while such Governmental Limitation is in effect and shall be deemed to constitute full performance by Production Company of its obligations respecting the payment of compensation. The foregoing-notwithstanding, if at such time as the Governmental Limitation is no longer in effect there is compensation remaining unpaid to Director, Production Company shall cooperate with Director in connection with the processing of any applications relative to the payment of such unpaid compensation and Production Company shall pay such compensation to Director at such times as Production Company is legally permitted to do so.

(c) Garnishment/Attachment: If Production Company shall be required, because of the service of any garnishment, attachment, writ of execution, or lien, or by the terms of any contract or assignment executed by Director, to withhold, or to pay to any other Party all or any portion of the compensation due Director, the withholding or payment of such compensation or any portion thereof in accordance with the requirements of any such attachment, garnishment, writ of execution, lien, contract or assignment shall not be construed as a breach by Production Company.

(d) Overpayment/Offset: If Production Company makes any overpayment to Director for any reason or if Director is indebted to Production Company for any reason, Director shall pay Production Company such overpayment or indebtedness on demand, or at the election of Production Company, Production Company may deduct and retain for its own account an amount equal to all or any part of such overpayment or indebtedness from any sums that may be due or become due or payable by Production Company to Director or for the account of Director and such deduction or retention shall not be construed as a breach by Production Company.

## 28. MISCELLANEOUS:

(a) Relationship: This agreement between the parties does not constitute a joint venture or partnership of any kind.

(b) Cumulative Rights and Remedies: All rights, remedies, licenses, undertakings, obligations, covenants, privileges and other property granted herein shall be cumulative, and Purchaser may exercise or use any of them separately or in conjunction with any one or more of the others.

(c) Waiver: A waiver by either party of any term or condition of this agreement in any instance shall not be deemed or construed to be a waiver of such term or condition for the future, or any subsequent breach thereof.

(d) Severability: If any provision of this agreement as applied to either party or any circumstances shall be adjudged by a court to be void and unenforceable, such shall in no way affect any other provision of this agreement, the application of such provision in any other circumstance, or the validity or enforceability of this agreement.

(e) Governing Law: This agreement shall be construed in accordance with the laws of the State of _____ applicable to agreements which are executed and fully performed within said State.

(f) Arbitration: This Agreement shall be interpreted in accordance with the laws of the State of _____, applicable to agreements executed and to be wholly performed therein. Any controversy or claim arising out of or in relation to this Agreement or the validity, construction or performance of this Agreement, or the breach thereof, shall be resolved by arbitration in accordance with the rules and procedures of the American Film Marketing Association, as said rules may be amended from time to time with rights of discovery if granted by the arbitrator. Such rules

CONTRACTS
FOR THE
FILM AND
TELEVISION
INDUSTRY

182

and procedures are incorporated and made a part of this Agreement by reference. If the American Film Marketing Association shall refuse to accept jurisdiction of such dispute, then the parties agree to arbitrate such matter before and in accordance with the rules of the American Arbitration Association (AAA) under its jurisdiction in _____ before a single arbitrator familiar with entertainment law. The parties shall have the right to engage in pre-hearing discovery in connection with such arbitration proceedings. The parties agree hereto that they will abide by and perform any award rendered in any arbitration conducted pursuant hereto, that any court having jurisdiction thereof may issue a judgment based upon such award and that the prevailing party in such arbitration and/or confirmation proceeding shall be entitled to recover its reasonable attorneys' fees and expenses. The arbitration will be held in _____ and any award shall be final, binding and non-appealable. The Parties agree to accept service of process in accordance with AFMA or AAA Rules.

(g) Captions: Captions are inserted for reference and convenience only and in no way define, limit or describe the scope of this agreement or intent of any provision.

(h) Entire Understanding: This agreement contains the entire understanding of the parties relating to the subject matter, and this agreement cannot be changed except by written agreement executed by the party to be bound.

IN WITNESS WHEREOF, the parties hereto have signed this Agreement as of the day and year first above written.

_____

(Name)

_____

Producer)

_____

("Production Company")

_____

("Director")

_____

Social Security Number

# DIRECTOR'S TELEVISION SERIES EMPLOYMENT AGREEMENT
## (To employ a DGA Director)

THIS AGREEMENT is made and entered into as of _____ between _____ ("Producer") and _____ ("Director"). The parties hereto agree as follows:

**1. ENGAGEMENT:**  Producer hereby employs Director, and Director accepts such employment, upon the terms and conditions herein contained and subject to the terms of the Basic Agreement (as hereinafter defined) to provide the services of Director to Producer as the director of a thirty (30) minute program presently entitled "_____" (the "Program") of the television series entitled "_____" ("Series"). Director shall render services in connection with rehearsals, production, photography, trailers, promotionals, and other film or tape material to be exhibited in connection with the Program, and otherwise in connection therewith until Producer secures a fully edited composite print thereof satisfactory to Producer.

**2. COMMENCEMENT OF SERVICES:**  Director shall render exclusive services to Producer commencing on or about _____ or such other date as Producer and Director shall mutually determine, and said services shall continue for a period (the "minimum guarantee period" herein) of not less than _____ days until the completion of Director's services hereunder. Principal photography is presently scheduled to begin on or about _____. A day's work by Director in connection with preparation, rehearsals and cutting need not run consecutively with other work days or with shooting dates.

**3. COMPENSATION:**  As full and complete consideration for all undertakings of Director and the services to be rendered by Director, and the results and proceeds thereof, and all rights and materials herein purchased, granted and agreed to be granted, and upon the condition that Director shall fully and faithfully perform all of Director's obligations hereunder and shall fully and faithfully complete all services which may be required of Director hereunder, Producer shall pay to Director, and Director agrees to accept, the following compensation:

(a) The sum of _____ Dollars for the minimum guarantee period hereunder (which sum represents scale compensation for three (3) days of prep and five (5) days of shooting); in the event Producer requires Director to render services (other than services which Producer is entitled to require pursuant to the Basic Agreement without additional payment) beyond the minimum guarantee period, Producer shall pay Director the sum of _____ Dollars for each day Director so renders services to Producer beyond the minimum guarantee period. The guaranteed compensation shall be payable upon completion of principal photography and any additional compensation shall be payable on Producer's regular payday of the week following completion of principal photography.

(b) Producer shall have the unlimited right (i) to rerun the Program and Series on television, (ii) make foreign telecasts thereof, (iii) release the Program and Series theatrically outside the United States and Canada and (iv) release the Program and Series in supplemental markets anywhere in the world. In the event Producer exercises any of such rights, Director shall receive therefor additional compensation only to the extent and in the minimum amounts

CONTRACTS
FOR THE
FILM AND
TELEVISION
INDUSTRY

184

required by the applicable provisions of the Basic Agreement. If the Program is included with other Series programs in a film given a foreign theatrical release the foreign theatrical residual payment required by the Basic Agreement will be divided equally among the directors of the programs so released. There shall be no theatrical exhibition of the Program in the United States or Canada without Director's written consent.

**4. TRANSPORTATION:** Producer shall provide Director with transportation to and from the set during the term of Director's engagement hereunder.

**5. CUTTING AUTHORITY:** _____ shall have final cutting authority.

**6. NOTICES:** The addresses of the parties for notices hereunder shall be:

Director:                                    _____
                                             (Director)

                                             _____
                                             (Address)

                                             _____


Producer:                                    _____
                                             (Producer)

                                             _____
                                             (Address)

                                             _____


with a copy to:                              _____

                                             _____

                                             _____

All payments due or payable to Director from Producer herein may be made by check to Director or agent at the above address and the receipt by such agent shall be good and valid discharge of all such indebtedness.

**7. REFERENCE:** The terms and conditions under which Producer has employed Director to provide services hereunder are those set forth in this Principal Agreement and in the Additional Series Directing Terms (herein the "Additional Terms") attached hereto and by this reference made a part hereof. Wherever the words "this agreement", "herein", "hereunder", "hereby", or similar words are used, those terms shall refer to this Principal Agreement and the Additional Terms attached hereto. Any word or phrase used in this Principal Agreement which is defined in said Additional Terms shall be deemed to be used and defined in accordance with the definitions set forth in the Additional Terms. In the event of any express inconsistency between the terms of this Principal Agreement and said Additional Terms, the terms of this Principal Agreement shall control.

IN WITNESS WHEREOF, the parties hereto have executed this Agreement the day and year first above written.

_____
(Producer)

_____
(Director)


# ADDITIONAL DIRECTING EMPLOYMENT TERMS

**A. Basic Agreement.** As used herein, "Basic Agreement" shall mean either the Director's Guild of America, Inc. Basic Agreement of 1993 or any agreement in extension or replacement thereof.

**B. Performance of Services.** Director shall render all services required hereunder at _____ (Performance City) or its environs, at such studio or otherwise as Producer may from time to time designate, or such other place or places as reasonably required by Producer from time to time during the term hereof. Director shall render all services under the supervision, direction and control of Producer, as exercised by Producer from time to time, and Director shall perform all services in a diligent and conscientious manner, and to the best of Director's ability, Director to comply promptly and faithfully with all reasonable instructions, directions, requests, rules and regulations (including those relating to matters of artistic taste and judgment) made or issued by Producer. Director shall also render as required by Producer all of the services usually and customarily rendered by persons employed or otherwise rendering services of the type and nature to be rendered by Director hereunder in the preparation and the production of motion pictures, television motion pictures, and television programs in the motion picture and television industries. Director's services shall be rendered solely and exclusively to Producer during the period beginning with commencement of Director's services as specified in Paragraph 2 hereof through the delivery of Director's final cut or master videotape recording of each Series program for which Director is employed hereunder. No services rendered for Director's own account or for any third party shall in any way interfere with Director's performance of any such services at such times and places as Producer may require pursuant to the terms hereof.

**C. Services Unique.** The rights granted to Producer and the services to be rendered by Director hereunder are of a special, unique, unusual, extraordinary and intellectual character, giving them peculiar value, the loss of which cannot be reasonably or adequately compensated in damages; a material breach by Director hereunder or the material failure by Director to render services hereunder would cause Producer irreparable injury and damage. Accordingly, Producer shall be entitled to seek injunctive or other equitable relief to prevent such breach and to prevent Director from performing services for himself or any person other than Producer, and for such other relief as to which Producer may be entitled; resort to any such equitable relief shall not, however, be construed as a waiver of any other rights or remedies to which Producer may be entitled for damages, suspension, termination or otherwise.

CONTRACTS
FOR THE
FILM AND
TELEVISION
INDUSTRY

186

## D. Rights and Materials.

1. Producer shall own in perpetuity all rights of whatever kind and character, throughout the world and in any and all languages, in and to the results and proceeds of Director's services hereunder, including without limitation to the generality of the foregoing, each Series program, all material, themes, ideas, operations, products, titles, composition, works, writings, "gags", "business", dialogue, and all other matter (all of the foregoing also included in the term "materials" herein) written suggested, composed, created, prepared, submitted, or interpolated by Director for or in connection with the services to be rendered by Director hereunder. In connection with the foregoing, Director expressly agrees that Producer shall be entitled to and hereby acquires the maximum rights permitted to be obtained by employers and purchasers of materials under applicable guild or union agreements. All said materials shall automatically become the property of Producer, and Director hereby transfers and agrees to transfer and assign to Producer all said rights and materials, it being understood that Producer for this purpose shall be deemed to be the author thereof, Director acting hereunder for this purpose entirely as Producer's employee-for-hire. Producer shall have the right to obtain all copyrights and copyright renewals, and any other protections whatsoever therefor.

2. Producer shall have the right, but not the obligation, to use, adapt, change, revise, delete from, add to or rearrange each Series program, the materials, or any part thereof, and to combine same with other works or materials of Director or of others, and to vend, copy, publish, reproduce, record, transmit, broadcast by radio and/or television, perform, photograph with or without sound, including spoken words, dialogue and music synchronously recorded, and to communicate the same by any means now known or hereafter devised, either publicly and for profit, or otherwise; Director waives throughout the world the benefit of any law, doctrine or principle known as "Droit Moral", or "moral rights of authors" or any similar law, doctrine or principle however denominated.

Producer and Director, on Producer's and Director's own behalf and on behalf of their successors in title, licensees and assigns hereby assign to Producer in perpetuity all rental and lending rights (whether implemented pursuant to the EC Rental and Lending Rights Directive or otherwise) to which Director may now be or hereafter may become entitled to therefrom. Producer and Director agree, on Producer's and Director's own behalf and on behalf of their successors in title, licensees and assigns, not to institute, support, maintain or permit directly or indirectly any litigation or proceedings instituted or maintained on the ground the Producer's (or its designee's) exercise of the rights granted to Producer in the Series program in any way constitutes an infringement or violation of any such rental or lending right as aforesaid. To the extent (if any) that any part of the compensation payable to the Director is required by any legislation to be specifically attributed to any such rights as are herein set out in order to constitute full, equitable, proper and adequate remuneration therefor, then the Producer, and the Director agree that ten percent (10%) of such compensation shall be deemed attributed thereto. Nothing herein shall prevent the Producer on behalf of the Director from receiving any monies collected on behalf of authors by any bona fide collection societies in respect of such rights provided that neither the Producer nor any assignees or licensees of the Producer shall have any obligation to make any payments to the Director or to such collecting societies in respect of such rights or to collect and/or pay to the Director any amounts in relation thereto.

3. Director shall, at Producer's request, execute, verify, acknowledge and deliver to Producer or procure the execution, verification, acknowledgment and delivery to Producer of such assignments, documents or other instruments which Producer may from time to time deem reasonably necessary or desirable to evidence, establish, maintain, protect, enforce or defend its rights hereunder to fully effectuate and carry out the intent and purposes of this Agreement and to convey to Producer those rights in and to the materials to be supplied to Producer by Director hereunder. If Director shall fail to execute, acknowledge or deliver to Producer any agreements, quitclaims or other instruments reasonably required by Producer hereunder, then Producer is hereby irrevocably appointed Director's attorney-in-fact (which agency shall be deemed coupled with an interest) with full right, power and authority to execute, acknowledge, verify and deliver the same in the name of and on behalf of Director.

**E. Representations and Warranties.**  Director hereby represents, warrants and agrees as follows:

1. Director is free to enter into this Agreement and is not subject to any obligation or disability which will to the best of Director's knowledge, prevent or interfere with Director fully keeping and performing all of the agreements, covenants and conditions to be kept or performed by Director hereunder, and Director has not made nor will not make any agreement, commitment, grant or assignment, or will do, or omit to do, any act or thing which shall interfere with or impair the complete enjoyment of the rights granted and the services to be rendered to Producer.

2. Any and all materials furnished, suggested and/or delivered to Producer by Director hereunder, and all parts thereof, shall be wholly original with Director except for materials in the public domain, and shall not be copied in whole or in part from any other work or materials (except that submitted to Director by the Producer as a basis for such materials), and neither the materials nor the use thereof shall infringe upon or violate any right of privacy of or constitute a libel, slander, or any unfair competition against, or infringe upon or violate the copyright, common law rights, literary, dramatic, photoplay, rights of privacy or publicity, or any other rights of any person, firm, corporation or other entity.

3. Director is, or agrees to become, and will remain throughout the term hereof a member in good standing of the properly designated labor organization or organizations (as defined and determined under applicable law) representing persons performing services of the type and character that are to be performed by Director hereunder. Producer may, but shall not be obligated to, deduct from the compensation payable to Director hereunder and pay to such guild or union any dues or assessments which such guild or union informs Producer are owed by Director.

4. Director represents that Director is aware that it is a criminal offense under the Federal Communications Act of 1934, as amended, ("Communications Act") for any person, in connection with the production or preparation of any television program to accept or pay any money, service, or other valuable consideration for the inclusion of any plug, reference or product identification or other matter as a part of such program unless such acceptance or payment is disclosed in the manner required by law. Director further understands that it is Producer's policy not to knowingly permit the acceptance or payment of any such consideration and that any such acceptance or payment

CONTRACTS
FOR THE
FILM AND
TELEVISION
INDUSTRY

188

will be cause of immediate dismissal, it being Producer's intention that each Series program shall be capable of being broadcast without the necessity of any disclosure or announcement which would otherwise be required by Section 317 or Section 508 of the Communications Act. Director represents, warrants and agrees that Director has not paid or accepted, and will not pay or accept any money, service or other valuable consideration for the inclusion of any plug, reference or product identification or any other matter in any Series program, and that Director has no knowledge of any information relating to any Series program which is required to be disclosed by Director under Section 508 of the Communications Act. Director will promptly deliver to Producer, upon request, such affidavits and/or statements as Producer may require with respect to said Section 508.

5. Director shall indemnify and hold Producer, any station or network telecasting the Series, each sponsor and its advertising agency, and the shareholders, directors, officers, agents, employees, successors, licensees and assigns of any of the foregoing harmless from and against any and all liability, loss, damage, costs, charges, claims, actions, causes of action, recoveries, judgments, penalties and expenses, including attorneys' fees, which they or any of them may suffer by reason of: the use of any materials furnished or services rendered by Director hereunder; any claims for compensation by Director and/or claims for payment by any third party relating in any way to Director and/or any breach or alleged breach of any representation, warranty or agreement made by Director in this Agreement. Producer shall indemnify Director with respect to material furnished to Director by Producer to the same extent as Director is indemnifying Producer hereunder.

**F. Insurance.** Producer may secure in its own name or otherwise, and at its own expense, life, health, accident, cast or other insurance covering Director, or Director and others and Director shall not have any right, title or interest in or to any such insurance. If Director shall be required to assist Producer to procure such insurance, Director shall submit to such medical and other examinations; and sign such applications and other instruments in writing, as may be reasonably required by Producer and any insurance company to which application for such insurance shall be made. Director represents and warrants that Director knows of no physical defect or other reason that would prevent Producer from obtaining insurance on Director without payment of extra premium and without exclusions. If Producer is unable to so obtain insurance on Director without payment of extra premium and without exclusions, Producer shall have the right to terminate this Agreement on or before thirty (30) days after Director shall have failed to pass a physical examination or otherwise qualify for such insurance as provided hereinabove.

**G. Controls and Publicity.** As between Director and Producer, Producer shall have full and exclusive budgetary, financial, business and creative control over each Series program. Director shall not at any time without Producer's prior written approval had and obtained in each case (whether before, during or after the term hereof) release or authorize any information, advertising or publicity relating to the engagement hereunder, the programs hereunder, Producer or Producer's personnel or operations; provided, however, that nothing herein contained shall preclude incidental mention of the Program in personal publicity relating primarily to Director, which is not derogatory to Producer or Producer's personnel or operations, the Program or Series.

**H. Name and Likeness.**  Director grants to Producer, its licensees, distributors, any station or network broadcasting the Series, or any sponsor or advertising agency of any of the foregoing, the non-exclusive right to display, reproduce, and make any other uses of Director's name, likeness, voice, biography, photograph and picture, such uses to be made, however, only in connection with Director's services hereunder, and the advertising or exploitation of the Series, the literary material upon which the Series is based, or of any of Producer's rights hereunder, and for commercial advertising or publicity or other commercial exploitation in connection with the Program or Series, any licensee or distributor of the Program, any station or network broadcasting the Series or any sponsor or advertising agency of the foregoing or Director's services for Producer; in any such advertising or publicity or other commercial exploitation, Director shall not be represented as directly endorsing any such product, commodity or service, without Director's consent. Unless Director shall appear as an actor in the Program, in advertising and publicity relating to the Program, Producer shall not represent Director as appearing therein as an actor.

**I. Interruption.**  If Director fails, refuses or is unable for any reason whatsoever to render any of Director's material services hereunder or to perform any of Director's material obligations hereunder, or if Producer's development and/or production of any Series program hereunder is interrupted or materially interfered with by reason of any governmental law, ordinance, order or regulation, or by reason of fire, flood, earthquake, labor dispute, lock-out, strike, accident, act of God or public enemy or by reason of any other cause, thing or occurrence of the same or any other nature not within Producer's control, Producer shall have the right: (i) to terminate this Agreement (whether or not Producer has theretofore suspended the Agreement as hereinafter provided) and Producer shall have no further obligation to Director hereunder, or, (ii) at Producer's option, to suspend this Agreement for a period equal to the duration of any such failure, refusal, or inability or the occurrence of any of the foregoing events, and no compensation shall be paid or become due to Director hereunder for such period; provided, however, that if Producer shall terminate this Agreement on account of the occurrence of a so-called "force majeure" and shall thereafter resume production of the Program, Producer shall offer to re-engage Director to complete the Program at such times as Producer may require therefor. No suspension shall relieve Director of Director's obligations hereunder as and when required by Producer under the terms hereof, except during the continuance of a disability of Director. If this Agreement and Director's services hereunder are suspended by reason of any disability, default or force majeure, Producer's then current obligation, if any, to use Director's services (and/or make the applicable payments to Director pursuant to Paragraph 3(a) of the Principal Agreement) shall be reduced by one (1) Series program for each Series program produced while Director's services remain suspended. Unless this Agreement shall have been previously terminated as provided hereinabove, any such suspension shall end as soon as the cause of such suspension ceases, and all time periods and dates hereunder shall be extended by a period equal to the period of such suspension.

**J. Preemption and Cancellation.**  Notwithstanding anything contained herein to the contrary, Producer shall have the further right to suspend, cancel and/or terminate this Agreement, or suspend production or broadcast of any Series program hereunder without liability or payment to Director at any time under such circumstances that the contract for the production or broadcasting of any Series program is terminated, canceled or suspended, by reason of force

CONTRACTS
FOR THE
FILM AND
TELEVISION
INDUSTRY

190

majeure. If any Series program hereunder is suspended or canceled, or if the Contract is suspended terminated or canceled, as a result of the illness or other incapacity of the producer or a principal star, the services of Director hereunder shall likewise be suspended, canceled or terminated, as the case may be, without any further liability or payment to Director, unless Producer receives reimbursement from the network or the sponsor or its advertising agency, in which case Director shall receive compensation hereunder on a prorated basis to the extent received by Producer. Notwithstanding anything to the contrary contained in this Paragraph J, Producer may terminate the Agreement pursuant to this Paragraph J only if agreements for the services of principal cast members who have not completed their services in connection with the Program shall likewise be terminated.

**K. Termination by Director.** Notwithstanding any contrary provision hereof, or the operation of law, this Agreement shall not be terminated because of a breach by Producer of any of the terms, provisions or conditions contained herein unless and until Director has given Producer written notice of any such breach and Producer has not within a period of thirty (30) days after receipt of such notice from Director, commenced to cure such breach.

**L. Failure to Utilize Services or Produce or Release Series.** Producer shall have no obligation to make, produce, release, telecast, distribute, advertise or otherwise exploit any Series program, whether or not containing the services and/or materials to be delivered to Producer by Director hereunder, or to use the Director's services or the rights granted hereunder in connection therewith or otherwise, and Producer is hereby and shall be released from any obligation for any such failure of Producer so to do; nothing in this Paragraph L shall, however, be deemed to relieve Producer of the obligation to pay to Director the compensation due Director pursuant to the terms of this Agreement.

**M. Credit.** Producer shall accord to Director screen credit on positive prints of each Series program which is directed substantially in its entirety by Director hereunder in accordance with the terms of the Basic Agreement. Subject to the foregoing, Producer shall determine in its sole discretion, the manner, form, size, style, nature and placement of such credit. No casual or inadvertent failure of Producer to comply with the provisions hereof with respect to credit, no failure of any other person to comply with its agreement with Producer relating to such credit and/or no error or omission in giving credit due to acts of third persons, or where the exigencies of time make the giving of credit impracticable, shall constitute a breach of this Agreement by Producer. In the event of a breach of this Agreement with respect to credit, Director's remedies, if any, shall be limited to the right to recover damages in an action at law, and in no event shall Director be entitled to terminate or rescind this Agreement, revoke any of the rights herein granted or to enjoin or restrain the distribution or exhibition of any Series program.

**N. Notices.** All notices, accountings and payments ("Notices") which either Producer or Director shall be required to give, make or serve hereunder shall be in writing and shall be served by United States mail if both parties are located within its territorial boundaries or by overnight air courier if either party is outside of the territorial United States or by telegraph or cable or by telephonic facsimile or personal delivery as provided herein. Service of any notice, statement or other paper by either party shall be deemed complete if and when the same is personally delivered to such party, upon receipt by such party of a telegraph or cable or telephonic facsimile, or upon its deposit in the continental United States in the United States mail, postage or toll prepaid registered or certified mail, return receipt requested, and addressed to the party which is the recipient at its address herein or by overnight courier outside of the continental United States, prepaid and addressed as aforesaid. Any party hereto may change its address for the purpose of receiving notices, demands and other communications as herein provided by a written notice given in the manner aforesaid to the other party or parties hereto. If the last date on which a notice is required under this Agreement shall fall on a Saturday, Sunday, or a day (a "closed day" herein) on which the department of the sending party that is responsible for sending such notice shall not be open for business, then (notwithstanding any other provision hereof) such last date shall be deemed postponed until the first day that shall not be a Saturday, Sunday, or closed day.

### O. Miscellaneous.

1. No waiver by either party hereto of any failure by the other party to keep or perform any covenant or condition of this Agreement shall be deemed to be a waiver of any preceding or succeeding breach of the same, or any other covenant or condition. Neither the expiration of this Agreement nor any other termination (whether by Producer's election or otherwise) shall affect the ownership by Producer of the materials to be prepared and delivered to Producer by Director hereunder or the results and proceeds of the services rendered by Director according to the terms and provisions of this Agreement, or alter any of the rights or privileges granted Producer, or any warranty or undertaking on the part of Director in connection therewith.

2. Producer shall have the right to lend Director's services or to assign this Agreement to any person who shall assume Producer's obligations under this Agreement, but no such lending or assignment shall relieve Producer of its obligations hereunder. Any breach by such person, however, of any of the terms of this Agreement shall not constitute a breach by Producer of its obligations and covenants under this Agreement, nor shall Director have the right to terminate this Agreement by reason of any such breach by such person, unless and until Director shall have given Producer notice of any such breach and Producer shall have not cured such breach within ten (10) business days following receipt of such notice from Director. If Producer does not cure such breach as aforesaid, Director may elect to be released from the obligation to render further services to such person. Director shall not have the right to assign this Agreement or any of Director's rights hereunder.

3. The remedies herein provided shall be deemed cumulative and the exercise of any one shall not preclude the exercise of or be deemed a waiver of any other remedy, nor shall the specification of any remedy hereunder exclude or be deemed a waiver of any rights or remedies at law, or in equity, which may be available to Producer, including any rights to damages or injunctive relief. All rights granted to Producer are irrevocable and without right of rescission by Director or reversion to Director under any circumstances whatsoever, and if Producer elects to terminate (or purports to terminate) this Agreement (and even if such termination or purported termination is ultimately determined by a court to have been without proper or legal cause or it is ultimately determined by such court that the Producer committed any material breach of this Agreement), Director's rights and remedies in any event whatsoever shall be strictly limited, if otherwise available,

CONTRACTS
FOR THE
FILM AND
TELEVISION
INDUSTRY

192

to the recovery of damages, and in no event shall Director have the right to rescind this Agreement, revoke any of the rights herein granted, or enjoin or restrain the production, distribution or exhibition of any Series program or any remake, sequel, television program or motion picture based thereon.

4. This Agreement shall be construed, interpreted and enforced in accordance with, and governed by, the laws of the State of _____ applicable to agreements executed and to be wholly performed within the State of _____. Nothing contained in this Agreement shall be construed so as to require the commission of any act or the payment of any compensation which is contrary to law or to require the violation of the Basic Agreement or any other written agreement between Producer and the Directors Guild of America, Inc. or any other guild or union applicable guild or union agreement applicable hereto and which may from time to time be in effect and by its terms controlling with respect to this Agreement; in the event there shall be any conflict between any provision of this Agreement and any such applicable law, or applicable guild or union agreement, the latter shall prevail, and the provision or provisions of this Agreement affected shall be modified to the extent (but only to the extent) necessary to remove such conflict and permit compliance with such law or applicable guild or union agreement, and as so modified this Agreement shall continue in full force and effect.

5. Producer shall have the right to the maximum extent permissible under the Basic Agreement, to apply all compensation paid to Director under this Agreement as a credit against any and all amounts which may be required under the Basic Agreement to be paid to Director for Director's services, the results and proceeds thereof, the rights granted by Director hereunder and the exercise thereof and for any other reasons whatsoever; provided, however, except as expressly provided to the contrary in this Agreement, Producer shall not apply any such overscale against any compensation that may become due and payable to Director hereunder on account of television reruns, theatrical exhibitions, foreign telecasting and supplemental uses of any Series program. If, pursuant to the Basic Agreement, Director is entitled to any payment in addition to or greater than those set forth herein, then any such additional or greater payment made by Producer shall, except to the extent expressly prohibited by the Basic Agreement, be considered as an advance against and deducted from any sum which may subsequently become payable to Director hereunder. If in determining the payments to be made hereunder there is required any allocation of the compensation paid to Director as between Director's various services, Director agrees to be bound by such allocation as may be made by Producer in good faith.

6. This instrument constitutes the entire agreement between the parties and cannot be modified except by a written instrument signed by Director and an authorized officer of Producer. No officer, employee or representative of Producer has any authority to make any representation or promise in connection with this Agreement or the subject matter hereof which is not contained herein, and Director agrees that Director has not executed this Agreement in reliance upon any such representation or promise.

7. The headings of paragraphs hereof are inserted only for the purpose of convenient reference; such headings shall not be deemed to govern, limit, modify, or in any manner affect the scope, meaning or intent of the provisions of this Agreement or any part or portion thereof; nor shall they otherwise be given any legal effect. This document may be executed in one or more separate counterparts, each of which, when so executed, shall be deemed an original.

Such counterparts shall, together, constitute and be one and the same instrument. Unless the context otherwise requires, the masculine gender throughout this Agreement includes the feminine and neuter, and the use of the singular with respect to Director includes the plural.

8. Unless required by the Basic Agreement, no additional compensation whatsoever shall accrue or be payable to Director, including without limitation to the generality of the foregoing, for any services rendered by Director at night, on Sundays or holidays, or after the expiration of any number of hours of service in any period.

9. Producer may deduct and withhold from the compensation payable to Director hereunder any amounts required to be deducted and withheld under the provisions of any statute, regulation, ordinance, order and any and all amendments thereto hereafter enacted requiring the withholding or deduction of compensation. If, pursuant to Director's request or authorization, Producer shall make any payments or incur any charges for Director's account, Producer shall have the right to deduct from any compensation payable to Director hereunder any charges so paid or incurred, but such right of deduction shall not be deemed to limit or exclude any other rights of credit or recovery or any other remedies that Producer may have; nothing hereinabove set forth shall be deemed to obligate Producer to make any such payments or incur any such charges.

10. If Producer is directed, by virtue of service of any garnishment, levy, execution or judicial order, to apply any amounts payable hereunder to any person, firm, corporation or other entity or judicial or governmental officer, Producer shall have the right to pay any such amounts in accordance with such directions, and Producer's obligations to Director shall be discharged to the extent of such payments; if because of conflicting claims to amounts payable hereunder, Producer becomes a party to any judicial proceeding affecting payment or ownership of such amounts, Director shall reimburse Producer for all costs, including attorneys' fees, incurred in connection therewith.

# CHAPTER 5

# COLLABORATION

## WRITER COLLABORATION

Many writers begin a collaboration with great promise only to discover later that the partnership is not working. Not only has time been wasted, but difficult questions may arise as to ownership of work that has been created. The breakup may engender animosity, making it difficult to resolve these issues. If ownership of the embryonic story is unclear, neither party may safely use it. Thus, writers are well advised to enter a written collaboration agreement beforehand.

Negotiating a collaboration agreement is also useful because it forces the parties to resolve important issues before they invest a lot of time and effort in the partnership. If the relationship is not going to work, it is best to know as early as possible.

CONTRACTS
FOR THE
FILM AND
TELEVISION
INDUSTRY

196

# WRITER COLLABORATION AGREEMENT

This Agreement between _____, residing at _____, (herein called Writer A), and _____, residing at _____, (herein called Writer B).

## WITNESSETH

The parties desire to collaborate in the writing of a screenplay, on the terms hereinafter set forth.

NOW THEREFORE, in consideration of the promises, and of the mutual undertakings herein contained, and for other good and valuable considerations, the parties agree as follows:

**1.** The parties hereby undertake to collaborate in the writing of a certain original feature-length screenplay (herein called the Screenplay or Work) about _____, and provisionally entitled _____.

**2.** The parties shall collaborate in the writing of the work and upon completion thereof shall be the joint owners of the work sharing all rights equally.

**3.** The parties contemplate that they will complete the manuscript of the Screenplay by _____. However, failure to complete the screenplay by such date shall not be construed as a breach of this Agreement on the part of either party.

**4.** If, prior to the completion of the work, either party shall voluntarily withdraw from the collaboration, then the other party shall have the right to complete the work alone or in conjunction with another collaborator or collaborators, and in such event the percentage of ownership, as hereinbefore provided in paragraph 2, shall be revised by mutual agreement in writing or, failing such agreement, by arbitration in accordance with the procedures hereinafter prescribed.

**5.** If, prior to the completion of the Work, there shall be a dispute of any kind with respect to the Work, then either party may terminate this Collaboration Agreement by written notice to the other party, and should they fail to agree upon the terms of such termination agreement, they shall submit the dispute for arbitration in accordance with the procedures hereinafter prescribed.

**6.** Any contract for the sale or other disposition of the Work, where the Work has been completed by the Parties in accordance herewith, shall require that the story and writing credits shall be equally shared by the parties, unless the parties agree otherwise.

**7.** Neither party shall sell, or otherwise voluntarily dispose of the Work, or his share therein, without the written consent of the other, which consent, however, shall not be unreasonably withheld.

**8.** Both parties agree that each shall be responsible for their own expenses incurred in the preparation of the Work.

**9.** The parties agree that all income received from the world-wide sale of motion picture and/or television (all markets and media) rights (including but not limited to all sequel, remake and television spin-off rights, novelization, merchandising, play, radio and audio rights) to the screenplay shall be shared equally.

**10.** Should the Work be sold or otherwise disposed of and, as an incident thereto, the Parties be employed to revise the Work, the total compensation provided for in such employment agreement shall be shared equally by the parties.

**11.** If either party shall be unavailable for the purposes of collaborating on such revision, then the Party who is available shall be permitted to do such revision and shall be entitled to the full amount of compensation in connection therewith.

**12.** If either party hereto shall desire to use the Work, or any right therein or with respect thereto, in any venture in which such Party shall have a financial interest, whether direct or indirect, the Party desiring so to do shall notify the other Party of that fact and shall afford such other Party the opportunity to participate in the venture in the proportion of such other Party's interest in the Work. If such other Party shall be unwilling to participate in such venture, the Party desiring to proceed therein shall be required to pay such other Party an amount equal to that which such other Party would have received if the Work or right, as the case may be, intended to be so used had been sold to a disinterested person at the price at which the same shall last have been offered, or if it shall not have been offered, at its fair market value which, in the absence of mutual agreement of the Parties, shall be determined by arbitration.

**13.** The copyright in the Work shall be obtained in the names of both parties, and shall be held jointly by them.

**14.** If either party (herein called the First Party) desires to transfer his rights to a third person, he shall give written notice by registered mail to the other party (herein called the Second Party) of his intention to do so.

> (a) In such case the Second Party shall have an option for a period of 30 days to purchase the First Party's share at a price and upon such terms indicated in the written notice.

> (b) If the Second Party fails to exercise his option in writing within the aforesaid period of 30 days, or if, having exercised it, he fails to complete the purchase upon the terms stated in the notice, the First Party may transfer his rights to the third person at the price and upon the identical terms stated in the notice; and he shall forthwith send to the Second Party a copy of the contract of sale of such rights, with a statement that the transfer has been made.

> (c) If the First Party fails for any reason to make such transfer to the third person, and if he desires to make a subsequent transfer to someone else, the Second Party's option shall apply to such proposed subsequent transfer.

**15.** Nothing herein contained shall be construed to create a general partnership between the parties. Their relation shall be one of collaboration on a single work.

**16.** This agreement shall continue for the life of the copyright of the work.

**17.** If either party dies before the completion of the screenplay, the survivor shall have the right to complete the same, to make changes in the text previously prepared, to negotiate and contract for sale or production and for the disposition of any of the subsidiary rights, and generally to act with regard thereto as though he were the sole author, except that (a) the name of the decedent shall always receive credit as agreed herein; and (b) the survivor shall cause the decedent's share of the proceeds to be paid to his estate, and shall furnish to the estate true copies of all contracts made by the survivor pertaining to the Work.

**18.** If either party dies after the completion of the screenplay, the survivor shall have the right to negotiate and contract for sale and/or production (if not theretofore arranged) and for the disposition of any of the subsidiary rights, to make

CONTRACTS
FOR THE
FILM AND
TELEVISION
INDUSTRY

198

revisions in any subsequent drafts, and generally to act with regard thereto as if he were the sole author, subject only to the conditions set forth in subdivisions (a) and (b) of clause 14.

**19.** Any controversy or claim arising out of or relating to this agreement or any breach thereof shall be settled by arbitration in accordance with the Rules of the American Arbitration Association; and judgment upon the award rendered by the arbitrators may be entered in any court having jurisdiction thereof. The prevailing party shall be entitled to reimbursement for costs and reasonable attorney's fees.

**20.** This agreement shall inure to the benefit of, and shall be binding upon, the executors, administrators and assigns of the parties.

**21.** This agreement constitutes the entire understanding of the parties.

**22.** This agreement is governed by and construed in accordance with the laws of the State of _____.

**23.** If any provision of this Agreement or the application thereof to any Person or circumstance shall be invalid or unenforceable to any extent, the remainder of this Agreement and the application of such provisions to other persons or circumstances shall not be affected thereby and shall be enforced to the greatest extent permitted by law.

IN WITNESS WHEREOF, the parties hereunto set their respective hand and seal this _____.


_____               _____
          Writer A                                      Writer B

A joint venture is a type of partnership. You should choose your partners carefully as you may be liable for their acts that are within the scope of the partnership.

General partnerships should be distinguished from limited partnerships. In a general partnership the parties share control over the enterprise. In a limited partnership, one or more limited partners (i.e., investors) provide financing but do not exercise control over the management of the enterprise. Limited partners have limited liability as well. Limited partnership agreements are discussed in greater detail in Chapter 7.

The following joint venture agreement is between two individuals to develop and produce projects for television. Since they jointly manage the enterprise they are general partners.

## JOINT VENTURE AGREEMENT

THIS JOINT VENTURE AGREEMENT is effective as of _____ by and between _____ (hereafter _____) ("First Party Short Name") and _____ (hereafter _____) ("Second Party Short Name") (individually or collectively referred to hereinafter as "Partner" or "Partners" respectively).

NOW, THEREFORE, it is mutually agreed by and between the parties hereto as follows:

**1. PURPOSE:** _____ (First Party Short Name) and _____ (Second Party Short Name) hereby enter into a joint venture (the "Venture") for the term hereinafter set forth for the purpose of completing production and exploiting an original motion picture currently entitled "_____" (the "Picture") based on an original script by _____ (the "Screenplay"). Said screenplay, and/or Picture and all ancillary rights therein and thereto are hereinafter sometimes collectively referred to as the "Property."

**2. TERM:** The term of the Venture shall commence as of the effective date of this Agreement and, unless sooner terminated in accordance with the provisions hereof, shall continue for the longer of: (a) the duration of any and all copyrights owned by the Venture in connection with the Property, or (b) the aggregate term of any and all agreements relating to the Property (the "Term").

**3. NAME AND STATUTORY COMPLIANCE:** The name of the Venture shall be the "_____." Upon execution of this Agreement, the Partners may sign and cause to be filed and published in Los Angeles a Certificate of Fictitious Business Name indicating that the Venture will be conducting business under said name.

**4. TITLE:** Any and all property and assets of the Venture as well as all intangible rights, including without limitation, all copyrights, trade names and trademarks, in and to the Screenplay, the Picture and all other forms of exploitation of the Property, and all ancillary, merchandising, music and book publishing rights, shall be owned by and title held in the name of the Venture or its corporation.

CONTRACTS
FOR THE
FILM AND
TELEVISION
INDUSTRY

200

**5. PRINCIPAL OFFICE:** The location of the principal office of the Venture shall be _____, or shall be at such other place or places in California as the Partners shall from time to time determine.

**6. NAME AND RESIDENCE OF EACH PARTNER:**

(a) _____: _____.

(b) _____: _____.

**7. CONTRACTS AND AGREEMENTS:**

(a) All contracts or agreements to be entered into by, on behalf of, or for the benefit of the Venture must be signed by all Partners hereto, it being understood that no Partner shall have the right to bind the Venture with respect to the Property without the express written consent of the other Partner(s). It is understood that if any contract or agreement is entered into by a Partner without the express written consent of the other Partner(s), the Partner purporting to enter into such unauthorized contract or agreement on behalf of the Venture will indemnify and hold harmless the non-contracting Partner(s) from all claims, liabilities, damages and costs (including attorneys' fees and court costs) arising out of or pertaining to such unauthorized contract or agreement.

(b) The proceeds of any contracts entered into by any officer, director or shareholder of any Partner hereto for personal services of such person as a writer, producer, director or otherwise shall belong solely to such Partner.

**8. CAPITAL CONTRIBUTIONS; ADDITIONAL CONTRIBUTIONS.**

(a) It is acknowledged _____ (First Party Short Name) has contributed approximately $_____ in capital needed to produce the Picture; _____ (Second Party Name) has contributed capital of $_____. Another $_____ is needed to complete the film. Both parties have contributed services.

(b) The Partners shall not be obligated to make any additional contributions to the capital of the Venture. If a need for additional capital arises, each Partner may contribute whatever portion of the total sum required that each elects to contribute, in its sole discretion.

(c) In furtherance of Subclause 8(a) above, _____ (First Party Short Name) hereby assign, transfer and convey to the Venture all their respective rights, titles and interests including copyrights and copyright rights and all extensions and renewals thereof, in and to the original Screenplay presently entitled "_____," pursuant to the terms of that Assignment attached hereto as Exhibit "A" and by this reference incorporated herein and made a part hereof.

**9. ALLOCATION OF PROFITS AND LOSSES; TAX CREDITS AND DEDUCTIONS:**

(a) The net profits or net losses of the Venture shall be allocated, credited or charged as the case may be, to the Partners in (specify; e.g., equal shares of fifty percent (50%) each). The terms "net profits" and "net losses" as used herein shall be defined as gross receipts received by the Venture from any and all sources in connection with the Screenplay, the Picture, the Property and all uses thereof and ancillary rights thereto (including without limitation, merchandising, music and publishing), less the aggregate of all costs, charges, fees and expenses of the

Venture including, without limitation, third party gross or net profit participations. For purposes of computing net profits and net losses only the costs and expenses approved by both Partners and incurred by any Partner directly on behalf of the Property or the Venture shall be a charge against and shall reduce the gross receipts of the Venture in calculating net profits or net losses of the Venture.

(b) Any and all tax credits and/or deductions to which the Venture shall become entitled shall be allocated equally between the Partners in shares of fifty percent (50%) each.

## 10. BOOKS, RECORDS, BANK ACCOUNTS, CHECKING:

(a) At all times during the term hereof, the Venture shall keep or cause to be kept, at the principal place of business of the Venture or at such other place as the Venture may determine, books and accounting records for the business and operations of the Venture. Such books shall be open to inspection by the Partners, or their authorized representatives, during reasonable working hours. The accounting for Venture purposes, including the determination of "net profits" and "net losses," shall be in accordance with generally accepted accounting principles consistently applied. The Venture shall engage the services of an accountant who shall be selected with the mutual approval of both parties.

(b) There shall be maintained for each Partner a capital account and an income account. Each Partner's distributive share of profits and losses, and monthly and end-of-the-year withdrawals not previously posted shall be credited or debited to the respective Partner's income account as of the close of the calendar year. Thereafter, any debit or credit balance remaining in the income account of a Partner shall be debited, or credited, as the case may be, to his respective capital account.

(c) The Venture shall be on a calendar year basis for accounting purposes (the "fiscal year"). As soon after the close of each fiscal year as is reasonably practical, a full and accurate accounting shall be made of the affairs of the Venture as of the close of each fiscal year. On such accounting being made, the net profit or the net loss sustained by the Venture during such fiscal year shall be ascertained and credited or charged, as the case may be, in the books of account of the Venture in the proportions hereinabove specified.

(d) From time to time, but no less than annually, the Venture shall make distributions from the capital of the Venture which shall be in excess of the reasonable needs of the Venture for working capital and reserves as mutually determined by the Partners in accordance with Clause 16(a); provided, however, that so long as any Partner has any indebtedness or other outstanding obligations to the Venture, any distribution that would otherwise be made shall first be applied toward any such indebtedness or other obligations.

(e) All funds of the Venture shall be deposited in an account or accounts in the name of the Venture at such bank or banks as may from time to time be selected by the Venture. All withdrawals from any such account or accounts shall be made by check or other written instrument which shall require the signature of a representative of _____ (First Party) and the signature of a representative of _____ (Second Party).

## 11. MANAGEMENT AND RESPONSIBILITIES OF THE PARTIES: The Partners shall have equal power, authority and control over all creative, business, financial and legal matters in connection with the Venture and the development,

CONTRACTS
FOR THE
FILM AND
TELEVISION
INDUSTRY

202

production and exploitation of the Property, and all subsidiary and ancillary rights thereto and all exploitation thereof including, without limitation, decisions regarding the budget, the motion picture studio and/or distributor, the name of the Screenplay and the Picture, and director, cast, producer, music, writers, and the consideration for any rights granted or services rendered hereunder by Partners and others, and all decisions regarding the foregoing shall be made only by the unanimous agreement of the Partners. The foregoing provisions are not intended to prevent or prohibit any partner from engaging in discussions with third parties with respect to distribution of the Picture, provided the Partner fully discloses such discussions and the parties thereto to the other Partner and consults with same. It is further agreed that, in accordance with Clause 7(a), neither Partner shall have no right to legally bind the Venture to commitments or contractual arrangements with any such motion picture distributor on behalf of the Venture or with regard to the Property without the express written consent and signature of both Partners.

## 12. CREDITS:

(a) Provided a Picture is produced and subject to the requirements of the WGA Minimum Basic Agreement if it applies, _____ (Script Writer) shall be accorded writing credit on positive prints of the Picture, in the main titles, on a separate card, and in paid ads and publicity concerning the Picture in substantially the following form:

"Written by _____"

_____ and _____ will receive credit as Producers.

(c) Each of the aforementioned producers shall each be accorded equal credit on positive prints of the Picture in the main titles and in all advertising and promotion in respect of the Picture as producers of the Picture.

(d) Credit on other forms of works embodying the Property including, but not limited to, television programs and novelizations, shall be substantially the same as set forth in Clauses 12(a), 12(b) and 12(c) above, unless agreed otherwise by the Partners.

(e) No casual or inadvertent failure of the Venture to comply with the provisions of this Section, and no failure of others to comply with their obligations to the Venture shall constitute a breach of this Agreement by the Venture. The rights and remedies of each of the aforementioned credited parties in the event of a breach of this clause by the Venture shall be limited to their rights, if any, to recover damages in an action at law and in no event shall they be entitled by reason of any such breach to terminate this Agreement or to enjoin or restrain the production, distribution or exhibition of any production (motion picture, television, or otherwise) produced pursuant to this Agreement.

## 13. WARRANTIES, INDEMNIFICATION:

(a) Each Partner hereby warrants and represents to the other(s) that it:

(1) Has the right and capacity to enter into this agreement;

(2) Shall not encumber or sell any property, assets or intangible rights of the Venture without the written consent of the other Partner(s);

(3) Shall not assign, mortgage, hypothecate or encumber his, her or its interest in the Venture without the written consent of the other Partner(s);

(4) Shall not loan any funds or extend the credit of the Venture to any person or entity without the written consent of the other Partner(s);

(5) Shall not incur any cost, expense, liability or obligation in the name or on the credit of the Venture without the written consent of the other Partner(s);

(6) Each Partner hereby indemnifies and holds harmless the other Partner from and against any and all claims, liabilities, damages and costs (including but not limited to reasonable attorneys' fees and court costs) arising from any breach by such Partner of any representation, warranty or agreement made by such Partner hereunder.

**14. EXCLUSIVITY:** None of the Partners shall be exclusive to the Venture and each Partner may develop other properties and engage in other activities in the motion picture and television industries separate and apart from the Venture and the other Partners. However, it is agreed by the Partners that each Partner shall devote as much time as shall be reasonably necessary to fulfill his, her or its duties and obligations in connection with the Venture and the Screenplay, Picture or Property, subject, however, to their availability.

**15. DISSOLUTION AND TERMINATION OF THE VENTURE:**

(a) The Venture shall be dissolved and terminated and its business wound up upon the first to occur of the following:

(1) The expiration of the term referred to in Clause 2, above;

(2) Mutual agreement of the Partners;

(3) Operation of law;

(4) Material breach of this Agreement by any Partner(s), which breach is not cured within (e.g., fifteen (15) days) after written notice thereof from the non-defaulting Partner(s); provided, however, it is understood that only the non-defaulting Partner(s) shall have the right to terminate the Venture pursuant to this Clause (a)(4). Such termination shall not release the defaulting Partner(s) from any obligations or liabilities to the other Partner(s), whether pursuant to the provisions of this Agreement or at law or in equity.

(b) Upon termination of the Venture, the business of the Venture shall be wound up and assets and properties of the Venture shall be liquidated. Upon the happening of any one of the events mentioned in Clause 15(a) hereof, the Venture shall engage in no further business, other than that necessary to protect the assets of the Venture, wind-up its business and distribute its assets as provided herein.

**16. DISTRIBUTIONS:**

(a) Distributions Other than Upon Liquidation: Distributions of available cash shall be made at such times and in such amounts as in the discretion of the Partners, the business, the affairs and the financial circumstances of the Venture permit. Notwithstanding the foregoing, revenue from the Picture shall be distributed in accordance with Exhibit B ("Sample Worksheet") attached.

CONTRACTS
FOR THE
FILM AND
TELEVISION
INDUSTRY

204

(b) Distribution of Assets on Dissolution and Liquidation: Upon any dissolution and liquidation of the Venture, the assets of the Venture shall be liquidated in an orderly manner (subject, however, to the terms of Clause 16(c) hereof), with a view toward maximizing the proceeds from such liquidation, and the proceeds thereof shall be distributed in the following order of priority:

(1) The expenses of liquidation and the debts of the Venture, other than debts owing to the Partners, shall be paid;

(2) Debts owing to the Partners, if any, shall be paid;

(3) Distribution shall be made to the Partners of amounts equal to their respective capital account balances, if any, which shall be made in the ratio of their respective capital account balances;

(4) Any funds remaining after the amounts described in the foregoing Clauses (1), (2) and (3) have been paid shall be distributed to the Partners in the proportion in which the Partners share the net profits of the Venture at the time of such distribution.

If the Partners have not sold the assets of the Venture, except as otherwise provided in Clause 16(c) hereof, within two (2) years following dissolution, then there shall be distributed to the Partners as tenants in common, subject to the foregoing Subclauses (1), (2), (3) and (4) of this Clause 16(b), undivided interests in the assets of the Venture, as valued and constituted on that date.

(c) However, it is understood and agreed that upon dissolution of the Venture, if all the rights in the Property have not been disposed of by the Venture prior to such dissolution, then any and all copyrights and copyright rights ancillary thereto of the Venture in and to the Screenplay and the Picture shall be promptly transferred to and belong in shares of fifty percent (50%) to _____ (First Party Short Name) and fifty percent (50%) to _____ (Second Party Name), respectively, as tenants in common, and in furtherance thereof the Partners hereto agree to promptly execute all necessary and proper assignments and/or other documents to effectuate said transfer.

**17. GAIN OR LOSS DURING DISSOLUTION:** Any gain or loss arising out of the disposition of assets of the Venture during the course of dissolution shall be borne by the Partners in the same proportions as such gain or loss was shared by the Partners hereunder immediately prior to the dissolution.

**18. OPPORTUNITIES AND CONFLICTS OF INTEREST:**

(a) Any of the Partners may engage or possess an interest in any other business venture of every kind, nature and description, including ventures or enterprises which may be competitive in nature with the Venture, and neither the Venture nor any of the Partners shall have any rights in and to said business ventures, or to the income or profits derived therefrom.

(b) No Partner shall be obligated to offer any investment or business opportunities to the other Partners or to the Venture. Any Partner may invest or otherwise participate in such opportunities without notice to the Venture or to the other Partners, without affording the Venture or the other Partners an opportunity of participating in same and without any liability whatsoever to the Venture or to any other Partner. Each Partner hereby waives any right he may have against the other Partner(s) for capitalizing on information learned as a consequence of his connection with the affairs of the Venture.

## 19. DEATH, INCAPACITY, DISABILITY OF A PARTNER:

(a) Upon the death, legal incapacity or total disability of a Partner leaving the other Partner(s) surviving, this joint venture shall not dissolve but shall continue as a limited partnership with the successor(s) in interest of such deceased, incapacitated or disabled Partner(s) as [a] limited partner(s) thereof, which limited partner shall not be entitled to vote on partnership matters or participate in the management of the partnership business except that such limited partners' written approval and signature shall be required for any sale or other disposition of the Property.

(b) If in the opinion of legal counsel for the deceased Partner(s), the joint venture interest of such deceased, incapacitated or disabled Partner(s) cannot be converted to a limited partnership interest without adverse tax consequences, then upon the death, incapacity or disability of such Partner(s), this joint venture shall not dissolve but shall continue with the remaining Partner(s) and the legal representative(s) or successor(s) in interest of such deceased, incapacitated or disabled Partner(s), which legal representative or successor(s) in interest shall thereafter be deemed [a] Class B Partner(s) in the Venture. Such Class B Partner(s) shall be entitled to the same economic rights, preferences as to distribution, capital and profits interest in the Venture as was the deceased, incapacitated or disabled Partner(s), including the right to approve all withdrawals; provided, however, that such Class B Partner(s) shall not be entitled to vote on Venture matters or to participate in the management of the Venture business, except that such Class B [Partner's/Partners'] written approval and signature shall be required for any sale or other disposition of the Property.

## 20. MISCELLANEOUS:

(a) Notices: All such notices which any party is required or may desire to serve hereunder shall be in writing and shall be served by personal delivery to the other parties or by prepaid registered or certified mail addressed to the parties at their respective addresses as set forth in Clause 6 hereof, or at such other address as the parties may from time to time designate in writing upon the books of the Venture. Notice by mail shall be deemed received one (1) day after deposit in the United States mail.

(b) Arbitration: This Agreement shall be interpreted in accordance with the laws of the State of _____, applicable to agreements executed and to be wholly performed therein. Any controversy or claim arising out of or in relation to this Agreement or the validity, construction or performance of this Agreement, or the breach thereof, shall be resolved by arbitration in accordance with the rules and procedures of AFMA, as said rules may be amended from time to time with rights of discovery if requested by the arbitrator. Such rules and procedures are incorporated and made a part of this Agreement by reference. If AFMA shall refuse to accept jurisdiction of such dispute, then the parties agree to arbitrate such matter before and in accordance with the rules of the American Arbitration Association under its jurisdiction in _____ before a single arbitrator familiar with entertainment law. The parties shall have the right to engage in pre-hearing discovery in connection with such arbitration proceedings. The parties agree hereto that they will abide by and perform any award rendered in any arbitration conducted pursuant hereto, that any court having jurisdiction thereof may issue a judgment based upon such award and that the prevailing party in such arbitration and/or confirmation proceeding shall be entitled to recover its reasonable attorneys' fees and expenses. The arbitration will be held in _____ and any award shall be final, binding and non-appealable. The Parties agree to accept service of process in accordance with the AFMA Rules.

CONTRACTS
FOR THE
FILM AND
TELEVISION
INDUSTRY

206

(c) This Agreement shall be construed, interpreted and enforced in accordance with the laws of the State of _____ applicable to agreements executed and to be wholly performed within such state.

(d) Nothing contained in this Agreement shall be construed so as to require the commission of any act or the payment of any compensation which is contrary to law or to require the violation of any guild or union agreement applicable hereto which may, from time to time, be in effect and by its terms controlling of this Agreement. If there is any conflict between any provision of this Agreement and any such applicable law or guild or union agreement and the latter shall prevail, then the provisions of this Agreement affected shall be modified to the extent (but only to the extent) necessary to remove such conflict and permit such compliance with law or guild or union agreement.

(e) No waiver by any party hereof of any failure by any other party to keep or perform any covenant or condition hereof shall be deemed a waiver of any preceding or succeeding breach of the same or any other covenant or condition.

(f) This Agreement may not be amended or changed except by a written instrument duly executed by each of the Partners.

(g) Each Partner shall execute and deliver any and all additional papers, documents and other instruments and shall do any and all further acts and things reasonably necessary in connection with the performance of his, her or its obligations hereunder to carry out the intent of the Venture.

(h) The remedies accorded herein or otherwise available to the Partners shall be cumulative and no one such remedy shall be exclusive of any other and the exercise of any one shall not preclude the exercise or be deemed a waiver of any other remedy nor shall the specification of any remedy exclude or be deemed to be a waiver of any right or remedy at law or in equity which may be available to a partner including any rights to damages or injunctive relief.

(i) Any and all consents and agreements provided for or permitted by this Agreement shall be in writing and a signed copy thereof shall be filed and kept with the books of the Venture.

(j) This Agreement contains the sole and only agreement of the Partners relating to the Venture and correctly sets forth the rights, duties and obligations of each to the other(s) as of its date. Any prior agreements, promises, amendments, negotiations or representations not expressly set forth in this Agreement are of no force and effect.

(k) No Partner shall sell, assign, mortgage, hypothecate or encumber his or her interest, or any portion thereof, in the Venture without the prior written consent of all Partners.

IN WITNESS WHEREOF, this Agreement is executed as of the date and year first above written.

"(First Party Name)":

_____

"(Second Party Name)":

_____

CONTRACTS
FOR THE
FILM AND
TELEVISION
INDUSTRY

208

# DISSOLUTION

When partners decide to dissolve a partnership they may need to resolve outstanding issues, including the division of partnership property.

If the partners have a written partnership agreement, that agreement should be looked to for the terms by which the partnership should be dissolved. However, parties may not have a written agreement, or the agreement may not address dissolution. In this case the partners will have to negotiate an agreement to dissolve the partnership.

## AGREEMENT TO DISSOLVE JOINT VENTURE

This Agreement between _____ (herein called _____) (Partner 1 Name), residing at_____, and _____ (herein called _____) (Partner 2 Name), at _____ is for the dissolution of the joint venture entered into between the parties on _____, pursuant to an agreement signed by the parties on that date. The joint venture has produced a completed _____ entitled _____ (herein "_____").

1. The parties hereby dissolve their joint venture.

2. Any and all remaining assets of the joint venture including future income from the sale or licensing of the _____ (with the exception of the copyright to the _____ and the raw footage), shall be liquidated, and the proceeds realized from the liquidation shall be distributed according to the following order of priority:

First, to payments of all outstanding joint venture expenses, if any, including obligations, royalties, debts, salaries, and taxes, and expenses necessary to wind up the joint venture.

Second, to the parties according to the following formula:

(a) Revenues up to the first $_____, shall be split equally (50/50) between the parties, then

(b) revenues shall be divided _____% to _____ (Partner 2 Name) and _____% to _____ (Partner 1 Name) until the cost of production has been recouped, then

(c) after the cost of production has been recouped, all additional revenues shall be split 50/50 between the parties.

3. Upon the request of either party, a complete and final audit of the books, records, and accounts of the joint venture shall be conducted, and all final adjustments between the parties shall be made on the basis of such audit.

4. If, after the termination of the joint venture, any claim, liability, or expense shall be asserted against the joint venture which was not used in computing the profits and losses of the joint venture and which is a proper item of computation, the parties shall bear any such claim, liability, or expense equally.

**5.** The copyright in the _____ and all raw footage shot for the _____ shall be owned by the parties as tenants in common and held in the names of both parties jointly.

**6.** Neither party shall sell, or otherwise voluntarily dispose of their copyright to the _____, or his share therein, without the written consent of the other, which consent, however, shall not be unreasonably withheld.

**7.** The parties agree that all income received from the world-wide exploitation of the _____ (all markets and media including but not limited to all sequel, remake and television spin-off rights, novelization, merchandising, play, radio and audio rights) shall be shared equally.

**8.** Should the _____ be sold, licensed or otherwise disposed of and, as an incident thereto, the Parties be employed to revise the Work, the total compensation provided for in such employment agreement shall be shared equally by the parties.

**9.** If either party shall be unavailable for the purposes of collaborating on such revision, then the Party who is available shall be permitted to do such revision and shall be entitled to the full amount of compensation in connection therewith.

**10.** If either party hereto shall desire to use the _____, or any right therein or with respect thereto, in any venture in which such Party shall have a financial interest, whether direct or indirect, the Party desiring so to do shall notify the other Party of that fact and shall afford such other Party the opportunity to participate in the venture in the proportion of such other Party's interest in the _____. If such other Party shall be unwilling to participate in such venture, the Party desiring to proceed therein shall be required to pay such other Party an amount equal to that which such other Party would have received if the _____ or right, as the case may be, intended to be so used had been sold to a disinterested person at the price at which the same shall last have been offered, or if it shall not have been offered, at its fair market value which, in the absence of mutual agreement of the Parties, shall be determined by arbitration.

**11.** If either party (herein called the First Party) desires to transfer his copyright to a third person, he shall give written notice by registered mail to the other party (herein called the Second Party) of his intention to do so.

(a) In such case the Second Party shall have an option for a period of 30 days to purchase the First Party's share at a price and upon such terms indicated in the written notice.

(b) If the Second Party fails to exercise his option in writing within the aforesaid period of 30 days, or if, having exercised it, he fails to complete the purchase upon the terms stated in the notice, the First Party may transfer his rights to the third person at the price and upon the identical terms stated in the notice; and he shall forthwith send to the Second Party a copy of the contract of sale of such rights, with a statement that the transfer has been made.

(c) If the First Party fails for any reason to make such transfer to the third person, and if he desires to make a subsequent transfer to someone else, the Second Party's option shall apply to such proposed subsequent transfer.

**12.** Nothing herein contained shall be construed to create a partnership between the parties.

CONTRACTS
FOR THE
FILM AND
TELEVISION
INDUSTRY

210

**13.** Any controversy or claim arising out of or relating to this agreement or any breach thereof shall be settled by arbitration in accordance with the Rules of the American Arbitration Association; and judgment upon the award rendered by the arbitrators may be entered in any court having jurisdiction thereof. The prevailing party shall be entitled to reimbursement for costs and reasonable attorney's fees.

**14.** This agreement shall inure to the benefit of, and shall be binding upon, the executors, administrators and assigns of the parties.

**15.** This agreement constitutes the entire understanding of the parties.

**16.** This agreement is governed by and construed in accordance with the laws of the State of _____.

**17.** If any provision of this Agreement or the application thereof to any Person or circumstance shall be invalid or unenforceable to any extent, the remainder of this Agreement and the application of such provisions to other persons or circumstances shall not be affected thereby and shall be enforced to the greatest extent permitted by law.

**18.** The parties agree to execute such further documents and instruments as they may reasonably request in order to effectuate the terms and intentions of this agreement, and in the event either party is unable to execute any such documents or instruments, each appoints the other as their irrevocable attorney in fact to execute any such documents and instruments, provided that said documents and instruments shall not be inconsistent with the terms and conditions of this agreement. The rights under this Clause constitute a power coupled with an interest and are irrevocable.

**19.** This agreement expresses the entire understanding between the parties and both agree that no oral understandings have been made with regard thereto. This agreement may be amended only by written instrument signed by both parties. Each party acknowledges that it has not been induced to enter this agreement by any representations or assurances, whether written or oral, and agree that each has not received any promises or inducements other than as herein set forth. The provisions hereof shall be binding upon each party's heirs, executors, administrators and successors.


AGREED TO AND ACCEPTED


_____Date:_____
(Partner 1 Name)

_____Date:_____
(Partner 2 Name)

In a co-production agreement, one or more partners agree to co-produce a project. Here is a fairly simple agreement for the production of a cable television show.

## CO-PRODUCTION AGREEMENT

This letter confirms the understanding between _____ ("First Producer"), at _____, and _____ ("Second Producer") at _____, with respect to co-production of a television in a series about _____ tentatively titled _____ (The "Series"). The pilot program is tentatively titled _____.

**1. FINANCING:** _____ (Second Producer) will use its best efforts to obtain financing for the production financing for the Series and shall exercise sole and exclusive control over the disbursement of monies for all production, marketing and distribution expenses. _____ shall arrange for the facilities, equipment and personnel needed for the production of the Series, within the limits of the budget as set forth in Exhibit A, attached hereto. Nothing in this agreement shall obligate _____ to produce the Series.

**2. SERVICES PROVIDED:** _____ (First Producer) shall provide consultative and administrative services and shall serve as liaison with artists, museums and galleries and enlist their support and participation in the Series. _____ (First Producer) shall:

a) Procure historical data, photographs, audio tapes and literature from artists and organizations participating in the Series,

b) Procure a signed depiction and location release at no expense to _____ (Second Producer) on forms supplied by _____ (Second Producer) for each museum and any persons appearing in the Series.

c) Use his best efforts to arrange for the sale of the broadcast, cable, home video and ancillary rights to the Series in the United States and foreign territories, and

d) Use his best efforts to recruit advertising sponsors for the Series.

**3. COMPENSATION:** As full and complete consideration for his services, _____ (First Producer) shall be entitled to receive 25 percent of all net profits derived from the episodes he serves as co-producer of and in which he performs that function. Net profits shall be that amount of revenue remaining after all production, marketing and distribution expenses (and a reasonable reserve) have been recouped and accounted for in accordance with industry custom and practice.

At _____ (First Producer)'s option, he may invest any amounts due him under this agreement for the production of future episodes of the Series. In the event he does contribute such amounts, he will be entitled to a greater share of net profits from the episodes he contributes financing to in accordance with the following formula:

CONTRACTS
FOR THE
FILM AND
TELEVISION
INDUSTRY

212

For every one percent of the entire budget _____ (First Producer) contributes, he shall be entitled to one-quarter percent increment in his share of net profits, but in no event shall (First Producer)'s share of profits exceed a total of 40%.

By way of example, if _____ (First Producer) contributes $4,000 to the production of a future episode produced on a budget of $10,000, then _____ would have contributed 40% of the entire budget and would be entitled to an additional 10% of net profits as well his customary 25% of net profits for a total of 35% of net profits.

In calculating _____'s share according to the abovementioned formula, contributions shall be rounded to the nearest percentile.

Profits shall be payable annually.

**4. CREDIT:** For each episode which the partner's co-produce, on a single card following the introduction of the episode, the credit shall read: "_____.

**5. COPYRIGHT:** _____ (Second Producer) shall be the sole copyright holder of the Series. _____ (First Producer)'s contribution shall be considered a work-for-hire for all services performed for the Series.

**6. ACCOUNTING:** _____ (First Producer) shall have the right to inspect and copy the books and records maintained by _____ (Second Producer) at all times upon reasonable notice. At _____ (First Producer)'s request, _____ (Second Producer) shall retain a Certified Public Accountant to prepare an annual financial report for all expenditures and revenues from the Series. _____ (Second Producer) shall provide _____ (First Producer) with quarterly accounting statements from the time the Series begins to produce revenue.

**7. ASSIGNMENT:** Neither party may assign their rights and obligations pursuant to this Agreement without the prior written consent of the other.

**8. AGENCY:** The parties are entering into this Agreement as independent contractors, and neither party shall have the right to bind the other without the express written consent of the party to be bound.

**9. WARRANTIES:** _____ (First Producer) warrants and represents that he is free to enter into this agreement; and that to the best of his knowledge and belief all the rights and releases necessary for production of the Series have been or will be secured; and that the production of this Series will not violate or infringe the rights of any person, company or corporation. Both parties agree that they shall not accept any promotional consideration unless disclosed and approved by the other party. Both parties agree to hold each other harmless and indemnify each other for any breach of the warranties in this paragraph, including claims, damages and reasonable attorney's fees.

**10. BREACH:** In the event _____ (First Producer) breaches his obligations under this agreement, _____ (Second Producer) shall have the right to terminate this agreement after _____ (Second Producer) gives written notice to _____ (First Producer) of his breach, and _____ (First Producer) fails to cure the breach within 30 days of his receipt of said notice. In the event of an uncured breach, _____ (First Producer) shall continue to be entitled to receive compensation for episodes previously produced but shall not receive any compensation from future episodes produced. In the event _____ (Second Producer) breaches its obligations under this agreement, _____ (First Producer) shall be entitled to monetary damages but no injunctive relief.

**11. ARBITRATION:** This Agreement shall be interpreted in accordance with the laws of the State of _____, applicable to agreements executed and to be wholly performed therein. Any controversy or claim arising out of or in relation to this Agreement or the validity, construction or performance of this or the breach thereof, shall be resolved by arbitration in accordance with the rules and procedures of AFMA, as said rules may be amended from time to time with rights of discovery if requested by the arbitrator. Such rules and procedures are incorporated and made a part of this Agreement by reference. If AFMA shall refuse to accept jurisdiction of such dispute, then the parties agree to arbitrate such matter before and in accordance with the rules of the American Arbitration Association (AAA) under its jurisdiction in _____ before a single arbitrator familiar with entertainment law. The parties shall have the right to engage in pre-hearing discovery in connection with such arbitration proceedings. The parties agree hereto that they will abide by and perform any award rendered in any arbitration conducted pursuant hereto, that any court having jurisdiction thereof may issue a judgment based upon such award and that the prevailing party in such arbitration and/or confirmation proceeding shall be entitled to recover its reasonable attorney's fees and expenses. The arbitration will be held in _____ and any award shall be final, binding and non-appealable. The Parties agree to accept service of process in accordance with the AFMA or AAA Rules.

**12. ENTIRE UNDERSTANDING:** This Agreement contains the entire understanding of the parties with respect to the subject matter hereof; it may not be changed or amended except in writing signed by the parties; and it shall be construed and governed in accordance with the laws of the State of _____. This Agreement shall inure to the benefit of, and shall be binding upon, the successors, heirs, executors and administrators of the parties.

AGREED TO AND ACCEPTED:

_____     Date: _____
(Second Producer)

_____     Date: _____
(First Producer)

**EXHIBIT A**
**BUDGET**

_____

*Handwritten notes:*

If Agree to form an LLC with David L. Tannen

Is profits to be received by 4 receive 18% ct. Per (out not profit) is

mike 25 / 15
David 25 / 10

30

13. Agreement to continue in the event of the death or disability of one of the parties, the other party shall have the right to finish the production

Vekden content for OF2

14. The parties agree to form an ~~corporation~~ LLC in the state of PA using David L. Tannen as attorney for the film. ^& associate producer

15. Location — is responsible for securing locations for the filming of Bloodsucking Friend 2. This is subject to clearance of the locations for filming or clearing

David L. Tannen, attorney & Assoc. Pro

# CHAPTER 6

# MUSIC

## SOUNDTRACKS

A producer can create a soundtrack either by obtaining the right to use existing music (e.g., a popular song), or by commissioning an original musical score (i.e., hire a composer to create something new for the movie), or a combination of both.

## BUYING EXISTING MUSIC

Music is a work of authorship protected under copyright law. Determining ownership in music can be complex since several persons may share a copyright. For example, the composer may own the copyright to the composition, the lyricist may own the copyright to the lyrics, the musicians may own the copyright to their performances, and the record label may own the copyright to the recording. A film producer must determine which parties have ownership interests in each song and then license the appropriate right from those parties.

Low-budget independent producers often run out of money by the time they reach post-production. They can economize by using songs by unknown songwriters that are available for little or no money. Fledgling songwriters often want to gain visibility and stature by having their music in a movie. The producer should keep in mind that a song performed in a movie that is broadcast can generate royalties for the songwriter (through ASCAP or BMI). Thus songwriters have a financial incentive to have their music on a soundtrack even if they do not receive a fee from the producer.

CONTRACTS
FOR THE
FILM AND
TELEVISION
INDUSTRY

216

Another way for a producer to reduce music costs is to use music in the public domain. One must make sure that all rights are in the public domain. Let's say a low-budget filmmaker decides to put Beethoven's Fifth Symphony on his soundtrack. He purchases a copy of the Boston Symphony Pops recording of Beethoven's Fifth. While the composition is in the public domain, this particular recording may not be. The filmmaker is free to use Beethoven's composition, but he will have to find a recording in the public domain, or hire musicians to make his own recording.

To produce a new recording, a producer will have to strike a deal with a recording studio, musicians and/or vocalists. AFofM, AFTRA and SAG collective bargaining agreements will apply to films made by Guild signatories. A star artist may receive $20,000 or more as a fee, as well as royalties based on the retail price of the soundtrack album. If the artist is exclusive to a record label, its permission will be needed.

If a producer wants to put recorded pre-existing music (not in the public domain) on a soundtrack, a Master Use License will be needed from the record company that owns the recording.[1] Fees range from several hundred dollars for use of a short excerpt to tens of thousands of dollars for the work of a superstar. The artist may have approval rights over licensing his music to another, in which case the artist's permission must also be obtained. Re-use payments to musicians and performers will be required if the recording was made by union members.

To use an existing musical composition on television, a Television Music Rights License will be needed. This license is often obtained from The Harry Fox Agency which represents many music publishers.

## COMMISSIONING AN ORIGINAL SCORE

The producer must take care in hiring a composer/lyricist or songwriter. The agreement between the parties will determine whether the artist is deemed an employee-for-hire or an independent contractor, which in turn will determine who is the author for copyright purposes. There can be joint ownership of a musical score (a participation agreement). Permission may also be needed from a record company if you use an artist under contract to them.

The producer will usually want the work to be considered one that is "made-for-hire," so that he automatically owns the copyright. The composer will be entitled to a fee for his work and royalties from non-movie uses of his music.[2] A top songwriter may demand to share the copyright under a co-publishing agreement. The expenses of recording the soundtrack are borne by the producer.

---

[1] A producer who has obtained synchronization and performance licenses from the artist's publisher could make its own sound-alike recording if the artist's record label refuses to grant a license to use its recording. That is, the producer could create his own recording that sounds exactly like the original as long as it was not copied from the original. See, Soundtrack Music by Lionel S. Sobel, Chapter 184A, Entertainment Industry Contracts, Volume 4, Matthew Bender.

[2] Composer's royalties from soundtrack albums are typically 50% of the mechanical license fees paid the studio by the record company that releases the album. Also, the composer will receive 50% of the public performance fees collected by the agencies ASCAP or BMI, which is paid directly to the composer by his agency. Additionally, the composer will receive a royalty from the sale of sheet music and in some circumstances may receive a royalty for conducting and/or producing the soundtrack album.

For low-budget movies a composer may wear several hats.[3] He may write, arrange, orchestrate, conduct and perform the music. A composer may even agree to produce and deliver a finished master recording at his own expense. Some producers minimize costs by using non-union musicians or electronic synthesizers.

Occasionally an artist anxious to break into movie composing will compose a soundtrack or song on speculation. Here the producer is not obligated to pay for the work unless he uses it.

A producer could also proceed under a step deal. The songwriter[4] is paid a modest up-front payment for composing the song and then the producer decides if he wants to use it. If the producer uses the song, he will pay an additional fee. If he doesn't use the song, the writer will retain all rights to it. In that event, the producer may seek reimbursement of the up-front payment if the song ever generates income.

When a popular artist is commissioned to provide a song, the studio will pay him a creative fee for his services. The deal can be structured by providing the artist with a fund that includes payment for all writing and recording expenses. Thus the artist is paid a flat fee and is responsible for delivering the song and master and paying all recording expenses. Such a deal limits the studio's liability for recording costs, and can provide greater compensation to the artist if expenses can be kept low.

Complications arise with popular songwriters because many have entered agreements granting a publisher the exclusive right to the songwriter's services. Both the publisher and the studio, which may have its own music publishing arm, will want copyright ownership and management of a song written for a movie. The parties will need to reach an agreement unless the artist has already fulfilled his songwriting contract.

Similarly, a soundtrack artist may be exclusive to a record label for recordings over a term of years or for several albums. The recording company may demand a royalty from the film studio in return for granting permission to use the artist on the soundtrack. Often the label and the artist share royalties.

Assuming all necessary permissions have been obtained from the artist's record label, a soundtrack recording agreement will be used to employ an artist. The agreement will give the studio both the right to use the song on the soundtrack and the right to include it on a soundtrack album.

Since several artists may contribute material to a soundtrack, each will want to ensure that they receive a fair deal compared to the others. An artist will often ask for a "Most Favored Nations" clause, which guarantees the artist as favorable terms as those given any other artist.

An artist may also seek to limit a studio's recoupment of recording costs and advances to those expenses directly incurred by that artist. Thus, the artist's royalty will not be reduced by expenses attributable to others. If the studio agrees to such a provision, it must maintain a separate accounting for each artist.

---

[3] Composers are not unionized. However, the American Federation of Musicians represents orchestrators and conductors, a role often performed by composers in delivering soundtracks.

[4] The songwriter creates a song for the soundtrack while the composer creates an entire score. The employment agreements are similar.

CONTRACTS
FOR THE
FILM AND
TELEVISION
INDUSTRY

218

# DISTRIBUTION OF THE SOUNDTRACK ALBUM

A motion picture studio will negotiate an agreement with a record label for the production and distribution of the soundtrack album. Record companies can earn significant revenue from such releases and will pay the studio a royalty and often an advance as well. Record companies prefer soundtracks with major artists and pop songs rather than orchestral performances.

The royalty will range from 10 to 19 percent of the retail price, although the studio will pay a portion to musical artists. The record company may ask the studio to put up matching funds for promotion. The studio will want the album's release to coincide with the film's release.

## COMPOSER AGREEMENT
## (LOW-BUDGET FEATURE)

_____ 19___

_____
(Composer Name)

_____
(Address)

_____

Dear _____:

This letter, when signed by you (the "Composer"), will confirm our mutual agreement whereby _____, (the "Producer") has engaged you as an employee for hire to render certain services and to furnish a complete and original musical score (the "Work") for the Motion Picture _____ (the "Picture").

Producer agrees to pay composer as full compensation, for all services required of him/her in connection with the Picture and for all the rights granted by the Composer, upon condition that the Composer shall fully and faithfully perform all the services required of him/her hereunder, the sum of _____ dollars and other valuable consideration including one VHS copy of the Picture with musical score and a credit in the picture.

Producer employs Composer to write, compose, orchestrate, perform, record and submit to Producer music suitable for use as the complete background score for the Picture. Composer shall bear the full cost of any musicians, studio or equipment rental, guild or union fees or any other costs incurred in preparing the work except for tape stock costs.

The Composer grants the Producer the irrevocable perpetual nonexclusive right to use and license others to use his/her name and likeness in any advertising promotion or exploitation of the Picture and Work.

The Composer agrees that Producer may perpetually use or authorize others to use any of the rights herein granted for commercial advertising or publicity in connection with any product, commodity or service manufactured, distributed or offered by the Producer or others, provided such advertising refers to the Picture, or to the Composer's employment by the Producer.

Composer warrants that all material written, composed, prepared or submitted by him/her during the term hereof or any extension of it, shall be wholly original with him/her and shall not be copied in whole or in part from any other work, except that submitted to the Composer by the Producer as a basis for such material. The Composer further warrants that said material will not infringe upon the copyright, literary, dramatic or photoplay rights of any person. Composer warrants and agrees to indemnify and hold Producer and Producer's officers, shareholders, employees, successors and assigns, harmless from and against any claim, demand, damage, debt, liability, account, reckoning, obligation, cost, expense, lien, action and cause of action (including the payment of attorneys' fees and costs incurred) arising out of any breach or failure of any of Composer's warranties, representations, agreements or covenants herein contained.

The Composer further agrees that all the material which he/she may write, compose, prepare or submit under this agreement shall be the sole property of the Producer as a work-for-hire. All of the material shall be written, composed, prepared and submitted by him/her as the employee of the Producer, and not otherwise. The Producer shall be the author and first proprietor of the copyright, and the Composer shall have no right, title or interest in the material. In the event that any of proceeds of Composer's work are not considered a work for hire, then Composer's copyright to such work is hereby assigned to Producer. Producer shall have the right to obtain copyrights, patents and/or other protection therefor. The Composer further agrees to execute, verify, acknowledge, and deliver any documents which the Producer shall deem necessary or advisable to evidence, establish, maintain, protect, enforce or defend its rights and/or title in or to the said material or any part of it. Producer shall have the right, but not the duty, to use, adapt, edit, add to, subtract from, arrange, rearrange, revise and change said material or any part of it, and to vend, copy, publish, reproduce, record, transmit, broadcast by radio and/or television, perform, photograph with or without sound, including spoken works, dialogue and/or music synchronously recorded, and to communicate the same by any means now known or from now on devised, either publicly and for profit, or otherwise.

Producer, its successors and assigns, shall in addition to the Composer's services be entitled to and own in perpetuity, solely and exclusively, all of the results and proceeds of said services and material, including all rights throughout the world of production, manufacture, recordation and reproduction by any art or method, whether now known or from now on devised, and whether such results and proceeds consist of literary, dramatic, musical, motion picture, mechanical, or any other form of work, theme, idea, composition, creation or product.

The Composer shall at the request of the Producer execute such assignments or other instruments as the Producer may deem necessary or desirable to evidence, establish or defend his/her right or title in the Work. The Composer hereby appoints the Producer the true and lawful attorney-in-fact of the Composer irrevocably to execute, verify, acknowledge and deliver any such instruments or documents which the Composer shall fail or refuse to execute.

CONTRACTS
FOR THE
FILM AND
TELEVISION
INDUSTRY

220

Producer will have and is hereby granted the complete control of the publication of all or any of the musical material written by the Composer hereunder. Producer agrees, however, that in the event it publishes the musical material or causes the musical material to be published by a third party, Producer shall pay to the composer the following fees:

(a) Ten cents (.10) per copy for each piano copy of the Composition and for each orchestration of the Composition printed, published and sold in the United States and Canada by Publisher or its licensees, for which payments have been received by Publisher, after deduction of returns.

(b) Ten percent (10%) of the wholesale selling price upon each printed copy of each other arrangement and edition of the Composition printed, published and sold in the United States and Canada by Publisher or its licensees, for which payment has been received, after deduction of returns, except that in the event the Composition shall be used or caused to be used, in whole or in part, with one or more other compositions in a folio, album or other publication, Composer shall be entitled to receive that proportion of said royalty which the Composition shall bear to the total number of compositions contained in such folio, album or other publication for which royalties are payable.

(c) Fifty percent (50%) of any and all net sums actually received (less any costs for collection) by Publisher in the United States from the exploitation in the United States and Canada by licensees of Publisher of mechanical rights, electrical transcription and reproducing rights, motion picture and television synchronization rights and all other rights (except printing and public performance rights) in the Composition, whether such licensees are affiliated with, owned in whole or in part by, or controlled by Publisher.

(d) Composer shall receive his/her public performance royalties throughout the world directly from his/her own affiliated performing rights society and shall have no claims at all against Publisher for any royalties received by Publisher from any performing rights society which makes payment directly (or indirectly other than through Publisher) to writers, authors and composers.

(e) Fifty percent (50%) of any and all net sums, after deduction of foreign taxes, actually received (less any costs of collection) by Publisher in the United States from sales, licenses and other uses of the Composition in countries outside of the United States and Canada [other than the public performance royalties as hereinabove mentioned in paragraph (d)] from collection agents, licensees, subpublishers or others, whether same are affiliated with, owned in whole or in part by, or controlled by Publisher.

(f) Publisher shall not be required to pay any royalties on professional or complimentary printed copies of the Composition which are distributed gratuitously to performing arts, orchestra leaders and disc jockeys or for advertising, promotional or exploitation purposes. Furthermore, no royalties shall be payable to Composer on consigned copies of the Composition unless paid for, and not until an accounting therefore can properly be made.

Notwithstanding anything to the contrary contained in this Agreement, Producer, its lessees, licensees and all other persons permitted by Producer to distribute, exhibit or exploit any picture in connection with which any material written, prepared or composed by Composer hereunder is used, shall have the free and unrestricted right to use any such material and to make mechanical reproductions of it without the payment of any sums at all, and in no event shall Composer be permitted or entitled to participate in any rentals or other forms of royalty received by Producer, its licensees or any other persons permitted by Producer to use any such material or mechanical reproductions of it in connection with the exhibition, distribution, exploitation or advertising of any present or future kind of motion picture, nor shall Producer be obligated to account to Composer for any sums received by Producer from any other persons from the sale or licensing or other disposition of any material written, created, or composed by Composer hereunder in connection with the exhibition, distribution, exploitation or advertising of any motion picture. Without limiting the foregoing, Composer shall not be entitled to any portion of any synchronization fee due to the use of the material or any portion of it in motion pictures produced by Producer or by any of its subsidiaries, affiliates or related companies.

Provided Composer fully and satisfactorily renders his/her services pursuant to the terms and conditions of this Agreement, and that all of the original music contained in the Picture as released is the product of Composer's services, Producer shall accord Composer billing on a separate card as follows: "_____," (Composer's Credit) or a phrase substantially similar thereto on the positive prints of said Picture. Except as set forth in the preceding sentence, all other matters about billing shall be decided in Producer's sole discretion.

If Producer, its successors or assigns shall exercise their right hereunder to make, distribute and sell, or authorize others to make, distribute and sell, commercial phonograph records (including, without limitation, discs of any speed or size, tape and wire demos and any and all other demos, whether now known or unknown, for the recording of sound) embodying the material for the Picture and if said records contain Composer's performance as a conductor, they shall pay or cause to be paid to Composer in connection with it a reasonable royalty as is customarily paid in the industry to be negotiated in good faith.

Composer's sole remedy for any breach or alleged breach hereof shall be an action at law for damages, if any. In no event shall Composer have the right to rescind this Agreement or any of the rights granted hereunder nor to seek or obtain injunctions or other equitable relief restraining or enjoining the production, exhibition or exploitation of any motion pictures based upon or using any portion of the Work.

Nothing contained in this Agreement shall be deemed to require Producer or its assigns to publish, record, reproduce or otherwise use the Work or any part of it, whether in connection with the Picture or otherwise.

This instrument is the entire Agreement between the parties and cannot be modified except by a written instrument signed by the Composer and an authorized officer of the Producer.

This Agreement shall be deemed to have been made in the State of _____ and its validity, construction and effect shall be governed by and construed under the laws and judicial decisions of the State of _____ applicable to agreements wholly performed therein.

Very truly yours,

By:_____
(Production Company Representative)

_____
(Production Company)

CONTRACTS
FOR THE
FILM AND
TELEVISION
INDUSTRY

222

**ACCEPTED AND AGREED TO:**

_____

Composer

I hereby certify that I wrote the material hereto attached, as an employee of _____, pursuant to an agreement dated _____, in performance of my duties thereunder, and in the regular course of employment, and that said _____ (Production Company), is the author of it and entitled to the copyright therein and thereto, with the right to make such changes therein and such uses of it, as it may determine as such author.

IN WITNESS WHEREOF, I have hereto set my hands this _____.

_____

(Composer Name)

# TV MUSIC RIGHTS

This license is used to obtain the right to use a composition in a television program. It only grants the right to record the composition on the soundtrack of the program. In other words, it does not grant the licensee any right to use a prior recording.

## TV MUSIC RIGHTS LICENSE

**1.** In consideration of the payment of $\_\_\_\_\_, and upon the payment of it to the undersigned, the undersigned does hereby grant to Licensee the non-exclusive, irrevocable right and license to record the following copyrighted musical composition(s) (the "Compositions") in synchronization or timed-relation with a picture produced by Licensee (the "Picture") for television broadcast and exhibition only, and known as:

Title of television program: _____
Composition: _____
Composer: _____
Publisher: _____
Length of Composition & Manner of Use:  \_\_\_\_\_ minutes; _____

**2.** This is a license to record only, and the exercise of the recording rights herein granted is conditioned upon performance of the Composition(s) over television stations having valid licenses from the copyright owner ("the Owner"), or from the person, firm, corporation or other entity having the legal right to issue performance rights licenses for the Owner in the respective territories in which the Composition(s) shall be performed. The Composition(s) shall not be used in any manner and media or be recorded for any other purpose, except those specifically set forth herein, without the express written consent of the Owner. No sound recordings produced pursuant to this license are to be manufactured, sold and/or used separately from the Picture; and the Picture shall not be exhibited in or televised into theaters or other public places of amusement where motion pictures are customarily exhibited.

**3.** This license is granted for the following territory: _____

**4.** This license shall end on \_\_\_\_\_. Upon such date rights herein granted shall immediately cease and end, and the right derived from this license to make or authorize any further use or distribution of the Picture with the licensed music shall also cease and end upon such date.

**5.** This license cannot be assigned or transferred without the express consent of the undersigned in writing.

**6.** The undersigned warrants, on behalf of the principal for whom the undersigned is acting, that it is the owner of the recording rights herein licensed, and this license is given without other warranty or recourse, except to repay the consideration paid for this license if said warranty shall be breached. The undersigned's warranty is limited to the amount of consideration paid for this license; and the undersigned further reserves all rights and uses in and to the Composition(s) not herein specifically granted.

CONTRACTS
FOR THE
FILM AND
TELEVISION
INDUSTRY

224

_____

(Publisher)

**AGREED AND ACCEPTED:**

_____

(Producer Name)

# USE OF COMPOSITION AND RECORDING

The following agreement permits the licensee to use a composition and a recording of that composition on the soundtrack of a motion picture. The license includes the right to use the music for promotional purposes and for a soundtrack album.

## SYNCHRONIZATION/PERFORMING/MASTER USE AND MECHANICAL LICENSE

THIS SYNCHRONIZATION/PERFORMING/MASTER USE AND MECHANICAL LICENSE is made and entered into as of _____, by and between _____ ("Licensor") at _____ and _____ ("Licensee"), at _____. The parties hereby agree as follows:

**1. GRANT OF RIGHTS:** Licensor hereby irrevocably grants to Licensee the non-exclusive right to include in the photoplay tentatively entitled "_____" (the "Film") and in promoting, advertising and publicizing of the Film that certain musical compositions written and owned by Licensor (the "Compositions") and the recording of an instrumental and vocal performance thereof owned by Licensor (the "Recording"). This license shall continue in perpetuity and be effective for any and all media, whether now known or hereafter devised, throughout the universe. The license shall include, but shall not be limited to, the following:

a. Use of the compositions, and any recording and any performance thereof, in synchronized or timed relation to the Film and any remake or remakes thereof for exploitation in any and all media now known or hereafter devised (including, but not limited to, audio-visual devices), including the recording and distribution of the Film on videocassette, videodisc, by television (including cable, pay-TV, and broadcast TV), electronic publishing rights, theatrical and non-theatrical exhibition, and in advertisements in-context and out-of-context, trailers, "music videos" and other promotional and ancillary uses of the Film or such other audio-visual work.

b. Use of the compositions, any recording and any performance thereof, on a soundtrack album including CD's and tapes ("Album") and to manufacture, sell, distribute and advertise copies of the Album embodying the Compositions and Recordings by any methods and in any configurations now known or hereafter devised; for the release of same under any trademarks, trade names or label; to perform the Compositions and Recordings publicly; and to commit to public performance thereof by radio and/or television, or by any other media now known or hereafter devised, and to permit any other person, corporation or other entity to do any or all of the foregoing. Licensor shall have the right to release the Recording as a so-called single ("Single").

c. Right to make, import and export copies of the Composition and Recording in the Film.

CONTRACTS
FOR THE
FILM AND
TELEVISION
INDUSTRY

226

**2. NAME AND LIKENESS:** Licensor hereby grants to Licensee the irrevocable universewide right, in perpetuity, to use and permit others to use Licensor's name, voice, approved photograph, likeness and biographical material concerning Licensor in connection with the Film, Album and any phonograph records derived therefrom and any promotions and advertisements thereof. Any photograph, likenesses or biographical material submitted or furnished by Licensor to Licensee shall be deemed approved, and, promptly following the execution of this Agreement, Licensor shall submit to Licensee a reasonable assortment of approved photographs, likenesses and biographical materials for use by Licensee in connection herewith. All such materials submitted by Licensee to Licensor for approval (which approval shall not be unreasonably withheld) shall be deemed given in the event Licensor fails to submit written objections thereto within five (5) days after the applicable photographs, likenesses and/or biographical materials have been submitted to Licensor for approval.

**3. RE-RECORDING:** Licensee shall have the right to re-record, edit, mix and re-mix, dub and re-dub the Recording in Licensee's sole discretion, and nothing contained herein shall be construed to obligate Licensee to employ Licensor in connection with same.

**4. COMPENSATION:**

(a)   Provided Licensor fully performs all material obligations under this Agreement, and in full consideration of all rights granted herein, Licensee shall pay or cause to be paid to Licensor, within thirty (30) days of the initial commercial release of the Film, the sum of $_____.

(b)   It is specifically understood and agreed that the sums set forth in this Clause 4 and the record royalties set forth in Clause 5 below shall constitute payment in full to Licensor, and to all persons or entities deriving or claiming rights through either Licensor.

**5. ROYALTIES:**

(a)   With respect to the exploitation of the Recording if embodied on the Album or other phonograph records derived therefrom, Licensee shall pay to Licensor a basic royalty at the rate of _____ percent (the "Basic Album Rate") of the suggested retail list price ("SRLP") in respect of net sales of Albums sold through normal retail channels in the United States in the form of black vinyl discs, cassettes, CD and any other configuration, pro-rated by multiplying the applicable royalty rate by a fraction, the numerator of which is the number one (1), and the denominator of which is the total number of master recordings, including the Recording, contained on the Album (the "Licensor Fraction").

(b)   The royalty payable to Licensor hereunder for singles, budget records, foreign record sales and other sales of records or exploitations of the Master shall be reduced and pro-rated in the same proportion that the basic United States Album rate payable to Licensee in respect of the Album (the "Basic Distributor Rate") is reduced or pro-rated pursuant to Licensee's agreement with the applicable Distributor, provided that with respect to such sales of records or exploitations of the Master for which Licensee receives a royalty which is computed as a flat fee or as a percentage of the Distributor's net receipts from such use, Licensor's royalty hereunder in respect of such sale or use shall be equal to the amount of Licensee's flat fee or net receipts, multiplied by the product of the following:

Basic Album Rate

_____ X   Licensor Fraction

Basic Distributor Rate

(c)    Except as otherwise provided in this Agreement, Licensor's royalties hereunder shall be computed, determined, calculated and paid to Licensor on the same basis (e.g., packaging deductions, free goods, reserves, definition of suggested retail list price, percentage of sales, discounts, returns policy, taxes, etc.) and at the same times as royalties are paid to Licensee by the applicable Distributor.

(d)    Notwithstanding anything to the contrary contained in this Agreement, (i) Licensor shall not be entitled to receive any record royalties at all with respect to records sold prior to the recoupment of all Recording Costs for the Album, if any, and Conversion Costs from the royalties otherwise payable to Licensor hereunder; and (ii) following such recoupment Licensor's royalties shall be credited to Licensor's account hereunder solely in respect of records thereafter sold which embody the Recording. The term "Recording Costs" shall mean all direct costs incurred by Licensee in the course of producing and recording any master recordings, including the Recording embodied on the Album and including, without limitation, the cost of studio time, musician fees, union payments, instrument rentals, producer's fees and advances and the costs of tape, editing, mixing, re-mixing and mastering and other similar costs customarily regarded as recording costs in the phonograph record industry. The term "Conversion Costs" shall mean all direct costs incurred in connection with the conversion of the Recording from use in the Film to use in the Album including, without limitation, new-use, re-use, re-mixing, and re-editing costs and all other costs which are now or hereafter recognized as conversion costs in the phonograph record and motion picture industries.

(e)    Licensor shall be deemed to have consented to all royalty statements and all other accounts rendered by Licensee, unless specific objection in writing, stating the basis thereof, is given by Licensor to Licensee within one (1) year from the date such statement is rendered. During this one (1) year period, Licensor may, at its expense, but not more than once annually, audit the books and records of Licensee, solely in connection with royalties payable to Licensor pursuant to this Agreement, provided such audit is conducted by a reputable certified public accountant, during business hours and upon reasonable written notice. Licensor shall be foreclosed from maintaining any action, claim or proceeding against Licensee in any forum or tribunal with respect to any statement or accounting rendered hereunder unless such action, claim or proceeding is commenced against Licensee in a court of competent jurisdiction within one (1) year after the date on which Licensee receives Licensor's written objection.

(f)    Licensee shall account to Licensor upon a semiannual basis within 90 days of June 30 and December 31. Licensee shall have the right to rely upon Distributor's accounting and statements.

(g)    Licensor shall be entitled to inspect such books and records of Licensee relating to the Album during regular business hours and shall be entitled to audit such books and records of Licensee relating to the Album upon reasonable notice to Licensee and provided that not more one (1) audit is conducted every calendar year and further provided that such audit shall last not more than thirty (30) consecutive business days once begun and does not interfere with Licensee's normal operations. Within Thirty (30) days of the completion of the audit, Licensor will furnish Licensee with a copy of said audit. All audit expenses shall be borne by the Licensor.

CONTRACTS
FOR THE
FILM AND
TELEVISION
INDUSTRY

228

## 6. CREDITS:

(a)    If the Recording and/or Composition is contained in the Film, Licensee shall accord Licensor a credit in substantially the following form in the end titles of release prints of the Film approximately adjacent to the titles of the Compositions and Recordings:

"WRITTEN BY _____"

"PERFORMED BY _____"

The type, size, shape, color, placement, duration and all other characteristics of the credit shall be at Licensee's sole and absolute discretion. Without limiting the generality of the foregoing, such credit may be shared with and/or adjacent to credits relating to other contributors to the Recording and/or the Compositions.

(b)    No casual or inadvertent failure by Licensee or any failure by a third party to comply with the provisions of this Clause 6 shall constitute a breach of this Agreement.

**7. WARRANTIES:**  Licensor, on its own and on Licensor's behalf, hereby warrants and represents that:

(a)    it has the full right, power and authority to enter into this Agreement and to grant all rights granted herein, that it is not under, nor will it be under, any disability, restriction or prohibition with respect to its rights to fully perform in accordance with the terms and conditions of this Agreement and that there shall be no liens, claims or other interests which may interfere with, impair or be in derogation of the rights granted herein;

(b)    the Album shall be freely available for use by Licensee, the Single(s) and other phonograph records derived therefrom and in the Film in any and all media (whether now known or hereafter devised) in which the Film is to be distributed (and in any and all publicizing, promoting and advertising therefor), throughout the universe including, without limitation, in theaters, free and pay television, in home video devices, and in radio, television and theatrical trailers, without further payment by Licensee, except as set forth herein;

(c)    any party who may be entitled to Licensor's exclusive recording services shall have given a written waiver of such rights in connection with Licensee's exploitation of the Recording as herein provided;

(d)    Licensee shall not be required to make any payments of any nature for, or in connection with, the acquisition, exercise or exploitation of rights by Licensee pursuant to this Agreement except as specifically provided in this Agreement;

(e)    Neither the Recording, nor the Compositions nor any other material supplied by Licensor will violate or infringe upon any common law or statutory right of any person, firm or corporation including, without limitation, contractual rights, copyrights, and rights of privacy.

(f)    Licensor owns or controls 100% of the Recording and the Composition.

**8. INDEMNITY:** Licensor hereby agrees to indemnify Licensee, Licensee's successors, Licensee's, distributors, sub-distributors and assigns, and the respective officers, directors, agents and employees of each of the foregoing, from and against any damages, liabilities, costs and expenses, including reasonable attorneys' fees actually incurred, arising out of or in any way connected with any claim, demand or action inconsistent with this Agreement or any warranty, representation or agreement made by Licensor herein.

**9. REMEDIES FOR BREACH:** Licensor's rights and remedies in the event of a breach or alleged breach of this Agreement by Licensee shall be limited to an action at law for damages, if any, and in no event shall Licensor be entitled by reason of any such breach or alleged breach to enjoin, restrain, or to seek to enjoin or restrain, the distribution or other exploitation of the Film, Album, Single, or other work which may embody the Recording and Licensee shall not have the right to rescind this Agreement. This Agreement shall not be deemed to give any right or remedy to any third party whatsoever unless the right or remedy is specifically granted by the parties hereto in writing to the third party. Licensor shall execute any further documents necessary to fully effectuate the intent and purposes of this Agreement.

**10. ASSIGNMENT:** Licensee shall have the right, at Licensee's election, to assign any of Licensee's rights hereunder, in whole or in part, to any person, firm or corporation including, without limitation, any distributor or subdistributor of the Film, Album or other phonograph records derived therefrom, or other work which may embody the Master. Licensor shall not assign rights without Licensee's prior written consent and any attempted assignment without such consent shall be void and shall transfer no rights to the purported assignee.

**11. ENTIRE AGREEMENT:** This Agreement sets forth the entire understanding of the parties thereto relating to the subject matter hereof and supersedes all prior agreements, whether oral or written, pertaining thereto. No modification, amendment, or waiver of this Agreement or any of the terms or provisions hereof shall be binding upon Licensor or Licensee unless confirmed by a written instrument signed by authorized officers of both Licensor and Licensee. No waiver by Licensor or Licensee of any terms or provisions of this Agreement or of any default hereunder shall affect their respective rights thereafter to enforce such term or provision or to exercise any right or remedy upon any other default, whether or not similar.

**12. RIGHT TO CURE:** No failure by Licensee to perform any of Licensee's obligations hereunder shall be deemed a breach hereof, unless Licensor gives Licensee written notice of such failure and Licensee fails to cure such nonperformance within thirty (30) days after Licensee's receipt of such notice.

**13. NOTICES:** All notices hereunder shall be sent certified mail, return receipt requested, or delivered by hand to the applicable address set forth below, unless and until written notice, via registered mail, to the contrary is received by the applicable party.

If to Licensee: _____ (Licensee), _____ (Licensee Address); courtesy copies to _____, _____.

If to Licensor: _____, _____.

Notwithstanding the foregoing, all accounting statements and payments may be sent by regular mail. Except as required by law, the date of mailing of such notice shall be deemed the date upon which such notice was given or sent.

CONTRACTS
FOR THE
FILM AND
TELEVISION
INDUSTRY

230

**14. APPLICABLE LAW:** This Agreement has been entered into in the State of _____, and its validity, construction, interpretation and legal effect shall be governed by the laws of the State of _____ applicable to contracts entered into and performed entirely within the State of _____.

**15. ARBITRATION:** Any controversy or claim arising out of or relating to this Agreement or any breach thereof shall be settled by arbitration in accordance with the Rules of the American Arbitration Association. The parties select expedited arbitration using one arbitrator as the sole forum for the resolution of any dispute between them. The venue for arbitration shall be _____. The arbitrator may make any interim order, decision, determinations, or award he deems necessary to preserve the status quo until he is able to render a final order, decision, determination or award. The determination of the arbitrator in such proceeding shall be final, binding and non-appealable. Judgment upon the award rendered by the arbitrator may be entered in any court having jurisdiction thereof. The prevailing party shall be entitled to reimbursement for costs and reasonable attorney's fees.

IN WITNESS WHEREOF, the parties hereto have executed this Agreement as of the year and date first above written.

"Licensor"

_____

(Licensor)

Accepted And Agreed To:

"Licensee"

_____

(Licensee)

# SOUNDTRACK RECORDING AGREEMENT

This agreement is used to employ an Artist (through the Artist's loan-out company) to provide vocal and musical services to make a master sound recording that will be owned by the producing company, and may be used on the soundtrack of a motion picture and in a soundtrack album.

## SOUNDTRACK RECORDING AGREEMENT
### (Loan-out format)

THIS AGREEMENT, is made as of _____ by and between _____ ("Company") and _____ (Lender) f/s/o _____ (Artist) in connection with a master sound recording (the "Master") embodying the musical composition entitled _____ (the "Composition "), for possible inclusion in the theatrical motion picture presently entitled _____ (the "Picture"), and in a soundtrack album (the "Album") and any other phonograph records to be derived therefrom. In consideration of the mutual covenants made herein, Company and Artist hereby agree as follows:

**1. SERVICES TO BE PROVIDED:** Company hereby employs Lender to cause Artist to render Artist's vocal and/or musical services to record the Master for possible inclusion in the Picture. Artist shall comply with all of Company's instructions and requests in connection with Artist's services hereunder. Artist shall render such services upon the terms and conditions set forth herein and in accordance with a production schedule to be designated by Company in its sole discretion.

**2. TERM:** The term of this Agreement shall commence as of the date hereof and shall continue thereafter until such time as Artist has fully rendered all of Artist's services required hereunder.

**3. OWNERSHIP:**

(a) All results and proceeds of Artist's services hereunder shall constitute or contribute to a work specially ordered or commissioned by Company for use as part of a motion picture or other audio-visual work and accordingly, all such results and proceeds shall constitute a "work-made-for-hire" (as such term is defined in the United States Copyright Act of 1976). Company shall own the Master, together with the performances embodied thereon and all copyrights therein and thereto, and all the results and proceeds of Artist's services hereunder throughout the universe in perpetuity, free of any and all claims by Lender, Artist or any person, corporation or other entity deriving any rights from Lender or Artist.

(b) Without limiting the generality of clause 3(a) hereof, Company shall have the exclusive, perpetual and worldwide right, but not the obligation, to use and perform the Master, and the results and proceeds of Artist's services hereunder:

(i) in synchronization with the Picture and any other audio-visual works for exploitation in any and all media now known or hereafter devised (including, but not limited to, audio-visual devices), and in advertisements, in-context and out-of-context, trailers, "music videos" and other promotional and ancillary uses of the Picture or such other audio-visual work; and

CONTRACTS
FOR THE
FILM AND
TELEVISION
INDUSTRY

232

(ii) to manufacture, sell, distribute and advertise the Album and any other phonograph records embodying the Master by any methods and in any configurations now known or hereafter devised; for the release of same under any trademarks, tradenames or label; to perform the Album and any other phonograph records derived therefrom publicly; and to commit to public performance thereof by radio and/or television, or by any other media now known or hereafter devised, all upon such terms and conditions as Company may approve, and to permit any other person, corporation or other entity to do any or all of the foregoing.

**4. NAME AND LIKENESS:** Lender hereby grants to Company the irrevocable worldwide right, in perpetuity, to use and permit others to use Lender's or Artist's name, voice, approved photograph, likeness and biographical material concerning Artist in connection with the Picture, Master, Album and any other phonograph records derived therefrom and any promotions and advertisements thereof. Any photograph, likenesses or biographical material submitted or furnished by Lender or Artist to Company shall be deemed approved, and, promptly following the execution of this Agreement, Lender shall submit to Company a reasonable assortment of approved photographs, likenesses and biographical materials for use by Company in connection herewith. All such materials submitted by Company to Lender for approval (which approval shall not be unreasonably withheld) shall be deemed given in the event Lender fails to submit written objections thereto within five (5) days after the applicable photographs, likenesses and/or biographical materials have been submitted to Lender for approval.

**5. RE-RECORDING:** Company shall have the right to re-record, edit, mix and re-mix, dub and re-dub the Master in Company's sole discretion, and nothing contained herein shall be construed to obligate Company to employ Artist in connection with same.

**6. COMPENSATION:**

(a) Provided Lender and Artist fully perform all their material obligations under Clause 1 above, and in full consideration of all rights granted herein, Company shall pay or cause to be paid to Lender, upon the later to occur at the date of the full completion of all of Lender's or Artist's services hereunder, or the date of Lender's and Artist's execution hereof, an amount equal to the minimum scale amount specified for Artist's recording services hereunder in any applicable union collective bargaining agreements. The provisions of any applicable union collective bargaining contract between Company and any labor organization which are required by the terms of such contract to be included in this Agreement shall be deemed incorporated herein.

(b) It is specifically understood and agreed that the sums set forth in this Clause 6 and the record royalties set forth in Clause 7 below shall constitute payment in full to Lender and Artist, and to all persons or entities deriving or claiming rights through either Lender and/or Artist.

**7. ROYALTIES:**

(a) With respect to the exploitation of the Master if embodied on the Album or other phonograph records derived therefrom, Company shall pay or cause any phonograph record distributor ("Distributor") of the Album, Single or phonograph records derived therefrom, to pay to Lender a basic royalty at the rate of _____ percent (the "Basic Album Rate") of the applicable suggested retail list price ("SRLP") in respect of net sales of Albums sold through normal retail channels in the United States in the form of black vinyl discs and cassettes, pro-rated by multiplying the applicable royalty rate by a fraction, the numerator of which is the number one (1), and the denominator of which is the total number of master recordings, including the Master, contained on the Album (the "Lender Fraction").

(b) The royalty payable to Lender hereunder for singles, budget records, compact discs, foreign record sales and other sales of records or exploitations of the Master shall be reduced and pro-rated in the same proportion that the basic United States Album rate payable to Company in respect of the Album (the "Basic Distributor Rate") is reduced or pro-rated pursuant to Company's agreement with the applicable Distributor, provided that with respect to such sales of records or exploitations of the Master for which Company receives a royalty which is computed as a flat fee or as a percentage of the Distributor's net receipts from such use, Lender's royalty hereunder in respect of such sale or use shall be equal to the amount of Company's flat fee or net receipts, multiplied by the product of the following:

$$\frac{\text{Basic Album Rate}}{\text{Basic Distributor Rate}} \quad X \quad \text{Lender Fraction}$$

(c) Except as otherwise provided in this Agreement, Lender's royalties hereunder shall be computed, determined, calculated and paid to Lender on the same basis (e.g., packaging deductions, free goods, reserves, definition of suggested retail list price, percentage of sales, discounts, returns policy, taxes, etc.) and at the same times as royalties are paid to Company by the applicable Distributor.

(d) Notwithstanding anything to the contrary contained in this Agreement, (i) Lender shall not be entitled to receive any record royalties at all with respect to records sold prior to the recoupment of all Recording Costs and Conversion Costs from the royalties otherwise payable to Lender hereunder; and (ii) following such recoupment Lender's royalties shall be credited to Lender's account hereunder solely in respect of records thereafter sold which embody the Master. The term "Recording Costs" shall mean all direct costs incurred in the course of producing and recording the Master hereunder including, without limitation, the cost of studio time, musician fees, union payments, instrument rentals, producer's fees and advances and the costs of tape, editing, mixing, re-mixing and mastering and other similar costs customarily regarded as recording costs in the phonograph record industry. The term "Conversion Costs" shall mean all direct costs incurred in connection with the conversion of the Master from use in the Picture to use in the Album and other phonograph records derived therefrom including, without limitation, new-use, re- use, re-mixing, and re-editing costs and all other costs which are now or hereafter recognized as conversion costs in the phonograph record and motion picture industries.

(e) Lender shall be deemed to have consented to all royalty statements and all other accounts rendered by Company, unless specific objection in writing, stating the basis thereof, is given by Lender to Company within one (1) year from the date such statement is rendered. During this one (1) year period, Lender may, at its expense, but not more than once annually, audit the books and records of

CONTRACTS
FOR THE
FILM AND
TELEVISION
INDUSTRY

234

Company, solely in connection with royalties payable to Lender pursuant to this Agreement, provided such audit is conducted by a reputable certified public accountant, during business hours and upon reasonable written notice. Lender shall be foreclosed from maintaining any action, claim or proceeding against Company in any forum or tribunal with respect to any statement or accounting rendered hereunder unless such action, claim or proceeding is commenced against Company in a court of competent jurisdiction within one (1) year after the date on which Company receives Lender's written objection.

## 8. CREDITS:

(a) If the Master is contained in the Picture, Company shall accord Artist a credit in substantially the following form in the end titles of release prints of the Picture approximately adjacent to the titles of the Composition:

"WRITTEN BY _____"

"PERFORMED BY _____"

The type, size, shape, color, placement, duration and all other characteristics of the credit shall be at Company's sole and absolute discretion. Without limiting the generality of the foregoing, such credit may be shared with and/or adjacent to credits relating to other contributors to the Master and/or the Composition.

(b) No casual or inadvertent failure by Company or any failure by a third party to comply with the provisions of this Clause 8 shall constitute a breach of this Agreement.

## 9. WARRANTIES: Lender, on its own and on Artist's behalf, hereby warrants and represents that:

(a) it has the full right, power and authority to enter into this Agreement and to grant all rights granted herein, that it is not under nor will it be under, any disability, restriction or prohibition with respect to its rights to fully perform in accordance with the terms and conditions of this Agreement and that there shall be no liens, claims or other interests which may interfere with, impair or be in derogation of the fights granted herein;

(b) the Master shall be freely available for use by Company in the Album, the Single(s) and other phonograph records and in the Picture in all media (whether now known or hereafter devised) in which the Picture is to be distributed (and in any and all advertising therefor), throughout the world including, without limitation, in theaters, free and pay television, in home video devices, and in radio, television and theatrical trailers, without further payment by Company, except as set forth herein;

(c) any party who may be entitled to Artist's exclusive recording services shall have given a written waiver of such rights in connection with Company's exploitation of the Master as herein provided;

(d) Company shall not be required to make any payments of any nature for, or in connection with, the acquisition, exercise or exploitation of rights by Company pursuant to this Agreement except as specifically provided in this Agreement;

(e) neither Lender nor Artist shall, prior to the date five (5) years after the delivery of the Master, produce or re-record or authorize the production or re-recording of the Composition or any portion thereof for any third party; and

(f) neither the Master, nor the Composition nor any other material supplied by Artist will violate or infringe upon any common law or statutory right of any person, firm or corporation including, without limitation, contractual rights, copyrights, and rights of privacy.

**10. INDEMNITY:** Lender hereby agrees to indemnify Company, Company's successors, licensees, distributors, sub-distributors and assigns, and the respective officers, directors, agents and employees of each of the foregoing, from and against any damages, liabilities, costs and expenses, including reasonable attorneys' fees actually incurred, arising out of or in any way connected with any claim, demand or action inconsistent with this Agreement or any warranty, representation or agreement made by Lender and/or Artist herein.

**11. UNIQUE SERVICE:** Lender acknowledges that the services performed by Artist hereunder and the rights hereunder granted are of a special, unique, extraordinary and unusual character which gives them a peculiar value, the loss of which cannot be reasonably or adequately compensated in damages in an action of law, and that any default by Lender and/or Artist will cause Company irreparable harm and injury. Lender agrees that Company shall be entitled to seek injunctive and other equitable relief in addition to Company's remedies at law, in the event of any default by Artist.

**12. REMEDIES FOR BREACH:** Lender's rights and remedies in the event of a breach or alleged breach of this Agreement by Company shall be limited to Lender's right, only, to recover damages in an action at law and in no event shall Lender be entitled by reason of any such breach or alleged breach to enjoin, restrain, or to seek to enjoin or restrain, the distribution or other exploitation of the Picture, Album, Single, or other work which may embody the Master. This Agreement shall not be deemed to give any right or remedy to any third party whatsoever unless the right or remedy is specifically granted by the parties hereto in writing to the third party. Lender shall execute any further documents necessary to fully effectuate the intent and purposes of this Agreement.

**13. ASSIGNMENT:** Company shall have the right, at Company's election, to assign any of Company's rights hereunder, in whole or in part, to any person, firm or corporation including, without limitation, any distributor or subdistributor of the Picture, Album or other phonograph records derived therefrom, or other work which may embody the Master. Lender shall not assign rights without Company's prior written consent and any attempted assignment without such consent shall be void and shall transfer no rights to the purported assignee.

**14. ENTIRE AGREEMENT:** This Agreement sets forth the entire understanding of the parties thereto relating to the subject matter hereof and supersedes all prior agreements, whether oral or written, pertaining thereto. No modification, amendment, or waiver of this Agreement or any of the terms or provisions hereof shall be binding upon Lender or Company unless confirmed by a written instrument signed by authorized officers of both Lender and Company. No waiver by Artist or Company of any terms or provisions of this Agreement or of any default hereunder shall affect their respective rights thereafter to enforce such term or provision or to exercise any right or remedy upon any other default, whether or not similar.

**15. RIGHT TO CURE:** No failure by Company to perform any of Company's obligations hereunder shall be deemed a breach hereof, unless Lender gives Company written notice of such failure and Company fails to cure such nonperformance within thirty (30) days after Company's receipt of such notice.

CONTRACTS
FOR THE
FILM AND
TELEVISION
INDUSTRY

236

**16. NOTICES:** All notices hereunder shall be sent certified mail, return receipt requested, or delivered by hand to the applicable address set forth below; unless and until written notice, via registered mail, to the contrary is received by the applicable party.

If to Company:_____ (Production Company), _____ (Production Company Address).

Courtesy copies to: _____, _____.

If to Lender: _____, _____.

Notwithstanding the foregoing, all accounting statements and payments may be sent by regular mail. Except as required by law, the date of mailing of such notice shall be deemed the date upon which such notice was given or sent.

**17. APPLICABLE LAW:** This Agreement has been entered into in the State of _____, and its validity, construction, interpretation and legal effect shall be governed by the laws of the State of _____ applicable to contracts entered into and performed entirely within the State of _____. The _____ Courts only will have jurisdiction in any controversies regarding this Agreement; and, any action or other proceeding which involves such a controversy will be brought in the courts located within the State of _____, and not elsewhere. Any process in any action or proceeding commenced in the courts of the State of _____ arising out of any such claim, dispute or disagreement, may, among other methods, be served upon Lender by delivering or mailing the same, via registered or certified mail, addressed to Lender at the address first above written or such other address as Lender may designate at the address first above written or such other address as Lender may designate pursuant to clause 16 hereof. Any such delivery or mail service shall be deemed to have the same force and effect as personal service within the State of _____. This Agreement shall not become effective until signed by Lender and countersigned by a duly authorized officer of Company.

IN WITNESS WHEREOF, the parties hereto have executed this Agreement as of the year and date first above written.

"COMPANY"

_____

(Production Company Representative)

_____

(Production Company Representative Title)

_____

(Production Company)

Accepted And Agreed To:

"LENDER"

By:_____

(Lender Representative)

# INDUCEMENT AGREEMENT

In order to induce _____ ("Company") to enter into the foregoing agreement ("Agreement") with_____, the undersigned hereby:

(a) acknowledges that he/she has read and is familiar with all the terms and conditions of the Agreement;

(b) assents to the execution of the Agreement and agrees to be bound by those provisions of the Agreement that relate to the undersigned in any way, including the services to be rendered thereunder by the undersigned and restrictions imposed upon the undersigned in accordance with the provisions of the Agreement;

(c) acknowledges and agrees that Company shall be under no obligation to make any payments to the undersigned or otherwise, for or in connection with this inducement and for or in connection with the services rendered by the undersigned or in connection with the rights granted to Company thereunder and the fulfillment of the undersigned's obligations pursuant to the Agreement, and that the undersigned shall look solely to _____ for payment of any sums due him in connection with his/her services under the Agreement.


_____
Artist

# CHAPTER 7

# FINANCING

A variety of methods are used to finance independent films. Some of the most common vehicles are: 1) bank loans collateralized by distributor pre-sale agreements, 2) bank loans based on the borrower's creditworthiness, and 3) equity investments by filmmaker or others.

In financing through pre-sales, a buyer pre-buys movie distribution rights for a territory(s) before the film has been produced. For example, a German distributor might buy the right to distribute a film throughout Germany. The filmmaker then uses such contracts as collateral to borrow from a bank. Some banks have offered gap and super-gap financing wherein the bank lends more than the value of the contracts. Here the bank makes a loan based on projections of how much revenue it expects the distributor to obtain from selling unsold territories.

Investors have a number of vehicles they can use to share the risk and rewards of a motion picture project. Investors can be limited partners in a partnership, passive members of a limited liability company (LLC), or shareholders in a corporation.

Loans can be either secured or unsecured. The borrower is obliged to repay the loan, even if the motion picture fails to generate revenue.

## PRESALE AGREEMENTS

If the buyer's commitment to purchase is sufficiently firm, and the buyer financially solid, a bank may be willing to lend the producer money to make a film based on the strength of the paper (i.e., the value of the contract). A contract that merely says a buyer will consider purchasing a film upon completion is not strong enough

CONTRACTS
FOR THE
FILM AND
TELEVISION
INDUSTRY

240

to lend against. Banks want to be assured that the buyer will purchase the film as long as it meets minimum technical standards, even if the film is an artistic or commercial disappointment. The bank will likely insist on a completion bond to insure that there are sufficient funds to complete production. The terms of a pre-sale agreement are similar to the terms of the acquisition agreement discussed in Chapter 9.

## INVESTOR FINANCING

Another method used to fund production is through investors. Investors usually want limited liability. That is, they don't want to be financially responsible for any over-budget costs, or liability from an injury on the set. They want their potential loss limited to the extent of their investment.

When investments are made by individuals or companies that do not manage the enterprise they are investing in, their interests are called securities. Security interests include the interests of "silent partners," limited partners, passive investors or stockholders. These individuals all share a common characteristic: they are putting money into an endeavor or business but they are not running it. State and federal security laws are designed to protect these investors by ensuring that the people managing the business (e.g., the general partners, managing members of an LLC or officers of a corporation) do not defraud investors by giving them false or misleading information about the business, or by failing to disclose information that a reasonably prudent investor would want to know before making an investment.

In a limited partnership agreement the limited partners (i.e., the investors) have limited liability and limited control over the enterprise. If they begin to manage the enterprise they will lose their limited liability. The enterprise is managed by one or more general partners. General partners (i.e., the producers) are fully liable.

Sometimes, general partners will establish a corporation that they control to serve as the general partner. This is one way to limit a producer's personal liability. In the event of a lawsuit, the corporation's assets may be vulnerable but not the assets of the producer. The courts will not consider the corporation a separate legal entity, however, if the transaction is deemed a sham designed only to insulate the owners from liability.

The courts will consider a corporation to be a separate legal entity if it operates like one. The company must be adequately capitalized and corporate formalities need to be observed. There should be no commingling of corporate and personal funds. The company must maintain separate books, records, and bank accounts, and it must hold periodic board of director meetings. Furthermore, all contracts for the making of the movie should be entered into on behalf of the corporation, and not by the producers personally.

A relatively new vehicle for producing motion pictures is the Limited Liability Company or LLC. A limited liability company combines aspects of the corporate and partnership forms of conducting business without some of the drawbacks. Like shareholders of a corporation, members of an LLC are not personally liable for the debts and obligations of the LLC. Like a partnership, an LLC may not be subject to income tax. Profits and losses can be passed through to members.

The interests of corporate shareholders, limited partners and passive members of an LLC are considered securities (investments), and their offering is subject to state and federal laws. These laws are complex and have strict requirements. A single technical violation can subject general partners to liability. Therefore, it is important that filmmakers retain an attorney with experience in both securities and entertainment law. This is an area where filmmakers should never attempt to do it themselves.

The law requires that securities be registered with state and/or federal governments. Registration is too time-consuming and expensive for most low-budget filmmakers. Filmmakers can avoid the cost and expense of securities registration only if they qualify for one or more exemptions.

State registration can be avoided by complying with the requirements for limited offering exemptions under state law. These laws are often referred to as "Blue Sky" laws. They were enacted after the stock market crash that occurred during the Great Depression. They are designed to protect buyers from being duped into buying securities that are worthless—backed by nothing more than blue sky.

The above mentioned federal and state exemptions restrict offerors in several important respects. For example, sales may be limited to thirty-five purchasers, the purchasers may need to have a pre-existing relationship with the issuer (or investment sophistication adequate to understand the transactions), the purchasers cannot purchase for resale, and no advertising or general solicitation is permitted.

A "pre-existing relationship" is defined as any relationship consisting of personal or business contacts of a nature and duration such as would enable a reasonably prudent purchaser to be aware of the character, business acumen and general business and financial circumstances of the person with whom the relationship exists.

The "offering" is usually comprised of several documents. There is a prospectus or limited offering memorandum, a proposed limited partnership agreement (or proposed LLC operating agreement), which becomes effective upon funding, and an investor questionnaire used to determine if the investor is qualified to invest. The prospectus is similar to a business plan in that it discloses the essential facts an investor needs to determine whether they want to invest in the project. The offerer of the security interests will be liable if there are any misrepresentations in the prospectus or any omissions of material facts.

Other documents may need to be filed with the federal and state government. For example, a Certificate of Limited Partnership may need to be filed with the Secretary of State to establish the partnership. To form an LLC, Articles of Organization (form LLC-1) must be filed with the Secretary of State.

In California, a notice of the transaction and Consent to Service of Process must be filed with the Department of Corporations. If a fictitious name is used for the enterprise, a DBA (Doing Business As) notice may need to be published and filed. If the transaction is subject to federal law, a Reg. D form will need to be filed with the Securities and Exchange Commission (SEC) soon after the first and last sales.

Once a corporation, limited partnership, or LLC is formed, the shareholders/partners/members will need to abide by all the state and federal laws regulating these entities as well as their own bylaws/partnership agreement/operating agreement.

CONTRACTS
FOR THE
FILM AND
TELEVISION
INDUSTRY

242

# FINDERS

Producers sometimes use intermediaries, or finders, to help them raise funds. Finders are subject to the same state and federal restrictions as the offeror. Here is a sample finder agreement.

## FINDER AGREEMENT

THIS AGREEMENT, made and entered into as of _____, by and between _____ (Finder) and _____ (Producer) with respect to the following facts:

A. Producer owns, controls or otherwise has the right to produce a screenplay tentatively entitled _____ ("Picture") written by _____.

B. Finder is a company engaged in financing and distribution activities in the motion picture business.

C. The parties want to enter an agreement whereby Finder would be encouraged to introduce Producer to third parties (herein collectively referred to as the "Financier" or "Financiers"), who may be interested in lending for, investing in, or in any other way financing all or a portion of development, production and/or distribution of the Picture.

WHEREFORE, for good and valuable consideration, the parties agree as follows:

**1. SERVICES; TERM:** Commencing on the date hereof, and continuing until the earlier of (a) termination by either party of this Agreement, or (b) the concluding of an agreement between Producer (or any designee, assignee, transferee, or other successor-in-interest of Producer in or to the Screenplay and/or Picture, collectively referred to hereinafter as "Producer") and a Financier, Finder shall use its best efforts to introduce Producer to parties who may be interested in financing, investing or lending money with respect to the production of the Picture or otherwise in becoming a Financier. The foregoing period of time is hereinafter referred to as the "Term."

**2. COMPENSATION:** If at any time during the Term or any time thereafter, Producer enters into any agreement with any Financier to invest in, lend for, or finance production and/or distribution of the Picture, then Finder shall receive an amount equal to five percent of the amount of any funds, credits or other consideration paid or lent by Financiers to Producer and used by Producer in the development and Production of the Picture, provided, that the amounts paid to Finder shall not exceed a total of $_____. Moreover, if Finder obtains ninety percent (90%) or more of the total financing needed to produce the Picture, _____ (Finder) shall receive "Executive Producer" credit. Finder shall receive his/her Commission when Producer has the right to use the amounts provided by financier(s).

**3. NO OBLIGATION:** Nothing in this agreement shall obligate Producer to enter into an agreement with any Financiers.

**4. NO SALE OF SECURITIES:** Finder agrees not to sell or offer to sell securities related to investing in the development and/or production of the Picture. Finder agrees to indemnify and hold Producer harmless from all damage and expense (including reasonable attorneys' fees) upon a breach or claim of breach of this provision.

**5. RELATIONSHIP OF THE PARTIES:** Finder is an independent contractor and shall not act as an employee, agent or broker of Producer.

**6. FINDER'S REPRESENTATIONS AND WARRANTIES:**

Finder represents and warrants to Producer that the following statements are true and correct in all respects:

A. Finder is in the business of arranging financing and international distribution of motion pictures, has substantial experience in said business, is not insolvent or in any danger of insolvency or bankruptcy, and is not in dissolution proceedings.

B. Finder represents and warrants to Producer that Finder has the full and complete authority to enter into this agreement, and that there is no outstanding claim or litigation pending against Finder.

If Finder breaches any of its warranties and representations, or otherwise breaches this agreement, Producer, in addition to its other equitable and legal remedies, may rescind this agreement and recover any reasonable amounts expended by Producer in developing or exploiting this property with Finder, and reasonable attorney fees. Finder shall at all times indemnify and hold Producer, its licensees, assignees, officers, employees and agents harmless against and from any and all claims, damages, liabilities cost and expenses, including reasonable attorney fees arising out of any breach or alleged breach by Finder of any of representation, warranty or other provision hereof.

**7. ADDITIONAL DOCUMENTS:** Finder agrees to execute, acknowledge and deliver to Producer and to procure the execution, acknowledgment and delivery to Producer of any additional documents or instruments which Producer may reasonably require to fully effectuate and carry out the intent and purposes of this agreement.

**8. ARBITRATION:** Any controversy or claim arising out of or relating to this Agreement or the validity, construction or performance of this Agreement or the breach thereof, shall be resolved by arbitration according to the rules and procedures of the American Arbitration Association, as they may be amended. Such rules and procedures are incorporated herein and made a part of this Agreement by reference. The parties agree that they will abide by and perform any award rendered in any such arbitration and that any court having jurisdiction may issue a judgment based upon the award. Moreover, the prevailing party shall be entitled to reimbursement of reasonable attorney fees and costs.

**9. ASSIGNMENT:** Finder shall not have the right to assign this agreement or any part hereof.

**10. SECTION HEADINGS:** The headings of paragraphs, sections and other subdivisions of this agreement are for convenient reference only. They shall not be used in any way to govern, limit, modify, construe this agreement or any part or provision thereof or otherwise be given any legal effect.

CONTRACTS
FOR THE
FILM AND
TELEVISION
INDUSTRY

244

**11. ENTIRE AGREEMENT:** This agreement contains the full and complete understanding and agreement between the parties with respect to the within subject matter, and supersedes all other agreements between the parties whether written or oral relating thereto, and may not be modified or amended except by written instrument executed by both of the parties hereto. This agreement shall in all respects be subject to the laws of the State of _____ applicable to agreements executed and wholly performed within such State.

AGREED TO AND ACCEPTED:


_____

"Finder"



_____

"Producer"

Loans can be secured or unsecured. A secured loan is supported or backed by security or collateral. When one takes out a car or home loan, the loan is often secured by the car or home. If the person who takes out the loan (the debtor) fails to pay back the loan, the creditor may take legal action to have the collateral sold and the proceeds applied to repay the loan.

An unsecured loan has no particular property backing the loan. Credit card debt and loans from family or friends are often unsecured. If a debtor defaults on an unsecured loan, the creditor can sue for repayment and force the sale of the debtor's property to repay the loan. If the debtor has many debts, however, the sale of the property may not be sufficient to satisfy all the creditors. In such a case, the creditors may end up receiving only a small portion of the money owed to them. Thus, a secured creditor is in a much stronger position to receive repayment. In the event of a default, designated property (the secured property) will be sold and all the proceeds will be applied first to repay the secured creditor's debt. Unsecured creditors will have to share whatever is left over.

The advantage of a loan, from a legal point of view, is that the transaction can be structured in a simple and inexpensive manner. A simple promissory note, such as the ones in this chapter, can be used. Since a loan is a debt, and not a security, state and federal security laws do not apply. Thus, there is no need to prepare a prospectus (or limited offering memorandum) or comply with the complex laws dealing with the issuance of securities. Keep in mind that if the agreement between the parties is labeled a "loan," but in reality the money is being given as an investment, then the courts will likely view the transaction as an investment. Giving a creditor a "piece of the back-end," or otherwise giving the creditor some equity in the project, may result in the transaction being characterized as an equity investment.

The difference between a loan and an investment has to do with risk. With a loan, the principal, and whatever interest is charged, must be repaid regardless of whether the film is a flop or a hit. The creditor does not share in the upside of a hit project. If the project is a flop, the creditor is still entitled to be repaid his money. In other words, the creditor does not share in the risk of the endeavor. Of course, there is some risk with a loan because loans may not be repaid, especially unsecured loans. That risk is minimal, however, compared to the risk taken by an investor.

An investor shares in both the potential rewards as well as the risks of failure. If the movie is a hit, the investor is entitled to receive his investment back and share in the proceeds. Of course, if the movie is a flop, the investor may lose his entire investment. The producer has no obligation to repay the investor his loss.

## PROMISSORY NOTES

A promissory note is used when one party borrows money from another. The borrower agrees to repay the loan according to the terms of the promissory note. If the note is unsecured, there is no collateral other than the promise of the borrower to pay back the loan.

CONTRACTS
FOR THE
FILM AND
TELEVISION
INDUSTRY

246

As a debt instrument, a promissory note is not a security. The borrower is entitled to a return of his money plus interest. If the movie is a hit, the borrower just gets back his loan plus interest. Because loans to producers are risky, it can be difficult to finance a motion picture on the basis of a loan unless there is some collateral backing the loan. Such collateral could be real estate, stocks or another asset that is pledged or mortgaged. This will entitle the borrower to collect against the asset if the loan is not repaid.

Excessive interest may violate various usury laws. The legal rate of interest is currently ten percent per year. Banks and certain financial institutions are allowed to charge a higher rate of interest.

# PROMISSORY NOTE

Date: _____      $_____ (Loan Amount)

**FOR GOOD AND VALUABLE CONSIDERATION**, receipt of which is hereby acknowledged, I, _____, ("Payor") for myself individually promise to pay to _____ ("Payee") or order, at _____, or at such other place as a Payee may designate, the sum of _____ dollars ($_____) plus interest at the rate of _____ percent per annum payable at a minimum of _____ dollars per year. In any given month, a minimum of _____ dollars shall be paid in payments of no more than two payments per month in the amount of no less than _____dollars per payment. Once _____ dollars has been paid in any given year, no additional payments need be paid during the course of that calendar year. There is no penalty for making additional payments.

If the payor fails to make payments as provided, then payee shall provide written notice to Payor who shall have ten (10) days from the date of such notice to cure the default.

Payments hereunder shall continue until the total principal amount and any interest due is paid.

The obligation to pay money hereunder shall be secured by all of my right, title and interest in _____ in which I have any interest.

This promissory note is executed in connection with an agreement dated _____.

This promissory note is payable in lawful money of the United States of America. Should any action be commenced to enforce the terms hereof, such shall be by arbitration before a single arbitrator in _____ (City), _____ (State), pursuant to the rules of the American Arbitration Association. The prevailing party shall be entitled to recover all reasonable attorneys' fees and costs incurred. Service on Payor can be by any method approved by the Code of Civil Procedure of the State of _____ and by mailing any Demand for Arbitration to Payor at _____ or any update of those addresses supplied to Payee by Payor. Payor will not defend such arbitration on any grounds other than whether Payor has been fully credited for the payments which Payor has made to Payee.

(Payor)

_____

CONTRACTS
FOR THE
FILM AND
TELEVISION
INDUSTRY

248

# NOTES WITH A GUARANTEE

Repayment of this promissory note is guaranteed by another person or company. If the borrower fails to repay the loan, the lender can proceed against the guarantor for repayment.

## PROMISSORY NOTE WITH GUARANTEE

_____ (City), _____ (State)

For value received, _____ (Maker) of _____ (Maker Address), herein referred to as Maker, promises to pay to the order of _____ (Lender) of _____ (Lender Address), his/her successors and assigns, herein referred to as Holder, the sum of _____ (Total Amount) in installments as follows: $_____ (First Installment Amount) by _____ (Due date for first installment), _____ (Installment amount), per month to be applied against the remaining balance of $_____ commencing with the second payment of _____, on, the third payment of $_____ on _____, the fourth payment of $_____ on _____ and a fifth payment of $_____ on _____, together with a delinquency charge on each installment in default for ten days in an amount equal to ten percent (10%) of such installment but not less than ten dollars ($10.00). The obligation to make these payments shall be discharged when they are received by Holder or his attorney.

1.   Acceleration of Maturity: In the event of default in the payment of any of the installments or interest when due as herein provided, time being of the essence hereof, Holder may without notice or demand declare the entire principal sum then unpaid immediately due and payable. Further, if Maker should at any time fail in business or become insolvent, or commit an act of bankruptcy, or if any writ of execution, garnishment, attachment or other legal process is issued against any deposit account or other property of Maker, or if any assessment for taxes against Maker, other than taxes on real property, is made by the federal or state government, or any department thereof, or if Maker fails to notify Holder of any material change in his financial condition, all of the obligations of Maker shall, at the option of Holder, become due and payable immediately without demand or notice.

2.   Any controversy or claim arising out of or relating to this agreement or any breach thereof shall be settled by arbitration in accordance with the Rules of the American Arbitration Association for expedited arbitration before an arbitrator; and judgment upon the award rendered by the arbitrators may be entered in any court having jurisdiction thereof. The prevailing party shall be entitled to reimbursement for costs and reasonable attorney's fees. The determination of the arbitrator in such proceeding shall be final, binding and non-appealable. This agreement is entered into, and shall be construed and interpreted in accordance with the laws of the State of _____.

3.   Collection Costs: Maker shall pay a reasonable collection charge should this note be referred to a collection agency.

4.   Waiver of Rights by Maker: Maker hereby waives presentment, demand, protest, notice of dishonor and/or protest and notice of non-payment.

**5.** Interest on Unpaid Amounts: All sums remaining unpaid on the agreed or accelerated date of maturity of the last installment shall thereafter bear interest at the rate of ten percent per year.

In Witness whereof, this note and agreement has been executed at _____ (City), _____ (State) on _____ (Date of execution).

_____
Maker

## GUARANTEE

_____, "Guarantor" hereby guarantees payment of the above. Guarantor agrees that the Holder may proceed against Guarantor directly and independently of the borrower, and that the cessation of the liability of the Maker for any reason other than full payment, or any extension, renewal, forbearance, change of rate of interest, or acceptance, release, or substitution of security, or any impairment or suspension of the Holder's remedies or rights against the Maker, shall not in any way affect the liability of Guarantor.

Dated: _____

GUARANTOR

_____

STATE OF                          )
                                 ) ss.:
COUNTY OF                         )

On the _____ day of _____, 199__, before me personally came _____ to me known and known to be the individual described in and who executed the foregoing instrument, and he/she did duly acknowledge to me that he/she executed the same.

_____
Notary Public

# CHAPTER 8

# PRODUCTION

Before going into production, a producer will need to negotiate a number of important agreements in order to fully secure all rights to his motion picture. Work-for-hire agreements must be in writing and signed by both parties **before** work commences in order for the producer to own the initial copyright to the work.

If a producer does not adequately secure the necessary rights to his picture, and all its component parts (e.g., underlying script, music, and stock footage), the producer will not have a clean "chain of title." Without proper documentation showing a clean chain of title, the producer will not be able to secure Errors & Omissions (E&O) insurance. Most distributors will decline to distribute a picture without such insurance. No distributor wants to acquire distribution rights to a picture, expend funds to market it, and then find himself a defendant in a lawsuit brought by a third party. In some circumstances, the third party may be able to obtain an injunction halting distribution of the motion picture.

There are three main areas of concern in regard to securing a clean chain of title. First, depiction releases should be obtained from all actors appearing in the picture. Second, written licenses should be secured for any copyrightable matter incorporated in the picture (e.g., music, stock footage). Third, work-for-hire agreements should be signed before work begins for anyone making a creative contribution to the picture (e.g., editor, cinematographer). In prior chapters we covered the various contracts used to acquire rights from actors, writers, directors and composers. In this chapter, we will cover the agreements needed to secure rights from producers, crew members, special effects artists and real property owners.

CONTRACTS
FOR THE
FILM AND
TELEVISION
INDUSTRY

252

# PRODUCTION SERVICES

Sometimes a financier desires to contract with another company to provide most or all of the production services necessary to produce a motion picture. By contracting with another company, the financier may be seeking to protect itself from any liability arising from the production. Since the production services company is usually a separate legal entity, the financier should not be liable if, for instance, an actor is hurt on the set. After the motion picture has been produced, the agreement often provides that all rights to the motion picture are assigned to the financier.

While the financing company may want to insulate itself from liability, it may well want to maintain tight fiscal and creative control over the production. It is not unusual for the financier to insist that it must approve the budget, cash flow schedule and all major creative decisions. Moreover, the financier may have takeover rights which permit it to take over production of the motion picture under certain conditions.

Here is an agreement between two companies, one which provided financing, the other which supervised the logistics of production. In this case, the service company is being used to insulate the financing company from liability. The service company is only entitled to be reimbursed the cost of production.

# PRODUCTION SERVICES AGREEMENT

THIS PRODUCTION SERVICES AGREEMENT is entered into as of _____, between _____, a _____ (State of Incorporation) corporation ("Financier") and _____, a _____(State of Incorporation) corporation ("Service Company"), and is made with reference to the following facts.

WHEREAS, Financier owns the right to produce and exploit a theatrical motion picture (the "Picture") based on the original screenplay entitled "_____" ("Screenplay") written by _____; and

WHEREAS, Financier has requested Service Company to supervise the production of the Screenplay in the State of _____; and

WHEREAS, to that end, Service Company has arranged for the directing services of _____, and the producing services of _____, all in accordance with a mutually approved budget and a production schedule which have been previously approved by Financier and Service Company; and

WHEREAS, Financier desires to finance and arrange for the production of the Picture, and Service Company desires to furnish the services set forth herein on the terms and conditions hereinafter set forth.

NOW, THEREFORE, in consideration of the promises and for other good and valuable consideration, receipt of which is hereby acknowledged, the parties hereto agree as follows:

## 1. Production of the Picture

(a) Subject to the terms and conditions hereinafter set forth, Financier agrees to furnish or cause a third party to furnish to Service Company, on a mutually approved cash flow schedule ("Cash Flow Schedule"), the amount of financing which Service Company represents will be required to finance the production of the Picture, and Service Company shall use all sums advanced hereunder for the sole purpose of furnishing the production services for the Picture in accordance with the approved screenplay, budget and production schedule, subject only to deviations therefrom caused by the exigencies of production and approved in writing by Financier. All obligations of Financier shall be subject to Financier first obtaining a completion bond from a reputable company, which in form and substance shall be subject to Financier's approval. All sums advanced hereunder shall be deposited in a production account that has been designated, approved and controlled by Financier, and until such funds have been expended in the production of the Picture such funds shall be and remain the sole and exclusive property of Financier.

(b) Delivery shall be complete when Service Company delivers to Financier in accordance with this Agreement all physical elements of the Picture, and which Financier reasonably requires to cause the Picture to be distributed throughout the world.

(c) Financier shall have the right of designation and approval in relation to all business, creative and other elements, including without limitation, cast, director, production personnel, music, locations, film laboratories, sound stages, post production facilities and all expenditures and other production matters in connection with the Picture, subject only to third party approvals and controls which are consented to by Financier and are contained in said third parties' written contract.

CONTRACTS
FOR THE
FILM AND
TELEVISION
INDUSTRY

254

(d) Service Company shall perform all of its obligations hereunder to the best of its ability and in a workmanlike manner. Upon the first to occur of: (i) delivery of the Picture hereunder, (ii) Financier's exercise of takeover rights hereinafter set forth, or (iii) Financier's request following completion of the Picture, Service Company shall irrevocably and without further action assign and transfer to Financier all of Service Company's rights in and to all past, present and future "elements" of the Picture and all rights and benefits actually acquired by Service Company pursuant to any agreements with third parties in a form substantially as set forth in Exhibit "A" annexed hereto and made a part hereof. Service Company shall execute Exhibit "A" upon execution of this Agreement and hereby authorizes Financier to date it upon the occurrence of any of the foregoing events. As used herein, the term "elements" shall include, without limitation, all literary material written for the Picture, if any, acquired by Service Company, all stills, artwork and designs used in connection with the Picture, all film clips, recordings, trailers, sound tracks, and all other tangible and intangible property relating to the Picture, and all rights in and to the foregoing, exercisable throughout the universe, in perpetuity, and all subsidiary, ancillary and related rights, performing rights, publishing rights, merchandising and commercial tie-up rights, and the right to use the names, likenesses, and voices of all persons rendering services in connection with the Picture. Service Company shall include in its contracts with third parties engaged to render services on the Picture a provision that the results and proceeds of all the services rendered in connection with the Picture shall upon rendition automatically be the sole property of Service Company. Service Company's rights under any Agreement in connection with the Picture shall be freely assignable and upon Financier's request, Service Company agrees to execute, acknowledge and deliver such assignments and other documents and instruments as may be necessary or appropriate to evidence Financier's acquisition of rights hereunder. The Picture shall contain such production or presentation or release credit to Financier as Financier shall determine. Additionally, the end titles shall contain a copyright notice in the following form: "Copyright _____ (Copyright year), _____ (Copyright Holder). All rights reserved", or such other notice as Financier shall designate.

(e) Upon Financier's acquisition of all right, title and interest in and to the Picture as provided above, Financier shall assume, or cause the distributor of the Picture to contractually adhere to, the executory obligations of all contracts undertaken by Service Company in the normal course of business to produce the Picture.

(f) If Service Company shall fail to execute any instrument or document which Financier may reasonably require to implement any term hereof or to perfect its rights hereunder, Financier shall have the right to execute such document or instrument on Service Company's behalf, such right being an irrevocable power coupled with an interest.

**2. Production Contracts.** All contracts for personnel, studio hire, purchase of goods and services, laboratory work and all other licenses, contracts and obligations in connection with the production of the Picture by Service Company, shall be made and entered into by Service Company in its own name as principal and not as agent for Financier and no obligations whatsoever shall be imposed upon Financier thereunder. All such contracts or undertakings shall be consistent with the provisions of this Agreement and industry custom and practice. Such contracts and undertakings shall not be terminated, canceled, modified or rescinded in any manner which would or might prejudice the rights of Financier hereunder. All such contracts shall be assignable to Financier without restriction. Service Company shall have all responsibilities of an employer with respect to those personnel locally engaged by Service Company in the United States, including those arising under any present or future legal requirements relating to Workers' Compensation, insurance, social security, tax withholding, pension, health and welfare plans under any legal requirements or any applicable collective bargaining agreement, if any, although upon delivery of the Picture and completion of all obligations required hereunder of Service Company, Financier shall assume or cause the distributor of the Picture to assume such obligations and hold Service Company harmless therefrom. Service Company shall use due care in the selection and purchase of any items to be used in connection with the production of the Picture and shall assign Financier on demand all rights which Service Company shall obtain, by warranty and otherwise, from the supplier of such items.

**3. Insurance.** Service Company shall carry and pay for appropriate insurance consistent with the requirements of Financier to cover all customary risks in connection with the performance of its obligations hereunder only with respect to those persons engaged in the United States, including without limitation, public liability, cast, and Workers' Compensation, which insurance shall specifically name Financier as an insured party (and beneficiary), and (as a condition to any payment hereunder) shall furnish Financier with certificates of insurance stating and certifying the amount and type of insurance and that Financier is an insured party thereunder and with copies of all said policies.

**4. Contract Price.** Except as provided in Paragraph 15 below, on the condition that Service Company fully and completely performs all of its obligations hereunder, Financier shall pay Service Company for services rendered an amount equal to financing required to produce and deliver the Picture hereunder.

**5. Production Schedule.** It is of the essence of this Agreement that Service Company furnish the production services respecting services and the Picture and all other elements required hereunder in accordance with the mutually approved production schedule ("Production Schedule").

**6. Distribution.** The Picture shall be distributed in such manner as Financier shall determine in its sole discretion.

**7. Service Company Representations and Warranties.** Service Company hereby represents, warrants and agrees as follows:

(a) Service Company is a corporation, duly organized and existing under the laws of the State of\_\_\_\_\_, and has the right to grant all rights granted herein, and is free to enter into and fully perform this Agreement.

(b) No liens, encumbrances, attachments or other matters constituting or possibly constituting any impediment to the clear marketable title and unrestricted commercial exploitation or disposition of the Picture or any rights therein or pertaining thereto shall be permitted to occur which shall or may arise by reason of any acts, omissions or activities of Service Company in connection with the performance or enforcement of this Agreement, or attachments by Service Company in connection with any litigation which Service Company shall be plaintiff against Financier or any other party whatsoever. Service Company will not create, make, cause or permit any lien, encumbrance, pledge (except as may be required by a film processing laboratory), hypothecation or assignment of or claim against the Picture, or any rights therein, or upon the copyrights thereof,

CONTRACTS
FOR THE
FILM AND
TELEVISION
INDUSTRY

256

or upon the literary material upon which the Picture is based, or the release, distribution, exploitation or exhibition rights therein, or upon any proceeds therefrom or any other rights, interests or property therein or pertaining thereto.

(c) Service Company shall at all times indemnify, defend, and hold harmless Financier, and the partners, officers, directors, employees, licensees, shareholders, subsidiaries, and agents of each of the foregoing, and their heirs, executors, administrators, successors and assigns, from and against any and all claims, damages, liabilities, actions, causes of action, costs and expenses, including reasonable attorneys' fees, judgments, penalties of any kind or nature whatsoever arising out of (i) Service Company's production and delivery of the Picture; (ii) any act or omission by Service Company or any person whose services or facilities shall be furnished by Service Company in connection with the Picture; and (iii) any breach by Service Company of any representation, warranty or agreement made by Service Company hereunder.

**8. Good Faith Assurance.** Neither party has nor will without the other's prior written consent: (i) enter into any agreement, commitment or other arrangement, grant any rights or do any act or thing which could or might prevent or interfere with the production and completion of the Picture or prevent or impede the performance of all of the respective party's obligations hereunder; (ii) do or fail to do any act which might or could interfere with or otherwise prevent such party from fully complying with all of the terms hereof; or (iii) engage in any conduct inconsistent with this Agreement or the other party's rights hereunder. The foregoing shall not be interpreted as impairing or preventing Financier's absolute right to abandon production of the Picture at anytime and/or to refrain from or cause the termination of the distribution of the Picture, all as provided in greater detail in Paragraph 15 below.

**9. Default.** Service Company specifically waives all rights and remedies, if available to Service Company, of rescission, injunction, restraint and specific performance and agrees in this regard that it shall have no right to revoke, terminate or rescind any rights acquired by Financier hereunder nor to restrain production, completion or distribution of the Picture and shall have no right to compel specific performance of any of Financier's obligations hereunder. Service Company understands and agrees that its sole remedy hereunder shall be for monetary damages, if any, in the event of breach by Financier.

**10. Security Interest.** As security for the delivery of the Picture hereunder, Service Company hereby mortgages, sells, assigns, pledges, hypothecates, and sets over to Financier as collateral all of Service Company's right, title and interest, if any, in and to the following:

(a) The Picture, in whatever form it may now exist or hereafter exist, including the negative, sound material and copyright thereto.

(b) The literary, dramatic and music material upon which the Picture is based or to be based, including without limitation, the Screenplay and all of Service Company's right, title and interest in and to the copyrights to the foregoing.

(c) All of Service Company's right, title and interest in and to any properties or things of value pertaining to rights, contract rights, claims, properties and material set forth in (a) and (b) above, whether now in existence or hereafter acquired by Service Company.

(d) Any other rights Service Company may have in or relating to the Picture.

It is intended that the security granted above is and shall be a "security interest" as such term is defined in the Uniform Commercial Code and Service Company hereby agrees to execute and deliver a financing statement in form and substance which complies with the Uniform Commercial Code of any and all states which Financier may hereafter require. Service Company hereby authorizes Financier or its representative to file such financing statement(s) and to execute any continuation statements as well as to perform any and all other acts Financier may deem appropriate to perfect and continue Financier's security interest in the collateral. Service Company warrants and represents that there shall be no lien or charge or encumbrance in whole or in part upon the collateral (other than a customary laboratory lien for processing services, a lien to secure obligations under a Collective Bargaining Agreement) or proceeds derived therefrom which are equal or superior to the lien and security interest above granted and that Financier's security interest shall at all times be and remain a first and continuing lien and security interest on the collateral until Financier is repaid the entire sum herein elsewhere provided. Service Company shall at all times keep Financier advised as to the location of all collateral herein pledged.

**11. Takeover Rights.** At any time after the occurrence of any of the events hereinafter set forth, Financier shall have the right, to be exercised in its sole and exclusive discretion, to either issue directions and instructions regarding production of the Picture, or to take over production of the Picture. The events entitling Financier to exercise the aforesaid rights shall be the following:

(a) If the projected cost of production in Financier's good faith judgment reasonably appears to exceed the approved budget by 5% (excluding over budget costs that are reimbursed by insurance, or caused by force majeure or a direct consequence of a third party breach of contract that is not induced or encouraged by Service Company);

(b) An event which might permit a takeover by the company issuing the completion bond;

(c) Service Company fails to substantially carry out any instructions which Financier may issue to Service Company in keeping herewith; or

(d) Service Company breaches any of the material terms and conditions hereof.

If Financier exercises its right to issue directions and instruction in keeping with the foregoing, Service Company shall fully and faithfully abide by and follow all such instructions issued in connection with the production of the Picture and Service Company shall have no further creative approval and/or other production rights concerning production, post-production and/or distribution of the Picture. If Financier exercises its takeover rights as aforesaid, Service Company shall immediately do all that is necessary to place at Financier's disposal and under Financier's control, all persons, production funds and other items of and concerning production of the Picture. For such purpose, Service Company hereby irrevocably constitutes and appoints Financier as Service Company's attorney-in-fact with full power of substitution and revocation, to act in Service Company's name and stead to make withdrawals from any production account or other bank

CONTRACTS
FOR THE
FILM AND
TELEVISION
INDUSTRY

258

accounts relating to the Picture and to expend funds from such account and to further carry out and fully perform, at Financier's discretion, any and all agreements or to modify, amend, compromise or terminate any such contract and to further engage or discharge personnel and to acquire, release and dispose of any equipment, real or other property relating to the Picture and to endorse, collect and deposit any checks or other instruments payable to Service Company as a result of the Picture and in general to do any and all acts which Service Company could have otherwise have done had Financier not exercised its takeover rights. Service Company specifically acknowledges that if Financier takes over the Picture in keeping with the foregoing, Financier may abandon the Picture or complete production as Financier may at such time determine. Notwithstanding the foregoing to the contrary, Financier's rights concerning production of the Picture shall be subject to creative and other approvals and controls that are contained in those agreements between Service Company and third parties that were entered with Financier's knowledge which are not terminated by Financier.

**12. Force Majeure.** The date for performance of either party's obligations hereunder shall be postponed to the extent any event of force majeure delays the commencement of production or the performance of the obligations of either party hereunder.

**13. Status of Parties.** The parties hereto expressly agree, each for the other, that the relationship between them hereunder is that of two principals dealing with each other as independent contractors for the sole and specific purpose that Service Company shall produce and deliver the Picture, subject to the terms and conditions of this Agreement. At no time, past, present or future, shall the relationship of the parties herein be deemed or intended to constitute a relationship with the characteristics of an agency, partnership, joint venture, or of a collaboration for the purposes of sharing any profits or ownership in common. Neither party shall have the right, power or authority at any time to act on behalf of, or represent, the other party, but each party hereto shall be separately and entirely liable for its own respective debts in all respects. This Agreement is not for the benefit of any person who is not a party signatory hereto or specifically named as a beneficiary herein. Financier may assign or license its rights hereunder in whole or in part to any person, firm or corporation. Except for assignment to Financier, Service Company may not assign or license any of its rights or obligations hereunder, or under any agreement entered into by Service Company with any third party. Subject to the foregoing, the provisions hereof shall be binding upon and inure to the benefit of the parties hereto and their respective heirs, personal representatives, administrators, executors, successors and assigns, and any past, present or future parent, subsidiary or affiliate company.

**14. Notices.** Any and all notices, communications and demands required or desired to be given hereunder by either party hereto shall be in writing and shall be validly given or made if served either personally or if deposited in the United States mail, certified or registered, postage prepaid, return receipt requested. If such notice or demand be served personally, service shall be conclusively deemed made at the time of such personal service. If such notice or demand be served by registered or certified mail in the manner herein provided, service shall be conclusively deemed made two business days after the deposit thereof in the United States mail addressed to the party to whom such notice or demand is to be given as hereinafter set forth:

Financier: _____
          (Financier)

         _____
          (Address)

         _____

Service Company: _____
          (Service Company)

         _____
          (Address)

         _____

Any party hereto may change its address for the purpose of receiving notices or demands as herein provided by a written notice given in the manner aforesaid to the other party hereto, which notice of change of address shall not become effective, however, until the actual receipt thereof by the other party.

**15. Abandonment.** Financier shall have no obligation to finance, release, broadcast, distribute, complete production of, not abandon or otherwise exploit the Picture, provided Financier indemnifies Service Company against any loss from contracts entered into with Financier's prior consent and knowledge.

**16. Miscellaneous.**

(a) This Agreement shall be construed, interpreted and enforced in accordance with and shall be governed by the laws of the State of _____ applicable to agreements entered into and wholly to be performed therein. In the event of any conflict between any provisions hereof and any applicable laws to the contrary, the latter shall prevail, but this Agreement shall be deemed modified only to the extent necessary to remove such conflicts.

(b) Each of the parties hereto shall execute and deliver any and all additional documents, and shall do any and all acts and things reasonably required in connection with the performance of the obligations undertaken hereunder and to effectuate the extent of the parties thereto.

(c) This Agreement constitutes the entire agreement of the parties hereto and supersedes all oral and written agreements and understandings made or entered into by the parties hereto prior to the date hereof. No amendment, change or modification of this Agreement shall be valid unless it is made in writing and signed by both parties hereto, and any waiver of a failure to perform or breach shall not operate to waive any subsequent failure to perform or breach.

(d) The captions appearing at the commencement of the paragraphs hereof are descriptive only and for convenience in reference to this Agreement and should there be any conflict between any such heading and the paragraph at the head of which it appears, the paragraph thereof and not such heading shall control and govern in the construction of this Agreement.

CONTRACTS
FOR THE
FILM AND
TELEVISION
INDUSTRY

260

IN WITNESS WHEREOF, the parties hereto have executed this Agreement as of the date and year first above written.

FINANCIER:


By:_____
    (Financier Representative)


Service Company:



By:_____
    (Service Company Representative)

## EXHIBIT A
## CERTIFICATE OF AUTHORSHIP

The undersigned hereby certifies and agrees that for one dollar ($1.00) and other good and valuable consideration, receipt of which is hereby acknowledged, _____ (Service Company) ("Producer") has employed my services as a writer in connection with a proposed motion picture entitled, _____ (the "Picture"), and that except for existing literary material which Producer instructs me to use as a basis for writing hereunder, all literary material of whatever kind or nature written or to be written, furnished or to be furnished, by me as well as all of the results and proceeds of my writing services in connection with the Picture (all such literary material, and all such results and proceeds thereof being referred to collectively herein as the "Material") submitted and to be submitted by me in connection with the Picture was and/or will be solely written and/or created by me as original material and that for copyright purposes, the Material shall be written and/or created by me as a work-made-for-hire, specially ordered or commissioned by Producer for use as part of a motion picture within the meaning of the 1976 Copyright Act, and Producer shall be deemed the sole author of the Material and owner of all rights of every kind or nature, whether now known or hereafter devised (including, but not limited to, all copyrights and extensions and renewals of copyrights) in and to the Material, as well as the right to make such changes in the Material and such uses of the Material, throughout the Universe, as Producer may from time to time determine as such author.

I warrant and represent that I have the right to execute this document and, except to the extent that it is based upon material assigned to me by Producer to be used as the basis therefor, that the Material is or shall be original with me, does not and shall not defame or disparage any person or entity or infringe upon or violate the rights of privacy, publicity or any other rights of any kind or nature whatsoever of any person or entity and is not the subject of any litigation or of any claim that might give rise to litigation. I acknowledge that I have been fully compensated for all services performed in connection with the Picture, and that there are no further obligations owed to me by Producer or its assignees. I shall defend (with counsel acceptable to Producer), indemnify and hold harmless Producer, any corporations comprising Producer, its and their employees, officers, agents, assigns and licensees from and against any and all liability, claims, costs, damages and expenses (including reasonable attorneys' fees and court costs) arising out of or in connection with a breach of the foregoing covenants, warranties and representations.

I agree to execute any documents and to do any other acts as may be reasonably required by Producer or its assignees or licensees to further evidence or effectuate Producer's rights as set forth in this Certificate of Authorship. Upon my failure promptly to do so, I hereby appoint Producer as my attorney-in-fact for such purposes (it being acknowledged that such appointment is irrevocable and coupled with an interest) with full power of substitution and delegation.

I further acknowledge that (i) in the event of any breach hereunder by Producer, I will be limited to my remedy at law for damages, if any, and will not have the right to terminate or rescind this Certificate or to enjoin the distribution, advertising or exploitation of the Picture, (ii) nothing herein shall obligate Producer to use my services or the results of proceeds thereof in the Picture or to produce, advertise or distribute the Picture, (iii) this Certificate shall be

CONTRACTS
FOR THE
FILM AND
TELEVISION
INDUSTRY

262

governed by the laws of the State of _____ applicable to agreements executed and to be performed entirely therein, and (iv) this Certificate constitutes the entire agreement between the parties to the within subject matter and cannot be modified except by a written instrument signed by the parties hereto.

I hereby waive all rights of "droit moral" or so-called "moral rights of authors" or any similar rights or principles of law which I may now or later have in the Material or to my services.

Producer's rights with respect to the Material and/or my services are irrevocable and may be freely assigned and licensed and its rights shall be binding upon me and inure to the benefit of any such assignee or licensee.

I have caused this document to be executed on _____.

_____

Signature

STATE OF                               )
                                       ) ss:
COUNTY OF                              )

On the___day of _____, 19__, before me personally came _____ to me known and known to be the individual described in and who executed the foregoing instrument, and he/she did duly acknowledge to me that he/she executed the same.

_____

Notary Public

Casting directors help producers select actors for their productions. Casting directors often know the interests and availability of name-actors, and they can screen through numerous candidates for the lesser roles. An experienced casting director may have better access to agents and actors than a fledgling producer.

The following casting director agreement is structured so as to hire a casting director as an independent contractor. It can be difficult to determine in many instances whether a casting director should be categorized as an independent contractor or as an employee. While the hiring party may prefer to hire the casting director as an independent contractor, and thus avoid calculating and withholding taxes, the IRS prefers to categorize a hired party as an employee. Recently the IRS has begun cracking down on production companies that improperly pay employees as independent contractors. Employers can be subject to substantial tax penalties.

The more control the production company exercises over how the casting director does his job, the more likely the casting director will be considered an employee. If the casting director works out of his own office, supplies tools of the trade, and/or is incorporated, the IRS is more likely to accept his classification as an independent contractor.

## CASTING DIRECTOR EMPLOYMENT AGREEMENT
## (Independent Contractor)

This Agreement ("Agreement") is made as of this the _____ (Date of Agreement), by and between _____ ("Production Company") whose offices are located at _____ and _____ ("Contractor") whose offices are located at _____.

**1. SERVICES & TERM:** The Production Company shall employ Contractor as Casting Director for the motion picture tentatively entitled "_____" (hereinafter referred to as "Picture"). Contractor's services shall include casting all speaking roles (approximately 20 roles) and shall commence within two (2) weeks either side of the first above stated date and shall continue for a maximum of _____ consecutive weeks. Contractor's services will be non-exclusive to the Production Company (provided that any services she may perform for third parties shall not interfere in a material manner with the services required hereunder) until completion of all required services in connection with casting and all customary follow-up services, including without limitation documentation of the deals made as approved by the Production Company. If the services of Contractor are required beyond _____ weeks, Contractor be paid additional compensation at the rate of $_____ per week.

Contractor is authorized to utilize the services of assistants in providing casting services for the Picture. The assistants shall be employed during the same time and for the same length of time as Contractor.

**2. STATUS OF PARTIES:** It is expressly acknowledged by the parties hereto that Contractor is an "independent contractor" and nothing in this Agreement is intended or shall be construed to create with Production Company an employer/

CONTRACTS
FOR THE
FILM AND
TELEVISION
INDUSTRY

264

employee relationship, a joint venture relationship, or a lease or landlord/tenant relationship, or to allow Production Company to exercise control or direction over the manner or method by which Contractor performs her services which are the subject matter of this Agreement; provided always that the services to be provided hereunder by Contractor shall be provided in a manner consistent with professional standards governing such services and the provisions of this Agreement. Contractor understands and agrees that Production Company will not withhold on behalf of Contractor pursuant to this Agreement any sums for income tax, unemployment insurance, social security, or any other withholding pursuant to any law or requirement of any governmental body relating to Contractor or make available to Contractor any of the benefits afforded to employees of Production Company and that all such payments, withholding, and benefits, if any, are the sole responsibility of Contractor. In the event the Internal Revenue Service or any other governmental agency should question or challenge the independent contractor status of Contractor, Production Company shall have the right to participate in any discussion or negotiation occurring with such agency or agencies, irrespective of who or by whom such discussion or negotiation is initiated.

**3. COMPENSATION:** For services provided in connection with the Picture contingent on Contractor providing all the contracted services and not being in default, Contractor shall receive the total sum of $_____ (Compensation), payable as follows:

(a)    $_____ (First Payment), _____ (First Payment Date);

(b)    $_____ (Second Payment), on _____ (Second Payment Date); and

(c)    $_____ (Third Payment), on _____ (Third Payment Date).

**4. PAYMENTS:** All payments made by the Production Company to Contractor shall be made to Contractor at the above stated address or at such other address of which Contractor shall advise the Production Company in writing. The compensation set forth in paragraph includes any and all compensation for the services of Contractor's assistants.

**5. OWNERSHIP:** Production Company is not obligated to actually utilize Contractor's services or the results and proceeds thereof. However, the Production Company shall own exclusively and perpetually throughout the universe all rights in and to the results and proceeds of such services as such services relate to the Picture and the exclusive perpetual right to use all or any part thereof as the Production Company may desire throughout the universe in connection with the Picture or otherwise. This includes but is not limited to all rights under copyright.

**6. CREDITS:** On the condition that Contractor renders all services required of her hereunder, Contractor shall be entitled to screen credit on a single card in the main titles (if other production credits appear in the main titles) in the position immediately following the final credit given to acting talent and preceding any other credit that may be given for casting.

**7. DOCUMENTATION:** Contractor will not be responsible for drafting any actor contracts, but will provide deal memos.

**8. CONTRACT CONSULTATION:** Any and all deals that fall within any of the following four (4) categories must have prior approval by the Production Company before the deal may be finalized: Deals in which an actor receives (1) over scale or more; (2) main title credit; (3) inclusion in paid ads; (4) any bonus, deferred or contingent compensation.

**9. OFFICE:** The Production Company shall provide office space for Contractor which is suitable for the purpose of rendering casting services for the Picture. Production Company shall reimburse Contractor her reasonable out-of-pocket expenses incurred by Contractor not to exceed a total of $300.00. There shall be no reimbursement for any travel expenses.

**10. SUSPENSION/PREMATURE TERMINATION:** If for any reason Contractor is unable to perform or comply with any of the material terms or conditions hereof ("Contractor's Incapacity").

(a) Suspension: The Production Company shall have the right, upon notice to Contractor, to suspend the rendition of services by Contractor and the running of time hereunder, which suspension shall begin as of the commencement date set forth in such notice and shall continue so long as Contractor's Incapacity shall continue and for such additional time thereafter as the Production Company requires to prepare for the recommencement of Contractor's services.

(b) Termination: If Contractor's Incapacity continues for a period in excess of five (5) days (aggregate or otherwise) during the performance of Contractor's services hereunder, then the Production Company shall have the right to terminate this Agreement upon written notice thereof to Contractor, which termination shall be effective as of the effective date set forth in such notice.

(c) In the event of any suspension or termination under this Clause 10 or Clause 11, Contractor will be compensated on a pro-rata basis for the amount if time worked.

**11. FORCE MAJEURE:**

(a) Suspension: If, by reason of fire, earthquake, labor dispute or strike, act of God or public enemy, any municipal ordinance, any state or federal law, governmental order or regulation, or other cause beyond Production Company's control which would excuse Production Company's performance as a matter of law, Production Company is prevented from or hampered in the pre-production or production of the Picture, or if, by reason of the closing of substantially all theatres in the United States, Production Company's production of the Picture is postponed or suspended, or if, by reason of any of the aforesaid contingencies or any other cause or occurrence not within Production Company's control, including but not limited to the death, illness or incapability of any principal member of the cast or Director of the Picture, the preparation or production of the Picture is interrupted or delayed and/or, if Production Company's normal business operations are interrupted or otherwise interfered with by virtue of any disruptive events which are beyond Production Company's control ("Production Company Disability"), then Production Company may postpone the commencement of or suspend the rendition of services by Contractor and the running of time hereunder for such time as the Production Company Disability shall continue; and no compensation shall accrue or become payable to Contractor hereunder during the period of such suspension. Such suspension shall end upon the cessation of the cause thereof.

CONTRACTS
FOR THE
FILM AND
TELEVISION
INDUSTRY

266

(b) Termination:

(i) Production Company Termination Right: If a Production Company Disability continues for a period in excess of four (4) weeks, Production Company shall have the right to terminate this Agreement upon written notice to Contractor.

(ii) Contractor's Termination Right: If a Production Company Disability results in compensation being suspended hereunder for a period in excess of four (4) weeks, Contractor shall have the right to terminate this Agreement upon written notice to Production Company.

**12. ARBITRATION:** This Agreement shall be interpreted in accordance with the laws of the State of _____, applicable to agreements executed and to be wholly performed therein. Any controversy or claim arising out of or in relation to this Agreement or the validity, construction or performance of this Agreement, or the breach thereof, shall be resolved by arbitration in accordance with the rules and procedures of AFMA, as said rules may be amended from time to time with rights of discovery if requested by the arbitrator. Such rules and procedures are incorporated and made a part of this Agreement by reference. If AFMA shall refuse to accept jurisdiction of such dispute, then the parties agree to arbitrate such matter before and in accordance with the rules of the American Arbitration Association (AAA) under its jurisdiction in _____ before a single arbitrator familiar with entertainment law. The parties shall have the right to engage in pre-hearing discovery in connection with such arbitration proceedings. The parties agree hereto that they will abide by and perform any award rendered in any arbitration conducted pursuant hereto, that any court having jurisdiction thereof may issue a judgment based upon such award and that the prevailing party in such arbitration and/or confirmation proceeding shall be entitled to recover its reasonable attorneys' fees and expenses. The arbitration award shall be final, binding and non-appealable. The Parties agree to accept service of process in accordance with the AFMA or AAA Rules.

IN WITNESS WHEREOF, the parties hereto have signed this Agreement as of the day and year first above written.

_____              _____
(Production Company)               (Contractor)


By: _____               _____
(Production Company Representative)   (Contractor)

Its: _____              _____
(Representative Title)             Social Security Number:

Below-the-line employees (i.e., the crew) are typically hired using a short form employment agreement. The following agreement is more detailed than most crew deal memos. It includes a work-for-hire clause stating that the results and proceeds of the employee's work are owned by the Employer. Thus, the agreement could be used to hire personnel that make a creative contribution (e.g., editor, cinematographer).

## CREW DEAL MEMO
## SALARIED ON-CALL
## EXEMPT EMPLOYEES

PRODUCTION COMPANY: _____
(Name of Production Company)

_____
(Address of Production Company)

MOTION PICTURE: "_____"

START DATE: _____

POSITION: _____

EMPLOYEE NAME: _____

ADDRESS: _____

PHONE: Home: _____ Work: _____

SOCIAL SECURITY NUMBER: _____ FED I.D. NUMBER: _____

*********************
(items below to be completed by production company only)

WEEKLY RATE: $ _____

RENTALS: _____
EMPLOYEE BOX AND EQUIPMENT IS SOLE RESPONSIBILITY
OF EMPLOYEE. PRODUCTION COMPANY ASSUMES NO RESPONSIBILITY FOR SAME.

OTHER TERMS: _____

_____

_____

(continued)

CONTRACTS
FOR THE
FILM AND
TELEVISION
INDUSTRY

268

# SALARIED/ON CALL
# EXEMPT EMPLOYEES
# TERMS AND CONDITIONS OF EMPLOYMENT

**1. PAYMENT OF WAGES:** Wages shall be paid to all employees no later than Friday following the week in which services were performed. Pay date may be delayed by reason of an intervening federal or state holiday. Employment is for a 6-day work week.

**2. EXEMPT EMPLOYEES:** Exempt employees shall not be beneficiary of additional overtime, turnaround or other hourly payments except as expressly provided in this deal memo.

**3. NIGHTS, WEEKENDS, HOLIDAYS, WORK TIME:** Unless expressly provided elsewhere in this deal memo, no increased or additional compensation shall accrue or be payable to employee for the rendering of services at night or on weekends or holidays, or after the expiration of any particular number of hours of service in any period.

**4. MEALS:** The Production Company will provide meal breaks and/or food service at approximately six (6) hour intervals.

**5. IMMIGRATION REFORM AND CONTROL ACT OF 1986 (IRCA):** Employment (or the engagement of services) hereunder is subject to employee providing the requisite documents required by IRCA and completing and signing the required Form I-9 pursuant to IRCA Section 274a.2. Employee shall comply with the immigration verification employment eligibility provisions required by law.

**6. CAR INSURANCE:** Employee is responsible for liability and collision insurance and deductibles on her/his personal vehicle used in conjunction with their employment.

**7. ALCOHOL/DRUGS:** Use of alcohol or drugs during hours of employment will result in employee's immediate termination.

**8. PURCHASES:** Employee will be held personally responsible for purchases, rentals and expenses not approved in advance by production.

**9. EXCLUSIVITY:** Employee's services are on an exclusive basis to the production of the motion picture (the "Picture") referred to in this deal memo for such period of time as required unless otherwise specified in this deal memo.

**10. CREDIT:** Unless otherwise specified in this deal memo, screen credit is at Production Company's discretion subject to employee's performing all services required through completion of term.

**11. TERM:** Unless expressly provided elsewhere in this agreement, employee's employment hereunder shall not be for a "run of the show" or for any guaranteed period of employment. Production reserves the right to discharge employee at any time, subject only to the obligation to pay the balance of any guaranteed compensation due. Production Company will attempt to notify employees a minimum of twenty-four (24) hours in advance of layoff. This agreement is subject to immediate suspension and/or termination (at Production's election) without further obligation on the part of Production in the event of any incapacity or default of employee or in the case of any suspension, postponement or interference with the production by reason of labor controversy, strike, earthquake, act of God, governmental action, regulation, or decree or for any other customary force majeure reason.

**12. NO WAIVER:**  The terms and conditions of this deal memo are binding on Production Company and employee and shall not be waived or altered by any method. Any added conditions on the front of this deal memo inconsistent with these conditions of employment shall be null and void.

**13. WORK-FOR-HIRE:**  Production Company shall be the owner of all of the results and proceeds of employee's services, including any copyright, trademark and any other intellectual property rights in any work or property created by Employee, or anyone under Employee's direction. Employee acknowledges that Employee's work is a "work made for hire" within the scope of Employee's employment, and therefore Employer shall be the author and copyright owner of any work created under this agreement. In the event that any of proceeds of Employee's work are not considered a work for hire, then Employee's copyright to such work is hereby assigned to Employer.

**14. PUBLICITY:**  Employee shall not directly or indirectly circulate, publish or otherwise disseminate any news story, article, book or other publicity concerning the Picture, or employee's or others' services without Production Company's prior written consent, provided that employee may issue personal publicity mentioning the Picture so long as such references are not derogatory. Employee has permission to show a videotape of Picture in connection with seeking future employment. Employer shall have the right to use employee's name, voice, picture and likeness in connection with the Picture, the advertising and publicizing thereof, and any promotional films or clips respecting the Picture without additional compensation therefore.

**15. ARBITRATION:**  This Agreement shall be interpreted in accordance with the laws of the State of _____, applicable to agreements executed and to be wholly performed therein. Any controversy or claim arising out of or in relation to this Agreement or the validity, construction or performance of this Agreement, or the breach thereof, shall be resolved by arbitration in accordance with the rules and procedures of AFMA, as said rules may be amended from time to time with rights of discovery if requested by the arbitrator. Such rules and procedures are incorporated and made a part of this Agreement by reference. If AFMA shall refuse to accept jurisdiction of such dispute, then the parties agree to arbitrate such matter before and in accordance with the rules of the American Arbitration Association under its jurisdiction in _____ before a single arbitrator familiar with entertainment law. The parties shall have the right to engage in pre-hearing discovery in connection with such arbitration proceedings. The parties agree hereto that they will abide by and perform any award rendered in any arbitration conducted pursuant hereto, that any court having jurisdiction thereof may issue a judgment based upon such award and that the prevailing party in such arbitration and/or confirmation proceeding shall be entitled to recover its reasonable attorneys' fees and expenses. The arbitration will be held in _____ and any award shall be final, binding and non-appealable. The Parties agree to accept service of process in accordance with the AFMA Rules.

EMPLOYEE ACCEPTS ALL CONDITIONS OF EMPLOYMENT AS DESCRIBED ABOVE

AGREED TO AND ACCEPTED:

EMPLOYEE SIGNATURE: _____ DATE: _____

PRODUCTION COMPANY SIGNATURE: _____ DATE: _____

CONTRACTS
FOR THE
FILM AND
TELEVISION
INDUSTRY

270

# PRODUCER EMPLOYMENT

The producer's job is often divided into "Executive Producer" and "Line Producer." The "Executive Producer" is the dealmaker, the financier. She may be producing a variety of projects at once. She will often hire a "Line Producer" to work for her. The line producer is in charge of logistics for the shoot. She will hire the crew, order supplies, and equipment and make sure the director has everything he needs to make the film. During production, a line producer will work on one film at a time.

Some producers call themselves "independent producers." While they may not be tied to one studio, most are not entirely independent. They may have to rely on studios to finance and distribute their pictures.

Producer deals can be structured in different ways. When a studio funds development and production, the studio will pay the producer a fee from the production budget and give her a percentage of net profits. Often "net profits" are defined in such a way that the producer is unlikely to see any revenue unless the picture is a smash hit.

On the other hand, if a producer funds development herself and/or production (i.e., using presale agreements or investor money), and the producer has a desirable film, she may be able to negotiate a much better deal. This so-called Negative Pick-up Deal, discussed in Chapter 9, is more likely to return profits to the producer. However, the producer may have to share this revenue with investors.

Producer credits can be misleading. Sometimes people who don't produce, receive a producing credit. That is because the Producers' Guild is not recognized as a union or a guild by the studios. The studios consider producers as part of management and have refused to enter into a collective bargaining agreement with them.

The collective bargaining agreements with the DGA and WGA, on the other hand, severely restrict the studio's ability to allocate credit. Since studios can assign producer credits as they please, they can give such credits as perks to those who have not earned them.

Producer deals vary a great deal in their compensation and terms. Here is a sample line producer contract for a low-budget feature film.

# PRODUCER EMPLOYMENT AGREEMENT

THIS AGREEMENT is made and entered into as of the _____, by and between _____ (hereinafter "Production Company"), and _____ (hereinafter "Employee").

This Agreement is entered into with reference to the following facts:

A. Production Company intends to produce a theatrical motion picture (hereinafter the "Picture") based upon that certain screenplay tentatively entitled "_____," (hereinafter the "Screenplay") which Picture is intended for initial theatrical exhibition.

B. Production Company wishes to utilize the services of Employee as a producer in connection with the production and delivery of the Picture upon the terms and conditions herein contained.

ACCORDINGLY, IT IS AGREED AS FOLLOWS:

**1. ENGAGEMENT:** Subject to events of force majeure, default, or the disability or death of Employee, Production Company hereby engages the services of Employee, and Employee agrees to render exclusive services as a producer, in connection with the production of the Picture upon the terms and conditions herein contained. Subject to Production Company's final approval, Employee shall supervise the testing of persons proposed for the cast, scouting for shooting locations, assembling the crew, the supervision of the photography of the Picture, assisting in the supervision of the editing, and sound mixing, assisting in the selection of music, assisting in the supervision of the final dubbing and scoring, the supervision of all other post-production requirements of the Picture, the delivery of the final answer print and all other customary delivery items to Production Company and its principal distributors, foreign and domestic, and perform such other services as are reasonably required by Production Company and are usually and customarily performed by producers in the motion picture industry. Employee will report to such place(s) as are reasonably designated by Production Company, and will be available at all times and for such periods of time as are reasonably designated by Production Company. Employee will advise Production Company of Employee's whereabouts so that Employee may be reached at any reasonable hour of the night or day. During the term of employment, Employee will render his services at all places and at all times reasonably required by Production Company, including nights, Saturdays, Sundays, and holidays.

**2. TERM:** Employee shall render the services required of him as set forth in paragraph 1 hereof during the period commencing on _____, and continuing thereafter for such time as pre-production, principal photography, and customary post-production and delivery of the Picture as required by Production Company. It is contemplated that principal photography of the Picture will commence approximately on _____ and, subject to extension for events beyond Production Company's control and other events of force majeure, Employee's exclusive services shall not be required beyond _____, but he shall nevertheless supervise the delivery of the Picture hereunder.

**3. COMPENSATION:** In consideration for all of the services to be rendered by Employee hereunder and for all of the rights granted by Employee to Production Company, and on condition that Employee is not in default hereunder, and subject to the terms and conditions specified herein, Production Company agrees to pay Employee, and Employee agrees to accept:

CONTRACTS
FOR THE
FILM AND
TELEVISION
INDUSTRY

272

(a) Fixed Compensation: $_____. Said sum to be divided into weekly installments and paid over the course of pre-production, production and post production.

(b) Deferred Compensation: In addition to the Fixed Compensation payable under Clause 3(a), subject to the production and release of the Picture, and subject to the performance of all obligations of Employee, the Employee shall receive and an amount equal to $_____ per week, in first position of all contingent deferments payable out of no more than fifty percent (50%) of the Production Company's gross revenues from the Picture, after the investors in the Picture have recouped their entire investment plus ten percent, and after recoupment of all production and financing costs and recoupment of loans, and after any deferments payable to any laboratories, post-production services and the cost of becoming a signatory to any Guild agreements. The aforesaid payment shall be deferred and paid pro rata with all similar deferments.

(c) Contingent Compensation: In addition to the Fixed and Deferred Compensation payable above, subject to the production and release of the Picture and subject to the performance of Employee's obligations hereunder, Employee shall be entitled to receive as Contingent Compensation an amount equal to _____ percent of one hundred percent of the Net Profits of the Picture, if any (and after deducting the cost of becoming signatory to any Guild agreements).

(d) Net Profits Definition: All income actually received by Production Company from the exploitation of the Picture after deducting all expenses and deferments incurred by Production Company in connection with the financing (including all interest and fees owed), pre-production, production, post-production, investor recoupment, marketing, distribution and exploitation of the Picture; this shall also include any attorneys' fees and expenses incurred by Production Company in connection with the Picture. Also included within the Net Profits definition is a one percent (1%) deduction of the Production Company's gross income for Production Company operating expenses.

**4. SERVICES:** At all times during the term of Employee's services hereunder, Employee will promptly and faithfully comply with all of Production Company's reasonable instructions, directions, requests, rules and regulations. Employee will perform his services conscientiously and to the full limit of his talents and capabilities when wherever reasonably required or desired by Production Company and in accordance with Production Company's reasonable instructions and directions in all matters, including those involving artistic taste and judgment. Employee will perform such service as Production Company may reasonably require of him, and as customarily and usually rendered by and required of producers employed to produce low-budget theatrical motion pictures in the motion picture industry.

Production Company will provide Employee with a copy of the work print on videocassette. Employee agrees not to show this work print to any distributor or sales rep without Production Company's prior written consent, and Employee will not show the work print to anyone else without the prior consent of Production Company.

**5. INSURANCE:** Employee agrees that Production Company may at any time or times, either in Production Company's name or otherwise, but at Production Company's expense and for Production Company's own benefit, apply for, and take out life, health, accident, and other insurance covering Employee whether independently or together with others in any reasonable amount which Production Company may deem necessary to protect Production Company's interests hereunder. Production Company shall own all rights in and to such insurance and in the cash values and proceeds thereof and Employee shall not have any right, title, or interest therein. Employee agrees to the customary examinations and correctly preparing, signing and delivering such applications and other documents as may be reasonably required.

**6. CONTROL:** Production Company shall have complete control of the production of the Picture including, but not limited to, all artistic controls and the right to cut, edit, add to, subtract from, arrange, rearrange, and revise the Picture in any manner. Production Company shall not be obligated to make any actual use of Employee's services or to produce or to release or to continue the distribution or release of the Picture once released.

**7. RIGHTS:** In addition to Employee's services as a producer, Production Company shall be entitled to and shall own all of the results and proceeds thereof throughout the world in perpetuity (including, but not limited to, all rights throughout the world of production, public performance, manufacture, television, recordation, and reproduction by any art or method, whether now known or hereafter devised, copyright, trademark and patent) whether such results and proceeds consist of literary, dramatic, musical, motion picture, mechanical or any other form of works, ideas, themes, compositions, creations, or products and without obligation to pay any fees, royalties or other amounts except those expressly provided for in this Agreement. Specifically, but without in any way limiting the generality of the foregoing, Production Company shall own all rights of every kind and character in and to any and all acts, poses, plays and appearances of any and all kinds which Employee may write, suggest, direct or produce during the term hereof (provided, however, that any assignment will not reduce Production Company's obligations to Employee in regard to compensation and credit). In the event that Production Company shall desire to secure separate assignments of any of the foregoing, Employee agrees to execute them upon Production Company's request therefore. All rights granted or agreed to be granted to Production Company hereunder shall vest in Production Company immediately and shall remain vested in Production Company and Production Company's successors and assigns whether this Agreement expires in normal course or whether Employee's engagement hereunder is sooner terminated for any cause or reason. Production Company shall have the right to use and authorize others to use the name, voice and likeness of Employee, and any results and proceeds of his services hereunder, to advertise and publicize the Picture including, but not limited to, the right to use the same in the credits of the Picture, in trailers, in commercial tie-ups, and in all other forms and media of advertising and publicity including merchandising, publications, records and commercial advertising and publicity tie-ups derived from or relating to the Picture.

**8. REPRESENTATIONS, WARRANTIES & INDEMNITY:**

(a) Employee represents and warrants that all material of every kind authored, written, prepared, composed, and/or submitted by Employee hereunder for or to Production Company shall be wholly original with him, and shall not infringe or violate the right of privacy of, or constitute libel against, or violate any copyright, common law right or any other right of any person, firm or corporation. The foregoing warranties shall not apply to any material not authored, written, prepared, composed or submitted by Employee, but shall apply to all material, incidents and characterizations which Employee may add to or incorporate in or cause to be added to or incorporated in such material.

CONTRACTS
FOR THE
FILM AND
TELEVISION
INDUSTRY

274

Employee further represents and warrants that Employee is free to enter into this Agreement and to render the required services hereunder and that Employee is not subject to any obligations or disability which will or might interfere with Employee's fully complying with this Agreement; that Employee has not made, and will not make any grant or assignment which might interfere with the complete enjoyment of the rights granted to Production Company hereunder; and that Employee will not at any time render any services or do any acts which shall derogate from the value of Employee's services rendered pursuant to this Agreement or which shall interfere with the performance of any of Employee's covenants or obligations pursuant to this Agreement. Employee hereby indemnifies Production Company, its successors, assigns, licensees, officers and employees, and hold it harmless from and against any and all liability, losses, damages and expenses (including attorneys' fees) arising out of (i) the use of any materials furnished by Employee for the Picture, or (ii) any breach by Employee of any warranty or agreement made by Employee hereunder.

(b) Production Company represents and warrants that Production Company has the right to enter into this Agreement, and to render the required obligations hereunder, and that Production Company is not subject to any other obligations or disabilities which will or might interfere with Production Company's fully complying with this Agreement; that Production Company has not made, and will not make any grant or assignment which might interfere with the complete enjoyment of the compensation granted to Employee hereunder; that Production Company has secured all necessary financing to make all payments hereunder, and complete the Picture as budgeted; and that Production Company will not at any time render any services or do any acts which shall derogate from the value of Production Company's obligations pursuant to this Agreement, or which shall interfere with the performance of any of Production Company's covenants or obligations pursuant to this Agreement. Production Company hereby indemnifies Employee and his successors and assigns, and holds them harmless from and against any and all liability, losses, damages, and expenses (including reasonable attorneys' fees) arising out of any breach by Production Company of any warranty or agreement made by Production Company hereunder.

**9. CREDIT:** Provided that Employee shall fully and completely keep and perform all of his obligations and agreements hereunder, and if the Picture has been produced substantially with the use of Employee's services hereunder, Employee shall receive a producing credit on the positive prints and/or tape for the Picture in the main titles thereof, and in all paid advertisements (subject to customary distributor exclusions). Employee's credit shall be in the same size and prominence as _____ and placed in all media in which his name appears. Credit shall read "Produced by _____." If an attribution is used, only company name may appear in print media. Credit on all prints will appear in the main titles in second or third position from last credit in the same size as the largest credit, other than film title or presentation credit (which could include production company name). Nothing herein shall be deemed to restrict Production Company from granting co-producer, associate producer, executive producer or similar producer credits to others.

No casual or inadvertent failure to comply with the provisions of this paragraph or failure of any third party to comply with same shall be deemed to be a breach of this Agreement by Production Company. In the event of a failure or omission by Production Company constituting a breach of its credit obligations under this Agreement, Employee's rights shall be limited to the right, if any, to seek damages at law, and Employee shall not have any right in such event to rescind this Agreement or any of the rights granted to Production Company hereunder, or to enjoin the distribution, exhibition, or other exploitation of the Picture or the advertising or publicizing thereof. Production Company shall, however, upon receipt of written notice of any such breach of its credit obligations, cure such breach on a prospective basis on materials to be created in the future.

**10. CONTINGENCIES:** If Employee shall become incapacitated or prevented from fully performing his services hereunder by reason of illness, accident, or mental and physical disability and/or if the production of the Picture is hampered or interrupted or interfered with for any event or reason beyond the control of Production Company or any other event of force majeure (hereinafter collectively referred to as "incapacity"), Production Company shall have the right to suspend Employee's services and the compensation payable to Employee during the continuance of any such incapacity. In the event any such incapacity continues for a period of seven (7) consecutive days or for an aggregate period of twenty-one (21) days, Production Company shall have the right to terminate Employee's engagement hereunder. In the event that Employee should fail, refuse or neglect other than because of incapacity to perform any of his required services hereunder, Production Company shall have the right at any time to suspend Employee's services and the compensation payable to Employee during the continuance of such default, and Production Company shall have the right at any time to terminate Employee's engagement hereunder by reason of such default.

**11. NO RIGHT TO CONTRACT:** Employee acknowledges and agrees that he has no right or authority to and will not employ any person to serve in any capacity, nor contract for the purchase or rental of any article or material, nor make any commitment or agreement whereby Production Company shall be required to pay any monies or other consideration or which shall otherwise obligate Production Company, without Production Company's express prior written consent.

**12. ASSIGNMENT:** Production Company may transfer and assign this Agreement or all or any of its rights hereunder to any person, firm or corporation, but no such assignment or transfer shall relieve Production Company of its executory obligations hereunder. This Agreement shall inure to the benefit of Production Company's successors, licensees and assigns. Employee shall not assign or transfer this Agreement, or any of his rights or obligations hereunder, it being understood that the obligations and duties of Employee are personal to Employee, and any purported assignment shall be void. Employee may, however, assign his right to receive any monies hereunder.

**13. LIMITATION OF REMEDY:** All rights assigned by this Agreement shall be irrevocable under all or any circumstances and shall not be subject to reversion, rescission, termination or injunction. Employee agrees that he shall not have the right to enjoin the exhibition, distribution or exploitation of any motion picture produced hereunder or to enjoin, rescind or terminate any rights granted to Production Company hereunder. Employee further agrees that Employee's sole remedy in the event of any default by Production Company hereunder, including the failure by Production Company to pay Employee any consideration payable to Employee pursuant hereto, or to accord Employee credit (to the extent that Production Company is obligated to accord Employee such credit) pursuant hereto, shall be an action at law for damages and/or for an accounting (if applicable). At all times, the Production Company shall have all rights and remedies which it has at law or in equity, pursuant hereto or otherwise.

CONTRACTS
FOR THE
FILM AND
TELEVISION
INDUSTRY

276

**14. NOTICES:** All notices or payments which Production Company may be required to give or make to Employee hereunder may be delivered personally or sent by certified or registered mail or telegraph, or by fax to Employee at _____.

All notices which Employee may wish to give to Production Company hereunder may be delivered personally or sent by certified or registered mail or telegraph, or fax, to Production Company at _____. The date of delivery, or attempted delivery, as the case may be, of any notice or payment hereunder shall be deemed to be the date of service of such notice or payment.

**15. SECTION HEADINGS:** The headings of paragraphs, sections or other subdivisions of this Agreement are for convenience in reference only. They will not be used in any way to govern, limit, modify, construe or otherwise be given any legal effect.

**16. ARBITRATION:** This Agreement shall be interpreted in accordance with the laws of the State of _____, applicable to agreements executed and to be wholly performed therein. Any controversy or claim arising out of or in relation to this Agreement or the validity, construction or performance of this Agreement, or the breach thereof, shall be resolved by arbitration in accordance with the rules and procedures of AFMA, as said rules may be amended from time to time with rights of discovery if requested by the arbitrator. Such rules and procedures are incorporated and made a part of this Agreement by reference. If AFMA shall refuse to accept jurisdiction of such dispute, then the parties agree to arbitrate such matter before and in accordance with the rules of the American Arbitration Association (AAA) under its jurisdiction in _____ before a single arbitrator familiar with entertainment law. The parties shall have the right to engage in pre-hearing discovery in connection with such arbitration proceedings. The parties agree hereto that they will abide by and perform any award rendered in any arbitration conducted pursuant hereto, that any court having jurisdiction thereof may issue a judgment based upon such award and that the prevailing party in such arbitration and/or confirmation proceeding shall be entitled to recover its reasonable attorneys' fees and expenses. The arbitration will be held in _____ and any award shall be final, binding and non-appealable. The Parties agree to accept service of process in accordance with AFMA or AAA Rules.

**17. ENTIRE AGREEMENT:** This Agreement represents the entire understanding between the parties hereto with respect to the subject matter hereof, and this Agreement supersedes all previous representations, understandings or agreements, oral or written, between the parties with respect to the subject matter hereof, and cannot be modified except by written instrument signed by the parties hereto. This Agreement shall be governed by and construed in accordance with the laws of the State of _____, and the exclusive venue for resolution of any dispute arising out of, or in connection with this Agreement shall be in _____, _____.

AGREED TO AND ACCEPTED:

_____

"Employee"

AGREED TO AND ACCEPTED:

"Production Company"

By: _____
   (Production Company Signer)

# TELEVISION SERIES PRODUCER AGREEMENT

This Agreement (the "Agreement") entered into on _____ (Agreement Date), together with all attached schedules and exhibits, shall constitute the terms and conditions of the agreement between _____ ("Company") and _____ (Producer Name) ("Producer").

**1. SERVICES.** Company hereby engages Producer to render exclusive producing and consulting services to Company during the Term hereof. Producer will render such services when, where and as reasonably required by Company and will comply with all reasonable directions of Company relative thereto. The services to be rendered by Producer hereunder include, but are not limited to, producing and consulting services with respect to the development and production of all programming of Company at the reasonable instruction of Company.

Producer's primary responsibilities will be (i) executive producing the television series entitled "_____," including consulting on key creative elements, scheduling, casting, selection and supervision of key crew and post-production.

**2. TERM:**

(a) Initial Term: This Agreement will commence on _____ and will terminate one year later ("Initial Term"), unless sooner terminated, suspended or extended in accordance with the terms provided for herein.

(b) Extended Term: Company will have an exclusive and irrevocable option, exercisable in writing on or before a date which is at least _____ days prior to the end of the Initial Term, to extend this Agreement for an additional _____ year period ("Extended Term"), unless sooner terminated, suspended or extended in accordance with the terms provided for herein.

The Initial Term and the Extended Term, to the extent exercised and in effect, are collectively referred to herein as the "Term."

**3. EXCLUSIVITY:** During the Term, Producer agrees to render his/her services solely and exclusively for Company or Company's designee, and will not perform services for any other person or business in connection with any other entertainment industry project without the prior written consent of Company.

**4. COMPENSATION:**

(a) Base Salary: Subject to Company's rights as set forth in this Agreement, in the event of Producer's death, default, disability or an event of force majeure, as full and complete compensation for all services rendered and the rights granted by Producer to Company hereunder, Company agrees to pay Producer and Producer agrees to accept a salary of $_____ for the Initial Term with increases of _____ percent and _____ percent respectively for the second and third years after the Initial Term, if Company exercises the options described in Paragraph 2(b) above.

The Base Salary will be payable in equal monthly installments on Company's standard payroll day.

(b) Additional Consideration: Subject to Company's rights as set forth in this Agreement, in the event of Producer's death, default, disability or an event of force majeure, in addition to the Base Salary payable to Producer as set forth above, Producer will be entitled to receive the following sums set forth below in this Paragraph 4(b).

CONTRACTS
FOR THE
FILM AND
TELEVISION
INDUSTRY

278

Residuals:

(i) With respect to all programming on which Producer renders his services hereunder, Producer will be entitled to receive additional compensation of $_____ for each episode of the series.

The foregoing constitute one-time payments for each episode of any series for which Producer renders services hereunder.

(ii) The residuals, less any applicable deductions required by law will be payable within thirty (30) days following the initial exploitation of the series episodes.

(iii) The residuals will be payable to Producer during and after the expiration of the Term of this Agreement. Such residuals will be payable to Producer after the expiration of the Term at the same time and in the same manner as if such were payable during the Term.

(c) Fringe Benefits: Subject to Company's rights as set forth in this Agreement, in the event of Producer's death, default, disability or an event of force majeure, Producer will be entitled to the following fringe benefits, which benefits will terminate upon the expiration of the Term hereof or the termination of Producer's services as provided for herein:

(i) Medical Insurance: Producer will be eligible to participate in Company's medical and health plan or other similar benefit plans generally made available to other employees of Company in accordance with the terms thereof, as such terms may change from time to time and subject to Producer cooperating with and successfully passing any medical examinations required in connection with such benefits.

(ii) Life Insurance: Provided Producer qualifies for life insurance at normal premium rates, Company will pay for the premiums on a $750,000 term life insurance policy during the Term.

(iii) Office: Company will provide Producer with a suitable, furnished office for Producer's sole use wherever Company maintains its principal offices, prepaid parking, and will employ a secretary or an assistant reasonably approved by Producer for Producer's sole use at a salary approved by Company.

(iv) Expenses: Producer will be regularly reimbursed (no less frequently than monthly) for all necessary and reasonable business expenses incurred by Producer in the scope of Producer's engagement hereunder upon submission of itemized expenses (together with original receipts wherever possible) in the manner and at the time specified by Company. If any expenses are substantial or exceed the parameters of Company's normal expense reimbursement procedures, Producer will obtain the approval of Company prior to incurring such expense.

(v) Business Travel: When required by Company to render services at an overnight location outside of Producer's city of residence, Company will provide or reimburse Producer for the cost of round-trip, business class transportation and business class hotel accommodations in accordance with Company policy with respect to such matters.

(vi) Car Allowance: Company will provide Producer with a monthly car allowance during the Term in the amount of $_____, payable on a monthly basis.

**5. CAPACITY TO CONTRACT:** Producer will have no right or authority to and will not employ any person in any capacity, nor contract for the purchase or rental on behalf of Company of any materials nor incur any obligations on behalf of Company whereby Company is required to pay any monies or incur liability, without the prior consent of Company. Notwithstanding the foregoing, Company agrees that Producer will have the right to employ persons and make obligations on behalf of Company provided such elements are contained within a budget previously approved by Company.

**6. CREDIT:** Subject to Company's rights as set forth in this Agreement, in the event of Producer's death, disability, default or an event of force majeure, Company will accord Producer an on-screen credit as Producer or Executive Producer, as the case may be. The credit will be contiguous with the other producer credits. If Producer creates a story for an episode, subject to the requirements of the Writers Guild of America Basic Agreement, Producer will receive "Story By" credit on such episode. All other matters with respect to such credits will be within Company's sole discretion. No casual or inadvertent failure to comply with the provisions of this Paragraph 6, nor any failure by third parties to comply with their agreement with Company, will constitute a breach of this Agreement by Company.

**7. NAME AND LIKENESS:** Company and its successors, licensees and assigns will have the non-exclusive and perpetual right, but not the obligation, to use and license the use of Producer's name, photograph, approved likeness and biographical data ("Name and Likeness") for the following: (a) in billing and credits with respect to any series produced during the Term; (b) in publicizing Producer's services hereunder or the results and proceeds of all Producer's services hereunder in connection with any series produced during the Term, which right may be exercised by Company or any distributor, network, sponsor, advertising agency or licensee of exhibition rights in the series; (c) in connection with the publication or other exploitation of ancillary products derived from any series produced hereunder; and (d) in connection with all publicity related to the series and the general business of Company. Producer will give prior notice to and coordinate with Company any and all publicity and interviews in connection with Producer's services hereunder.

**8. STANDARD TERMS:** Attached as Exhibit A hereto and deemed a part hereof are Company's Standard Terms and Conditions of Agreement, which Standard Terms and Conditions are deemed a part hereof and are binding on the parties.

IN WITNESS WHEREOF, the parties hereto have executed this Agreement as of the day and year first above written.

AGREED TO & ACCEPTED:

COMPANY                                                      PRODUCER


_____            _____
(Production Company Signer)                      (Producer Signer)

CONTRACTS
FOR THE
FILM AND
TELEVISION
INDUSTRY

280

# EXHIBIT "A"
## STANDARD TERMS AND CONDITIONS

**1. DEFINITIONS:**

(a) "Person" means any individual, partnership, corporation, trust, joint venture, unincorporated association or other entity.

(b) "Company" means _____ (Production Company Name).

(c) "Property" means the characters and other intellectual property now or hereafter developed by Company and all productions produced, distributed and/or owned by Company.

(d) "Term" refers to the minimum rights period pursuant to which a Property is exploited.

**2. PAYMENT:** Producer's compensation will be payable in accordance with Company's customary payroll practice and will constitute full compensation for all of Producer's services performed hereunder. All payments made to Producer as salary or otherwise will be subject to such definitions, withholdings and limitations as shall from time to time be required by law, governmental regulations or orders, as well as any agreements between Company and Producer.

**3. VACATION:** Producer will be entitled to annual paid vacations in accordance with the vacation policy of Company.

**4. DEATH OR DISABILITY:**

(a) In the event of Producer's death during the Term, this Agreement will terminate and Company will be obligated to pay Producer's estate only that portion of Base Salary and Additional Consideration, if any, earned and accruing to Producer pursuant to Paragraph 4 of the Special Terms, through the date of termination.

(b) In the event that Producer is substantially unable to perform the services required hereunder as the result of physical or mental disability, as determined by Company (including consultation with Producer's physician, if any) and such disability continues for a period of six consecutive weeks, Company will have the right, at its option, to terminate Producer's employment hereunder upon ten days' written notice at any time after the six-week period, so long as the disability is continuing at the time of such notice, and Company will be obligated to Producer for only that portion of the Base Salary and Additional Compensation, if any, earned and accruing to Producer pursuant to Paragraph 6 of the Special Terms, through the date of termination.

**5. FORCE MAJEURE:** In the event that Company sells or otherwise transfers substantially all of its business assets to an unrelated third party or suspends substantially all of its business operations as a result of an event of force majeure (i.e., the interruption of Company's normal business operations caused by any disruptive event including, but not limited to, a labor dispute or strike which is beyond Company's control) and if such event of force majeure continues for a period of eight consecutive weeks, effective as of the date of the commencement of the event of force majeure, then Company may terminate Producer's services hereunder and Company will be obligated to pay Producer only that portion of the

Base Salary and Additional Compensation, if any, earned and accruing to Producer pursuant to Paragraph 4 of the Special Terms through the date of termination. Notwithstanding the foregoing, if Company terminates Producer's services pursuant to this Paragraph and at any time during the Term hereof recommences its business operations and if Producer is available when Company requires his/her services, then Producer will be offered the opportunity to render services to Company as provided herein for the balance of the previous engagement in accordance with the terms and conditions of this Agreement, and such offer will be accepted, if at all, in writing by Producer within three (3) business days after the offer is received, and, if not, the offer will be deemed rejected.

**6. INSURANCE:** Company has the right to secure in its own name or otherwise, and at its own expense, life, health, accident and other insurance covering Producer. Producer will have no right, title or interest in and to such insurance. Producer will assist Company in procuring such insurance by submitting to examinations and by signing such applications and other instruments as may be reasonably be required by the insurance carrier to which application is made for any such insurance. Producer's own physician may be present at any such examinations, at Producer's sole cost and expense, provided that Producer's physician will not interfere with any such examination.

**7. WARRANTIES:** Producer warrants and represents that:

(a) Producer has the right to enter into this Agreement and to grant to Company any and all rights and services set forth herein.

(b) Producer is not subject to any obligation or disability which will or might prevent or interfere with the performance by Producer of all of the covenants, conditions, and agreements to be performed and observed by Producer hereunder, and Producer has not made nor will make any contractual or other commitments which would inhibit the full performance of this Agreement by Producer.

(c) This Agreement is not subject to any claim against Company or any of its affiliates for fees or commissions by any of Producer's agents or personal representatives or any other person, firm or corporation.

(d) All material created, added and/or otherwise contributed by Producer pursuant to this Agreement (collectively the "Material") is wholly original with Producer and no part thereof is taken from, based upon, or adapted from any other literary material, dramatic work or television program (other than material fully cleared by Producer or in the public domain) and the full use of the Material, or any part thereof, as herein granted will not, to the best of Producer's knowledge, in any way violate or infringe upon any copyright belonging to any person or entity or constitute a libel or defamation of, or an invasion of the rights of privacy of or otherwise violate or infringe upon any other right or rights whatsoever of any person or entity.

(e) To the best of Producer's knowledge, there is no outstanding claim or litigation pending against the title or ownership of the Material or any part thereof or in the rights therein.

(f) Producer has not assigned nor licensed to any other person or entity or in any manner encumbered or hypothecated any of the rights herein granted to Company with respect to the Material, nor has Producer agreed to do so.

CONTRACTS
FOR THE
FILM AND
TELEVISION
INDUSTRY

282

The foregoing warranties and representations are made by Producer to induce Company to execute this Agreement. Producer hereby indemnifies and agrees to hold Company, its affiliates, successors and assigns, and their officers, employees, directors, agents and licensees, harmless against any and all claims, liabilities, damages, costs and expenses (including reasonable attorneys' fees) arising out of or in connection with a breach or alleged breach by Producer of any of the warranties, representations or agreements contained in this Agreement.

Company similarly indemnifies and holds Producer harmless against any and all claims, liabilities, damages, costs and expenses (including reasonable attorneys' fees) arising out of or in connection with a breach or alleged breach by Company of any of its warranties, representations or agreements contained in this Agreement.

Company agrees to make application to add Producer as an additional insured under Company's errors and omissions insurance policy with respect to all projects in connection with which Producer renders services pursuant to this Agreement, subject to the terms, conditions and restrictions of said policy, including any deductible or policy limits, provided that (i) the inclusion of Producer on such policy will not relieve Producer in any way from producer's representations, warranties and indemnities contained herein, and (ii) Company will not be responsible to producer if its insurance carrier refuses such application.

**8. OWNERSHIP:**  The results and proceeds of Producer's services hereunder including, without limitation, in connection with the Property, are and shall be deemed a work-made-for-hire as an employee of Company. Company will exclusively own all now known or hereafter existing rights of every kind throughout the universe in perpetuity, and in all languages, the results and proceeds of the Materials that Producer has furnished hereunder, free and clear of any claims by Producer (or anyone claiming under or on behalf of Producer) of any kind or character whatsoever for all now known or hereinafter invented uses, media and forms including, without limitation, all copyrights thereof in and to motion picture, home video, television, sequel, remake and allied rights therein. The foregoing is inclusive of a full assignment to Company thereof. If under any applicable law the fact that the Property is a work-made-for-hire is not effective to place authorship and ownership of the Property and all rights therein in Company, then to the fullest extent allowable and for the full term of protection otherwise accorded to Producer under such applicable law, including without limitation, for the full term of any copyrights, Producer hereby assigns and transfers to Company all right, title and interest of Producer in the Property. Producer agrees to execute such further instruments as Company may from time to time reasonably deem necessary or desirable to evidence, establish, maintain, perfect, protect, enforce or defend its right, title or interest in or to the Property.

**9. EQUITABLE RELIEF:**  Producer acknowledges that the services to be rendered by Producer under the terms of this Agreement, and the rights and privileges granted to Company by Producer herein, are of a special, unique, extraordinary and intellectual character which gives them a peculiar value, the loss of which cannot be reasonably or adequately compensated in damages in any action at law, and that a breach by Producer of any of the provisions contained in this Agreement will cause Company irreparable injury and damage. Producer acknowledges that Company is entitled to the remedies of injunction, special performance and other equitable relief for a breach of this Agreement by Producer. Such right of equitable relief will not act as a waiver of any other rights or remedies available to Company.

In the event of breach of this Agreement by Company, Producer acknowledges and agrees that under no circumstances will Producer be entitled to injunctive or equitable relief, nor will Producer have the right to rescind this agreement, Producer's sole remedy in the event of such breach is limited to an action at law to recover monetary damages.

## 10. TERMINATION:

(a) Company may terminate this agreement and Producer's engagement hereunder at any time for cause. For purposes of this agreement, the term "cause" will mean conviction of Producer for any felony or any lesser crime involving the property of Company, willful misconduct or gross negligence by Producer in connection with the performance of Producer's duties hereunder. Upon termination of this agreement for cause, Company will only be obligated to pay Producer that portion of the Base Salary and Additional Compensation, if any, earned and accruing to Producer pursuant to Paragraph 4 of the Special Terms, through the date of termination of Producer's engagement. In the event the "cause" can be cured by producer, Company will afford Producer a two business day period from the date of written notice thereof to effect the cure, and this Agreement may not be terminated during such two business day period.

(b) Company will have the right to terminate Producer's employment at any time without cause. In the event Producer's services are terminated by Company other than for cause, death or disability prior to the completion of the Term, Producer will receive the Base Salary for the balance of the Term, payable in equal installments no less frequently than semimonthly.

**11. SUCCESSORS:** This Agreement will be binding upon and inure to the benefit of the parties hereto and their respective successors and assigns, but Producer will not have the right to assign Producer's interest in this agreement, any rights under this agreement or any duties imposed under this agreement nor will Producer have the right to pledge, hypothecate or otherwise encumber Producer's right to receive compensation hereunder without the prior consent of Company.

**12. NOTICES:** All notices, statements or other documents which either party may be required or will desire to give to the other hereunder must be in writing and will be given either by personal delivery, registered or certified mail (postage prepaid) or facsimile and will, except as herein expressly provided, be deemed given hereunder on the date delivered, faxed or forty-eight (48) hours after the date of mail. The addresses of the parties are as set forth below:

Producer:      _____
                (Producer Name)

                _____
                (Address)

                _____

Company:      _____
                (Production Company Name)

                _____
                (Address)

                _____

CONTRACTS
FOR THE
FILM AND
TELEVISION
INDUSTRY

284

**13. ARBITRATION:** This Agreement shall be interpreted in accordance with the laws of the State of _____ applicable to agreements executed and to be wholly performed therein. Any controversy or claim arising out of or in relation to this Agreement or the validity, construction or performance of this Agreement, or the breach thereof, shall be resolved by arbitration in accordance with the rules and procedures of the American Film Marketing Association, as said rules may be amended from time to time with rights of discovery if requested by the arbitrator. Such rules and procedures are incorporated and made a part of this Agreement by reference. If the American Film Marketing Association shall refuse to accept jurisdiction of such dispute, then the parties agree to arbitrate such matter before and in accordance with the rules of the American Arbitration Association under its jurisdiction in _____ before a single arbitrator familiar with entertainment law. The parties shall have the right to engage in pre-hearing discovery in connection with such arbitration proceedings. The parties agree hereto that they will abide by and perform any award rendered in any arbitration conducted pursuant hereto, that any court having jurisdiction thereof may issue a judgment based upon such award and that the prevailing party in such arbitration and/or confirmation proceeding shall be entitled to recover its reasonable attorneys' fees and expenses. The arbitration will be held in _____ and any award shall be final, binding and non-appealable. The Parties agree to accept service of process in accordance with the AFMA Rules.

**14. ENTIRE AGREEMENT; AMENDMENT; NO WAIVER:** This Agreement contains the entire understanding between the parties with respect to Producer's engagement by Company and supersedes all existing agreements, whether written or oral, between the parties hereto. This Agreement cannot be amended, except in writing, subscribed thereto by Producer and Company. The failure of a party to insist upon strict adherence to any term, condition or other provision of this Agreement will not be considered a waiver or deprive that party of the right to insist upon strict adherence to that term or any other term, condition or other provision of the Agreement.

# MAKE-UP AND SPECIAL EFFECTS AGREEMENT

This agreement (hereinafter referred to as the "Agreement") is entered into this the _____ (Date), by and between _____ (the "Production Company") and _____ (the "Special Effects Contractor").

Said parties hereby agree as follows:

## 1. SERVICES TO BE PROVIDED:

(a) The Production Company hereby engages the Special Effects Contractor and the Special Effects Contractor hereby agrees to provide the services necessary or required to design, originate, create, develop, construct, maintain and otherwise produce for the Production Company the special and make-up effects (collectively, the "Effects") required by the Production Company for its "_____" character in the motion picture entitled "_____" (the "Picture"). The Effects will be available for demonstration to the Production Company as required in order that the Effects will be completed not later than _____.

The Special Effects Contractor shall maintain the Effects after completion of photography thereof in the condition then existing, subject to reasonable wear and tear for a period of at least five (5) years and shall not destroy the Effects without first providing the Production Company with the opportunity to determine whether it desires to continue storing and/or maintaining such Effects at a facility other than that of the Special Effects Contractor.

(b) The Special Effects Contractor shall also furnish the services of _____(the "Artist") and other trained personnel (the "Crew") in order to complete second unit photography of the Effects for the Picture. Thereafter, if the Production Company requires the Artist's services, such services shall be subject to the Artist's professional availability (provided that the Artist shall use reasonable efforts to be available as and when requested by the Production Company).

(c) The Effects required by the Production Company have been discussed in detail between the Special Effects Contractor and the Production Company. The Special Effects Contractor and the Artist shall originate, design, create, develop, construct and, if necessary, repair the Effects in accordance with such discussions, the screenplay submitted to the Special Effects Contractor, the activity description provided by the Special Effects Contractor and approved by the Production Company, and all drawings submitted by the Production Company, as the foregoing may by mutual approval be revised (collectively, the "Plans"). The Special Effects Contractor and the Artist shall consult with the Production Company concerning matters relative to the design and specifications of the Effects and will comply with requests and suggestions of the Production Company to insure that the Effects will achieve the creative and dramatic effects desired. The Production Company shall have the right to view from time to time the progress of the Effects prior to delivery, but all such viewings shall be set up by appointment.

## 2. TIME FOR PERFORMANCE:
The services of the Special Effects Contractor, Artist and Crew shall commence on _____ and shall continue until completion, delivery and photography of the Effects.

## 3. DELIVERY:
The Special Effects Contractor and the Artist shall deliver each item of the Effects to the Production Company (or, at Production Company's

CONTRACTS
FOR THE
FILM AND
TELEVISION
INDUSTRY

286

discretion, ready the Effects for pickup by the Production Company) in accordance with Clause 1 above, subject to delays due to force majeure events. All delivery charges will be directly billed to the Production Company.

**4. COMPENSATION:** Provided the Special Effects Contractor and Artist are not in material breach of this Agreement and have rendered all services required by the Production Company hereunder, the Production Company shall pay the Special Effects Contractor for all such services and rights:

(a) $_____, to be advanced in installments as follows:

$_____ upon execution of this Agreement;

$_____ upon delivery of the photographs of the Effects thereof to the Production Company;

$_____ upon the theatrical release of the Picture in the domestic marketplace.

(b) An amount equal to _____ percent of the Production Company's merchandising net profits derived from exploitation of the Effects; provided, however, that if the Effects shall be used in any merchandising item with another character or characters and any royalty shall be payable on account of the use of such other character or characters then the percentage of such net profits payable to the Special Effects Contractor hereunder shall be reduced by the amount of such other royalty to not less than two percent (2%). As used herein "merchandising net profits" shall mean the Production Company's gross receipts from exploitation of the Effects in merchandising less the aggregate of (i) the Production Company's direct out-of-pocket manufacturing and licensing costs actually incurred and paid (it being agreed that costs incurred but not yet paid may be deducted, provided that if any such cost is not paid within one (1) year from the time incurred its deductibility will be reversed until such time as such cost is actually paid), if any, and (ii) a distribution fee for the Production Company equal to forty percent (40%) of its gross receipts.

The Production Company shall account to the Special Effects Contractor on a quarterly basis for one (1) year and thereafter semi-annually, within thirty (30) days after the close of each accounting period; provided, however, that if the Production Company's merchandising licensee shall account to the Production Company on a less frequent basis then the Production Company shall account to the Special Effects Contractor on such basis, and provided further that if pursuant to any such accounting a payment of less than One Hundred Dollars ($100) shall be due to the Special Effects Contractor, the Production Company shall not be required to provide such accounting. Any payment due to be paid to the Special Effects Contractor pursuant to this clause shall accompany such statement.

Any statement not objected to by the Special Effects Contractor in writing within eighteen (18) months after its dispatch shall be deemed conclusive and binding upon said Special Effects Contractor. The Special Effects Contractor may, at his expense and on reasonable notice, audit the Production Company's books and records relating to merchandising of the Effects not more than once each year. In relation to any such audit, the Special Effects Contractor may make copies of such books and records at the place they are kept and shall receive copies of the results of any audit of the Production Company's licensees.

(c) To the extent that changes required by the Production Company in the Plans cause a material increase in the cost of manufacturing the Effects, the Special Effects Contractor shall promptly notify the Production Company in writing of the approximate amount of such increase and the Production Company and the Special Effects Contractor shall in good faith determine an appropriate increase in the compensation payable to the Special Effects Contractor pursuant to clause 4(a) above.

(d) For set operations in connection with photography of the Effects, the Production Company will pay (i) an amount equal to Screen Actors Guild ("SAG") scale compensation to and for such Crew as may be required by the Special Effects Contractor and approved by the Production Company for set operations and (ii) SAG Pension and Health and Welfare Plan contributions from the employer for said services.

## 5. OBLIGATIONS OF SPECIAL EFFECTS COORDINATOR:

(a) The Special Effects Contractor shall furnish and be solely responsible for the cost of:

(i) All pre-production labor incurred by the Special Effects Contractor for his administrative and production employees, including, but not limited to, hourly wages and employer contributions required by law or applicable collective bargaining agreements;

(ii) All materials and supplies used by the Special Effects Contractor hereunder;

(iii) Except as otherwise specifically provided in this Agreement, any and all other incurred expenses including, but not limited to, local transportation costs (rental or leasing of vehicles and repair and maintenance of same), shop rental, utilities, insurance, rental, repair, and maintenance of tools and equipment and any and all other costs, fixed or otherwise, required by the Special Effects Contractor to perform the services required hereunder;

(iv) The salaries of the Artist and Crew for all services required hereunder during photography of the Picture, including retakes and added scenes, except as provided in clause 4(d) above.

(b) All personnel necessary for the design, creation, production and delivery of the Effects shall be the Special Effects Contractor's employees or independent contractors and the Special Effects Contractor shall have all duties and responsibilities of an employer, including but not limited to payment of compensation to its employees, payroll deduction and withholdings, employer's taxes and worker's compensation insurance.

## 6. WARRANTIES AND INDEMNIFICATION:

(a) The Special Effects Contractor hereby represents and warrants that:

(i) No Claims: The Effects shall be free from any and all claims, liens, judgments, or suits of any nature, and that no portion of the Effects will impair or interfere with the Production Company's production, distribution or

CONTRACTS
FOR THE
FILM AND
TELEVISION
INDUSTRY

288

other exploitation of the Picture or any other rights granted to the Production Company hereunder, and that in connection with the services rendered by the Special Effects Contractor, said Special Effects Contractor will not knowingly violate or infringe upon the trademark, trade name, copyright, patent, literary right or any other right of any other person, firm or corporation; and

(ii) Condition: The Effects, when completed, will be suitable for the purposes intended, and will not contain any materials, defects, or devices which could cause personal injury or other health hazards to persons using the Effects as contemplated hereunder or working in proximity with the Effects.

(b) The Special Effects Contractor shall indemnify and hold harmless the Production Company, its successors, assigns and licensees and the officers, directors, shareholders, employees and representatives of any of the foregoing from and against any and all costs, liability, damages and expenses (including but not limited to reasonable attorneys' fees) arising by reason of the breach of any of the foregoing representations or warranties. The Production Company shall indemnify and hold harmless the Special Effects Contractor and its officers, directors, shareholders, employees and representatives from and against any and all cost, liability, damages and expense (including but not limited to reasonable attorneys' fees) arising by reason of any material contained in the Picture.

**7. OWNERSHIP OF EFFECTS:** All rights to the Effects and the design thereof shall be the property of the Production Company and shall be created by the Special Effects Contractor as a work-for-hire in order that the Production Company shall have all copyright, trademark and other proprietary rights in the Effects. However, the Production Company shall not disclose to any third party mechanical details concerning the design, construction or manufacture of the Effects except (i) for merchandising purposes and (ii) if motion pictures are produced in addition to the Picture and the Production Company and Special Effects Contractor do not enter into an agreement pursuant to which the Special Effects Contractor will provide the services of the Artist and Crew for such additional motion pictures, such details may be disclosed to any person(s) engaged to design, construct, operate or maintain the Effects for such additional motion pictures, it being agreed that the Production Company and the Special Effects Contractor will consult in the selection of any such person(s) but the Production Company's decision shall be determinative.

**8. OWNERSHIP OF PROCEEDS:** The Production Company shall be entitled to and shall solely and exclusively own all proceeds of the services of the Special Effects Contractor, Crew and Artist hereunder, including all rights throughout the universe of copyright, trademark, patent, production, manufacture, recordation, reproduction, transcription, performance, broadcast, and exhibition by any art or method now known or hereafter devised. All of the proceeds of the services rendered hereunder are works specifically ordered by the Production Company and the Production Company shall have the free and unrestricted right to use and exploit the Effects in any manner whatsoever as the Production Company may designate in its sole discretion.

**9. POSSESSION OF EFFECTS:** Notwithstanding the provisions above relating to ownership of the Effects and the proceeds thereof the Special Effects Contractor shall retain physical possession of the Effects in trust for the Production Company after completion of photography thereof (i) for safekeeping of the Effects and (ii) for use on its premises by the Special Effects Contractor as part of its portfolio of motion picture special effects work. The Production Company and Special Effects Contractor hereby represent that they both recognize that the Effects are to be constructed and operated with the several loaned parts that are more particularly described and identified on the accompanying Exhibit "A," which is attached hereto and incorporated herein by reference as if recited verbatim in this Agreement. As such, after completion of photography of the Picture, the loaned parts listed on Exhibit "A" are to remain the property of the Special Effects Contractor, and any reference to the Effects thereafter shall be represented by the Effects without such loaned parts.

**10. SUBSEQUENT PRODUCTIONS:** If the Production Company elects to produce or cause the production of other motion pictures (whether produced for initial theatrical or television release) in addition to the Picture, the Production Company and the Special Effects Contractor shall negotiate in good faith with respect to such services and compensation as may be required by the Production Company in connection with its use of the Effects. The Production Company and the Special Effects Contractor hereby represent and agree that the Effects are to be designed and built to last through the completion of photography of the Picture. As such, the Special Effects Contractor cannot guarantee the condition of the Effects after photography of the Picture. If the Production Company and the Special Effects Contractor fail to reach agreement concerning any such subsequent production(s), then the Production Company may engage the services of any other person(s) to refurbish, add to, maintain, modify and/or operate the Effects, it being agreed that the Production Company and the Special Effects Contractor will consult in the selection of any such person(s) but the Production Company's decision shall be determinative.

**11. PUBLICITY AND CREDIT:**

(a) Publicity: The Production Company shall have the sole and exclusive right to issue publicity concerning the Effects. Notwithstanding the foregoing, the Special Effects Contractor may mention the fact that the Artist is performing services in connection with the Picture so long as such (i) is not an advertisement for the Picture, (ii) does not contain language which is derogatory in nature, and (iii) does not disclose confidential information.

(b) Screen Credit: If the Special Effects Contractor and Artist are not in material breach of this Agreement and a substantial portion of the Effects created pursuant to this Agreement are utilized in a recognizable manner in the Picture, the Special Effects Contractor shall be accorded credit on the Picture on screen as follows:

"SPECIAL EFFECTS BY _____"

(c) Other Credits: Except as specifically provided above, all aspects of the credit to be accorded pursuant to this clause, including, without limitation, the size, style of type and position shall be determined by the Production Company in its discretion.

**12. INSURANCE:** The Special Effects Contractor shall maintain at all times while any employees of the Special Effects Contractor are rendering services hereunder, workers' compensation insurance, unemployment insurance and state disability insurance as required by _____ law and any applicable collective bargaining agreement. In connection with workers' compensation insurance, the Special Effects Contractor is furnishing the Artist's and the Crew's services to the

CONTRACTS
FOR THE
FILM AND
TELEVISION
INDUSTRY

290

Production Company, thus, for the purposes of any and all applicable workers' compensation statutes, no employment relationship exits between the Artist and the Crew on the one hand and the Production Company on the other since the Special Effects Contractor is the "general employer" of the Artist and Crew and the Production Company is merely their "special employer" as such terms are understood and used within the context of workers' compensation law.

The rights, if any, of the Artist and/or any of the Crew's heirs, executors, administrators, successors and assigns, against the Production Company or its employees, successors, assigns, parent, subsidiaries, affiliates, officers, directors, agents or licensees, relating to any injury, illness, disability or death arising out of or occurring during the course of the rendition of services hereunder are governed by and limited to those provided under such workers' compensation statutes, and neither the Production Company nor its employees, successors, assigns, parent, subsidiaries affiliates, officers, directors, agents, or licensees shall have any other obligation or liability by reason of any such injury, illness, disability or death. If the applicability of any workers' compensation statutes to the engagement of the Artist's and/or the Crew's services hereunder is dependent upon, or affected by, any election on their part or on the part of the Special Effects Contractor, such election may be made in favor of such application, it being expressly understood that such remedies and liabilities afforded hereunder are no less nor greater than those enjoyed by the Artist and the Crew had they been employed by the Production Company directly.

**13. PARKING AND WORKING SPACES:** If the Special Effects Contractor is required to provide services away from the Special Effects Contractor's facility located at _____, the Production Company shall provide (a) one parking space for the Artist; and (b) a work space, which shall be a room if at a studio or, if on location, a work space in a truck which is sufficient to accommodate the Special Effects Contractor's needs.

**14. MISCELLANEOUS PROVISIONS:**

(a) Assignment: The Production Company may transfer or assign this Agreement or all or any part of its rights hereunder to any person, firm or corporation, and this Agreement shall inure to the benefit of and be binding upon the heirs, successors and assigns of either of the parties hereto. No such transfer or assignment, however, shall relieve the Production Company of its obligations to the Special Effects Contractor hereunder unless the transferee or assignee shall be a member company of the Motion Picture Association of America ("MPAA") and such company shall assume in writing such obligations. The Special Effects Contractor may assign its right to receive revenues hereunder, but otherwise it shall not assign any of its obligations or rights relating to this Agreement.

(b) Notices: All notices (and statements and payments, if applicable) shall be in writing and shall be given by the parties personally or by mailing (postage prepaid), or by telegraphing same to the appropriate party at the addresses set forth below:

For the Special Effects Contractor:     _____
                                        (Contractor)

                                        _____
                                        (Contractor Address)

For the Production Company:             _____
                                        (Production Company)

                                        _____
                                        (Production Company Address)

The date of receipt of such personal delivery, mailing or telegraphing shall be presumed to be not later than two (2) days following submission of such notice, statement or payment, properly addressed to the applicable carrier.

(c) Governing Law: This Agreement shall be governed by the laws of the State of _____ applicable to agreements entered into and to be wholly performed therein.

(d) Additional Documents: The parties hereby agree to execute such additional document(s) as may be reasonably necessary or desirable in order for either of such parties to enforce their respective rights hereunder.

(e) Entire Agreement: This Agreement expresses the binding and entire agreement between the Production Company and the Special Effects Contractor and shall replace and supersede all prior arrangements and representations, either oral or written, as to the subject matter hereof.

(f) Arbitration: Any controversy or claim arising out of or in relation to this Agreement or the validity, construction or performance of this Agreement, or the breach thereof, shall be resolved by arbitration in accordance with the rules and procedures of AFMA, as said rules may be amended from time to time with rights of discovery if requested by the arbitrator. Such rules and procedures are incorporated and made a part of this Agreement by reference. If AFMA shall refuse to accept jurisdiction of such dispute, then the parties agree to arbitrate such matter before and in accordance with the rules of the American Arbitration Association under its jurisdiction in _____ before a single arbitrator familiar with entertainment law. The parties shall have the right to engage in pre-hearing discovery in connection with such arbitration proceedings. The parties agree hereto that they will abide by and perform any award rendered in any arbitration conducted pursuant hereto, that any court having jurisdiction thereof may issue a judgment based upon such award and that the prevailing party in such arbitration and/or confirmation proceeding shall be entitled to recover its reasonable attorneys' fees and expenses. The arbitration will be held in _____ and any award shall be final, binding and non-appealable. The Parties agree to accept service of process in accordance with the AFMA Rules.

Executed at _____, _____ as of the date first above written.

SPECIAL EFFECTS CONTRACTOR

_____
(Contractor)

PRODUCTION COMPANY

_____
on behalf of

_____
(Production Company)

## EXHIBIT "A"
## LIST OF LOANED PARTS

CONTRACTS
FOR THE
FILM AND
TELEVISION
INDUSTRY

292

## ON LOCATION

Filmmakers who shoot on location without securing a release may be subject to liability. Filmmakers don't have a First Amendment right to trespass or invade the rights of others.

Even if a landowner doesn't bring suit, a filmmaker should secure releases for every location. Without such documents it may be difficult to purchase Errors and Omissions (E&O) insurance and survive the scrutiny of a distributor's legal department. Location agreements should be sought from landowners or land possessors when shooting on private property and from the appropriate government entity when shooting on public property. Make sure that the person signing the release has authority to grant such permission.

Location agreements don't necessarily cost much. In a small community which filmmakers rarely visit, the arrival of a movie crew can generate a lot of excitement. Residents may offer the use of their property for little or no money. On the other hand, in Los Angeles, movie crews have worn out their welcome in many neighborhoods. Residents are annoyed by the traffic congestion and noise that accompanies a shoot. Homeowners may have had their property damaged by prior film crews. These homeowners are more aware of how much the studios are willing to pay for locations. They may demand top dollar, which can amount to several thousand dollars per day.

# LOCATION AGREEMENT

Agreement entered into this _____, by and between _____ ("Production Company") and _____ ("Grantor").

**1. IDENTITY OF FILMING LOCATION:** Grantor hereby agrees to permit Production Company to use the property located at _____ ("Property") in connection with the motion picture currently entitled _____ ("Picture") for rehearsing, photographing, filming and recording scenes and sounds for the Picture. Production Company and its licensees, sponsors, assigns and successors may exhibit, advertise and promote the Picture or any portion thereof, whether or not such uses contain audio and/or visual reproductions of the Property and whether or not the Property is identified, in any and all media which currently exist or which may exist in the future in all countries of the world and in perpetuity.

**2. RIGHT OF ACCESS:** Production Company shall have the right to bring personnel and equipment (including props and temporary sets) onto the Property and to remove same after completion of its use of the Property hereunder. Production Company shall have the right but not the obligation to photograph, film and use in the Picture the actual name, if any, connected with the Property or to use any other name for the Property. If Production Company depicts the interior(s) of any structures located on the Property, Grantor agrees that Production Company shall not be required to depict such interior(s) in any particular manner in the Picture.

**3. TIME OF ACCESS:** The permission granted hereunder shall be for the period commencing on or about _____ and continuing until _____. The period may be extended by Production Company if there are changes in the production schedule or delays due to weather conditions. The within permission shall also apply to future retakes and/or added scenes.

**4. PAYMENT:** For each day the Production Company uses the location, it shall pay Grantor the sum of $_____ in consideration for the foregoing.

**5. ALTERATIONS TO LOCATION:** Production Company agrees that (with Grantor's permission) if it becomes necessary to change, alter or rearrange any equipment on the Property belonging to Grantor, Production Company shall return and restore said equipment to its original place and condition, or repair it, if necessary. Production Company agrees to indemnify and hold harmless Grantor from and against any and all liabilities, damages and claims of third parties arising from Production Company's use hereunder of the Property (unless such liabilities, damages or claims arise from breach of Grantor's warranty as set forth in the immediately following sentence) (and from any physical damage to the Property proximately caused by Production Company, or any of its representatives, employees, or agents). Grantor warrants that it has the right and authority to enter this Agreement and to grant the rights granted by it herein. Grantor agrees to indemnify and hold harmless Production Company from and against any and all claims relating to breach of its aforesaid warranty.

**6. NO KICKBACKS FOR USE:** Grantor affirms that neither it nor anyone acting for it gave or agreed to give anything of value to any member of the production staff, anyone associated with the Picture, or any representative of Production Company, or any television station or network for mentioning or displaying the name of Grantor as a shooting location on the Property, except the use of the Property, which was furnished for use solely on or in connection with the Picture.

CONTRACTS
FOR THE
FILM AND
TELEVISION
INDUSTRY

294

**7. BILLING CREDIT:** Grantor acknowledges that any identification of the Property which Production Company may furnish shall be at Production Company's sole discretion and in no event shall said identification be beyond that which is reasonably related to the content of the Picture.

**8. RELEASE:** Grantor releases and discharges Production Company, its employees, agents, licensees, successors and assigns from any and all claims, demands or causes of actions that Grantor may now have or may from now on have for libel, defamation, invasion of privacy or right of publicity, infringement of copyright or violation of any other right arising out of or relating to any utilization of the rights granted herein.

The undersigned represents that he/she is empowered to execute this Agreement for Grantor.

IN WITNESS WHEREOF, the parties have hereunto set their names and signatures:

PRODUCTION COMPANY:

_____

GRANTOR:

_____

# CHAPTER 9

# DISTRIBUTION

## THE ACQUISITION/DISTRIBUTION AGREEMENT

Some motion pictures are not produced by the company that distributes them. These independently produced projects may use investors, or rely on pre-sale distribution deals (selling of various foreign distribution rights), to finance production. The producer enters an acquisition/distribution agreement with a distributor for release of the picture. This agreement is often referred to as a Negative Pick-up Deal.

While the terms of these deals vary, the studio/distributor typically pays for all distribution, advertising and marketing costs. The studio and producer share profits. Because the producer has taken the risk of financing production, he may obtain a better definition of net profits than if the distributor financed production. Profits may be split fifty/fifty between the studio and producer without deduction of a distribution fee. Of course, the independent producer takes a chance. If the film turns out poorly, no distributor may want it. In that case the producer may incur a substantial loss.

In a negative pick-up deal, the distributor will often agree to give the producer an advance on his share of profits. This money is paid after the distribution agreement is made but before distribution. The producer can use this money to repay investors. Producers want to obtain as large an advance as possible because they know they may never see anything on the back end of the deal (i.e., no profits).

The distributor wants to pay as small an advance as possible, and usually resists giving an amount greater than the cost of production. If the distributor has a definition of "net profits" that allows many deductions, or engages in creative

CONTRACTS
FOR THE
FILM AND
TELEVISION
INDUSTRY

296

accounting, profit participants are unlikely to see any "net profits." Consequently, a shrewd producer wants a large advance. The producer may also want to retain distribution rights to other territories, and keep revenue from those territories from being cross-collateralized.[1]

Negative pick-up deals can be negotiated before, during, or after production. Often distributors become interested in a film after seeing it at a film festival and observing audience reaction.

## FILMMAKER'S CHECKLIST

Here is a list of some of the issues that filmmakers need to address in order to protect their interests. The ability of the filmmaker to improve the terms of a distribution deal will depend on the desirability of their motion picture and whether the filmmaker is able to interest multiple buyers and create competition for the film.

This list should not be considered exhaustive. There are other items a filmmaker may want to include, such as clauses dealing with advances, guarantees, and reservation of rights.

*1. NO CHANGES: The film should not be edited, nor the title changed, without the filmmaker's prior approval. Editing for censorship purposes, television broadcast and changes made for a foreign release, such as translating the title, are permissible.*

*2. MINIMUM ADVERTISING SPECIFIED: The contract should specify in writing the minimum amount the distributor will spend on advertising and promotion of the motion picture. The distributor should make a commitment to pay for the creation of a poster, one-sheet and trailer if these items have not been created.*

*3. EXPENSES LIMITED: There should be a floor and a ceiling on expenses. Market expenses (the cost to attend film markets) should be limited to the first year of release and capped per market. Promotional expenses should be limited to direct out-of-pocket costs spent to promote the motion picture and should specifically exclude the distributor's general overhead and staff expenses.*

*4. TERM: The term should be a reasonable length, perhaps up to ten years, but not in perpetuity. The filmmaker should be able to regain rights to the motion picture if the distributor gives up on it. Thus, it is best to have a short initial term, such as two years, and a series of automatic rollovers if the distributor returns a certain amount of revenue to the filmmaker. If these performance milestones are not met, all rights would automatically revert to the filmmaker.*

---

[1] Cross-collateralized means the monies earned from several markets are pooled. For example, let's say your picture made one million dollars in England and lost one million dollars in France. If those territories were cross-collateralized, and you were entitled to a percentage of the net revenue, you would get nothing. On the other hand, if the territories were not cross-collateralized, you would get your percentage of the English revenues and the distributor would absorb the loss incurred in France.

**5. INDEMNITY:** *Filmmaker should be indemnified (receive reimbursement) for any losses incurred by filmmaker as a result of distributor's breach of the terms of the agreement, violation of third party rights, and for any changes or additions made to the motion picture.*

**6. POSSESSION OF NEGATIVE:** *Distributor should receive a lab access letter rather than possession of the original negative and other original elements. Distributor should not be permitted to remove masters from the laboratory.*

**7. ERRORS AND OMISSIONS (E&O) POLICY:** *While it is generally the filmmaker's responsibility to purchase an E & O insurance policy, distributors are often willing to advance the cost of this insurance and recoup the cost from gross revenues. In such an event, the filmmaker should be added as an additional named insured on the policy.*

**8. TERMINATION CLAUSE:** *If the distributor defaults on its contractual obligations, the filmmaker should have the right to terminate the contract, and regain rights to license the film in unsold territories as well as obtain money damages for the default. Filmmaker should give distributor fourteen days prior written notice of default before exercising the right to termination.*

**9. RIGHT TO INSPECT BOOKS AND RECORDS:** *Distributor should maintain complete books and records with regard to all sales and rental of the motion picture. Filmmaker should receive quarterly (or monthly) producer statements with any payment due filmmaker. Filmmaker should have the right to examine the books and records of distributor during reasonable business hours on ten days' notice.*

**10. LATE PAYMENTS/LIEN:** *All monies due and payable to filmmaker should be held in trust by distributor for filmmaker. Filmmaker should be deemed to have a lien on filmmaker's share of revenue. Distributor should pay filmmaker interest on any amounts past due.*

**11. LIMITATION ON ACTION:** *Filmmaker should have at least three years from receipt of any financial statement, or discovery of any accounting irregularity, whichever is later, to contest accounting errors and file a Demand for Arbitration.*

**12. ASSIGNMENT:** *It is best to prohibit assignment unless Filmmaker consents. If assignment is permitted, Distributor should not be relieved of its obligations under the original contract.*

**13. FILMMAKER DEFAULT:** *Distributor should give Filmmaker fourteen days' written notice of any alleged default by filmmaker, and an additional ten days to cure such default, before taking any action to enforce its rights.*

**14. WARRANTIES:** *Filmmaker's warranties in regard to infringement of third party rights should be to the best of the filmmaker's knowledge and belief, not absolute.*

CONTRACTS
FOR THE
FILM AND
TELEVISION
INDUSTRY

298

*15. SCHEDULE OF MINIMUMS:* *For distributors who license foreign rights (known as international distributors or foreign sales agents) there should be a schedule of minimum license fees per territory. The distributor is not permitted to license the motion picture in each territory for less than the minimum without the prior approval of the Filmmaker.*

*16. ARBITRATION CLAUSE:* *Every contract should contain an arbitration clause ensuring that all contractual disputes are subject to binding arbitration with the prevailing party entitled to reimbursement of legal fees and costs. The arbitration award should be final, binding and non-appealable. AFMA will now arbitrate entertainment industry disputes involving non-AFMA companies. The AFMA personal guarantee Rider can be used to bar a company's chief executive from attending future American Film Markets if the company refuses to pay an arbitration award.*

I have provided two versions of a theatrical acquisition/distribution agreement. The Filmmaker Friendly version has terms more favorable than the standard terms generally offered by distributors. The distributor friendly version sets forth the terms generally proposed by distributors.

# THEATRICAL ACQUISITION/DISTRIBUTION AGREEMENT
## (Filmmaker Friendly)

_____
(Date of Agreement)

_____
(Production Company)

_____
(Production Company Representative)

_____
(Production Address)

_____
(Production Company City State & Zip)

_____
Tel.

_____
Fax.

Re: "_____"
(Motion Picture Title)

Agreement made and entered into as of _____ by and between _____, ("Distributor") at _____, and _____, ("Producer"). In consideration of their respective covenants, warranties and representations, together with other good and valuable consideration, Distributor and Producer hereby agree as follow:

**1. PICTURE:** Producer will deliver to Distributor the documentation, advertising and physical materials (the "Materials") set forth in the attached Delivery Schedule, relating to the _____ (Motion Picture Format) Motion Picture, currently entitled: "_____" (the "Picture")

**2. RIGHTS GRANTED:**

a) Producer hereby grants to Distributor the irrevocable, right, title and interest in and to the distribution of the Picture, its sound, and music in the territory (as hereinafter defined) including without limitation, the sole, exclusive, and irrevocable right and privilege, under Producer's copyright and otherwise, to distribute, license and otherwise exploit the Picture, its image sound and music, for the term (as hereinafter defined) throughout the territory (as hereinafter defined) for Theatrical, Home Video, and Television media.

Such rights do not include the rights to produce other motion Pictures, or sequels, or remakes of the Picture or any right to produce television series, mini series, or programs or other so-called ancillary rights (herein called "Reserved Rights").

Without limiting the generality of the foregoing, or any other rights granted to Distributor elsewhere in this agreement, Producer hereby grants to Distributor the following rights:

CONTRACTS
FOR THE
FILM AND
TELEVISION
INDUSTRY

300

i) Theatrical Rights: All rights in and to the manufacture, distribution, exhibition, marketing and other exploitation of the Picture its sound and music, by and relating to the projection of visual images contained on positive film prints of any size or kind (including 35mm and 16mm) whether in movie theaters, drive-ins or any other venues (herein the "Theatrical Rights") throughout the territory for the term.

ii) Home Video Rights: All rights in and to the manufacture, distribution, exploitation and non-theatrical, non-admission free home use exhibition of the Picture, its sound and music (whether by sale or by rental) by means of any and all forms of videocassette, videodisc, video cartridge, tape or other similar device ("Videogram") now known or hereafter devised and designed to be used in conjunction with a reproduction apparatus which causes a visual image (whether or not synchronized with sound) to be seen on the screen of a television receiver or any comparable device now known or hereafter devised, including DVD (the "Home Video Rights" or "Video Rights").

iii) Free Television Rights: All rights in and to the distribution, exhibition, marketing and other exploitation of the Picture, its sound, and music by free television utilizing means other than those provided for in Paragraph 1(A) hereinabove and including without limitation, free television, by network, or syndicated UHF or VHF broadcast (the "Free Television Rights").

iv) Pay Television/Pay Per View: All rights in and to the distribution, exhibition, marketing and other exploitation of the Picture, its sound and music by means of "Pay Television" as that expression is commonly understood in the motion Picture industry, and including without limitation, cable, wire or fiber of any material, "over-the-air pay", all forms of regular or occasionally scrambled broadcast, master antenna, and multi-channel multi-point distribution, satellite transmission and radio (for purposes of simulcast only), all on a subscription, pay-per-view, license, rental, sale or any other basis ("the Pay Television Rights").

b) Advertising:  Distributor shall have the exclusive right throughout the territory during the Term to advertise and publicize (or have it subdistributors advertise and publicize) the Picture by any and all means, media and method whatsoever, including, by means of the distribution, exhibition, broadcasting and telecasting of trailers of the Picture, or excerpts from the Picture prepared by Distributor or others, subject to any customary restrictions upon and obligations with respect to such rights as are provided for in the contracts in relation to the production of the Picture.

c) Title: Distributor shall have the right to use the present title of the Picture. Subdistributors may change the title for distribution in their territories.

d) Editing:

i) Distributor in its discretion will have the right to: incorporate into the Picture preceding and/or following the main and end titles of the Picture and Trailers thereof, and in all advertising and publicity relating thereto, in such manner, position, form and substance as Distributor may elect, Distributor's trademark, logo and presentation announcement, and the designation of Distributor as the distributor of the Picture: any re-edit of the credit sequence will be at Distributor's expense.

ii) Distributor's right to edit hereunder specifically exclude the rights to make alterations whatsoever to the original negative and the Video Master of the Picture, to which Distributor shall have lab access (irrevocable for the term of this Agreement) for duplication purposes only.

iii) Distributor hereby indemnifies Producer for any losses incurred as a result of any liability arising from Distributor's editing, adding, or changing material in the Picture .

e) Licensing: Distributor has the right to grant licenses and other authorizations to one or more third parties to exercise any or all of said rights and privileges provided herein, for any and all territories throughout the territory. The Maximum term for any license granted by Distributor shall be twelve (12) years (15 years for Germany).

f) Territorial Minimums: Producer and Distributor have established mutually agreed minimum guarantee amounts per territory (hereinafter "Territorial Minimums"). Nothing contained herein or in the schedule of Territorial Minimums shall be deemed to require Distributor in fact to obtain any such Territorial Minimum(s), but, rather, it is the intention of the parties hereto that Distributor may not enter into an agreement for an amount less than the applicable Territorial Minimum without first obtaining Producer's approval. The Territorial Minimums for the Picture are set forth in Schedule A, attached.

g) No Further Rights: This agreement confers no right on the part of the Producer to use, or authorize others to use the Picture or any of the rights granted Distributor, within the Territory, which is not authorized by the Distributor hereunder, except Producer shall have the right to exhibit the Picture in festivals, industry screenings and screenings for non-profit and/or educational purposes.

**3. RESERVED RIGHTS:** All other rights not expressly written herein, including but not limited to electronic publishing, print publication, music publishing, live-television, radio and dramatic rights are reserved to the Producer.

**4. TERRITORY:** The territory (herein "Territory") for which rights are granted to Distributor consists of the World (in all languages and in all formats) with the exception of the United States, its territories, possessions & military bases, and English-speaking Canada.

**5. TERM:** The rights granted to Distributor under this Agreement will commence on the date of this Agreement and continue thereafter for two years (the "Initial Term"). If Distributor pays Producer $200,000 or more in the Initial Term, Distributor shall automatically have the right to extend the term for another two year term "a Subsequent Term"). During this Subsequent Term (and additional subsequent terms if extended), Distributor shall have the option of extending the term for additional two year periods (up to a total term of no more than ten years) if the following thresholds are met:

Initial Term: If $200,000 has been paid to Producer , then Distributor may extend the term for another two years (the First Extended Term).

First Extended Term: If $300,000 cumulatively has been paid to Producer during the Initial and First Extended Term, then Distributor may extend the term another two years (Second Extended Term).

CONTRACTS
FOR THE
FILM AND
TELEVISION
INDUSTRY

302

Second Extended Term: If $400,000 cumulatively has been paid to Producer during the Initial, First and Second Extended Term, then Distributor may extend the term for another two years (the Third Extended Term).

Third Extended Term: If $500,000 cumulatively has been paid to Producer during the Initial, and First through Third Extended Term, then Distributor may extend the term for another two years (the Fourth Extended Term).

**6. ADVERTISING:** Distributor will consult in good faith with Producer on marketing plans before any artwork is commissioned and the marketing campaign has begun. Producer will supply to Distributor advertising and marketing materials as set forth on the attached delivery schedule "Schedule A."

### 7. COPYRIGHT:

Producer represents and warrants that the Picture is, and will be throughout the Term, protected by copyright. Each copy of the Picture will contain a copyright notice conforming to and complying with the requirements of the United States Copyright Act as amended from time to time.

### 8. PRODUCTION COSTS:

As between Producer and Distributor: Producer is and will be responsible for and has paid or will pay all production costs, taxes, fees and charges with respect to the Picture and/or the Materials except as provided herein. As used herein, "production costs" will include all costs incurred in connection with the production of the Picture and the Materials, including payments to writers, producers, directors, artists, and all other persons rendering services in connection with the Picture and/or the materials, all costs and expenses incurred in acquiring rights to use music in connection with the Picture,) including synchronization, performance and mechanical reproduction fees and union residuals.

**9. PRODUCER'S REPRESENTATION AND WARRANTIES:** Producer warrants and represents to Distributor, to the best of Producer's knowledge and belief, as follows:

a) Producer has full right, power and authority to enter into and perform this Agreement and to grant to Distributor all of the rights herein granted and agreed to be granted to Distributor.

b) Producer has acquired, or will have acquired prior to the delivery of the Picture hereunder, and will maintain during the term all rights in and to the literary and musical material upon which the Picture is based or which are used therein and any other rights necessary and required for the exploitation of the Picture, as permitted hereunder.

c) Neither the Picture nor the Materials nor any part thereof, nor any literary, dramatic or musical works or any other materials contained therein or synchronized therewith, nor the exercise of any right, license or privilege herein granted, violates or will violate, or infringes or will infringe, any trademark, trade name, contract, agreement, copyright,(whether common law or statutory), patent literary, artistic, dramatic, personal, private, civil, or property right or right of privacy or "moral right of author", or any law or regulation or other right whatsoever of, or slanders or libels, any person, firm, corporation or association.

d) Producer has not sold, assigned, transferred or conveyed and will not sell, assign, transfer or convey, to any party, any right, title or interest in and to the Picture or any part thereof, or in and to the dramatic, musical or literary material upon which it is based, adverse to or derogatory of or which would interfere with the rights granted to Distributor, and has not and will not authorize any other party to exercise any right or take any action which will derogate from the rights herein granted or purported to be granted to Distributor.

e) Producer will obtain and maintain all necessary licenses for the production, exhibition, performance, distribution, marketing and exploitation of the Picture and/or the Materials, including, without limitation, the synchronization and performance of all music contained therein, throughout the Territory during the term for any and all purposes contemplated hereunder. Producer further represents and warrants that as between the Producer and Distributor, the performing rights to all musical compositions contained in the Picture and/or the Materials will be controlled by Producer to the extent required for the purposes of the Agreement and, that no payments will be required to be made by Distributor to any third party for the use of such music in the Materials or on television or in Videogram embodying the Picture other than Guild required residual payments (or, if any such music payments are required, Producer will be solely responsible therefor).

f) Producer represents and warrants all artists, actors, musicians and persons rendering services in connection with the production of the Picture or the materials have been or will be paid by Producer the sums required to be paid to them under applicable agreements, and the sums required to be paid pursuant to any applicable pension or similar trusts required thereby will be made by Producer, in a due and timely manner.

g) It is understood that the Producer has not obtained errors and omissions insurance. However, if demand is made by a sublicensee/distributor, for a certificate of errors and omissions insurance as indicated above, Distributor will advance such cost and recoup the expense from Gross receipts. Producer shall be added as an additional named insured on any E & O policy.

h) The Picture was shot on _____ film. The Picture and the television/airline version (when available) have a running time of _____ minutes and the Picture should receive an MPAA rating no more restrictive than "R." It is understood that the Picture has not received or applied for an MPAA rating. If and when it becomes necessary to receive an MPAA rating, Producer shall promptly perform any and all additional editing necessary in order to secure said MPAA rating. The expense of securing of such rating shall be advanced by Distributor and recouped from Gross receipts.

i) At the time of delivery of the Picture to Distributor, the Picture will not have been exhibited anywhere in the Territory for commercial reasons, with the exception of festivals or industry screenings.

## 10. DISTRIBUTOR'S WARRANTIES:

a) Distributor warrants that it is solvent and not in danger of bankruptcy. Distributor has the authority to enter into this agreement and there are and, to the best of Distributor's knowledge and belief, will be no claims, actions, suits, arbitrations, or other proceedings or investigations pending or threatened against or affecting the Distributors ability to fulfill its obligations under this agreement,

CONTRACTS
FOR THE
FILM AND
TELEVISION
INDUSTRY

304

at law or in equity, or before any federal, state, county, municipal or other governmental instrumentality or authority, domestic or foreign. Distributor warrants that all payments from sub-distributors and other Distributors will be by check, wire transfer, letter of credit or money order payable in the name of Distributor. If cash is accepted, a copy of license agreement with the amount of the deposit will be sent to Producer. Distributor further warrants that Distributor will not accept any other consideration, whether cash, discounts on Distributors for other films, favors of any kind, or any other form of consideration, from any sub-distributor or Distributor in return for licensing the Picture, unless such consideration is approved by Producer.

**11. INDEMNITY:** Each party hereby agrees to defend, indemnify and hold harmless the other (and its affiliates, and its and their respective successors, assigns, distributors, officers, directors, employees and representatives) against and for any and all claims, liabilities, damages, costs and expenses (including reasonable attorney's fees and court costs) arising from or related to any breach by the indemnifying party of any of its undertakings, representations or warranties under this Agreement, and/or arising from or related to any and all third party claims which, if proven, would be such breach. Each party agrees to notify the other in writing of any and all claims to which this indemnity will apply, and to afford the indemnifying party the opportunity to undertake the defense of such claim(s) with counsel approved by the indemnified party (which approval will not be unreasonably withheld), subject to the right of the indemnified party to participate in such defense at its cost. In no event shall any such claim be settled in such a way as which would adversely affect the rights of the indemnified party in the Picture without such party's prior written consent; provided, however, that Producer hereby consents to any settlement entered into under any of the following circumstances: (i) the applicable insurance authorized the settlement; (ii) the settlement relates to a claim for injunctive relief which has remained unsettled or pending for a period of 30 days or longer which otherwise interferes with Distributor's distribution of the Picture hereunder; or (iii) the settlement is for not more than $10,000.00. All rights and remedies of the parties hereunder will be cumulative and will not interfere with or prevent the exercise of any other right or remedy which may be available to the respective party.

**12. DELIVERY MATERIALS:** The Picture will be delivered as follows:

a) On or before _____ Producer will deliver to Distributor the materials specified in Exhibit A hereto, accompanied by a fully executed lab access letter (irrevocable for the term) for access to the Master materials. If any said materials are not acceptable to Distributor, Distributor will notify the Producer of any technical problems or defects within (10) business days, and Producer will promptly replace the defective materials at Producers' sole expense. Distributor shall have no right to terminate this Agreement unless and until Producer has failed to cure any such defects within thirty (30) days after notice thereof from Distributor. If no objection is made within ten business days of delivery of an item, the item will be deemed acceptable. If Distributor creates its own artwork and trailers for the Picture, Ownership of these materials shall vest in Producer, and Producer shall have the right to use said materials at any time for the Domestic release of the picture, and anywhere in the Universe after the term of this Agreement expires. Any artwork or copyrightable material commissioned by Distributor shall be created pursuant to a written contract, signed before the material is created, which states the work is a work-for-hire and that Producer is owner of all rights.

b) Producer will concurrently with the delivery of the materials deliver to Distributor a list of contractual requirements for advertising credits to persons who rendered services or furnished materials for such Picture and a list of any restrictions.

c) All materials delivered to Distributor shall be returned to Producer within 30 days of the end of the term.

d) Time is of the essence hereof.

**13. ADVANCE/GUARANTEE:**

There shall be non-refundable advance of $_____, payable on execution of this agreement.

**14. ALLOCATION OF GROSS RECEIPTS:** As to proceeds derived from Distributor's exploitation of all rights outlined in Paragraph 2, division of the Gross receipts will be made, as follows;

a) From the Distributors exploitation of Theatrical, Television, Home Video and any other Granted Rights, Distributor shall deduct and retain twenty percent (20%) of Gross receipts.

From the remaining revenues Distributor shall recoup any advance and all recoupable expenses related to the prints, marketing, advertising and sale of the Picture. The net proceeds shall be paid to Producer.

b) Gross Receipts: As used herein, the term "Gross Receipts" shall mean all monies actually received by and credited to Distributor less any refunds, returns, taxes, collection costs and manufacturing or duplication costs. Distributor may receive advances, guarantees, security deposits, and similar payments from persons or companies licensed by Distributor to subdistribute or otherwise exploit the Picture. Notwithstanding Distributors receipt of such monies, if any, and notwithstanding anything to the contrary contained herein, no such monies will be deemed to be Gross receipts hereunder unless and until such monies are earned or deemed forfeited, or become non-returnable.

c) Deductions from Gross Receipts shall be taken in the following order:

1) Distribution fee (20%)

2) Recoupment of any advance and any recoupable Delivery Expenses incurred by Distributor

3) Recoupment of any recoupable Market and Promotional Expenses incurred by Distributor.

4) Net Proceeds shall be paid to Producer.

**15. RECOUPABLE EXPENSES:** As used herein, the term expenses and/or recoupable expenses shall mean all of Distributor's actual expenses on behalf of the Picture limited as follows:

(i) Market Expenses: These expenses include all direct out-of-pocket costs to attend film markets such as AFM, Cannes and MIFED. Such expenses include airfare, hotel, shipping, telephone and staff expenses incurred to attend a film market. Such expenses shall be recoupable for the first year of distribution only, and only for those markets in which Distributor is actively participating (i.e., Distributor attends,

CONTRACTS
FOR THE
FILM AND
TELEVISION
INDUSTRY

306

rents a suite and is actively selling the Picture). Distributor may recoup a total of $3,500 per market attended with an overall cap of no more than $10,000 overall market cap for the year. Distributor agrees to attend no less than three (3) markets during the first year of distribution. Should the distribution term extend beyond one year, no market expenses shall be recoupable during the second and any subsequent years, unless the parties agree otherwise in writing.

(ii) Promotional Expenses: These expenses include the cost of preparing posters, one-sheets, trailers and advertising. Distributor agrees to spend no less than $25,000 and no more than $40,000 on promotional expenses. These expenses are limited to direct out-of-pocket expenses actually spent on behalf of the Picture. At Producer's request, Distributor shall provide receipts for each and every expense or forgo recoupment. Recoupable promotional expenses do not include any of Distributor's general office, overhead, legal or staff expenses or any of the aforementioned Market Expenses. Distributor agrees to spend the minimum necessary to adequately promote the Picture, including preparation of a trailer, poster, one-sheet, videocassette and customary promotional material, if these items have not been supplied by Producer. Distributor will use its best efforts to promote the Picture, and will promote the Picture in a no less favorable manner than any of Distributor's other films.

(iii) Delivery Expenses: Delivery Expenses are the direct out of pocket costs incurred by Distributor to manufacture any of the film or video deliverables (as listed on Exhibit A) which Producer did not supply. Delivery Expenses also include the direct out-of-pocket costs incurred between markets for shipping, duplicating, delivery of marketing materials (i.e. screeners) to foreign buyers, and phone and fax calls. At Producer's request, Distributor shall provide receipts for each and every expense or forgo recoupment. Recoupable Delivery Expenses do not include any of Distributor's general office, overhead, legal or staff expenses or any of the aforementioned Promotional or Market Expenses.

**16. CONTRACTS:** Distributor will use exclusively AFMA deal memos and model contracts. Distributor will provide copies of all Deal Memos and contracts to Producer within 14 days of their execution.

**17. PACKAGE SALES:** The Picture may be included in any of Distributor's package of motion pictures provided that Distributor shall make a fair and reasonable allocation of the package price to each of the pictures in the package, and provided that the price allocated to Producer's Picture shall be at least the minimum set forth in Schedule A, attached.

**18. LATE PAYMENTS/LIEN:** Producer shall hold a lien and security interest on the gross receipts and distribution contracts for the Picture. All monies due Producer shall be paid in accordance with this agreement. Distributor shall pay Producer interest at three percent over prime per month on any amounts thirty (30) days past due.

**19. SECURITY INTEREST:** As security for payment of Producer's share of gross revenues hereunder, Distributor hereby grants and assigns a lien and security interest in all of Distributor's right, title and interest in and to (i) all rights granted to Distributor in the Picture and its underlying material, (ii) all film elements, video tapes, sound elements, and other physical materials of any kind to be used in the exploitation of the Picture by Distributor from exploitation of the Picture by Distributor, (iii) all proceeds realized by Distributor from exploitation of the Picture, to which Producer is entitled as Producer's share of Gross revenues hereunder.

With respect to said security interest, Producer shall have all the rights, power and privileges of a secured party under the Uniform Commercial Code as the same may be amended from time to time. Distributor agrees to sign and deliver to Producer all such financing statements and other instruments as may be legally necessary for Producer to file, register and or record such security interests.

### 20. DEFAULT/TERMINATION:

a) Distributor Default: If it is found and proven that Distributor has defaulted on its obligations under this agreement, upon notification of that fact from Producer, Distributor will have thirty (30) days to cure said default. If the default is not cured within the allotted period, the Producer will have the right to initiate arbitration.

b) Producer Default: Distributor shall notify Producer in writing of any alleged default hereunder. Producer shall have thirty (30) days to correct alleged default before Distributor initiates arbitration.

c) Termination Rights: No failure by either party hereto to perform any of its obligations under this Agreement shall be deemed to be a material breach of this Agreement until the non-breaching party has given the breaching party written notice of its failure to perform and such failure has not been corrected within thirty (30) business days from and after the giving of such notice. In the event of an uncured material breach, either party shall be entitled to terminate this Agreement (subject to arbitration) by written notice to the other party, obtain monetary damages and other appropriate relief and, in the case of Producer, regain all of its rights in the Picture subject to existing executory contracts and licenses respecting Picture.

Producer shall have the right to terminate this Agreement and cause all rights herein conveyed to Distributor to revert to Producer subject, however, to third party agreements conveying rights in the Picture (in respect to which Producer shall be deemed an assignee of all of Distributor's rights therein in respect to the Picture), by written notice to Distributor in the event that Distributor files a petition in bankruptcy or consents to an involuntary petition in bankruptcy or to any reorganization under Chapter 11 of the Bankruptcy Act. Notwithstanding anything to the contrary which may be contained in the preceding sentence, in the event that Distributor files a petition in bankruptcy or consents to an involuntary petition in bankruptcy or to any reorganization under Chapter 11 of the Bankruptcy Act, Producer shall not be entitled to terminate this Agreement if thereafter: (1) Distributor shall segregate Producer's share of the moneys that Distributor receives in connection with the Picture and place the moneys into a separate trust account and that such moneys shall not be commingled with Distributor's other funds, and Producer's share of such moneys shall become Producer's property immediately upon the collection by Distributor and (2) this procedure is approved by the Bankruptcy Court. In connection with the foregoing, Distributor hereby grants to Producer a security interest in the Picture and the right to receive moneys from the exploitation of the Picture ("Security Interest"). Producer may by written notice to Distributor execute against the Security Interest if and only if Distributor files a petition in bankruptcy or consents to an involuntary bankruptcy or a reorganization under Chapter 11 and Producer is entitled to terminate this Agreement in accordance with the other provisions of this Paragraph.

### 21. ACCOUNTINGS:

a) Distributor will render or cause to be rendered to Producer and his attorney, _____, quarterly accounting statements commencing 45 days after the first quarter after the initial release of the Picture takes place in any portion of the

CONTRACTS
FOR THE
FILM AND
TELEVISION
INDUSTRY

308

territory, for the first year of this agreement. Thereafter, quarterly statements will be made within forty-five (45) days after the last day of Distributor's then current fiscal accounting period. All monies due and payable to Producer pursuant to this Agreement will be paid simultaneously with the rendering of such statements. A copy of every statement shall be sent to: _____ c/o _____, _____, _____, with the original and any payments sent to _____ at _____. Payments shall be made payable to "_____."

b) Producer will be deemed to have consented to all accountings rendered by Distributor or its assignees, or successors and all such statements will be binding upon Producer unless specific objections in writing, stating the basis thereof, is given by Producer.

c) Distributor shall keep and maintain at its office in _____ (City), _____ (State), until expiration of the Term and for a period of five (5) years thereafter, complete detailed, permanent, true and accurate books of account and records relating to the distributing and exhibition of the Picture, including, but not limited to, detailed collections and sales by country and/or buyer, detailed billings thereon, detailed playdates thereof, detailed records of expenses that have been deducted from collections received from the exploitation of the Picture, and the whereabouts of prints, trailers, accessories and other material in connection with the Picture. Records shall be kept in accordance with Generally Accepted Accounting Principles (GAAP). Producer shall be entitled to inspect such books and records of Distributor relating to the Picture during regular business hours and shall be entitled to audit such books and records of Distributor relating to the Picture upon 10 business days' written notice to Distributor and provided that not more one audit is conducted every twelve months during each calendar year and further provided that such audit shall last not more than ten consecutive business days once begun and does not interfere with Distributor's normal operations. Within Thirty (30) days of the completion of the audit, Producer will furnish Distributor with a copy of said audit. In the event that the audit discloses that Producer has been underpaid $5,000.00 or more, Distributor shall reimburse Producer for all audit costs. Otherwise, all audit expenses shall be borne by Producer.

d) Relationship Between Parties: Distributor will hold the Producer's portion of Gross receipts in trust for Producer. This agreement will not constitute a partnership or joint venture between Distributor and Producer, and neither of the parties will become bound or liable because of any representations, acts or omissions of the other party hereto.

**22. NOTICES:** All notices, correspondence, writings and statements shall be forwarded to the address and numbers as follows: _____, _____, _____. Fax: _____ with a courtesy copy to _____, _____. Fax: _____. Fax receptions shall be deemed an acceptable mode of acceptance of all notices, writings and statements unless otherwise agreed. In all instances hard copies will follow all telephonic or fax correspondence. Both parties reserve the right to change the address of service at any time with notice in writing to the receiving party.

**23. ASSIGNMENT:** This agreement will be binding upon and will enure to the benefit of the parties hereto and their respective successors and permitted assigns. Producer may assign its rights to payment of monies. Distributor may not assign its rights without the prior written consent of Producer, provided that nothing herein will prevent Distributor from assigning its rights to a successor company that may arise from Distributor merging, being acquired or partnering with another company.

**24. ARBITRATION AND JURISDICTION:** This Agreement shall be interpreted in accordance with the laws of the State of _____, applicable to agreements executed and to be wholly performed therein. Any controversy or claim arising out of or in relation to this Agreement or the validity, construction or performance of this Agreement, or the breach thereof, shall be resolved by arbitration in accordance with the rules and procedures of the American Film Marketing Association, as said rules may be amended from time to time with rights of discovery if requested by the arbitrator. Such rules and procedures are incorporated and made a part of this Agreement by reference. If the American Film Marketing Association shall refuse to accept jurisdiction of such dispute, then the parties agree to arbitrate such matter before and in accordance with the rules of the American Arbitration Association under its jurisdiction in _____ before a single arbitrator familiar with entertainment law. The parties shall have the right to engage in pre-hearing discovery in connection with such arbitration proceedings. The parties agree hereto that they will abide by and perform any award rendered in any arbitration conducted pursuant hereto, that any court having jurisdiction thereof may issue a judgment based upon such award and that the prevailing party in such arbitration and/or confirmation proceeding shall be entitled to recover its reasonable attorneys’ fees and expenses. The arbitration will be held in _____ and any award shall be final, binding and non-appealable. The Parties agree to accept service of process in accordance with AFMA Rules. The parties further agree that if an arbitration award is awarded against Distributor, and Distributor fails to pay the award after it is confirmed by a court, the AFMA market barring rule will apply against _____ as an officer of Distributor, and _____ agrees to sign the AFMA Rider attached to this agreement (attached as Exhibit B).

**25. ENTIRE AGREEMENT:** This Agreement is intended by the parties hereto as a final expression of their Agreement and understanding with respect to the subject matter hereof and as a complete and exclusive statement of the terms thereof (unless amended in writing by both parties) and supersedes any and all prior and contemporaneous agreements and understanding thereto. This Agreement will be understood in all respects to lay under the jurisdiction of _____ law and the laws of the United States of America. All parties agree that because of the specialized interest of this Agreement pertaining to entertainment that it is in both parties' interests that confirmation of any arbitration award, and any other matters of law, be submitted to the jurisdiction of the U.S. District for the Central district of _____, or the Superior Courts in _____ County. The parties waive their rights to transfer such actions to any other jurisdictions and will be bound by the decisions of such courts.

In the event of any conflict or action between the parties the prevailing party shall be entitled to recoup its reasonable attorney fees and court costs and expenses from the non-prevailing party.

Paragraph headings in this Agreement are used for convenience only and will not be used to interpret or construe the provisions of this Agreement.

CONTRACTS
FOR THE
FILM AND
TELEVISION
INDUSTRY

310

IN WITNESS WHEREOF, the parties have executed this agreement as of the date hereof.

_____

(Distribution Company)

By:_____

Its:_____

ACCEPTED AND AGREED:

_____

on behalf of

_____

(Production Company)

# EXHIBIT "A"
## DELIVERY REQUIREMENTS

Delivery of the Picture shall consist of Licensor making delivery, at Licensor's expense, to Licensee (at the address specified below) of all items set forth below to the location(s) designated below (or as may hereafter be designated by Licensee). Access to all "access" delivery items referred to in this Exhibit shall be deemed complete when designated items are delivered to Licensee and/or placed in a lab or vault in _____ with a Lab Access Letter put on file so that Licensee may fulfill its obligations under this agreement or any sublicensing agreement. Delivery items shall be delivered to the following:

_____

(Distribution Company)

_____

(Distribution Address)

## I. PICTURE ITEMS

### 1. Original Picture and Soundtrack Negative:

Access to the following:

(a) Original Picture Negative: The original first-class completely edited color 16mm Picture negative, fully timed and color corrected.

(b) Original Optical Soundtrack Negative: A first-class completely edited 16mm optical sound-track negative (including combined dialogue, sound effects and music made from the original magnetic print master described in Paragraph 5 below conforming to the original negative and answer print. The Sound track is to be in Stereo.

(c) 16mm Low Contrast Print: One (1) first class 16mm composite low contrast print fully timed and color corrected, manufactured from the original action negative and final sound track, fully titled, conformed and synchronized to the final edited version of the Picture.(if available)

(d) Color Interpositive Protection Master: One (1) color corrected and complete interpositive Master of the Picture, conformed in all respects to the Answer Print for protection purposes without scratches or defects.(if available)

(e) Color Internegative/Dupe Negative: One(1) 35mm Internegative manufactured from the color interpositive protection Master conformed in all respects to the delivered and accepted Answer Print without scratches or defects.(if available)

The elements listed in subparagraphs (a) (b) (c) (d) and (e) above are to be without scratches or injury, so that clear first class composite positive prints can be made therefrom in order to properly exhibit and perform the Picture, and to properly produce the recorded sound of the Picture and the musical compositions included in the score thereof in synchronism with the photographic action in the Picture.

CONTRACTS
FOR THE
FILM AND
TELEVISION
INDUSTRY

312

**2. Interpositive Masters of the Textless Background:**

Access to the following :

(a) Master Negative

(b) One set of first class completely edited color corrected 16mm interpositives or fine grains (made from the original Picture negative described in Paragraph 1(a) above) (if available).

(c) Access to corresponding daily prints (to be held with outake trims) of the following:

    (i) all main titles and end title backgrounds, without lettering;

    (ii) background of any forewords and/or scenes carrying superimposed titles, without lettering (if available); and

    (iii) backgrounds of any inserts, without lettering, where text must be replaced in foreign languages (if available).

(d) in addition, one overlay title 16mm internegative (first-class completely edited color) of main and end titles and any forewords (if available). Should the text of any titles and/or inserts as photographed for theatrical release printing extend beyond the "Safe Title Area" for television (as specified by the Society of Motion Picture and Television Engineers), then Licensor shall provide Licensee with access to an alternate original 16mm negative of each such title and/or insert, photographed to the precise length and with the same lettering style and background of the theatrical title and/or insert, photographed to the precise length and with the same lettering style and background of the theatrical title or insert and which can be printed by normal laboratory procedure within the limits of the "Safe Title Area" for television.

**3. Videotape Master:** Access to a Videotape master of the original motion Picture and television version thereof, meeting the specifications set forth in section III of this Exhibit.

**4. Answer Print:** Access to one (1) first class 16mm answer print, fully timed and color corrected, manufactured from the original action negative and original optical sound track negative, fully titled, conformed and synchronized to the final version of the Picture.

**5. M & E Track:** Access to one (1) 16mm state of the art magnetic sound track master including the music track and the 100% fully-filled effects track on separate channels where the effect track contains all effects including any effects recorded on the dialogue track. This M & E track shall also include a third separate dialogue guide track with no Spanish dialogue in the M & E tracks. If the Picture is to be released with Stereophonic sound, Licensor shall deliver an additional 16mm stereophonic dubbing four-channel magnetic soundtrack minus any Spanish dialogue or narration, for use as an M & E track with surrounds if surrounds were recorded and in Dolby if the Picture is in Ultra-Stereo.

**6. Magnetic Print Master:** Access to one (1) 16mm 3-Track Stereo magnetic master of the dubbed soundtrack of the Picture on 1000' reels from which the Optical sound track negative was made.

**7. Sound Tracks:** Access to the separate dialogue tracks, sound effects tracks, and music tracks, each recorded on 16mm magnetic tracks from which the magnetic print master was made ,

**8. Complete Materials to Create Trailer:** delivery of the following:

(a)  A Beta SP Sub-master of the entire film.

(b)  Continuity Script: delivery of Two (2) copies of the dialogue cutting continuity (in English), being an accurate transcript of dialogue, narration and song vocals and description of action of the trailer as finally edited for release, conforming to the format of release scripts used by Licensee, from which such scripts may be printed. each scene to be numbered. margin of 2 ½" on the left side of the page. Masters to be typed so text will appear when printed on pages with dimensions of 11"x 8 ½".

**9. Music Masters/Tracks/Dubbing Set-Up Sheets:**

(a)  Access to the uncut original music masters in the form (e.g., number of tracks) in which they were recorded or , at Licensee's election, a first generation copy thereof of selected takes of each musical sequence of the Picture, regardless of whether such selected takes are in the Picture;

(b)  Access to the synchronized magnetic tracks of music, sound effects and dialogue, as set up for dubbing; and

(c)  Copies of Dubbing set-up sheets (e.g. all "cue sheets")

**10. Outakes and Trims:** If requested, access to all unused takes and trims and all other film including without limitation soundtrack (whether negative, positive or magnetic) produced for or used in the process of preparing the Picture, whether or not actually used in the Picture.

**11. List of Scenes for Stock Footage:**

**12. TV/Airline Version:** If requested, a D2 NTSC video master of a TV/Airline version of the Picture, fully edited and/or dubbed with appropriate cover footage and dialogue so as to conform with U.S. network television broadcast standards. Master shall conform to specifications as set forth in Section III of this Exhibit.

**13. Unrated Version: None**

**14. Subtitled Version: None**

**15. Closed Captioned Version: Intentionally Omitted**

## II. DOCUMENTATION

**1. Continuity Script:** Two (2) copies of the dialogue cutting continuity (in Spanish and English), being an accurate transcript of dialogue, narration and song vocals and description of action of the trailer as finally edited for release, conforming to the format of release scripts used by VideoTime, from which such scripts may be printed, each scene to be numbered, margin of 2 ½" on the left side of the page. Masters to be typed so text will appear when printed on pages with dimensions of 11"x 8 ½".

CONTRACTS
FOR THE
FILM AND
TELEVISION
INDUSTRY

314

**2. Spotting List: Intentionally Omitted**

**3. Title Sheets:** One (1) typewritten list of all words appearing visually in the Picture suitable for use in translating such words into another language.

**4. Music Cue Sheets:** Two (2) copies of a music cue sheet showing the particulars of all music contained in the Picture, including the sound equipment used, the title of each composition, names of composers, publishers, and copyright owners, the usages (whether instrumental-visual, vocal, vocal-visual, or otherwise), the place and number of such uses showing the footage and running time for each cue, the performing rights society involved, and any other information customarily set forth in music cue sheets.

**5. Dubbing Restrictions:** A statement of any restrictions as to the dubbing of the voice of any player including dubbing dialogue in a language other than the language in which the Picture was recorded.

**6. Copyright Information:** Detailed information as to the copyright proprietor(s) of the Picture and appropriate copyright notice to be affixed to reproductions of the Picture and packaging of such reproductions, as well as copies of all copyright registrations, assignments of copyrights, and/or copyright licenses in Licensor's possession (or in the possession of Licensor's agents or attorney) pertaining to the Picture or any component element thereof (including but not limited to copies of all synchronization and performance licenses pertaining to music contained in the Picture).

**7. Insurance:** It is understood that the Licensor has not obtained errors and omissions insurance. However, if demand is made by a sublicensor/distributor, a certificate of errors and omissions insurance naming _____ and those entities designated by Licensee for exploitation of its rights hereunder as additional insured and otherwise in accordance with the provisions of the agreement to which this Exhibit is attached ($1,000,000.00 for single claim; $3,000,000 aggregate.), will be paid out of the proceeds of the sale/license agreement.

**8. Chain of Title:** Copies of all certificates of authorship. Licenses, contracts, assignments and the written permissions from the proper parties interest, establishing Licensor's "Chain of Title" with respect to the Picture and all elements thereof and permitting Licensor, and its assigns to use any musical, literary, dramatic and other material of whatever nature used by Licensor in the Production of the Picture, together with Copyright and Title search reports and Opinion prepared either by Thompson &Thomson, Dennis Angel, Esq. and/or Brylawski, Cleary & Leeds. "Chain of Title" materials must be suitable for filing with the United States Library of Congress and reasonably suitable to Licensor's primary lender indicating that Grantor has full right, title and interest in and to the Picture and all underlying property.

**9. Copyright Mortgage:** If applicable

**10. UCC Financing Statement:** Not Applicable

**11. UCC Search:** Not Applicable

**12. Technical Crew:** Intentionally Omitted

**13. Screen Credit Obligations:** Three (3) copies of the Screen Credit Obligations: for all individuals and entities affiliated with the Picture

**14. Paid Ad Credit Obligations:** Three (3) copies of the Paid Advertising Credit obligations for all individuals and entities affiliated with the Picture.

**15. Billing Block:** Three (3) copies of the approved credit block to be used in paid advertising of the Picture.

**16. Name and Likeness Restrictions:** Three (3) copies of all name and likeness restrictions and/or obligations pertaining to all individuals and entities affiliated with the Picture.

**17. Talent Agreements:** If required, all contracts of the cast, director, cinematographer, screenwriter(s),producer(s) and author(s), (or other owner of the underlying material, if applicable) including their respective Agent's name and phone number.

**18. Certificate of Origin:** One Certificate of Origin of the Picture.

**19. Notarized Assignment of Rights:** Intentionally Omitted

**20. Music License and Composer Agreement:** Copies of Music Licenses (synchronization and mechanical) and composers agreement.

**21. Publicity and Advertising Materials:**

(a) Color Slides: At least 100 color slides (16 MM color transparencies) and any available prints of black and white still photographs and accompanying negatives, and at least Twenty Five color still photographs and accompanying negatives depicting different scenes from the Picture, production activities, and informal poses, the majority of which depict the principal members of the cast. Each slide shall be accompanied by a notation identifying the persons and events depicted and shall be suitable for reproduction for advertising and publicity purposes. Where a player has still approval, Licensor shall furnish licensee with only approved photos and shall provide an appropriate written clearance from the player.

(b) Synopses: One (1) copy of a brief synopsis in the English Language, and in such other Language as such synopsis exists, (one typewritten page each) of the story of the Picture.

(c) The statement of credits applicable to the Picture including verification of the writing credits by the appropriate writers guild and photocopy excerpts of all of Licensor's obligations (taken from the actual contract) to accord credit on the screen, in advertising and on recordings; and excerpts as to any restrictions as to use of name and likeness.

(d) Cast: One (1) copy of a list indicating the name of the character portrayed by each player and a complete description of the character.

(e) Crew: One (1) copy of a list indicating each member of the crew and the function.

(f) Titles: One (1) typewritten list of the main credits and end titles of the Picture.

(g) Miscellaneous: At least one (1) copy of all advertisements, paper accessories, and other advertising materials, if any, prepaid by Licensor or by any other party in connection with the Picture. Art elements and transparencies necessary to make proofs thereof.

CONTRACTS
FOR THE
FILM AND
TELEVISION
INDUSTRY

316

(h) Press books: 200 Press books, including biographies (one to three type-written pages in length) of key members of cast, individual producer, director, cinematographer and screenwriter.

(i) Production Notes: If requested, a copy of the production notes of the Picture prepared by the unit publicist, including items relating to: underlying work (original screenplay, book, etc), places where the Picture was photographed, anecdotes about the production of background of the Picture.

**22. Editor's Script notes and Editors Code Book:** Intentionally Omitted

**23. Final Shooting Script:** If requested, one (1) copy of the final shooting script of the Picture.

**24. MPAA Rating Certificate:**

It is understood that the Picture has not received or applied for an MPAA rating. If and when it becomes necessary to receive a MPAA rating, Licensor shall make application for the rating and recoup expense from sales/licensing revenues.

**25. Shooting Script: Intentionally Omitted.**

**26. Laboratory List:** A List of the names and addresses of all Laboratories used and to be used for production and post-Production of the Picture (including, without limitation, sound Labs, optical Labs, special effects Labs etc., and a list of all physical elements of the Picture in the Possession of each such Laboratory.

**27. Title Report:** One current (no more than 60 days old) title report showing that the title of the Picture is available for use without infringing any other person or entity's rights.

**28. Copyright Report:** Intentionally Omitted

**29. Copyright Certificate:** Two (2) Mexican Copyright Registration Certificates (stamped by authorized authorities) (if applicable) and Two (2) U.S. Copyrights (stamped by the library of Congress). If the copyright application has not yet been received from the Library of Congress, then Licensor shall deliver a copy of the Application PA form, along with a copy of the cover letter and two (2) copies of the Copyright Certificate to _____ when received from the Library of Congress. If application has not been made _____ shall apply for the U.S. copyright at Licensors expense.

### III. VIDEO SPECIFICATIONS

### 1. TYPE OF VIDEO TAPE.

1.1 The Master Videotapes (to be made only from the original 16mm low contrast print, inter-positive or internegative ) of the Picture and the Television Version are to be of Broadcast quality D2 NTSC format tape (and access to D2 Pal Format tape), containing the M&E tracks 3m 479, in two parts.

### 2. VIDEO SPECIFICATIONS:

2.1 Peak luminance must not exceed 100 IRE.

2.2 Pedestal level must be 7.5 IRE for all signals.

2.3 Peak chrominance level must not exceed 110 IRE.

2.4 Color burst must be present at all times, including stereochrome recordings.

2.5 Color subcarrier phase must be continuous across edits (color frame edits).

2.6 Stability is requested in both the sync and control track signals.

2.7 Great care must be taken to achieve the highest possible video S/N (SNR).

2.8 Video signal timings must meet EIA standards.

## 3. Audio Specifications.

3.1 The Picture must be recorded in Stereo.

3.2 The audio test signal during color bars must be a 1kHz tone at zero db (zero db = 4dbm) on both audio channels.

3.3 The Audio recording level must be well balanced between the two VTR audio channels.

3.4 There will be no audio modulation during "run out."

3.5 Great care must be taken to achieve the highest possible audio S/N ration.

3.6 Channel 1 of video masters shall contain Stereo left of the final sound track and channel 2 shall contain Stereo right of the final soundtrack.

3.7 Channel 3 of video masters will contain M&E left and channel 4 will contain M&E right.

## 4. TIME CODE SPECIFICATIONS

4.1 The SMPTE time code must be of the drop mode.

4.2 The first frame of Program material must have SMPTE time code of 00:00:00:00.

4.3 The recording level of the SMPTE time code is zero (0) VU.

## 5. FILM TO TAPE TRANSFER.

5.1 The program material must be transferred from negative or internegative, or low contrast print with Interlock for the highest quality.

5.2 The film must be ultrasonically cleaned, inspected, and evaluated prior to the transfer process.

5.3 Action or audio break-up between reels is unacceptable.

5.4 Anamorphic kinescope prints must be panned and scanned to insure maximum letterbox and pan positions for monitor viewing.

5.5 "T.O.P.S.Y." scene by scene color correction is desirable. Cynamic gain, gamma, and color enhancement should be applied where required.

5.6 The head and tail of the master videotape must be structured as follows:

CONTRACTS
FOR THE
FILM AND
TELEVISION
INDUSTRY

318

5.7 Textless background shall be attached to the tail of each feature master. AT 23:53:30:00 non drop SMPTE time code must begin with 75% color bars and 1kHz tone oscillated to both audio channels At 23:54:30:00 black bursts must run with no modulation until the begging of program material at 00:00:00:00, with three (3) minutes of black prior to beginning of Program.

Black bursts must be initiated for a minimum of 10 minutes at end of program material. No audio Modulation.

## 6. ASPECT RATIOS.

The Picture shall not be in an aspect ration other than the standard theatrical 1:85 to 1 without Licensor's prior written consent. No elements shall be "letter boxed" without Licensee's written consent.

## 7. QUALITY CONTROL REQUIREMENTS.

_____ shall, at its own option and its own cost, perform one quality control test on each element supplied by Licensor. Licensor shall be liable for the cost of all quality control tests after the initial quality control test of all elements replaced because of failure to conform to Licensee's technical quality requirements.

# EXHIBIT B

## AFMA RIDER TO
## INTERNATIONAL DISTRIBUTION AGREEMENT

Licensor: _____

Distributor: _____

Picture: _____

Territory: _____

Date: _____

The Undersigned, in order to induce the Licensor to enter into the "Agreement" with the Distributor for the Picture in the Territory with the date and Contract Reference Code listed above, executes this Rider to the Agreement and agrees and confirms as follows:

### 1. Arbitration:

The Undersigned agrees that the Undersigned shall be a party respondent in any arbitration and related court proceedings which may be originally brought or brought in response by the Licensor against the Distributor under the Agreement. The Undersigned shall have the right to raise in such proceedings only those defenses available to the Distributor. No failure of Licensor to resort to any right, remedy or security will reduce or discharge the obligations of the Undersigned. No amendment, renewal, extension, waiver or modification of the Agreement will reduce or discharge the obligation of the Undersigned. The Undersigned waives all defenses in the nature of suretyship, including without limitation notice of acceptance, protest, notice of protest, dishonor, notice of dishonor and exoneration. Subject to Paragraph 2 below, any award or judgment rendered as a result of such arbitration against the Distributor shall be deemed to be rendered against the Undersigned. In the event that Licensor shall obtain an award for damages against Distributor, Licensor shall receive a similar award against the Undersigned.

### 2. Remedies:

Notwithstanding anything in this Rider, in the event of an award against the Distributor, Licensor shall have no remedy against the Undersigned other than the remedy provided under the Market Barring Rule of the American Film Marketing Association. In that regard, the Undersigned hereby agrees to be bound by the provisions of the Market Barring Rule with respect to the Agreement, as though the Undersigned were the Distributor. Licensor confirms that its only remedy against the Undersigned in the event of breach of the Agreement by, and an arbitration award for damages against, the Distributor shall be application of the Market Barring Rule, to the same extent that the Market Barring Rule may be applied against the Distributor. Licensor waives any and all other remedies of every kind and nature which it may have with respect to the Undersigned's inducements and agreements herein.

CONTRACTS
FOR THE
FILM AND
TELEVISION
INDUSTRY

320

## 3. Assignment:

This Rider will inure to the benefit of and be fully enforceable by Licensor and its successors and assigns.

## 4. Governing Law:

This Rider will be governed by and interpreted in accordance with the Agreement, including without limitation the arbitration provisions, governing law, and forum provisions therein stated.

The Undersigned confirms that service of arbitration notice, process, and other papers shall be made to the Undersigned at the address first set forth in the Agreement pertaining to Distributor, unless otherwise set forth below.

WHEREFORE, the Undersigned and the Licensor hereby execute this Rider as of the date first set forth above.

THE "UNDERSIGNED"


_____
(Distribution Company Representative)


_____
(Distribution Company)

# SCHEDULE A

### Schedule of Minimums

| Territory | Minimum Acceptable |
|---|---|
| **ENGLISH SPEAKING** | |
| United States | |
| Eng. Canada | |
| Fr. Canada | |
| UK | |
| Australia/New Zealand | |
| South Africa | |
| East Africa | |
| West Africa | |
| West Indies | |
| | |
| **EUROPE** | |
| Germany/Austria | |
| Switzerland | |
| France | |
| Italy | |
| Spain | |
| Benelux | |
| Scandinavia | |
| Iceland | |
| Portugal | |
| Greece | |

CONTRACTS
FOR THE
FILM AND
TELEVISION
INDUSTRY

322

| Territory | Minimum Acceptable |
|---|---|
| **FAR EAST** | |
| Japan | |
| Korea | |
| Taiwan | |
| Hong Kong | |
| Singapore | |
| Brunei | |
| Malaysia | |
| Indonesia | |
| Phillippines | |
| Thailand | |
| India | |
| Sri Lanka | |
| Pakistan | |
| China | |
| | |
| **LATIN AMERICA** | |
| Arg/Par/Uru | |
| Brazil | |
| Mexico | |
| Chile | |
| Colombia | |
| Venezuela | |
| C. America | |
| Ecuador | |
| Peru/Bolivia | |
| Dominican Rep. | |

| Territory | Minimum Acceptable |
|---|---|
| **MIDDLE EAST** | |
| Leb/Middle East | |
| Turkey | |
| Israel | |
| | |
| **EAST EUROPE** | |
| Bulgaria | |
| Czech | |
| Hungary | |
| Poland | |
| Croatia | |
| Serbia | |
| CIS | |
| Rumania | |

CONTRACTS
FOR THE
FILM AND
TELEVISION
INDUSTRY

324

# THEATRICAL ACQUISITION/DISTRIBUTION AGREEMENT
## (Distributor Friendly)

Agreement dated _____ between _____ ("Production Company") at _____ and _____ ("Distributor"), with offices at _____.

**1. PICTURE:** The term "Picture" refers to the Theatrical Motion Picture set forth in Schedule "A" hereof.

**2. TERRITORY AND TERM:**

(a) Territory: The territory covered hereby ("Territory") is set forth in Schedule "A."

(b) Distribution Term: The term of this Agreement and the rights granted Distributor hereunder for each country or place of the Territory shall be the period of time specified in Schedule "A" ("Distribution Term"). The term of this Agreement shall commence on the date hereof and expire upon the expiration of the Distribution Term as extended unless sooner terminated as provided herein.

**3. RIGHTS GRANTED:**

(a) Grant: Production Company hereby grants to Distributor throughout the Territory the exercise of all rights of theatrical, television (free, pay and syndication) and home video (cassette and disc) exhibition and distribution with respect to the Picture and Trailers thereof, and excerpts and clips therefrom, in any and all languages and versions, including dubbed, subtitled and narrated versions. The rights granted herein shall include without limit the sole and exclusive right:

(i) Titles: To use the title or titles by which the Picture is or may be known or identified.

(ii) Music and Lyrics: To use and perform any and all music, lyrics and musical compositions contained in the Picture and/or recorded in the soundtrack thereof in connection with the distribution, exhibition, advertising, publicizing and exploiting of the Picture;

(iii) Versions: To make such dubbed and titled versions of the Picture, and the Trailers thereof, including without limitation cut-in, synchronized and superimposed versions in any and all languages for use in such parts of the Territory as Distributor may deem advisable.

(iv) Editing: To make such changes, alterations, cuts, additions, interpolations, deletions and eliminations into and from the Picture and trailer subject to prior written approval of Production Company and Director as Distributor may deem necessary or desirable, for the effective marketing, distribution, exploitation or other use of the Picture.

(v) Advertising and Publicity: To publicize, advertise and exploit the Picture throughout the Territory during the Distribution Term, including without limitation the exclusive right in the Territory for the purpose of advertising, publicizing and exploiting the Picture to:

(A) Literary Material: Publish and to license and authorize others to publish in any language and in such forms as Distributor may deem advisable, synopses, summaries, adaptations, novelizations, and stories of and excerpts from the Picture and from any literary or dramatic material included in the Picture or upon which the Picture is based in book form and in newspapers, magazines, trade periodicals, booklets, press books and any other periodicals and in all other media of advertising and publicity whatsoever not exceeding 7,500 words in length taken from the original material;

(B) Radio and Television: Broadcast by radio and television for advertising purposes and to license and authorize others to so broadcast, in any language, any parts or portions of the Picture not exceeding five minutes in length, and any literary or dramatic material included in the Picture or upon which the Picture was based alone or in conjunction with other literary, dramatic or musical material; and

(C) Names and Likenesses: Use, license and authorize others to use the name, physical likeness and voice (and any simulation or reproduction of any thereof) of any party rendering services in connection with the Picture for the purpose of advertising, publicizing or exploiting the Picture or Distributor, including commercial tie-ins.

(vi) Use of Name and Trademarks: To use Distributor's name and trademark and/or the name and trademark of any of Distributor's licensee's on the positive prints of the Picture and in Trailers thereof, and in all advertising and publicity relating thereto, in such a manner, position, form and substance as Distributor or its licensees may elect.

(vii) Commercials: To permit commercial messages to be exhibited during and after the exhibition of the Picture.

(viii) Trailers: To cause trailers of the Picture and prints thereof and of the Picture to be manufactured, exhibited and distributed by every means, medium, process, method and device now or hereafter known.

(b) Grant of Other Rights: Production Company hereby grants to Distributor throughout the Territory the sole and exclusive right, license and privilege to exercise all literary publishing rights, live television rights, merchandising rights, music publishing rights, soundtrack recording rights, radio rights, additional motion picture rights, remake rights and sequel motion picture rights subject to the terms and conditions of the agreements pursuant to which Production Company acquired the foregoing rights with respect to the literary, dramatic and/or musical material used by Production Company in connection with the Picture. Production Company agrees that at the request of Distributor, Production Company will execute and deliver to Distributor for recordation purposes a separate document pursuant to which Production Company confirms the transfer and assignment to Distributor of said rights.

(c) Rights Free and Clear: The above-stated rights are granted by Production Company to Distributor without qualification and are free and clear from any and all restrictions, claims, encumbrances or defects of any nature and Production Company agrees that it will not commit or omit to perform any act by which any of these rights, licenses, privileges and interests could or will be encumbered, diminished or impaired, and that Production Company will pay or discharge, and will hold Distributor harmless from, any and all claims that additional payments are due anyone by reason of the distribution, exhibition, telecasting, of re-running of the Picture or the receipt of its proceeds. Production Company further agrees that during the Distribution Term (as extended) with respect to each country or place, Production Company shall neither exercise itself nor grant to any third party the rights granted to Distributor pursuant to the terms hereof.

CONTRACTS
FOR THE
FILM AND
TELEVISION
INDUSTRY

326

(d) Production Company's Reservation of Rights: Production Company reserves for its use non-theatrical distribution.

(e) Credits: The statements of credits required to be given pursuant to Exhibit "A" shall conform to Distributor's standard credit provisions for comparable talent, including without limitation Distributor's standard art work title provisions as set forth in Exhibit "A," attached hereto.

## 4. PRODUCTION COMPANY'S WARRANTIES AND REPRESENTATIONS:
Production Company represents and warrants to Distributor, its successors, licensees and assigns as follows:

(a) Quality: The Picture is completely finished, fully edited and titled and fully synchronized with language dialogue, sound and music and in all respects ready and of a quality, both artistic and technical, adequate for general theatrical release and commercial public exhibition.

(b) Content: The Picture consists of a continuous and connected series of scenes, telling or presenting a story, free from any obscene material and suitable for exhibition to the general public.

(c) Unrestricted Right to Grant: Production Company is the sole and absolute owner of the Picture, the copyright pertaining thereto and all rights associated with or relating to the distribution the absolute right to grant to and vest in Distributor, all the rights, licenses and privileges granted to Distributor under this Agreement, and Production Company has not heretofore sold, assigned, licensed, granted, encumbered or utilized the Picture or any of the literary or musical properties used therein in any way that may affect or impair the rights, licenses and privileges granted to Distributor hereunder and Production Company will not sell, assign, license, grant or encumber or utilize the rights, licenses and privileges granted to Distributor hereunder.

(d) Discharge of Obligations: All the following have been fully paid or discharged or will be fully paid and discharged by Production Company or by persons other than Distributor:

(i) All claims and rights of owners of copyright in literary, dramatic and musical rights and other property or rights in or to all stories, plays, scripts, scenarios, themes, incidents, plots, characters, dialogue, music, words, and other material of any nature whatsoever appearing, used or recorded in the Picture;

(ii) All claims and rights of owners of inventions and patent rights with respect to the recording of any and all dialogue, music and other sound effects recorded in the Picture and with respect to the use of all equipment, apparatus, appliances and other materials used in the photographing, recording or otherwise in the manufacture of the Picture;

(iii) All claims and rights with respect to the use, distribution, exhibition, performance and exploitation of the Picture and any music contained therein throughout the Territory, and

(e) No Infringement: To the best of Production Company's knowledge and belief neither the Picture nor any part thereof, nor any materials contained therein or synchronized therewith, nor the title thereof, nor the exercise of any fight, license or privilege herein granted, violates or will violate or infringe or will infringe any trademark, trade name, contract, agreement, copyright (whether common law or statutory), patent, literary, artistic, dramatic, personal, private, civil or property right or right of privacy or "moral rights of authors" or any other right whatsoever of or slanders or libels any person, firm, corporation or association whatsoever. In connection therewith, Production Company shall supply Distributor with a script clearance in a form acceptable to Distributor.

(f) No Advertising Matter: The Picture does not contain any advertising matter for which compensation, direct or indirect, has been or will be received by Production Company or to its knowledge by any other person, firm, corporation or association.

(g) No Impairment of Rights Granted: There are and will be no agreements, commitments or arrangements whatever with any person, firm, corporation or association that may in any manner or to any extent affect Distributor's rights hereunder or Distributor's share of the proceeds of the Picture. Production Company has not and will not exercise any right or take any action which might tend to derogate from, impair or compete with the rights, licenses and privileges herein granted to Distributor.

(h) Contracts: All contracts with artists and personnel, for purchases, licenses and laboratory contracts and all other obligations and undertakings of whatsoever kind connected with the production of the Picture have been made and entered into by Production Company and by no other party and no obligation shall be imposed upon Distributor thereunder and Production Company shall indemnify and hold Distributor harmless from any expense and liability thereunder. All such contracts are in the form customarily in use in the Motion Picture industry and are consistent with the provisions of this Agreement, particularly with reference to the warranties made by Production Company and the rights acquired by Distributor hereunder. Said contracts shall not, without Distributor's prior written consent, be terminated, canceled, modified or rescinded in any manner which would adversely affect Distributor's rights hereunder.

(i) All Considerations Paid: All considerations provided to be paid under each and all the agreements, licenses or other documents relating to the production of the Picture have been paid in full, or otherwise discharged in full, and there is no existing, outstanding obligation whatsoever, either present or future, under any of said contracts, agreements, assignments or other documents, unless disclosed in Schedule "A".

(j) Full Performance: All terms, covenants and conditions required to be kept or performed by Production Company under each and all of the contracts, licenses or other documents relating to the production of the Picture have been kept and performed and will hereafter be kept and performed by Production Company and there is no existing breach or other act of default by Production Company under any such agreement, license or other document, nor will there be any such breach or default during the term hereof.

(k) No Release/No Banning: Neither the Picture nor any part thereof has been released, distributed or exhibited in any media whatsoever in the Territory nor has it been banned by the censors of or refused import permits for any portion of the Territory.

(l) Valid Copyright: The copyright in the Picture and the literary, dramatic and musical material upon which it is based or which is contained the Picture will be valid and subsisting during the Distribution Term (as extended) with respect to each country or place of the Territory, and no part of any thereof is in the public domain.

CONTRACTS
FOR THE
FILM AND
TELEVISION
INDUSTRY

328

(m) Peaceful Enjoyment: Distributor will quietly and peacefully enjoy and possess each and all of the rights, licenses and privileges herein granted or purported to be granted to Distributor throughout the Distribution Term (as extended) for each country or place of the Territory without interference by any third party.

(n) Guild-Union-Performing Rights Society - Participation payments: Any payments required to be made to any performing rights society or to any body or group representing authors, composers, musicians, artists, any other participants in the production of the Picture, publishers or other persons having legal or contractual rights of any kind to participate in the receipts of the Picture or to payments of any kind as a result of the distribution or exhibition of the Picture and any taxes thereon or on the payment thereof will be made by Production Company or by the exhibitors and need not be paid by Distributor.

(o) Music Performing Rights: The Performing rights to all musical compositions contained in the Picture are: (i) controlled by the American Society of Composers, Authors and Publishers (ASCAP), Broadcast Music, Inc., (BMI) or similar organizations in other countries such as the Japanese Society of Rights of Authors and Composers (JASEAC), the Performing Right Society Ltd. (PRS), the Society of European Stage Authors and Composers (SESAC), the Societe des Auteurs Compositeurs Et Editeurs de Musique (SACEM), Gesellscraft fur Misikalische Auffuhrungs und Mechanische Vervielfaltigunsrechte (GEMA) or their affiliates, or (ii) in the public domain in the Territory, or (iii) controlled by Production Company to the extent required for the purposes of this Agreement and Production Company similarly controls or has licenses for any necessary synchronization and recording rights.

(p) Television Restriction: The Picture will not be exhibited in or telecast in or cablecast in or into the Territory during the Distribution Term for each country or place of the Territory by any one other than Distributor or its licensees.

(q) Authority Relative to this Agreement: Production Company has taken all action necessary to duly and validly authorize its signature and performance of this Agreement and the grant of the rights, licenses and privileges herein granted and agreed to be granted.

(r) Financial Condition: Production Company is not presently involved in financial difficulties as evidenced by its not having admitted its inability to pay its debts generally as they become due or otherwise not having acknowledged its insolvency or by its not having filed or consented to a petition in bankruptcy or for reorganization or for the adoption of an arrangement under Federal Bankruptcy Act (or under any similar law of the United States or any other jurisdiction, which relates to liquidation or reorganization of companies or to the modification or alteration of the rights of creditors) or by its not being involved in any bankruptcy, liquidation, or other similar proceeding relating to Production Company or its assets, whether pursuant to statute or general rule of law, nor does Production Company presently contemplate any such proceeding or have any reason to believe that any such proceeding will be brought against it or its assets.

(s) Litigation: To Production Company's knowledge, there is no litigation, proceeding or claim pending or threatened against Production Company which may materially adversely affect Production Company's exclusive rights in and to the Picture, the copyright pertaining thereto or the rights, licenses and privileges granted to Distributor hereunder.

**5. INDEMNITY:** Production Company does hereby and shall at all times indemnify and hold harmless Distributor, its subdistributors and licensees, its and their officers, directors and employees, and its and their exhibitors, licensees and assignees, of and from any and all charges, claims, damages, costs, judgments, decrees, losses, expenses (including reasonable attorneys' fees), penalties, demands, liabilities and causes of action, whether or not groundless, of any kind or nature whatsoever by reason of, based upon, relating to, or arising out of a breach or claim of breach or failure of any of the covenants, agreements, representations or warranties of Production Company hereunder or by reason of any claims, actions or proceedings asserted or instituted, relating to or arising out of any such breach or failure or conduct or activity resulting in a breach or claim of breach. All rights and remedies hereunder shall be cumulative and shall not interfere with or prevent the exercise of any other right or remedy which may be available to Distributor. Upon notice from Distributor of any such claim, demand or action being advanced or commenced, Production Company agrees to adjust, settle or defend the same at the sole cost of Production Company. If Production Company shall fail to do so, Distributor shall have the right and is hereby authorized and empowered by Production Company to appear by its attorneys in any such claim, demand or action, to adjust, settle, compromise, litigate, contest, satisfy judgments and take any other action necessary or desirable for the disposition of such claim, demand or action. In any such case, Production Company, within 20 days after demand by Distributor, shall fully reimburse Distributor for all such payments and expenses, including reasonable attorneys' fees. If Production Company shall fail so to reimburse Distributor, then, without waiving its right to otherwise enforce such reimbursement, Distributor shall have the right to deduct the said amount of such payments and expenses, or any part thereof, from any sums accruing under this Agreement or any other agreement, to or for the account of Production Company. Also, in the event of any matter to which the foregoing indemnity relates, Distributor shall have the right to withhold from disbursements to or for the account of Production Company a sum which in Distributor's opinion may be reasonably necessary to satisfy any liability or settlement in connection with such matter, plus a reasonable amount to cover the expenses of contesting or defending such claim and shall have the further right to apply the amount withheld to the satisfaction of such liability or settlement and to reimbursement of such expenses.

## 6. COPYRIGHT:

(a) Ownership: Production Company warrants that Production Company has not heretofore transferred its ownership in and to all copyrights pertaining to the Picture throughout the world, including without limitation the rights to secure copyright registration anywhere in the world with respect to all copyrights in the Picture and to secure any renewals and extensions thereof wherever and whenever permitted. Production Company warrants that upon delivery of the Picture to Distributor, Production Company will own all copyrights in the Picture throughout the world for the full period of copyright and all extensions and renewals thereof. The negative of the Picture shall contain a copyright notice complying with all statutory requirements of the copyright laws of the United States or any country which is a party to the Berne Union or Universal Copyright Convention, such notice to appear in the main or end titles of the Picture. Production Company and Distributor shall not have the right to change the copyright notice contained in the Picture.

CONTRACTS
FOR THE
FILM AND
TELEVISION
INDUSTRY

330

(b) Defense of Copyright: Distributor hereby agrees to take all reasonable steps to protect such copyrights from infringement by unauthorized parties and in particular, at the request of Production Company, to take such action and proceedings as may be reasonable to prevent any unauthorized use, reproduction, performance, exhibition or exploitation by third Parties of the Picture or any part thereof or the material on which it is based which may be in contravention of the exclusive rights granted to Distributor in respect to the Picture.

For the purpose of permitting Distributor to defend and enforce all rights and remedies granted to Distributor hereunder, and to prevent any unauthorized use, reproduction, performance, exhibition or exploitation of the Picture or any part thereof or the material on which it is based, Production Company hereby irrevocably appoints Distributor its sole and exclusive attorney-in-fact, to act in Production Company name or otherwise. Distributor agrees (consistent with commercially acceptable practices in the Motion Picture industry), in its own name or in the name of Production Company, to take all reasonable steps to enforce and protect the rights, licenses and privileges herein granted, under any law and under any and all copyrights, renewals and extensions thereof, and to prevent the infringement thereof, and to bring, prosecute, defend and appear in suits, actions and proceedings of any nature under or concerning all copyrights in the Picture and to settle claims and collect and receive all damages arising from any infringement of or interference with any and all such rights, and in the sole judgment of Distributor exercised in good faith to join Production Company as a party plaintiff or defendant in such suit, action or proceeding. Production Company hereby irrevocably appoints Distributor as its sole and exclusive attorney-in-fact, during the Term of this Agreement, with full and irrevocable power and authority to secure, register, renew and extend all copyrights in the Picture and all related properties upon each thereof becoming eligible for copyright, registration, renewal and extension.

(c) Limitation of Liability: Distributor shall not be liable, responsible or accountable in damages or otherwise to Production Company for any action or failure to act on behalf of Production Company within the scope of authority conferred on Distributor under this Clause 6, unless such action or omission was performed or omitted fraudulently or in bad faith or constituted wanton and willful misconduct or gross negligence.

**7. ERRORS AND OMISSIONS INSURANCE:** As provided in Exhibit A, Producer shall obtain and maintain or cause to be obtained and maintained throughout the Distribution Term (as extended), Motion Picture Distributor Errors and Omissions insurance in a form acceptable to Distributor, from a qualified insurance company acceptable to Distributor naming Distributor and Production Company and each and all the parties indemnified herein as additional named insureds. The amount and coverage shall be for a minimum of $1,000,000/$3,000,000 with respect to any one or more claims relating to the Picture or if Distributor pays an advance, the amount of the advance, whichever shall be greater. The policy shall provide for a deductible no greater than $10,000 and thirty (30) days notice to Distributor before any modification, cancellation or termination.

**8. INSTRUMENTS OF FURTHER ASSURANCE:** Production Company shall execute and deliver to Distributor, promptly upon the request of Distributor therefore, any other instruments or documents considered by Distributor to be necessary or desirable to evidence, effectuate or confirm this Agreement, or any of its terms and conditions.

**9. NO DISTRIBUTOR REPRESENTATIONS AND WARRANTIES:** Production Company acknowledges and agrees that Distributor makes no express or implied representation, warranty, guaranty or agreement as to the gross receipts to be derived from the Picture or the distribution, exhibition or exploitation thereof, nor does Distributor guarantee the performance by any subdistributor, licensee or exhibitor of any contract for the distribution, exhibition or exploitation of the Picture, nor does Distributor make any representation, warranty, guaranty or agreement as to any minimum amount of monies to be expended for the distribution, advertising, publicizing and exploitation of the Picture. Production Company recognizes and acknowledges that the amount of gross receipts which may be realized from the distribution, exhibition and exploitation of the Picture is speculative, and agrees that the reasonable business judgment exercised in good faith of Distributor and its subdistributors and licensees regarding any matter affecting the distribution, exhibition and exploitation of the Picture shall be binding and conclusive upon Production Company.

**10. DISTRIBUTION AND EXPLOITATION OF THE PICTURE:** Distributor shall have the complete, exclusive and unqualified control of the distribution, exhibition, exploitation and other disposition of the Picture (directly or by any subdistributor or licensee) in the media granted to Distributor hereunder throughout the Territory during the Distribution Term with respect to each country or place, in accordance with such sales methods, plans, patterns, programs, policies, terms and conditions as Distributor in its reasonable business judgment may determine proper or expedient. The enumeration of the following rights of distribution and exploitation shall in no way limit the generality or effect of the foregoing:

(a) Terms: Distributor may determine the manner and terms upon which the Picture shall be marketed, distributed, licensed, exhibited, exploited or otherwise disposed of, and all matters pertaining thereto and the decision of Distributor on all such matters shall be final and conclusive. Production Company shall have no control whatsoever in or over (i) the manner or extent to which Distributor or its subdistributors or licensees shall exploit the Picture, (ii) the terms and provisions of any licenses granted by Distributor to third Parties or (iii) to the sufficiency or insufficiency of proceeds from the Picture.

(b) Refrain from Distribution, Exhibition or Exploitation. Distributor may refrain from the release, distribution, re-issue or exhibition of the Picture at any time, in any country, place or location of the Territory, in any media, or in any form. Production Company acknowledges that there is no obligation to exploit the soundtrack recording rights or music publishing rights or merchandising rights or literary publishing rights, it being agreed that Distributor may elect to exercise any or all of said rights as Distributor in its sole business judgment exercised in good faith may determine.

(c) "Outright Sales": Distributor may make outright sales of the Picture as Distributor in good faith may determine. Only net monies actually received and earned by Distributor with respect to outright sales of the Picture shall be included within gross film rentals.

(d) Contracts and Settlements: Distributor may distribute the Picture under existing or future franchise or license contracts, which contracts may relate to the Picture separately or to the Picture and one or more other Motion Pictures distributed by or through Distributor. Distributor may, in the exercise of its reasonable business judgment, exercised in good faith, make, alter or cancel contracts with

CONTRACTS
FOR THE
FILM AND
TELEVISION
INDUSTRY

332

exhibitors, subdistributors and other licensees and adjust and settle disputes, make allowances and adjustments and give credits with respect thereto.

(e) Means of Release: Distributor may exhibit or cause the Picture to be exhibited in theaters or other places owned, controlled, leased or managed by Distributor. Distributor may enter into any agreement or arrangement with any other major distributor for the distribution by such other major distributor of all or a substantial portion of Distributor's theatrical motion pictures. Distributor may also enter into any agreement or arrangement with any other major distributor or any other party for the handling of the shipping and inspection activities of Distributor's exchanges or the handling of other facilities in connection with the distribution of motion pictures.

(f) Time of Release: The initial release of the Picture in any part of the Territory shall commence on such date or dates as Distributor or its subdistributors or licensees in their respective sole judgment and discretion may determine. Such releases shall be subject to the requirements of censorship boards or other governmental authorities, the availability of playing time in key cities, the securing of the requisite number of motion picture copies, and delays caused by reason of events of force majeure or by reason of any cause beyond the control of Distributor or its subdistributors or licensees. If any claim or action is made or instituted against Distributor or any of its subdistributors or licensees as to the Picture, Distributor or such subdistributors or licensees shall have the right to postpone the release of the Picture (if it has not then been released) or to suspend further distribution thereof (if it has been released) until such time as such claim or action shall have been settled or disposed of to the satisfaction of Distributor or such subdistributors or licensees.

(g) Duration of Release: Distribution of the Picture shall be continued in the Territory or any part thereof in which it is released by Distributor or its licensees only for _____ years. Distributor shall not be obligated to reissue the Picture at any time in the Territory but shall have the right to do so from time to time within the term as it may deem desirable.

(h) Withdrawal of the Picture: Should Distributor or its subdistributors or licensees deem it inadvisable or unprofitable to distribute, exhibit or exploit the Picture in the Territory or any part thereof, Distributor or its subdistributors or licensees shall have the right to withhold or withdraw the Picture from such Territory or any part thereof.

(i) Banning of Release: If by reason of any law, embargo, decree, regulation or other restriction of any agency or governmental body, the number or type of motion pictures that Distributor is permitted to distribute in the Territory or any part thereof is limited, then Distributor may in its absolute discretion determine which motion pictures then distributed by Distributor will be distributed in the Territory or any part thereof, and Distributor shall not be liable to Production Company in any manner or to any extent if the Picture is not distributed in the Territory or any part thereof by reason of any such determination.

(j) Collections: Distributor shall in good faith every six months audit, check or verify the computation of any payments and press for the collection of any monies which, if collected, would constitute gross receipts. There shall be no responsibility or liability to Production Company for failure to audit, check, or verify or to collect any monies payable.

(k) Advertising: Distributor agrees to commit a minimum of $_____ with respect to the advertising and publicity of the Picture.

(l) Expenses: Distributor may incur any expenses which Distributor, in the good faith exercise of its reasonable business judgment, deems appropriate with respect to the Picture or the exercise of any of Distributor's rights hereunder.

(m) No Preferential Treatment: Anything herein contained to the contrary notwithstanding, Production Company agrees that nothing herein shall require Distributor to prefer the Picture over any other motion picture distributed by Distributor or shall restrict or limit in any way Distributor's full right to distribute other motion pictures of any nature or description whether similar or dissimilar to the Picture.

**11. IMPORT PERMITS:** Distributor shall be under no duty to obtain any necessary licenses and permits for the importation and distribution of the Picture in any country or locality nor to utilize for the Picture any licenses or permits available to Distributor in limited quantity. Production Company shall on request use its best efforts to secure for Distributor any such licenses or permits. Distributor shall be entitled to the benefit of all import and/or export licenses and/ or quotas and/ or similar benefits of Production Company with respect to the Picture which would entitle the Picture to be imported into any country or territory.

**12. MOTION PICTURE PRINTS:** Distributor shall be entitled to obtain such prints, dupe negatives and master prints of the Picture which Distributor shall deem advisable for distribution of the Picture in the Territory. All such prints shall remain the property of Distributor.

**13. CENSORSHIP OR FORCE MAJEURE:**

(a) Adjustment of Advance: If Distributor is required to pay or advance to Production Company any fixed or other sum before it is collected from the distribution of the Picture, and Distributor is unable to distribute the Picture in any country or area of the Territory for any reason, including without limitation, censorship, import restriction, force majeure or failure to secure permits, the fixed payment or advance shall be reduced by the amount reasonably allocable to such country or area. The amount allocable to such country or area shall be the amount indicated in Schedule "A" or in the absence of such indication in Schedule "A", or if the country or area where distribution is prevented is one to which no allocation is made or which is a part of a country or area for which an overall allocation is made, then a reasonable allocation shall be made by Distributor for such country or area in which distribution is prevented. If the Picture is classified as unsuitable for children under 18 years of age or suitable for adults only in any country or area, the fixed payment or advance payable for such country or area shall be reduced by _____ percent.

(b) Adjustment of Distribution Expenses: If Distributor is for any reason unable to distribute the Picture in any country or area of the Territory and Distributor has incurred any Distribution Expenses in connection with the distribution of the Picture in such country or area, Producer will on demand reimburse Distributor therefore or, at Distributor's election, Distributor shall be repaid by Production Company from any sum thereafter due from Distributor to Production Company.

**14. DISTRIBUTOR'S DEFAULT:** Production Company shall not be entitled to bring any action, suit or proceeding of any nature against Distributor or its

CONTRACTS
FOR THE
FILM AND
TELEVISION
INDUSTRY

334

subdistributors or licensees, whether at law or in equity or otherwise, based upon or arising in whole or in part from any claim that Distributor or its subdistributors or licensees has in any way violated this Agreement, unless the action is brought within one (1) year from the date of Production Company's discovery of such alleged violation. It is agreed that if Distributor breaches this Agreement and fails to begin to remedy such breach within a period of thirty (30) days after receipt by Distributor of written notice from Production Company specifying the alleged breach and fails to cure such breach within sixty days thereafter, or if after delivery of the Picture, Distributor shall fail to make any payments at the time and in the manner provided and Production Company has given Distributor ten (10) days' written notice to that effect, then in either of such events, Production Company shall have the right to proceed against Distributor for monies due to Production Company in accordance with any and all remedies available to Production Company both at law and in equity. In no event, however, shall Production Company have any right to terminate or rescind this Agreement, nor shall the rights acquired by Distributor under this Agreement be subject to revocation, termination or diminution because of any failure or breach of any kind on the part of Distributor or its subdistributors or licensees. In no event shall Production Company be entitled to an injunction to restrain any alleged breach by Distributor or its subdistributors or licensees of any provisions of this Agreement.

**15. ASSIGNMENT:** This agreement will be binding upon and will enure to the benefit of the parties hereto and their respective successors and permitted assigns. Producer may assign its rights to payment of monies. Distributor may not assign its rights without the prior written consent of Producer, provided that nothing herein will prevent Distributor from assigning its rights to a successor company that may arise from Distributor merging, being acquired or partnering with another company.

**16. ARBITRATION AND JURISDICTION:** This Agreement shall be interpreted in accordance with the laws of the State of _____, applicable to agreements executed and to be wholly performed therein. Any controversy or claim arising out of or in relation to this Agreement or the validity, construction or performance of this Agreement, or the breach thereof, shall be resolved by arbitration in accordance with the rules and procedures of the American Film Marketing Association, as said rules may be amended from time to time with rights of discovery if requested by the arbitrator. Such rules and procedures are incorporated and made a part of this Agreement by reference. If the American Film Marketing Association shall refuse to accept jurisdiction of such dispute, then the parties agree to arbitrate such matter before and in accordance with the rules of the American Arbitration Association (AAA) under its jurisdiction in _____ before a single arbitrator familiar with entertainment law. The parties shall have the right to engage in pre-hearing discovery in connection with such arbitration proceedings. The parties agree hereto that they will abide by and perform any award rendered in any arbitration conducted pursuant hereto, that any court having jurisdiction thereof may issue a judgment based upon such award and that the prevailing party in such arbitration and/or confirmation proceeding shall be entitled to recover its reasonable attorney's fees and costs. The arbitration will be held in _____ and any award shall be final, binding and non-appealable. The Parties agree to accept service of process in accordance with the AFMA or AAA Rules.

**17. WAIVER:** No waiver of any breach of any provision of this Agreement shall constitute a waiver of any other breach of the same or any other provision hereof, and no waiver shall be effective unless made in writing.

**18. RELATIONSHIP OF PARTIES:** Nothing herein contained shall be construed to create a joint venture or partnership between the parties hereto. Neither of the parties shall hold itself out contrary to the terms of this provision, by advertising or otherwise nor shall Distributor or Production Company be bound or become liable because of any representations, actions or omissions of the other.

**19. ASSIGNMENT:** Distributor may assign this Agreement to and/or may distribute the Picture through any of its subsidiaries, parents, or affiliated corporations or any agent, instrumentality or other means determined by Distributor, provided that Distributor shall not thereby be relieved of the fulfillment of its obligations hereunder. Production Company may assign the right to receive payment hereunder to any third party; provided, however, that Production Company shall not be permitted to assign any of its obligations hereunder.

**20. NOTICES:** All notices from Production Company or Distributor to the other, with respect to this Agreement, shall be given in writing by mailing or telegraphing the notice prepaid, return receipt requested, and addressed to Distributor or Production Company, as appropriate, at the address set forth in the preamble hereof. A courtesy copy of any notice to Production Company shall be sent to _____, and a courtesy copy of any notice to Distributor shall be sent to _____.

**21. GOVERNING LAW:** This Agreement shall be governed by the laws of the State of _____, without giving effect to principles of conflict of laws thereof.

**22. CAPTIONS:** The captions of the various paragraphs and sections of the Agreement are intended to be used solely for convenience of reference and are not intended and shall not be deemed for any purpose whatsoever to modify or explain or to be used as an aid in the construction of any provisions.

**23. AMENDMENTS IN WRITING:** This Agreement cannot be amended, modified or changed in any way whatsoever except by a written instrument duly signed by authorized officers of Production Company and Distributor.

**24. ENTIRE AGREEMENT:** This Agreement, which is comprised of the general terms above ("Main Agreement") and the attached Schedule and Exhibits, represents the entire agreement between the parties with respect to the subject matter hereof and this Agreement supersedes all previous representations, understandings or agreements, oral or written, between the parties regarding the subject matter hereof.

By signing in the spaces provided below, the parties accept and agree to all the terms and conditions of this Agreement as of the date first above written.

_____
(Production Representative)

_____

Its: _____ (Production Representative Title)
("Production Company")

_____
(Distributor Representative)

_____

Its: _____ (Distribution Representative Title)
("Distributor")

CONTRACTS
FOR THE
FILM AND
TELEVISION
INDUSTRY

336

**EXHIBIT A**

(Delivery List)

**SCHEDULE "A"**

("Main Agreement") dated _____ between _____ ("Distributor") and _____ ("Production Company").

**1. Picture:**

a) Specifications:

Title: _____
Individual Producer: _____
Principal Cast: _____
Director: _____
Technical Specifications: _____
Color: _____
Running Time: _____
MPAA Rating: _____

b) Delivery: The _____ language version of the Picture shall be delivered to Distributor no later than _____ and complete delivery pursuant to the requirements of Clause 4 of the Main Agreement shall be completed no later than _____.

c) Terms of the Essence: All the provisions of this clause 1 of this Schedule "A" are of the essence of this Agreement. If Production Company does not comply with any of the material provisions of this Clause 1, Distributor, may at its option, terminate this Agreement upon written notice to Production Company at any time prior to compliance by Production Company without any liability on the part of Distributor and Production Company shall promptly repay to Distributor all monies paid hereunder together with interest thereon at an annual percentage rate of _____ plus an administrative charge of _____% on said annual percentage rate.

**2. Territory:** The territory shall be _____ (including ships and airplanes flying flags of the countries of the Territory or served therefrom, military installations in and of the countries of the Territory and all countries cinematographically associated with the countries of the Territory).

**3. Distribution Term:** The Distribution Term for each of the Territory shall commence from the date hereof and continue for a period expiring _____ of years thereafter from the first exhibition of the Picture in each country of the Territory.

**4. Minimum Guarantee (Advance):** Provided Production Company has furnished to Distributor documentation establishing Production Company's distribution rights to the Picture in the Territory, Distributor shall pay to Production Company a Minimum Guarantee advance of $_____.

**5. Interest on the Minimum Guarantee (Advance):** Interest on the Minimum Guarantee shall be calculated and charged as set forth in Exhibit "_____" attached hereto.

**6. Division of Net Profits/Adjusted Gross Receipts/Gross Proceeds:** The Net Profits/Gross Receipts/Gross Proceeds as defined in Exhibit "_____" attached shall be paid as follows:

(*specify*)

**7.Trailers and Advertising Accessories:** Revenue derived from trailers and advertising accessories shall be excluded from Gross Receipts. Distributor shall pay all such costs and retain all revenue derived therefrom for its account.

**8. Television Rights:** All television distribution rights, including, without limitation, pay, pay-per-view, satellite and free, are reserved by Production Company; however, Production Company agrees these rights will not be exercised in the Territory by Production Company or its licensees nor will the picture be announced or advertised for such television exhibition in the territory during the Distribution Term (the period commencing upon the date hereof and continuing for a period expiring _____.

_____

"Distributor"

By:_____

Its:_____


_____

"Production Company"

By:_____

Its:_____

CONTRACTS
FOR THE
FILM AND
TELEVISION
INDUSTRY

338

# CERTIFICATE OF AUTHORSHIP

A certificate of authorship is a common delivery item given to the distributor by the producer. The certificate of authorship certifies the identity of the copyright owner of the script. This document is one of the documents that make up the "chain-of-title," which are the contracts that vest all rights in a motion picture in the producer. Note that under American copyright law, the copyright owner of a work-for-hire is the employer unless the parties agree otherwise. Thus, the producer will generally be the copyright owner of a script written for the producer. If the script was written by the writer on his own behalf, and then "sold" to a producer, the initial copyright owner would be the writer. In this instance, the producer would require the writer to assign or transfer the motion picture rights to the script to the producer.

## CERTIFICATE OF AUTHORSHIP

The undersigned hereby certifies and agrees that for one dollar ($1.00) and other good and valuable consideration, receipt of which is hereby acknowledged, _____ ("Producer") has employed my services as a writer in connection with a proposed motion picture entitled, _____ (the "Picture"), and that except for existing literary material which Producer instructs me to use as a basis for writing hereunder, all literary material of whatever kind or nature written or to be written, furnished or to be furnished, by me as well as all of the results and proceeds of my writing services in connection with the Picture (all such literary material, and all such results and proceeds thereof being referred to collectively herein as the "Material") submitted and to be submitted by me in connection with the Picture was and/or will be solely written and/or created by me as original material and that for copyright purposes, the Material shall be written and/or created by me as a work-made-for-hire, specially ordered or commissioned by Producer for use as part of a motion picture within the meaning of the 1976 Copyright Act, and Producer shall be deemed the sole author of the Material and owner of all rights of every kind or nature, whether now known or hereafter devised (including, but not limited to, all copyrights and extensions and renewals of copyrights) in and to the Material, as well as the right to make such changes in the Material and such uses of the Material, throughout the Universe, as Producer may from time to time determine as such author.

I warrant and represent that I have the right to execute this document and, except to the extent that it is based upon material assigned to me by Producer to be used as the basis therefor, that the Material is or shall be original with me, does not and shall not defame or disparage any person or entity or infringe upon or violate the rights of privacy, publicity or any other rights of any kind or nature whatsoever of any person or entity and is not the subject of any litigation or of any claim that might give rise to litigation. I acknowledge that I have been fully compensated for all services performed in connection with the Picture, and that there are no further obligations owed to me by Producer or its assignees. I shall defend (with counsel acceptable to Producer), indemnify and hold harmless Producer, any corporations comprising Producer, its and their employees, officers, agents, assigns and licensees from and against any and all liability, claims, costs, damages and expenses (including reasonable attorneys' fees and court costs) arising out of or in connection with a breach of the foregoing covenants, warranties and representations.

I agree to execute any documents and to do any other acts as may be reasonably required by Producer or its assignees or licensees to further evidence or effectuate Producer's rights as set forth in this Certificate of Authorship. Upon my failure promptly to do so, I hereby appoint Producer as my attorney-in-fact for such purposes (it being acknowledged that such appointment is irrevocable and coupled with an interest) with full power of substitution and delegation.

I further acknowledge that (i) in the event of any breach hereunder by Producer, I will be limited to my remedy at law for damages, if any, and will not have the right to terminate or rescind this Certificate or to enjoin the distribution, advertising or exploitation of the Picture, (ii) nothing herein shall obligate Producer to use my services or the results of proceeds thereof in the Picture or to produce, advertise or distribute the Picture, (iii) this Certificate shall be governed by the laws of the State of _____ applicable to agreements executed and to be performed entirely therein, and (iv) this Certificate constitutes the entire agreement between the parties to the within subject matter and cannot be modified except by a written instrument signed by the parties hereto.

I hereby waive all rights of "droit moral" or so-called "moral rights of authors" or any similar rights or principles of law which I may now or later have in the Material or to my services.

Producer's rights with respect to the Material and/or my services are irrevocable and may be freely assigned and licensed and its rights shall be binding upon me and inure to the benefit of any such assignee or licensee.

I have caused this document to be executed on _____.


_____
Writer



STATE OF _____  )
                                      ) ss:
COUNTY OF _____  )

On the _____ day of _____, 19\_\_\_, before me personally came _____ to me known and known to be the individual described in and who executed the foregoing instrument, and he/she did duly acknowledge to me that he/she executed the same.


_____
Notary Public

CONTRACTS
FOR THE
FILM AND
TELEVISION
INDUSTRY

340

# CERTIFICATE OF ORIGIN

A certificate of origin is a standard delivery item for international distribution. The certificate is evidence of the country of origin of a motion picture.

## CERTIFICATE OF ORIGIN

Date:_____

To whom it may concern:

This is to certify that the feature motion picture currently entitled "_____" ("Picture") starring _____, directed by _____, and produced by _____ ("Licensor") is an _____ production. The Picture has a running time of _____ minutes.

The Licensor has granted to _____ ("_____"), throughout the world (excluding the United States and Canada) the sole and exclusive right to enter on Licensor's behalf into distribution agreements regarding the distribution, exhibition and license of the Picture and to advertise and publicize the Picture.

On the basis of the foregoing, it is requested that the Picture be treated as an _____ production for distribution, exhibition and importation purposes.

LICENSOR: _____

BY:_____
    (Production Company Representative)

STATE OF                    )
                            ) ss.
COUNTY OF                   )

On _____, 199__, before me personally appeared _____ who proved to me on the basis of satisfactory evidence to be the person whose name is subscribed to the within instrument and acknowledged to me that she executed the same in her authorized capacity, and that by her signature on the instrument the person, or the entity upon behalf of which the person acted, executed the instrument.

WITNESS my hand and official seal.

_____
Notary Public in and for said
County and State

# SHORT FORM ASSIGNMENT

An assignment agreement is used to transfer rights. A writer who has written a screenplay, for example, may need to transfer the motion picture rights to a producer. The short form is often used for registration with the copyright office so that a minimal amount of information is placed on the public record. The parties may not want to disclose, for instance, the amount of compensation paid to the writer. Typically, a more detailed agreement is entered into between the parties. The short-form agreement will serve as a summary of the parties' agreement.

## SHORT-FORM ASSIGNMENT

KNOW ALL MEN BY THESE PRESENTS that, in consideration of One Dollar ($1.00) and other good and valuable consideration, receipt of which is hereby acknowledged, the undersigned _____, ("Assignor") does hereby sell, grant, convey and assign unto _____ ("Assignee"), its successors, assigns and licensees forever, all right, title and interest including but not limited to the exclusive worldwide Motion Picture and allied rights of Assignor in and to that certain literary work, to wit: "_____," and all drafts, revisions, arrangements, adaptations, dramatizations, translations, sequels and other versions of the Literary Property which may heretofore have been written or which may hereafter be written with the sanction of Assignor.

Dated this _____.

_____
("Assignor")


AGREED TO:

_____
("Assignee")

CONTRACTS
FOR THE
FILM AND
TELEVISION
INDUSTRY

342

# REVENUE PARTICIPANT DEFINITIONS

Producers often license motion picture rights to distributors under terms which provide that the producer is entitled to share in the revenues or net profits earned from a motion picture. The terms that define how much the participant will receive are often complex and lengthy, and in the case of "net profit" participants, the subject of considerable controversy. Some of the definitions are so skewed in favor of the distributor that profits are illusory. A relative handful of top stars and directors are able to negotiate a share in a studio's gross revenues. Gross revenue participants often receive significant payments.

The term "Gross Receipts" is usually defined to include rental payments from all exhibitors and revenue derived from other markets such as television, foreign sales, cable, home video and merchandising. Profit participants with a "piece of the gross" share in gross revenue, although a few deductions, such as taxes, may be allowed. Only the most desirable talent has the negotiating clout to obtain a piece of the gross revenue. Studios dislike gross deals because gross participants share in revenue from a picture even if the studio has not earned its investment back.

Suppose a studio has given a star ten percent of the gross revenues from a motion picture. If the film's gross from all sources is $50 million, and if the film's production, marketing and distribution costs total $50 million, the distributor has broken even. The star, however, is due $5 million dollars (which may be in addition to whatever he received as an up-front payment). So the studio is losing money while the star is making a bundle. To avoid this situation, studios prefer to pay participants only after the studio recoups at least some expenses. When the participant is allowed to share in revenue after a limited amount of deductions, such as the expenses of advertising and print duplication costs, the arrangement is called an ADJUSTED GROSS or MODIFIED GROSS deal.

Filmmakers and studios have devised all kinds of variations to these deals. For instance, a participant's piece of the gross might not be payable until the movie grosses two or three times its negative cost. The parties could also agree to split off revenue from some media (e.g., home video) into a separate revenue pool and pay a portion of these funds to the participants.

The least desirable deal from the profit participant's point of view, is a "NET PROFIT"[2] deal. Here so many deductions are allowed that what is left is often zero or less. Although the net profit participant may not see any money from his POINTS, or percentage of profits, the studio may make a "profit" because it receives thirty to forty percent of the gross as a distribution fee. This commission is usually far more than the actual costs the studio incurs to distribute a motion picture. Thus the release of a picture may be very profitable to the studio although there are no "profits" for the participants.

Net profits, if there are any, are often shared fifty/fifty between the studio and the producer. While net profit participants typically receive their pieces of the profit pie from the producer's half, net profits are customarily defined in terms of the whole (one hundred percent). We say the writer is entitled to five percent of one hundred percent (5% of 100%) of the net profits. This means the writer is entitled to five

---

[2] A "net profit" deal does not represent anyone's economic net profit but is simply a net amount determined by a contract formula.

percent of all the net profits, although his percentage comes from the producer's half. Parties define net profits this way to avoid ambiguity. If the contract simply said the writer was entitled to five percent of the net profits, the question might arise, is he due five percent of the producer's half (which would amount to five percent of fifty percent) or is he entitled to five percent of the whole?

There is more room for accounting disputes when a participant is entitled to a piece of the net because the studio is allowed to deduct various marketing expenses as well as interest, distribution, overhead fees, and payments to gross profit participants. Thus, even without any creative accounting, a net profit participant is unlikely to see any profits.

CONTRACTS
FOR THE
FILM AND
TELEVISION
INDUSTRY

344

## ADJUSTED GROSS

The terms of adjusted gross deals vary. Here is one studios' provision that allows for participation in the gross after "break-even." Note that "break-even" is defined in such a manner as to allow the studio to deduct the cost of production, distribution fees and distribution expenses. Thus, this definition is not much better than a "net profit" definition.

## DEFINITION OF GROSS RECEIPTS AFTER BREAKEVEN

**1. Definition of Parties:** "Studio" means _____, a \_\_\_\_\_ (Incorporation State) corporation, and its subsidiaries engaged in the business of distributing motion pictures for exhibition in theatres and for broadcasting over television stations, but shall not include any other persons, firms or corporations licensed by Studio to distribute motion pictures in any part of the world. Nor shall such term include: any person, firm or corporation distributing the Picture for purposes other than exhibition in theatres or by television stations; exhibitors or others who may actually exhibit the Picture to the public; radio or television broadcasters; cable operators; manufacturers, wholesalers or retailers of video discs, cassettes or similar devices; book or music publishers; phonograph record producers or distributors; merchandisers, etc., whether or not any of the foregoing are subsidiaries of Studio. As used herein, a "subsidiary" of Studio refers to an entity in which Studio has at least a 50% interest.

"Participant" means the party under the foregoing agreement who or which is entitled to participate in the gross receipts of the Picture in excess of breakeven, and the successors and permitted assigns of such party.

**2. Breakeven:** As between Studio and Participant, the Picture shall be deemed to have reached "breakeven" at such time as the gross receipts (as defined in 3 hereof) of the Picture shall equal the following:

(a) Studio's distribution fees set forth in 4 hereof.

(b) Studio's expenses in connection with the distribution of the Picture, as set forth in 5 hereof.

(c) The cost of production of the Picture, plus an amount equal to interest thereon, all as provided for in 9 hereof, and plus such other costs, if any, as may have been incurred in connection with the financing of the cost of production of the Picture. Said interest and other costs shall be recouped before said cost of production.

**3. "Gross Receipts"** of the Picture means the aggregate of:

(a) All film rentals actually received by Studio from parties exhibiting the Picture in theatres and on television where Studio distributes directly to such parties (hereinafter referred to as "exhibitors"),

(b) Where Studio grants theatrical distribution rights to a subdistributor on a basis requiring it to account to Studio with respect to film rentals, either: (i) the film rentals received by such subdistributor from exhibitors which Studio accepts for the purpose of its accountings with such subdistributor; or (ii) Studio's share (actually received) of film rentals received by such subdistributor; whichever Studio elects from time to time as to each subdistributor.

(c) In respect of licenses of exhibition or distribution rights by means of video discs, cassettes or similar devices, an amount equal to 20% of (i) the gross wholesale rental income therefrom and (ii) the gross wholesale sales income therefrom less a reasonable allowance for returns.

(d) All amounts actually received by Studio from the following: (i) trailers (other than trailers advertising television exhibitions of the Picture); (ii) licenses of theatrical distribution rights for a flat sum; (iii) licenses of exhibition or distribution rights other than those referred to in (a), (b), (c) and (d) (ii) of this 3, specifically including licenses to cable operators; (iv) the lease of positive prints (as distinguished from the licensing thereof for a film rental); and from the sale or licensing of advertising accessories, souvenir programs and booklets; and (v) recoveries by Studio for infringement of copyrights of the Picture.

(e) All monies actually received by Studio on account of direct subsidies, aide or prizes relating specifically to the Picture, net of an amount equal to income taxes based thereon imposed by the country involved, if any. If local laws require use of such monies as a condition to the grant of such subsidy or aide, such monies shall not be included in gross receipts until actually used.

(f) All amounts required to be included under Exhibits "1," "2" and "3" hereof.

All costs incurred in connection with any of the foregoing shall be deemed and treated as recoupable distribution expenses. In no event shall rentals from the exhibition of the Picture which are contributed to charitable organizations be included in gross receipts.

Notwithstanding anything herein contained, after the Picture shall be deemed to have reached "breakeven" as defined in 2 above, gross receipts shall be as defined and this Exhibit shall otherwise be modified as set forth in Schedule 1 attached hereto and incorporated herein by this reference.

**4. Distribution Fees:** Studio's distribution fees shall be as follows:

(a) _____% of the gross receipts of the Picture derived by Studio from all sources in the United States and Canada.

(b) _____% of the gross receipts of the Picture derived by Studio from all sources in the United Kingdom.

(c) _____% of the gross receipts of the Picture derived by Studio from all sources other than those referred to in (a) and (b) above.

(d) Notwithstanding the foregoing; (i) with respect to sums included in the gross receipts pursuant to 3(b)(ii) and 3(d)(ii) hereof, Studio's distribution fee shall be 15% of such sums; (ii) if Studio shall license the exhibition of the Picture on free television, the aforesaid percentages as to amounts received and collected by Studio from sources in the United States, shall be 30% if collected from a network for national network telecasts in prime time; and 35% in all other instances; and, as to amounts received and collected by Studio from sources outside the United States 40%; (iii) no distribution fee shall be charged on gross receipts referred to in 3(e) hereof.

CONTRACTS
FOR THE
FILM AND
TELEVISION
INDUSTRY

346

All distribution fees shall be calculated on the full gross receipts without any deductions or payments of any kind whatsoever, except as specifically hereinafter provided.

Notwithstanding anything herein contained, it is agreed that for the accounting period in which the Picture shall first reach breakeven, the distribution fees for the purpose of calculating breakeven shall be calculated only on that portion of the gross receipts in respect of such accounting period which is equal to the sum of the following:

(a) An amount equal to the sums specified in subparagraphs (b) and (c) of paragraph 2 of this Exhibit which are recouped or paid in respect of such accounting period; and

(b) An amount equal to the distribution fees on gross receipts equal to the sum of said deductible items, plus the distribution fees on gross receipts equal to such distribution fee.

**5. Distribution Expenses:** Studio's deductible distribution expenses in connection with the Picture shall include all costs and expenses incurred in connection with the distribution, advertising, exploitation and turning to account of the Picture of whatever kind or nature, or which are customarily treated as distribution expenses under customary accounting procedures in the motion picture industry. If Studio reasonably anticipates that additional distribution expenses will be incurred in the future, Studio may, for a reasonable time, set up appropriate reserves therefor. Without limiting the generality of the foregoing, the following particular items shall be included in distribution expenses hereunder:

(a) The cost and expense of all duped and dubbed negatives, sound tracks, prints, release prints, tapes, cassettes, duplicating material and facilities and all other material manufactured for use in connection with the Picture, including the cost of inspecting, repairing, checking and renovating film, reels, containers, cassettes, packing, storing and shipping and all other expenses connected therewith and inspecting and checking exhibitors' projection and sound equipment and facilities. Studio may manufacture or cause to be manufactured as many or as few duped negatives, positive prints and other material for use in connection with the Picture as it, in its sole discretion, may consider advisable or desirable.

(b) All direct costs and charges for advertisements, press books, artwork, advertising accessories and trailers (other than (i) prints of trailers advertising free television exhibition of the Picture, and (ii) the trailer production costs which are included in the cost of production of the Picture), advertising, publicizing and exploiting the Picture by such means and to such extent as Studio may, in its uncontrolled discretion, deem desirable, including, without limitation, pre-release advertising and publicity, so-called cooperative and/or theatre advertising, and/or other advertising engaged in with or for exhibitors, to the extent Studio pays, shares in, or is charged with all or a portion of such costs and all other exploitation costs relating to such theatre exhibition. Any re-use fees and costs of recording and manufacturing masters for phonograph records, which Studio shall advance in order to assist in the advertising and exploitation of the Picture, shall be treated as costs hereunder to the extent unrecouped by the record company. Where any Studio advertising or publicity employee (other than an executive supervisory employee) or facility is used for the Picture, the salary of such employee and the cost of such facility (while so used for the Picture) shall be direct costs hereunder. Any costs and charges referred to in this (b) (and not included in the cost of production of the Picture), expended or incurred prior to delivery of the Picture, shall be included in direct costs under this (b). There shall also be included as an item of cost a sum equal to 10% of all direct costs referred to in this (b) to cover the indirect cost of Studio's advertising and publicity departments, both domestic and foreign.

(c) All costs of preparing and delivering the Picture for distribution (regardless of whether such costs are the salaries and expenses of Studio's own employees or employees or parties not regularly employed by Studio), including, without limitation, all costs incurred in connection with the production of foreign language versions of the Picture, whether dubbed, superimposed or otherwise, as well as any and all costs and expenses in connection with changing the title of the Picture, recutting, re-editing or shortening or lengthening the Picture for release in any territory or for exhibition on television or other media, or in order to conform to the requirements of censorship authorities, or in order to conform to the peculiar national or political prejudices likely to be encountered in any territory, or for any other purpose or reason. The costs referred to in this (c) shall include all studio charges for facilities, labor and material, whether or not incurred at a studio owned or controlled by Studio.

(d) All sums paid or accrued on account of sales, use, receipts, income, excise, remittance and other taxes (however denominated) to any governmental authority assessed upon the negatives, duplicate negatives, prints or sound records of the Picture, or upon the use or distribution of the Picture, or upon the revenues derived therefrom, or any part thereof, or upon the remittance of such revenues, or any part thereof; any and all sums paid or accrued on account of duties, customs and imposts, costs of acquiring permits, "Kontingents," and any similar authority to secure the entry, licensing, exhibition, performance, use or televising of the Picture in any country or part thereof, regardless of whether such payments or accruals are assessed against the Picture or the proceeds thereof or against a group of motion pictures in which the Picture may be included or the proceeds thereof. In no event shall the deductible amount of any such tax (however denominated) imposed upon Studio, be decreased (nor the gross receipts increased) because of the manner in which such taxes are elected to be treated by Studio in filing net income, corporate franchise, excess profits or similar tax returns. Subject to the foregoing, (i) Studio's own United States federal and state income taxes and franchise taxes based on Studio's net income; and (ii) income taxes payable to any country or territory by Studio based on the net earnings of Studio in such country or territory and which is computed and assessed solely by reason of the retention in such country or territory by Studio of any portion of the gross receipts shall not be deductible hereunder.

(e) Expenses of transmitting to the United States any funds accruing to Studio from the Picture in foreign countries, such as cable expenses, and any discounts from such funds taken to convert such funds directly or indirectly into U.S. dollars.

(f) All costs and expenses, including reasonable attorneys' fees, loss, damage or liability suffered or incurred by Studio in connection with: any action taken by Studio (whether by litigation or otherwise) in copyrighting, protecting and enforcing the copyright of, and other rights and sources of revenue to be derived from, the Picture; reducing or minimizing the matters referred to in (d) and (e) above, the collection of film rentals, and other sums due Studio from exhibitors,

CONTRACTS
FOR THE
FILM AND
TELEVISION
INDUSTRY

348

subdistributors and others in respect of the Picture or to recover monies due pursuant to any agreement relating to the distribution or the exhibition of the Picture; checking attendance and exhibitors' receipts; preventing and/or recovering damages for unauthorized exhibition or distribution of the Picture, or any impairment of, encumbrance on or infringement upon, the rights of Studio in and to the Picture; prosecuting and defending actions under the antitrust laws, communications laws, and federal, state and local laws, ordinances and regulations (including censorship) affecting the exhibition and/or distribution of the Picture and/or the ability of Studio to derive revenue from the Picture and its component parts and by-products; and auditing of books and records of any exhibitor, subdistributor or licensee.

(g) Royalties payable to manufacturers of sound recording and reproducing equipment and dues and assessments of, and contributions by Studio to, AMPTP, MPAA, MPEA, the Academy of Motion Picture Arts and Sciences and other trade associations or industry groups comprised of a substantial number of motion picture producers and/or distributors, but only for purposes relating to the production, distribution, export, import, advertising, exploitation and general protection and/or promotion of motion pictures.

(h) In the event any person shall make a claim relating to the Picture against Studio or any of its licensees, which claim, in Studio's judgment, is of sufficient merit to constitute a reasonable probability of ultimate loss, cost, damage or expense, Studio may deduct under this (h) such amount as Studio may deem necessary to cover any loss, cost, damage or expense which may be suffered as a result thereof. Studio shall have the right to settle and pay any such claim. After the settlement of any such claim, or after the final judicial determination thereof, the amount previously deducted hereunder shall be adjusted accordingly with the next accounting statement rendered hereunder. Nothing herein contained shall be construed as a waiver of any of Participant's warranties contained in this Agreement, or a waiver of any right or remedy at law or otherwise which may exist in favor of Studio, including, but not limited to, the right to require Participant to reimburse Studio on demand for any liability, cost, damage or expense arising out of, or resulting from, any breach by Participant of any warranty, undertaking or obligation by Participant, or any right on the part of Studio to recoup or recover any such cost or expense out of Participant's share of any monies payable hereunder, rather than treating such costs or expenses as distribution expenses.

(i) All amounts paid or payable to or for the benefit of actors, writers, composers, directors and others, pursuant to applicable collective bargaining agreements and/or any law or governmental regulation or decree now or hereafter in force by reason of, and/or as a condition or consideration for, any exhibition, use, re-use, rerun, performance, sale, license and/or distribution of the Picture and/or copies of all or any part thereof, on television, supplemental markets, or otherwise (all herein called "residuals"), together with all taxes, pension fund contributions and other costs paid or payable in respect of such residuals, and in respect of participations in the gross receipts and net profits of the Picture; provided, however, that if Participant or any principal stockholder of Participant, or any heirs, executors, administrators, successors or assigns of Participant, or any such stockholder, are entitled, either directly or by way of participation in any pension fund, to any such residuals, or to compensation for services rendered beyond any guaranteed period referred to in the foregoing agreement, the amount payable on account thereof shall be treated as an advance against Participant's share of the net profits hereunder.

(j) The cost of all insurance (to the extent that the same is not included in the cost of production of the Picture) covering or relating to the Picture, including, but not limited to, errors and omissions insurance and all insurance on negatives, positive prints, sound materials or other physical property, it being understood, however, that Studio shall not be obligated to take out or maintain any such insurance.

(k) If Studio shall proceed under 3(b)(i) hereof, all items deducted by the subdistributor as distribution expenses, and which Studio accepts for the purpose of its accountings with such subdistributor, shall be treated as Studio's expenditures under the corresponding subdivision of this 5.

**6. Film Rentals:** "Film Rentals" shall be determined after all refunds, credits, discounts, allowances and adjustments granted to exhibitors, whether occasioned by condemnation by boards of censorship, settlement of disputes or otherwise. Until earned, forfeited or applied to the Picture, neither advance payments nor security deposits shall be included in film rentals. No cost (regardless of how incurred, paid or allowed) of Studio's share of cooperative and/or theater advertising shall be deducted in determining film rentals. Where allowances are granted and paid on account of Studio's share of cooperative theatre or joint advertising, such payments shall not be deducted in determining film rental, and where Studio's share of cooperative theater or joint advertising is deducted by the exhibitor Studio's share of cooperative theater or joint advertising shall be added back into the film rental received from such exhibitor, and all such costs, payments, discounts and allowances shall be treated as distribution expenses. Wherever Studio exhibits the Picture in a theatre or over a television station owned or controlled by Studio, or licenses the Picture or rights connected therewith to theaters, television stations or other agencies in which Studio has an interest, directly or indirectly, or to which Studio is obligated to pay a fixed sum for exhibiting the Picture or for the use of its premises or facilities, Studio shall include in the film rentals of the Picture such sums, determined in good faith, as may be reasonable and consistent with Studio's usual practice in such matters.

**7. Allocations:** Wherever Studio (i) receives from any license either a flat sum or a percentage of the receipts, or both, for any right to a group of motion pictures (including the Picture) under any agreement (whether or not the same shall provide for the exhibition, lease or delivery of positive prints of any of said motion pictures) which does not specify what portion of the license payments apply to the respective motion pictures in the group (or to such prints or other material, if any, as may be supplied), or (ii) receives foreign currency under 8 hereof relating to a group of motion pictures (including the Picture), then in any and all such situations Studio shall include in, or deduct from, the gross receipts, as the case may be, such sums, determined in good faith, as may be reasonable and consistent with Studio's usual practice in such matters. All costs described in 5 hereof (and, after breakeven, all deductible items set forth in Schedule 1 hereto) shall be fairly apportioned to the Picture if incurred or expended on an industry basis, or in conjunction with other motion picture producers and/or distributors, or with respect to the Picture and other motion pictures distributed by Studio.

**8. Foreign Receipts:** No sums received by Studio relating to the Picture shall be included in gross receipts hereunder unless and until such sums have been (i) received by Studio in U.S. dollars in the United States; or (ii) used by Studio for the

CONTRACTS
FOR THE
FILM AND
TELEVISION
INDUSTRY

350

production or acquisition of motion pictures or television films which can be lawfully removed from the country or territory involved, in which event they shall be included in gross receipts for the accounting period during which an amount (computed at the official or unofficial rate of exchange, as Studio may elect) equal to the amount expended for such production or acquisition, plus interest thereon, as herein provided, has been recouped by Studio (in excess of normal distribution fees and distribution expenses) from distribution thereof outside the country or territory involved; or (iii) used by Studio for acquisition of tangible personal property which can be and is lawfully exported from the country or territory involved, in which event the U.S. dollar equivalent of the currency utilized to acquire such property shall be included in gross receipts hereunder for the accounting period during which such property was so exported, such U.S. dollar equivalent to be computed at the official or unofficial rate of exchange, as Studio may elect, in effect on the date of export. Studio will, promptly after receipt of a written request from Participant (but not more frequently than annually) advise Participant in writing as to foreign revenues not included in gross receipts as aforesaid, and Studio shall, at the written request and expense of Participant (subject to any and all limitations, restrictions, laws, rules and regulations affecting such transactions), deposit into a bank designated by Participant in the country involved, or pay to any other party designated by Participant in such country, such part thereof as would have been payable to Participant hereunder. Such deposits or payments to or for Participant shall constitute due remittance to Participant, and Studio shall have no further interest therein or responsibility therefor. Studio makes no warranties or representations that any part of any such foreign currencies may be converted into U.S. dollars or transferred to the account of Participant in any foreign country. In no event shall Studio be obligated to apply gross receipts of any country not actually received by Studio in U.S. dollars in the United States to the recoupment of any costs or expenses incurred with respect to the Picture (or, after breakeven, of any deductible items set forth in Schedule 1 hereto) in any other country.

### 9. Cost of Production; Interest:

(a) The "cost of production" of the Picture means the total direct cost of production of the Picture, including the cost of all items listed on Studio's standard Delivery Schedule, computed and determined in all respects in the same manner as Studio then customarily determines the direct cost of other motion pictures distributed and/or financed by it, plus Studio's overhead charge. The determination of what items constitute direct charges and what items are within said overhead charge shall be made in all respects in the same manner as Studio customarily determines such matters. The full amount of all direct costs of production of the Picture (whether payable in cash, deferred or accrued) shall be included in the direct cost of the Picture at the time liability therefor is incurred or contracted, regardless of whether the same has actually been paid to the party or parties entitled thereto at the time involved. Deferments and participations in gross receipts of the Picture consented to by Studio (however defined) shall be treated as direct costs of production, whether the same shall be in a definite amount or based on a percentage of the gross receipts, and whether the same are fixed obligations or are contingent upon receipts of the Picture; provided, however, contingent participations based on a percentage of gross receipts as defined in the applicable agreement shall not be included in the direct cost of production beyond recoupment under 2(c) hereof.

(b) Studio's overhead charge shall be in an amount equal to _____% of the direct cost of production of the Picture, with the understanding that any production facilities, equipment or personnel supplied by Studio or by a studio owned or controlled by Studio, or in which Studio has a substantial financial interest (and which are not furnished within the overhead charge), shall be supplied at Studio's usual rental rates charged for such items, and such charges shall be treated as direct costs of production of the Picture and shall bear said _____% overhead charge. Studio's overhead charge shall accrue and be included in the cost of production of the Picture concurrently with the incurring of the respective items of direct cost to which it applies.

(c) The amount equal to interest provided for in 2(c) hereof shall be calculated at a rate per annum equal to _____% of the rate announced from time to time by the First National Bank of Boston as its prime rate on unsecured loans to its preferred customers. Said amount shall be calculated from the respective dates that each item is charged to the Picture until the close of the accounting period during which the cost of production is recouped under 2(c) hereof, except that interest on deferred amounts shall be calculated from the date of payment.

(d) Concurrently with delivery to Participant of the first earnings statement hereunder, Studio will (subject to revisions and correction) deliver to Participant an itemized summary of the cost of production of the Picture. Participant shall have the right to audit such statement in accordance with 11 hereof.

(e) If the final cost of production shall exceed the budgeted cost by 5% or more, then for the purposes of 2(c) hereof there shall be added to the actual cost of production of the Picture an amount equal to the amount by which the final direct cost exceeds 105% of the budgeted direct cost. For the purposes of this subdivision (e), the final direct cost shall not include costs incurred solely by reason of force majeure events, union increases not reflected in the budget, and overbudget costs incurred at the request of an officer of Studio having the rank of Vice President or higher over the written objection of Participant.

**10. Earnings Statements:** Studio shall render to Participant periodic statements showing, in summary form, the appropriate calculations under this Agreement. Statements shall be issued for each calendar quarter until the Picture has been in release for 4 years from and including the quarter in which the Picture was first released, and thereafter annually. Each such quarterly or annual period, as the case may be, is herein referred to as an "accounting period." No statements need be rendered for any accounting period during which no receipts are received. Statements rendered by Studio may be changed from time to time to give effect to year-end adjustments made by Studio's Accounting Department or Public Accountants, or to items overlooked, to correct errors and for similar purposes. If Studio shall extend credit to any licensee with respect to the Picture and if such credit has been included in the gross receipts, and if, in the opinion of Studio, any such indebtedness shall be uncollectible, the uncollected amount may be deducted in any subsequent earning statement. Should Studio make any overpayment to Participant hereunder for any reason, Studio shall have the right to deduct and retain for its own account an amount equal to any such overpayment from any sums that may thereafter become due or payable by Studio to Participant or for Participant's account, or may demand repayment from Participant, in which event Participant shall repay the same when such demand is made. Any U.S. dollars due and payable to Participant by Studio pursuant to any such statement shall be paid to Participant simultaneously with the rendering of such statement; provided, however, that all amounts payable to Participant hereunder shall be subject to all laws and regulations now or hereafter in existence requiring deductions or withholdings for

CONTRACTS
FOR THE
FILM AND
TELEVISION
INDUSTRY

352

income or other taxes payable by or assessable against Participant. Studio shall have the right to make such deductions and withholdings and the payment thereof to the governmental agency concerned in accordance with its interpretation in good faith of such laws and regulations, and shall not be liable to Participant for the making of such deductions or withholdings or the payment thereof to the governmental agency concerned. In any such event Participant shall make and prosecute any and all claims which it may have with respect to the same directly with the governmental agency having jurisdiction in the premises. The right of Participant to receive, and the obligation of Studio to account for, any share of the gross receipts of the Picture shall terminate if the Picture has been made available for exhibition on syndicated television in the U.S.A., and if the first earnings statement issued thereafter shows a deficit under 2 hereof such that at least $500,000 of gross receipts would be required before Participant would be entitled to receive any gross receipts hereunder. In the event a new medium of exhibition shall thereafter be developed and there shall be substantial exhibition and distribution of the Picture by such new medium which is likely to generate gross receipts of $500,000 or the amount of the deficit, whichever is larger, Participant may audit Studio's records for the purpose of determining whether the Picture has earned, or is likely to earn, any gross receipts in excess of breakeven, and if, as a result of such audit, it is determined by mutual agreement, or in the event of dispute appropriate legal proceedings, that the Picture has earned, or is likely to earn, gross receipts in excess of breakeven as herein defined, accountings hereunder and payments, if required, shall be reinstated.

**11. Accounting Records re Distribution; Audit Rights:** Studio shall keep books of account relating to the distribution of the Picture, together with vouchers, exhibition contracts and similar records supporting the same (all of which are hereinafter referred to as "records"), which shall be kept on the same basis and in the same manner and for the same periods as such records are customarily kept by Studio. Participant may, at its own expense, audit the applicable records at the place where Studio maintains the same in order to verify earnings statements rendered hereunder. Any such audit shall be conducted only by a reputable public accountant during reasonable business hours in such manner as not to interfere with Studio's normal business activities. In no event shall an audit with respect to any earnings statement commence later than 24 months from the rendition of the earnings statement involved; nor shall any audit continue for longer than 30 consecutive business days; nor shall audits be made hereunder more frequently than once annually; nor shall the records supporting any earnings statement be audited more than once. All earnings statements rendered hereunder shall be binding upon Participant and not subject to objection for any reason unless such objection is made in writing, stating the basis thereof and delivered to Studio within twenty-four (24) months from rendition of the earnings statement, or if an audit is commenced prior thereto, within thirty (30) days from the completion of the relative audit. If Studio, as a courtesy to Participant, shall include cumulative figures in any earnings or other statement, the time within which Participant may commence any audit or make any objection in respect of any statement shall not be enlarged or extended thereby. Participant's right to examine Studio's records is limited to the Picture, and Participant shall have no right to examine records relating to Studio's business generally or with respect to any other motion picture for purposes of comparison or otherwise; provided, however, that where any original income or expense document with third parties relates to the Picture and to other motion pictures, Participant shall have the right to examine the entire document without deletions therefrom.

**12. Ownership:** Participant expressly acknowledges that Participant has and will have no right, title or interest of any kind or character whatsoever in or to the Picture, and no lien thereon or other rights in or to the gross receipts or net profits of the Picture; and that the same shall be and remain Studio's sole and exclusive property, and Studio shall not be obligated to segregate the same from its other funds, it being the intent and purpose hereof that the gross receipts in excess of breakeven of the Picture are referred to herein merely as a measure in determining the time and manner of payment to Participant; and that Studio shall not be deemed a trustee, pledgeholder or fiduciary. Participant shall have no right, title or interest of any kind or character whatsoever in or to the literary, dramatic or musical material upon which the Picture is based, or from which it may be adapted; and Studio shall have the sole and exclusive right to utilize, sell, license or otherwise dispose of all or any part of its rights in such material upon such terms and conditions as it may deem advisable, all without consulting or advising Participant and without accounting to Participant in any manner with respect thereto.

**13. Distribution:** As between Participant and Studio, Studio shall have complete authority to distribute the Picture and to license the exhibition thereof throughout the world in accordance with such sales methods, policies and terms as it may, in its uncontrolled discretion, determine. Studio shall have the broadest possible latitude in the distribution of the Picture, and the exercise of its judgment in good faith in all matters pertaining thereto shall be final. Studio has not made any express or implied representation, warranty, guarantee or agreement as to the amount of proceeds which will be derived from the distribution of the Picture, nor has Studio made any express or implied representation, warranty, guarantee or agreement that there will be any sums payable to Participant hereunder, or that the Picture will be favorably received by exhibitors or by the public, or will be distributed continuously. In no event shall Studio incur any liability based upon any claim that Studio has failed to realize receipts or revenue which should or could have been realized. Studio may distribute the Picture either itself or through such distributors, subdistributors and other parties as Studio may, in its uncontrolled discretion, determine, and Studio may refrain from releasing and/or distributing the Picture in any territory for any reason whatsoever. Studio may license the Picture or rights connected therewith to any and all theatres or other agencies in which Studio may have an interest directly or indirectly upon such terms and rentals as Studio may deem fair and proper under the circumstances. Nothing herein contained shall be construed as a representation or warranty by Studio that it now has or will hereafter have or control any theatres or agencies in the United States or elsewhere.

**14. Sale of Picture:** Studio shall have the right at any time after completion of the Picture to sell, transfer or assign all or any of its rights in and to the Picture and the negative and copyright thereof. Any such sale, transfer or assignment shall be subject to Participant's rights hereunder, and upon the purchaser, transferee or assignee assuming performance of this agreement in place and stead of Studio, Studio shall be released and discharged of and from any further liability or obligation hereunder. No part of any sale price or other consideration received by, or payable to, Studio shall be included in the gross receipts hereunder and Participant shall have no rights in respect of any thereof.

**15. Assignments, etc.:** Participant shall have the right to sell, assign, transfer or hypothecate (all herein called "assign") all or any part of Participant's right to receive the monies payable to Participant hereunder. Any such assignment shall be subject to all pertinent laws and governmental regulations and to the rights

CONTRACTS
FOR THE
FILM AND
TELEVISION
INDUSTRY

354

of Studio hereunder. In the event of any such assignment by Participant, a Notice of Irrevocable Authority and Distributor's Acceptance in Studio's usual form shall be executed by Participant and by the transferee and delivered to Studio. If at any time more than three parties shall be entitled to receive payments, which under the terms hereof are to be paid to or for the account of Participant, Studio may, at its option, require that all such parties execute and deliver an agreement in Studio's usual form appointing a disbursing agent for all such parties.

## Schedule 1

**1. "Gross Receipts"** of the Picture means the aggregate of:

(a) All film rentals actually received by Studio from parties exhibiting the Picture in theatres and on television where Studio distributes directly to such parties (hereinafter referred to as "exhibitors");

(b) In respect of licenses of exhibition or distribution rights by means of video discs, cassettes or similar devices, an amount equal to 20% of (i) the gross wholesale rental income therefrom and (ii) the gross wholesale sales income therefrom less a reasonable allowance for returns;

(c) All sums actually received by Studio from grants or licenses of distribution rights in and to the Picture (in any and all gauges of film, tape and other material) from sources other than those referred to in (a) and (b) above;

(d) All net earnings of Studio from trailers of the Picture (other than trailers advertising the television exhibition of the Picture); and the lease of positive prints, tapes and other material (as distinguished from the licensing thereof for a film rental); and from the sale or licensing of advertising accessories, souvenir programs and booklets;

(e) All net sums derived by Studio from distribution of the Picture on a "road show", "reissue" and "four wall" basis, as such terms are commonly understood in the motion picture industry, whether on fixed or percentage engagements. The term "net sums" means Studio's receipts less all advertising, publicity and other distribution costs incurred directly in connection therewith;

(f) All amounts required to be included under Exhibits X, Y and Z hereof, less the aggregate of:

(i) All sums paid or accrued on account of sales, use, receipts, income, excise, remittance and other taxes (however denominated) to any governmental authority assessed upon the negatives, duplicate negatives, prints or sound records of the Picture, or upon the use or distribution of the Picture, or upon the revenues derived therefrom, or any part thereof, or upon the remittance of such revenues, or any part thereof; any and all sums paid or accrued on account of duties, customs and imposts, costs of acquiring permits, "Kontingents," and any similar authority to secure the entry, licensing, exhibition, performance, use or televising of the Picture in any country or part thereof, regardless of whether such payments or accruals are assessed against the Picture or the proceeds thereof or against a group of motion pictures in which the Picture may be included or the proceeds thereof. In no event shall the deductible amount of any such tax (however denominated) imposed upon Studio, be decreased (nor the gross receipts increased) because of the manner in which such taxes are elected to be treated by Studio in filing net income, corporate franchise, excess profits or similar tax returns. Subject to the foregoing, (i) Studio's own United States federal and state income taxes and franchise taxes based on Studio's net income; and (ii) income taxes payable to any country or territory by Studio based on the net earnings of Studio in such country or territory and which is computed and assessed solely by reason of the retention in such country or territory by Studio of any portion of the gross receipts shall not be deductible hereunder.

(ii) Expenses of transmitting to the United States any funds accruing to Studio from the Picture in foreign countries, such as cable expenses and any discounts from such funds taken to convert such funds directly or indirectly into U.S. dollars.

(iii) The cost of reducing or minimizing the matters referred to in (i) or (ii) above, which costs shall be fairly apportioned to the Picture if done on an industry basis or with respect to motion pictures distributed by Studio generally.

(iv) All costs of cooperative or other advertising or promotion (excluding trade and institutional advertising or promotion) incurred in connection with exhibitions of the Picture in theatres (or other places where an admission is charged) where Studio pays, shares in or is charged with all or a portion of the promotional or advertising costs relating to any such exhibitions.

(v) All amounts paid or payable to or for the benefit of actors, writers, composers, directors and others, pursuant to applicable collective bargaining agreements and/or any law or governmental regulations or decree now or hereafter in force by reason of, and/or as a condition or consideration for, any exhibition, use, reuse, rerun, performance, sale, license and/or distribution of the Picture and/or copies of all or any part thereof, on television, supplemental markets, or otherwise (all herein called "residuals"), together with all taxes, pension fund contributions and other costs paid or payable in respect of such residuals, and in respect of participations in the gross receipts and net profits of the Picture; provided, however, that if Participant or any principal stockholder of Participant, or any heirs, executors, administrators, successors or assigns of Participant, or any such stockholder, are entitled, either directly or by way of participation in any pension fund, to any such residuals, or to compensation for services rendered beyond any guaranteed period referred to in the foregoing agreement, the amount payable on account thereof shall be treated as an advance against Participant's share of the gross receipts hereunder, and conversely, any gross receipts paid to Participant hereunder shall (to the extent permissible under applicable collective bargaining agreements) constitute an advance against such residuals payable to or for the benefit of Participant or any principal stockholder of Participant, or any such heirs, executors, administrators, successors or assigns.

(vi) Dues and assessments of and contributions by Studio to AMPTP, MPAA, MPEA, the Academy of Motion Picture Arts and Sciences, and other trade associations or industry groups comprised of a substantial number of motion picture producers and/or distributors, but only for purposes relating to the production, distribution, export, import, advertising, exploitation and general protection, including actions under the antitrust laws, and/or promotion of motion pictures.

In no event shall rentals from the exhibition of the Picture which are contributed to charitable organizations be included in gross receipts. If Studio reasonably anticipates taxes, residuals, uncollectible accounts, or any matters relating to the Picture, which, if and when determined, will be deductible hereunder, Studio may, for a reasonable time, set up appropriate reserves therefor.

CONTRACTS
FOR THE
FILM AND
TELEVISION
INDUSTRY

356

**2. Film Rentals:** In paragraph 6 of the foregoing Exhibit, for purposes of computing gross receipts under this Schedule 1, the third and fourth sentences are deleted, and the following substituted: Where the film rental is computed on the basis of box-office receipts of the Picture, any expenses incurred in checking attendance and/or receipts of such engagements shall be deducted in determining film rentals hereunder. There shall be deducted from film rentals expenses incurred in the collection thereof.

### Music Publishing Income

In the event the party entitled to share in gross receipts or net profits of the Picture under the foregoing agreement is not entitled to share directly in publishing revenues, there shall also be included in gross receipts of the picture:

A sum equal to _____% of the "publisher's share" of mechanical reproduction and performing fees received in U.S. currency by Studio's subsidiary or affiliated publisher with respect to music and lyrics written specifically for and synchronized in the picture as released, provided such publisher is vested with all rights therein and all of the "publisher's share" of the receipts therefrom, and provided the party entitled to share in gross receipts or net profits of the picture under the foregoing agreement is not entitled to receive composers' or lyricists' royalties in respect of such music or lyrics. The "publisher's share" of mechanical reproduction fees shall be the full amount paid by the licensee, less composers' share of such fees and less the charges of the publisher or any agent, trustee or administrator acting for the publisher for the collection of such fees, not to exceed 5% thereof. Mechanical reproduction fees do not include synchronization fees.

The "publisher's share" of performing fees shall be the net amount actually received by the publisher from any performing rights society in respect of the music and lyrics involved; or, if Studio or the publisher shall administer the collection of all or any part of performance fees, the full amount of all performance fees collected by Studio or the publisher, less the composer's share of such fees and all reasonable costs and expenses in administering the collection of such fees.

If the agreement or Exhibit to which this Exhibit is attached provides for distribution fees, no distribution fees shall be charged on amounts included in gross receipts pursuant to this Exhibit.

### Sound Track Record Income

In the event the party entitled to share in the gross receipts or net profits of the picture under the foregoing agreement is not entitled to receive any artists' royalties in respect of phonograph records derived from the sound track of the picture, then Studio agrees to include in the gross receipts of the picture royalties on sound track records, as herein defined, computed at the applicable royalty rate.

As used herein:

The term "sound track records" means and refers to phonograph records, tapes, or other sound recordings which contain either (i) portions of the sound track transferred directly to phonograph record masters from sound records which form a part of the sound track of the picture; or (ii) sound recordings recorded separately but utilizing substantially the same musical score, parts and instrumentation, and essentially the same artists, music and/or dialogue and/or sound effects as is contained in the sound track of the picture; or (iii) a combination of (i) and (ii). Sound track records do not, however, include any recordings produced solely for the purpose of advertising and exploiting the picture and copies of which are not distributed to the public.

The term "applicable royalty rate" means and refers to the following percentages of the prevailing retail price but in no event more than the net royalty actually received and retainable by Studio for its own account with respect to the sale of any particular copies: 5% of 90% in respect of sound track records sold in the United States; 2 ½% of 90% in respect of sound track records sold outside the United States except that as to sound track records sold pursuant to mail order or "club" plans, the royalty rate shall be one-half of the rate otherwise applicable.

If any sound track records contain selections from other sources, the applicable royalty rate hereunder shall be prorated on the basis of the total number of minutes of selections from the sound track compared to the total number of minutes on such records.

In determining the net royalty retainable by Studio, all royalties payable to artists, conductors and other third parties in respect to such sound track records shall be deducted from the aggregate royalty payable to Studio under the applicable distribution agreement.

The term "prevailing retail price" means and refers to the price generally prevailing in the country of manufacture or sale (as determined by the Record Company), less all taxes, duties and charges for containers.

There shall be deducted from amounts included in gross receipts hereunder a pro rata share of re-use fees and costs of recording and manufacturing masters advanced by Studio or the Record Company. Sales shall be determined on the basis of the number of records sold and for which the Record Company has been paid in U.S. currency, after allowing for all returns, cancellations, exchanges, applicable discounts, etc. and reasonable reserves which may be established therefor. No sums shall be included in gross receipts with respect to records given away or sold at less than the Record Company's cost or for promotional purposes, or as sales inducements or otherwise.

If the agreement or Exhibit to which this Exhibit is attached provides for distribution fees, no distribution fees shall be charged on amounts included in gross receipts pursuant to this Exhibit.

### Merchandising Income

In the event the party entitled to share in gross receipts or net profits of the picture under the foregoing agreement is not entitled to share directly in merchandising revenue, there shall be included in gross receipts of the picture:

(a) A sum equal to 50% of all license fees (in excess of all royalties and participations) received by Studio directly as a result of the exercise by Studio itself of merchandising license rights. If, however, Studio shall sublicense or subcontract any of such merchandising license rights, Studio shall include in the gross receipts hereunder, at its election, either a sum equal to (i) 85% of the net sums (in excess of all royalties and participations) received from such sub-licensee; or (ii) 50% of such sub-licensee's license fees from the exercise of such licensing rights (from which there shall be deducted all royalties and participations), and out of the remaining 50% thereof Studio shall pay and discharge the fees of its sublicensee.

CONTRACTS
FOR THE
FILM AND
TELEVISION
INDUSTRY

358

(b) If the publication rights to the underlying literary material were owned or controlled by the party entitled to share in gross receipts or net profits of the picture under the foregoing agreement (herein called "participant") prior to the execution of this agreement, and were acquired by Studio pursuant to or in connection with this agreement, then (i) all net sums received by Studio from non-affiliated or nonsubsidiary publishers from the publication of such underlying literary material and of novelizations of the screenplay of the picture, and (ii) a sum equal to 5% of the net receipts of Studio's subsidiary or affiliated publishers from the publication of such material and novelizations, less, in either case, royalties paid out of (i) or (ii) to the writers of such material and novelizations.

If the agreement or Exhibit to which this Exhibit is attached provides for distribution fees, no distribution fees shall be charged on amounts included in gross receipts pursuant to this Exhibit.

# NET PROFITS

Each studio can define the term "net profits" as it likes. Here is one distributor's definition:

## NET PROFIT DEFINITION

**1. *Definition of Parties:*** "Distributor" means _____ (Distribution Company Name), a _____ corporation, and its subsidiaries engaged in the business of distributing motion pictures for exhibition in theatres and for broadcasting over television stations, but shall not include any other persons, firms or corporations licensed by Distributor to distribute motion pictures in any part of the world. Nor shall such term include: any person, firm or corporation distributing the Picture for purposes other than exhibition in theatres or by television stations; exhibitors or others who may actually exhibit the Picture to the public; radio or television broadcasters; cable operators; manufacturers, wholesalers or retailers of video discs, cassettes or similar devices; book or music publishers; phonograph record producers or distributors; merchandisers, etc., whether or not any of the foregoing are subsidiaries of Distributor. As used herein, a "subsidiary" of Distributor refers to an entity in which Distributor has at least a 50% interest.

"Participant" means the party under the attached agreement who or which is entitled to participate in the gross receipts or net profits of the Picture, and the successors and permitted assigns of such party.

**2. *Net Profits:*** As between Distributor and Participant, the "net profits" of the Picture means an amount equal to the excess, if any, of the gross receipts (as defined in 3 hereof) of the Picture over the aggregate of the following, which shall be deducted in the order listed:

(a) Distributor's distribution fees set forth in 4 hereof.

(b) Distributor's expenses in connection with the distribution of the Picture, as set forth in 5 hereof.

(c) The cost of production of the Picture, plus an amount equal to interest thereon, all as provided for in 9 hereof, and plus such other costs, if any, as may have been incurred in connection with the financing of the cost of production of the Picture. Said interest and other costs shall be recouped before said cost of production.

(d) All contingent amounts consented to by Producer and not included in the cost of production of the Picture payable to Participant or any third party based upon, or computed in respect of, the gross receipts of the Picture (as defined in the relevant agreements), or any portion thereof.

Net profits shall be determined as of the close of each accounting period provided for in 10 hereof.

**3. *Gross Receipts:*** As used herein, the term "gross receipts" means the aggregate of:

(a) All film rentals actually received by Distributor from parties exhibiting the Picture in theatres and on television where Distributor distributes directly to such parties (hereinafter referred to as "exhibitors").

CONTRACTS
FOR THE
FILM AND
TELEVISION
INDUSTRY

360

(b) Where Distributor grants theatrical distribution rights to a subdistributor on a basis requiring it to account to Distributor with respect to film rentals, either: (i) the film rentals received by such subdistributor from exhibitors which Distributor accepts for the purpose of its accountings with such subdistributor; or (ii) Distributor's share (actually received) of film rentals received by such subdistributor; whichever Distributor elects from time to time as to each subdistributor.

(c) In respect of licenses of exhibition or distribution rights by means of video discs, cassettes or similar devices, an amount equal to 20% of (i) the gross wholesale rental income therefrom and (ii) the gross wholesale sales income therefrom less a reasonable allowance for returns.

(d) All amounts actually received by Distributor from the following: (i) trailers (other than trailers advertising television exhibitions of the Picture); (ii) licenses of theatrical distribution rights for a flat sum; (iii) licenses of exhibition or distribution rights other than those referred to in (a), (b), (c) and (d) (ii) of this 3, specifically including licenses to cable operators; (iv) the lease of positive prints (as distinguished from the licensing thereof for a film rental); and from the sale or licensing of advertising accessories, souvenir programs and booklets; and (v) recoveries by Distributor for infringement of copyrights of the Picture.

(e) All monies actually received by Distributor on account of direct subsidies, aid or prizes relating specifically to the Picture, net of an amount equal to income taxes based thereon imposed by the country involved, if any. If local laws require use of such monies as a condition to the grant of such subsidy or aid, such monies shall not be included in gross receipts until actually used.

(f) See Exhibits "1," "2" and "3" attached hereto.

In no event shall rentals from the exhibition of the Picture which are contributed to charitable organizations be included in gross receipts.

**4. *Distribution Fees:*** Distributor's distribution fees shall be as follows:

(a) _____% of the gross receipts of the Picture derived by Distributor from all sources in the United States and Canada.

(b) _____% of the gross receipts of the Picture derived by Distributor from all sources in the United Kingdom.

(c)_____% of the gross receipts of the Picture derived by Distributor from all sources other than those referred to in (a) and (b) above.

(d) Notwithstanding the foregoing; (i) with respect to sums included in the gross receipts pursuant to 3(b)(ii) and 3(d)(ii) hereof, Distributor's distribution fee shall be 15% of such sums; (ii) if Distributor shall license the exhibition of the Picture on free television, the aforesaid percentages as to amounts received and collected by Distributor from sources in the United States, shall be _____% if collected from a network for national network telecasts in prime time; and 35% in all other instances; and, as to amounts received and collected by Distributor from sources outside the Untied States 40%; (iii) no distribution fee shall be charged on gross receipts referred to in 3(e) or 3(f) hereof.

All distribution fees shall be calculated on the full gross receipts without any deductions or payments of any kind whatsoever.

**5. *Distribution Expenses:*** Distributor's deductible distribution expenses in connection with the Picture shall include all costs and expenses incurred in connection with the distribution, advertising, exploitation and turning to account of the Picture of whatever kind or nature, or which are customarily treated as distribution expenses under customary accounting procedures in the motion picture industry. If Distributor reasonably anticipates that additional distribution expenses will be incurred in the future, Distributor may, for a reasonable time, set up appropriate reserves therefor. Without limiting the generality of the foregoing, the following particular items shall be included in distribution expenses hereunder:

(a) The cost and expense of all duped and dubbed negatives, sound tracks, prints, release prints, tapes, cassettes, duplicating material and facilities and all other material manufactured for use in connection with the Picture, including the cost of inspecting, repairing, checking and renovating film, reels, containers, cassettes, packing, storing and shipping and all other expenses connected therewith and inspecting and checking exhibitors' projection and sound equipment and facilities. Distributor may manufacture or cause to be manufactured as many or as few duped negatives, positive prints and other material for use in connection with the Picture as it, in its sole discretion, may consider advisable or desirable.

(b) All direct costs and charges for advertisements, press books, artwork, advertising accessories and trailers (other than (i) prints of trailers advertising free television exhibition of the Picture, and (ii) the trailer production costs which are included in the cost of production of the Picture), advertising, publicizing and exploiting the Picture by such means and to such extent as Distributor may, in its uncontrolled discretion, deem desirable, including, without limitation, pre-release advertising and publicity, so-called cooperative and/or theatre advertising, and/or other advertising engaged in with or for exhibitors, to the extent Distributor pays, shares in, or is charged with all or a portion of such costs and all other exploitation costs relating to such theatre exhibition. Any re-use fees and costs of recording and manufacturing masters for phonograph records, which Distributor shall advance in order to assist in the advertising and exploitation of the Picture, shall be treated as costs hereunder to the extent unrecouped by the record company. Where any Distributor advertising or publicity employee (other than an executive supervisory employee) or facility is used for the Picture, the salary of such employee and the cost of such facility (while so used for the Picture) shall be direct costs hereunder. Any costs and charges referred to in this (b) (and not included in the cost of production of the Picture), expended or incurred prior to delivery of the Picture, shall be included in direct costs under this (b). There shall also be included as an item of cost a sum equal to 10% of all direct costs referred to in this (b) to cover the indirect cost of Distributor's advertising and publicity departments, both domestic and foreign.

(c) All costs of preparing and delivering the Picture for distribution (regardless of whether such costs are the salaries and expenses of Distributor's own employees or employees or parties not regularly employed by Distributor), including, without limitation, all costs incurred in connection with the production of foreign language versions of the Picture, whether dubbed, superimposed or otherwise, as well as any and all costs and expenses in connection with changing the title of the Picture, recutting, re-editing or shortening or lengthening the Picture for release in any territory or for exhibition on television or other media, or in order to conform to the requirements of censorship authorities, or in order to conform to the peculiar national or political prejudices likely to be

CONTRACTS
FOR THE
FILM AND
TELEVISION
INDUSTRY

362

encountered in any territory, or for any other purpose or reason. The costs referred to in this (c) shall include all studio charges for facilities, labor and material, whether or not incurred at a studio owned or controlled by Distributor.

(d) All sums paid or accrued on account of sales, use, receipts, income, excise, remittance and other taxes (however denominated) to any governmental authority assessed upon the negatives, duplicate negatives, prints or sound records of the Picture, or upon the use or distribution of the Picture, or upon the revenues derived therefrom, or any part thereof, or upon the remittance of such revenues, or any part thereof; any and all sums paid or accrued on account of duties, customs and imposts, costs of acquiring permits, "Kontingents," or and any similar authority to secure the entry, licensing, exhibition, performance, use or televising of the Picture in any country or part thereof, regardless of whether such payments or accruals are assessed against the Picture or the proceeds thereof or against a group of motion pictures in which the Picture may be included or the proceeds thereof. In no event shall the deductible amount of any such tax (however denominated) imposed upon Distributor, be decreased (nor the gross receipts increased) because of the manner in which such taxes are elected to be treated by Distributor in filing net income, corporate franchise, excess profits or similar tax returns. Subject to the foregoing, (i) Distributor's own United States federal and state income taxes and franchise taxes based on Distributor's net income; and (ii) income taxes payable to any country or territory by Distributor based on the net earnings of Distributor in such country or territory and which is computed and assessed solely by reason of the retention in such country or territory by Distributor of any portion of the gross receipts shall not be deductible hereunder.

(e) Expenses of transmitting to the United States any funds accruing to Distributor from the Picture in foreign countries, such as cable expenses, and any discounts from such funds taken to convert such funds directly or indirectly into U.S. dollars.

(f) All costs and expenses, including reasonable attorneys' fees, loss, damage or liability suffered or incurred by Distributor in connection with: any action taken by Distributor (whether by litigation or otherwise) in copyrighting, protecting and enforcing the copyright of, and other rights and sources of revenue to be derived from, the Picture; reducing or minimizing the matters referred to in (d) and (e) above, the collection of film rentals; and other sums due Distributor from exhibitors, subdistributors and others in respect of the Picture or to recover monies due pursuant to any agreement relating to the distribution or the exhibition of the Picture; checking attendance and exhibitors' receipts; preventing and/or recovering damages for unauthorized exhibition or distribution of the Picture, or any impairment of, encumbrance on or infringement upon, the rights of Distributor in and to the Picture; prosecuting and defending actions under the antitrust laws, communications laws, and federal, state and local laws, ordinances and regulations (including censorship) affecting the exhibition and/or distribution of the Picture and/or the ability of Distributor to derive revenue from the Picture and its component parts and by-products; and auditing of books and records of any exhibitor, subdistributor or licensee.

(g) Royalties payable to manufacturers of sound recording and reproducing equipment and dues and assessments of, and contributions by Distributor to, AMPTP, MPAA, MPEA, the Academy of Motion Picture Arts and Sciences and other trade associations or industry groups comprised of a substantial number of motion picture producers and/or distributors, but only for purposes relating to the production, distribution, export, import, advertising, exploitation and general protection and/or promotion of motion pictures.

(h) In the event any person shall make a claim relating to the Picture against Distributor or any of its licensees, which claim, in Distributor's judgment, is of sufficient merit to constitute a reasonable probability of ultimate loss, cost, damage or expense, Distributor may deduct either this (h) or such amount as Distributor may deem necessary to cover loss, cost, damage or expense which may be suffered as a result thereof. Distributor shall have the right to settle and pay any such claim. After the settlement of any such claim, or after the final judicial determination thereof, the amount previously deducted hereunder shall be adjusted accordingly with the next accounting statement rendered hereunder. Nothing herein contained shall be construed as a waiver of any of Participant's warranties contained in this Agreement, or a waiver of any right or remedy at law or otherwise which may exist in favor of Distributor, including, but not limited to, the right to require Participant to reimburse Distributor on demand for any liability, cost, damage or expense arising out of, or resulting from, any breach by Participant of any warranty, undertaking or obligation by Participant, or any right on the part of Distributor to recoup or recover any such cost or expense out of Participant's share of any monies payable hereunder, rather than treating such costs or expenses as distribution expenses.

(i) All amounts paid or payable to or for the benefit of actors, writers, composers, directors and others, pursuant to applicable collective bargaining agreements and/or any law or governmental regulation or decree now or hereafter in force by reason of, and/or as a condition or consideration for, any exhibition, use, re-use, rerun, performance, sale, license and/or distribution of the Picture and/or copies of all or any part thereof, on television, supplemental markets, or otherwise (all herein called "residuals"), together with all taxes, pension fund contributions and other costs paid or payable in respect of such residuals, and in respect of participations in the gross receipts and net profits of the Picture; provided, however, that if Participant or any principal stockholder of Participant, or any heirs, executors, administrators, successors or assigns of Participant, or any such stockholder, are entitled, either directly or by way of participation in any pension fund, to any such residuals, or to compensation for services rendered beyond any guaranteed period referred to in the foregoing agreement, the amount payable on account thereof shall be treated as an advance against Participant's share of the net profits hereunder.

(j) The cost of all insurance (to the extent that the same is not included in the cost of production of the Picture) covering or relating to the Picture, including, but not limited to, errors and omissions insurance and all insurance on negatives, positive prints, sound materials or other physical property, it being understood, however, that Distributor shall not be obligated to take out or maintain any such insurance.

(k) If Distributor shall proceed under 3(b)(i) hereof, all items deducted by the subdistributor as distribution expenses, and which Distributor accepts for the purpose of its accountings with such subdistributor, shall be treated as Distributor's expenditures under the corresponding subdivision of this 5.

**6. *Film Rentals:*** "Film Rentals" shall be determined after all refunds, credits, discounts, allowances and adjustments granted to exhibitors, whether occasioned by condemnation by boards of censorship, settlement of disputes, or otherwise. Until earned, forfeited or applied to the Picture, neither advance

CONTRACTS
FOR THE
FILM AND
TELEVISION
INDUSTRY

364

payments nor security deposits shall be included in film rentals. No cost (regardless of how incurred, paid or allowed) of Distributor's share of cooperative and/or theater advertising, shall be deducted in determining film rentals. Where allowances are granted and paid on account of Distributor's share of cooperative theatre or joint advertising, such payments shall not be deducted in determining film rental, and where Distributor's share of cooperative theater or joint advertising is deducted by the exhibitor Distributor's share of cooperative theater or joint advertising shall be added back into the film rental received from such exhibitor, and all such costs, payments, discounts and allowances shall be treated as distribution expenses. Wherever Distributor exhibits the Picture in a theatre or over a television station owned or controlled by Distributor, or licenses the Picture or rights connected therewith to theatres, television stations or other agencies in which Distributor has an interest directly or indirectly, or to which Distributor is obligated to pay a fixed sum for exhibiting the Picture or for the use of its premises or facilities, Distributor shall include in the film rentals of the Picture such sums, determined in good faith, as may be reasonable and consistent with Distributor's usual practice in such matters.

**7.** *Allocations:* Wherever Distributor (i) receives from any license either a flat sum or a percentage of the receipts, or both, for any right to a group of motion pictures (including the Picture) under any agreement (whether or not the same shall provide for the exhibition, lease or delivery of positive prints of any of said motion pictures) which does not specify what portion of the license payments apply to the respective motion pictures in the group (or to such prints or other material, if any, as may be supplied), or (ii) receives foreign currency under 8(ii) or 8(iii) hereof relating to a group of motion pictures (including the Picture), then in any and all such situations Distributor shall include in, or deduct from, the gross receipts, as the case may be, such sums, determined in good faith, as may be reasonable and consistent with Distributor's usual practice in such matters. All costs described in 5 hereof shall be fairly apportioned to the Picture if incurred or expended on an industry basis, or in conjunction with other motion picture producers and/or distributors, or with respect to the Picture and other motion pictures distributed by Distributor.

**8.** *Foreign Receipts:* No sums received by Distributor relating to the Picture shall be included in gross receipts hereunder unless and until such sums have been (i) received by Distributor in U.S. dollars in the United States, or (ii) used by Distributor for the production or acquisition of motion pictures or television films which can be lawfully removed from the country or territory involved, in which event they shall be included in gross receipts for the accounting period during which an amount (computed at the official or unofficial rate of exchange, as Distributor may elect) equal to the amount expended for such production or acquisition, plus customary interest thereon, has been recouped by Distributor (in excess of normal distribution fees and distribution expenses) from distribution thereof outside the country or territory involved; or (iii) used by Distributor for acquisition of tangible personal property which can be and is lawfully exported from the country or territory involved, in which event the U.S. dollar equivalent of the currency utilized to acquire such property shall be included in gross receipts hereunder for the accounting period during which such property was so exported, such U.S. dollar equivalent to be computed at the official or unofficial rate of exchange, as Distributor may elect, in effect on the date of export. Distributor will, promptly after receipt of a written request from Participant (but not more frequently than annually) advise Participant in writing as to foreign revenues not included in gross receipts as aforesaid, and Distributor shall, at the written request and expense of Participant (subject to any and all limitations, restrictions, laws, rules and regulations affecting such transactions), deposit into a bank designated by Participant in the country involved, or pay to any other party designated by Participant in such country, such part thereof as would have been payable to Participant hereunder. Such deposits or payments to or for Participant shall constitute due remittance to Participant, and Distributor shall have no further interest therein or responsibility therefor. Distributor makes no warranties or representations that any part of any such foreign currencies may be converted into U.S. dollars or transferred to the account of Participant in any foreign country. In no event shall Distributor be obligated to apply gross receipts of any country not actually received by Distributor in U.S. dollars in the United States to the recoupment of any costs or expenses incurred with respect to the Picture in any other country.

### 9. *Cost of Production; Interest:*

(a) The "cost of production" of the Picture means the total direct cost of production of the Picture, including the cost of all items listed on Distributor's standard Delivery Schedule, computed and determined in all respects in the same manner as Distributor then customarily determines the direct cost of other motion pictures distributed and/or financed by it, plus Distributor's overhead charge. The determination of what items constitute direct charges and what items are within said overhead charge shall be made in all respects in the same manner as Distributor customarily determines such matters. The full amount of all direct costs of production of the Picture (whether payable in cash, deferred or accrued) shall be included in the direct cost of the Picture at the time liability therefor is incurred or contracted, regardless of whether the same has actually been paid to the party or parties entitled thereto at the time involved. Deferments and participations in gross receipts of the Picture consented to by Distributor (however defined) shall be treated as direct costs of production, whether the same shall be in a definite amount or based on a percentage of the gross receipts, and whether the same are fixed obligations or are contingent upon receipts of the Picture; provided, however, contingent participations based on a percentage of gross receipts as defined in the applicable agreement shall not be included in the direct cost of production beyond recoupment under 2(c) hereof.

(b) Distributor's overhead charge shall be in an amount equal to _____% of the direct cost of production of the Picture, with the understanding that any production facilities, equipment or personnel supplied by Distributor or by a studio owned or controlled by Distributor, or in which Distributor has a substantial financial interest (and which are not furnished within the overhead charge) shall be supplied at Distributor's usual rental rates charged for such items, and such charges shall be treated as direct costs of production of the Picture and shall bear said _____% overhead charge. Distributor's overhead charge shall accrue and be included in the cost of production of the Picture concurrently with the incurring of the respective items of direct cost to which it applies.

(c) The amount equal to interest provided for in 2(c) hereof shall be calculated at a rate per annum equal to _____% of the prime commercial rate of First National Bank of Boston from time to time in effect. Said amount shall be calculated from the respective dates that each item is charged to the Picture until the close of the accounting period during which the cost of production is recouped under 2(c) hereof, except that interest on deferred amounts shall be calculated from the date of payment.

CONTRACTS
FOR THE
FILM AND
TELEVISION
INDUSTRY

366

(d) Concurrently with delivery to Participant of the first earnings statement hereunder, Distributor will (subject to revisions and correction) deliver to Participant an itemized summary of the cost of production of the Picture. Participant shall have the right to audit such statement in accordance with 11 hereof.

**10.** *Earnings Statements:* Distributor shall render to Participant periodic statements showing, in summary form, the appropriate calculations under this Agreement. Statements shall be issued for each calendar quarter until the Picture has been in release for 4 years from and including the quarter in which the Picture was first released, and thereafter annually. Each such quarterly or annual period, as the case may be, is herein referred to as an "accounting period." No statements need be rendered for any accounting period during which no receipts are received. Statements rendered by Distributor may be changed from time to time to give effect to year-end adjustments made by Distributor's Accounting Department or Public Accountants, or to items overlooked, to correct errors and for similar purposes. If Distributor shall extend credit to any licensee with respect to the Picture, and if such credit has been included in the gross receipts, and if, in the opinion of Distributor, any such indebtedness shall be uncollectible, the uncollected amount may be deducted in any subsequent earning statement. Should Distributor make any overpayment to Participant hereunder for any reason, Distributor shall have the right to deduct and retain for its own account an amount equal to any such overpayment from any sums that may thereafter become due or payable by Distributor to Participant or for Participant's account, or may demand repayment from Participant, in which event Participant shall repay the same when such demand is made. Any U.S. dollars due and payable to Participant by Distributor pursuant to any such statement shall be paid to Participant simultaneously with the rendering of such statement; provided, however, that all amounts payable to Participant hereunder shall be subject to all laws and regulations now or hereafter in existence requiring deduction or withholdings for income or other taxes payable by or assessable against Participant. Distributor shall have the right to make such deductions and withholdings and the payment thereof to the governmental agency concerned in accordance with its interpretation in good faith of such laws and regulations, and shall not be liable to Participant for the making of such deductions or withholdings or the payment thereof to the governmental agency concerned. In any such event Participant shall make and prosecute any and all claims which it may have with respect to the same directly with the governmental agency having jurisdiction in the premises. The right of Participant to receive, and the obligation of Distributor to account for, any share of the net profits of the Picture shall terminate if the Picture has been made available for exhibition on syndicated television in the U.S.A., and if the first earnings statement issued thereafter shows a deficit under 2 hereof which would require in excess of $500,000 of gross receipts before Participant would be entitled to receive any net profits hereunder. In the event a new medium of exhibition shall thereafter be developed and there shall be substantial exhibition and distribution of the Picture by such new medium which is likely to generate gross receipts of $500,000 or the amount of the deficit, whichever is larger, Participant may audit Distributor's records for the purpose of determining whether the Picture has earned, or is likely to earn, any net profits, and if, as a result of such audit, it is determined by mutual agreement, or in the event of dispute appropriate legal proceedings, that the Picture has earned, or is likely to earn, net profits as herein defined, accountings hereunder and payments, if required, shall be reinstated.

**11. *Accounting Records re Distribution; Audit Rights:*** Distributor shall keep books of account relating to the distribution of the Picture, together with vouchers, exhibition contracts and similar records supporting the same (all of which are hereinafter referred to as "records"), which shall be kept on the same basis and in the same manner and for the same periods as such records are customarily kept by Distributor. Participant may, at its own expense, audit the applicable records at the place where Distributor maintains the same in order to verify earnings statements rendered hereunder. Any such audit shall be conducted only by a reputable public accountant during reasonable business hours in such manner as not to interfere with Distributor's normal business activities. In no event shall an audit with respect to any earnings statement commence later than twenty-four (24) months from the rendition of the earnings statement involved; nor shall any audit continue for longer than thirty (30) consecutive business days; nor shall audits be made hereunder more frequently than once annually; nor shall the records supporting any earnings statement be audited more than once. All earnings statements rendered hereunder shall be binding upon Participant and not subject to objection for any reason unless such objection is made in writing, stating the basis thereof, and delivered to Distributor within twenty-four (24) months from rendition of the earnings statement, or if an audit is commenced prior thereto, within thirty (30) days from the completion of the relative audit. If Distributor, as a courtesy to Participant, shall include cumulative figures in any earnings or other statement, the time within which Participant may commence any audit or make any objection in respect of any statement shall not be enlarged or extended thereby. Participant's right to examine Distributor's records is limited to the Picture, and Participant shall have no right to examine records relating to Distributor's business generally or with respect to any other motion picture for purposes of comparison or otherwise; provided, however, that where any original income or expense document with third parties relates to the Picture and to other motion pictures, Participant shall have the right to examine the entire document without deletions therefrom.

**12. *Ownership:*** Participant expressly acknowledges that Participant has and will have no right, title or interest of any kind or character whatsoever in or to the Picture, and no lien thereon or other rights in or to the gross receipts or net profits of the Picture; and that the same shall be and remain Distributor's sole and exclusive property, and Distributor shall not be obligated to segregate the same from its other funds, it being the intent and purpose hereof that the net profits or gross receipts after moving breakeven, as the case may be, of the Picture are referred to herein merely as a measure in determining the time and manner of payment to Participant; and that Distributor shall not be deemed a trustee, pledgeholder or fiduciary. Participant shall have no right, title or interest of any kind or character whatsoever in or to the literary, dramatic or musical material upon which the Picture is based, or from which it may be adapted; and Distributor shall have the sole and exclusive right to utilize, sell, license or otherwise dispose of all or any part of its rights in such material upon such terms and conditions as it may deem advisable, all without consulting or advising Participant and without accounting to Participant in any manner with respect thereto.

**13. *Distribution:*** As between Participant and Distributor, Distributor shall have complete authority to distribute the Picture and license the exhibition thereof throughout the world in accordance with such sales methods, policies and terms as it may, in its uncontrolled discretion, determine. Distributor shall have the broadest possible latitude in the distribution of the Picture, and the exercise of its

CONTRACTS
FOR THE
FILM AND
TELEVISION
INDUSTRY

368

judgment in good faith in all matters pertaining thereto shall be final. Distributor has not made any express or implied representation, warranty, guarantee or agreement as to the amount of proceeds which will be derived from the distribution of the Picture, nor has Distributor made any express or implied representation, warranty, guarantee or agreement that there will be any sums payable to Participant hereunder, or that the Picture will be favorably received by exhibitors or by the public, or will be distributed continuously. In no event shall Distributor incur any liability based upon any claim that Distributor has failed to realize receipts or revenue which should or could have been realized. Distributor may distribute the Picture either itself or through such distributors, subdistributors and other parties as Distributor may, in its uncontrolled discretion, determine, and Distributor may refrain from releasing and/or distributing the Picture in any territory for any reason whatsoever. Distributor may license the Picture or rights connected therewith to any and all theatres or other agencies in which Distributor may have an interest directly or indirectly upon such terms and rentals as Distributor may deem fair and proper under the circumstances. Nothing herein contained shall be construed as a representation or warranty by Distributor that it now has or will hereafter have or control any theatres or agencies in the United States or elsewhere.

**14.** *Sale of Picture:* Distributor shall have the right at any time after completion of the Picture to sell, transfer or assign all or any of its rights in and to the Picture and the negative and copyright thereof. Any such sale, transfer or assignment shall be subject to Participant's rights hereunder, and upon the purchaser, transferee or assignee assuming performance of this agreement in place and stead of Distributor, Distributor shall be released and discharged of and from any further liability or obligation hereunder. No part of any sale price or other consideration received by, or payable to, Distributor shall be included in the gross receipts hereunder and Participant shall have no rights in respect of any thereof.

**15.** *Assignments, etc.:* Participant shall have the right to sell, transfer or hypothecate (all herein called "assign") all or any part of Participant's right to receive the monies payable to Participant hereunder. Any such assignment shall be subject to all pertinent laws and governmental regulations and to the rights of Distributor hereunder. In the event of any such assignment by Participant, a Notice of Irrevocable Authority and Distributor's Acceptance in Distributor's usual form shall be executed by Participant and by the transferee and delivered to Distributor. If at any time more than three parties shall be entitled to receive payments, which under the terms hereof are to be paid to or for the account of Participant, Distributor may, at its option, require that all such parties execute and deliver an agreement in Distributor's usual form appointing a disbursing agent for all such parties.

### Music Publishing Income

There shall also be included in gross receipts of the picture:

A sum equal to _____% of the "publisher's share" of mechanical reproduction and performing fees received in U.S. currency by Distributor's subsidiary or affiliated publisher with respect to music and lyrics written specifically for and synchronized in the picture as released, provided such publisher is vested with all rights therein and all of the "publisher's share" of the receipts therefrom, and provided the party entitled to share in gross receipts or net profits of the picture under the foregoing agreement is not entitled to receive composers' or lyricists' royalties in respect of such music or lyrics. The "publisher's share" of mechanical reproduction fees shall be the full amount paid by the licensee, less composers' share of such fees and less the charges of the publisher or any agent, trustee or administrator acting for the publisher for the collection of such fees, not to exceed 5% thereof. Mechanical reproduction fees do not include synchronization fees.

The "publisher's share" of performing fees shall be the net amount actually received by the publisher from any performing rights society in respect of the music and lyrics involved; or, if Distributor or the publisher shall administer the collection of all or any part of performance fees, the full amount of all performance fees collected by Distributor or the publisher, less the composer's share of such fees and all reasonable costs and expenses in administering the collection of such fees.

If the agreement or Exhibit to which this Exhibit is attached provides for distribution fees, no distribution fees shall be charged on amounts included in gross receipts pursuant to this Exhibit.

## Sound Track Record Income

In the event the party entitled to share in the gross receipts or net profits of the picture under the foregoing agreement is not entitled to receive any artists' royalties in respect of phonograph records derived from the sound track of the picture, then Distributor agrees to include in the gross receipts of the picture royalties on sound track records, as herein defined, computed at the applicable royalty rate.

As used herein:

The term "sound track records" means and refers to phonograph records, tapes, CD's or other sound recordings which contain either (i) portions of the sound track transferred directly to phonograph record masters from sound records which form a part of the sound track of the picture; or (ii) sound recordings recorded separately but utilizing substantially the same musical score, parts and instrumentation, and essentially the same artists, music and/or dialogue and/or sound effects as is contained in the sound track of the picture; or (iii) a combination of (i) and (ii). Sound track records do not, however, include any recordings produced solely for the purpose of advertising and exploiting the picture and copies of which are not distributed to the public.

The term "applicable royalty rate" means and refers to the following percentages of the prevailing retail price but in no event more than the net royalty actually received and retainable by Distributor for its own account with respect to the sale of any particular copies—5% of 90% in respect of sound track records sold in the United States; 2 1/2% of 90% in respect of sound track records sold outside the United States—except that as to sound track records sold pursuant to mail order of "club" plans, the royalty rate shall be one-half of the rate otherwise applicable.

If any sound track records contain selections from other sources, the applicable royalty rate hereunder shall be prorated on the basis of the total number of minutes of selections from the sound track compared to the total number of minutes on such records.

In determining the net royalty retainable by Distributor, all royalties payable to artists, conductors and other third parties in respect to such sound track records shall be deducted from the aggregate royalty payable to Distributor under the applicable distribution agreement.

CONTRACTS
FOR THE
FILM AND
TELEVISION
INDUSTRY

370

The term "prevailing retail price" means and refers to the price generally prevailing in the country of manufacture or sale (as determined by the Record Company), less all taxes, duties and charges for containers.

There shall be deducted from amounts included in gross receipts hereunder a pro rata share of re-use fees and costs of recording and manufacturing masters advanced by Distributor or the Record Company. Sales shall be determined on the basis of the number of records sold and for which the Record Company has been paid in U.S. currency, after allowing for all returns, cancellations, exchanges, applicable discounts, etc. and reasonable reserves which may be established therefor. No sums shall be included in gross receipts with respect to records given away or sold at less than the Record Company's cost or for promotional purposes, or as sales inducements or otherwise.

If the agreement or Exhibit to which this Exhibit is attached provides for distribution fees, no distribution fees shall be charged on amounts included in gross receipts pursuant to this Exhibit.

## Merchandising Income

In the event the party entitled to share in gross receipts or net profits of the picture under the foregoing agreement is not entitled to share directly in merchandising revenue, there shall be included in gross receipts of the picture:

(a) A sum equal to 50% of all license fees (in excess of all royalties and participations) received by Distributor directly as a result of the exercise by Distributor itself of merchandising license rights. If, however, Distributor shall sublicense or sub-contract any of such merchandising license rights, Distributor shall include in the gross receipts hereunder, at its election, either a sum equal to (i) 85% of the net sums (in excess of all royalties and participations) received from such sub-licensee; or (ii) 50% of such sub-licensee's license fees from the exercise of such licensing rights (from which there shall be deducted all royalties and participations), and out of the remaining 50% thereof Distributor shall pay and discharge the fees of its sub-licensee.

(b) If the publication rights to the underlying literary material were owned or controlled by the party entitled to share in gross receipts or net profits of the picture under the foregoing agreement (herein called "participant") prior to the execution of this agreement, and were acquired by Distributor pursuant to or in connection with this agreement, then (i) all net sums received by Distributor from nonaffiliated or nonsubsidiary publishers from the publication of such underlying literary material and of novelizations of the screenplay of the picture, and (ii) a sum equal to 5% of the net receipts of Distributor's subsidiary or affiliated publishers from the publication of such material and novelizations, less, in either case, royalties paid out of (i) or (ii) to the writers of such material and novelizations.

If the agreement or Exhibit to which this Exhibit is attached provides for distribution fees, no distribution fees shall be charged on amounts included in gross receipts pursuant to this Exhibit.

# TELEVISION BROADCAST DISTRIBUTION

Television stations and networks can attract high viewer ratings by broadcasting movies. The broadcasting networks' appetite for movies depends on several factors. The networks consider the comparative cost of buying made-for-television movies and the kinds of ratings they can be expected to generate. Another factor to consider is how well a theatrical movie performed at the box office, and whether it has been previously distributed on pay cable television.

## TELEVISION DISTRIBUTION AGREEMENT

_____
(Name of Licensor)

_____
(Street address of Broadcasting Company)

_____
(Licensor city state & zip)

Summary

Name of Licensee: _____

Address of Licensee: _____

_____

Picture or Pictures: _____

Number of Runs: _____

Duration of License: _____

License Fee Per Picture: $_____

Total License Fee: $_____

Payments: (a) First payment of $_____ on or before _____; and (b) _____ monthly payments of $_____ commencing on _____ until the total license fee of $_____ has been paid.

This application for a license was executed by the Licensee on _____. Upon acceptance thereof by a duly authorized officer of the Licensor, this application shall constitute a license for the telecast of the aforesaid Picture or Series on the terms and conditions set forth above and in the Schedule hereto annexed and made a part hereof.

CONTRACTS
FOR THE
FILM AND
TELEVISION
INDUSTRY

372

(Company Name)

By _____
Authorized Officer

Accepted:

Date _____

(Name of Licensor)

By _____
Authorized Officer

## Schedule of Terms and Conditions

**1. License:** Subject to the prompt payment of the license fees above specified and the due performance by the Licensee of all its obligations hereunder, the Licensor hereby grants to the Licensee, and the Licensee hereby accepts, a limited license to exhibit and broadcast over the facilities of the television station specified in the foregoing Summary the motion picture or the motion pictures therein specified (herein called the Pictures), and to reproduce recorded sound in connection therewith, for the period of time and the maximum number of runs therein specified, and for no other use or purpose.

**2. Payment of License Fees:** The Licensor shall pay the license fees specified in the Summary at the time or times therein set forth, without offset, deduction, counterclaim or credit for any claim that the Licensee may have or assert against the Licensor, regardless of whether or not the Licensee has exhibited all the Pictures available to it.

**3. Licensor's Warranties:** The Licensor represents and warrants to the Licensee that:

(a) The performing rights in all musical compositions contained in the Pictures (i) are controlled by the American Society of Composers, Authors and Publishers (ASCAP) or Broadcast Music, Inc. (BMI); or (ii) are in the public domain; or (iii) are controlled by the Licensor;

(b) With respect to music controlled by ASCAP or BMI, the Licensor has obtained the necessary licenses for the inclusion thereof in the Pictures, and the exhibition of the Pictures via television;

(c) The Pictures and the prints thereof to be furnished by the Licensor to the Licensee will be free and clear of any and all liens or encumbrances; and

(d) The Licensor has the full right to grant this license.

**4. Licensor's Indemnity:** The Licensor shall indemnify the Licensee against any and all damage or expense (including reasonable attorneys' fees) that the Licensee may suffer or incur as a result of the breach of any of the Licensor's warranties, subject to the following:

(a) The Licensor's indemnity shall not apply unless it is given (i) prompt written notice of any claim; and (ii) full control of the defense thereof, through its own counsel; and (iii) the right to settle the same.

(b) The Licensee shall cooperate fully with the Licensor in the defense or settlement of any claim.

(c) The Licensor's liability on the warranty set forth in subdivision (d) of clause 3 shall be limited as provided in clause 16.

**5. Delivery:** The Licensor shall deliver to the Licensee a positive synchronized 16 mm print of each Picture scheduled for exhibition.

(a) Delivery to the Licensee's premises, or to its agent, or to a common carrier, or to the U. S. Post Office, or to any shipping agent designated by the Licensee, shall be deemed due delivery; and the Licensor shall not be liable for any loss or delay attributable to any intervening agency.

(b) The Licensee shall bear the expenses of delivery.

(c) Unless the Licensee designates a mode of delivery, the Licensor shall have the right to select the same.

(d) The Licensor's failure to deliver any of the Pictures shall not constitute a default hereunder, but the license fee hereunder shall be reduced proportionately in the ratio that the number of runs of each undelivered Picture bears to the total number of runs for all Pictures covered by this agreement.

(e) The Licensor at its own election may substitute a product deemed by it to be equivalent to the Pictures without reduction of the license fee.

**6. Examination of Prints:** Upon receipt of each positive print, the Licensee shall promptly examine the same to determine whether it is physically suitable for exhibition. If the print is unsuitable, the Licensee shall give immediate notice thereof to the Licensor, specifying the particular defect; and upon receipt of such notice the Licensor shall furnish a substitute print, or in lieu thereof, a print of another Picture that the Licensor deems equivalent. Unless the Licensor receives a notification in writing as to a defect at least 48 hours prior to the scheduled play date, a print received by the Licensee shall be deemed accepted as satisfactory.

**7. Restrictions on Cutting:** The Licensee shall telecast the Pictures in the form submitted by the Licensor, and shall not modify, add to or take from the same without the Licensor's written consent. Among other things, the Licensee shall telecast the screen credits and the Licensor's release credit as incorporated in the prints of the Pictures. The Licensee shall have the right to insert commercials at points selected by it, provided that, prior to redelivery, it restores each print to its original condition.

**8. Play Dates:** If no specific play dates are designated in the Summary, the Licensee shall, from time to time but at least 14 days in advance of any play date, furnish to the Licensor a list of the Pictures that the Licensee intends to telecast, together with the proposed telecast date.

(a) The Licensor shall have the right to designate a particular one of the Pictures to be shown on the proposed telecast date, except that it shall not designate a Picture that may have been previously shown by the Licensee during the term of this agreement.

(b) Not later than 10 days after the end of every month during the term of this agreement, the Licensee shall deliver to the Licensor a list of the Pictures that it telecast during the preceding month.

CONTRACTS
FOR THE
FILM AND
TELEVISION
INDUSTRY

374

(c) If a scheduled telecast does not take place by reason of the pre-emption of the scheduled time, or for any reason beyond the Licensee's control, the Licensee shall notify the Licensor thereof within 24 hours after the scheduled play date.

(d) If the Licensee fails to notify the Licensor as aforesaid, or if it fails to telecast any Picture on the play date for any other reason, it shall be charged with the license fee for the scheduled telecast.

**9. Maximum Runs:** When the Licensee reaches the maximum number of runs permitted under this license, its right to telecast the Pictures shall forthwith terminate, and the unpaid balance of the total agreed license fee for all the Pictures shall immediately become due and payable. The Licensee's failure to complete the maximum number of runs on or before the expiration date indicated in the Summary shall not extend the term of this license, nor shall it relieve the Licensee of its obligation to pay the total agreed license fee upon the expiration date.

**10. Licensee's Covenants:** The Licensee covenants that:

(a) It will not telecast the Pictures except over the facilities of the station specified in the Summary. If such station suspends its operation for any reason, and the Licensee selects a substitute station, such substitute shall be subject to the Licensor's approval, which shall not be unreasonably withheld.

(b) It will not telecast the Pictures beyond any cut-off dates or in excess of the maximum number of permitted runs; and

(c) It will not permit or allow the Pictures entrusted to it to be exhibited or telecast by any other party.

**11. Advertising Materials:** The Licensor shall make available at reasonable cost to the Licensee [or to any sponsor of the television broadcasts of the Pictures, or to the advertising agencies of such sponsors], any advertising or promotional material owned by the Licensor that is available for distribution.

(a) No advertising, promotional or display material originated by the Licensee or the sponsor of the Pictures or the sponsor's advertising agency shall be used without the Licensor's prior written consent, which shall not be unreasonably withheld.

(b) Any advertising material used by the Licensee that may be copyrightable shall be registered for copyright by the Licensee in the Licensor's name.

(c) The Licensee shall not in any event use, for the purpose of a commercial tie-in or tie-up, the name or likeness of any person (producer, director, star, supporting players, and the like) appearing in or connected with the Picture.

**12. Advertising Credits:** The Licensee shall comply with all the Licensor's instructions with respect to the requisite advertising credits, and shall indemnify the Licensor against any damage or expense (including reasonable attorneys' fees) that the Licensor may suffer or incur by reason of the Licensee's failure to observe such instructions.

**13. Advertising Practices:** All advertising utilized by the Licensee in connection with the exhibition of the Pictures shall be in accordance with the code requirements of the National Association of Broadcasters, as well as the applicable orders and regulations of any governmental agency.

**14. Return of Prints:** Within 48 hours after the broadcast thereof, the Licensee shall return each positive print to the Licensor or to such place or places as the Licensor may from time to time direct. Sundays and holidays shall not be included in the computation of the aforesaid period.

(a) The cost of transportation shall be borne by the Licensee.

(b) Each print shall be returned in good condition, ordinary wear and tear excepted, on the reels and in the containers in which it was received.

(c) If the Licensee fails to return a print as aforesaid, it shall be automatically charged with the laboratory cost of replacing the same, and it shall pay the charge forthwith to the Licensor.

(d) If the Licensee claims that a print has been lost or destroyed, it shall furnish an affidavit to that effect, sworn to by one of its officers.

(e) All prints shall remain the property of the Licensor.

**15. Taxes:** The Licensee shall bear all taxes now or hereafter in effect that are or may be (I) imposed or based upon the Licensee's exhibition, possession or use of the prints of the Pictures, or upon the grant of this license or the exercise thereof; or (ii) measured by the license fees, however determined, paid or payable hereunder.

(a) The word "taxes" as herein used shall include, without limitation, taxes, fees, assessments, charges, imposts, levies and excises, whether designated as sales, gross income, gross receipts, personal property, storage, use, consumption, licensing, compensating, excise or privilege taxes.

(b) To the extent that such taxes are paid by the Licensor, the Licensee shall reimburse the Licensor therefor on demand; and upon its failure to do so, the Licensor shall have all the remedies herein provided for the collection of unpaid license fees, in addition to whatever other remedies it may have by law.

**16. Substitution:** If the Licensor's right to grant this license with respect to any Picture is challenged by any third party, the Licensor may, at its option, either substitute a picture that it deems to be equivalent, or terminate this agreement with respect to such Picture. If the Licensor elects to terminate:

(a) The total license fee specified in the Summary shall be reduced proportionately in the ratio that the number of projected runs of the Picture involved bears to the total number of runs of all the Pictures.

(b) The Licensee shall and does waive all claims for damages that may arise from such termination, other than a claim for a refund of all prepaid exhibition fees.

**17. Licensee's Default:** If the Licensee fails to make payment of the license fees or any part thereof when due, or if it defaults in any of its other obligations hereunder, and fails to make payment or to remedy its default within [10] days after notice from the Licensor, or if the Licensee is adjudicated a bankrupt or becomes insolvent or makes an assignment for the benefit of creditors, or if a receiver, liquidator or trustee is appointed for its assets or affairs, the Licensor shall have the right, in addition to whatever other remedies it may have by law, to terminate this license wholly or in part by written notice to the Licensee, in which event the entire unpaid balance of the total agreed license fee for all the Pictures shall immediately become due and payable.

CONTRACTS
FOR THE
FILM AND
TELEVISION
INDUSTRY

376

**18. Force Majeure:** If the Licensor is delayed in or prevented from making delivery of the Pictures as herein provided, by reason of any act of God, labor difficulties, injunctions, judgments, adverse claims, fire, flood, transportation tie-up, public disaster or any other cause beyond its control, or if the Licensee is delayed in or prevented from telecasting the Pictures or returning the positive prints thereof as herein provided by reason of any of the aforesaid contingencies, neither party shall be liable to the other for the delay or failure so to perform; and the term of this license shall be deemed extended for a period equal to the duration of the contingency.

**19. Licensor's Right to Assign:** The Licensor shall have the right to hypothecate, pledge or assign this license to obtain loans thereon. The Licensee recognizes that lenders may be induced to advance substantial sums to the Licensor on the security of this license. Accordingly the Licensee shall pay to any assignee all moneys due to the Licensor without offset, deduction, counterclaim or credit for any claim that the Licensee may have against the Licensor.

**20. No Assignment by Licensee:** This license shall not be assigned by the Licensee without the Licensor's written consent, nor shall it be assignable by operation of law insofar as the Licensee is concerned.

**21. Arbitration:** Any controversy or claim arising out of or relating to this agreement or any breach thereof shall be settled by arbitration in accordance with the Rules of the American Arbitration Association (AAA); The parties select expedited arbitration using one arbitrator, to be a disinterested attorney specializing in entertainment law, as the sole forum for the resolution of any dispute between them. The venue for arbitration shall be _____. The arbitrator may make any interim order, decision, determinations, or award he deems necessary to preserve the status quo until he is able to render a final order, decision, determination or award. The determination of the arbitrator in such proceeding shall be final, binding and non-appealable. Judgment upon the award rendered by the arbitrator may be entered in any court having jurisdiction thereof. The prevailing party shall be entitled to reimbursement for costs and reasonable attorney's fees.

**22. General Provisions:** The following provisions shall apply:

(a) This license shall not be modified or waived in whole or in part except in writing.

(b) A waiver by either party of any breach or default by the other party shall not be construed as a waiver of any other breach or default.

(c) Any notices given or required to be given hereunder shall be in writing, and shall be sent by certified mail, return receipt requested, to the parties at their respective addresses shown in the Summary.

(d) This license is complete, and embraces the entire understanding of the parties.

# INTERNATIONAL TELEVISION DISTRIBUTION

The following agreement provides for distribution of a motion picture to television markets worldwide. The major television markets include MIP, MIP-COM, and NATPE.

The principal difference between this agreement and the theatrical acquisition/distribution agreements, is the media covered. This agreement is designed for a distributor that sells to television broadcasters and home video sub-distributors worldwide. It does not contemplate the licensing of theatrical rights. With minor modifications, the agreement could be used for the sale of a television series.

## INTERNATIONAL TV DISTRIBUTION AGREEMENT

THIS AGREEMENT made as of this _____, BETWEEN: _____ (hereinafter called the "Producer"); AND _____, at _____ (herein called the "Distributor"). WHEREAS the Producer has the exclusive right to distribute and otherwise exploit the television Motion Picture entitled "_____" (hereinafter called the "Motion Picture"); AND WHEREAS the Producer wishes to appoint Distributor the sole and exclusive distributor of the Motion Picture in the Territory as herein defined; NOW THEREFORE THIS AGREEMENT WITNESSETH that in consideration of the mutual covenants contained in this agreement, the parties agree as follows:

### 1.00 GRANT OF RIGHTS

1.01 Producer grants to Distributor the sole and exclusive right to distribute, sub-distribute, license, reproduce for servicing all agreements entered into hereunder, and market (collectively "distribute") the Motion Picture in all languages and in the media, territories (the "Territories") and for the term (the "Term") described in Schedule "A" annexed hereto. The agreement shall thereafter renew itself automatically for further periods of one (1) year, which renewal periods shall be subject to the right of termination by either party by the giving of ninety (90) days' written notice prior to the expiry of the Term or any renewal period.

1.02 The rights granted to Distributor include the following rights:

(i) Distribution Rights: The right to distribute the Motion Picture in all of the granted media which shall include; the right to distribute the Motion Picture on all forms of television now known or hereafter devised including, without limitation, free, pay, closed circuit, Direct Broadcast Satellite, CATV, syndicated or otherwise; the right to distribute the Motion Picture in the home video market. Distributor shall have the right to arrange distribution of the Motion Picture in multimedia, CD-ROM, interactive media and the Internet, for a period of 18 months from the date of this Agreement, provided that any such distribution shall be subject to the prior written approval of the Producer. All other media, including but not limited to, theatrical, print and electronic publishing, radio, dramatic, non-theatrical, direct marketing, merchandising and music publishing rights to the soundtrack are reserved to Producer.

CONTRACTS
FOR THE
FILM AND
TELEVISION
INDUSTRY

378

(ii) Versions: To make such dubbed, sub-titled and close captioned versions of the Motion Picture and any promotional materials for use in such parts of the Territory as Distributor may deem advisable.

(iii) Distributor is granted the right to make such changes, alterations, cuts, additions, interpolations, deletions and eliminations into and from the Motion Picture and any promotional materials as (a) may be required by any duly authorized censorship authority or industry organization; (b) as may be required for distribution of the Motion Picture for use in any form of television or on airlines; and (c) to repackage the Motion Picture or parts thereof for distribution in the home video market. The credits, English-language title, and copyright notice shall not be changed or deleted unless approved by Producer and such approval shall not be unreasonably withheld. No other changes will be made without the prior approval of Producer.

(iv) Advertising and Publicity: To create and issue by way of broadcast or otherwise by any means or authorize others to do so, publicity in connection with the Motion Picture (including the names, photographs, likenesses, biographies, acts, poses, voices and other sound effects, as well as transcriptions, films and other reproductions thereof, of the director(s), musicians, writers, composers, author, all members of the cast and all other persons rendering services in connection with the Motion Picture), and to use clips and stills from the Motion Picture and in connection therewith, to use Distributor's name and trademark and/or the name and trademark of any of Distributor's licensees. Not later than delivery of the Motion Picture, Producer will advise Distributor in writing of any customary restriction on such rights contained in any agreement entered into with the above-noted personnel and Distributor agrees to abide by such customary restriction.

(v) Claims: The right in the name of Distributor or otherwise to institute and prosecute all actions or proceedings which Distributor may deem necessary for the purpose of establishing, maintaining or preserving any of the rights herein granted or purported to be granted to Distributor and similarly to defend any action or proceeding which may be brought against Distributor or assigns with respect to the Motion Picture or any of the right herein granted or purported to be granted to Distributor or which in any manner questions or disputes any of the rights of Distributor in and to the said Motion Picture or any of the rights herein granted to it at Distributor's sole expense, provided however that all recoveries from such dispute constitute Gross Receipts and all expenses incurred in connection therewith shall constitute Direct Distribution Costs.

## 2.00 DISTRIBUTOR'S BUSINESS JUDGMENT

2.01 The Distributor agrees to use reasonable good faith efforts to distribute the Motion Picture in good faith in accordance with sound business policies.

2.02 The Producer hereby expressly understands, acknowledges and agrees that the Distributor has not made and does not make any representation or warranty with respect to the amount of the license fees or other amounts which will or may be earned from the exploitation of the Motion Picture.

## 3.00 DISTRIBUTION FEES, COSTS AND EXPENSES

3.01 As consideration for its services, Distributor shall retain as its sole and exclusive property the distribution fees equal to the percentage of Gross Receipts as set out in Schedule A" (the "Distribution Fees").

3.02 "Gross Receipts" shall be defined to mean all monies actually received by Distributor or its sub-distributors arising from the exploitation of the Motion Picture. Gross Receipts do not include taxes paid, collection costs incurred, and any payment for duplication or manufacturing of materials.

3.03 After the termination or expiry of this Agreement, Distributor shall nevertheless be entitled to receive Distribution Fees and recoupment of Direct Distribution Costs due to it in respect of all agreements ("Original Agreements") made by or on behalf of the Distributor between the dates of the commencement and termination of rights granted to Distributor hereunder from exploitation of the Motion Picture in the Territory.

3.04 "Direct Distribution Costs" means all reasonable and verifiable costs incurred in connection with the promotion, distribution, exploitation, licensing or sale of the Motion Picture. Such expenses include, long distance phone charges, photocopying, fax, shipping and courier charges, clearance and brokerage fees, warehouse and handling charges, insurance, transcoding, pro-rata share of market expenses, bank transfer charges, promotional material duplication (i.e. slides and black & white prints), any direct publicity or promotional costs (e.g. cost of creation of advertising materials, paid advertising), taxes and duties including withholding taxes (but excluding Distributor's income taxes), copyright registrations and searches (if required). Such expenses shall not exceed 10% of Gross Receipts and shall be net of any third party contributions, such as Telefilm IMAF Funds. Duplication of screening cassettes and program master tapes, PAL duplication, dubbing, and foreign language versionning expenses shall be excluded from the 10% expense cap.

3.05. Limit on Recoupable Expenses. As used herein, the term expenses and/or recoupable expenses shall mean all of Distributor's Direct Distribution Costs actually spent on behalf of the Motion Picture limited as follows:

(i) Market Expenses: These expenses include all costs to attend film markets such as MIP, MIP-COM and NATPE. Such expenses may include airfare, hotel, shipping, and telephone expenses incurred to attend a film market. Such expenses shall be recoupable for the first year of distribution only, and only for those markets in which Distributor is actively participating (i.e., Distributor attends, has a booth, and attempts to sell the Motion Picture). Distributor may recoup a total of $1,500 per market attended with an overall cap of no more than $5,000 overall market cap for the year. Distributor agrees to attend no less than three (3) markets during the first year of distribution. Should the distribution term extend beyond one year, no market expenses shall be recoupable during the second and any subsequent years.

(ii) Promotional Expenses: These expenses include the cost of preparing posters, one-sheets, trailers and advertising. Distributor agrees to spend no less than $15,000 and no more than $50,000 on promotional expenses. These expenses are limited to direct out-of-pocket expenses actually spent on behalf of the Motion Picture. At Producer's request, Distributor shall provide receipts for each and every expense or forgo recoupment. Recoupable promotional expenses do not include any of Distributor's general office, overhead, legal or staff expenses or expenses for attendance at any market. Distributor agrees to spend the minimum necessary to adequately promote the Film, including preparation of a one-sheet, videocassettes and customary promotional material, if these items have not been supplied by Producer. Distributor will use its best efforts to promote the Motion

CONTRACTS
FOR THE
FILM AND
TELEVISION
INDUSTRY

380

Picture, and will promote the Motion Picture in a no less favorable manner than any of Distributor's other films.

## 4.00 APPLICATION OF GROSS RECEIPTS

4.01 Gross Receipts shall be allocated as follows:

(i) Firstly to payment of Distribution Fees;

(ii) Secondly to recoupment of Direct Distribution Costs, as limited by paragraphs 3.04 and 3.05.

(iii) The balance will be paid to Producer.

Any tax credits for withholding taxes shall be given to Producer.

## 5.00 REPORTS AND ACCOUNTING

5.01 Distributor shall deliver to Producer at Producer's address set forth above, a written statement relating to the Gross Receipts received and Direct Distribution Costs deducted during the period to which the statement pertains. Such statements shall be delivered quarterly. Producer's share of Gross Receipts shall be forwarded by cheque with such reports. Distributor shall report blocked funds in accordance with paragraph 5.04. At Producer's Request, Distributor shall promptly supply Producer with a copy of any license agreement under which any third party acquires any rights to the Motion Picture.

5.02 Any statement and report submitted to Producer by Distributor hereunder shall be binding upon Producer and not be subject to any objection for any reason if not disputed in writing within three years after such statement or report shall have been delivered to Producer.

5.03 Distributor shall keep and maintain at its offices in the City of _____, complete and accurate books of account and records relating to the distribution, exploitation and licensing of the Motion Picture. Said books of account and records shall be kept and maintained under a standard system customarily used in the television industry in accordance with generally accepted accounting principles. Throughout the Term and for a period of one year after the expiration or sooner termination of either thereof, but not more than once in each calendar year, Producer shall have access for the purposes of conducting an audit, upon giving 5 business days' notice to Distributor, and during customary business hours to all said books and records insofar as they relate to the previous two years of distribution, exhibition and exploitation of the Motion Picture. Producer and its agent shall have the right to make extracts or copies therefrom. Producer acknowledges that this agreement and the books of account and records of the Distributor contain confidential trade information. Neither the Producer nor the Producers' representatives shall reveal or use on the Producer's behalf or on behalf of any other person any facts or information arising from this agreement or any inspection of the Distributor's book of accounts and records hereunder. In the event that an audit discloses that Producer has been underpaid five percent (5%) or more, Distributor shall reimburse Producer for all audit costs. Otherwise, all audit expenses shall be borne by the Producer.

5.04 Gross Revenues which are frozen, blocked or incapable of being remitted from a territory (the "Blocked Territory") shall be placed in Distributor's bank account in the Blocked Territory and the Distributor shall notify Producer to such effect. Upon written request by Producer, Producer's share of Gross Revenues shall, at Producer's cost, be transferred to Producer's bank account in the Blocked Territory and in its currency. Such notice and transfer shall satisfy Distributor's obligation to pay and remit such Gross Revenue.

## 6.00 PRODUCER'S REPRESENTATIONS AND WARRANTIES

6.01 Producer represents and warrants, to the best of its knowledge and belief, and agrees as follows:

(a) Producer is duly organized under the laws of the State of _____, has the full, complete and unrestricted right and power to enter into this Agreement and grant, sell, assign, transfer and convey to the Distributor all rights and licenses herein contained for the Term and in the Territory and in any manner or form whatsoever herein granted; it has taken all necessary action to authorize the execution and delivery of this Agreement and the same does not and will not violate any other agreement to which Producer is a party.

(b) Producer owns or controls all the licenses, property and all other rights herein granted including, without limitation, all rights of copyright throughout the Territory, musical synchronization rights, still photo rights, videotape and film footage licences and other appropriate rights and licenses for constituent elements of the Motion Picture together with the right to use the same in publicizing, advertising and exploiting the Motion Picture. Producer shall at Distributor's request deliver to Distributor copies of all such documents as are evidence of Producer's chain of title or evidence that such rights are in the public domain.

(c) Producer has not and will not sell, assign, convey or encumber any of the rights herein granted to Distributor and Producer will not do or commit any act or thing that is in derogation of the rights herein granted to Distributor and the rights granted hereunder are free of any claims, liens or encumbrances in favor of any person whatsoever. Producer has not entered into, and will not enter into, any agreement which is inconsistent with any of the provisions of this Agreement and will not exercise any right to take any action which conflicts with, prejudices or derogates from the rights herein granted to Producer. There are no claims, demands or actions instituted, pending or threatened against the Motion Picture (other than Producer's obligations to pay Guild and union residuals and contingent compensation, which obligations will be satisfied by Producer) which if adversely determined, would impair or prevent the exercise by Distributor of its rights hereunder.

(d) Neither the Motion Picture nor any part thereof (including the music, sound and dialogue synchronized therewith), nor the exercise by any authorized party of any rights granted to the Distributor hereunder, will violate or infringe upon the trademark, tradename, copyright, patent, literary, artistic, personal, private, civil or property right or the right to privacy or any other right of any person, firm or corporation. The Motion Picture and the publicity materials delivered by Producer will not contain any material which is libelous, slanderous or defamatory.

(e) Producer has or will obtain a waiver of moral rights from all writers, composers and other persons having moral rights with respect to the Motion Picture.

(f) Producer has obtained, or will obtain on a timely basis and by no later than delivery of the Motion Picture:

CONTRACTS
FOR THE
FILM AND
TELEVISION
INDUSTRY

382

(i) licenses or grants of authority to use the results of the services of performers, musicians and other persons connected with the production of the Motion Picture which are sufficient to permit Distributor to exercise all the rights granted under this Agreement; and

(ii) the consent of persons to use their names, voices, likenesses and biographies for the purposes of advertising and exploiting the Motion Picture.

(g) The Producer has obtained the synchronization and performing rights in the music contained in the Motion Picture and the Producer warrants that in respect of the uses granted hereunder that said rights are either:

(i) controlled by a performing rights society having jurisdiction in the Territory; or
(ii) in the public domain; or
(iii) owned or controlled by Producer.

(h) The Producer has not and will not itself nor has it nor will it authorize any other party during the Term to produce, distribute or exhibit any television or home video production based in whole or in part upon underlying literary material or real life incidents or material and will not itself nor will it authorize any other party to exercise any right to take action which would tend to derogate from or compete with the rights herein granted or agreed to be granted to Distributor.

(i) Distributor, in the exercise of its rights hereunder will not be requested to make any payment to any third party involved in the production of the Motion Picture or who rendered services in connection therewith, or any music performance fees, or to or on account of any union, guild or other collective bargaining agent because of any exploitation by Distributor, and any such payments shall be borne solely by Producer, and Distributor shall have no responsibility whatsoever with respect thereto.

(j) The Motion Picture when delivered will be completely finished, fully edited and titled and fully synchronized with language dialogue, sound and music and in all respects ready and of a technical quality, adequate for network television exhibition.

6.02 Distributor represents and warrants that Distributor is duly incorporated under the laws of the Province of Ontario, has the full, complete and unrestricted right and power to enter into this Agreement; it has taken all necessary action to authorize the execution and delivery of this Agreement and the same does not and will not violate any other agreement to which Producer is a party. Distributor further warrants that it is not insolvent or in danger of bankruptcy, and all payments from Licensees of the Motion Picture will be by check or money-order payable in the name of Distributor, and Distributor will not accept any other consideration, whether cash, discounts on distribution of other films, favors of any kind, or any other form of consideration, from any Licensee in return for licensing the Motion Picture.

6.03 The representations and warranties contained in this agreement shall survive the execution, delivery, suspension and termination of this agreement.

## 7.00 INDEMNIFICATION

7.01 Distributor shall defend, indemnify and hold harmless Producer, its officers, directors and employees from and against any demand, claim, action, liability, damages, cost and expense (including reasonable legal fees) arising out of or in connection with Distributor's breach of any of the representations, warranties or provisions contained in this agreement; provided that Producer shall promptly notify Distributor of any such demand, claim etc. and that Distributor has the right to participate in the defense and approve any settlement thereof. If Distributor elects not to consent to any settlement approved by Producer, Producer may nevertheless enter into such settlement, reserving all of its rights of indemnification hereunder as against Distributor; and nothing shall be construed as a waiver by Distributor of Distributor's right to defend against a claim by Producer for costs, damages or losses arising out of such settlement.

7.02 Producer shall defend, indemnify and hold harmless Distributor, its sub-distributors and licensees and its and their respective officers, directors and employees from and against any demand, claim, action, liability, damages, cost and expense (including reasonable legal fees) arising out of or in connection with Producer's breach of any of the representations, warranties or provisions contained in this agreement; provided that Distributor shall promptly notify Producer of any such demand, claim etc. and that Producer shall have the right to participate in the defense and approve any settlement thereof. If Producer elects not to consent to any settlement approved by Distributor, Distributor may nevertheless enter into such settlement, reserving all of its rights of indemnification hereunder as against Producer; and nothing shall be construed as a waiver by Producer of Producer's right to defend against a claim by Distributor for costs, damages or losses arising out of such settlement.

## 8.00 ERRORS AND OMISSIONS INSURANCE

8.01 Distributor may purchase an Errors and Omissions (E&O) Insurance policy which may be maintained for a period of three years (or such longer period as is required by any party to whom Distributor licenses the Motion Picture) in a form and for a period acceptable to Distributor from a qualified insurance company acceptable to Distributor naming Distributor and each and all of the parties indemnified herein as additional named insureds. The amount and coverage shall be for a minimum of One Million Dollars ($1,000,000) with respect to one occurrence and Three Million Dollars ($3,000,000) in the aggregate. The policy shall provide for ten (10) days' written notice to Distributor in the event of any modification, cancellation or termination. Distributor shall advance the cost of any E & O insurance policy purchased, and shall recoup such cost from Gross Receipts. Producer shall be added as an additional named-insured on any E & O insurance policy. The limits on recoupable expenses do not apply to any payments for E & O insurance.

## 9.00 DELIVERY

9.01 At its expense, Producer shall effect delivery ("Delivery") of the Motion Picture to Distributor at Distributor's head office.

9.02 Delivery shall consist of making physical delivery of all Delivery Items listed in Schedule "B" to Distributor's head office, provided that for any original film or video master materials Distributor shall be given a lab access letter; and

9.03 Distributor shall have the right to inspect and examine all Delivery Items, documentation and publicity and advertising materials tendered as Delivery hereunder and shall advise Producer within 10 business days after Delivery if and wherein the same is not complete, whereupon Producer shall promptly deliver to Distributor the items of which it failed to make Delivery of in the

CONTRACTS
FOR THE
FILM AND
TELEVISION
INDUSTRY

384

first instance. Acceptance by Distributor of less than all the items required for Delivery and/or release of the Motion Picture prior to Delivery of all items required shall in no event be construed to be a waiver by Distributor of Producer's obligation to deliver any item not delivered. Distributor shall have thirty days after delivery of any delivery item to raise any objection to its quality; if Distributor does not raise an objection within thirty days it shall waive its right to object. Distributor agrees to acknowledge complete Delivery if so requested by Producer. The cost of any item of Delivery required hereunder supplied by Distributor shall be charged to Producer's share of the Gross Receipts, if any, including any and all advances or guarantees paid hereunder, if any. Producer agrees that Distributor shall be the sole judge of the adequacy of Delivery, which judgement shall be exercised reasonably.

## 10.00 DEFAULT

10.01 This agreement may be terminated by either party upon written notice if:

(a) either party breaches a material provision of this agreement and fails to remedy such breach within 14 business days after written notice thereof by the other party;

(b) any representation or warranty made herein shall be found to be false, incorrect or misleading in any material respect, by omission or otherwise.

## 11.00 NOTICES

11.01 Any notice, payment, request or other communication required or permitted to be given hereunder by either of the parties to the other of them shall be given, made or communicated, as the case may be, by personally delivering the same, by telex, telegram or electronic facsimile transfer, or by registered or certified mail, first-class, postage prepaid, return receipt requested, addressed to the recipient as follows:

TO THE PRODUCER: _____ (Producer Name), _____ (Producer Address)

With a courtesy copy to: _____, _____, Phone: _____, FAX: _____.

TO THE DISTRIBUTOR: _____ (Distributor Name), _____ (Distributor Address)

or to such other place or address or addresses as either party hereto may designate from time to time by giving notice as herein provided. Any notice, request, payment or other communication shall be deemed to have been given, made or communicated, as the case may be, at the time that the same is personally delivered, or on the first business day next following the date upon which the same is dispatched by telex, telegram or electronic facsimile transfer or, if by registered or certified mail as aforesaid, on the third (3rd) business day (excluding Saturdays, Sundays, statutory holidays or periods during which strikes, lockouts or other occurrences interfere with normal mail service) next following the date when same is so mailed.

## 12.00 GENERAL PROVISIONS

12.01 Nothing contained in this Agreement shall constitute a partnership or joint venture between the parties. Neither party shall become liable by any representation, act or omission of the other contrary to the provisions of this Agreement.

12.02 The parties agree to execute and deliver such further documents and perform and cause to be performed such further acts as may be necessary or desirable in order to give full effect to this Agreement.

12.03 This Agreement constitutes the entire agreement between the parties regarding the Motion Picture.

12.04 The failure at any time to require performance of any provision of this Agreement shall not affect the full right to require such performance at any later time. The waiver of a breach of any provision shall not constitute a waiver of the provision or of any succeeding breach.

12.05 Should any provision of this Agreement be held to be void, invalid, or inoperative, the remainder of this Agreement shall be effective as though such void, invalid or inoperative provision had not been contained in this Agreement.

12.06 Neither party may assign this Agreement without the prior written consent of the other provided that Distributor may appoint subdistributors and assign rights hereunder in the normal course, and Producer may assign its right to monies.

12.07 Time is of the essence with respect to all provisions of this Agreement.

12.08 Arbitration and Jurisdiction: This Agreement shall be interpreted in accordance with the laws of the State of _____, applicable to agreements executed and to be wholly performed therein. Any controversy or claim arising out of or in relation to this Agreement or the validity, construction or performance of this Agreement, or the breach thereof, shall be resolved by arbitration in accordance with the rules and procedures of AFMA, as said rules may be amended from time to time with rights of discovery if requested by the arbitrator. Such rules and procedures are incorporated and made a part of this Agreement by reference. If AFMA shall refuse to accept jurisdiction of such dispute, then the parties agree to arbitrate such matter before and in accordance with the rules of the American Arbitration Association under its jurisdiction in _____ before a single arbitrator familiar with entertainment law. The parties shall have the right to engage in pre-hearing discovery in connection with such arbitration proceedings. The parties agree hereto that they will abide by and perform any award rendered in any arbitration conducted pursuant hereto, that any court having jurisdiction thereof may issue a judgment based upon such award and that the prevailing party in such arbitration and/or confirmation proceeding shall be entitled to recover its reasonable attorneys' fees and expenses. The arbitration shall be final, binding and non-appealable. The arbitration will be held in _____ and any award shall be final, binding and non-appealable. The Parties agree to accept service of process in accordance with AFMA Rules.

## 13.00 MISCELLANEOUS

13.01 Distributor will consult with Producer in good faith on marketing plans before artwork is commissioned and the marketing of the Motion Picture has begun.

13.02 PAYMENTS/LATE PAYMENTS/LIEN: All monies due and payable to Filmmaker should be held in trust by Distributor. Filmmaker shall have a lien on Gross Receipts. All checks shall be made payable to "_____." A copy of all producer reports and notices shall be sent to Producer and _____. All monies due

CONTRACTS
FOR THE
FILM AND
TELEVISION
INDUSTRY

386

Producer shall be paid when due. Distributor shall pay Producer interest at 10 percent per annum on any amounts more than 15 days past due.

13.03 ALLOCATION OF PACKAGE REVENUE: If the Motion Picture is included in a package with other motion pictures sold to a buyer, then the price allocated to the Motion Picture shall be on the basis of a reasonable allocation of revenues in light of the commercial worth of all the motion pictures in the package. Whenever the Motion Picture is sold as part of a package, Distributor shall disclose the licensee fee allocated to each motion picture in the package.

13.04 Distributor and Producer hereby establish minimum guarantee amounts per territory (hereinafter "Territorial Minimums") as set forth on the attached schedule. Nothing contained herein or in the schedule of Territorial Minimums shall be deemed to require Distributor in fact to obtain any such Territorial Minimum(s), but, rather, it is the intention of the parties hereto that Distributor may not enter into an agreement for an amount less than the applicable Territorial Minimum without first obtaining Producer's approval.

13.05 RETURN OF ADVERTISING MATERIALS: After termination all advertising materials and the right to use same to promote the Motion Picture, will revert to Producer. Any artwork or copyrightable material commissioned by Distributor shall be created pursuant to a written contract which states the work is a work-for-hire and that Producer is owner of all rights therein. If under the applicable copyright for the country in which any such work is created, ownership cannot be vested in Producer as a work-for-hire, then Distributor shall have the creator of any work assign all rights to Producer in a written instrument which shall be executed no later than when the work is delivered.

IN WITNESS WHEREOF, the parties have executed this Agreement.

_____

PRODUCER


_____

DISTRIBUTOR

# SCHEDULE "A"

Motion Picture: _____ - feature length Motion Picture

Territories: _____

Rights: Rights - as set out in 1.02(i)

Term: The term shall be _____ years, and if Distributor pays Producer $100,000 (U.S.) in Net Receipts, or more, in that two year period, Distributor shall automatically receive another two year term ("the first renewal period"). If Distributor pays Producer an additional $100,000 (U.S.) or more during the first renewal period, then Distributor shall receive an additional three (3) year extension. Distributor shall not license film to any third party licensee for a term in excess of 12 years without the prior approval of Producer.

Distributor commission: _____% of Gross Receipts, the remainder after deduction of recoupable expenses, to Producer.

# SCHEDULE "B"

Materials To Be Supplied:

(a) A lab access letter for one of the following technically acceptable formats: Digital, Betacam, D2, D1, or Betacam SP NTSC and PAL standard sub-masters of the Motion Picture, duplicated directly from Producer's master. Such videotape shall be accompanied by separate music and effects audio tracks. If M&E track is unavailable Producer is to supply an alternative technically acceptable digital audio format, including but not limited to DAT and DA88, with fully mixed M&E tracks and without voice or narration. The above items must also be accompanied by a technical evaluation report, indicating such items are technically acceptable for broadcast. Producer must deliver Materials within 14 days of any confirmed offers.

(b) Story synopsis, press kits and one sheets.

(c) Music cue sheets and production cue sheet.

(d) Selection of 12 black & white stills and 12 colour transparencies.

(e) Cast and crew bios.

(f) "As broadcast" script from the Motion Picture.

(g) Intentionally deleted

(h) A ¾" video-cassette of the Motion Picture (or 15 VHS copies) to be used for screening purposes.

(i) If Canada forms part of the Territory, certificate of certification from the CAVCO that Motion Picture are certified Canadian Videotape Productions pursuant to the Income Tax Act (Canada) or a "C" or "SR" number issued by the CRTC.

CONTRACTS
FOR THE
FILM AND
TELEVISION
INDUSTRY

388

# Schedule of Minimums

| Territory | Minimum Acceptable |
|---|---|
| **ENGLISH SPEAKING** | |
| United States | |
| Eng. Canada | |
| Fr. Canada | |
| UK | |
| Australia/New Zealand | |
| South Africa | |
| East Africa | |
| West Africa | |
| West Indies | |
| | |
| **EUROPE** | |
| Germany/Austria | |
| Switzerland | |
| France | |
| Italy | |
| Spain | |
| Benelux | |
| Scandinavia | |
| Iceland | |
| Portugal | |
| Greece | |
| | |

| Territory | Minimum Acceptable |
|-----------|--------------------|
| **FAR EAST** | |
| Japan | |
| Korea | |
| Taiwan | |
| Hong Kong | |
| Singapore | |
| Brunei | |
| Malaysia | |
| Indonesia | |
| Phillippines | |
| Thailand | |
| India | |
| Sri Lanka | |
| Pakistan | |
| China | |
| | |
| **LATIN AMERICA** | |
| Arg/Par/Uru | |
| Brazil | |
| Mexico | |
| Chile | |
| Colombia | |
| Venezuela | |
| C. America | |
| Ecuador | |
| Peru/Bolivia | |
| Dominican Rep. | |
| | |

CONTRACTS
FOR THE
FILM AND
TELEVISION
INDUSTRY

390

| Territory | Minimum Acceptable |
|---|---|
| **MIDDLE EAST** | |
| Leb/Middle East | |
| Turkey | |
| Israel | |
| | |
| **EAST EUROPE** | |
| Bulgaria | |
| Czech | |
| Hungary | |
| Poland | |
| Croatia | |
| Serbia | |
| CIS | |
| Rumania | |
| | |

# SECURITY AGREEMENT

A filmmaker who enters into a distribution agreement may want to secure his right to share in revenue generated from his picture. He can accomplish this by having the distributor give him a "secured interest." A secured party is a person in whose favor there is a security interest. The other party—the one who owes the obligation— is often referred to as the "debtor."

The granting of a security interest is usually set forth in the distribution agreement. The "collateral" that secures the contract is usually the distributor's right to distribute the motion picture including any rights it may have in film elements (e.g., master tapes) and any proceeds realized from the exploitation of its rights.

If the distributor goes bankrupt, a filmmaker who has a security interest may have preference when the distributor's assets are sold to pay creditors. As a secured creditor, the filmmaker will be paid before unsecured creditors. To put it simply, if the distributor goes bankrupt, the assets of the distributor are liquidated, and if there are insufficient funds to pay all the creditors, a security interest will enable the filmmaker to have preference over unsecured vendors (e.g., the stationary supply store). In most instances, the filmmaker only has preference in regard to revenue generated from his picture.

In addition to a clause in the distribution agreement that grants the filmmaker a security interest, the parties will often execute a separate security agreement, and a short form security agreement along with form UCC-1. In order to perfect one's security interest one must record it with the Secretary of State and the Copyright Office.

Note that distributors who provide production financing or pay advances to producers, may want to protect their own interests by holding onto and recording their own security interests. In this case, the collateral would be the film elements.

CONTRACTS
FOR THE
FILM AND
TELEVISION
INDUSTRY

392

# SECURITY AGREEMENT

This Security Agreement is made as of the_____, by and between _____ ("Debtor") and _____ ("Secured Party") with reference to the following facts:

A. Debtor and Secured Party have entered into a Distribution Agreement dated as of _____, regarding among other things, the assignment by Secured Party to Debtor of certain exclusive rights of distribution and exploitation in the motion picture entitled "_____" (the "Picture") in designated media and non-exclusive incidental rights necessary to exploit the Picture (collectively such rights are referred to hereinafter as the "Rights"), all as more fully set forth in the Distribution Agreement.

B. The parties desire to secure the right of Secured Party to the Rights upon the terms and conditions of this Security Agreement.

NOW THEREFORE, the parties agree as follows:

1. COLLATERAL: The "Collateral" is any and all of the following:

a. Intangibles: All of the Debtor's right, title and interest in and to the Rights in the Picture as more fully set forth in the Distribution Agreement dated as of _____.

b. Tangibles: All of the Debtor's right, title and interest in and to all film elements, videotapes, sound elements, paperwork, and other physical materials of any kind ("Materials") to be used in the exploitation of the Rights in the Picture, and

c. Proceeds: All proceeds, realized by Debtor from exploitation of the Rights or the Materials in the Picture, to which secured Party is entitled under the provisions of the Distribution Agreement.

2. SECURITY INTEREST: In order to induce Secured Party to enter into the Distribution Agreement and to secure Secured Party's right to receive the Producer's Share of Net Proceeds as defined in the Distribution Agreement, Debtor grants and assigns to Secured Party a continuing security interest in the Collateral.

3. RESORT TO SECURITY INTEREST: Secured Party may resort to its Security Interest in the Collateral if, as provided in the Distribution Agreement Debtor fails to pay Secured Party proceeds in the form of Producer's share of Gross Receipts received by Debtor, if any, from the exploitation of the Picture to which Secured Party is entitled.

4. RIGHTS AND REMEDIES OF SECURED PARTY: Secured Party and its assignees will have all the rights and remedies of a secured party under the California Commercial Code as it may be amended from time to time and under applicable law.

5. DEBTOR'S WARRANTIES AND REPRESENTATIONS: Debtor warrants and represents to Secured Party that:

a. Debtor has the right and authority to execute and deliver this Security Agreement;

b. No other security interest has been granted by Debtor in the Collateral which might interfere with or have priority over the Security Interest granted in this Agreement;

c. There are no other agreements or understandings of Debtor which interfere with the rights granted to Secured Party in this Security Agreement or the Distribution Agreement.

6. NOTICES: All notices under this Agreement will be in writing and delivered by regular mail to the following addresses:

TO SECURED PARTY:      _____

_____

_____

A COURTESY COPY TO:      _____

_____

_____

TO DEBTOR:      _____

_____

_____

Each party may change its place for notice by written notice duly given in accordance with the Distribution Agreement.

7. FURTHER ASSURANCES: Each party upon the reasonable request of the other, will execute such other documents as are required to perfect or release the Security Interest, including the attached UCC-1 Financing Statement and Short-Form Security Agreement.

8. GOVERNING LAW: This Security Agreement will be governed by the laws of the State of _____.

IN WITNESS WHEREOF, the parties have executed this Security Agreement as of the date first written Above in _____, _____.

SECURED PARTY                 DEBTOR

_____                 _____


_____                 _____

_____                 _____

CONTRACTS
FOR THE
FILM AND
TELEVISION
INDUSTRY

394

# SHORT-FORM SECURITY AGREEMENT

For valuable consideration, receipt of which is acknowledged, _____ ("Debtor") grants and assigns to _____ ("Secured Party") a continuing Security Interest in and to the "Collateral" described in the following paragraph with regard to the motion picture currently entitled "_____" upon the terms and conditions to that certain Security Agreement between the parties dated as of the same date as this Short-Form Security Agreement.

The "Collateral" is any and all of the following:

a. Intangibles: All of Debtor's right, title, and interest in and to the Rights in the Picture as more fully set forth in the Distribution Agreement dated as of _____.

b. Tangibles: All of Debtor's right, title, and interest in and to all film elements, videotapes, sound elements, paperwork, and other physical materials of any kind ("Materials") to be used in the exploitation of the Rights in the Picture, and

c. Proceeds: All proceeds realized by Debtor from exploitation of the Rights or the Materials in the Picture, to which Secured Party is entitled under the provisions of the Distribution Agreement.

IN WITNESS WHEREOF, the parties have executed this Short-Form Security Agreement as of _____, at _____, _____.

_____
Debtor

_____

_____
Secured Party

_____

# DISTRIBUTOR ASSUMPTION AGREEMENT (SAG)

The Screen Actor's Guild (SAG) is the union that represents actors. Even independent filmmakers who make low-budget "non-union" films, often want to employ SAG actors. That is because most experienced actors are members of SAG, or its sister union AFTRA. Since producers can choose which unions to sign with (or not sign with), an independent producer can use a non-WGA writer and a non-DGA director yet employ SAG actors.

In contracting with independent producers, SAG is concerned that its union members receive their share of residuals. Residuals are additional payments due to actors if a motion picture is used in ancillary markets. For instance, if a motion picture intended for an initial theatrical release is subsequently distributed in the home video and cable television markets, the producer will be required to share the revenue he receives from exploiting his film in these ancillary markets by making additional payments (called residuals) to the actors. Today these so-called ancillary markets, generate more money than the theatrical market. Indeed, there would be few movies made today if the producer did not expect revenue from ancillary markets.

Because of the high turnover of independent production companies, SAG is concerned that its members might not receive their residuals. If a producer doesn't pay residuals due actors, SAG can commence an action against the producer. By the time the law catches up with the producer, however, the money may be gone and the producer out of business. In order to better secure its member's residuals, SAG requires producers to have their distributors sign an assumption agreement. If a distributor signs this agreement, the distributor will make residual payments directly to SAG (instead of paying the producer who in turn pays SAG).

The problem facing independent producers is that some distributors refuse to sign the SAG assumption agreement. SAG insists that the independent producer agree to have its distributor sign an assumption agreement in order for the producer to become a union signatory and employ SAG actors. At the time the producer signs the agreement with SAG, the producer may not know who will distribute the motion picture. After the movie is made, the producer may find that his distributor of choice refuses to sign the assumption agreement. The producer is left with the dilemma of whether to violate his contract with SAG or forego distribution of his film.

CONTRACTS
FOR THE
FILM AND
TELEVISION
INDUSTRY

396

# DISTRIBUTOR'S ASSUMPTION AGREEMENT (SAG)

In consideration of the execution of a DISTRIBUTION AGREEMENT between _____ ("Producer") and the undersigned Distributor, Distributor agrees that the motion picture presently entitled _____ (the "Picture") is subject to the Screen Actors Guild Codified Basic Agreement of 1995, 1992, 1989, 1986, 1983 or 1980 (strike those which are not applicable) for Independent Producers ("Basic Agreement") covering theatrical motion pictures and particularly to the provisions of (strike those of the following clauses (1), (2) or (3) which are not applicable):

(1) Section 5 thereof, pertaining to additional compensation payable to performers when theatrical motion pictures, the principal photography of which commenced after October 6, 1980 and which are covered by said Section, are released to free television, and Section 34 pertaining to applicable pension and health contributions, if any are required;

(2) Section 5.1 thereof, pertaining to additional compensation payable to performers when theatrical motion pictures, the principal photography of which commenced after June 30, 1971 but prior to July 1, 1984 and which are covered by said Section, are released in Supplemental Markets and Section 34 pertaining to applicable pension and health contributions, if any are required; and

(3) Section 5.2 thereof, pertaining to additional compensation payable to performers when theatrical motion pictures, the principal photography of which commenced after July 1, 1984 and which are covered by said Section, are released in Supplemental Markets and Section 34 pertaining to applicable pension and health contributions, if any are required.

Distributor is distributing or licensing the Picture for distribution (select one)

_____ in perpetuity (i.e., for the period of copyright and any renewals thereof)

_____ for a limited term of _____ years

in the following territories and media (indicate those that are applicable):

## Territory:

_____ Domestic (the U.S. and Canada, and their respective possessions and territories)

_____ Foreign (the world excluding the U.S. and Canada and their respectivepossessions and territories)

_____ Other (please describe): _____

## Media:

_____ All

_____ Home Video

_____ Pay Television

_____ Free Television

_____ Other (please describe: _____)

See Description, attached hereto "A" and Incorporated herein by reference

Distributor hereby agrees, expressly for the benefit of the Screen Actors Guild, herein called SAG, as representative of the performers whose services are included in the Picture, when the Picture is telecast on free television or exhibited in Supplemental Markets (as applicable), to make the additional compensation payments required under the Basic Agreement, if any, and the pension and health contributions required thereby, if any, with respect to the territories, media and term referred to above as provided in the applicable Sections referred to hereinabove (all such payments are collectively hereinafter referred to as "Residuals'). Distributor, for and on behalf of the Producer, shall make all Social Security, withholding, unemployment insurance and disability insurance payments required by law with respect to the additional compensation referred to in the preceding sentence.

It is expressly understood that the right of Distributor to license the Picture for exhibition on free television or in Supplemental Markets (as applicable), or to exhibit or cause or permit the Picture to be exhibited on free television or in Supplemental Markets (as applicable), shall be subject to and conditioned upon the prompt payment of Residuals with respect to the territories, media and term referred to above in accordance with said applicable Sections. It is agreed that SAG, in addition to all other remedies, shall be entitled to injunctive relief against Distributor in the event such payments are not made.

To the extent that Producer has executed a security agreement and financing statement in SAG's favor in the Picture and related collateral as defined in the SAG-Producer Security Agreement ("SAG Security Interest"), Distributor agrees and acknowledges that Distributor's rights in the Picture acquired pursuant to the Distribution Agreement (to the extent those rights are included in the collateral covered by the Security Agreement) are subject and subordinate to the SAG Security Interest. SAG agrees that so long as Residuals with respect to the Picture for the territories, media and term referred to above are timely paid in accordance with said applicable Sections that SAG will not exercise any rights under the SAG Security Interest which would in any way interfere with the rights of the Distributor to distribute the Picture and receive all revenues from such distribution.

SAG further agrees that if it exercises its rights as a secured party, it will dispose of collateral which encompasses any of Distributor's rights or interests in, or physical items relating to, the Picture, only to a transferee which agrees in writing to be bound by SAG's obligations under this Assumption Agreement.

Within a reasonable time after the expiration of each calender quarter, but not exceeding sixty (60) days, Distributor will furnish or cause to be furnished to SAG a written report showing the gross receipts during the preceding quarter from the distribution of the Picture by Distributor on free television or in Supplemental Markets (as applicable), with respect to which Distributor is required to make payments hereunder, (whether distributed by the Distributor or through another distributor), and showing the date of the first exhibition on television or in Supplemental Markets (as applicable), and whether such exhibition was on network television and, if so, whether in prime time.

Distributor shall also make available for inspection by SAG all Distributor's statements delivered to Producer insofar as they relate to such gross receipts. SAG shall have the right at reasonable times and on reasonable notice to examine the books and records of Distributor as to such gross receipts pertaining to such

CONTRACTS
FOR THE
FILM AND
TELEVISION
INDUSTRY

398

distribution on free television or in Supplemental Markets (as applicable) of the Picture. If Distributor shall fail to make such payments as and when due and payable, Distributor shall pay late payment damages as specified in Section 5, 5.1 or 5.2, whichever is applicable, of the Basic Agreement.

In the event of any sale, assignment or transfer of Distributor's distribution or exhibition rights in the Picture, Distributor shall remain liable for the Residuals unless Distributor obtains an executed Distributor's Assumption Agreement from such purchaser, assignee or transferee and SAG approves in writing the financial responsibility of the party obtaining such rights. SAG agrees that it will not unreasonably withhold its approval of the financial responsibility of any such purchaser, assignee or transferee. In the event SAG is notified that such purchaser, Assignee or transferee is a Qualified Distributor, then the financial responsibility of such purchaser, assignee or transferee shall be deemed automatically approved on the date SAG receives written notice of the assumption of obligations hereunder by the Qualified Distributor. Nothing herein shall release Producer of its obligations under the Basic Agreement or any other agreement between Producer and SAG.

If SAG does not approve in writing the financial responsibility of the party obtaining such rights, this DISTRIBUTOR'S ASSUMPTION AGREEMENT shall remain effective and binding upon Distributor, and Distributor shall be obligated to pay Residuals which accrue during the term for those territories and media for which it was granted distribution rights and all extensions and renewals. Such obligations shall be subject to Section 6.C. of the Basic Agreement. The Distributor shall have the right, at its election, to cause to be immediately submitted to arbitration, pursuant to the provisions of Section 9 of the Basic Agreement, the issue of whether SAG has unreasonably withheld the approval of the financial responsibility of such purchaser, assignee or transferee for payments due hereunder.

Distributor and SAG hereby agree that all disputes based upon, arising out of or relating to this Assumption Agreement, other than SAG's entitlement to injunctive or other equitable relief, shall be submitted to final and binding arbitration in accordance with the arbitration provisions contained in the Basic Agreement. Notwithstanding the foregoing, Distributor agrees and acknowledges that SAG is not precluded by this or any other provision of this Assumption Agreement from obtaining from a court injunctive relief or any other legal remedy at any time prior to arbitration or issuance of an arbitration award. The right to obtain injunctive relief from a court shall be applicable whether an arbitration proceeding has or has not been initiated, and further, without limitation, shall be applicable in conjunction with a proceeding to confirm and enforce an arbitration award against Distributor.

THIS DISTRIBUTOR'S ASSUMPTION AGREEMENT SHALL BE GOVERNED BY AND CONSTRUED IN ACCORDANCE WITH THE LAWS OF THE STATE OF CALIFORNIA AND THE UNITED STATES, AS THE SAME WOULD BE APPLIED BY A FEDERAL COURT IN CALIFORNIA WITHOUT REGARD TO PRINCIPLES OF CONFLICTS OF LAWS. SAG and Distributor agree that any arbitration or legal action or proceeding brought to interpret or enforce the provisions of this Distributor's Assumption Agreement (including an action to compel arbitration or a petition to enforce, confirm or vacate an arbitration award) shall be held or brought, in the Guild's sole discretion, in Los Angeles County, California, or in

New York County, New York. Distributor irrevocably submits to the jurisdiction of the federal and state courts therein. Distributor irrevocably waives any objection which it may now or hereafter have to the venue of any suit, action or proceeding, arising out of or relating to the Assumption Agreement brought in the State of California or in the State of New York and hereby irrevocably waives any claim that any such suit, action or proceeding in the State of California or the State of New York has been brought in an inconvenient forum. Notwithstanding the foregoing, SAG, at its option may bring a legal action or proceeding in the courts of any country or place where Distributor or any of its assets may be found and, by execution and delivery of this Assumption Agreement, Distributor irrevocably submits to the jurisdiction of the courts of such places. Further, Distributor consents to service of process by personal delivery or by certified or registered mail, return receipt requested, or by first class mail addressed to Distributor's general counsel or if none is designated below, to Distributor's representative identified below, or by any other method permitted by law. Notice will be deemed to have been duly given or made (a) immediately upon personal delivery or (b) if sent by mail, five (5) days from the date of mailing within the United States of America or seven (7) days from the date of mailing across national borders.

Date: _____

DISTRIBUTOR: _____

Address: _____

_____

By: _____
(Signature)

_____
(Please print name)

Title: _____
(Please insert title)

Distributor's Representative or General Counsel:

_____

CONTRACTS
FOR THE
FILM AND
TELEVISION
INDUSTRY

400

# HOME VIDEO DISTRIBUTION

The so-called "ancillary" markets of home video and cable television actually generate more revenue than the "primary" theatrical market. Home video and cable distribution are less risky and more profitable than theatrical distribution. The distributor does not have to pay for duplication of film prints, shipping to theaters and expensive advertising.

Because the right to distribute to ancillary markets is so desirable, it is difficult to interest a distributor in a theatrical release without giving it the ancillary markets in the same territory.

Some movies and programming are made for release directly to home video or cable. Exercise, children, and specialty programs, for example, have successfully recouped their costs and generated significant profits without a theatrical release. The following agreement is for a series of specialty programs made for home video and cable distribution only.

# HOME VIDEO LICENSING AGREEMENT

This Agreement between _____, residing at _____ (herein called "Licensor"), and _____, (herein called "Distributor"), a _____ corporation, is for the licensing to the domestic (United States and English-speaking Canada) home video market for the program "_____," (herein "Program") a collection of titles as set forth in Schedule "A", which is owned by Licensor.

1. Licensor licenses his interest in the program to Distributor for distribution to the domestic (U.S. & Canada) home video market ("Licensed Territory") for a term of _____ years and one month from the date this agreement is executed by both parties.

2. Licensor hereby grants Distributor the exclusive and irrevocable right, license and privilege in the Licensed territory (Domestic only) and in the Licensed Field (home video only) to manufacture Videograms (videocassettes, Videodiscs, DVD's and similar devices) of the program and to sell, lease, license, rent, distribute, reproduce, perform, exploit, advertise and otherwise market such Videograms during the term hereof. Distributor promises to use its efforts to market and distribute the program.

3. Distributor shall reproduce and incorporate the Program into Videograms in its entirety in the form delivered by Licensor to Distributor, with no titles, credits, copyright notices, or other material changed, added to, omitted or edited without Licensor' prior written approval, which shall not be unreasonably withheld.

4. All rights not expressly granted hereunder are reserved to Licensor including the use of any Videograms for viewing in any place of public assembly where an admission fee is charged, for broadcasting by television or cable, whether free or pay for public exhibition in the traditional non-theatrical market, sequels and remakes, or for theatrical exhibition. Distributor shall only have the right to distribute the Program to the domestic home video market, to be used for exhibition on a television set for private home use only.

5. Licensor is not in any way obliged to license to Distributor any new programs Licensor may produce in the future.

6. Distributor shall cause to be stamped or imprinted on the Videograms or their packaging enclosures a statement substantially to the effect that: "The copyright proprietor has licensed the material contained herein for noncommercial private use only, and prohibits any other use, copying or reproduction in whole or in part."

7. For each Video Gram of the program sold, rented or otherwise vended in the Licensed Territory during the Term, Distributor shall pay Licensor a royalty equal to _____% of such Gross Receipts as Distributor derives therefrom. "Gross Receipts" shall be defined, computed, paid and accounted for in accordance with the provisions of Schedule "B" attached and incorporated by this reference. Gross receipts shall include any and all income received from the exploitation of the Program regardless of source.

8. Distributor shall bear all costs and obligations with respect to the distribution of the Program, including but not limited to all salaries, royalties, license fees, service charges, laboratory charges and the like. Licensor shall have no obligation for past, current or future salaries, royalties, residuals, deferments, license fees, service charges, laboratory charges or similar charges.

9. Distributor shall maintain complete books and records with respect to all Videograms sold, leased, licensed or rented. Distributor will render to Licensor, on a quarterly basis, a written statement of Licensor's royalties following the conclusion of each quarterly accounting period and shall be accompanied by payment of any amount shown to be due Licensor.

10. Licensor shall have the right to examine the books and records of Distributor to the extent they pertain to the Program. Such examination shall be made during reasonable business hours, upon reasonable advance notice, at the regular place of business of Distributor where such books and records are to be maintained.

11. In any instance where revenues are earned or deductions allowed with regard to a group of films or video programs including the Program, Distributor shall make such allocations as are determined by Distributor in good faith, and gross receipts hereunder shall only include the amounts allocated to the Program.

12. All monies due or payable to Licensor shall be deemed held in trust by Distributor for Licensor. Licensor shall be deemed to have a lien or claim on the gross receipts. Distributor's obligation shall include interest at the legal rate of interest (currently 10% per annum) on any amounts due Licensor when such amounts are 30 days or more past due.

13. Distributor may only assign its obligations under this agreement to a person, corporation or other entity purchasing substantially all of the assets of the Distributor or into which Distributor shall be merged and which assumes Distributor's obligations hereunder. Licensor shall be entitled to assign its right to receive monies hereunder. No assignment shall relieve the assignor of its obligations to the other party hereunder.

15. Nothing herein contained shall be construed to create a partnership or joint venture by or between the Distributor and Licensor or to make either the agent of the other. Each party agrees not to hold itself out as a partner or agent of the

CONTRACTS
FOR THE
FILM AND
TELEVISION
INDUSTRY

402

other or to otherwise state or imply by advertising or otherwise any relationship that is contrary to the terms of this agreement. Neither party shall become liable or bound by any representation, act, omission or agreement of the other. All matters involving the distribution, lease, exhibition, sale, licensing and reissuing of the program, shall be exercised by the Distributor in accordance with its sound business judgment.

16. This agreement shall inure to the benefit of, and shall be binding upon, the executors, administrators and assigns of the parties.

17. If any provision of this Agreement or the application thereof to any Person or circumstance shall be invalid or unenforceable to any extent, the remainder of this Agreement and the application of such provisions to other persons or circumstances shall not be affected thereby and shall be enforced to the greatest extent permitted by law.

18. The parties agree to execute such further documents and instruments as each may reasonably request in order to effectuate the terms and intentions of this agreement, and in the event either party is unable to execute any such documents or instruments, each appoints the other as their irrevocable attorney in fact to execute any such documents and instruments, provided that said documents and instruments shall not be inconsistent with the terms and conditions of this agreement. The rights under this Clause constitute a power coupled with an interest and are irrevocable.

19. This agreement expresses the entire understanding between the parties and both agree that no oral understandings have been made with regard thereto. This agreement may be amended only by written instrument signed by both parties. Each party acknowledges that it has not been induced to enter this agreement by any representations or assurances, whether written or oral, and agree that each has not received any promises or inducements other than as herein set forth.

20. This Agreement shall be interpreted in accordance with the laws of the State of _____, applicable to agreements executed and to be wholly performed therein. Any controversy or claim arising out of or in relation to this Agreement or the validity, construction or performance of this Agreement, or the breach thereof, shall be resolved by arbitration in accordance with the rules and procedures of AFMA, as said rules may be amended from time to time with rights of discovery if requested by the arbitrator. Such rules and procedures are incorporated and made a part of this Agreement by reference. If AFMA shall refuse to accept jurisdiction of such dispute, then the parties agree to arbitrate such matter before and in accordance with the rules of the American Arbitration Association under its jurisdiction in _____ before a single arbitrator familiar with entertainment law. The parties shall have the right to engage in pre-hearing discovery in connection with such arbitration proceedings. The parties agree hereto that they will abide by and perform any award rendered in any arbitration conducted pursuant hereto, that any court having jurisdiction thereof may issue a judgment based upon such award and that the prevailing party in such arbitration and/or confirmation proceeding shall be entitled to recover its reasonable attorney's fees and expenses. The arbitration will be held in _____ and any award shall be final, binding and non-appealable. The Parties agree to accept service of process in accordance with the AFMA or AAA Rules.

AGREED TO AND ACCEPTED

_____     Date:_____
(Licensor)

_____
(Distributor Representative)

                                    Date:_____
(Distributor)

    IN WITNESS WHEREOF, the parties hereunto set their respective hand and seal this _____.


_____

# CHAPTER 10

# MERCHANDISING

Movie merchandising can generate substantial revenue. Some movies have generated more gross revenues from retail sales of movie-related merchandise than the amount of money exhibitors have taken in at the box office.

Studios usually do not manufacture film-related products themselves. They license the right to sell these products to other companies (the "Licensee"). In most instances there is no risk to the studio (the "Licensor") because the licensees incur all manufacturing and distribution expenses. The studio receives an advance per product, and royalty payments, often between five and ten percent of gross revenues from sales to retailers (i.e., the wholesale price). If the movie flops and the products don't sell, the manufacturer incurs the loss.

Musicals such as *Saturday Night Fever*, *Grease*, *Flashdance*, and *Dirty Dancing*, earn substantial revenues from sales of soundtrack albums. Moreover, a hit song can effectively promote a film.

Keep in mind that few films lend themselves to extensive merchandising efforts. While *Jurassic Park* can spin off numerous toys, posters and other items, a film like *Sleepless in Seattle*, has limited merchandising potential other than the soundtrack album.

CONTRACTS
FOR THE
FILM AND
TELEVISION
INDUSTRY

406

# MERCHANDISING AGREEMENT

AGREEMENT made _____ between _____ ("Licensor") and _____ ("Licensee") with respect to certain merchandising rights in the motion picture entitled: _____ (the "Picture").

## 1. LICENSE:

(a) Grant of License: Licensor grants to Licensee for the term of this Agreement, subject to the terms and conditions herein contained, and Licensee hereby accepts, the exclusive right, license and privilege to utilize the names, characters, artists' portrayal of characters, likenesses and visual representations as included in Picture (collectively the "Property") solely and only in connection with the manufacture, advertising, distribution and sale of the article or articles specified in Schedule "A" attached hereto and by this reference made a part hereof (such articles being referred to herein as "Licensed Products") under the terms and conditions stated herein. Licensee agrees that it will not utilize the Property in any manner not specifically authorized by this Agreement.

(b) Limited Grant: Nothing in this Agreement shall be construed to prevent Licensor from granting any other licenses for the use of the Property in any manner whatsoever, except that Licensor agrees that, except as provided herein, it will grant no other licenses effective during the term of this Agreement, for use in the Licensed Territory of the Licensed Product(s). Licensor specifically reserves all rights not herein granted, including, without limitation, premium rights. For purposes of this Agreement, premium rights shall mean use of the Property in such manner as to identify it with a particular product or service other than the Licensed Products. It is clearly understood that the Licensed Products may not be sold for use, or be used as, premiums, self-liquidators, containers, or for any secondary use without the prior written consent of the Licensor.

## 2. TERRITORY:

The license hereby granted extends only to the territory described in Schedule "B," attached hereto and by this reference made a part hereof (hereinafter: Licensed Territory"). Licensee agrees that it will not make, or authorize, any use, direct or indirect, of the Licensed Products or Property in any other area, and that it will not knowingly sell articles covered by this Agreement to persons who intend or are likely to resell them in any other area, to the extent this prohibition is permitted by law.

## 3. LICENSE PERIOD (THE "TERM"):

The License granted hereunder shall be effective and terminate as of the dates specified in Schedule "C," attached hereto and by this reference made a part hereof unless sooner terminated in accordance with the terms and conditions hereof.

## 4. EXCLUSION:

Anything in this Agreement to the contrary notwithstanding, Licensee's rights hereunder shall not include the right to, and Licensee hereby warrants that it will not, use the Property for any endorsement, including but not limited to the Licensed Product(s).

## 5. PAYMENT:

(a) Guaranteed Minimum Compensation: Licensee shall pay to Licensor, as Guaranteed Minimum Compensation under this Agreement, not less than the minimum amount specified for the respective period of time set forth in Schedule "D" (attached hereto and by this reference made a part hereof) and such Guaranteed

Minimum Compensation shall be paid in a manner and at the time specified in said Schedule "D."

(b) Percentage Compensation: Licensee agrees to pay Licensor a sum equal to the percentage specified in Schedule "E" in connection with the distribution of any units of the Licensed Products covered by this Agreement (hereinafter "Percentage Compensation") whether to third parties, to its affiliated, associated or subsidiary companies or otherwise, whether or not billed. A Percentage Compensation shall also be paid by Licensee to Licensor on all Licensed Products distributed by Licensee to any of its affiliated, associated or subsidiary companies. The amount payable to Licensor under this sub-clause 5(b) shall be reduced by the amount of any advance paid to Licensor pursuant to Schedule "D."

**6. PERIODIC STATEMENTS:** Within thirty (30) days after the initial shipment of the Licensed Products covered by this Agreement, and on the tenth day of each month thereafter, Licensee shall furnish to Licensor complete and accurate statements, certified to be accurate by Licensee, showing the number, description and sales price of the Licensed Products distributed and or sold by Licensee during the preceding month, including a statement of any returns made during the preceding month. Such statements shall be furnished to Licensor whether or not any of the Licensed Products have been sold during the month for which such statements are due. Percentage Compensation as provided in Schedule "E" shall be payable by the Licensee simultaneously with the rendering of statements. Receipt or acceptance by Licensor of the statements furnished pursuant to this Agreement or of any sums paid hereunder shall not preclude Licensor from questioning the correctness thereof at any time, and if any inconsistencies or mistakes are discovered in such statements or payments, they shall immediately be rectified and the appropriate payments made by Licensee. Time is of the essence with respect to all payments hereunder.

**7. BOOKS AND RECORDS:** Licensee agrees to keep accurate books of account and records covering all transactions relating to the License hereby granted and Licensor and its duly authorized representatives shall have the right upon reasonable advance notice to an examination of said books of account and records and of all other documents and material, whether in the possession or under the control of Licensee or otherwise, with respect to the subject matter and the terms of this Agreement and shall have free and full access thereto for said purpose of making extracts and or copies therefrom. All books of account and records shall be kept available for at least two (2) years after the expiration or termination of this License, and Licensee agrees to permit inspection thereof by Licensor during such two (2) year period as well. The receipt or acceptance by Licensor of any of the statements furnished pursuant to this Agreement or of any Percentage Compensation paid hereunder (or the cashing of any checks paid hereunder) shall not preclude Licensor from questioning the correctness thereof at any time prior to the date two (2) years after the conclusion of the term of this Agreement, and if any inconsistencies or mistakes are discovered in such statements or payments, they shall immediately be rectified and the appropriate payments made by Licensee. Payment shall be made in United States funds. Domestic taxes payable in the Licensed Territory shall be Licensee's responsibility. If any such examination shows an under reporting and or payment in excess of five percent (5%) of the total amount reported and or paid for any twelve (12) month period and if that underpayment is acknowledged by Licensee or is affirmed by litigation or arbitration, then Licensee shall pay the costs of such examination and or litigation, including, without limitation, attorneys' fees with respect thereto.

CONTRACTS
FOR THE
FILM AND
TELEVISION
INDUSTRY

408

## 8. COPYRIGHT AND TRADEMARK NOTICES:

(a) Copyright and Trademark Notices: Licensee shall cause to be imprinted irremovably and legibly on all Licensed Products and on at least the principal face of all packaging, enclosure materials and advertising materials for the Licensed Products the complete copyright notice: © (name of copyright owner date of copyright) (The year of the copyright notice shall be the year in which the latest revision of the respective Licensed Products, packaging, enclosure or advertising is first placed on sale, sold or publicly distributed by the Licensee under the authority from Licensor).

Licensee shall also cause to be imprinted irremovably and legibly on all Licensed Products and on at least the principal face of all packaging, enclosure materials and advertising materials for the Licensed Products the appropriate trademark notice, either "TM" or "R" as Licensor shall determine, and shall affix the notice as specified by Licensor.

(b) Copyright Samples, Approval and Registration:

(i) Prior to the production of any particular Licensed Product or of any packaging, enclosure, promotion and advertising therefor, Licensee shall deliver, at Licensee's expense to Licensor the following;

(a) a complete set of art work and sketches and actual samples, if available of the applicable Licensed Product;

(b) its packaging, enclosures, promotional materials and advertising; for Licensor's written approval of the copyright and trademark form and of the manner and style of use of the Property. Once Licensor approves the trademark or copyright notice, Licensee will not deviate from the Licensor-approved notice. Licensee shall make such deliveries to Licensor each time a new Licensed Product, packaging, enclosure, promotion or advertising is to be produced. Public sale and distribution will not be made until Licensor's approval pursuant to this Subclause 8(b) is received.

(ii) Promptly after the first public sale or distribution, Licensee shall deliver, at Licensee's expense, five (5) complete prototypes of each Licensed Product, packaging, enclosure, promotion and advertising for copyright and trademark registration at Licensor's discretion and expense; however, Licensor has no obligation to obtain such registration(s). Licensee will advise Licensor in writing of the date of first public sale and distribution. Copyrights and trademarks in all such material shall be owned by Licensor.

## 9. LICENSOR'S APPROVAL OF LICENSED PRODUCTS, ADVERTISING, CONTAINERS, MATERIALS:

The quality and style of the Licensed Products as well as any carton, container, packing or wrapping material shall be subject to the express written approval of Licensor prior to distribution and sale thereof. Each and every tag, label, imprint or other device used in connection with any Licensed Products and all advertising, promotional or display material bearing the Property and or Licensed Products shall be submitted by Licensee to Licensor for express written approval prior to use by Licensee. Such approval may be granted or withheld as Licensor in its sole discretion may determine. Licensee shall, before selling or distributing any of the Licensed Products, furnish to Licensor free of cost, for its express written approval, three (3) prototype samples of (a) each Licensed Product, (b) each type of carton, container, packing and wrapping material used with each Licensed Product, (c) each and every tag, label, imprint or other device used in connection with any Licensed Product, and (d) all advertising, story board, script, promotional or display material bearing the Property and or Licensed Products.

Said samples shall be sent to Licensor by means permitting certification of receipt at the mailing address stated in the notice clause herein. Failure by Licensor to approve in writing any of the samples furnished to Licensor within two weeks from the date of submission thereof shall be deemed approval thereof. After samples have been approved pursuant to this clause, Licensee shall not depart therefrom in any respect without the express prior written approval of Licensor. The prototypes shall conform to the requirements of Clause 8.

**10. PROTECTION OF LICENSOR'S RIGHTS AND INTERESTS:** Licensor and Licensee agree that Licensee's utilization of the Property upon or in connection with the manufacture, distribution and sale of the Licensed Products is conditioned upon Licensor's protection of its rights and obtaining the goodwill resulting from such use. Licensee agrees to protect Licensor's rights and goodwill as set forth hereinbelow and elsewhere in this Agreement.

(a) Good Will and Protection:

(i) Licensee recognizes the great value of the publicity and goodwill associated with the Property and, in such connection, acknowledges that such goodwill exclusively belongs to Licensor and that the Property has acquired a secondary meaning in the mind of the purchasing public. Licensee further acknowledges that all rights in any additional material, new versions, translations, rearrangements, or other changes in the Property which may be created by or for Licensee, shall be and will remain the exclusive property of Licensor and the same shall be and will remain a part of the Property under the terms and conditions of this Agreement.

(ii) Licensee shall assist Licensor and or Licensor's authorized agents to all reasonable extent requested by Licensor in obtaining and maintaining in Licensor's name any and all available protection of Licensor's rights in and to the Property; specifically, Licensee agrees to sign documents, give testimony, provide exhibits, provide facts and otherwise cooperate with Licensor and its agents in obtaining registrations, assignments, certificates and the like evidencing Licensor's rights in the Property. Pursuant to the foregoing, Licensee shall assign over to Licensor, at Licensor's request, formal and absolute title subject to the License granted herein, to any protectable new version, variation, revision, arrangement of compilation of the Property, ownership of which shall be absolute in Licensor.

(iii) Licensor may, if it so desires, and in its reasonable discretion, commence or prosecute any claims or suits against infringement of its right in the Property and may, if it so desires, join Licensee as a party in such suit. Licensee shall notify Licensor in writing of any activities which Licensee believes to be infringements or utilization by others of the Property or articles of the same general class as the Licensed Products, or otherwise. Licensor shall have the sole right to determine whether or not any action shall be undertaken as a result of such activity and shall have sole discretion in the accommodation or settlement of any controversies relating thereto. Licensee shall not institute any suit or take any action with

CONTRACTS
FOR THE
FILM AND
TELEVISION
INDUSTRY

410

respect to any such infringement or imitation without first obtaining the written consent of Licensor to do so.

(b) Indemnification By Licensee: For purposes of this Subclause 10(b) "Indemnified Parties" refer to Licensor, and _____ (name of copyright owner if other than Licensor), their parents, subsidiaries and affiliates, and co-producers and co-venturers of Licensor and _____ and the performers and other personnel in or associated with the Property and Licensees of rights relating to the Property, and the person or firm whose rights are being licensed hereunder and, where applicable, sponsors of the Property and their respective advertising agencies, and officers, directors, employees and agents of each of the foregoing and all persons connected with and or employed by them and each of them.

Except for the rights licensed hereunder by Licensor to Licensee, Licensee hereby indemnifies and shall hold harmless the Indemnified Parties and each of them from and against the costs and expenses of any and all claims, demands, causes of action and judgments arising out of the unauthorized use of any patent, process, method or device or out of infringement of any copyright, trade name, patent or libel or invasion of the right of privacy, publicity, or other property right, or failure to perform, or any defect in or use of the Licensed Products, the infringement or breach of any other personal or property right of any person, firm or corporation by Licensee, its officers, employees, agents or anyone, directly or indirectly, acting by, through, on behalf of, pursuant to contractual or any other relationship with Licensee in connection with the preparation, manufacture, distribution, advertising, promotion and or sale of the Licensed Products and or any material relating thereto and or naming or referring to any performers, personnel, marks and or elements. With respect to the foregoing indemnity, Licensee shall defend and hold harmless Indemnified Parties and each of them at no cost or expense to them whatsoever, including but not limited to attorneys' fees and court costs. Licensor shall have the right but not the obligation to defend any such action or proceeding with attorneys of its own selection.

(c) Product Liability Insurance: Licensee shall obtain and maintain at its sole cost and expense throughout the term standard Product Liability Insurance, the form of which must be acceptable to Licensor, from a qualified insurance company licensed to do business in the State of _____ naming Licensor and each and all the Indemnified Parties described in Subclause 10(b) above, as additional named insureds, which policy shall provide protection against any and all claims, demands and causes of action arising out of any defects or failures to perform, alleged or otherwise, in the Licensed Products or any material used in connection therewith or any use thereof. The amount of coverage shall be a minimum of One Million Dollars ($1,000,000) combined single limit for each single occurrence for bodily injury and One Hundred Thousand Dollars ($100,000) for property damage. The policy shall provide for thirty (30) days' notice to Licensee and Licensor from the insurer by Registered Mail, return receipt requested, in the event of any modification, cancellation or termination. Licensee agrees to furnish Licensor a certified copy of the policy providing such coverage within thirty (30) days after the date of this Agreement and in no event shall Licensee manufacture, distribute or sell the Licensed Products prior to receipt by Licensor of such evidence of insurance.

(d) Advertiser's Liability Insurance: Licensee shall obtain and maintain at its sole cost and expense throughout the term standard Advertiser's Liability Insurance, the form of which must be acceptable to Licensor, from a qualified insurance company licensed to do business in the State of _____ naming Licensor and each and all of the Indemnified Parties described in Subclause 10(b) above as additional named insureds. The amount and coverage shall be a minimum of Five Hundred Thousand Dollars\One Million Dollars ($500,000\$1,000,000). The policy shall provide for thirty (30) days' notice to Licensee and Licensor from the insurer by Registered Mail, return receipt requested, in the event of any modification, cancellation or termination. Licensee agrees to furnish Licensor a certified copy of the policy providing such coverage within thirty (30) days after the date of this Agreement and in no event shall Licensee manufacture, distribute or sell the Licensed Products prior to receipt by Licensor of such evidence of insurance.

(e) No Licensor Warranty: Licensor makes no warranty or representation as to the amount of gross sales or net sales or profits Licensee will derive hereunder. Licensor makes no warranty or representation concerning the quality of the Property or that production of the Property will be completed or that the Property will be released. Licensor shall not be under any obligation whatsoever to continue the distribution of the Property or to continue to use any element of the Property. If the Property is not completed, and release thereof not commenced in the United States within one (1) year after the date of this Agreement, by reason of fire, earthquake, labor dispute, lockout, strike, act of God or public enemy, any local, state, federal, national or international law, governmental order or regulation, or any other cause beyond Licensor's control, including but not limited to the death, illness or incapacity of the director or of any principal member of the cast of the Property, this Agreement shall terminate at the expiration of said one (1) year period and Licensor's only liability shall be to return to Licensee the unrecouped portion, if any, of the Guaranteed Minimum Compensation theretofore paid by Licensee to Licensor after the expiration of said one (1) year period, in which event Licensor shall make said refund within thirty (30) days after receiving said demand.

## 11. SPECIFIC UNDERTAKINGS OF THE PARTIES:

(a) Licensor warrants, represents and agrees that:

> (1) It has certain ownership rights in and has the right to grant licenses to utilize the names (including the name of the Picture), characters, artists' portrayal of characters, likenesses and visual representations as included in the Picture and to grant the rights to the Property granted Licensee in this agreement.

(b) Licensee warrants, represents and agrees that:

> (1) It will not dispute the title of Licensor in and to the Property or any copyright or trademark pertaining thereto, nor will it attack the validity of the License granted hereunder.

> (2) It will not harm, misuse or bring into dispute the Property or any part thereof;

> (3) It will manufacture, sell and distribute the Licensed Products in an ethical manner and in accordance with the terms and intent of this Agreement;

> (4) It will not incur any costs chargeable to Licensor;

CONTRACTS
FOR THE
FILM AND
TELEVISION
INDUSTRY

412

(5) It will not enter into any sublicense or agency agreement for the sale or distribution of the Licensed Products;

(6) It will not enter into any agreement relating to the Property for commercial tie-ups or promotions, or otherwise with any person or entity engaged, in whole or in part, in the production of motion pictures or television without the prior written consent of Licensor. Licensee's advertising on television is not subject to the provisions of this subclause;

(7) It will manufacture, sell and distribute Licensed Products of a high standard and of such quality, style and appearance as shall be reasonably adequate and suited to their exploitation to the best advantage and to the protection and enhancement of the Property and the good will pertaining thereto; that such articles will be manufactured, packaged, sold and distributed and advertised in accordance with all applicable (whether national, federal, state, provincial or local) laws: and that the policy of sale, distribution and or exploitation by Licensee shall be of high standard and at the best advantage of the Property and that the same shall in no manner reflect adversely upon the good name of Licensor, or the Property;

(8) It will diligently and continuously solicit sales of the Licensed Products and actively offer the Licensed Products for sale, and make distribution in order to meet orders for the articles covered by this Agreement;

(9) It will sell and distribute the articles covered by this Agreement outright at a competitive price and not for more than the price generally and customarily charged the trade by Licensee, and only to the public by direct mail order sales, to jobbers, wholesalers and distributors for sale and distribution to retail stores and merchants, and to retail stores and merchants for sale and distribution direct to the public. Licensee shall not, without prior written consent of Licensor, sell or distribute such article to jobbers, wholesalers, distributors, retail stores or merchants whose sales or distribution are or will be made for publicity or promotional tie-up purposes, premiums, giveaways or similar methods of merchandising. If any sale is made at a special price to any of Licensee's parents, affiliates or subsidiaries or to any other person, firm or corporation related in any manner to Licensee or its officers, directors or major stockholders, a Percentage Compensation shall be paid on such sale based upon the price generally charged the trade by Licensee.

Notwithstanding anything to the contrary contained herein, Licensed Products may only be sold through required distribution channels for ultimate use by the consumer and may not be sold in quantity or otherwise for any distribution method or device not contemplated by this Agreement.

(10) It will not grant exclusivity to any purchaser without the written consent of Licensor. In addition, Licensee will not require any purchaser to purchase assortments containing merchandise other than that licensed hereunder in order to obtain the articles which are the subject of this License.

(11) It will coordinate the release, promotion, and distribution and sales activities for the Licensed Products with the release of the Property in such manner as Licensor shall request.

## 12. TERMINATION:

(a) If Licensee files a petition in bankruptcy or is adjudicated a bankrupt or if a petition in bankruptcy is filed against Licensor or if Licensee becomes insolvent or makes an assignment for the benefit of its creditors or an arrangement pursuant to any bankruptcy law or if Licensee discontinues its business or if a receiver is appointed for it or its business, the License granted hereunder, without notice, shall terminate automatically (upon the occurrence of any such event).

(b) If Licensee shall violate any of its obligations or conditions under the terms of this Agreement, Licensor shall have the right to terminate the License herein granted upon fourteen days' notice in writing, and such notice of termination shall become effective, unless Licensee shall completely remedy the violation and satisfy Licensor that such violation has been remedied within the fourteen day period.

(c) If the License granted hereunder is terminated in accordance with the provisions of Sub clauses 12(a) or 12(b), all compensation theretofore accrued shall become due and payable immediately to Licensor, and Licensor shall not be obligated to reimburse Licensee for any payment theretofore paid by Licensee to Licensor.

## 13. FINAL STATEMENT UPON TERMINATION OR EXPIRATION: As soon as practical after termination or expiration of this Agreement, but in no event more than 30 days thereafter, Licensee shall deliver to Licensor a statement indicating the number and description of Licensed Products which Licensee has on hand (or in process of manufacture) as of (a) sixty (60) days prior to the end of the Term of this Agreement, or (b) fourteen days after receipt from Licensor of a notice terminating this Agreement (in the event no such notice was given, fourteen days after the occurrence of any event which terminates this Agreement) whichever shall be applicable.

## 14. DISPOSAL OF STOCK UPON EXPIRATION: Upon expiration of the term of this Agreement, Licensee shall have the right, pursuant to the provisions hereof, to dispose of all Licensed Products, theretofore manufactured at the time of the expiration of the License granted hereunder, for a period of 90 days after the date of such expiration subject to the condition that Licensee pays to Licensor all compensation accrued to such time and delivers to Licensor a report in the form required by Clause 6 above to such time. Notwithstanding anything to the contrary contained herein, Licensee shall not sell or dispose of any Licensed Products if this Agreement was terminated for any cause set forth in Clause 12 above.

## 15. EFFECT OF TERMINATION OR EXPIRATION: Upon expiration of the License granted hereunder or the earlier termination thereof, all rights granted to Licensee hereunder shall forthwith revert to Licensor, and Licensee thereafter, directly or indirectly, shall not use or refer to, except as provided in Clause 14, above, the Property or any name, character, trademark or designation which in Licensor's reasonable opinion is similar to the Property, in connection with the manufacture, sale or distribution of products of the Licensee. Licensee shall upon the expiration or termination turn over to Licensor all molds and other materials which reproduce the Licensed Products, or give Licensor satisfactory evidence of their destruction.

Licensee hereby agrees that at the expiration or termination of this Agreement for any reason, Licensee will be deemed automatically to have assigned, transferred and conveyed to Licensor any and all copyrights, trademark or service mark rights, goodwill or other right, title or interest in and to the merchandising

CONTRACTS
FOR THE
FILM AND
TELEVISION
INDUSTRY

414

of the Property which may have been obtained by Licensee or which may have vested in Licensee in pursuance of any endeavors covered hereby. Licensee will execute, and hereby irrevocably appoints Licensor its attorney-in-fact (acknowledging that such power is coupled with an interest) to execute, if Licensee fails or refuses to do so, any instruments requested by Licensor to accomplish or confirm the foregoing. Any such assignment, transfer or conveyance shall be without consideration other than the mutual covenants and considerations of this Agreement. Also, upon expiration or termination of this Agreement, Licensor shall be free to license to others the right to use the Property in connection with the manufacture, sale and distribution of the Licensed Products,

### 16. REMEDIES OF LICENSOR:

(a) Licensee acknowledges that the failure of the Licensee to cease the manufacture, sale or distribution of Licensed Products except as herein permitted upon the expiration or earlier termination of the License granted hereunder or the failure of Licensee to fulfill its obligations specified in Clauses 4, 5, 6, 8, 9, 10, and 11, will result in immediate and irremediable damage to Licensor and to the rights of any other licensee of the Property. Licensee acknowledges that Licensor has no adequate remedy at law for any such failure referred to or referenced to in this Clause and in the event of any such failure, Licensor shall be entitled to equitable relief by way of temporary and permanent injunctions, in addition to such other further relief as any court of competent jurisdiction may deem just and proper.

(b) If Licensor uses any remedy afforded by this Clause, Licensor shall not be deemed to have elected its remedy or to have waived any other rights or remedies available to it under this Agreement, or otherwise.

### 17. FORCE MAJEURE: Licensee shall be released from its obligations hereunder in the event that governmental regulations or conditions arising out of a state of national emergency or war, or causes beyond the control of Licensee render performance by Licensee hereunder impossible. The release of obligations under this Clause shall be limited to a delay in time for Licensee to meet its obligations for a period not to exceed three (3) months, and if there is any failure to meet such obligations after that period, Licensor shall have the absolute right to terminate this Agreement upon fourteen days' notice in writing. Such notice of termination shall become effective if Licensor does not completely remedy the violation within the same fourteen day period and satisfy Licensor that such failure has been remedied.

### 18. RESERVATION OF RIGHTS. Licensor reserves all rights pertaining to the Property, except as specifically granted herein to Licensee.

### 19. NOTICES:

(a) All notices to be given to Licensor hereunder and all statements and payments to be sent to Licensor hereunder shall be addressed to Licensor at (address of Licensor) or at such other address as Licensor shall designate in writing from time to time. Licensee shall send a courtesy copy of each notice hereunder to Licensor's attorney, _____. All notices to be given to Licensee hereunder shall be addressed to it at _____, or at such other address as Licensee shall designate in writing from time to time. Licensor shall send a courtesy copy of each notice hereunder to Licensee's attorney, _____. All notices shall be in writing and shall either be served by Certified or Registered Mail Return Receipt Requested, or telegraph, all charges prepaid. Except as provided herein, such notices shall be deemed given when mailed or delivered to a telegraph office, all charges prepaid, except that notices of change of address shall be effective only after the actual receipt thereof.

(b) Submission: All submissions pursuant to Clauses 8 and 9 shall be forwarded by personal delivery or mail, all charges prepaid by Licensee pursuant to the provisions of Subclause 19(a) above.

**20. WAIVER, MODIFICATION, ETC.:** No waiver, modification or cancellation of any term or condition of this Agreement shall be effective unless executed in writing by the party charged therewith. No written waiver shall excuse the performance of any act other than those specifically referred to therein. Licensor makes no warranties to Licensee except those specifically expressed herein.

**21. NO PARTNERSHIP, ETC.:** This Agreement does not constitute and shall not be construed as constituting an agency, a partnership or joint venture between Licensor and Licensee. Neither party hereto shall hold itself out contrary to the terms of this Clause, and neither Licensor nor Licensee shall become liable for any representation, act or omission of the other contrary to the provisions hereof. This contract shall not be deemed to give any right or remedy to any third party whatsoever unless said right or remedy is specifically granted by Licensor in writing to such third party.

**22. NON-ASSIGNABILITY:** The license granted hereunder is and shall be personal to Licensee, and shall not be assignable by any act of Licensee or by operation of law. Licensee shall not have Licensed Products manufactured for Licensee by a third party unless Licensee first obtains Licensor's approval in writing and unless the third party enters into an agreement with Licensor not to supply Licensed Products to anyone other than Licensee. Any attempt by Licensee to grant sub-licenses or to assign or part with possession or control of the License granted hereunder or any of Licensee's rights hereunder shall constitute a material breach of this Agreement. Licensor shall have the right to assign this Agreement, in which event Licensor shall be relieved of any and all obligations hereunder, provided such assignee shall assume this Agreement and all rights and obligations hereunder in writing.

**23. GOVERNING LAW:** This Agreement shall be deemed to have been made in, and shall be construed in accordance with the laws of the State of _____, and its validity, construction, interpretation and legal effect shall be governed by the laws of the State of _____ applicable to contracts entered into and performed entirely therein.

**24. HEADINGS:** The headings used in connection with the clauses and subclauses of this Agreement are inserted only for the purpose of reference. Such headings shall not be deemed to govern, limit, modify, or in any other manner affect the scope, meaning, or intent of the provisions of this Agreement or any part thereof, nor shall such headings otherwise be given any legal effect.

**25. ENTIRE AGREEMENT:** This Agreement sets forth the entire understanding of the parties hereto relating to the subject matter hereof. No modification, amendment, waiver, termination or discharge of this Agreement, or of any of the terms or provisions hereof shall be binding upon either party hereto unless confirmed by a written instrument signed by Licensee and Licensor. No waiver by Licensor or Licensee of any term or provision of this contract or of any default here under shall affect the other's respective rights thereafter to enforce such term or provision or to exercise any right or remedy in the event of any other default whether or not similar.

CONTRACTS
FOR THE
FILM AND
TELEVISION
INDUSTRY

416

**26. SEVERABILITY:** If any provision of this Agreement shall be held void, voidable, invalid, or inoperative, no other provision of this Agreement shall be affected as a result thereof, and, accordingly, the remaining provisions of this Agreement shall remain in full force and effect as though such void, voidable, invalid, or inoperative provision had not been contained herein.

**27. RIGHTS AND REMEDIES CUMULATIVE:** Except as otherwise provided in this contract, all rights and remedies herein or otherwise shall be cumulative and none of them shall be in limitation of any other right or remedy.

**28. EXECUTION OF AGREEMENT:** This contract shall not be effective until signed by a duly authorized officer of Licensee and countersigned by a duly authorized officer of Licensor.

**29. SPECIFIC ARRANGEMENT:** If there is any specific arrangement between the parties, such specific situation shall be embodied in Schedule "F", attached hereto and by this reference made a part of this Agreement.

IN WITNESS WHEREOF, the parties hereto have signed this Agreements of the day and year first above written.

AGREED TO AND ACCEPTED:

LICENSOR:

_____

By:_____

LICENSEE:

_____

By:_____

SCHEDULES ANNEXED TO LICENSE AGREEMENT BETWEEN _____ (Licensor) and _____ (Licensee) dated _____.

Schedule "A" LICENSED PRODUCTS.

Schedule "B" LICENSED TERRITORY.

Schedule "C" LICENSE PERIOD:

Effective commencement date: _____

Termination date: _____

Schedule "D" GUARANTEED MINIMUM COMPENSATION:

The Guaranteed Minimum Compensation under this Agreement shall be _____ dollars payable upon execution of this Agreement. Such payment shall be an advance against the Percentage Compensation attributable to gross sales made by Licensee during the period for which the Guaranteed Minimum Compensation is due. The payment of Guaranteed Minimum Compensation shall be non-refundable.

Schedule "E" PERCENTAGE COMPENSATIONS:

The Percentage Compensation under this Agreement shall be _____% (Royalty) of the current wholesale price of the Licensed Products based on one hundred percent (100%) of the articles sold.

Schedule "F" SPECIAL ARRANGEMENT.

APPROVED:

_____

By:_____

LICENSEE:

_____

By:_____

CONTRACTS
FOR THE
FILM AND
TELEVISION
INDUSTRY

418

# PRODUCT PLACEMENT

Manufacturers often want to have their products shown in films in order to boost sales. The companies are willing to supply samples of their products, and sometimes money and promotions, in return for placement of a product in a film. Some manufacturers have in-house departments that arrange these placements. Other companies use product placement agents. These agents may represent products from several manufacturers.

The law does not necessarily require that a filmmaker obtain a release to show a product in a film. Assuming you don't disparage the product, it is unlikely a manufacturer could successfully sue simply because its product was shown without consent.

If the product is momentarily on the screen and not identifiable, you need not bother to get a release.[1] No director who shoots a scene in a supermarket is going to obtain releases for every product that passes by in the background. Still, a release never hurts even if not legally required. Remember distributors and insurance carriers like to see releases for every identifiable product.

# PRODUCT RELEASE

_____
(Date)

_____
(Company Representative)

_____
(Company)

_____
(Address)

_____

Re: _____ (Picture)

Dear _____:

When countersigned by you, on behalf of _____ ("Company"), this letter will confirm that Company has agreed to, and hereby does grant, to _____ ("Producer") the right to use its product _____, including any related logo(s) and trademark(s) (collectively, the "Product") in the theatrical motion picture presently entitled _____ (the "Picture"). Company acknowledges that the Picture may be exhibited and exploited worldwide, in all languages and in all media now known or hereafter devised in perpetuity.

Producer agrees that the Product will not be used in a disparaging manner. Company hereby warrants and represents that it has the right and authority to grant the rights granted herein, that the consent of no other person or company is required to enable Producer to use the Product as described herein, and that

---

[1] You should always have a lawyer review your script before production to determine what releases may be required.

such use will not violate the rights of any kind of any third parties. Company agrees to indemnify and hold harmless Producer, its officers, shareholders, assignees and licensees, and each of their successors-in-interest from and against any and all liabilities, damages and claims (including attorneys' fees and court costs) arising out of (i) any breach of Company's warranties, (ii) Producer's use of the Product, as provided herein, and/or (iii) the rights granted herein.

The sole remedy of Company for breach of any provision of this agreement shall be an action at law for damages, and in no event shall Company seek or be entitled to injunctive or other equitable relief by reason of any breach or threatened breach of this Product Release agreement, or for any other reason pertaining hereto, nor shall Company be entitled to seek to enjoin or restrain the exhibition, distribution, advertising, exploitation or marketing of the Picture.

Your countersignature below will confirm this Agreement.

Sincerely,

_____

By:_____ on behalf of
Producer

AGREED TO AND ACCEPTED:

"COMPANY"

_____          Date: _____

By:_____ on behalf of
Company

# CHAPTER 11

# RETAINER AND AGENCY AGREEMENTS

## ATTORNEYS

California requires lawyers to have written fee agreements with their clients whenever the client's total expense, including fees, will likely exceed $1,000 (Business & Professions Code § 6148). A written fee agreement protects the client because it explains how the lawyer charges for services.

The agreement must disclose the lawyer's hourly rate and other charges, the general nature of legal services to be provided, and the respective responsibilities of the lawyer and client under the agreement.

As of January 1, 1993, California requires all California lawyers to disclose to their clients whether or not they have errors and omissions insurance (i.e., malpractice insurance) and the policy limits if coverage is less than $100,000 per claim, $300,000 in the aggregate.

If the lawyer fails to comply with the above requirements, the fee agreement becomes voidable at the client's option. In that case the lawyer would be entitled to reimbursement of a "reasonable" fee.

Lawyers are regulated and subject to discipline by their state bar. They have an elaborate set of ethical rules governing their behavior. For example, an attorney should not simultaneously represent clients with conflicting interests unless the clients are aware of the conflict and give their written consent.

Lawyers have a fiduciary duty to their clients. This means the lawyer should be putting the client's interests first, ahead of what is convenient or profitable for the attorney.

Before retaining an attorney, you should carefully review the retainer agreement. The rate an attorney charges is often negotiable and many attorneys

CONTRACTS
FOR THE
FILM AND
TELEVISION
INDUSTRY

422

charge a lesser rate to low-budget filmmakers. Some large firms, however, may not consider it worth their while to take on a small client.

An attorney's hourly rate is not always a good measure of how much the client will pay for services. That is because an experienced attorney who charges $350 an hour who is able to draft a contract in an hour may prove less expensive than a novice who charges $150 an hour but needs four hours to complete the task, and then may not do it correctly.

When hiring an entertainment attorney, it is advisable to retain someone who specializes in the field. A real estate attorney may think it exciting to dabble in entertainment law but he may not have the specialized knowledge that an experienced entertainment attorney possesses. Within the entertainment arena, some attorneys handle a lot of litigation while others may restrict their practice to transactional work (i.e., dealmaking & drafting contracts).

# ATTORNEY-CLIENT RETAINER AGREEMENT

This ATTORNEY-CLIENT FEE CONTRACT ("Contract") is entered into by and between the undersigned, _____ ("Client"), and _____ ("Attorney").

**I. CONDITIONS.** This Contract will not take effect, and Attorney will have no obligation to provide legal services, until Client returns a signed copy of this Contract and pays the deposit called for under paragraph 3.

**2. SCOPE AND DUTIES.** Client hires Attorney to provide legal services in connection with entertainment counseling, negotiation and contracts. Attorney shall provide those legal services reasonably required to represent Client and shall take reasonable steps to keep Client informed of progress and to respond to Client's inquiries. Attorney's services will not include litigation of any kind, whether in court, in administrative hearings or before government agencies or judicial arbitration. Client shall be truthful with Attorney, cooperate with Attorney, keep Attorney informed of developments, abide by this Contract, pay Attorney's bills on time and keep Attorney advised of Client's address, telephone number and whereabouts.

**3. DEPOSIT.** Client will deposit $_____ by _____ (Deposit Date). The sum will be deposited in a trust account, to be used to pay costs and expenses and fees for legal services. Client hereby authorizes Attorney to withdraw sums from the trust account to pay the costs and/or fees Client incurs. Any unused deposit at the conclusion of Attorney's services will be refunded.

**4. LEGAL FEES.** Client agrees to pay for legal services at the following rates: Attorney: $_____/hour; law clerks/paralegal $_____/hour; secretarial $_____/ hour. Attorney charges in minimum units of ten minutes. Attorney's billable time includes phone conferences with client and with third parties on client's behalf. Other arrangements:

**5. COSTS AND EXPENSES.** In addition to paying legal fees, Client shall reimburse Attorney for all reasonable expenses incurred by Attorney, including long distance telephone calls, messenger fees, postage, photocopying ($.25 per page), faxes ($.50 cents per page local, $1.00 per page long distance, $2.00 per page international), parking, and mileage at 29 cents per mile. Attorney shall obtain Client's consent before incurring any cost in excess of $200.

**6. STATEMENTS.** Attorney shall send Client periodic statements for fees and costs incurred. Client shall pay Attorney's statements within 10 days after each statement's date. Client may request a statement at intervals of no less than 30 days. Upon Client's request Attorney will provide a statement within 10 days. Statements unpaid for more than 30 days are subject to a late charge at the legal rate of interest.

**7. DISCHARGE AND WITHDRAWAL.** Client may discharge Attorney at any time. Attorney may withdraw with Client's consent or for good cause. Good cause includes Client's breach of this Contract, Client's refusal to cooperate with Attorney or to follow Attorney's advice on a material matter or any other fact or circumstance that would render Attorney's continuing representation unlawful or unethical. Attorney has the right to discontinue work if Client has failed to pay attorney in accordance with this agreement.

**8. CONCLUSION OF SERVICES.** When Attorney's services conclude, all unpaid charges shall become immediately due and payable. After Attorney's services

CONTRACTS
FOR THE
FILM AND
TELEVISION
INDUSTRY

424

conclude, Attorney will, upon Client's request, deliver Client's file to Client, along with any Client funds or property in Attorney's possession. Attorney shall have no obligation to retain Client's files beyond one year after services conclude.

**9. LIEN.** Client hereby grants Attorney a lien on any and all monies due client, claims or causes of action that are the subject of Attorney's representation under this Contract. Attorney's lien will be for any sums due and owing to Attorney at the conclusion of Attorney's services. The lien will attach to any recovery Client may obtain, whether by arbitration award, judgment, settlement or otherwise. Said recovery shall be deposited in Attorney's Trust Fund account whereupon attorney shall deduct any sums due attorney and pay the balance to Client.

**10. CONFLICT OF INTEREST:** Whenever an attorney represents two or more people at the same time with regard to the same matter, the Attorney is obligated to advise those people that there is a potential for conflict of interest. Such a conflict might arise, for instance, if Attorney negotiates a deal for a filmmaker with a co-producer or distributor who is also a client. Attorney has advised Client(s) of the following terms of the provisions of Section 3-310 of the California State Rules of Professional Conduct:

(a) If a member has or had a relationship with another party interested in the representation, or has an interest in its subject matter, the member shall not accept or continue such representation without all affected clients' informed written consent.

(b) A member shall not concurrently represent clients whose interests conflict, except with their informed written consent.

Attorney has advised Client(s) of the following provisions of California Evidence Code section 962 relating to the attorney-client privilege:

"Where two or more clients have retained or consulted a lawyer upon a matter of common interest, none of them, nor the successor in interest of any of them, may claim a privilege under this article as to a communication made in the course of that relationship when such communication is offered in a civil proceeding between one of such clients (or his successor in interest) and another of such clients (or his successor in interest)."

Notwithstanding such joint representation and any actual or potential conflict of interest, Client(s) hereby consents to Attorney's joint representation provided Attorney discloses same beforehand. Furthermore, Client(s) acknowledge and agree that at no time will Attorney's representation be construed, claimed or deemed to be a breach of a fiduciary relationship, a conflict of interest or a violation of any other obligation to Client(s). Client(s) agree that at no time shall Client(s) claim or contend that Attorney should be disqualified from representing any Client in connection with any matter, related or unrelated.

**11. ARBITRATION:** If any dispute arises between Client(s) and Attorney, the dispute shall be resolved by binding arbitration in _____ County in accordance with the rules of the State Bar of _____, before a single arbitrator selected in accordance with those rules or the rules of any local Bar Association within _____ County which is operating under the auspices of the State Bar or, if none, in accordance with the arbitration laws of _____. The arbitrator shall have the discretion to order that the cost of arbitration, including arbitrator's fees, or other costs, and reasonable attorneys' fees, shall be borne by the losing party.

**12. DISCLAIMER OF GUARANTEE/INSURANCE.** Nothing in this Contract and nothing in Attorney's statements to Client will be construed as a promise or guarantee about the outcome of Client's matter. Attorney makes no such promises or guarantees. Attorney's comments about the outcome of Client's matter are expressions of opinion only. Attorney maintains errors and omissions insurance.

**13. EFFECTIVE DATE.** This Contract will take effect when Client has performed the conditions stated in paragraph 1, but its effective date will be retroactive to the date Attorney first provided services. The date at the beginning of this Contract is for reference only. Even if this Contract does not take effect, Client will be obligated to pay Attorney the reasonable value of any services Attorney may have performed for Client. The provisions of this agreement concerning legal fees, conclusion of services, withdrawal, lien and arbitration shall survive the discharge or withdrawal of attorney. This contract has been entered into in the City of _____, County of _____.

_____ _____

(CLIENT)                              (ATTORNEY)

Date: _____          Date: _____

CONTRACTS
FOR THE
FILM AND
TELEVISION
INDUSTRY

426

# AGENTS

An agent differs from an attorney in several important respects. First, the agent is a salesperson whose primary role is to find employment for his clients. An agent spends a lot of time surveying the town to determine what potential buyers (i.e., studios, producers) are seeking and then tries to fill their needs from his client list. While a lawyer might help a client find work, the lawyer's primary role is to negotiate deals and protect the legal rights of the client. Lawyers don't systematically cover the town the way agents do.

Second, agents work on a contingent fee basis. In California, agents are limited to a ten percent commission. For instance, if an agent sells a client's screenplay for $50,000, the agent would receive a fee of $5,000. Lawyers, on the other hand, usually work on an hourly basis, often charging $300 or more for each hour of their time. Some law firms charge clients a percentage, often five percent, for their services. This type of deal, however, is usually offered only to clients who work on a steady basis.

From the client's point of view, the advantage of a contingent fee is that it allows the client to avoid any expense unless and until a deal is closed. The agent or attorney has a strong incentive to conclude the deal. On the other hand, if an attorney only spends a few hours on a deal, a contingent fee may amount to a much larger fee than had the attorney billed on an hourly basis.

Agents may negotiate routine deals for clients without the assistance of a lawyer. More complex matters require an attorney. Clients may want both an agent and an attorney to look out for their interests. Lawyers may be more aggressive than agents. As salespeople, agents may be reluctant to push too hard because they know they need to return to the same buyer next week to sell him another project or client.

California and some other states license talent agents. In those states, one cannot perform the function of a talent agent without obtaining a license. An agent who engages in wrongdoing may lose his license. Personal managers, on the other hand, are not licensed. They are not supposed to solicit work for their clients, but they often do so nevertheless. In such a case, the personal manager is in a vulnerable position because the client may be able to revoke the representation agreement and not pay the manager.

Agents may enter into franchise agreements with one or more talent guilds. These franchise agreements take precedence over any agreement between the agent and a guild member. The franchise agreements require agents to provide talent with certain minimum terms. For example, talent may have the right to terminate the agency agreement if the agent is unable to secure any offers of employment within a set period.

Agents don't always enter into written representation agreements with their clients. They may depend on a handshake only. This may be acceptable to the client since the agent's conduct is regulated by the state and one or more guilds. Moreover, a written agreement doesn't guarantee that an agent will find the client work. From a practical point of view, if an agent is unable to secure work there is no sense in continuing the relationship for either party.

The agency agreement defines the fields in which the agent will represent the client. A client involved in multi-disciplinary activities may need several agents. For example, the client may sign a New York literary agent to represent her in publishing, a Hollywood talent agent for screenwriting, and a personal appearance agent for live performances. Some agencies cover several fields while others specialize in one. For instance, one agency may specialize in dancers, another in television commercials. While a person may have several agents, the agents will usually insist on exclusivity within their respective fields.

## SAG MOTION PICTURE / TELEVISION AGENCY CONTRACT

THIS AGREEMENT, made and entered into at _____, by and between _____, a talent agent, hereinafter called the "Agent", and _____, _____ (social security number) hereinafter called the "Actor".

WITNESSETH:

1. The Actor engages the Agent as his agent for the following fields as defined in Screen Actors Guild Codified Agency. Regulations, Rule 16(g) and the Agent accepts such engagement:

[Mark appropriate space(s)]

☐ Theatrical Motion Pictures ☐ Television Motion Pictures

If television motion pictures are included herein for purposes of representation and if during the term of this agency contract the Actor enters into a series or term employment contract for services in television motion pictures, under which he agrees also to render services in program commercials or spots, this agency contract shall include representation of the Actor in connection with his employment in said commercials, and representation of the Actor in said commercials shall not be deemed included in any separate agency contract which the Actor may have entered into covering commercials.

This contract is limited to motion pictures in the above-designated field(s) and to contracts of the Actor as an actor in such motion pictures, and any reference herein to contracts or employment whereby Actor renders his services refers to contracts or employment in such motion pictures unless otherwise specifically stated.

2. The term of this contract shall be for a period of _____ commencing _____.

3. (a) The Actor agrees to pay to the Agent as commissions a sum equal to _____% (Commission) of all moneys or other consideration received by the Actor, directly or indirectly, under contracts of employment (or in connection with his employment under said employment contracts) entered into during the term specified in Paragraph (2) or in existence when this agency contract is entered into except to such extent as the Actor may be obligated to pay commissions on such existing employment contract to another agent. Commissions shall be payable when and as such moneys or other consideration are received by the Actor, or by any-

CONTRACTS
FOR THE
FILM AND
TELEVISION
INDUSTRY

428

one else for or on the Actor's behalf. Commission payments are subject to the limitations of Rule 16(g).

(b) Commissions on compensation paid to Actors for domestic reruns, theatrical exhibition, foreign exhibition or supplementary market exhibition of television motion pictures are subject to the provisions of Rule 16(g).

(c) Commissions on commercials included herein under paragraph (1) above shall be subject to the rules governing commercials provided by Rule 16(g).

(d) No commissions shall be payable on any of the following:

(i) Separate amounts paid to Actor not as compensation but for travel or living expenses incurred by Actor;

(ii) Separate amounts paid to Actor not as compensation but as reimbursement for necessary expenditures actually incurred by Actor in connection with Actor's employment, such as for damage to or loss of wardrobe. special hairdress, etc.;

(iii) Amounts paid to Actor as penalties for violations by Producer of any of the provisions of the SAG collective bargaining contracts, such as meal period violations, rest period violations, penalties or interest on delinquent payments;

(iv) Sums payable to Actors for the release on free television or for supplemental market exhibition of theatrical motion pictures produced after January 31, 1960, under the provisions of the applicable collection bargaining agreement providing for such payment; however, if an Actor's individual theatrical motion picture employment contract provides for compensation in the event the motion picture made for theatrical exhibition is exhibited over free television or in supplemental market exhibition, in excess of the minimum compensation payable under the applicable collective bargaining agreement in effect at the time the employment contract was executed, commissions shall be payable on such compensation.

(v) Sums payable to Actors for foreign telecasting on free television of television motion pictures and commercials under the provisions of the applicable collective bargaining agreements; however, if an individual Actor's contract provides for compensation in excess of minimum under the applicable collective bargaining agreements in effect at the time of employment, commissions shall be payable on such sums.

(vi) On any employment contract which is in violation of SAG collective bargaining agreements. For example, employment contracts providing for "free days", "free rehearsal", "free looping", "a break in consecutive employment", etc., shall not be commissionable. This paragraph is not subject to SAG waiver.

(vii) On any employment contract for television motion pictures which provide for any prepayment or buyout of domestic or foreign residuals or theatrical release, or supplemental market fees, other than those permitted by the appropriate SAG collective bargaining agreement, unless such provisions of individual employment contracts are expressly approved by SAG.

(e) Any moneys or other consideration received by the Actor, or by anyone for or on his behalf, in connection with any termination of any contract of the Actor by virtue of which the Agent would otherwise be entitled to receive commission, or in connection with the settlement of any such contact, or any litigation arising out of any such contract, shall also be moneys in connection with which the Agent is entitled to the aforesaid percentage; provided, however, that in such event the Actor shall be entitled to deduct attorney's fees, expenses and court costs before computing the amount upon which the Agent is entitled to his percentage. The Actor shall also be entitled to deduct reasonable legal expenses in connection with the collection of moneys or other consideration due the Actor arising out of an employment contract in motion pictures before computing the amount upon which the Agent is entitled to his percentage.

(f) The aforesaid percentage shall be payable by the Actor to the Agent during the term of this contract and thereafter only where specifically provided herein and in the Regulations.

(g) The Agent shall be entitled to the aforesaid percentage after the expiration of the term specified in Paragraph (2) for so long a period thereafter as the Actor continues to receive moneys or other consideration under or upon employment contracts entered into by the Actor during the term specified in Paragraph (2) hereof, including moneys or other consideration received by the Actor under the extended term of any such employment contract, resulting from the exercise of an option or options under such an employment contract, extending the term of such employment contact, whether such options be exercised prior to or after the expiration of the term specified in Paragraph (2), subject, however, to the applicable limitations set forth in the Regulations.

(h) If during the period the Agent is entitled to commissions a contract of employment of the Actor be terminated before the expiration of the term thereof, as said term has been extended by the exercise of options therein contained, by joint action of the Actor and employer, or by the action of either of them, other than on account of Act of God, illness. or the like, and the Actor enters into a new contract of employment with said employer within a period of sixty (60) days, such new contract shall be deemed to be in substitution of the contract terminated as aforesaid, subject, however, to the applicable limitations set forth in the Regulations. No contract entered into after said sixty (60) day period shall be deemed to be in substitution of the contract terminated as aforesaid. Contracts of substitution have the same effect as contracts for which they were substituted; provided, however, any increase or additional salary, bonus or other compensation payable to the actor thereunder over and above the amounts payable under the contract of employment which was terminated shall be deemed an adjustment and, unless the Agent shall have a valid agency contract in effect at the time of such adjustment, the Agent shall not be entitled to any commissions on any such additional or increased amounts. In no event may a contract of substitution with an employer extend the period of time during which the Agent is entitled to commission beyond the period that the Agent would have been entitled to commission had no substitution taken place. A change in form of an employer for the purpose of evading this provision or a change in the corporate form of an employer resulting from reorganization or the like shall not preclude the application of these provisions.

(i) So long as the Agent receives commissions from the Actor, the Agent shall be obliged to service the Actor and perform the obligations of this agency contract with respect to the services of the Actor on which such commissions are based, unless the Agent is relieved therefrom under express provisions of the Regulations.

CONTRACTS
FOR THE
FILM AND
TELEVISION
INDUSTRY

430

(j) The Agent has no right to receive money unless the Actor receives the same, or unless the same is received for or on his behalf, and then only in the above percentage when and as received. Money paid pursuant to legal process to the Actor's creditors, or by virtue of assignment or direction of the Actor, and deductions from the Actor's compensation made pursuant to law in the nature of a collection or tax at the source, such as Social Security, Old Age Pension taxes, State Disability taxes or income taxes shall be treated as compensation received for or on the Actor's behalf.

4. Should the Agent, during the term specified in Paragraph (2), negotiate a contract of employment for the Actor and secure for the Actor a bona fide offer of employment, which offer is communicated by the Agent to the Actor in reasonable detail and in writing or by other corroborative action. which offer the Actor declines, and if, within sixty (60) days after the date upon which the Agent gives such information to the Actor, the Actor accepts said offer of employment on substantially the same terms, then the Actor shall be required to pay commissions to the Agent upon such contract of employment. If an agent engaged under a prior agency contract is entitled to collect commissions under the foregoing circumstances, the Agent with whom this contract is executed waives his commission to the extent that the prior agent is entitled to collect the same.

5. (a) The Agent may represent other persons who render services in motion pictures, or in other branches of the entertainment industry.

(b) Unless and until prohibited by the Actor, the Agent may make known the fact that he is the sole and exclusive representative of the Actor in the motion picture fields covered hereby. However, it is expressly understood that even though the Agent has not breached the contract the Actor may at any time with or without discharging the Agent, and regardless of whether he has legal grounds for discharge of the Agent, by written notice to the Agent prohibit him from rendering further services for the Actor or from holding himself out as the Actor's Agent, and such action shall not give Agent any rights or remedies against Actor, the Agent's rights under this paragraph continuing only as long as Actor consents thereto but this does not apply to the Agent's right to commissions. In the event of any such written notice to the Agent the 91-day period set forth in Paragraph (6) of this agency contract is suspended and extended by the period of time that the Agent is prohibited from rendering services for the Actor.

6. (a) If this is an initial agency contract and if actor fails to be employed and receive, or be entitled to receive compensation for ten (10) days' employment in the initial 151 days of the contract, provided further that if no bona fide offer of employment is received by the Actor within any consecutive period of 120 days during the initial 151 day period, or if during any other period of 91 days immediately preceding the giving of the notice of termination hereinafter mentioned in this paragraph, the Actor fails to be employed and receive, or be entitled to receive compensation for ten (10) days' employment, whether such employment is from fields under SAG's jurisdiction or any other branch of the entertainment industry in which the Agent may be authorized by written contract to represent the Actor, then either the Actor or Agent may terminate the engagement of the Agent hereunder by written notice to the other party, subject to the qualifications hereinafter in this paragraph set forth. Each day the Actor renders services or may be required to render services in motion pictures shall count as one (1) day's employment. For the purpose of determining what is a day's employment in other fields of the entertainment industry the following rules shall govern:

(i) Each separate original radio broadcast (including rehearsal time), whether live or recorded, and each transcribed program shall be considered a day's employment.

(ii) Each separate live television broadcast shall be considered a minimum of two (2) days' employment. However, each day spent in rehearsal over the minimum of two (2) days inclusive of the day of telecast, shall be considered an additional one-half (½) day's employment.

(iii) A rebroadcast, whether recorded or live, or by an off the line recording, or by a prior recording, or time spent in rehearsal for any employment in the radio broadcasting or radio transcription industry shall not be considered such employment. A retelecast of a live television program and a rerun of television motion picture entertainment film or commercial shall likewise not be considered such employment.

(iv) Each master phonograph record recorded by the Actor shall be one (1) day's employment.

(v) In all other branches of the entertainment industry, except as set forth above, each day the Actor renders services or may be required to render services for compensation shall count as one (l) day's employment.

(b) The 91 day period which is the basis of termination shall be extended by the amount of employment the Actor would have received from calls for his services in any other branch of the entertainment industry in which the Actor is a recognized performer and at or near the Actor's usual places of employment at a salary and from an employer commensurate with the Actor's prestige, which calls are actually received by the Agent and reported to the Actor in writing or by other corroborative action, when the Actor is in such a locality (away from his usual places of employment) that he cannot return in response to such a call, or when the Actor is unable to respond to such a call by reason of physical or mental incapacity or any other reason beyond his control, or by reason of another engagement in a field in which the Actor is not represented by the Agent; provided, however, that if the Actor is rendering services in another engagement in a field in which the Agent is authorized to represent the Actor, then the time spent in such engagement shall not be added to the 91 day period. Regardless of whether or not the Agent is authorized to represent the Actor on the legitimate stage, if the Actor accepts an engagement on the legitimate stage under a run of the play contract, the 91 day period which is the basis of termination shall be extended by the length of such run of the play contract including rehearsals. The 91 day period which is the basis of termination shall also be extended for any period of time during which the Actor has declared himself to be unavailable and has so notified the Agent in writing or by other corroborative action or has confirmed in writing or by other corroborative action a communication from the Agent to such effect.

(c) In the event that the Agent has given the Actor notice in writing or by other corroborative action of a bona fide offer of employment as an actor in any branch of the entertainment industry in which the Actor is a recognized performer at or near his usual place of employment at a salary and from an employer commensurate with the Actor's prestige (and there is in fact such an offer), which notice sets forth in detail the terms of the proposed employment and the Actor refuses or fails within a reasonable time after receipt of such notice to accept such proffered employment, then the period of guaranteed employment in said offer shall be deemed as

CONTRACTS
FOR THE
FILM AND
TELEVISION
INDUSTRY

432

time worked by the Actor in computing time worked with reference to the right of the Actor to terminate under the provisions of this paragraph.

(d) The Actor may not exercise the right of termination if at the time he attempts to do so:

The Actor is under a contract or contracts for the rendition of his services in the entertainment industry, in any or all fields in which the Agent is authorized by written contract to represent the Actor, which contract or contracts in the aggregate guarantee the Actor:

(i) compensation for such services of Seventy. Thousand ($70,000.00) Dollars or more, or

(ii) Fifty (50) or more days' employment, during the 91 days in question plus the succeeding 273 days after said 91 day period.

(e) Saturdays, Sundays and holidays are included in counting days elapsed during the 91 and 273 day periods provided.

(f) No termination hereunder shall deprive the Agent of the right to receive commission or compensation on moneys earned or received by the Actor prior to the date of termination, or earned or received by the Actor after the date of termination of the Agent's engagement, on contracts for the Actor's services entered into by the Actor prior to the effective date of any, such termination.

(g) Periods of lay-off, leave of absence, or any periods during which the Actor is not performing and is prohibited from rendering services for others in the motion picture field under and during the term of any motion picture employment contract shall not be deemed periods of unemployment hereunder. The "term of any motion picture employment contract" as used in this subparagraph shall not include any unexercised options.

(h) Where the Actor does not actually render his services for which he has been employed but nevertheless is compensated therefor, the same shall be considered as employment hereunder. This shall not apply to employment on live television shows, which employment is computed according to the formula set forth in subparagraph (a) (ii) hereof.

(i) If, at any time during the term of the agency contract, the production of motion pictures in general (as distinguished from production at one or more studios) should be suspended, thereupon the 91-day period herein mentioned shall be extended by the period of such suspension.

(j) If the Actor is under an employment contract which provides that any part of the Actor's guaranteed compensation shall be deferred or if said compensation is spread over a period prior or subsequent to the time of the actual performance of Actor's services under said employment contract, then for the purpose of determining the Actor's right to terminate under the provisions of subparagraph (d) hereof, the guaranteed compensation shall be deemed to have been paid to the actor during the period of the actual performance of Actor's services under said employment contract.

(k) Anything herein to the contrary notwithstanding, if the Agent submits to the Actor a bona fide offer of employment in writing or by other corroborative action, as defined in Paragraph (6) subparagraph (c), after the right of termination has accrued under Paragraph (6) but the Actor has not yet terminated the agency contract, and if the Actor thereafter terminates the agency contract pursuant to Paragraph (6) and thereafter accepts the offer within sixty (60) days of the date of submission of the offer to the Actor by the agent, the Actor shall the pay the Agent commission on the compensation received by the Actor pursuant to such offer.

(1) Other than in cases of initial agency contracts subject to the 151 day clause provided by the first paragraph of this paragraph (6), the right of termination provided by the 91 day termination provisions of this Paragraph (6), the Actor shall also have the right of termination beginning with the 82nd day of the 91-day period whenever it becomes apparent that the Agent will be unable to procure the required employment pursuant to this Paragraph (6) during such 91-day period. In considering whether it has become so apparent, the possibility that after the Actor exercises the right of termination, the Agent might preclude exercise of the right by compliance with subparagraphs (b), (c) or (d) hereof, shall be disregarded. To illustrate: If the Actor has had no employment for 82 days, Actor may terminate on the 82nd day, since only 9 days remain, and Agent cannot obtain 10 days' employment for the Actor in such period. If Actor received one day's employment in 83 days, Actor may terminate on the 83rd day, since only 8 days remain, and Agent cannot obtain 10 days' employment for Actor in such period.

(m) Employment at SAG minimum shall be deemed "employment" and/or "work" for purposes of this Paragraph (6).

7. Rule 16(g) of the Screen Actors Guild, Inc. which contains regulations governing the relations of its members to talent agents is hereby referred to and by this reference hereby incorporated herein and made a pan of this contract. The provisions of said Rule are herein sometimes referred to as the "Regulations" and the Screen Actors Guild, Inc. is herein sometimes referred to as "SAG."

8. The Agent agrees that during the term of this contract the following persons only shall have the responsibility of personally supervising the Actor's business and of servicing and being available to the Actor. The name of one of the persons shall be inserted in the Actor's own handwriting.

*(This italicized provision is a note from SAG to the Actor and not a part of the contract. If the Actor is executing this contract in reliance on the fact that a particular person is connected with the Agent, then the Actor should insert only such person's name in the space following. If the Actor is not executing this contract in reliance on such fact, then the Agent shall insert not more than one name, and the Actor shall insert one name.)*

The Agent upon request of the Actor, shall assign either one of such persons who may be available (and at least one of them always shall be upon reasonable notice from the Actor) and whom the Actor may designate to conduct negotiations for the Actor at such city or its environs and such person shall do so; it being understood that sub-agents employed by the Agent who are not named herein may handle agency matters for the Actor or may aid either of the named persons in handling agency matters for the Actor. In the event both of the persons above named shall cease to be active in the affairs of the Agent by reason of death,

CONTRACTS
FOR THE
FILM AND
TELEVISION
INDUSTRY

434

disability, retirement or any other reason, the Actor shall have the right to terminate this contract upon written notice to the Agent. The rights of the parties in such case are governed by Sections XI and XII of the Regulations.

9. The Agent agrees to maintain telephone service and an office open during all reasonable business hours (emergencies such as sudden illness or death excepted) within the city of _____, or its environs, throughout the term of this agreement and that some representative of the Agent will be present at such office during such business hours. This contract is void unless the blank in this paragraph is filled in with the name of a city at which the Agent does maintain an office to render services to actors.

10. If the Actor is employed under a series or term contract the Actor shall have the right to terminate this contract during the 30-day period immediately following any annual anniversary date of the series or term contract then in effect by giving the Agent 30-days' written notice of his intention to so terminate this contract. Exercise of this termination right shall not affect the Actor's commissions obligation hereunder.

11. Any controversy under this contract, or under any contract executed in renewal or extension hereof or in substitution hereof or alleged to have been so executed, or as to the existence, execution or validity hereof or thereof, or the right of either party to avoid this or any such contract or alleged contract on any grounds, or the construction, performance, nonperformance, operation, breach, continuance or termination of this or any such contract, shall be submitted to arbitration in accordance with the arbitration provisions in the Regulations regardless of whether either party has terminated or purported to terminate this or any such contract or alleged contract. Under this contract the Agent undertakes to endeavor to secure employment for the Actor. This provision is inserted in this contract pursuant to a rule of the SAG, a bona fide labor union, which Rule regulates the relations of its members to talent agents. Reasonable written notice shall be given to the Labor Commissioner of the State of California of the time and place of any arbitration hearing hereunder. The Labor Commissioner of the State of California, or his authorized representative, has the right to attend all arbitration hearings. The clauses relating to the Labor Commissioner of the State of California shall not be applicable to cases not failing under the provisions of Section 1700.45 of the Labor Code of the State of California.

12. Both parties hereto state and agree that they are bound by the Regulations and by all of the modifications heretofore or hereafter made thereto pursuant to the Basic Contract and by all waivers granted by SAG pursuant to said Basic Contract or to the Regulations.

13. (a) Anything herein to the contrary notwithstanding, if the Regulations should be held invalid, all references thereto in this contract shall be eliminated; all limitations of the Regulations on any of the provisions of this contract shall be released, and the portions of this contract which depend upon reference to the Regulations shall be deleted, and the provisions of this contract otherwise shall remain valid and enforceable.

(b) Likewise, if any portion of the Regulations should be held invalid, such holding shall not affect the validity of remaining portions of the Regulations or of this contract; and if the portion of the Regulations so held invalid should be a portion specifically referred to in this contract, then such reference shall be eliminated herefrom in the same manner and with like force and effect as herein provided in the event the Regulations are held invalid; and the provisions of this contract otherwise shall remain valid and enforceable.

Whether or not the Agent is the Actor's agent at the time this contract is executed. it is understood that in executing this contact each party has independent access to the Regulations and has relied exclusively upon his own knowledge thereof.

    IN WITNESS WHEREOF, the parties hereto have executed this agreement the _____ day of _____ , 19__.

                                _____

                                Actor

                                _____

                                Agent

                                By: _____

This talent agent is licensed by the Labor Commissioner of the State of California.

This talent agent is franchised by the Screen Actors Guild, Inc.

The form of this contract has been approved by the State Labor Commissioner of the State of California on January 11, 1991.

This form of contract has been approved by the Screen Actors Guild, Inc.

The foregoing references to California may be deleted or appropriate substitutions made in other states.

CONTRACTS
FOR THE
FILM AND
TELEVISION
INDUSTRY

436

# PRODUCER REPRESENTATIVE AGREEMENT

A producer representative, or producer rep, is a marketing and distribution consultant to the producer. The producer rep is also a salesperson who takes on the responsibility of finding a distributor for a film. This function may entail a variety of different tasks, depending on the nature of an independently made film.

For a film that has the potential for generating positive reviews and winning film festivals, it might mean orchestrating a festival strategy to get the film in the best festivals, preparing collateral materials (e.g. one-sheet, poster) and attending festivals to generate excitement about the film. For a more commercial film, the work might entail calling distribution executives and arranging screenings in L.A. and/or New York. The basic scenario in either case is to create competition among buyers for the film that will ultimately lead to a bidding contest. The Producer Rep can advise his client as to the relative strengths and weaknesses of different distributors and which distributors to avoid.

# REPRESENTATIVE AGREEMENT

This letter agreement ("Agreement") sets forth those basic terms you, _____ (Producer), _____ ("Owner"), and _____ ("Representative") have agreed upon with regard to your motion picture entitled "_____" ("Film").

**1. Term:** This Agreement shall be for a term ("Term") of one (1) year from the date of its complete execution; provided, however, that in the event Representative is in good faith negotiations with a distributor to license the Film, this Agreement shall automatically be extended for a period of 90 days. Upon expiration of the initial Term, Owner may terminate the Agreement on written notice at any time. Until such time as Owner terminates, the Term will be automatically extended.

**2. Exclusivity:** During the Term herein, Representative shall have the sole and exclusive right to perform those services set forth in Paragraph 3 below. Owner shall not circumvent or arrange for completion financing or distribution of the Film except through Representative. Notwithstanding the foregoing, nothing in his paragraph shall restrict Owner's own efforts respecting the arranging for completion financing, distribution and exploitation of the Film; provided however that any such efforts shall be made in consultation with Representative, shall not involve any third party acting in the role of Representative, shall be subject to all other terms of this Agreement, and any transactions which arise out of Representative's efforts shall be subject to Representative's fee as set forth in Paragraph 4 below.

**3. Services:** During the Term hereof, Representative shall utilize its good faith efforts to arrange distribution of the Film in all media throughout the world ("Territory") an in all versions. Representative shall have the exclusive right to contact and deal with distribution and/or foreign sales companies/entities with respect to the Film. Representative may also perform certain business affairs consultation services respecting distribution deals the fee for which shall be included in the fee for Representative's services set forth in Paragraph 4(a), below. Representative shall draft, review, negotiate and comment on distribution agreements. Notwithstanding any other provision contained within this Agreement, Owner shall have final approval over any and all financing/distribution agreement entered into with regard to the Film, which approval shall not be unreasonably withheld. Owner understands, acknowledges, and agrees that Representative may represent other filmmakers in similar capacities. Representative agrees to consult Owner at all reasonable times during negotiations.

**4. Consideration:** For and in consideration of Representative's services, Representative shall be paid:

a) A flat fee of _____ dollars ($_____) against _____ percent (_____%) of the gross revenues due Owner from the Film. As an example, a flat fee payment shall apply as an advance against a 15% commission. The commission shall be fifteen percent of one hundred percent (15% of 100%) of the gross license fees or other consideration (including without limitation any post-production, or completion funding, or other goods and services) derived from the worldwide exploitation of the Film. Gross revenues are all sums due Owner from all film and video distributors or other buyers from exploitation of the film in any and all markets and media received by Owner at any time. Owner shall provide and pay for any promotional materials and expenses needed to market the film. The aforesaid 15% contingency fee is not set by law and is negotiable between Representative and Client.

b) If credits on the negative of the film have not been set, or the Film is re-cut, Owner will add a credit in the Film, substantially as follows: "Producer Rep: _____."

**5. Expenses:** Representative also shall be reimbursed for his actual out-of-pocket costs and expenses incurred in connection with the Film including but not limited to long distance telephone calls, messenger and courier fees, postage, photocopying ($.15 per page), faxes ($.50 per page local, $1.00 per page long distance, $2.00 per page international), parking, festival entrance fees, screening room rentals, shipping of prints, and similar items, if any. No single expense in excess of two-hundred dollars ($200.00) shall be incurred without Owner's prior consent. Representative may require prepayment of expenses. Owner shall receive periodic billing statements for services and expenses.

**6. Warranties:** In connection with this Agreement, Owner hereby warrants and agrees that Owner presently owns all right, title and interest in the Film; that Owner has not heretofore, and will not hereafter during the term hereof assign, license, or encumber any rights in and to the Film inconsistent with the terms of this agreement; that the Film is free and clear of all liens, claims, and encumbrances; and that the Film does not libel, slander, defame or otherwise infringe in any manner on the rights of any third parties. Owner shall indemnify Representative for any claims, costs or expenses arising out of a breach of the foregoing representations and warranties. Further, Owner shall provide Representative with any and all underlying documentation necessary to complete financing and distribution agreements that may be negotiated with regard to the Film. Owner acknowledges that Owner has had an opportunity to consult with an attorney or other representative of Owner regarding the terms and conditions of this Agreement.

**7. Extension of Term/Contracts:** Notwithstanding the expiration of the Term as defined herein, should Owner enter into an agreement with any company, entity or person that Representative has contacted regarding the Film during the Term hereof, for the period of one (1) year after the expiration of the Term, Representative shall be entitled to its consideration as set forth in Paragraph 4.

CONTRACTS
FOR THE
FILM AND
TELEVISION
INDUSTRY

438

**8. Additional Documentation:**  This Agreement sets forth the basic terms and conditions of the Agreement contemplated by the parties hereto. In connection herewith, both parties agree to execute and complete any and all other documentation that may be reasonably necessary to effectuate the purposes and intent of this Agreement, however, this Agreement shall be binding on the parties hereto.

**9. Payments:**  Owner agrees that Representative shall receive all revenues due Owner from Distributors or licensees. Said funds shall be deposited in Representative's Client Trust Fund account, with Owner's share of the proceeds to be promptly remitted.

**10. Lien:**  Owner hereby grants Representative a lien on any and all gross revenues, claims and causes of action that are the subject to Representative's representation under this Agreement. Representative's lien will be for any sums due and owing to Representative hereunder, from the Film and from any recovery Owner may obtain, whether by arbitration award, judgment, settlement or otherwise. The provisions of this paragraph shall survive the discharge or withdrawal of Representative or termination of this Agreement.

**11. Disclaimer of Guarantee:**  Nothing in this Agreement and nothing in Representative's statements to Owner will be construed as a promise or guarantee about the outcome or the results of Representative's services hereunder. Owner understands and acknowledges that the motion picture business is risky, unpredictable, and subject to cultural trends and the whims and personal tastes of film buyers. Owner acknowledges that Representative makes no such promises or guarantees as to the results of his services hereunder. Representative's comments about the outcome or the results of Representative's services hereunder are expressions of opinion only.

**12. Arbitration and Jurisdiction:**  This Agreement shall be interpreted in accordance with the laws of the State of _____, applicable to agreements executed and to be wholly performed therein. Any controversy or claim arising out of or in relation to this Agreement or the validity, construction or performance of this Agreement, or the breach thereof, shall be resolved by arbitration in accordance with the rules and procedures of AFMA, as said rules may be amended from time to time (If AFMA shall refuse to accept jurisdiction of such dispute, then the parties agree to arbitrate such matter before and in accordance with the rules of the American Arbitration Association under its jurisdiction in _____ before a single arbitrator familiar with entertainment law). The arbitrator may make any interim order, decision, determinations, or award he deems necessary to preserve the status quo until he is able to render a final order, decision, determination or award. Such rules and procedures are incorporated and made a part of this Agreement by reference. The parties shall have the right to engage in pre-hearing discovery in connection with any arbitration proceedings. The parties agree hereby that they will abide by and perform any award rendered in any arbitration conducted pursuant hereto, that any court having jurisdiction thereof may issue a judgment based upon such award and that the prevailing party in such arbitration and/or confirmation proceeding shall be entitled to recover its reasonable attorneys' fees and expenses. The arbitration will be held in _____ and the award shall be final, binding and non-appealable. The Parties agree to accept service of process in accordance with AFMA or AAA Rules.

Please indicate your agreement with the foregoing by executing this letter in the space provided below and returning same to my office.

Very truly yours,

_____
(Producer Rep)


READ, APPROVED AND ACCEPTED:


(Producer)


_____


Date:_____

# CHAPTER 12

# GLOSSARY OF TERMS

***Above-the-Line Costs*** Portion of the budget which covers major creative participants (writer, director, actors and producer) including script and story development costs.

***Adaptations*** Derivative works. When a motion picture is based on a book, the movie has been adapted from the book.

***Adjusted Gross Participation*** Gross participation minus certain costs, such as cost of advertising and duplication. Also called "Modified Gross." If many deductions are allowed, the participant is essentially getting a "net profit" deal.

***Administrator*** Person appointed by a court to manage the assets of a deceased person.

***Advance*** Up-front payment that counts against monies that may be payable at some time in the future. Non-recoupable advances are payments that are not refundable even if future monies are never due.

***Affirm*** To ratify or approve.

***AFMA*** Trade organization for film distributors. Used to mean American Film Marketing Association, but this organization now just calls itself AFMA.

***Aforesaid*** Previously said.

***Amend*** Change, modify.

***Answer Print*** The first composite (sound and picture) motion picture print from the laboratory with editing, score and mixing completed. Usually color values will need to be corrected before a release print is made.

CONTRACTS
FOR THE
FILM AND
TELEVISION
INDUSTRY

442

**Art Theater**   Shows specialized art films, generally in exclusive engagements, rather than mass-marketed studio films.

**Aspect Ratio (A.R.)** The proportion of picture width to height.

**Assign**   Transfer.

**Assignee**   Person receiving property by assignment.

**Assignor**   Person giving or transferring property to another.

**Assigns**   Those to whom property has or may be assigned.

**Attorney-in-Fact**   Person authorized to act for another.

**Auteur**   A French term, the auteur theory holds that the director is the true creator or author of a film, bringing together script, actors, cinematographer, editor and molding everything into a work of cinematic art with a cohesive vision. Anyone who has worked on a movie knows what complete nonsense this theory is. Filmmaking is a collaborative endeavor and the director is only one of the contributors.

**Author**   Creator, originator. Under U.S. copyright law, the author may be the employer of the person who actually creates the work. See "work for hire."

**Back End**   Profit participation in a film after distribution and/or production costs have been recouped.

**Balance Stripe** A magnetic stripe on the film, which is on the opposite edge from the magnetic sound track.

**Below-The-Line Costs**   The technical expenses and labor including set construction, crew, camera equipment, film stock, developing and printing.

**Blind Bidding**   Requiring theater owners to bid on a movie without seeing it. Several states and localities require open trade screenings for each new release. Guarantees and advances may also be banned.

**Blow-Up**   Optical process of enlarging a film, usually from 16mm to 35mm.

**Box Office Gross**   Total revenues taken in at a movie theater box offices before any expenses or percentages are deducted.

**Box Office Receipts**   What the theater owner takes in from ticket sales to customers at the box office. A portion of this revenue is remitted to the studio/distributor in the form of rental payments.

**Break**   To open a film in several theaters simultaneously, either in and around a single city or in a group of cities, or on a national basis.

**Breakout**   To expand bookings after an initial period of exclusive or limited engagement.

**Cause Of Action**   The facts which entitle a person having a right to judicial relief against another.

**Cel**   A transparent sheet of cellulose acetate used as an overlay for drawing or lettering. Used in animation and title work.

**Color Correction**   Changing tonal values of colored objects or images by the use of light filters, either with a camera or a printer.

**Color Temperature**   The color in degrees Kelvin (K) of a light source. The higher the color temperature, the bluer the light, the lower the temperature, the redder the light.

**Completion Bond**   A form of insurance which guarantees completion of a film in the event that the producer exceeds the budget and is unable to secure additional funding. Completion bonds are sometimes required by banks and investors to secure loans and investments in a production. Should a bond be invoked, the completion guarantor will assume control over the production and be in a recoupment position superior to all investors. Do you really want an insurance company finishing your film?

**Consideration**   Usually money, but can be anything of value. The reason or inducement for a party to contract with another. The right, interest or benefit to one party, or the loss or forbearance of another. A necessary element for a contract to be binding.

**Contrast**   The density range of a negative or print. The brightness range of lighting in a scene.

**Convey**   To transfer or deliver to another.

**Covenant**   An agreement or promise to do something, or not do something.

**Cross Collateralization**   Practice by which distributors off-set financial losses in one medium or market against profits derived from others. For example, the rentals obtained from France are combined with those from Italy, and after the expenses for both are deducted, the remainder, if any, is profit. Filmmakers don't like to have the markets for their films cross-collateralized because it may reduce the amount of money they are likely to see.

**Crossover Film**   Film which initially is targeted for a narrow specialty market, that achieves acceptance in a wider market.

**Dailies (Rushes)**   Usually an untimed one-light print, made without regard to color balance, from which the action is checked and the best takes selected.

**Day and Date**   The simultaneous opening of two or more movie theaters in one or more cities.

**Day Player**   An actor who works a day at a time on a film. In other words, actors with bit parts.

**Deal Memo**   A letter or short contract.

**Decedent**   A deceased person.

CONTRACTS
FOR THE
FILM AND
TELEVISION
INDUSTRY

444

*Defamation*   A false statement that injures another's reputation in the community.

*Default*   Failure to perform.

*Deferred Payment*   Writers, directors, actors and others may take only part of their salary up-front in order to reduce the budget of the picture. The rest of their fee is paid from box-office and other revenues that may, or may not, accrue later.

*Depth Of Field*   The distance range between the nearest and farthest objects that appear in sharp focus.

*Development*   The process by which an initial idea is turned into a finished screenplay. Includes optioning the rights to an underlying literary property, and commissioning writer(s) to create a treatment, first draft, second draft, rewrite, and polish.

*Direct Advertising*   Direct outreach to consumers such as mailing flyers. Usually targeted to a specific interest group.

*Direct Broadcast Satellite (DBS)*   A satellite broadcast system designed with sufficient power so that inexpensive home satellite dishes can be used for reception.

*Display Advertising*   Advertising which features art work or title treatment specific to a given film, in newspaper and magazine advertising.

*Dissolve*   An optical or camera effect in which one scene gradually fades out at the same time that a second scene fades in.

*Distributor*   A company that markets a motion picture, placing it in theaters, advertising and promoting it. The major studios nowadays are mostly in the business of financing and distributing films, leaving production to smaller independent companies.

*Distribution Expenses*   Includes taxes, guild payments, trade association dues, conversion/transmission costs, collection costs, checking costs, advertising and publicity costs, re-editing costs, prints, foreign version costs, transportation and shipping costs, copyright costs, copyright infringement costs, insurance, royalties, and claims and lawsuits.

*Distribution Territories*   There are 33 principal distribution centers for pictures in the United States.

*Domestic Rights*   Usually defined as rights within U.S. and English-speaking Canada only.

*Double Distribution Fees*   Where distributor uses a sub-distributor to sell to a territory. If both distributors are allowed to deduct their standard fees, the filmmaker is less likely to see any money.

**Double-System Sound**   The recording of sound on tape and picture on film so that they can be synchronized during editing.

**Downbeat Ending**   A story that ends unhappily or in a depressing manner.

**Droit Moral**   French term for Moral Rights. A doctrine of artistic integrity that prevents others from altering the work of artists, or taking the artist's name off work, without the artist's permission. For example, the doctrine might prevent the buyer of a painting from changing it even though the physical item and the copyright to it has been transferred to the buyer.

**Dubbing**   The addition of sound (either music or dialogue) to a visual presentation through a recording process to create a sound track that can be transferred to and synchronized with the visual presentation.

**Dupe**   A copy negative, or duplicate negative.

**Edge Numbers**   Sequential numbers printed along the edge of a strip of film to designate the footage.

**Exclusive Opening**   A type of release whereby a film is opened in a single theater in a major city, giving the distributor the option to hold the film for a long exclusive run or move it into additional theaters based on the film's performance.

**Execute**   To complete; to sign; to perform.

**Executor**   A person appointed to carry out the requests in a will.

**Feature Film**   Full length, fictional films (not documentaries or shorts), generally for theatrical release.

**Film Noir**   Dark, violent, urban, downbeat films, many of which were made in the 40's and 50's.

**Film Rental**   The amount the theater owner pays the distributor for the right to show the movie. As a rough rule of thumb, this usually amounts to about half of the box-office gross.

**Final Cut**   The last stage in the editing process. The right to final cut is the right to determine the ultimate artistic control over the picture. Usually the studio or the financier of a picture retains the right to final cut.

**First-Dollar Gross**   The most favorable form of gross participation for the participant. Only a few deductions, such as checking fees, taxes, and trade association dues are deductible.

**First Money**   From the producers' point-of-view, the first revenue received from the distribution of a movie. Not to be confused with profits, first monies are generally allocated to investors until recoupment, but may be allocated in part or in whole to deferred salaries owed talent or deferred fees owed the film laboratory.

CONTRACTS
FOR THE
FILM AND
TELEVISION
INDUSTRY

446

***First Run***   The first engagement of a new film.

***Floors***   In distributor/exhibitor agreements, the minimum percentage of box office receipts the distributor is entitled to regardless of the theater's operating expenses. Generally decline week by week over the course of an engagement. Generally range from 70 to 25 percent.

***Force Majeure***   Superior or irresistible force. A Force Majeure clause in a contract may suspend certain obligations in the event the contract cannot be performed because of forces beyond the control of the parties such as a fire, strike, earthquake, war or Act of God.

***Foreign Sales***   Licensing a film in various territories and media outside the U.S. and Canada. Although Canada is a foreign country, American distributors typically acquire Canadian rights when they buy U.S. domestic rights.

***Four-Walling***   Renting a theater and its staff for a flat fee, buying your own advertising, and receiving all the revenue. The exhibitor is paid his flat fee regardless of performance and receives no split of box office receipts.

***FPM***   Feet per minute, expressing the speed of film moving through a mechanism.

***FPS***   Frames per second, indicating the number of images exposed per second.

***Front Office***   The top executives, the people who control the money.

***General Partners***   Management side of a limited partnership (the position usually occupied by the film's producers) which structures a motion picture investment and raises money from investors who become limited partners. General partners control all business decisions regarding the partnership.

***Grant***   To give or permit. To bestow or confer.

***Grantor***   The person who makes a grant. The transferor of property.

***Grass Roots Campaign***   Using flyers, posters, stickers and building word-of-mouth with special screenings for local community groups.

***Gross After Break-even***   The participant shares in the gross after the break-even point has been reached. The break-even point can be a set amount or determined by a formula.

***Gross Box-Office***   Total revenue taken in at theater box-office for ticket sales.

***Gross Participation***   A piece of gross receipts without any deductions for distribution fees or expenses or production costs. However, deductions for checking and collection costs, residuals and taxes are usually deductible. A "piece of the gross" is the most advantageous type of participation from the filmmaker or writer's point of view. In an audit, it is the most easily verified form of participation.

***Gross Receipts***   Studio/distributor revenues derived from all media, including film rentals, television sales, merchandising and ancillary sales.

*Heirs*  The persons who inherit property if there is no will.

*Hot*  Anyone whose last picture was a big hit, won an Academy Award or is being lionized by the media. A transitional state.

*House Nut*  Weekly operating expenses of movie theater.

*Hyphenates*  Persons who fulfill two or more major roles such as producer-director, writer-director or actor-director.

*In Perpetuity*  Forever.

*Incapacity*  Inability. Want of legal, physical or intellectual capacity. A minor, or a person committed to a mental institution, may be legally incapable of contracting with another.

*Indemnify*  Reimburse. To restore someone's loss by payment, repair or replacement.

*Interlock*  The first synchronous presentation of the workprint and the sound track (on separate films) by means of mechanical or electrical drive between the projector and the sound reproducer.

*Internegative*  A color negative made from a color positive.

*Interpositives*  A positive duplicate of a film used for further printing.

*Inure*  To take effect; to result.

*Invasion of Privacy*  A tort that encompasses a variety of wrongful behavior such as an unjustified appropriation of another's name, image or likeness; the publicizing of intimate details of another's life without justification; or intrusions into another's privacy by eavesdropping or surveillance in an area where a person has a reasonable expectation of privacy.

*Irrevocable*  That which cannot be revoked or recalled.

*Key Art*  Art work used in posters and ads for a movie.

*Letterbox*  A process of film-to-video transfer that maintains the original film aspect ratio by matting the top and the bottom of the screen with black bars. Standard TV's have an aspect ratio of 1.33 (4/3), while contemporary feature films have such aspect ratios of 1.66, 1.83, 1.85, 2.33 and 2.35. The more conventional transfer process is called Pan & Scan.

*Libel*  The written form of defamation. Compare to Slander, the spoken form of defamation.

*Licensee*  Person who is given a license or permission to do something.

*Licensor*  The person who gives or grants a license.

*Limited Partnership*  Instrument of investment commonly used to finance movies. General partners initiate and control the partnership, limited

CONTRACTS
FOR THE
FILM AND
TELEVISION
INDUSTRY

448

partners are the investors and have no control of the running of the partnership business and no legal or financial liabilities beyond the amount they have invested.

**Litigation**   A lawsuit. Proceedings in a court of law.

**M&E Track**   Music and Effects Track.

**Magnetic Track**   Audio recorded on a film or tape that has been coated with a magnetic recording medium.

**Master**   The final edited and complete film or videotape from which subsequent copies are made.

**Merchandising Rights**   Right to license, manufacture and distribute merchandise based on characters, names or events in a picture.

**Mini-Multiple**   Type of release which falls between an exclusive engagement and a wide release, consisting of quality theaters in strategic geographic locations, generally a prelude to a wider break.

**Multi-Tiered Audience**   An audience of different types of people who find the film attractive for different reasons, and who must be reached by different publicity, promotion or ads.

**Negative Cost**   Actual cost of producing a film through to the manufacture of a completed negative (does not include costs of prints or advertising). It may be defined to include overhead expenses, interest and other expenses which may inflate the amount way beyond what was actually spent to make the film.

**Negative Pickup**   A distributor guarantees to pay a specified amount for distribution rights upon delivery of a completed film negative by a specific date. If the picture is not delivered on time and in accordance with the terms of the agreement, the distributor has no obligation to distribute it. A negative pickup guarantee can be used as collateral for a bank loan to obtain production funds.

**Net Profit**   The amount of money left, if anything, after all allowable deductions are taken. This usually amounts to zero. Typically expressed in terms of 100% of net profits, although payable out of the producer's share.

**Novelization**   A book adapted from a motion picture.

**NTSC**   National Television System Committee. The standard for North America, Japan and several other countries, which is 525 lines, 60 fields/30 frames per second. Compare to PAL.

**Obligation**   A duty imposed by law, courtesy or contract.

**Off-Hollywood**   American independent films made outside the studio system.

**Officer**   Person holding office of trust or authority in a corporation or institution.

**On Spec**   Working for nothing on the hope and speculation that something will come of it.

**Optical Sound Track**   A sound track in which the sound record takes the form of density variations in a photographic image, also called a photographic sound track.

**Original**   A screenplay that has not been adapted from an article, book, play, old movie, etc.

**Original Material**   Not derived or adapted from another work.

**Overexposure**   A condition in which too much light reaches the film, producing a dense negative or a washed-out reversal.

**PAL**   Phase Alternation Line. The standard adopted by European and other countries, which is 625 Lines, 50 fields/25 frames per second. Compare to NTSC.

**Pan**   A horizontal movement of the camera.

**Pan & Scan**   Used to transfer a film to video for use on standard television because of the different image aspect ratio (the ratio of the width versus the height of the image). The transfer camera focuses on a portion of the total film image.

**Pari Passu**   Equitably, without preference.

**Platforming**   A method of release whereby a film is opened in a single theater or small group of theaters in a major territory and later expanding to a greater number of theaters. Compare with Letterbox and process.

**Player**   Actor.

**Playoff**   Distribution of a film after key openings.

**Positive Film**   Film used primarily for making master positives or release prints.

**Power Coupled with an Interest**   A right to do some act, together with an interest in the subject-matter.

**Print**   A positive picture usually produced from a negative.

**Pro Rata**   Proportionately.

**Processing**   A procedure during which exposed photographic film or paper is developed, fixed, and washed to produce either a negative image or a positive image.

**Quitclaim**   To release or relinquish a claim. To execute a deed of quitclaim.

**Raw Stock**   Motion picture film that has not been exposed or processed.

**Regional Release**   As opposed to a simultaneous national release, a pattern of distribution whereby a film is opened in one or more regions at a time.

CONTRACTS
FOR THE
FILM AND
TELEVISION
INDUSTRY

450

**Release Print**   A composite print made for general distribution and exhibition after the final answer print has been approved.

**Remake**   A new production of a previously produced film.

**Remise**   To remit or give up.

**Rescind**   Rescission. To abrogate, annul or cancel a contract.

**Right of Privacy**   The right to be left alone, and to be protected against a variety of intrusive behavior such as unjustified appropriation of one's name, image or likeness; the publicizing of intimate details of one's life without justification; unlawful eavesdropping or surveillance.

**Right of Publicity**   The right to control the commercial value and use of one's name, likeness and image.

**Roll-out**   Distribution of film around the country subsequent to either key city openings or an opening in one city, usually New York.

**Rough Cut**   A preliminary assemblage of footage.

**Run**   Length of time feature plays in theaters or territory.

**Sanction**   To assent, concur or ratify. To reprimand.

**Scale**   The minimum salary permitted by the guilds.

**Sequel**   A book or film that tells a related story that occurs later. A continuation of an earlier story usually with the same characters.

**Shooting Script**   A later version of the screenplay in which each separate shot is numbered and camera directions are indicated.

**Sleeper**   An unexpected hit. A film audiences fall in love with and make a success.

**Slicks**   Standardized ad mechanicals, printed on glossy paper, which include various sizes of display ads for a given film, designed for the insertion of local theater information as needed.

**Sound Track**   The portion of a film reserved for the sound.

**Specialized Distribution**   As opposed to commercial distribution, distribution to a limited target audience, in a smaller number of theaters, with a limited advertising budget and reliance upon publicity, reviews and word-of-mouth to build an audience for the picture.

**Stills**   Photographs taken during production for use later in advertising and/or publicity. Stills should be in a horizontal format, and should list such information as film title, producer/director and cast below the photo.

**Stock**   General term for motion picture film, especially before exposure. Film stock.

***Story Analyst or Reader***   A person employed by a studio or producer to read submitted scripts and properties, synopsize and evaluate them. Often young literature or film school graduates who don't know a great deal about story or filmmaking, but then again their bosses sometimes know even less.

***Story Conference***   A meeting at which the writer receives suggestions about how to improve his/her script.

***Stripe***   A narrow band of magnetic coating or developing solution applied to a motion picture film.

***Sub-Distributor***   In theatrical releases, distributors who handle a specific geographic territory. They are sub-contracted by the main distributor who co-ordinates the distribution campaign and marketing of all sub-distributors.

***Successors***   Persons entitled to property of a decedent by will or as an heir.

***Successors-in-Interest***   One who follows another in ownership or control of property.

***Survivor***   One who survives or outlives another.

***Synchronization***   The positioning of a sound track so that it is in harmony with, and timed to, the image portion of the film.

***Syndication***   Distribution of motion pictures to independent commercial television stations on a regional basis.

***Talent***   The word used to describe those involved in the artistic aspects of filmmaking (i.e., writers, actors, directors) as opposed to the business people.

***Target market***   The defined audience segment a distributor seeks to reach with its advertising and promotion campaign, such as teens, women over 30, yuppies, etc.

***Television Distribution Fee***   Typically 10-25% for U.S. Network broadcast sales, 30-40% for domestic syndication, and 45-50% for foreign distribution.

***Television Spin-Off***   A television series or mini-series based on characters or other elements in a film.

***Test marketing***   Pre-releasing a film in one or more small, representative markets before committing to an advertising campaign. The effectiveness of the marketing plan can thereby be assessed and modified as needed before the general release.

***Theatrical Distribution Fees***   Generally between 30% and 40% of gross film rentals.

***Trades***   The daily and weekly periodicals of the industry such as Variety and Hollywood Reporter.

CONTRACTS
FOR THE
FILM AND
TELEVISION
INDUSTRY

452

*Translation*　The reproduction of a book, movie, or other work into another language.

*Treatment*　A prose account of the story line of a film. Usually between 20 and 50 pages. Comes after outline and before first draft screenplay.

*Warranty*　A promise. An assurance by one party as to the existence of a fact upon which the other party may rely.

*Wide Release*　The release of a film in numerous theaters (800-2,000).

*Window*　Period of time in which a film is available in a given medium. Some windows may be open-ended, such as theatrical and home video, or limited, such as pay television or syndication.

*Work-for-Hire (or Work-made-for-hire)*　Under the Copyright law, this is either 1) a work prepared by an employee within the scope of employment; or 2) a specially ordered or commissioned work of a certain type (e.g., a motion picture, a contribution to a collective work), if the parties expressly agree so in a writing signed by both before work begins.

*Workprint*　A picture or sound-track print, usually a positive, intended for use in editing only so as not to expose the original elements to any wear and tear.

# APPENDIX

## SECTIONS OF THE CALIFORNIA CODE THAT ARE REFERRED TO IN THIS BOOK

### CIVIL CODE

**§ 36 Minors; contracts not disaffirmable**

(a) Contracts not disaffirmable. A contract, otherwise valid, entered into during minority, cannot be disaffirmed upon that ground either during the actual minority of the person entering into such contract, or at any time thereafter, in the following cases:

1. Necessaries. A contract to pay the reasonable value of things necessary for his support, or that of his family, entered into by him when not under the care of a parent or guardian able to provide for him or them, provided that these things have been actually furnished to him or to his family.

2. Artistic or creative services; judicial approval.

(A) A contract or agreement pursuant to which such person is employed or agrees to render artistic or creative services, or agrees to purchase, or otherwise secure, sell, lease, license, or otherwise dispose of literary, musical or dramatic properties (either tangible or intangible) or any rights therein for use in motion pictures, television, the production of phonograph records, the legitimate or living stage, or otherwise in the entertainment field, if the contract or agreement has been approved by the superior court in the county in which such minor resides or is employed or, if the minor neither resides in or is employed in this state, if any party to the contract or agreement has its principal office in this state for the transaction of business.

(B) As used in this paragraph, "artistic or creative services" shall include, but not be limited to, services as an actor, actress, dancer, musician, comedian, singer, or other performer or entertainer, or as a writer, director, producer, production executive, choreographer, composer, conductor, or designer.

3. Professional sports contracts; judicial approval. A contract or agreement pursuant to which such person is employed or agrees to render services as a participant or player in professional sports, including, but without being limited to, professional boxers, professional wrestlers, and professional jockeys, if the contract or agreement has been approved by the superior court in the county in which such minor resides or is employed or, if the minor neither resides in or is employed in this state, if any party to the contract or agreement has its principal office in this state for the transaction of business.

(b) Judicial approval; procedure; extent. The approval of the superior court referred to in paragraphs (2) and (3) of subdivision (a) may be given upon the petition of either party to the contract or agreement after such reasonable notice to the other party thereto as may be fixed by said court, with opportunity to such other party to appear and be heard; and its approval when given shall extend to the whole of the contract or agreement, and all of the terms and provisions thereof, including, but without being limited to, any optional or conditional provisions contained therein for extension, prolongation, or termination of the term thereof.

CONTRACTS
FOR THE
FILM AND
TELEVISION
INDUSTRY

454

## § 36.1 Contracts for particular services; trust or savings plan; net earnings; taxes

In any order made by the superior court approving a contract of a minor for the purposes mentioned in Section 36 of this code, the court shall have power, notwithstanding the provisions of any other statute, to require the setting aside and preservation for the benefit of the minor, either in a trust fund or in such other savings plan as the court shall approve, of such portion of the net earnings of the minor, not exceeding one-half thereof, as the court may deem just and proper, and the court may withhold approval of such contract until the parent or parents or guardian, as the case may be, shall execute and file with the court his or their written consent to the making of such order. For the purposes of this section, the net earnings of the minor shall be deemed to be the total sum received for the services of the minor pursuant to such contract less the following: All sums required by law to be paid as taxes to any government or governmental agency; reasonable sums expended for the support, care, maintenance, education and training of the minor; fees and expenses paid in connection with procuring such contract or maintaining the employment of the minor; and the fees of attorneys for services rendered in connection with the contract and other business of the minor.

## § 36.2 Continuing jurisdiction over, and termination of, minor's trust or savings plan

The superior court shall have continuing jurisdiction over any trust or other savings plan established pursuant to Section 36.1 and shall have power at any time, upon good cause shown, to order that any such trust or other savings plan shall be amended or terminated, notwithstanding the provisions of any declaration of trust or other savings plan. Such order shall be made only after such reasonable notice to the beneficiary and to the parent or parents or guardian, if any, as may be fixed by the court, with opportunity to all such parties to appear and be heard.

### § 1427 Obligation defined

OBLIGATION, WHAT. An obligation is a legal duty, by which a person is bound to do or not to do a certain thing.

### § 1428 Creation and enforcement

An obligation arises either from:

One—The contract of the parties; or,

Two—The operation of law.

An obligation arising from operation of law may be enforced in the manner provided by law, or by civil action or proceeding.

### § 1542 General release; extent

A general release does not extend to claims which the creditor does not know or suspect to exist in his favor at the time of executing the release, which if known by him must have materially affected his settlement with the debtor.

### § 1550 Essential elements

ESSENTIAL ELEMENTS OF CONTRACT. It is essential to the existence of a contract that there should be:

1. Parties capable of contracting;
2. Their consent;
3. A lawful object; and,
4. A sufficient cause or consideration.

## § 1607 Lawfulness of consideration

CONSIDERATION LAWFUL.  The consideration of a contract must be lawful within the meaning of Section 1667.

## § 1620 Express contract defined

EXPRESS CONTRACT, WHAT.  An express contract is one, the terms of which are stated in words.

## § 1624 Statute of frauds

The following contracts are invalid, unless they, or some note or memorandum thereof, are in writing and subscribed by the party to be charged or by the party's agent:

(a) An agreement that by its terms is not to be performed within a year from the making thereof.

(b) A special promise to answer for the debt, default, or miscarriage of another, except in the cases provided for in Section 2794.

(c) An agreement for the leasing for a longer period than one year, or for the sale of real property, or of an interest therein; such an agreement, if made by an agent of the party sought to be charged, is invalid, unless the authority of the agent is in writing, subscribed by the party sought to be charged.

(d) An agreement authorizing or employing an agent, broker, or any other person to purchase or sell real estate, or to lease real estate for a longer period than one year, or to procure, introduce, or find a purchaser or seller of real estate or a lessee or lessor of real estate where the lease is for a longer period than one year, for compensation or a commission.

(e) An agreement which by its terms is not to be performed during the lifetime of the promisor.

(f) An agreement by a purchaser of real property to pay an indebtedness secured by a mortgage or deed of trust upon the property purchased, unless assumption of the indebtedness by the purchaser is specifically provided for in the conveyance of the property.

(g) A contract, promise, undertaking, or commitment to loan money or to grant or extend credit, in an amount greater than one hundred thousand dollars ($100,000), not primarily for personal, family, or household purposes, made by a person engaged in the business of lending or arranging for the lending of money or extending credit. For purposes of this section, a contract, promise, undertaking or commitment to loan money secured solely by residential property consisting of one to four dwelling units shall be deemed to be for personal, family, or household purposes.

This section does not apply to leases subject to Division 10 (commencing with Section 10101) of the Commercial Code.

## § 1667 Unlawfulness defined

WHAT IS UNLAWFUL.  That is not lawful which is:

1. Contrary to an express provision of law;
2. Contrary to the policy of express law, though not expressly prohibited; or,
3. Otherwise contrary to good morals.

CONTRACTS
FOR THE
FILM AND
TELEVISION
INDUSTRY

456

BUSINESS & PROFESSIONS CODE

### § 6148 Contracts for services in cases not coming within § 6147; bills rendered by attorney; contents; failure to comply

(a) In any case not coming within Section 6147 in which it is reasonably foreseeable that total expense to a client, including attorney fees, will exceed one thousand dollars ($1,000), the contract for services in the case shall be in writing and shall contain all of the following:

(1) The hourly rate and other standard rates, fees, and charges applicable to the case.

(2) The general nature of the legal services to be provided to the client.

(3) The respective responsibilities of the attorney and the client as to the performance of the contract.

(4) A statement disclosing whether the attorney maintains errors and omissions insurance coverage applicable to the services to be rendered and the policy limits of that coverage if less than one hundred thousand dollars ($100,000) per occurrence up to a maximum of three hundred thousand dollars ($300,000) per policy term.

(b) All bills rendered by an attorney to a client shall clearly state the basis thereof. Bills for the fee portion of the bill shall include the amount, rate, basis for calculation, or other method of determination of the attorney's fees and costs. Bills for the cost and expense portion of the bill shall clearly identify the costs and expenses incurred and the amount of the costs and expenses. Upon request by the client, the attorney shall provide a bill to the client no later than 10 days following the request unless the attorney has provided a bill to the client within 31 days prior to the request, in which case the attorney may provide a bill to the client no later than 31 days following the date the most recent bill was provided. The client is entitled to make similar requests at intervals of no less than 30 days following the initial request. In providing responses to client requests for billing information, the attorney may use billing data that is currently effective on the date of the request, or, if any fees or costs to that date cannot be accurately determined, they shall be described and estimated.

(c) Failure to comply with any provision of this section renders the agreement voidable at the option of the client, and the attorney shall, upon the agreement being voided, be entitled to collect a reasonable fee.

(d) This section shall not apply to any of the following:

(1) Services rendered in an emergency to avoid foreseeable prejudice to the rights or interests of the client or where a writing is otherwise impractical.

(2) An arrangement as to the fee implied by the fact that the attorney's services are of the same general kind as previously rendered to and paid for by the client.

(3) If the client knowingly states in writing, after full disclosure of this section, that a writing concerning fees is not required.

(4) If the client is a corporation.

(e) This section applies prospectively only to fee agreements following its operative date.

# AUTOMATED CONTRACTS
# FOR THE FILM & TELEVISION INDUSTRY

60 "Fill in the blank" entertainment contracts for your computer. Covers most areas of film and television production. A valuable collection of sample entertainment contracts which can be completed by answering questions using a fill in the blank window that pops up. Information is then automatically inserted into the contract. View, make changes, import into your word processor and then print. Provides comprehensive help and a detailed glossary of terms. Includes all of the contracts from Mark Litwak's *Contracts for the Film & Television Industry, 2nd Edition*.

---

## ORDER FORM

---

Ship To:

_____

(Name)

_____

(Company)

_____

(Street Address)

_____

(City, State & Zip)

_____

(Telephone Number)

Please print clearly!

### System Requirements

Windows 3.1, 95/98, NT 4.0 or PowerMAC & one of the following JavaScript capable browsers including Netscape Navigator 3.05, 4.0 or Internet Explorer 4.01.

Contracts are available on CD-ROM or 3.5 inch High-Density disks.

Orders are shipped via UPS Ground. Prices are subject to change without notice. All sales are final. Allow 2-4 weeks for delivery. For faster service, include your Federal Express account number. Visa & MasterCard accepted.

| Qty | Description | Taxable | Unit Price | Total |
|-----|-------------|---------|------------|-------|
| | Contracts for the Film & Television Industry (CD-ROM) | | 149.95 | |
| | Contracts for the Film & Television Industry (Disk) | | 149.95 | |
| | | | Subtotal | |
| | | | Tax† | |
| | | | Shipping (UPS)* | 7.50 |
| | | | Total | |

†Sales Tax: California residents add 8 1/4% ($12.37 per item).

*Shipping fees vary for orders outside the United States. Please contact your local UPS to confirm correct shipping costs or call (310) 859-9595.

**MAIL ORDER TO:**
Hampstead Enterprises, Inc.
P.O. Box 3226
Santa Monica, CA 90408-3226
Order by Phone: 310-859-9595
Order by Fax:   310-859-0806

_____

VISA or MC #

_____

Expiration

**Order online: http://www.marklitwak.com**

# ABOUT THE AUTHOR

Mark Litwak is a veteran entertainment and multimedia attorney who represents numerous writers and independent filmmakers. He handles production legal work, drafting the contracts and clearances needed to produce motion pictures. He also functions as a producer's rep, assisting filmmakers in the marketing and distribution of their films. A lawyer for twenty-one years, he is Of Counsel to the Beverly Hills law firm of Berton & Donaldson.

Litwak is the author of five books, including *Reel Power: The Struggle for Influence and Success in the New Hollywood*, *Courtroom Crusaders*, *Dealmaking in the Film and Television Industry*, and *Litwak's Multimedia Producer's Handbook*. His *Dealmaking* book won the prestigious Krasna-Krausz Award for best book on the business of film. His *Contracts for the Film and Television Industry* has been published as a CD-ROM program.

A professor of entertainment and copyright law, Litwak has taught at the University of California Los Angeles, Loyola Law School, and the University of West Los Angeles. He has lectured before audiences of lawyers, filmmakers, and university students, including presentations for the American Bar Association, the American Film Institute, Century City Bar Association, Columbia University, New York University, the University of Southern California, The New School for Social Research, the Toronto Film Festival, San Francisco State University, and the Royal College of Art in London.

As an authority on the movie industry, he has been interviewed on more than fifty television and radio shows on such networks as ABC and CNN, and such shows as *The Larry King Show* and National Public Radio's *All Things Considered*.

For additional information about entertainment legal issues, visit Mark Litwak's website, Entertainment Law Resources, at **http://www.marklitwak.com**.